MW00474168

Gunkholing in the San Juan Islands

A Comprehensive Cruising Guide Encompassing Deception Pass to the Canadian Boundary

with Jo Bailey & Carl Nyberg

Ⓖ **'gunk•hol•ing'** *adj* : "a quiet anchorage, as in a cove used by small yachts (Random House);" where the anchor usually sinks into soft mud, or 'gunk'— thus 'gunkholing' applies to those who engage in this low-key, relaxed style of cruising (Bailey-Nyberg).

Published by San Juan Enterprises, Inc.
Seattle, Washington

Disclaimer: The charts, tables and illustrations contained in this book are not for navigation purposes, but are for reference or planning use only. Selected laws require all vessels to have on board, maintain, and use appropriate navigational charts and equipment. None of the material in this book is intended to replace nor substitute, any government or other navigation charts or other government publications, including *Notice to Mariners,* for current information regarding changes, additions and deletions to existing navigational materials.

San Juan Enterprises, Inc., and the authors offer this book as a general cruising guide about the cruising area, vessel outfitting, operation, and facilities and services. Experience, hands-on training and sources of written information beyond this book are necessary to engage in cruising safely. The reader is strongly advised to make use of all these sources prior to cruising.

San Juan Enterprises, Inc., and the authors do not guarantee or warrant information in this book to be complete, correct or current. The authors and publisher disclaim liability and responsibility to any person or entity with respect to any loss or damage caused, or alleged to be caused, directly or indirectly, by the use and/or interpretation of any of the information contained in this book.

The reader needs to understand that under no circumstances are the authors to be held responsible for any omissions, oversights or errors. This book is about cruising in this area as we know it or believe it to be.

GUNKHOLING IN THE SAN JUAN ISLANDS
The Comprehensive Cruising Guide Encompassing Deception Pass to the Canadian Boundary
With Joanne "Jo" Bailey and Carl Nyberg

Published by San Juan Enterprises, Inc.
3218 Portage Bay Place East
Seattle, Washington 98102
© 2000 by Joanne I. Bailey and Carl O. Nyberg
New & improved edition
All rights reserved
0 9 8 7 6 5 4 3 2 1

Manufactured in the United States of America
Printed in the United States of America

Final book design and layout by Sally Cox Bryan, Carl and Jo
Edited by Sally Cox Bryan
Photographs by Joanne Bailey, unless otherwise noted
Cover photograph: Fossil Bay in Sucia Island Marine State Park
Back photo: Authors Joanne & Carl, by Bill & Lisa Bailey

Library of Congress Cataloging-in-Publication Data
Library of Congress Catalog Card Number: 00130179
Bailey, Joanne and Nyberg, Carl
Gunkholing in the San Juan Islands: A Comprehensive Cruise Guide Encompassing Deception Pass to the Canadian Boundary
Joanne "Jo" Bailey and Carl Nyberg, New & improved Edition, Volume #1 in Gunkholing series
     Includes bibliographical references and index
     ISBN 0-944257-04-6
     1. Outdoor recreation—Washington (State)—San Juan Islands 2. Outdoor recreation—Washington (State)—San Juan Islands—Directories. 3. San Juan Islands (Wash.)—Guidebooks. 4. Marinas—Washington (State)—San Juan Islands—Guidebooks. I. Title.

Table of Contents

LEGEND

⚓ = ANCHORING   ☸ = UNDERWAY   Ⓖ = GUNKHOLE

🐚 = PUBLIC BEACH ACCESS   ➡ = CAUTION

Charts & Publications

Charts

	Chart #	Date	Name	Scale	Soundings
U.S	18400	08/30/97	Strait of Georgia & Strait of Juan de Fuca	1:200,000	Fathoms
	18421	03/21/98	Strait of Juan de Fuca to Strait of Georgia	1:80,000	Fathoms
			Drayton Harbor	1:30,000	Fathoms
	18423	06/18/94	Strip Chart: Bellingham to Everett, including		
			San Juan Islands	1:80,000	Fathoms
			Blaine	1:30,000	Fathoms
	18424	07/12/97	Bellingham Bay	1:40,000	Fathoms
			Bellingham Harbor	1:20,000	Fathoms
	18427	02/21/98	Anacortes to Skagit Bay	1:25,000	Fathoms
	18429	03/16/96	Rosario Strait—Southern Part	1:25,000	Fathoms
	18430	11/02/96	Rosario Strait—Northern Part	1:25,000	Fathoms
	18431	10/05/96	Rosario Strait to Cherry Point	1:25,000	Fathoms
	18432	08/15/92	Boundary Pass	1:25,000	Fathoms
	18433	04/20/91	Haro Strait—Middle Bank to Stuart Island	1:25,000	Fathoms
	18434	04/27/96	San Juan Channel	1:25,000	Fathoms
	18465	08/01/98	Strait of Juan de Fuca—Eastern Part	1:80,000	Fathoms
Br. Adm.	79	08/05/94	Strait of Georgia, Southern Part	1/200.000	Meters
Can.	3313	1995	Gulf Islands Chart Book	Varies	Meters
	3390	07/25/97	Fraser River	1/20,000	Meters
	3392	11/27/98	Roberts Bank	1/20,000	Meters
	3441	12/06/96	Haro Strait, Boundary Pass & Satellite Channel	1:40,000	Meters
	L/C 3461	12/02/94	Juan de Fuca Strait, Eastern Portion	1:80,000	Meters
	L/C 3462	10/23/98	Juan de Fuca Strait to Strait of Georgia	1:100,000	Meters

Maps

Washington State Public Lands Quadrangle Map, **Bellingham**   1:100,000

Washington State Public Lands Quadrangle Map, **Port Townsend**   1:100,000

Washington State Public Lands Quadrangle Map, **San Juan County** 1:100,000

Publications

NOAA Tidal Current Tables, Pacific Coast of North America & Asia

NOAA Tide Tables, West Coast of North & South America

NOAA United States Coast Pilot 7

Coast Guard Light List, Volume VI, Pacific Coast and Pacific Islands

Canadian Sailing Directions, Volume I

Current Atlas, Juan de Fuca Strait to Strait of Georgia

Canadian Tide and Current Tables, Volume 5

For You, Our Readers

Come Cruise with us through the new and improved *Gunkholing in the San Juan Islands* book.

Feel the wind in your hair and the salt spray on you face as we cruise together in the stunningly beautiful San Juans and other islands. We'll anchor serenely at the end of each day.

This book is for seasoned or novice mariners, residents or visitors, because you're enthusiastic about cruising, sailing or paddling adventures, we explore the greater San Juan Islands area of well over 800 islands. We visit some of the geographically similar and fascinating islands, but add the intriguing mainland shores from Deception Pass to Point Roberts, and many new gunkholes.

We'd like you with us as we plot our course through twelve chapters of information on what we consider one the greatest cruising areas in the world. There are many routes to the islands and the region dealt with in this book. From the Puget Sound region most pleasure boaters approach the islands by crossing the Strait of Juan de Fuca, often departing from Port Townsend. Others go up the "inside passage" east of Whidbey Island and through the Swinomish Channel or Deception Pass, while others reach the area from British Columbia.

We're glad you're with us and hope you'll enjoy *Gunkholing in the San Juan Islands.*

Welcome aboard once again!

Jo & Carl

About the Authors

Jo and Carl are both Seattle natives and their combined cruising of Puget Sound, the San Juans and British Columbia waters amounts to nearly a century in a variety of sailboats, including Carl's 50' yawl, Winsome; 24' schooner, Condor, and assorted dories and Port Madison prams; Jo's 8' El Toro, Wee Witch; 15' sloop, Naiad; 19' sloop, Winsome, and 29' sloop, Sea Witch. They currently cruise the 35' Chris Craft sloop, Scheherazade.

Acknowledgments

In addition to our families, with special thanks to Sally Cox Bryan (our angel, advisor and editor), are due to the following for helping us in so many different and special ways:

John Adams, John & Trish Aydelotte, Robin Bailey, John & Lauralee Brainard, Dick Britton, Ed Brighton, Dan Crookes, Sally & Bob Bryan, Howard & Pearl Calloway; David Castor, Nan & Jack Culver, Jon Daniel, Sue Anne Sanders, Larry Tuzeau, Neve, Russ, Leonard, Emery & all the crew at Captain's Nautical; Fred Elsethehagen, George & Betty Hansen, Polly Hanson, Tim Johnson, Jim Julius, Lloyd Keith, Ted Leche, Ken Lloyd, Peter McCorison, Ron Meng, Peter Roloff, Steve & Meredith Ross, Jim & Miki Straughan, Gus & Ellyn Swanson, Bill Watts, special San Juan Island friends: John & Louise Dustrude, Les & Betsy Gunther, Hugh & Joan Lawrence, Lee & Tal Sturdivant (always with a warm meal and extra room); Al & Lottie Wilding, National Ocean & Atmospheric Administration (NOAA), Museum of History & Industry, U.S. Coast Guard, Washington State Parks Department, Department of Natural Resources (Kathy Gunther, Sean Hewitt, Stan Kurowski & others), Department of Fisheries & Wildlife, Washington State Ferries and so many more.

Carl's Very Interesting Crossing of the Straits...

Seattle Yacht Club member Ed Kennel owned Sterling Hayden's 98-foot schooner *Gracie S* in the 1950's.

A group of powerboat guests from Queen City Yacht Club boarded *Gracie* in Seattle for a memorable cruise into the San Juans. Ship's company on this cruise were Ed Kennel, John Condon, John Levitt, John Adams, Rupert Broom, myself and "Rusty Plates," the latter a paid Seaman's Union cook. Condon and Levitt were regulars aboard *Gracie*. Adams, Broome and I all grew up on the water, sailed our own boats, and crewed on *Gracie* at every opportunity.

At 2 a.m. under full working rig the big schooner was between Dungeness Spit and Protection Island when the light airs turned abruptly to gale force. *Gracie* buried her rail, the dory floating while hanging in its davits. Except for Condon, Levitt and myself, most everyone else had turned in below, and were unexpectedly awakened.

Condon and Levitt immediately eased the main and fores'l sheets and *Gracie* began to charge ahead in the darkness. As Kennel, Adams and Broom came topside the main sheet was paid out until the mains'l luffed.

As the main's throat and peak halyards were paid out, the huge gaff and sail thrashed and settled onto the boom between the lazy jacks.

Main sheet then hauled in, preventer tackle attached, the main boom was secured amidships. *Gracie* plunged past Dungeness Light. Its flashing illuminated our sails. We altered course sailing briefly downwind, putting the jib in the lee of the fores'l. Adams and Broom lowered the jib, scrambled out on the bowsprit and secured the jib.

Finally, bound for Cattle Pass with only her stays'l and fores'l set *Gracie* surged on at a more comfortable angle. We watched the Dungeness light fade as the glimmer of Victoria, Smith Island and Cattle Point lights grew brighter.

My watch over, I went below to turn in. One of our guests nervously asked if we were going to be okay. I assured him it was "all in a day's work"—it was *Gracie's* kind of weather.

Some things are different under sail.

**Carl, Rupert Broom,
John Condon,
John Adams**

CRUISING NOTES

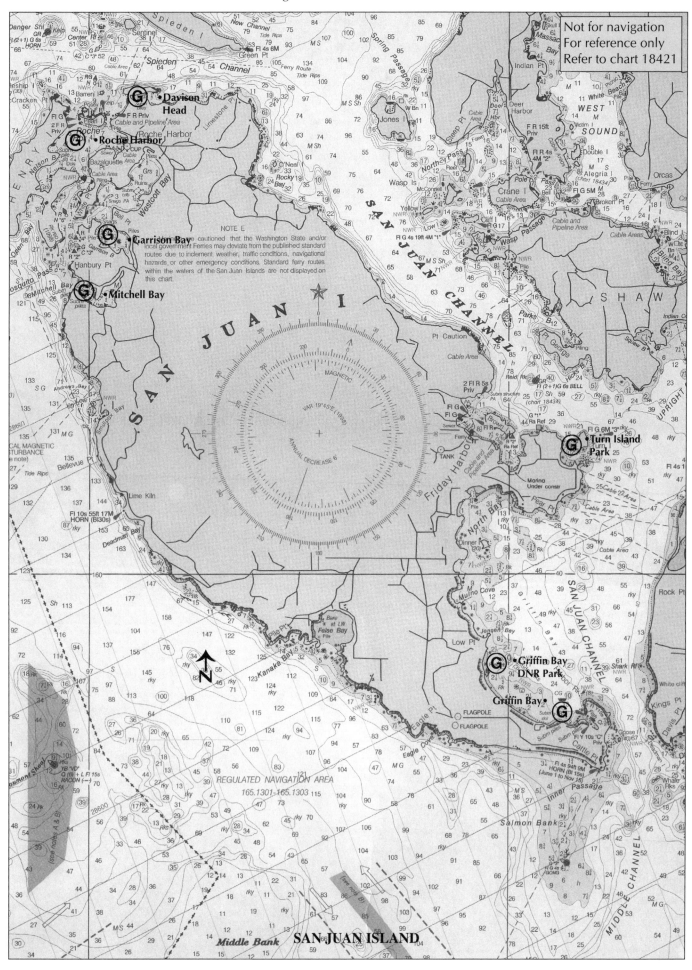

SAN JUAN ISLAND

Chapter 1
SAN JUAN ISLAND
ADJACENT ISLANDS & FRIDAY & ROCHE HARBORS

Charts & Publications for this Chapter

	Chart	Date	Title	Scale	Soundings
	U.S. 18421	03/21/98	Strait of Juan de Fuca to Strait of Georgia	1:80,000	Fathoms
	U.S. 18423	06/18/94	Strip Chart Bellingham to Everett, inc. San Juans C,D	1:80,000	Fathoms
			Page C, inset 5	1:40,000	Fathoms
			Page D, inset 7	1:20,000	Fathoms
			Page D, inset 8	1:25,000	Fathoms
☆	U.S. 18433	04/20/91	Haro Strait, Middle Bank to Stuart Island	1:25,000	Fathoms
☆	U.S. 18434	04/27/96	San Juan Channel	1:25,000	Fathoms
	CAN. 3313	07/28/95	Gulf Islands & Adjacent Waterways		
			Page 1, Juan de Fuca to Georgia Strait	1:200,000	Meters
			Page 6b	1:20,000	Meters
			Pages 5, 6, 22, 23	1:40,000	Meters
	CAN. 3441	12/06/96	Haro Strait, Boundary Pass & Satellite Channel	1:40,000	Meters
	CAN. L/C 3461	12/02/94	Juan de Fuca Strait, Eastern Portion	1:80,000	Meters
	CAN. L/C 3462	10/23/98	Juan de Fuca Strait to Strait of Georgia	1:80,000	Meters
	🐚		Washington State DNR Quad Map—San Juan County	1:100,000	

Compare your chart dates with those above. There may be discrepancies between chart editions.
☆ = Preferred chart for this chapter 🐚 = DNR & other public tideland information

SAN JUAN ISLAND OVERVIEW

San Juan is not quite the largest island in the archipelago. At 35,448.14 acres, it is second to Orcas which claims 36,431.91 acres, a difference of about one square mile. It feels urban when you step into downtown Friday Harbor, with shops and restaurants bustling with tourists. However, when you leave downtown and wander into the countryside or cruise along the remaining undeveloped beaches, the beauty and wonder of the island can still be found. The term "magical island" still applies.

Rocky beaches are rimmed with expensive, glass-fronted residences with commanding views. The island's waterfront, farmlands and hills are turning into developments of custom-built "mega-homes." San Juan has the largest population in the islands with over 6,000 permanent residents, the largest school district, and the most real estate offices of any island. It has the county seat, the only incorporated town, Friday Harbor, and boasts the only Whale Watching State Park in the U.S.

San Juan is the site of the infamous Pig War in the mid-1800s—the "non-war" that established Haro Strait as the boundary line between U.S. and Canadian islands. It is a beautiful island whose residents are now facing the challenge of metamorphosing from a sleepy country island to what many feel is the most desirable place to live in the United States.

Let's get on with our circumnavigation of the island with its fascinating cruising, geography and history which we'll delve into as we go. We cruise counterclockwise because we assume that perhaps you just crossed the Strait of Juan de Fuca and you're anxious to get "inside."

➡ **NOTE: Marine fuel** is available in the area covered in this chapter at:
- **Port of Friday Harbor**
- **Roche Harbor Resort**
- **Snug Harbor Marina Resort**
  in Mitchell Bay

San Juan locals

Cattle Point Light

⊕ **UNDERWAY,** we start at Cattle Point at the southeast tip of San Juan Island and go north in San Juan Channel with a stop in Griffin Bay.

Cattle Point Light is a most re-assuring sight as we reach the southern end of San Juan Island, we've made it across the Strait. The crossing can run the gamut from glass-smooth and clear, to foggy or gale-force winds with huge seas. It's never the same, always an adventure.

Cattle Point Light [Fl 4s 94ft 5 M] a flashing 4 second light 94 feet high visible 5 miles, has a horn that operates continuously from June 1 to November 15. The light is on a white octagonal tower on the barren bluff on the tip of the island, overlooking restless San Juan Channel which offers its own challenges, depending on the wind and currents.

Currents in the channel are taken from direct readings in the *Tidal Current Tables*. The **flood currents** run nearly north at 10° True and are sometimes predicted at well over 5 knots. **Ebb currents** run true south at 180° True and predictions can exceed 4 knots. "The average current velocity between Goose and Deadman islands is 2.6 knots on the flood and ebb, **however, maximum flood currents of 5 knots or more cause severe rips and eddies.**" (*Coast Pilot, 31st Edition*)

Problems arise approaching the channel if the wind is in opposition to current, especially with a strong southerly or southwesterly. We've seen waves well over 10 feet high in the channel during storms. Nearly everyone who uses the pass tells stories of strong winds and waves. We've also nearly "surfed" through the pass at over 7 knots in a small sailboat when we've had wind and current with us.

San Juan Channel from Cattle Point to the north end of the "hook" on the San Juan Island side is known as **Cattle Pass,** although that name is not charted. This is a place that demands the respect and caution of mariners.

Goose Island is less than 0.2 mile off San Juan and is surrounded by shoals and kelp. Between Cattle Point Light and Goose Island the shoreline is rocky with steep banks 10 to 20 feet high. Behind Goose Island is Cape San Juan, a residential development with a low bank shoreline.

About 0.4 mile north of Goose Island and across from Kings Point on Lopez, the channel opens up and we continue north. However, we're going to stay in this area for a bit and visit some great places.

> ➥ **NOTE:** If extreme weather conditions exist when approaching San Juan channel from the Strait, when a strong ebb current flows against a southwest wind, possible ports of refuge might be Aleck Bay or Mackaye Harbor on Lopez.

> ➥ **NOTE: Chart 18423** states CAUTION—Currents of 5 knots or more with severe rips and eddies occur in San Juan Channel between Goose Island off San Juan Island and Deadman Island off Lopez Island.

🐚 *Public Tidelands*

Unless otherwise noted, public tidelands are state-owned. Some may be leased and posted for aquaculture or other private use. When going ashore take the Public Lands Quad Map of San Juan County.

Public tidelands surround much of San Juan Island and we point them out as we go, but many are inaccessible.

🐚 **Cattle Point DNR Day-Use Picnic Area & Interpretive Site**

This park is onshore about 300 yards north of Cattle Point Lighthouse. This is a day-use site only, with picnic tables, restrooms, water, readerboards, hiking trails and some rather fascinating historical information for mariners. A concrete compass rose built into the rocks has guideposts to distant sights, with spectacular panoramic views of Iceberg Point on Lopez, Smith Island, Admiralty Inlet, Mount Rainier, Olympic Mountains and Juan de Fuca's passage west to the Pacific Ocean beyond the south end of Vancouver Island.

Not recommended for anchoring, the area can be approached by beachable boats, weather permitting. Cars, bikes or mopeds can be rented in Friday Harbor making it possible to visit here by land.

A trail leads down below the radio shack to a nice shore for beachcombing. It's also possible to hike out to Cattle Point Light, now automated, along grassy trails.

The foghorn is in front of the lighthouse and we advise you not stand there when it sounds—it will make your head ring.

The park is a dramatic place to watch storms in the Strait. When a gale is blowing, armies of breaking seas assault Iceberg Point and Long Island off Lopez to smash into the narrows of Cattle Pass. It's even more dramatic if the wind is against an ebb tide. Spume-crested waves 10 to 12 feet high stand briefly suspended in the roiling storm, and huge logs are tossed about like toothpicks onto the beach.

❧ **Public beach** surrounds Cattle Point from Eagle Cove on the Strait, east around the point and into Griffin Bay to about 1,000 yards south of Low Point. Almost all of this shoreline is part of San Juan Island National Historical Park. This means we can go ashore, walk the beaches and uplands in this terrific park. *(We do not advise going ashore or in to private moorages or on posted beaches.)*

Aid to Navigation, Circa 1920

Visible from the water is the old buff-colored, cinder-block building atop a rocky promontory at Cattle Point DNR park, all that remains of a wireless station manned by the U.S. Navy in the 1920s. The building housed the station power plant. Around 1921, mariners in these waters began benefitting from the newly-developed radio direction finders. Unlike the lighthouse, this aid could be used during the thickest fogs. Two or three strategically located stations were needed to fix the position of a ship, and throughout the 1920s Cattle Point served as one of these stations.

Here's how it worked: A mariner somewhere in the Strait of Juan de Fuca who needed help would send a Morse Code "QTE," meaning "What is my true bearing?" The Cattle Point operator then took a bearing on the call using a loop antenna mounted on an azimuth compass. The bearing was then radioed back to the ship's navigator. Additional bearings from two other stations at Smith Island and New Dungeness fixed the ship's position.

Later this process was revised and the land-based radio stations transmitted only continuous Morse code signals. Radio directional antennas were used aboard ships and small vessels to determine their positions, called RDF. Now modern radar and GPS electronics have replaced the radio direction finders.

⚓ **UNDERWAY AGAIN,** let's continue into Griffin Bay.

Harbor Rock, NWR, surrounded by shoals, is 100 yards off the tip of the little hook on San Juan at the north end of Cattle Pass. It is the turning point to enter Griffin Bay. We've gone between the rock and the island in about 4 fathoms. Fishing boats often cut a swath through the kelp here.

Griffin Bay is about three miles long from Harbor Rock north to Pear Point. It indents San Juan Island about 1.5 miles to the west, encompassing several charted shoals and rocks which seem to pop up in strange places when least expected. Two major parks are on the bay, San Juan Island National Historical Park's American Camp, and Griffin Bay Department of Natural Resources Campground. American Camp played a major role in the Pig War.

We explore the bay from south to north.

Fish Creek is a "non-creek" in the southeast corner of Griffin Bay, which almost bisects the end of the island. The creek was once a favored anchorage for fishers and others waiting out bad weather in the Strait of Juan de Fuca. It is now filled with private docks, boats and the homes of Cape San Juan residents.

Three [Fl Y 10 sec] flashing yellow 10 second lights on floats labeled "A," "B," "C," mark Cape San Juan Community Moorage.

Naming Cattle Point
Some 1,300 cattle and sheep were off-loaded from the British paddle-wheel freighter Beaver on December 13, 1853, in calm waters at what is now known as Cattle Point. Not to be confused with Cattle Point at Oak Bay in Victoria.

"Back Door" in Cattle Pass
If there are adverse currents in Cattle Pass, there can be a "back door" narrow pass with kelp and a charted depth of 5 feet at MLLW between Goose and San Juan islands that is sometimes ued by those with "local knowledge."

Naming San Juan Island
The island was named by Spanish explorer Francisco in 1791 as Isla y Archipielago (sic) de San Juan.

Between 1847 and 1859 it was shown as **San Juan Island** on British Admiralty charts; as **Bellevue** by the Hudson Bay Company, and **Rodgers Island** as named by Wilkes in 1841. (John Rodgers was a commodore in the U.S. Navy who commanded the "President" in the battle with "Little Belt" in 1811.)

Griffin Bay and San Juan Channel were named **Ontario Roads** by Wilkes in 1841. The name was for Lake Ontario where Captain Isaac Chauncey of the U.S. Navy served during the War of 1812.

Griffin Bay got its present name in an 1858 U.S. survey for Charles John Griffin, manager of the Hudson Bay Co. farm and fishing station near Cattle Point in the 1850s. The other names were never accepted by other cartographers. Griffin was held in high esteem by Englishmen, Americans and Indians.

San Juan was the name printed on British Admiralty charts of the area from 1859 through 1865, and it has remained ever since.

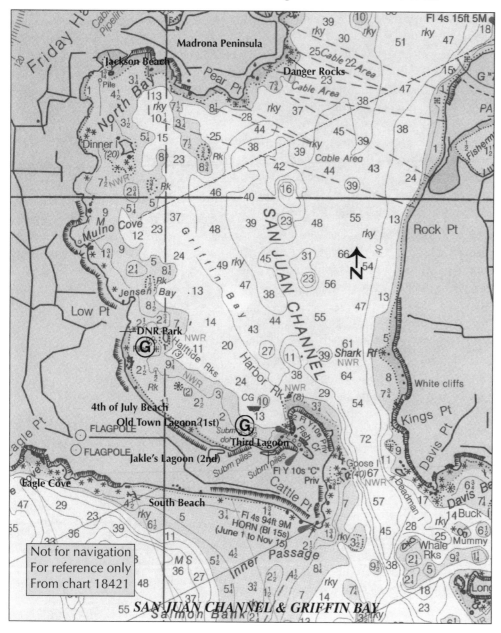

SAN JUAN CHANNEL & GRIFFIN BAY

Not for navigation
For reference only
From chart 18421

During the commercial fishing season large fish-buying barges, gillnetters and purse seiners anchor in the sheltered waters off the creek.

AMERICAN CAMP

American Camp covers 1,223 acres and 4.25 miles of shoreline at the southeast end of San Juan Island. The shoreline includes about 2.5 miles along South Beach on the Strait of Juan de Fuca, and just under 2 miles on the Griffin Bay side. No overnight camping is allowed in the park. Much of the park land is barren and wind-swept, especially on the south side facing the Strait. Some forested areas line Griffin Bay, and this is a marvelous place to see a variety of wildlife: eagles, herons, other birds, deer, rabbits, wild turkeys and perhaps a red fox at dusk or dawn.

The national historic park of American Camp commemorates the site of the encampment of American troops during the Pig War with England which took place between 1859 and 1872. While termed a "war," the only fatality was a pig, and the dispute was settled when a boundary was finalized between British Columbia and the U.S. after 13 years of joint occupation of San Juan Island by both countries.

National Wildlife Refuge

Many rocks and islands off San Juan Island are part of the San Juan Islands National Wildlife Refuge and Wilderness Area— NWR.

Mariners must stay 200 yards away from these rocks and islands. All refuge islands are closed to public access except Matia and Turn islands.

The Pig War

Now for San Juan Island's Pig War, "the war that wasn't." In the 1850s both British and American settlers were living on San Juan Island, but nobody knew which country owned the island. The Oregon Treaty of 1846 gave the U.S. undisputed possession of the Pacific Northwest south of the 49th parallel, with the boundary west "to the middle of the channel separating the continent from Vancouver's Island; and thence southerly through the middle of said channel, and of Fuca's straits to the Pacific Ocean."

But nobody knew which channel was "the channel" separating British-owned Vancouver Island from the U.S. mainland. Britain insisted the boundary ran through Rosario Strait, which would give all the San Juan Islands to the British. The Americans said the boundary was Haro Strait, which would give the islands to the U.S.

The British had a toehold on San Juan when the Hudson Bay Company

(HBC) established a salmon-curing station at Fish Creek in 1851, and later started a sheep ranch on the southeast end of the island.

By 1859, 25 Americans were settle on government claims, which the British considered illegal.

On the fateful morning of June 15, 1859, Lyman Cutlar, a Kentucky frontiersman-turned-settler, woke up to find a big pig rooting up his newly planted potatoes, and not for the first time. Cutlar grabbed his shotgun and with a blast, sent the pig to hog heaven. Unfortunately, the pig belonged to the Hudson Bay manager.

It turned into an immediate international crisis which set off enormous military build-ups by both sides. By August, 461 Americans were protected by the quickly built earthen redoubt (still standing) and 14 cannons. The redoubt, built on "the very apex of the slope," was promptly dubbed "Robert's Gopher Hole" after supervising engineer, Lt. Henry M. Robert.

Three British warships with troops sailed into Griffin Bay, ready for action. Capt. George E. Pickett ("Pickett's Charge" of Civil War fame) refused to withdraw even though he was outnumbered as the situation escalated and tempers flared. Robert L. Baynes, commander of British naval forces in the Pacific, was utterly appalled at the situation. He advised Gov. James Douglas in Victoria in no uncertain terms that he would not "involve two great nations in a war over a squabble about a pig."

Both sides backed off and matters went from boiling to simmering. The British Royal Marines set up camp on Garrison Bay on the island's northwest coast as the Americans stayed at the southeast end, the beginning of a 13 year joint military occupation of the island. Over time, men from both camps became friends and got together for horse races, parties and other social events. The "military road" across the island from one camp to the other was often used for social rather than military purposes.

Because of the joint occupation, land on the island could not be homesteaded and the most a settler could hope for was "squatter's rights."

In 1871, the U.S. and Great Britain signed the "Treaty of Washington" and the San Juan question was referred to Kaiser Wilhelm I of Germany.

On October 21, 1872, the Kaiser ruled in favor of the U.S., establishing the international boundary line through Haro Strait. San Juan Island officially became part of the United States. The Royal Marines withdrew in 1872 and American soldiers departed in 1874.

Peace was established without a battle, the only casualty was a pig.

(As we continue around the island we'll visit English Camp on Garrison Bay, pages 30-32. There's even more about the war and island history in our book titled **San Juan, the Pig War Island.***)*

Too many stolen spuds

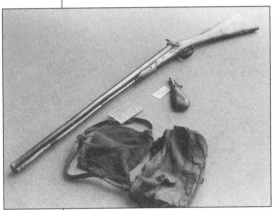
Gun that shot the pig

"Sleazy" San Juan Town

When two members of the U.S. Boundary Commission toured the islands in January 1860 to sort out the ambiguities in the Treaty of 1846, they were not impressed with San Juan Town on Old Town Lagoon.

"There are about 20 houses, one of them is occupied by a store keeper who keeps an exceedingly limited supply of goods; five or six are 'rum mills,' and the rest are vacant.

"The population of the place numbers about 30 or 40, the number being made up of ... white men, Chinamen and Indians. Whiskey drinking seems to be the principal occupation. There were not more than half a dozen respectable Americans in the place," wrote W.I. Warren.

🌸 **San Juan National Park** extends about two miles from Third Lagoon at its east end to about one mile south of Low Point at the northwest end. On the strait side the park runs from Eagle Cove to about 0.5 mile west of Cattle Point.

Griffin Bay is a great place to row ashore and spend time. Wear comfortable walking shoes, as there is much to see, with miles of trails and beaches to walk. The three lagoons in the park are not named on the charts but a park map calls them First, Second and Third Lagoons. We'll start at Third Lagoon and go west.

Looking east from across San Juan Channel to Mount Baker

Jakle's Lagoon

This is a low salt marsh, dominated by pickleweed, fleshy jaumea, salt-marsh sands-purry, and saltweed or fat hen.

As elevation increases, the salt marsh transitions to grasses, then to the bronze tops of Baltic Rush. Swamp rose begins at the upper edge of Baltic rush and gives way to upland grasses and forbs in the meadows above the lagoon. Snowberry and wild rose mix in large drifts on the hillsides south of the lagoon.

Mount Finlayson

The 290 foot hill near where Capt. George Pickett established American Camp, was named after Roderick Finlayson, one of the founders of Victoria and chief factor with Hudson Bay Co.

Robert's Rules of Order

*Lt. Henry M. Robert, later General Robert, left his mark on the world in 1876 when he created **Robert's Rules of Order,** a manual of parliamentary procedure. The book, which has gone through more than 30 printings, is still referenced by organizations in how to run their meetings successfully.*

Third Lagoon is the farthest east, nearest Fish Creek. "Submerged piles" are charted here. Trails from the beach lead south around Mount Finlayson, and west along an old road to the middle lagoon. It's an easy walk to the top of the 290 foot hill covered with scrub and grasses. On a clear day you can see east to Mount Baker, southeast to Mount Rainier, south across the Strait of Juan de Fuca to the Olympic Mountains, and west to Vancouver Island.

⚓ **Anchoring** is good in the southeast part of the bay in 2 to 5 fathoms with sand or mud bottom. It's well protected, except during winds from north to east.

Ⓖ It's a good **gunkhole,** depending on weather.

Jakle's Lagoon (Second Lagoon) is the middle lagoon in a wooded area which shelters deer and many birds, including raptors. Trails lead from here to the Mount Finlayson trail and to both other lagoons. It is a peaceful, lovely stop.

Old Town Lagoon (First Lagoon) is where old San Juan Town once stood. The town was the hub of the south end of the island in early days, when locals traded at the Katz Store. San Juan Island pioneer, Etta Egeland, born in 1897, said her aunt shopped at Katz's Store in Old Town.

"Previous to the big 1890 fire, the store and post office were on the right side of the lagoon, which is now filled up with driftwood. I did have the privilege of being entertained one time in Mr. Katz's very lovely home," she said.

Fourth of July Beach, west of First Lagoon, has a picnic ground, privy and beach. Small beach fires are allowed, but they must be five feet below the driftwood line.

For those energetic souls who love to walk, we suggest walking from the parking area near Old Town Lagoon to Pickett's Lane across to South Beach on the Strait, the longest public beach on San Juan Island at 2.5 miles. A multitude of shore birds frequent the incredible beach: terns, gulls, greater and lesser yellowlegs, plovers and bald eagles. If you're lucky you may see a pod of whales swim past. Tidal pools abound

Pioneer Etta Egeland

where rocks reach the beach near the park's west end. A privy and several picnic tables are at South Beach. It's a fantastic area for beachcombing, as heavy surf from the Strait washes all kinds of treasures ashore.

American Camp Visitors' Center and several other buildings are west of Pickett's Lane. The redoubt overlooks the entire area. A self-guiding interpretive trail leads through most of the sites of interest, including former officer's quarters, laundress's quarters and the Bellevue Farm (HBC) site.

The park is open year-round. From mid-June through Labor Day some park employees and volunteers dress in period clothes and demonstrate aspects of the life of American soldiers who occupied the site from 1859 to 1872. Tide pool walks and other programs are also scheduled.

A park map and guide can be picked up at the park office in Friday Harbor as well as at American and English camps, urges safety and stresses "visitors should exercise caution and common sense at all times. Look out for insecure footing on primitive trails and watch for overhanging branches and downed limbs." It advises that tree-climbing is dangerous and harmful for the trees. It also notes that rabbits have dug many holes in American Camp and stepping in one can be hazardous. Swimming isn't recommended at South Beach because of the cold water and strong currents.

Windswept American Camp

UNDERWAY AGAIN from Fourth of July Beach, we follow the shoreline west and then north, staying outside the 10 fathom curve, avoiding the rocks and shoals. This is a rather messy area, and should be navigated with care.

North Pacific Rock, NWR, is 600 yards off the beach at Old Town Lagoon, and within the 5 fathom curve. A 3 foot shoal is almost 600 yards due east of North Pacific Rock inside the 10 fathom curve. Another rock which bares at 4 feet is 500 yards northwest of North Pacific Rock inside the 5 fathom curve. The chart should help make this a bit less confusing, but as we said, it's messy.

Halftide Rocks, NWR, are 0.5 mile north of North Pacific Rock, and they are ugly. We saw them poking their ridges above the surface about 800 yards offshore. "Foul piling" are charted halfway between the rocks and shore.

GRIFFIN BAY DNR CAMPGROUND

This campsite is inshore of Halftide Rocks. Many recreational mariners in larger boats don't try to go here because of shallow water, making it ideal for small boats, kayaks and those who feel adventurous and want to get away from the crowds. We've gone in slowly, keeping well away from either side of Half Tide Rocks and the foul pilings, with the depth sounder on and a bow watch.

This park is a "boat-in-only" site that was built in 1984 after DNR assured neighbors on either side of the fenced campground that they wouldn't be bothered by campers. You can spot the DNR sign on shore as you approach. Mount Baker peeks over Lopez Island and all of San Juan Channel is there to be enjoyed. Sunrises are spectacular at Griffin Bay Park.

The park is well used by guided kayak tours out of Friday Harbor. It's on low bank waterfront with a lovely gravel beach that's good for beachcombing, playing and a great place for kids to run off steam.

Anchoring is possible in 2 fathoms in soft bottom.

(G) And yes, it's a **gunkhole** for some boats.

Griffin Bay Beaches

Some beautiful beaches line Griffin Bay, and many are public DNR lands, which means they can be visited below the high tide line if not otherwise posted or noted in the quad map.

North Pacific Rock

The rock was named after a steamer of the same name that struck it in the late 1800s.

Inhumane Smugglers

*Bryce Wood, former Friday Harbor resident and author of **San Juan Island—Coastal Place Names**, tells the tale of a smuggler who left some Chinese laborers "temporarily" on a rock in San Juan Channel as the "Feds" hunted for him.*

The hapless Asians were found much later, near starvation, apparently existing only on clams on a reef then named China Rock.

Wood, who meticulously researched his book, identifies the reef as "probably Halftide Rocks near the south end of Griffin Bay."

Naming Low Point

Rocky Low Point was named by the British. It faced the north end of the anchorage at the Hudson Bay Co. pier.

Naming Dinner Island

There are two theories on how the island got its name.

It may have been named by an early owner who swapped it for a meal in a Friday Harbor restaurant.

The more probable reason for the name is that members of a party from a British vessel landed on the rock and ate their dinner.

➡ **NOTE:** Fisherman Bay Sector Light dashed line discrepancy as charted on 18423 (1994) and 18434 (1996), shows the west sector line coincidentally intersecting a 5 foot rock shoal in Griffin Bay bearing 070°T to the light.

Light List (1999) #19560 indicates this sector line bearing to the light is 064°T as it is charted on 18400 (1997), 18421 (1998) and 18430 (1996). We believe this red sector line was intended only to keep traffic clear of Fisherman Bay peninsula rocks and shoals.

Note at 064° this dashed sector line passes about 500 yards south of the Griffin Bay Rock.

(See p. 50 for sector line discrepancy involving Lopez Rocks.)

Old Argyle

Argyle was named by the first white man to build in the area, a Scot named McDonald, who named the area after his home county. A post office was established at Argyle in 1873, and the name was changed to San Juan. The name reverted to Argyle in 1886 because the local folks always called it that.

⚙ **UNDERWAY AGAIN,** and we finish our tour of Griffin Bay.

Low Point, with its long spit and shoal beaches, is about 600 yards north of Griffin Bay DNR Park. Cruising along this shore it makes sense to stay outside the 10 fathom depth curve. There's just 4 feet of water over a charted rock 0.2 mile northeast of the point. A fair number of rocks line this area.

Jensen Bay, Mulno Cove and **Merrifield Cove** were all named after people who once owned the adjoining uplands.

Dinner Island is a jewel, 500 yards east of San Juan Island. The privately owned nine acre island is surrounded by shoals, especially off the south side. Some of the rocks around Dinner Island have their own names, given by locals: "Snack," "Tidbit," "Lunch," and "Supper" rocks.

Argyle is next, a small peninsula that was an established town during the 1870s with a post office and dock where steamers from Seattle and Port Townsend stopped. It's now residential. Shoal rocks are south of Argyle and west of Dinner Island.

North Bay includes the north part of Griffin Bay and goes all the way to Pear Point. Dominating the northwest corner of North Bay is the huge Friday Harbor Sand and Gravel Company. There is a large barge-loading dock along the shore. The peninsula, which includes Pear Point north and west around to Brown Island, is known locally as Madrona Peninsula, but the name is not charted.

Little Island at the end of Jackson Beach isn't an island, although it may have been one at one time. It is the location of the large J.J. Theodore Fish Cannery on the end of a spit.

Launch ramp, owned by the Port of Friday Harbor, is just north of the cannery on the inside of the spit. A large, fenced-off tide pool north of the cannery on the west side of the spit is a U.W. Biological Preserve.

🌿 **Jackson Beach,** unnamed on charts, is below the gravel company on the sandspit. This lovely bit of driftwood-covered beach, owned by the Port of Friday Harbor, is open to the public for picnicking, beachcombing, swimming, sunbathing and volleyball. A large private mooring buoy is off Jackson Beach. Picnic tables, privies and a volleyball net make this a popular local beach.

⚓ **Anchoring** is possible near Jackson Beach in 3 to 4 fathoms, rocky bottom. This is a weather-dependent anchorage and there is no protection from strong southerlies that may sweep up San Juan Channel. It's an okay anchorage in the daytime, but we wouldn't want to overnight here. Winds get too "iffy" this close to the Strait.

Cable areas from San Juan to Lopez are in North Bay and around Pear Point.

Continuing east around Madrona Peninsula, we pass many homes built among the trees as we pass the point. Between Pear Point and Danger Rock the shores are jumbled with rocks, for more than 0.1 mile offshore.

Danger Rock and its charted "foul shoal" extend 0.2 mile offshore.

Reef Point, NWR, about 0.4 mile north of Danger Rock, is mean. Waves have created threatening rocks and reefs off the point which are sometimes visible. We stay well outside the 20 to 30 fathom depth curve, just to be on the safe side.

Turn Rock, NWR, about 0.2 mile east of Turn Island, is a ledge about 100 yards across which bares at half tide, and we keep at least 100 yards off.

Turn Rock Light [Fl G 4s 18ft 6M "3"] a flashing green 4 second light 18 feet high visible 6 miles, is on a square green dayboard on the rock. This is a major navigation aid in San Juan Channel. The channel turns northwest here.

Currents around the Turn Rock area are very strong. Based on predictions at the south end of San Juan Channel, the currents here may be up to half the velocity of those predictions, or 2.5 knots, often much more. Flood current runs northwest up San Juan Channel, ebb current flows southeast. Backeddies can be helpful here.

TURN ISLAND MARINE STATE PARK

A favorite with local boaters, this island is another wonderful state marine park, just outside of Friday Harbor. On the chart it looks as though the island separated itself from San Juan Island like a perfect puzzle piece.

Turn was initially established by U.S. Fish and Wildlife Services as a game refuge. Since 1959, Washington State Parks has managed it for recreational use.

The main beach inshore of the three buoys has five campsites, picnic areas, firepits and privies. Two more campsites are on a beautiful beach on the low south point of the island, an area kayakers enjoy. The other campsites are above the gravel beach inside the tiny charted islet, which is joined by a tombolo to Turn Island at low tide.

Trails circle the island. On the eastern and north shores the paths are high and rocky with almost no beaches or paths to the water. The southeast end offers stunning views south down San Juan Channel. The center of the island is heavily forested with a 100 foot hill in the center. Cross-island trails offer glimpses of wildlife, including many different sea birds, raccoons, squirrels, rabbits and an occasional deer.

Massive shoulders of rock jut out of the ground. On the low hill above the buoy area are giant rounded rocks that look strangely out of place. They are smooth, as if they tumbled for some distance to wear off their edges. The result of glacial movements many millennia ago?

⚓ We consider anchoring here on a short-term basis only, because of the rocky bottom and strong currents. The three buoys here are often taken by early afternoon in summer in this popular park.

Ⓖ This is a great **gunkhole**, but be aware of currents.

Turn Island

Turn Island Marine State Park Facilities
➤ 35 acres, three miles of shoreline
➤ Three mooring buoys, $5 night
➤ Moorage limited to 3 consecutive nights
➤ Three miles of trails
➤ 10 campsites, picnic tables, fire pits, toilets, no water
➤ Activities: picnic, camp, fish, clam, scuba dive, hike, swim (brrr), enjoy

There is plenty of water around Turn Island, 5 to 8 fathoms, although there are shoals off the south and west shores which should be given wide berth. At minus tides this is a tremendous place to beachcomb and gather shellfish.

A pretty little bay between Turn and San Juan islands has a number of homes and boats on mooring buoys off San Juan. Turn Point road-end on San Juan, about 0.2 mile south of the charted flagpole, is a favorite place to launch kayaks and paddle the 0.2 mile across the water to Turn Island.

Merrifield Bay

It was named about 1875 for William Merrifield, probably an early settler. A USGS report stated the bay "affords summer anchorage for small craft."

Not Point Salsbury

Turn Island was originally mapped as a point of land on San Juan Island by the Wilkes Expedition in 1841 and was named Point Salsbury.

The island marked the need for vessels to make a fairly sharp change of course in navigating San Juan Channel.

Naming Brown Island

Naming Brown Island

The island was named by the Wilkes expedition in 1841 for John G. Brown, the mathematical instrument maker on the Vincennes, one of the expedition ships.

When developers bought Brown Island they changed the named to Friday Island, but it never took hold.

⚓ **UNDERWAY AGAIN,** we're bound for Friday Harbor.

Minnesota Reef, unnamed on charts, is a nasty reef with unforgiving jagged rocks ready to snag any who get too close. It's just a bit over 0.6 mile west of Turn Island on the north shore of San Juan Island and about 0.4 mile east of Brown Island. The reef is listed as #19595 in the *Light List*.

Minnesota Reef Daybeacon [G Bn Ra Ref] square green daybeacon with a radar reflector on a pile marks the reef.

Reid Rock Lighted Bell Buoy [Fl (2+1) G 6s Bell] a flashing green 6 second lighted bell buoy with green and red bands, marks a rock at 2 fathoms, 2 feet, which rises abruptly from 20 fathoms. It is charted in San Juan Channel 0.7 mile east of Brown Island and 0.5 mile west of Shaw. Kelp surrounds it much of the time. Currents can be quite strong here, but they are not noted in *Tidal Current Tables*.

Reid Rock Currents

Our late friend Bryce Wood, author of *Coastal Place Names and Cartographic Nomenclature,* spent many long hours in his dory at Reid Rock, trying to understand the swirling currents around the rock. When he told NOAA of his frustrations, they told him they had done the same thing and even with sophisticated instrumentation, couldn't predict currents at the rock.

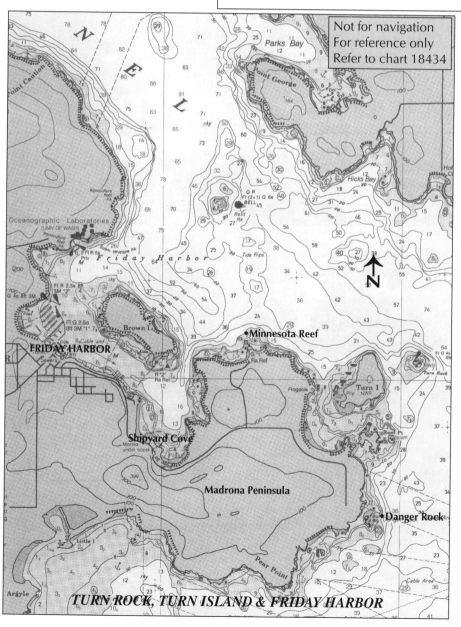

Not for navigation
For reference only
Refer to chart 18434

TURN ROCK, TURN ISLAND & FRIDAY HARBOR

Brown Island, private, tree covered and all residential, is about 0.5 mile long and about 0.24 mile wide, and forms the east shore of Friday Harbor.

The names get a little confusing here because there's the Town of Friday Harbor, the Port of Friday Harbor and the Harbor of Friday Harbor.

Harbor of Friday Harbor, between San Juan and Brown islands, is irregularly-shaped, about 1.25 miles long and about 0.25 mile wide.

A quick orientation of the harbor with its two entrances from San Juan Channel around the northwest or southeast ends of Brown Island.

U.W. Oceanographic Labs are on San Juan north of Brown Island.

Port of Friday Harbor Marina is on San Juan due west of the northwest end of Brown.

Washington State Ferry piers are charted just south of the marina.

Shipyard Cove, unnamed on charts, is the large cove at the harbor's south end.

Northwest Entrance is 650 yards wide shore to shore, the larger of the two.

Channel widths between the charted 3 fathom depth curves of San Juan and Brown is about 450 yards. This is reassuring when encountering ferries and other traffic.

Channel depths range from 30 fathoms at the entrance to about 8 fathoms east of the marina.

A charted 1 fathom, 3 foot shoal extending about 150 yards northwest of Brown Island is shown on 18434 (1996). The above shoal is in the vicinity of a 4 foot rocky shoal still charted on 18423 (1994). We believe the 4 foot shoal was removed in the mid-1980s.

Northwest Entrance Navigation Aids:

We start with the seaplane operation aids which are unique with this area and not otherwise common to cruising in general.

Quick Flashing Yellow Lights

QY displays are at three fixed locations in the harbor. They can be activated by one or more pilots during seaplane operations to alert mariners in the harbor of the approaching planes which are merging with vessel traffic in this often congested area.

QY lights fixed locations are at:
• UW Oceanographic Labs pier on San Juan
• North end of Brown Island on a small pier
• Marina north breakwater float near the flashing red entrance light "2."

Since their installation the QY displays have not been charted and have never been assigned their own *Light List* numbers describing their location or purpose. Hopefully this will happen in the near future plus suitable charted notations explaining their use and how they function.

Pilots activate the quick flashing yellow lights at all three locations simultaneously using a radio controlled signal. Duration of the QY flashing mode is about 1-1/2 minutes and can be extended at the pilot's discretion.

If any of the displays are flashing, mariners should assume seaplanes are active in the vicinity. The displays do not indicate the plane's location or final destination in the harbor.

Two [Fl R 5s] flashing 5 second red pier lights on piles are at the UW Labs.

Navigation Aids at the Port Of Friday Harbor Marina

Three aids are at the outer ends of two long, angled breakwater floats at the marina's north end, marking entrances to inside guest and permanent moorage.

North Breakwater Light [Fl G 4s 8ft 3M] flashing green 4 second light 8 feet high visible 3 miles, is on a square green dayboard on a pedestal at the northwest end of the north breakwater float at a narrow entrance to floats on the northwest side of the marina.

Marina Entrance Light 2 [Fl R 2.5s 8ft 3M "2"] flashing red 2.5 second light 8 feet high visible 3 miles, is on a triangular red dayboard on a pile on the southeast end of the north breakwater float at the central entrance.

Marina Entrance Light 1 [FL G 2.5s 8ft 3M "1"] flashing green 2.5 second light 8 feet high visible 3 miles, is on a square green dayboard on a pile on the north end of the south breakwater float at this central marina entrance.

Southeast Entrance to Friday Harbor by way of Shipyard Cove is the lesser used of the

Friday Harbor's Loss

Brown Island was offered to Friday Harbor by the owners for $25,000 decades ago. Town fathers turned it down, as there was no water supply on the island and they figured nobody would ever want to live there.

Now the residential 60 acre island with lovely homes on large lots gets water piped over from Friday Harbor and has about one mile of road. There's a community dock, swimming pool, tennis courts, volunteer fire department—and $25,000 today won't come close to buying anything on the island.

An island legend claims that during Prohibition speakeasies in Friday Harbor kept their booze hidden somewhere on Brown. Twice daily bartenders rowed to the small island and picked up their "supplies."

➡ **NOTE:** There is no public moorage or access at the UW Labs floats. In previous years they were open to the public for educational purposes.

Friday Harbor

Naming Friday Harbor

There are several different versions about the naming of the town.

*One is that a Kanaka (Hawaiian) sheepherder in the harbor spoke little English. When he was asked what **bay** it was, he misunderstood, thought he was asked what **day** it was, and replied "Friday."*

Another story is the Kanaka thought he was asked his name, and answered "Friday."

➡**NOTE:** When anchoring in Friday Harbor be aware of:
- Cables and pipelines
- Heavy vessel & ferry traffic
- Vessels should not anchor within 100 yards of marina floating breakwater because of danger of fouling anchor cables. *(Coast Pilot)*
- Ferry propellors thrust strong currents seaward while loading and unloading which can be potentially dangerous to small craft.
- Arriving ferries sound one long and two short blasts. Departing ferries sound one long blast, theoretically.

---

two channels, and is 200 yard wide shore-to-shore.

Channel width is about 150 yards between the 3 fathom depth curves of San Juan and Brown islands.

Channel depths of 20 fathoms extends a short distance into the cove. A rocky point is off San Juan and we favor the center of the channel.

Southeast Entrance Navigation Aids

The only charted aid besides Minnesota Reef daybeacon outside this entrance is on a shoal 100 yards south of Brown Island inside the entrance.

Brown Island Daybeacon [R "2" Ra Ref] is a triangular red dayboard on a multi-pile structure with a radar reflector marking a large shoal off the island's south shore. At low tide the shoal it guards may be visible. We stay south of it and round the island off the southern tip. A small marina for Brown Island residents is on the southwest side of the island.

We've now negotiated both entrances into the harbor of Friday Harbor, and before jumping ship and going ashore let's take a quick look at some harbor options and concerns.

Shipyard Cove Marina and **Jensen's Shipyard** are on pages 16 and 17.

Harbor depths are fairly constant at 6 to 8 fathoms, except in the south end where they reach 18 fathoms.

Currents in the harbor are estimated at one knot.

Cable and pipeline area between Brown and San Juan islands is signed and charted for about 500 yards northwest from the south end of Brown Island. Boats anchored in this area risk fouling their anchors on cables and pipelines unless they have extraordinary local knowledge, or an underwater metal detector.

⚓ **Anchoring** is possible in some places in the harbor of Friday Harbor, although it may be crowded. Holding ground is good with mud bottom.

Beaverton Bay, a small bay in the cove west of the Labs and north of the port marina, is used as an anchorage by some boats. The bottom is covered with eel grass and other slippery stuff on which the anchor can slide; it's less than 3 fathoms deep, and is vulnerable to wake from ferries and other vessels.

Shipyard Cove has some anchorage, but finding a spot between 5 and 10 fathoms may be difficult in summer when many boats are hunting for an anchorage. Those anchoring in the cove need to allow room for boats using south end marinas.

Launch ramp is in the cove immediately south and adjacent to Shipyard Cove Marina slips. Fee is five dollars each way.

Several private piers and floats are between the south end of the harbor and the ferry landing, including a Seattle Yacht Club outstation.

Capron's Landing has some transient moorage, Tel.: 360-378-4581.

Spring Street Landing, where tour boats dock, is west of the ferry dock.

The fuel float is next, and after that the marina.

Port of Friday Harbor

Port Of Friday Harbor Marina

The port has moorage for both recreational and commercial vessels.

Enter the marina between the north (BW-A) and south (BW-B) breakwaters or between the fuel dock and the west end of the south breakwater (BW-D). Visitors can tie temporarily on the inside or outside of the breakwaters and check with the harbormasters for a slip assignment.

Friday Harbor Facilities

➤ Guest moorage for at least 150 transient boats:
  • on "G" dock
  • inside "H" dock
  • north side "B" dock
  • foot of "C" dock
  • inside breakwaters B, C, D
  • outside breakwaters A, B, D
➤ Moorage rates:
  • May 1-June 30, 65¢ foot
  • July 1-Sept 30; 75¢ foot
  • Oct. 1-April 30, 55¢ foot
  • $1/foot reservation charge
➤ 30 amp power, 10¢ foot; water
➤ Fuel dock: gas, diesel, propane
➤ Restrooms, showers, laundry nearby
➤ Pumpout & porta-potty dump, garbage & recycling
➤ Marina office & Customs port-of-entry office at head of dock
➤ Fresh seafood market, fishing gear, bait on dock; scuba air
➤ San Juan Island Yacht Club moorage for members of reciprocal yacht clubs
➤ Nearby boat repair service, Jensen's shipyard; San Juan Canvas sail loft
➤ Sea plane terminal
➤ Nearby: tennis courts, picnic areas, launch ramp at Jackson Beach
➤ Monitors VHF Channel 66A
➤ Harbormasters: Tami Hayes/Ed Barrett
➤ Tel.: 360-378-2688/FAX: 360-378-6114
➤ Address: P.O. Box 889, Friday Harbor, WA 98250

PORT OF FRIDAY HARBOR MARINA

Entrance
BW-A
Entrance
H
G
F
E
C
BW-B
Seaplane dock
Main Float
BW-C
K
BW-D
Pump Out
L
Entrance
Spring St. Landing
Fuel Dock
Ferry Dock
B
W
Customs Office
BW=Breakwater
Port Office

Growing Town

Over 1,800 full time residents lived in Friday Harbor in 1995, the latest year there were population figures.

TOWN of FRIDAY HARBOR

The crowded shores of Friday Harbor are covered with homes, condos and moorages as we approach "downtown." In the summer especially, ferries seem to be constantly coming and going.

Friday Harbor is a wonderful place to visit, especially if you're from a big city. While Friday Harbor is "urban" for the San Juans, it's small-town friendly to visitors. Not only that, you can find everything you want here, plus some things you didn't even know you needed. It's easy walking everywhere within the town itself, making it great for families. There are restaurants, markets, gift shops, book stores, churches, marine stores, hardware stores, yarn shops, wine stores, galleries with local jewelry and paintings, and a movie theater with several first run shows.

What else to do and see in town? We'll share a couple of our favorite places. We suggest a visit to **Driftwood Drive-In**, the hub for locals, where we love to "drift in" because we usually find old friends there. It's not a drive-in, but it's the coffee stop for just about everyone, and their burgers are awesome.

The other "must-see" place is **Herb's Tavern**. It's been in existence forever, and you'll catch a lot of "local color." There are many other enjoyable restaurants and watering holes in town—try them!

You can rent cars, mopeds, bicycles, or take a tour bus around the island.

Friday Harbor Jazz Festival is in July and the **San Juan County Fair** is in August, with many other happenings all year round. There's also a community theater, health club with indoor swimming pool, golf course, medical and dental ser-

"Popeye," Friday Harbor's friendly seal

Watch the Whales

There are a variety of whale watching tours in the San Juans. San Juan Island Chamber of Commerce has brochures for whale tours with many departing from Friday Harbor.

San Juan Historical Museum

vices, U.W. Lab, veterinarians, state liquor store and real estate offices.

The Whale Museum is an absolute must if you have children, or even if you don't. There are displays and exhibits which depict the world of whales in photos, glass, stone, wood and bone. It's a center for environmental education and marine research, exciting to kids and adults. Educational programs let the public into the lives of the world's whales with workshops and publications which include *Gentle Giants of the Sea* for children in grades K-6. Research includes field studies investigating the natural history of local species. Sound-Watch program educates about effects people may have on resident orcas. It's a fabulous place.

The delightful **San Juan Historical Museum** is in the James King farmhouse, built in the late 1800s, a marvelous step back in time to experience island life as it was at the turn-of-the-century. The museum is the most northwestern in the continental U.S. The complex includes the original farmhouse, the first county jail, old log cabin, barn, milk house and carriage house. Each room is full of displays, photographs, authentic furnishings and memorabilia, and is important to those interested in local history, genealogy and researchers. It's an easy walk from the port docks or the ferry landing up Spring Street, and is worth the visit, especially for history buffs.

That's some of the fun and the reason we're here: to experience the ambiance of a small, friendly town with so many of the amenities of a large city—a town that depends on tourism, even though it sometimes wishes it didn't.

Shipyard Cove—South End Of Friday Harbor

The cove has long been home to shipyards and marinas.

Nourdine Jensen

Jensen's—the Legendary Shipyard

Albert Jensen & Sons Shipyard, the legendary yard thriving for close to a century, is in the cove. Son Nourdine Jensen runs the yard as he has for many years, and we visited with him.

"Dad moved to the island in 1910, had a mill in downtown Friday Harbor, and later moved here to the cove," Nourdine told us. "The yard built custom wooden boats, but now we're repairing boats, not building them."

The full service yard has a travel lift, machine shop and prop shop. They rebuild and repair engines, do woodworking and welding. The yard is not fancy, parts of it even a bit ramshackle, but Nourdine loves it the way it is, and so do islanders. Born in 1914, this legendary boat builder still puts in full days at the yard, although he now has others who help manage the place. When you're in the islands and need some work done on your boat, or want to do it yourself, check out Jensen's Shipyard. They have permanent moorage, but no transient tie-up space.

The yard was famous for the boats it built back in the early days, passenger and freight steamers, workboats, fishboats, and occasionally a classic yacht. Many of the boats are still plying northwest waters.

From World War II until about 1980, the yard turned out about 300 vessels. Some were designed by Nourdine's brother Ben, a naval architect, some were designed by well known northwest naval architects H.C. Hansen, Bill Garden and Ed Monk Sr., and some were designed by a "committee" of Nourdine and shipyard workers. Jensen's yard was among the first to introduce the trawler-type boat, good for fishing, recreation and transportation. The walls of Nourdine's office are covered with photos of Jensen boats.

One of Jensen's best known boats was built in 1912, the 80 foot cannery tender, *Neried.* She worked in the fish business for 82 years, and would have continued another 82 if she hadn't been lost off Alaska coast in 1994.

San Juan Sand and Gravel is behind the shipyard. We mentioned it earlier when we were in North Bay as it runs between North Bay and Friday Harbor. The mountain of gravel is being steadily reduced and barged off the island, most of it to British Columbia. The British may have lost the island to the Americans after the Pig War, but they're buying it back, rock by rock.

Shipyard Cove Marina is immediately west of Jensen's, an all private marina with no guest moorage.

Jensen Shipyard

A Bit Of San Juan Island History

Settlers, the opportunists and the losers, came to the island in the late 1850s and early 1860s for many reasons: some wanted to be where there was excitement, others were stranded after failed attempts to find the elusive gold in Fraser River valley, others were looking for work, some were hunting for a place to hide, some had jumped ship, and some were ready to get-rich-quick by supplying food and drink to the others.

The majority of the pioneers worked hard and played hard. But, there was a seamy side to island living: San Juan Island was described as the epitome of a wild and wicked western frontier town, with booze and brothels, murder and mayhem as a part of everyday life.

After the boundary decision had been finalized in 1872, San Juan Island farmers discovered their former principal market, Victoria, was not as lucrative as it had been because of duties now imposed. Islanders turned to Port Townsend and Bellingham to buy and sell. Steamer service to the island took on some regularity.

The town of Friday Harbor got off to a slow start, with competing San Juan Town and Argyle village on Griffin Bay, which both had post offices and steamer docks. These towns were far more active than Friday Harbor because they were closer to where the settlers lived.

In 1873, there were from 400 to 800 residents of newly-formed San Juan County, and Friday Harbor was destined to be the county seat. Ed Warbass, county auditor, staked out 160 acres on the shores of Friday Harbor for the new county offices.

In 1876, storekeeper Joseph Sweeney and Auditor John Bowman who replaced Warbass, bought 56 acres for 171 dollars in what later became downtown. Warbass was furious, vowed he would never live in Friday Harbor and bought 110 acres east of town called "Kwan Lama." His home was the first in the county built of sawed lumber.

In the early 1880s, Friday Harbor land finally began to sell: 20 dollars for waterfront lots and 10 dollars for any others. Businesses with back-room bars were encouraged, and Friday Harbor finally began to appeal to mainlanders. The county continued to grow and population began to climb, thanks to the many new babies being born in the islands.

Fishing was a major industry on San Juan and other islands, and a big cannery was where Cannery Landing shopping center is now. When huge amounts of fish were caught, school and businesses might close down so the whole town could assist in the canning process.

Friday Harbor fan

Jo was a liveaboard in Friday Harbor for 11 years while working as a reporter for local newspapers and as a free-lance writer, which accounts for the enthusiasm in this book about Friday Harbor—and all the islands.

Old Friday Harbor docks

Record number of salmon

Pioneer midwife Lucinda Boyce

Lucinda Boyce

One woman who was almost single-handedly responsible for getting hundreds of babies off to a good start was Lucinda Boyce, wife of the first sheriff, Stephen Boyce. Her career as a midwife began in the 1860s, and during the 57 years she lived in the islands she delivered between 500 and 600 babies, many of them born to Indian women who lived on the "outer islands." She made house calls to the other islands by boat, usually in an Indian canoe. Beryl Wade of Friday Harbor told about her grandmother whom she adored:

"She had a sense of humor that just never quit, and that was good, because Grandma had the most awful tasting potions you can imagine. For colds and congestion, there was goose grease and turpentine which was rubbed on your chest. For coughs, they put a few drops of kerosene on sugar. If you could stand it, you'd get over your cough. If there was danger of pneumonia, they slapped a mustard plaster on you.

"For measles there was sassafras tea, if you could hold it down. That was awful stuff. I remember pouring mine in the sewing machine drawer when no one was looking. For fever there was niter, which is either potassium nitrate or sodium nitrate. A good dose of salts was the cure for irregularity; harlem oil was used if you had kidney problems. Plain salt and water was for throats or bad eyes. You'd either wash your eyes or gargle, whichever was appropriate. But Grandma always had pockets in her aprons and dresses full of goodies for the children, candies and trinkets. Everyone loved her."

When Lucinda died in 1916 she left behind 10 children, 45 grandchildren, 28 great-grandchildren and a legacy of love and caring.

Before leaving Friday Harbor we need to mention a little about the fascinating complex on the north shore of the harbor, the University of Washington Oceanographic Laboratory, known locally as the Friday Harbor Labs.

University of Washington Oceanographic Laboratory

The Friday Harbor Labs were founded in 1903 by two young marine biologists, H.R. Foster and Trevor Kincaid. It was an ideal location for marine research as nearby sea depths ranged from shallow beaches to 200 fathoms, a natural laboratory just waiting for researchers.

The labs, which started out in the Friday Harbor fish cannery, has grown to nearly 500 acres on the north shore of town. It provides training for advanced students and independent researchers. Scientists and students come from practically every major university in the United States and from many universities around the world to study at the labs.

At this time they are not open to the public as they once were, although hopefully that will change, so that more people can share their findings.

UW Labs

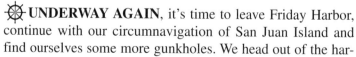

⚓ **UNDERWAY AGAIN**, it's time to leave Friday Harbor, continue with our circumnavigation of San Juan Island and find ourselves some more gunkholes. We head out of the harbor through the northwest entrance between Brown Island and the U.W. Labs, dodging ferries, tour boats, fish boats and seaplanes.

Point Caution is about 0.5 mile north of the entrance to Friday Harbor, with steep forested cliffs plunging into the sea. Currents up to 6 knots were indicated off this point in 1858. Since sailing vessels could have been carried into the cliffs as the water was too deep for anchoring, mariners were "cautioned," hence the name.

The shore from Point Caution north to Mineral Point is forested, rocky and privately owned. Bluffs rise 100 feet or more and island hills reach over 500 feet in places. There is little protection along here, although it is slightly less lumpy in a southerly blow than out in the main part of San Juan Channel. Substantial backeddies form downstream of Point Caution and other points in the channel.

Mineral Point, a small knob on San Juan Island southeast of Rocky Bay, is charted but not named. A small bay inside the point offers some protection from southerlies, but is very exposed to northerlies. Homeowners in the area often keep their boats in this bay during the summer.

Rocky Bay was obviously named for its many rocks, including an especially wicked one that bares at 4 feet about 300 yards off an unnamed point.

O'Neal Island covers 4.5 acres in Rocky Bay with rocks and shoals flanking its south shores. It was once used as a sheep range for a few weeks each year even though it has no fresh water.

Reuben Tarte County Park is on a tiny, rocky knoll about 0.5 mile north of O'Neal Island, with about 600 feet of waterfront. There is no anchorage and the knoll is surrounded by rocks. With care, kayakers can paddle in. The six acre park is a fine place for picnicking, and the view from the rocky point is magnificent. Scuba divers and birdwatchers find the area fascinating. The park is recognized from the water by the steep road that leads down to it. A portable toilet is the only facility.

Limestone Point at the northeast tip of San Juan Island is 1.2 miles north-northwest of O'Neal Island, or 0.7 mile north of Tarte Park. Charts show this northeast tip of the island with two points, one extends east into San Juan Channel. Limestone Point juts north into Spieden Channel. The 10 fathom curve around Limestone is from 200 to 400 yards offshore in places where shoals and rocks abound.

Spieden Channel, between San Juan and Spieden islands, is 0.6 mile wide and two miles long. Spieden Channel meets San Juan Channel at the east end, and Haro Strait at the west end.

Currents in Spieden are a factor to be reckoned with, especially by sailboats, slow powerboats and small boats. They're based on San Juan Channel predictions. The small print on the chart, "*Tide rips*," is scarcely adequate to describe the currents that often swirl around Limestone Point.

Flood currents average 1.8 knots and flow easterly at 085° True. The fastest predicted flood in 1999 was 3.64 knots, with six predictions of 3.5 knots or greater.

Ebb currents average 3.2 knots and flow westerly at 283° True. Fastest predicted ebb in 1999 was 5.4 knots, with 15 predictions of 5.04 knots or greater.

From Limestone Point west into Roche Harbor the shores are covered with waterfront homes with spectacular views across Spieden Channel.

Lonesome Cove is a small cove west of Limestone Point, with Lonesome Cove Resort. There are beach cabins and a pier, but moorage is for guests only.

Davison Head, a highly developed residential area, is about 1.2 miles west of Limestone Point. The outer third of the east facing cove between Davison Head and San Juan is used by residents of the area for moorage.

⚓ **Anchoring** may be possible in the cove if there is room among other anchored boats in 5 to 7 fathoms, mostly mud bottom. There is no public access.

Ⓖ This is a good **gunkhole.**

Barren Island, NWR, is west of Davison Head. The name is perfect for this absolutely barren 1.37 acre rock. It's 3 to 4 fathoms deep around the island.

Roche Harbor Junction Buoy [R G] nun buoy with red and green bands, is about 250 yards northwest of Barren Island in Spieden Channel. It marks a 1 fathom, 3 foot shoal about 300 yards east of the buoy.

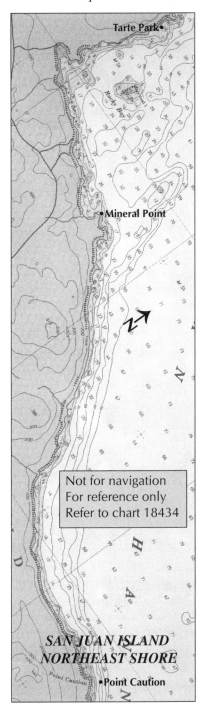

Not for navigation
For reference only
Refer to chart 18434

SAN JUAN ISLAND
NORTHEAST SHORE

Reuben Tarte Park
The park was named for the founder of Roche Harbor Resort & Marina in the early 1940s. The marina resort was originally called a Boatel.

➡ **NOTE: Time to change charts from 18434 to 18433** along the northeast shore of San Juan Island.

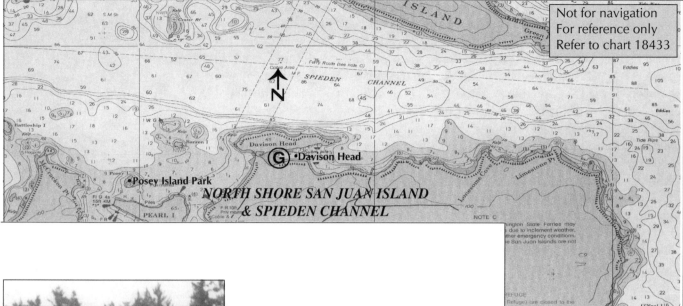

Not for navigation
For reference only
Refer to chart 18433

NORTH SHORE SAN JUAN ISLAND
& SPIEDEN CHANNEL

Non-Historic Outhouse

A wooden structure, histori-cally used as a "tidally flushed" outhouse on the west shore of Posey Island was turned down recently by the National Historic Register.

High tides and storms de-stroyed much of the structure's foundation in the winter of 1998, leaving it too unstable to use or to qualify for the historic desig-nation.

A modern composting toilet and a drainfield have been in-stalled recently.

Our cruising plan is that before entering the shelters of Roche Harbor, Westcott, Garrison and Nelson bays and Mosquito Pass via the Haro Strait-Spieden Channel "shortcut," we'll check out Posey, Pearl, Battleship and Henry islands. These islands have withstood millenniums of relentless tidal currents and the fury of storms in the Haro Strait and Spieden Channel area.

Then we'll investigate the three entrances, south around either the east or west sides Pearl Island or from the north through Mosquito Pass. The entrances are on pages 23-25, and details on the bays are on pages 25-35.

POSEY, PEARL, BATTLESHIP & HENRY ISLANDS

Posey Island, one acre in size, is a marine state park, but only for kayaks, canoes and other human-powered boats, primarily because the water surrounding the island is less than 1 fathom. It's possible to walk to Posey from Pearl Island at extreme low tides.

Posey is 0.4 mile south and west of the Roche Harbor Junction buoy, and 200 yards north of Pearl Island. The south side of this tiny island is the easiest place to land a small craft as reefs line the other shores. Sunsets from Posey are spectacular. The island use is classified as "heavy" by state parks. On an average summer weekend there are six to eight people overnight, plus another 10 for day-use. The island was first thought to be part of Pearl Island and was called either Spit or Split Point. During the Coast and Geodetic Survey they found that locals called it Posey Island as they picked wild flowers here. The name stuck and Posey it is. Several long-time San Juan islanders say they still find Easter (Avalanche or Fawn) lilies here.

Anchoring is not encouraged by State Parks in the shallows surrounding Posey.

Posey Island Marine State Park Facilities
➤ No mooring buoys, boats must be beached
➤ One acre, 1,000 feet shoreline
➤ Two picnic tables, composting toilet, fire ring, no water
➤ Sandy beaches
➤ Washington Water Trail Campsite, fees: $7 person or $20 annual pass
➤ Activities: paddle, beachcomb, camp, picnic, scuba dive, snorkel

Pearl Island forms the north shore of Roche Harbor and is covered with upscale vacation and year-round homes. It is 0.4 mile long and 0.2 mile wide. Roche Harbor can be entered either east or west of Pearl Island. *(See p. 23)*

Battleship Island, NWR, northwest of McCracken Point on Henry Island, is west of the west entrance into Roche Harbor. The 150 yard long island is one of the most aptly-named geographic features in the San Juan Archipelago. From a distance out in Spieden Channel or Haro Strait this island really does look like a battleship. Little bluffs look like superstructures and trees looks like masts. In morning and evening light, the illusion is especially dramatic.

Pearl, Homesteaded Early

The 39 acre island was homesteaded in the 1870s, but eventually became part of the Roche Harbor lime holdings.

William Pearl Chevalier is the first person known to have been born on the island, about 1895.

Pearl Island

The island was named by the Wilkes Expedition "for its shape and position."

Its shape is not round, and its position, nearly blocking the northern entrance to Roche Harbor, does not easily give credence to a pearl in an oyster.

"Battleship Ahead, Sir"

In 1904 President Theodore Roosevelt paid a visit to the Roche Harbor area. He ordered monuments to be placed at American and English camps to memorialize the two national forces contending for San Juan Island during the Pig War. He also ordered the battleship *Wyoming* to be present for the ceremony and expected a British battleship to show up.

As the *Wyoming* headed for the entrance to Roche Harbor, Cmdr. V.L. Cottman was called from his cabin by a crewman and told, "Battleship ahead, Sir."

Certain his British counterpart was arriving, the commander ordered, "Have the saluting crew go to their stations to fire a salute."

While the men waited at their cannons for the order to fire, the *Wyoming* neared the island. Only then did someone realize it was an island. Cmdr. Cottman quickly rescinded the order.

"If I had given the order to fire that salute I could never live it down for the rest of my days in the Navy—saluting an island for a battleship!" he said.

Battleship Island

Henry Island is the H-shaped, 2.5 miles long, one mile wide island separated from northwest San Juan by Mosquito Pass. The island has about 50 to 60 summer residents, and about five or six persons reside year-round. On extreme high tides, Henry is almost separated into two islands, which residents call "Little Henry" on the east side, and the much larger "Big Henry" on the west.

Nelson Bay on Henry indents from the northeast and **Open Bay** indents from the south.

McCracken Point is at the north tip of Henry with a nasty reef marked by kelp that bares at a 3 foot tide about 300 yards northwest of the point. The point is about 0.2 miles southeast of Battleship and it is possible to pass between them by staying in 7 fathoms, closer to the Battleship shore.

The west half of Henry (Big Henry) is about 2.2 miles long, from McCracken Point at the north end to Kellett Bluff at the south end. This entire west shore along Haro Strait is high and rocky with cliffs ranging from 213 feet at the north end to over 300 feet at the south and a 58 foot saddle in the center. A hill at the south end is charted with two different heights. Chart 18433 shows it as 305 feet and Chart 18421 shows it at 355 feet. Take your pick.

Haro Strait is the 16 mile long, north-south pass between San Juan and Vancouver islands. It runs from the Strait of Juan de Fuca at the south to Turn Point on Stuart Island where it meets Boundary Pass. Haro is heavily traveled by large commercial vessels bound for British Columbia and Alaska.

We cruise south in Haro Strait past Henry Island's bluffs and offshore rocks, staying outside the 10 fathom depth curve, sometimes 200 yards offshore.

Not really Wilkes' vessel

Fog off Kellett Bluff

An automatic fog bell, which sounded a warning every 15 seconds, was installed at Kellett after the British tramp steamer Intravelli ran into the bluff in a fog one November night in 1907. The bell is no longer indicated on charts or in the Light List.

Kellett Bluff, steep, rocky and easily visible from both north and south, is the southwest tip of the Henry Island. It is an important landmark for vessels going north to Boundary Pass and the Strait of Georgia or south to the Strait of Juan de Fuca. The bluff was described as a "high, rocky precipitous front," in the 1889 edition of the *Coast Pilot*. There is virtually no shore here, 100 foot cliffs dive straight down into the sea. Orca whales are often seen off this southwest side of Henry. In the summer of 1998 fires raged on federal land at Kellett Bluff.

Kellett Bluff Light [Fl 4sec 80ft 7M] flashing 4 second light 80 feet high visible 7 miles, is on a diamond-shaped dayboard with black and white sectors.

Currents swirl around Kellett Bluff on both the ebb and flood. The 1999 *Tidal Current Tables* lists the average **flood current** at 1.6 knots flowing north at 000° True. The fastest predicted flood was 3.7 knots, and there were 17 predictions of 3.4 knots or greater.

Ebb current average flow is listed at 2.1 knots and flows southerly at 170° True. The fastest predicted ebb in 1999 was 3.52 knots, and there were 14 predictions of 3.36 knots or greater.

Open Bay is east of Kellett Bluff, indenting Henry for about 0.7 miles with bluffs on both sides and low land at the head of the bay. Open Bay lives up to it's name and is open to strong southerlies off Haro Strait. There are about a dozen homes visible from the water and two private docks in the bay.

⚓ The bay is a **good anchorage** in north or east winds. We've anchored here in calm summer weather in 5 to 10 fathoms. For years there's been a huge old resident deadhead slowly meandering about the bay.

Ⓖ A sometimes gunkhole.

Little Henry Island is about 1.2 miles from north to south. North lobe forms the east shore of Nelson Bay and the south lobe forms the east shore of Open Bay.

Offshore of Henry's southeast point is a mess of shoals, with only 4 feet of water in among the rocks at MLLW, 0.2 mile south of the point. The shoals and point are at the southwest entrance to Mosquito Pass.

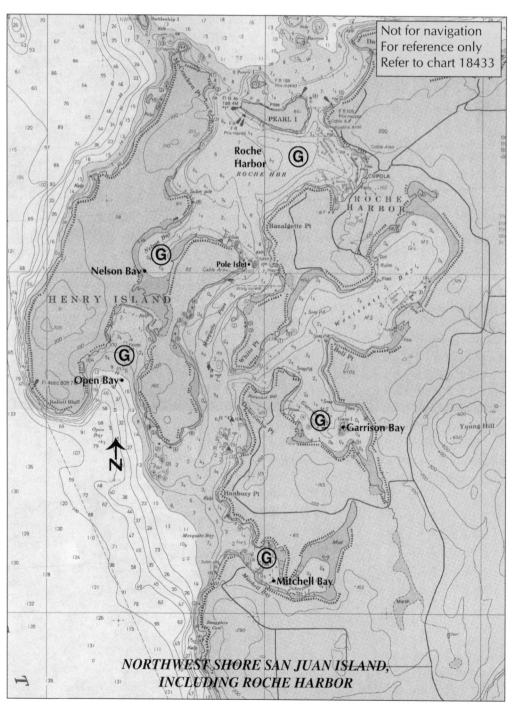

NORTHWEST SHORE SAN JUAN ISLAND, INCLUDING ROCHE HARBOR

This can also be good fishing, if you stay out of the rocks. It wasn't until February 1997 that an aid to navigation was placed here.

Mosquito Pass [G C "1"] green can buoy was placed of Henry Island at Lat. 48°34'45.1" N., Long. 123°10'53.1"W., according to Notice to Mariners #6, 04 02, 97. *(See sidebar)*

Now that we've cruised along the outside of Henry Island, we return to Roche Harbor and discuss its entrances, including Mosquito Pass.

Navigation Aids & Information about Entering Roche Harbor, Garrison & Westcott Bays

Three entrances lead into Roche Harbor, two from the north and one from the south. Any of these may also be used to enter Garrison and Westcott bays. This whole intriguing area was created when San Juan, Henry and Pearl islands emerged above sea level thousands of years ago, leaving seashells on the slopes of higher hills on San Juan.

The two entrances from the north are around either side of Pearl Island. From the south, the entrance is through Mosquito Pass.

(1) Pearl Island west entrance: The wider, deeper and preferred entrance from either Haro Strait or Spieden Channel is off the west side of Pearl, between Pearl and Henry. It is charted about 250 yards wide between the 3 fathom curves of the two islands. Controlling depths are charted at 6 fathoms, 4 feet on 18433, and 3 fathoms, 3 feet on 18423.

Two navigation aids are at this west entrance:

• **Pearl Island Light 1 [Fl G 4s 15ft 4M "1"]** flashing green 4 second light 15 feet high visible 4 miles, is on a square green dayboard on a skeleton tower off the west end of Pearl.

• **Pearl Island [F R pier lights (2)]** two fixed red lights on dolphins, privately maintained, are along the southwest shore of Pearl.

(2) Pearl Island east entrance: This narrower, shallower and potential "short-cut" from Spieden Channel into Roche Harbor at the east end of Pearl Island has a charted width of 75 feet between the 1 fathom, MLLW depth curves off Pearl and San Juan islands. Controlling channel depth is charted at 1 fathom, 4 feet on 18433, and 1 fathom, 1 foot on chart 18423.

Before entering the channel we note two navigation aids, both listed as "dock lights," one on San Juan and one on Pearl.

[F R 10ft, Priv. Maintd] fixed red, pile-mounted dock light 10 feet high, is charted on San Juan Island slightly northeast of the channel entrance. The *Light List* shows the name as North Roche Harbor Dock Light, which is somewhat confusing as the light is outside Roche Harbor and there are no lights identified as such on docks in the harbor.

Pearl Island Dock Light [F R 18ft Priv Maintd] fixed red private aid on a pile 18 feet high, is at the northeast corner of Pearl Island. It is less than 200 yards west of a rock which bares at 4 feet, MLLW. The rock itself is charted at approximately 75 yards off the northeast shore of Pearl. The rock is not in the middle of the channel, although at low tides it may appear that way from some locations. We've seen boats aground on the rock.

Cable and pipeline areas are between Pearl and San Juan islands in the pass.

➥ **NOTE:** Regarding placement of Mosquito Pass Green Can Buoy "1" off the southeast tip of Henry Island, we note some discrepancies.

Notice to Mariners #6 (LNM), 04 Feb. 1997, places the buoy at Latitude 48°34'45.1"N., Longitude 123°10'53.1" W.

Light List Volume VI 1998, #19724, give the approximate position of the buoy at Latitude 48°34'8" N., Longitude 123°10.9' W.

Plotting the position on chart 18433, according to the *LNM,* places the buoy about 430 yards south of Henry Island and 560 yards west of Hanbury Point on San Juan.

We note the charted position of the buoy on chart 18421, 3/24/98, shows it about 600 yards south of Henry and 600 yards west of Hanbury Point.

The buoy is presently shown on charts 18400 and 18421 and should be added to 18423 and 18433 when they are updated.

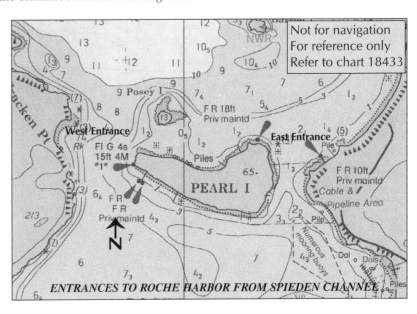

ENTRANCES TO ROCHE HARBOR FROM SPIEDEN CHANNEL

Delacombe Point

The point was named by Comm. Daniel Pender for Capt. William A. Delacombe, Royal Marines Light Infantry, who succeeded Capt. George Bazalgette in 1867 and commanded the Royal Marine Camp on San Juan until its evacuation in 1872.

White Point

This point was most likely named after Sub-Lt. James T.A. White who was attached to H.M.S. Zealous in 1869 for surveying service.

Mosquito Pass

The pass probably named by surveyors in the summer of 1857. They were apparently visited by mosquitoes from a salt marsh on Henry Island on the west side of the pass.

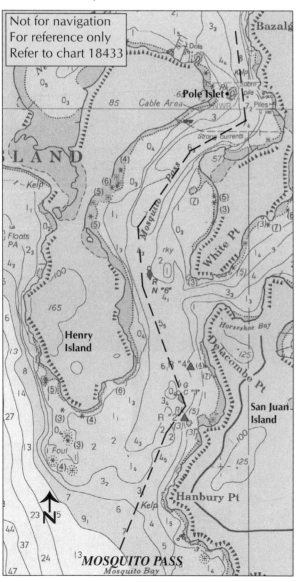

Now, aware of all of the above, we slip through the channel and have reached Roche Harbor through this "shortcut."

(3) Entering Roche Harbor from Haro Strait via Mosquito Pass

This is the 1.6 mile north-south pass separating San Juan and Henry islands. It runs between Hanbury Point just north of the entrance of Mitchell Bay to Bazalgette Point at Roche Harbor, and is used mainly by small craft.

The south entrance channel into Mosquito Pass is charted approximately 150 yards wide between the 3 fathom depth curves just west of Hanbury Point, then narrows to perhaps 100 yards in the vicinity of R "2" and G C "3." Midway through the pass we can enter Garrison and Westcott Bays through an unnamed channel off the pass. We visit them and Mitchell Bay on pages 29-37.

South-flowing ebb currents in the pass can exceed 2.5 knots, according to the *Canadian Current Atlas* and listings in *Washburne's Tables*. Residents say currents may run over 4 knots in extreme tidal conditions. Strong currents combined with strong southerly or westerly winds can cause steep waves close together, which can be uncomfortably violent and even dangerous. This condition is exacerbated as depths shoal from 100 fathoms to 10 feet within 0.7 mile at the Mosquito Pass south entrance, which is open to the long fetch of Haro and Juan de Fuca straits.

Mosquito Pass navigation aids & other information, from south to north:

• **[GC Buoy "1"]** green can buoy, is between 430 and 600 yards off the southeast lobe of Henry Island, marking a huge mess of rocks and shoals. It's about 600 yards west of Hanbury Point. *(P. 23)*

Before the buoy was in place (or if it should go off station), we maintain a bearing of 90° True (not necessarily a course) on Hanbury Point to keep south and clear of this area. We also tend to use line-of-site ranges to verify radar, dead reckoning or GPS course and position.

• **Daybeacon [R "2"]** triangular red dayboard with a red reflective border, is on a pile about 525 yards north of Hanbury Point marking a drying shoal. It's about 150 yards off a small unnamed nub on San Juan.

• **Buoy [G C "3"]** green can buoy, is charted approximately 150 yards north of R "2" and 300 yards off San Juan. It marks a 4 foot shoal and the west side of the narrow marked pass.

• **Daybeacon [R "4"]** triangular red dayboard with red reflective border on a pile, is charted 200 yards north of G "3" and 150 yards off San Juan. It marks the east side of the pass near a rock which bares at 4 feet above MLLW.

We are now midway through the pass and have reached the unnamed channel to the east which is the entrance into Westcott and Garrison bays, offering anchorages and interesting gunkholing. The passage is about 100 yards wide, and mid-channel it is 3 fathoms, 3 feet deep at MLLW.

Delacombe Point is the bluff on the south side of the entrance and **White Point** is the bluff on the north.

• **Buoy [R N "6"]** red nun buoy charted 630 yards north and slightly west of R "4," is 300 yards west of **White Point**. It's at the west edge of the 3 fathom depth curve off the point, and is the east edge of the pass.

On the San Juan side depths are now 6 to 7 fathoms in the 100 yard wide pass as it swings to the east. On the Henry Island side it's as shallow as 3 to 4 feet and rocky off the bay here. Speed limit buoys with "7 knots" and "No Wake" signs are very visible. Unfortunately, some faster vessels don't observe the slowdown, to the distress of nearby residents and to slower boats.

Pole Islet, NWR, charted but not named, is south of the Roche Harbor entrance into Mosquito Pass. The rocky islet is impassable on the west (Henry Island) side at low tide to any craft other than kayaks, rowboats and shallow draft powerboats, even though it looks like a shortcut. Local advice: "don't try it."

The narrowest part of the pass is between Pole Islet and San Juan where it's less than 100 yards wide. This is the area where "Strong currents" are indicated on the charts. Currents may run 4 to 5 knots or more in this area, with floods zigzagging north and the ebb zigzagging south.

Cable area is south of Pole Islet.

We pass **Bazelgette Point** on the east shore, pop out of Mosquito Pass and we've reached Roche Harbor from the south.

And now, finally, it's time to explore the northwest shores of San Juan Island.

ROCHE HARBOR

Historical Roche Harbor is a great natural harbor at the northwest corner of San Juan Island. Henry Island forms the west shore of the harbor and Pearl Island is the north shore. The irregularly-shaped harbor is about 1.1 miles east to west and 0.5 mile north to south.

Roche Harbor Resort and Marina, largest resort on San Juan, covers the southeast cove of Roche Harbor. The site of what once was the most valuable supply of high-grade lime in the world, the Roche Harbor Lime & Cement Company operated from 1886 until the mid-1950s. The "company town" was the veritable fiefdom of John S. McMillin, now a company-town-turned sophisticated resort.

The rest of the harbor is lined with waterfront homes and private moorages. The southwest portion of Roche Harbor ends in Nelson Bay on Henry. The bay indents the island less than 0.5 mile and depths are less than 3 fathoms. At the bay's east entrance is a Seattle Yacht Club outstation for members' use only. The large brick building at the club's facility was built as a private home in 1927.

Pole Islet
This little bit of land was named for tall poles set up by Indians where nets were attached to catch low-flying ducks. One pole was attached on the islet and the other pole was on the marshy point on Henry Island.

Bazalgette Point
The point was named for Capt. George Bazalgette, the first commander of the Royal Marine Camp on San Juan Island from 1860-67.

His name was variously misspelled as Bazelgette, Bazalgettil, Bazalgetti, Bagatelle and Bazalgene, but the chartmakers got it right.

*Roche Harbor Resort & Marina
(Courtesy Roche Harbor Resort)*

Naming Nelson Bay

This bay on Henry Island was named for Ole Nelson who lived in the shallow bay at the turn of the century, hence the name.

"Booze Bay"

This is the local name of the small unnamed bay on the east side of Henry Island north of Nelson Bay. Americans returning from B.C. sometimes anchored here to drink up remaining liquor before heading into Customs at Roche Harbor.

Naming Roche Harbor

The area was named after Lt. Richard Roche who had served as midshipman with Capt. Henry Kellett in 1846. He was a surveyor and colleague of Capt. George Henry Richards.

A USC&GS report of 1894 called it a perfect landlocked harbor:"Its shores are mostly rocky as the name would imply."

➥ **NOTE:** All of Roche Harbor is a **"No Wake"** zone, from McCracken Point off the northwest shore of Henry Island south into Mosquito Pass.

Our Lady of Good Voyage Chapel

⚓ **Anchoring is possible** in about 1 fathom in the center of Nelson Bay, being aware of weather, as strong southerlies sometimes blow over the isthmus between Nelson and Open bays.

Ⓖ Nelson Bay is a **possible gunkhole** in good weather.

Roche Harbor Marina has grown by leaps and bounds with ever expanding moorage floats, and no longer has "numerous mooring buoys" as charted. The homey "boatel" founded by Reuben Tarte in the late 1950s for his boating friends who cruised into Roche Harbor, now has 350 moorage slips. The boats keep getting larger and the marina keeps growing.

Customs clearance for returning Americans and arriving Canadians is at the outer dock of Roche Harbor Marina from mid-May to October.

⚓ **Anchoring** is possible throughout Roche Harbor in 5 to 7 fathoms, mud bottom. There is heavy boat traffic in the harbor all summer and space may be limited.

Ⓖ **Roche Harbor** is a **gunkhole**—if there is room.

Roche Harbor Marina Facilities

➤ Moorage for 350 boats: 650 feet of space for boats over 140 feet, and 36 slips for those over 60 feet, no mooring buoys
➤ Moorage rates: $1.10/foot mid-May thru Sept.; 60 cents/foot off-season
➤ Fee includes 30-50 amp power, water, free pumpout, garbage, access to swimming pool & tennis courts
➤ Fuel: diesel, gas, propane; mechanic
➤ Pumpout at four locations, three at fuel dock, travelling boat pumpout service
➤ Restrooms with 14 showers, including new, private facilities, laundry
➤ U.S. Customs port of entry mid-May to October
➤ Launch ramp, small boat rentals
➤ Groceries & marine supplies, authorized chart sales, gift shops, post office
➤ Restaurant, bar and cafe
➤ Swimming pool, tennis & Victorian gardens
➤ Whale watching tours
➤ Marina hosts various boat club rendezvous
➤ Hotel & cabin accommodations
➤ Nearby airport
➤ Activities: hike, sight-see, historical landmarks, swim, tennis, fish, shop
➤ Monitors VHF channel 78A
➤ Harbormaster: Kevin Carlton
➤ Tel.: 360-378-2155 Ext. 500, 800-451- 8910; FAX: 360-378-6809
➤ e-mail: http://www.rocheharbor.com
➤ P.O. Box 4001, Roche Harbor, WA 98250

A Brief History of Roche Harbor

Throughout the 11 years the British Marines were quartered at English Camp during the Pig War, their chief occupation was not patrolling the area to resist invasion by the Yankees, or even to fight off occasional raids by Haida tribes from B.C. Instead it was to keep busy quarrying the precious limestone and stoking fires under two primitive lime kilns they had installed at nearby Roche Harbor. Hudson Bay Company shipped barrels of top grade lime all over the world from the harbor.

After the British left, brothers Robert and Richard Scurr bought the rights to the quarry at Roche Harbor in 1881 and turned out lime, living in a small log cabin on the property. They sold the quarry to John S. McMillin in 1886, and it became the Tacoma & Roche Harbor Lime Company.

In a short time, the entrepreneur added 11 more kilns to the original two. To reduce the lime, the 13 kilns used 128 cords of firewood per day—cut from the 4,000 acres of timber on land attached to the lime works.

McMillin's was a feudal domain: a company town with trim little houses, a company store where supplies were paid for by scrip which was issued instead of money. The work force of about 800 was made up of Asians and Causcasians—the single men housed in barracks. The Asians were segregated into a cluster of houses known as "Jap Town," historically but not politically correct.

Although it was a company town, the community had a doctor, Victor Capron, and a Methodist chapel, which served weekdays as the school for workers' children.

McMillin built Hotel de Haro

Roche Harbor Store

in 1886. The ornate mansion still stands, and guests flock to the hotel where Presidents Theodore Roosevelt and William Howard Taft visited. The registration book with Roosevelt's signature can be viewed in the hotel. The building was built around a bunkhouse, and a portion of the wall has been removed to reveal the 14 inch thick cedar logs which make up the core of the hotel.

McMillin built a mausoleum in the forest, where his entire family is interred. It is reminiscent of an old Greek temple within Doric columns, with Masonic Order symbolism. The mausoleum, "Afterglow Vista," is open to the public. It's an easy walk to the fascinating mausoleum, a "must-see" while in Roche Harbor.

Limestone & Lime *(as defined by Webster)*

Limestone: "Rock consisting wholly or chiefly of calcium carbonate, originating principally from the calcareous remains of organisms, and yielding lime when heated."

Lime: "Calcium oxide, a white caustic solid prepared by calcining limestone … and used in making mortar and cement."

Hotel de Haro is still the centerpiece of Roche Harbor, overlooking the harbor and the formal gardens. Nine rustic cottages that were once home to lime company workers are now rented out to visitors. The Scurr brothers old log cabin is near the tennis courts and swimming pool.

The Methodist chapel was converted in the 1950s by the Reuben Tarte family to a Catholic chapel named "Our Lady of Good Voyage Church." Beautifully appointed, it is the only privately owned Catholic church north of the Mexican border. While Catholic services are held here, it is also used for many non-denominational weddings.

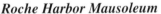

Roche Harbor Mausoleum

The refurbished old company store and office buildings now house shops and restaurants. The name Roche Harbor Lime & Cement Company is proudly painted across the store front. Bricks from the old kilns with names of brick manufacturers make up the "yellow brick road" in front of the hotel. Decaying and rusting towers still standing are part of the old lime kiln operations, and a loop hike along the road goes past rusted railroad tracks and machinery.

Each evening from mid-May through late September there is a ritualistic flag-lowering ceremony of U.S. and Canadian flags which is colorful and impressive. The performance is almost as famous as the resort itself. Even some jaded and

Hotel de Haro

world-weary travelers admit to reactions ranging from warmly bemused to a welling of patriotic spirit during the colors ceremony.

U.S. Customs at Roche Harbor

U.S. Customs officials have been at Roche Harbor since the late 1800s for good reason. Smuggling from British Columbia, particularly from Vancouver Island to Washington, has been going on practically since the first settlers arrived in the San Juans. Obscure coves and twisting channels provided ideal places to hide contraband shipments.

Customs officials early-on grumbled of "great and increasing evil" among island pioneers. They told of storekeepers whose Indian wives would paddle canoes across Haro Strait, returning at night with three to five tons of goods, and stash them where officials could not reach them.

In 1897, the Roche Harbor inspector complained, "Smugglers waltz up to the customs house in ballast, having left their stuff within easy reach in little harbors." They would clear customs, retrieve their concealed shipments and proceed with their business.

Even respected citizens were occasionally seduced into smuggling Canadian fleece. Shortly after shearing season customs officials watched the crossings to Stuart, Spieden and Henry islands, where some ranchers mixed the illegal sheep wool with their own.

Nowadays, customs officers keep a sharp eye out for drug smugglers, many of whom still operate the way smugglers did 100 years ago. Some bring their contraband to San Juan from Vancouver Island in personal watercraft (presently illegal in San Juan County) which can outrun the sheriff's boat, and others are actually running drugs in kayaks.

Carl on the Condor

Carl and the Condor

In 1939, Bill Garden designed my unique *Condor,* a 24 foot, flat-bottom, fin-keel, double-ended sharpie schooner, which I built at age 17. I cruised mostly single-handed before joining the Navy in 1942, and continued after WW II into the early 1950s.

During one of my early cruises the engine quit before reaching the San Juans. I continued under sail, at the whim and fancy of wind and devious currents. Sailing into Roche Harbor, I met the vintage caretaker. He gave me a tour of McMillin's former town, including lime kiln ruins, mausoleum, hotel and company store. He said workers had been required to rent company housing and purchase all their goods with company scrip at the company store or risk loss of their jobs.

The caretaker told of gigantic Indian salmon feasts for visiting dignitaries, tourists arriving by ships in years past, departures of large sailing ships laden with lime, going worldwide, all of which made Condor's engine-less adventures seem mundane.

Back on board—after studying the *Tidal Current Tables*—*Condor* drifted and sailed out of Roche with the current early the next morning and then through Johns Pass between Stuart and Johns islands. *(More adventures of Carl & Condor in Chapter 5)*

⚓ **UNDERWAY AGAIN, we're off to Westcott & Garrison bays.**
We left Roche Harbor and cruised about midway through Mosquito
Pass where a charted channel opens to the east, leading to Westcott Bay
in the northeast and Garrison Bay to the southeast. Both bays are sites
of ancient Indian villages, dating back at least 9,000 years, according to
islands' historian Wayne P. Suttles.

We pass through the unnamed channel between White and Delacombe points. Horseshoe Bay is on the south side, just inside Delacombe. This is a beautiful little bay, low bank and with many trees.

Westcott Bay is a treasure, a lovely, shallow bay less than 3 fathoms deep, rimmed by houses along the northwest shore. Island resident
and environmentalist Susan Meredith said, "It is the last major bay on
San Juan Island that has a relatively natural shoreline. The large marsh
and tidal flat at the inner end are important to the marine life of the
islands, and as such have been designated as a Marine Habitat Management Area Environment." She asks that boaters help keep these important waters clean by using the pumpout station at nearby Roche Harbor.

Westcott Bay Sea Farms is a remarkable island business on the eastern shore
of the bay about one mile in from the entrance. From the water, the view is of
hundreds of buoys surrounding a large sturdy dock, the only dock in Westcott Bay,
against a background of evergreen trees. The charted "Subm crib" with piles are the
location of the sea farms. Boaters in Westcott Bay are asked to maintain some
distance from the sea farms and to be certain not to pollute the pristine waters.

Condor under sail

Westcott Bay Ruins
   *On the northwest shore of
Westcott are charted "ruins,"
just outside the one fathom line.
These ruins are the unremark-
able remains of an old limestone quarry.*

Westcott Bay Sea Farms

This local industry produces top quality oysters, clams and mussels
which are sold across the U.S. and as far away as France and Hong Kong.

The oysters are grown in tiered, barrel-shaped nets suspended from
buoys. The key to the premier oysters and clams is the water, which is of
unusually high quality, and controls the health and taste of the seven million
oysters growing in the nets. Ideal conditions in the bay provide algae which
the oysters consume.

The Sea Farms produce all their own oyster spat in a hatchery complex,
and when they reach the size of a dime they are put in stacked trays in the
bay. Later they are sorted by size and put in the tiered nets until harvested.

Bill and Doree Webb started Westcott Bay Sea Farms in 1977 as a
family-run business, which has proven to be an island success. In January
1998, following Doree's death, the ownership was sold to a group of its
employees.

➡ **NOTE:** The state regularly
tests shellfish and if there is any
chance of PSP—Paralytic
Shellfish Poisoning commonly
know as "red tide"—the areas
are posted. Call the PSP hotline
at 1-800-562-5632 for current
information.

Westcott Bay Sea Farms

⚓ **Anchoring** is possible in Westcott
Bay in slightly more than 2 fathoms,
mud and sand bottom. It may be regu-
lated in the future. However, to help
save the environment we don't recommend anchoring here.

Susan Meredith Conversation
Susan Meredith is one of the
most experienced and well-known
kayakers, activists and authors in
the islands. She is an authority on
kayaking, whales, Henry Island,
(continued on next page)

➥ **NOTE:** The charted snags in Westcott and Garrison Bays do exist, although they may move around a bit.

Extraordinary octogenerian Susan Meredith

Overcrowding in the bays

More than 80 boats have been counted anchored in Westcott & Garrison Bays on 4th of July weekends.

Mosquito Pass, Westcott Bay and a myriad of other topics. Susan lives with husband Jim in a log cabin they built on Mosquito Pass in the late 1970s, perfect for launching their kayaks.

Susan, who turned 80 in 1998, has kayaked many of the northwest's rivers, around all of the larger San Juan islands, most of the west side of Vancouver Island, and Alaska's Yukon River from White Horse to Dawson.

"I love paddling around islands because I think it's boring to paddle in big open spaces." Back in the 1950s, they could camp anywhere, on almost any beaches, and they did. "We were welcomed wherever we stopped. People were interested in kayaks and invited us to camp. We were very careful of fires and tried to leave no sign we had been there. There were very few people living at most of the places we went."

Susan first paddled an Eskimo skin kayak, then a German Klepper foldboat until fiberglass became popular. She now paddles a fiberglass (low-tech) kayak, which, although not sleek "is large enough to wiggle around in and has room to carry enough stuff for a week or more camping. It handles beautifully in a following sea. I always have a life jacket and pump. And yes, I've tipped a lot, especially when running rivers."

In the fall of 1997, her book *Alaska's Search for a Killer,* a seafaring medical adventure, was published. She details her time along the Alaska coast from 1946-48 when as a bacteriologist and X-ray technician she worked on a survey determining the extent and location of the tuberculosis epidemic raging through Alaska.

We had a marvelous conversation with her one rainy fall day. The evening before she had gone kayaking and caught a rock cod for dinner, although even that is getting unusual as the pass is pretty well fished out. We can't begin to detail all of her favorite kayaking places, we promised we wouldn't, but one is out around Henry Island.

"I go around Henry when the weather's good because I love the beautiful cliffs, the bird rookeries and the cormorants. But there are no places to tuck in along Kellett Bluff where it can get very rough. I see whales out there quite a bit. It was pretty exciting once on a Mother's Day, and I thought, 'Oh, goody, whales!' Jim was in a canoe with a friend farther out, when all of a sudden a group of whales came zooming around this point. I usually aim a little toward shore when I see them because I'm chicken. We just sort of hung around the point because the tide was running. Then another group came from another direction and they were all milling around us. This big bull was going fast, his fin was up and he was getting so close to Jim, I could tell that if he went down his fin would hit Jim's canoe. But he flipped over on his side, went under the canoe and flipped back up. They looked down and saw the whale's eye right under them. That was a pretty neat experience for all of us," she said.

When she paddles in Spieden Channel, currents almost always seem to be setting west, especially near Danger Shoal, where it's "very confused."

She's lived on Mosquito Pass over 20 years and watched the increased boat traffic. "I don't even take my kayak out on three day weekends anymore, there are so many boats going through the pass, and they go so fast. We got the county to pass a 'No Wake, 7 knot speed limit.' If there are two or three boats going through it's not dangerous. But when 12 to 15 boats of all sizes are going in both directions it's just not safe, there's so much wake. Some boaters don't pay any attention to the signs. There are four buoys, a large sign on Pole Islet, and the sheriff patrols and issues speeding tickets on busy weekends."

She's a terrific role model for all ages.

⎈ **UNDERWAY AGAIN**, we leave Westcott Bay and go around **Bell Point** to enter Garrison Bay. There is a typical rock bank on the west shore with some scraggly evergreens and an attractive log house on top of the point. The cliff has weathered away exposing the root system of a large tree under the log house.

Garrison Bay is a lovely tree-lined bay with English Camp along the east shore and private homes along the south and west shores. Federal park land extends along the shore and inland from the marshes in south Garrison Bay, across to the marshy area in Westcott Bay, where a series of pilings mark the boundary. Garrison is virtually landlocked and well protected. Although the bay is about 0.7 mile long and 0.4 mile wide, only about half of that is usable with the rest either within the 1 fathom depth curve or foul and marshy.

Guss Island, an attractive half-acre island in the southeast part of the bay, with evergreen and madrona trees, is off-limits to visitors as it is an archeological site. A centuries-old Indian skull and bone fragments were found there in the early 1980s.

🐚 **One mile of public beach** lines Garrison Bay from Bell Point to the national park boundary at the south end of the bay. A dinghy float is about 300 yards north of the white blockhouse at the park.

ENGLISH CAMP, SAN JUAN ISLAND NATIONAL HISTORICAL PARK

English Camp is the counterpart of American Camp. The Brits picked a beautiful site. On entering the bay, the old two-story blockhouse on the shore comes in sight. At one time visitors could go inside and climb the stairs to look out the small holes in the second level—the kids loved it. After rebuilding a few years ago the upper floor was closed to the public. Park rangers said this was more likely a guardhouse for the sentries. Or perhaps the upstairs room was a brig for the unruly. Back in the days when we could go inside we could scarcely see out of those tiny slots. It was unlikely the building was used for defense. There wasn't room to see out at marauding settlers or Indians and at the same time shove a rifle through the slots.

There are still a few pilings on the beach, remnants of old docks built in the 1860s. The beach is covered with oyster and clam shells; this was the site of an early Indian camp and the shells are part of the midden. The remains of an Indian longhouse for more than 1,000 people, perhaps nearly 600

Westcott & Garrison bays— Gardens of Eden

Lummi Tribal lore records: "The first man, swet'an, came down from Heaven to a place on the north end of our island. It was the center of the universe. This man became the ancestor of the kale'gamis people.

"The kale'gamis were the original stock from which emanated the Lummi, Saanich and Songish."

Both Garrison and Westcott areas were the Lummis' "center of the universe," veritable Gardens of Eden for those early Indians.

English Camp on Garrison Bay

feet long by 60 feet wide, were found by surveyors in 1858. Archeological digs sponsored by the U.W. over the years have unearthed thousands of items from early Indian encampments, as well as unique finds from the marines of the Pig War era and early settlers.

⚓ **Anchoring** is possible within the shallow bay in depths of 1 to 2 fathoms, mud and sand bottom. It is not to advisable to anchor south or east of Guss Island because of the shallows. Any buoys in the bay are private.

Ⓖ **Garrison Bay** is a good, secure **gunkhole.**

English Camp Facilities

➤ Nearly 530 acres, 1.5 miles of shoreline
➤ Dinghy dock, picnic tables, no drinking water
➤ Restrooms, no showers
➤ Hiking trails
➤ Activities: hike, dig clams, visit historical displays, picnic, swim, gunkhole

---

Mid-1960s, John and Bill Bailey peer into the blockhouse

After anchoring and rowing to the dinghy float it's time for a delightful day ashore. We pack a lunch, camera and hiking sticks. A nearby hill with a wonderful view was the location of quarters for officers and their wives. Below the terraced site was a traditional formal English garden enclosed within a white picket fence, where, we presume, they sipped afternoon tea. The garden is open for viewing.

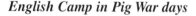

This was a pleasant time for the English officers and their wives. After all, the Pig War had turned into a non-war and they began to enjoy living on San Juan Island. It might not have been quite so pleasant for the enlisted men without their families, however, we understand it was fairly easy duty.

There are three reconstructed English Camp buildings in their original locations: a commissary near the beach, a tiny building that served as a hospital, and a barracks. The latter structure houses a photography exhibit of the day-to-day life of the soldiers stationed there during the Pig War era, and a self-operated laser disc show on park history.

English Camp's formal garden

A towering maple tree, claimed to be among the world's largest, is on shore between the buildings and the formal gardens. Above the gardens is the terraced bluff where officers' residences once stood. A monument commemorates Kaiser Wilhelm's decision to award San Juan Island to the U.S. instead of to the English.

English Camp in Pig War days

A peaceful trail heads north from the dinghy dock along the shore to Bell Point and the cove beyond, winding through evergreen and madrona trees, with picnic tables along the way. At low tide clam-digging is good and the clams are delicious. There are often posted closures, and rangers urge obeying the limits, or be ticketed.

Mount Young is the local name for 650 foot Young Hill, which energetic islanders like to think of as a mountain. The park extends inland north and east, including Mount Young. It's a favorite hiking area for islanders and visitors because of the fabulous panoramic views from the top. The hike is about a three-mile round trip from the beach. It's a good trail with signs from the parking lot through the woods, across West Valley Road and to English Cemetery, with its historic headstones enclosed within a picket fence. The cemetery was built in memory of seven members of the Royal Marine Light Infantry and one civilian who died here from 1860 to 1872. At least four of the men drowned and one was accidentally shot to death by his brother. From the summit on a clear day you feel you can see forever. The views are spectacular across the waters of Haro Strait to Vancouver Island. You'll be glad you walked to Mount Young, and it's all downhill on the trip back.

Carl at English Camp Cemetery

Early Visitors to Garrison Bay

Each spring and summer Native Americans beached their cedar canoes on the sandy shores at Garrison Bay, an active trading center more than 2,000 years ago. They traded their shells and jewelry for the tools and arrowheads of artisans from distant tribes. They set up their longhouse on the shore, picked salmon berries and salal, dug clams on the beach and camas roots in the woods.

They were following salmon: chinook and coho in spring, sockeye in summer. They strategically set up reefnets when the fish were on their spawning migration from the ocean to the Fraser River. They were the only peoples who fished by setting a net between two anchored canoes, waiting the right light, tide, calm surface, and then scooping fish from the net into the canoes. At the peak of the run they could catch several thousand fish.

Guss Island was owned by August Hoffmeister as part of his nearby farm in Garrison Bay. Hoffmeister stated in a petition in 1868, that he "keeps the suttlers (sic) store for the English Garrison," and he requested exemption from customs duties for the goods he sold to British Marines.

His request was rejected with the comment, "It is wonderful that there is scarcely an hour in the day when somebody's not clamouring (sic) to escape from the payment of customs duties."

⚓ **UNDERWAY AGAIN**, leaving Garrison Bay, we're headed back out through the channel and into Mosquito Pass once more. We turn south after we clear the 1 fathom shoal off Delacombe Point and continue south through the channel already described on page 24.

Hanbury Point is the northern boundary of **Mosquito Bay** off the entrance to Mitchell Bay, which we will visit shortly. But before we visit Mitchell Bay we have a bit more lore about Henry Island.

Henry Island Historical Bits

Indians reefnetted on Open Bay for many years. Old marine charts show an Indian camp here. Fishing shacks are still at the south end of Little Henry and reefnetters still fish off the west side of Open Bay.

The first homesteader on the island was Henry H. Edwards. The second, Henry Perkins, received a patent on Open Bay in 1886, after Henry Edwards had left. However, Henry Island was not named for either of these settlers, or even after Henry Kellett. Instead it was named after Midshipmen Wilkes Henry, a nephew of Commander Charles Wilkes who led the U.S. Exploring Expedition of 1838-42. Young Henry of the *U.S. Vincennes* was killed in a fight with Fiji natives on the shore of Malolo Island on July 24, 1840.

Camp Confusion

For many years the camp in Garrison Bay was known as English Camp. The name was changed to British Camp in the 1980s, and signs were made proclaiming the name change.

In 1992, the camp was once again named English Camp, and signs were made once again announcing the name change.

Barb (Nyberg) Hanna & Gale Nyberg dig clams at English Camp

Hanbury Point

The point was named after Ingham Hanbury, assistant surgeon at the Royal Marine Camp (English Camp) on San Juan from 1865-70. He had a distinguished career in the Royal Navy.

➡ **NOTE: Kellett Bluff** on Henry Island is a Marine Reserve area in the Voluntary Bottomfish "No Take" Zone program. Located on the southwest side of Henry Island, the area runs from the navigation light on the bluff north to the round marker, about 800 yards. All "no take" zones extend seaward 0.25 mile from the shoreline.

Kellett Bluff

This bluff on Henry Island was named "in honor of Captain Henry Kellett of the British Navy," by the skipper of the H.M.S. Pandora of the British Navy in 1847.

Somehow Wilkes missed naming this point in his 1841 expedition.

Historic Mitchell Bay log cabin

Smuggler's Cove is a little bay on the east side of Henry Island named for those bootleggers who long ago ran in there for shelter after crossing Haro Strait with contraband cargoes of opium, Chinese laborers or wool. Smuggler Jim Kelly's boat was boarded there in 1889 by Deputy Customs Inspector O.H. Culver who, facing Kelly's loaded revolver, uncovered no suspicious evidence and left the scene. Jim Kelly was unrelated to the more infamous smuggler Lawrence Kelly. *(See Ch. 11)*

Heirs of William Schultz, who had been plant superintendent at McMillin's staveless barrel factory, inherited 350 acres on Henry when Schultz died in 1925. He had a flock of sheep, and with a partner ran several fish traps near Henry.

Cleve VanderSluy, former town treasurer of Friday Harbor for many years, used to lease the entire island from the Schultz heirs, reefnetted off it and ran a couple of hundred sheep in the 1930s.

"At that time I could have bought the island for $16,000," he told us in 1995. "My wife and I lived on it, had a horse and wagon, and a gas-powered washing machine that we'd take down to the beach and wash clothes near a little spring. She didn't like it too much, but when World War II came along we gave it up and moved back into town."

A large brick house was built on Henry Island in 1927 by Frank Dever. It was later sought by a promoter who planned to use the property for a resort, but he departed the island so suddenly when his scheme to defraud was discovered that his dinner was left on the table. In 1946, the Henry Bresslers bought the house where they lived as driftwood artists, building lamps and tables from unusual wood picked up on the beach. They built a wharf in Mosquito Pass, naming their estate Driftwood Shores, which is now part of the Seattle Yacht Club outstation.

Over the years much of the island has been subdivided into summer home sites, and the island has electricity and water.

Water Party Time

Long-time friends and neighbors of Jo and Carl, Gus and Ellyn Swanson own a beautiful tract of land on the east side of Open Bay on Henry Island where the family has had a "compound" since 1956. They have kept their land as natural as possible.

Jo remembers one calm evening when a large party of friends departed from the shore on a raft towed by a small outboard boat to the entrance of Open Bay. The engine was shut down, and into the silence came the lovely strains of Handel's "Water Music" wafting across the water from a tape machine as we drifted with the current back into the bay.

Had the women been in long, white lace-trimmed gowns holding white parasols, and the men in white suits, instead of jeans and T-shirts, they could easily have been transported back into another century.

⚓ **UNDERWAY AGAIN,** we leave Mosquito Pass, turning southeast of Hanbury Point, pass through Mosquito Bay and head into Mitchell Bay.

MITCHELL BAY

Low-bank Mitchell Bay, about 0.3 mile long by 0.2 mile wide, is highly residential, with many homes, private piers and is the site of **Snug Harbor Marina Resort.** The bay is shallow, not much over 1 fathom deep at MLLW, with tideflats along the east and north shores.

A large well-charted rock and its shoal extend about 200 yards from the south shore at the entrance to the bay. All boats MUST stay north of the rock in the navigable channel which is less than 100 yards wide and 8 feet deep at low tide, said Dick Barnes, former owner of Snug Harbor Marina Resort. Even larger boats use this channel, and once through it you can head for the marina or anchor off.

⚓ **Anchoring** is possible throughout the shallow bay, mud-bottomed bay. All mooring buoys in the harbor are private.

Ⓖ The entire bay is a **good gunkhole** in most weather.

Snug Harbor Marina is along the south shore, just inside the rocky en-

Snug Harbor in Mitchell Bay

trance. Tie up at the gas dock or the outside float. If no one is there, walk to the office on shore and they'll assign a slip. Summers bring throngs of visitors for the weekend waterfront oyster barbecues.

Snug Harbor Marina Resort Facilities
➤ Guest moorage for approximately 20-30 boats
➤ Moorage fees minimum from $10 to $15 night
➤ 20-30 amp shore power, $2 night, water
➤ Fuel: gas at float, propane cannisters, kerosene at store
➤ Restrooms, showers, garbage, laundry by appointment
➤ Pump-out (coming soon)
➤ Boat & engine repairs
➤ Launch ramp, $15 round trip
➤ Marine supplies, hardware, bait & tackle, scuba air
➤ Basic store with groceries, ice, deli, coffee, gifts
➤ Waterfront cabins, camping
➤ Activities: fish, dig clams, swim, hike, play area, picnic, hot tub, kayak tours & rentals, whale watch excursions, scuba dive, bus and taxi service
➤ Harbormaster: Lance Rhinehart
➤ Tel.: 360-378-4762/FAX: 360-378-8859
➤ website: www.snugresort.com/e-mail: sneakaway@snugresort.com
➤ Address: 1997 Mitchell Bay Rd., Friday Harbor, WA 98250

➥ **NOTE:** Entering Mitchell Bay there is only one rule: **STAY NORTH OF THE ROCK**!

Mitchell Bay

It was probably named for Charlie Mitchell, an old Indian fisherman who lived there, wrote anthropologist Wayne P. Suttles. He said he was told that by Charlie Kahana in 1951.

Suttles also noted a Cowichan family named Mitchell once lived there.

There's been a marina in Mitchell Bay since at least the early 1960s, according to Dick, who bought the resort in the mid-1970s. They expanded it in the 1980s to its present capacity. Under new ownership, Snug Harbor has been extensively remodeled.

Strong winds seldom blow into Mitchell Bay as prevailing winds are south, southwest or east, usually not from the northwest, although once in a while bay residents are taken by surprise.

"If flags are blowing from the east we have 'flag waving weather,' low pressure, and we're trying to get sucked out to sea by all that cool, moist, stormy air," Dick said. "If it's blowing from the west it means high pressure and we call that 'halyard flopping weather.' Generally, any westerlies or nor'westerlies are in late May and early June when it blows pretty hard and we get a good surge. The rest of the time it's pretty much sou'easters, which usually miss the bay, so we're pretty protected.

"In winter we get nor'easters. The winter of 1991 was phenomenal with an Arctic freeze blast. There was hardly any snow,

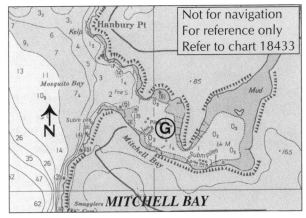

Not for navigation
For reference only
Refer to chart 18433

MITCHELL BAY

Snug Harbor Marina

but the ground froze two feet, we lost power and it was cold. The winter of 1996-97 we had pan ice on the water surface. We had enough people to scoop snow off docks and boats, and were really lucky we didn't have any more problems than we did."

Over the years Dick has seen many water birds wintering in the bay: harlequins, wood ducks, cormorants, buffleheads, different sizes of grebes and loons as there was a lot of herring. That's diminished because of the decline in herring spawning habitat. The fertility of the bay is still a wonder with seasonal highlights to be observed, especially fluorescent plankton in summer.

Dick left the marina in 1998. He owned it longer than anyone else, and managed it through 1998. It recently expanded and upgraded facilities, which are shifting from the early fish camp focus to a destination eco-tourism resort and "sneakaway retreat." The resort is involved in Nature Institute programs and tours which take people kayaking and whale watching.

Otters, herons, raccoons, wharf rats, eagles and fox are in the area. An eagle nest is about one-quarter mile from the resort campground and eaglets have been raised there for at least 20 years. An osprey visits Mitchell Bay.

An even shallower inner bay, entered through a channel between uncharted Pirates Point and the south shore, leads east and then turns north, where the entire bay north of a small island is drying mudflats. Known to early settler's as Upper Mitchell Bay, there are also homes and piers in here.

Mitchell Bay's Outer & Inner Harbors, Past & Present

Mitchell Bay actually consists of two bays, the outer bay where the resort and many homes are located, and a shallow inner harbor. We went past "Pirates Point" on the north shore and then were into the inner harbor where several boats were anchored. We gunkholed about in our skiff at high and low tides, and found it an intriguing place, lined with homes and piers. It's shallow, 1 fathom at the entrance and dry in the north. We went around the tiny charted island at high tide, but at low tide it is mudflats in the entire north end.

We never found out who owns the island, even local residents and the county weren't sure, but it was supposedly an Indian burial ground. Susan Meredith said she's kayaked into the bay and picnicked on the island. Numerous Indians lived around Mitchell Bay in the past, hunting, fishing and clam digging. There was a longhouse on the bay before settlers arrived. A home that originally belonged to Peter Kirk, for whom Kirkland was named, is in the outer bay. The house was barged into the bay from Kirkland in the early 1980s.

We were moored at Snug Harbor Marina during a nearly 50 mph easterly, and it was quite an experience. Winds howled, halyards banged, and waves in the bay were about one to two feet high, with tops blowing off the tiny white caps. Because of strong gusts, we tied to tires placed around the piling. This worked well and kept the boat from jerking on the float.

UNDERWAY AGAIN, and we head south along the west side of San Juan Island. We go around Mitchell Point (unnamed on the charts) keeping outside of the 10 fathom depth curve, and we're once again in Haro Strait.

It's over 12 miles from Mitchell Bay to Cattle Point at the south tip of the island

San Juan where?

As we've mentioned several times before in this tome, San Juan Island very nearly became part of Great Britain during the Pig War skirmishes. It wasn't until the "battle" over the U.S. and Canadian boundary was was solved in 1872 that San Juan officially became part of the U.S.

However, not every English schoolboy was taught this in history class.

In 1983, Queen Elizabeth and Prince Philip were visiting Victoria. Jo had credentials as a reporter on the Friday Harbor Journal, and was thrilled to board the royal yacht Britannia and meet the royal couple.

After shaking hands with both of them, the prince noted Jo's credentials showed she was from San Juan. "Is that San Juan, Puerto Rico?" he asked.

She then gave the surprised prince a quick history lesson he had never learned in school about the island that "got away" from the British Empire.

where we began this circumnavigation. These are fascinating, rugged, rock-bound shores, with high forested cliffs that bear the brunt of storms sweeping up Haro Strait from the Strait of Juan de Fuca. There are no places to put in along this coast, except for small boats. In the early days smugglers used the many tiny bays and coves along this shore to deposit their ill-gotten goods.

Smugglers Cove on San Juan (another Smugglers in addition to those on Henry, Shaw and other islands), is about 0.5 mile south of Mitchell Point, but is not a gunkhole. The name does conjure up images of the many various smugglers who used every nook on the west side of the island to land Chinese immigrants, wool, opium and booze. An island pioneer said she remembers hearing there was a cave in this cove where local Native Americans hid when the marauding Haidas came rampaging south. A cynic suggest the name was dreamed up by real estate developers to entice land sales to romantics.

❀ **Public tidelands** are along most of this west coast of San Juan Island. Most of the beaches are difficult to access from water as the shoreline is quite formidable and there's little upland access until we reach South Beach at the southeast end.

ANDREWS BAY & SAN JUAN COUNTY PARK

This is a fairly large open bight about 1.2 miles south of Smugglers Cove and is the site of the county park. The 15 acres of lovely, forested waterfront is a favorite with islanders and others who often see whales swimming past during spring and summer. It has long been a destination for bicyclists who find they've arrived in a peaceful and quiet wonderland after the ride across the island from Friday Harbor.

In 1894, the Coast and Geodetic office summed up the mariner's view of Andrews Bay: "It is merely an indentation and affords no shelter."

Low Island, NWR, is just offshore of the park, not to be confused with the Low islands in Griffin Bay and Wasp Passage.

Smallpox Bay is at the south end of the park.

San Juan County Park is popular with kayakers because of its proximity to **Lime Kiln State Park,** the state's only whale watching park. Kayakers paddle along this coast, hoping to spot whales. It's also a favorite with scuba divers who find dive sites near their camp sites. The park is showing deterioration and pollution caused by overuse of visitors, to the dismay of locals who find that at times there is scarcely any room for them.

Andrews Bay History

Back in the days when fishtraps were legal, this was one of the most productive areas for setting weirs. In one rig at the south end of Andrews Bay fishermen hauled in over 400,000 fish in one year. Workers' shanties were built along shore for those who tended the fish traps, but no trace of them remains. The bay got its name in the 1890s when map makers, who had run out of names of famous people, friends and relatives, started naming areas after the people who lived there. An elderly San Juan historian said she remembers somebody named Andrews who had a log cabin on that beach, but land records don't show anyone by that name holding a title, although there is an old log cabin.

Movie Magic

The movie "Practical Magic" was filmed at San Juan County Park in 1997 with most Islanders pleased with the project, which added a much needed infusion of money to county park coffers.

Naming Smallpox Bay

The bay was named, according to one source, after a tragic episode. In the 1860s, an unnamed boat anchored in the bay and two sick sailors were taken ashore and abandoned. They had smallpox.

The Indians who lived in this pleasant cove tried to take care of them. They had never coped with the disease and were terribly susceptible to it. The epidemic spread throughout their camp, and many of them died. In desperation, survivors burned their tents and belongings and migrated down the coast.

"The bay was earlier called Bivouac Cove by the surveyors of Capt. Henry Kellett's expedition in 1846. It may have been intended to designate the sheltered place where the small boats of the expedition should meet at day's end. It does not appear on any charts." (From Bryce Wood, Coastal Place Names and Cartographic Nomenclature)

Kayakers off the west side of San Juan, looking for whales

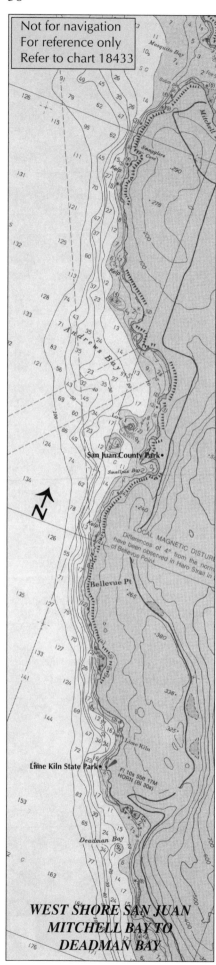

WEST SHORE SAN JUAN
MITCHELL BAY TO
DEADMAN BAY

The name "Andrews" was held by several local "black sheep." One was William Andrews, a bootlegger who "decided" to leave the island in 1917, possibly because his activities as a liquor dealer made it wise to leave before his time ran out.

Facilities at San Juan County Park

➤ Two mooring buoys in Smallpox Bay, fee $8/day
➤ Launch ramp in Smallpox Bay, no fee in 1998
➤ 18 campsites & one group campsite, reservations strongly recommended
➤ Fees charged for all camping, firewood & parking
➤ Commercial & non-profit groups should contact park superintendent in advance for special use permit application
➤ Picnic tables & fireplaces, water, restrooms
➤ Activities: beachcomb, scuba dive, kayak, camp, snorkel, whale watch, camp
➤ Park Superintendent phone: 360-378-8420

Bellevue Point is the next charted reference as we continue south. A local magnetic disturbance is charted near the point indicating "differences of 4°." It was discovered by Spanish explorer Juan Carrasco on June 29, 1790. The Spanish name is "Punta de Herrara."

Lime Kiln Bay & Lime Kiln Light are about 0.8 mile south of Bellevue Point. This area is fascinating for several reasons, including the light, which is the only navigational aid on the entire west coast of San Juan Island. There is no shelter in the bay, but from the water the ruins of old lime kilns and the old cookhouse in the bight north of the point can still be seen.

Lime Kiln Light [Fl 10s 55ft 17M, Horn (Bl 30s)] flashing 10 second light 55 feet high visible 17 miles, is on a tower on a fog signal building. The horn operates continuously, one blast every 30 seconds. For those who have just crossed the Strait of Juan de Fuca from Port Townsend or Port Angeles, or crossed Haro Strait from Victoria, the lighthouse means you're getting near a harbor in the San Juans.

LIME KILN STATE PARK

This is one of the newest and most unusual parks in the country, a dedicated whale watching park. The park's 2,550 feet of salt waterfront and 39 acres surrounding the lighthouse are there for the purpose of watching whales as they feed and frolic off the rocky cliffs in one of their favorite feeding areas. Anyone who has ever seen a whale close up knows it is a once-in-a-lifetime thrill.

There are close to 100 whales in three resident pods, J, K and L, who live within a 200 mile radius of San Juan Island. In 1999, authorities said there had been a noticeable decline in the whale population, possibly due to pollution.

Visitors to the park arrive by land as there is no good place to launch or land a boat. Views from this day-use park are magnificent. Each summer thousands of visitors drive or bicycle the narrow roads of San Juan to Lime Kiln Point Park to watch whales. Kayakers and whale watching boats cruise past.

State parks had plans to put in 30 campsites for walkers, bicyclists and small car camping. This was not acceptable to residents and the idea was dropped.

When the park was dedicated in 1985, few realized the impact whales and whale watching would have. The most concerned were those at Whale Museum in Friday Harbor. Since its founding in 1979 it has become internationally recognized for its environmental education and marine research.

Scores of whale watching cruises are based in Friday Harbor, Roche Harbor, Deer Harbor, West Sound, Rosario, Bellingham, Anacortes, Everett, and Seattle.

They cruise daily in spring and summer to view the giant mammals in their natural habitat. Kayak cruises off the west shore of the island usually have only one goal in mind: to view the whales.

Facilities at Lime Kiln State Park
➤ 10 picnic sites, 11 parking sites
➤ Two vault toilets
➤ Interpretive signs, hiking trails
➤ Interpretive programs by Whale Museum volunteers
➤ Activities: whale watch, birdwatch, scuba dive, snorkel, picnic, hike

Lime Kiln Light

Deadman Bay is south of Lime Kiln State Park, a beautiful little bay, currently owned by the Land Bank, although state parks had hoped to purchase it. The delightful beach, 100 feet below the winding county road, is a favorite with scuba divers and even a few hardy swimmers who occasionally brave the icy waters of the strait, especially on a hot day. Kayakers also stop at the bay for picnics or for a rest.

➡ NOTE: Whale watching guidelines are in the appendix, page 291.

Deadman Bay History

Obviously, the bay was named for a dead person, but there are conflicting ideas as to who it was, and how he got there.

Centenarian and island native, Etta Egeland of Friday Harbor, said an unnamed man criticized a Chinese cook at the Lime Kiln, and the cook killed the man with his knife in about 1890. The Chinese was helped to escape from San Juan Island by a farmer named Bailer, who hid him in a wagon until he found a vessel that was leaving Friday Harbor. Walter Arend, a retired Friday Harbor postmaster, said the name was used to identify the place where a man's body had drifted ashore.

Another version is that the first settler who died on the island was buried there. However, if it was 1890, that could never be, as by then a fair number of settlers had died on San Juan Island. Early Indian reefnetters had a summer village at Deadman Bay, long before it received that name.

Whales in Haro Strait
(Photo courtesy Whale Museum)

Pile Point is about three miles southeast of Lime Kiln Point along this forbidding rocky coast, where homes with incredible views encroach along the shores. There is a surveyor's monument with a bench mark at the point, which was the site of reefnetters summer villages years ago.

Captain George's Bay is a small bay, unnamed on charts, about 0.75 mile north of Pile Point. Agnes Nash (member of the pioneer Nash family) recalled that she and other children used to crawl to the edge of the hill above the bay to watch Indian 'potlatches.'

The name is probably connected in some way with a man called Captain George, the son of a Klallam man and a Samish woman who lived for a time at Fish Creek and was employed at American Camp." *(From Suttles, 1974)*

Kanaka Bay is a fairly large bay east of Pile Point, filled with rocks and tiny coves. It has long been used by small boats and fish boats.

Active Lime Kilns

Lime kilns were active in the late 1800s and early 1900s in the large bight just north of Lime Kiln Lighthouse. A wharf came out from the rocks to berth steamers picking up lime. Ruins of some buildings are still seen, including the cookhouse.

Attempts to develop the area over the years have failed.

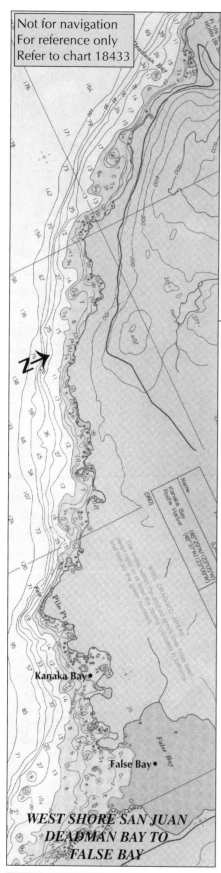

*WEST SHORE SAN JUAN
DEADMAN BAY TO
FALSE BAY*

Kanaka Bay

Pile Pt.

False Bay

➡ **NOTE** It's time to switch charts again in the Kanaka Bay-False Bay area. We change from 18433 to 18434.

Kanaka Bay History

Kanakas were Hawaiians brought to San Juan Island by the Hudson Bay Company in the mid-1850s to work for the company. After the Kanakas were dismissed in 1872 by HBC at the end of the Pig War, many of them settled in the area surrounding the bay named after them—Kanaka Bay. Pile Point was called Kanaka Point for many years. Indians camped in the coves of Kanaka Bay during the summer fishing season.

According to the autobiography of Lila Hannah Firth, born on the island in 1865, "there was quite a sheltered bay where boats could lie at anchor in any kind of bad storms." Historian Bryce Wood said the bay "is frequently used as an emergency anchorage by purse seiners and gill netters." This also looks like an ideal place for smugglers to dart in, off-load their contraband and pop back out into Haro Strait.

In another smuggling yarn, a number of Chinese hoping to enter the country, were found in the bottom of Lawrence Kelly's boat, sound asleep, as officials greeted the boat when it landed at Kanaka Bay. That was the end of their short-lived, illegal stay in the U.S.

Kanaka Bay in the "early days"

Homes at the edge of the bay have spectacular views of the Strait. At one time a large development was envisioned on the bay and an airplane landing strip was built above the bay. Between the landing strip and the shoreline are acres of rolling fields and low rock outcroppings.

We haven't mentioned it lately, but we stay well offshore along this coast, in the 10 to 40 fathom range.

False Bay is immediately east of Kanaka Bay, and it is extremely well named. A glance at the chart will verify it. At high tide it looks like a fairly extensive bay, but at low water it's all mudflats. Bryce Wood calls the name akin to such terms as Cape Flattery and Deception Pass. The bay apparently silted up over the millennia by a stream that drains a large part of the island. The bay is a University of Washington Biological Station.

Seven Unnamed Islets, NWR, are about 1 mile southeast of False Bay. This string of rocks extends south of the island for more than 0.2 mile.

Eagle Point is the next charted point, just under two miles southeast of False Bay, at the west end of Eagle Cove. It is all rocky cliffs.

Eagle Cove is a charming little cove east of Eagle Point and west of the boundary of American Camp National Historical Park.

There is good fishing just off this cove. It's long been a favorite place for sports and commercial fishers. There are rocks and kelp in the cove so it's not a recommended anchorage.

🌿 The shore is public and islanders use the beach for picnics, but it is a scramble from the road and is not protected from southerly winds.

We have reached the western end of American Camp, it's less than 2.5 miles to Cattle Point, and the glorious shores of South Beach are in view.

INNER PASSAGE

This is the shoal extending over the Salmon Bank to the buoy about 1.5 miles offshore.

Salmon Bank Lighted Gong Buoy "3" [Fl G 4s] flashing green 4 second lighted buoy, is 1.5 miles south of Cattle Point. Depths in this area range from 1 fathom, 3 feet, to 8 fathoms. Most recreational mariners have no problem with the depths through the passage.

A Washington State Ferry, which draws about 16 feet, ran aground in 1997 in Inner Passage. The skipper had taken it on a joyride without permission. He's no longer with the ferry system.

During fishing season, assuming there still will be fishing seasons, gillnetters and purse seiners are in clusters out here, all the way from the buoy to Kanaka Bay.

We've reached Cattle Point once again and have completed our circumnavigation of San Juan Island.

Looking east along South Beach past Cattle Point to Lopez Island

In **Chapter 2** we explore laid-back and lovely Lopez Island which has some excellent cruising and anchorages.

SOUTHEAST TIP OF SAN JUAN ISLAND & INNER PASSAGE

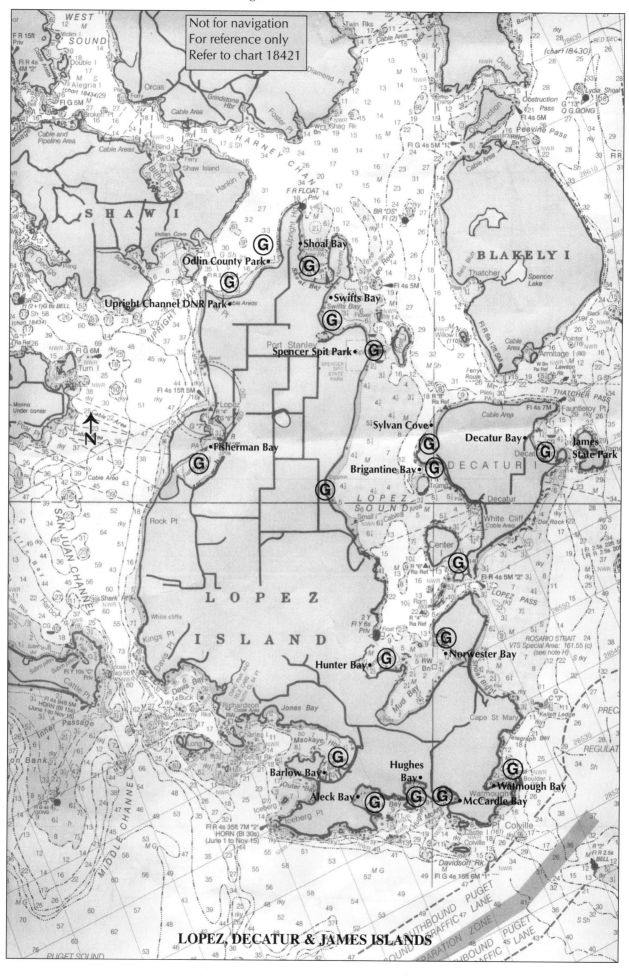

Not for navigation
For reference only
Refer to chart 18421

LOPEZ, DECATUR & JAMES ISLANDS

Chapter 2
LOPEZ ISLAND
Decatur, James & Adjacent Islands

Charts & Publications for this Chapter

Chart	Date	Title	Scale	Soundings
U.S. 18421	03/21/98	Strait of Juan de Fuca to Strait of Georgia	1:80,000	Fathoms
U.S. 18423 SC	06/18/94	Strip Chart Bellingham to Everett, inc. San Juan Islands		
		Pages A, C, D,	1:80,000	Fathoms
		Page D, inset 8	1:25,000	Fathoms
☆ U.S. 18429	03/16/96	Rosario Strait, Southern Part	1:25,000	Fathoms
☆ U.S. 18430	11/02/96	Rosario Strait, Northern Part	1:25,000	Fathoms
☆ U.S. 18434	04/27/96	San Juan Channel	1:25,000	Fathoms
U.S. 18465	08/01/98	Strait of Juan de Fuca, Eastern Part	1:80,000	Fathoms
CAN.L/C 3461	12/02/94	Juan de Fuca Strait, Eastern Portion	1:80,000	Meters
CAN.L/C 3462	10/23/98	Juan de Fuca Strait to Strait of Georgia	1:80,000	Meters
🐚		Washington State DNR Quad Map—San Juan County	1:100,000	

➥ *Compare your chart dates with those above. There may be discrepancies between chart editions.*
☆ *= Preferred chart for this chapter* 🐚 *= DNR & other public tideland information*

OVERVIEW of LOPEZ ISLAND

Lopez, the third largest island in the San Juan Archipelago and possibly the most picturesque of all, is fascinating and delightful. The southern rock-bound coast with its many bays, scattered islets and rocky shores, faces the Strait of Juan de Fuca, and may be the first island seen when crossing the Strait from the south. Storms sometimes slam into the rugged, steep-sided shores with fierce intensity.

Bluffs reach nearly 250 feet high along the south coast, and in some places cliffs soar 100 feet straight up above turbulent waters. It's not always the greatest place for mariners, although there are some anchorages along this shore which provide shelter, depending on wind and weather conditions. Fog tends to set in at the island's south end earlier and lasts longer than at the north end.

On the other hand, there is good cruising along other Lopez shores with sheltered bays, pleasant harbors and many good anchorages. Temperatures vary from north to south, with the north end often being warmer.

Prevailing winds in spring and summer are southwest, and in early spring can be nasty. In winter they're generally southeast, but occasionally a nor'easter blows through and can be ugly, as are winter easterlies.

On land, the nearly 19,000 acres that constitute Lopez encompasses fields, meadows, deep evergreen forests and rambling farms. Much of the island's population is concentrated in the Lopez Village and Fisherman Bay area. Others live along quiet shorelines, or perhaps you'll even meet a few gentle "woodsies" from the

➥**NOTE:** Marine fuel is available at two places on Lopez:
- **Lopez Islander** on Fisherman Bay, gas and diesel
- **Richardson Dock,** call first, 360-468-2275

Coast Guard on the Rocks

U.S. CUTTER GUARD ON ROCKS AT RICHARDSON

Old barn on Lopez

National Wildlife Refuge

Many rocks and islands off Lopez are part of the San Juan Islands National Wildlife Refuge & Wilderness Area, NWR.

Mariners must stay 200 yards away from these rocks and islands. All refuge islands are closed to public access except Matia and Turn islands.

Naming Iceberg Point

It was named in 1854 by George Davidson, a topographer with Lt. James Alden aboard the in the U.S. Coast Survey vessel Active. He named it because of "remarkable deep and smooth marks of glacial action."

island's hinterlands.

Inland on Lopez are many island sights fascinating to cruisers who walk or ride around the island on bikes, with a lovely old church and cemetery in the island's center, and a picturesque barn we couldn't resist.

What we love most about Lopez are the wonderful people. An island with the motto, "Wave, you're on Lopez," has our hearts. In fact, the "Lopez Wave" is a well-known feature of the island. Wave to everyone you see, resident or visitor.

Washington State Ferries connects Lopez to three other San Juan Islands and to Anacortes, with the ferry terminal located at the far north end of the island at Upright Head. There is no float or landing here, so cruisers who plan to pick up guests in the islands will find it far easier to meet them at Shaw, Orcas or Friday Harbor where there are mooring facilities near the ferry terminals.

Marinas, state and county waterfront parks are scattered around the island.

Many businesses and commercial enterprises are located in Lopez Village, about four miles south of the ferry landing and less than one mile from the moorages in Fisherman Bay. There are fire and aid departments, medical services, markets, museums, bakeries, churches, historical buildings, schools, art galleries, bed and breakfasts, a pharmacy, lumber yard and library. A golf course and San Juan County's oldest winery are also on the island.

Lopez Island church and cemetery

This chapter features the good cruising and anchorages around this lovely and laid-back island. Enough said, let's get cruising around Lopez.

⊕ **UNDERWAY,** we start at Iceberg Point and travel clockwise to circumnavigate lovely Lopez.

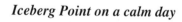
Iceberg Point on a calm day

Iceberg Point, bleak and windswept, is the most southwesterly point on Lopez Island, with grassy bluffs rising about 100 feet above waves often crashing against gigantic rocks. Less than 0.5 mile east of the point, the hills rise to 226 feet.

Iceberg Point Light [Fl R 4s 35ft 7M "2"] flashing red 4 second light 35 feet high, visibility 7 miles, is on a triangular red dayboard on a white square house, is not your typical looking lighthouse. It's a smudge of white with its flashing red light and a horn activated from June 1 to November 15. Rocks extend as much as 600 feet off the point. An unnamed rock east of Iceberg Point is charted as a National Wildlife Refuge.

Outer Bay is just inside Iceberg Point, as is **Iceberg Island,** 3.5 acres of rock. Charted rocks, reefs and kelpy shallows are scattered about the bay. A needle-shaped, snaggle-toothed rock in the bay's west end sticks up like a menacing spear. Even if there is virtually no wind, two to three foot seas roll in against the shore. We've seen boats anchor inside Iceberg Island, although friends who live nearby say they shouldn't.

There are a couple of other tiny bays where sailing friends said they've anchored briefly. It's much too "iffy" as an anchorage: on a lee shore with a hard bottom, exposure to westerlies and no safe place to hide.

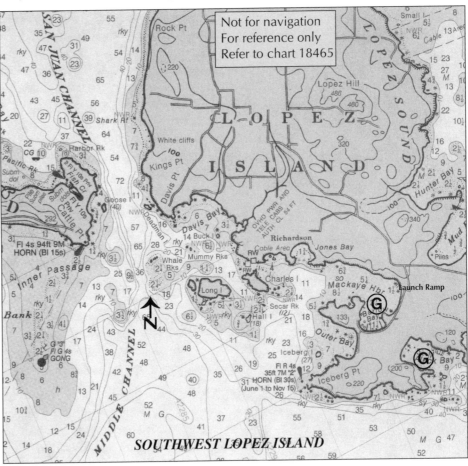

Not for navigation
For reference only
Refer to chart 18465

SOUTHWEST LOPEZ ISLAND

"Anchoring in Outer Bay is not good, in fact, it's a bad idea," said Ron Meng, our Lopez expert. The north shore of Outer Bay has steep cliffs rising to 128 feet, although the bay is surprisingly shallow, at 1 to 4 fathoms. A better place to escape the weather is around Johns Point and east into Mackaye Harbor and Barlow Bay.

※**Agate Beach County Park** is in Outer Bay, and holds a fascination for experienced scuba divers and kayakers who launch their craft after climbing down long stairs from a county road. In front of the 600 feet of park shoreline is a large moss-covered rock which joins the beach at low tide, a favorite climbing spot for youngsters. The two acre park has picnic tables and pit toilets, but no water.

Johns Point is a ragged, rocky shoreline with practically no beach. The bluff is steep with water 5 to 7 fathoms deep near the base of the cliffs. As we continue around into Mackaye Harbor there's a mess of rocks and some small bays on the north side of Johns. Carl anchored his 24 foot schooner *Condor* in several of these little pockets some 50 years ago.

A peninsula separates Mackaye from Barlow Bay, and there's development on the uplands with a private marina on the west shore.

Mackaye Harbor is home of the Lopez fishing fleet, smaller now than back in the heyday of commercial fishing. The harbor is about 0.4 mile wide by just under one mile long. Depths range from 1 to 9 fathoms as the harbor gently shoals into Barlow Bay and the east shore.

Barlow Bay has several long docks that have been here for years, as have old fishing camps. The western Fidalgo Docks are privately owned. Native American fishers bought the old Islands Fresh Seafood Dock, the longer, skinnier middle dock, where fishing boats moor in summer. The most

Astoria Puget Sound Canning

This company was located on John's Point peninsula in Mackaye Harbor from 1912-1930s. There were docks for loading nets, a bunkhouse, cookhouse, shed for making wire netting, field areas to store fishtrap pilings and ways to service purse seiners in the winter. No buildings remain today.

Barlow Bay

Lumpy Mackaye Harbor

*"We tucked in Mackaye Harbor on **Island Bird** in a sou'easter to wait it out. Waves came all the way around and rolled right in. Wasn't dangerous, but just very lumpy and lots of movement. We were surprised that the waves were opposite the way the wind was blowing," said John and Louise Dustrude, long-time San Juan Islanders and experienced mariners.*

Waves striking steep shorelines do bounce back. The angle of incidence equals the angle of refraction.

They owned the 29 foot sailboat for years, row extensively around the islands in beautiful gigs, and now do their gunkholing in a Fjord 33 motor sailer.

John Dustrude, intrepid mariner

Richardson Store

easterly dock has been proposed as a marina, but last we heard it's still undecided.

⚓ **Anchoring** is possible in Mackaye Harbor and Barlow Bay, 2 to 4 fathoms, soft and muddy bottom. We've anchored here at various times over the years. Since it is a commercial area we suggest anchoring away from fish boats which come in at all hours. Be sure to leave an anchor light on at night.

Ⓖ This is a reasonable **gunkhole.**

The eastern shore of the harbor is no-bank waterfront covered with driftwood. The county road is beyond the sandy beach. There are a few homes scattered here, but the outstanding building is the handsome, white Mackaye Harbor Inn, built in 1904. It is a bed and breakfast just across the road from the beach. For those folks who want a night of luxury off the boat, this might be the ticket. Reservations are a must. (*Tel. 360-468-2253/FAX 360-468-2393*)

🐚 **County launch ramp** in the northeast part of the bay was a gravel pit until it closed in the early 1980s. There is parking, but no other facilities at this single lane, concrete ramp, a popular spot for kayakers to put in. The ramp provides public access, and it's possible to anchor offshore, row in and walk to Islandale Market, about 0.5 mile away. Mackaye Harbor's north shore is pretty much all 100 foot high bluffs, starting near the launch ramp and continuing west to Jones Bay.

Jones Bay, private and rock strewn, is exposed to the Strait. A steep bluff with a few houses is behind the bay. Some private mooring buoys are in the bay, but it's not recommended as an anchorage.

RICHARDSON

As we round the bluff at the west side of Jones Bay and approach Richardson, we see a couple of houses on the low bluffs with fields behind. There are four conspicuous fuel tanks here and a small building on the pier. This is the major petroleum port for Lopez.

We Arrive at Richardson and Weep a Bit …

The sad thing about Mackaye Harbor is that the store at Richardson is gone. The well-loved store, which was an historic landmark, burned down in May of 1990 in a devastating fire that shocked all of Lopez Island.

The store, built on a pier over the water, was long a favorite stop for recreational and commercial mariners, and historically the first fuel stop in the islands. Not only that, Richardson Store had the greatest ice cream cones around. It was as close to being an old-fashioned general store as could be found in the Pacific Northwest, carrying everything from oxen yokes to food, fishing tackle and clothing. The store's motto was, "If you can't find it, you don't need it."

There was no float and mariners tied to the pier, climbing the ladder to the top— a dizzying 15 feet or so at low tide—and over the bull rail onto the dock. Richardson Store served not only cruisers, but the entire south end of Lopez and was a favorite stop for bicyclists who pedaled 12 miles from the ferry landing for a rest and an ice cream cone.

In 1985, the store was added to the National Register of Historic Places, and it burned down on it's 100th anniversary. Richardson store is a charming bit of island history, gone, but not forgotten.

Richardson Fire

An electrical fire started in the store during a gale in May 1990. When firefighters reached the store it could not be saved. Nearby residents were moved out of harm's way and firefighters were most concerned about keeping nearby gas tanks from blowing as the raging flames threatened ever closer. Tanks were watered down and it was 24 hours before the fire department was satisfied the fire was out.

"It was a tremendous loss to the island, and that is an understatement," said Hildegarde Goss who lives with husband Bill near Agate Beach.

The 1990 fire was not the first one for the Richardson Store. It burned in a major fire in the late 1800s and then was rebuilt at the pier.

The owners wanted to rebuild after the 1990, but learned they couldn't build on pilings and there wasn't enough land to build on shore. The store is gone, but the tanks are still used for off-loading fuel from large vessels. *(Mariners can buy fuel at Richardson by calling ahead: 360-468-2275.)*

Lopez Islanders are Unique
The San Juan Islander newspaper of 1901 commented on the People of Lopez:
"They are most hospitable and entertaining. It is a saying that no one on Lopez, be he stranger or friend, knocks in vain when seeking food or shelter."

Richardson "now," fuel tanks but no store

Richardson History

"The first town one approaches in going to San Juan County upon the steamer *Lydia Thompson* from Seattle is Richardson. The rugged and unpropitious shores which rise before the eye from the water's edge give little evidence of the fertile and productive acres of land which lay immediately inland, and which constitute an agricultural district than which (sic) heart could desire no better in the world. Thus, the unfavorable conditions which upon arrival seem to fill the mind are swept away in admiration for the opportunities and scenes of progress which are seen upon all sides within the forbidding pale." *(From the San Juan Islander)*

Richardson was settled in the 1870s by George Richardson. Fishing became the main industry for this southern extremity of Lopez.

"The leading industry at the town of Richardson is salmon fishing, conducted in Richardson Bay in front of the place. In fishing season the entire bay is filled with all kinds of fishing craft and the shores are lined with tents and huts of the fishermen …

"The fish running into Puget Sound through the Strait of Juan de Fuca strike this point first, and when fish are caught in no other locality they are caught here. During the past summer when a phenomenally large run was experienced in all places, one of the purseine (sic) outfits caught so many fish in one haul they were unable to lift the net and were compelled to let the fish go. A close estimate gives the approximate catch at this place for 1901 at over one million fish, not including many thousands of fish which were caught, and because of no market for them were dumped back into the sea, which would bring the total to about one million and a half."

The *San Juan Islander* also reported that N.O. Hodgson ran the general merchandise store, operated the wharf and sold firewood for steamboats. A blacksmith shop was located near Richardson, and there was talk of building a steel manufacturing plant. When Smith Island Lighthouse was manned by the Coast Guard, "coasties" relied on provisioning at Richardson during their lonely vigil.

Naming Lopez Island
It was named in honor of Gonzales Lopez de Haro, the Spanish discoverer.
He was the pilot for Lt. Alferez Quimper aboard **Princess Real,** who prepared the first chart of the Strait of Juan de Fuca in 1790.
Quimper turned south and sailed into what later was called Puget Sound.
Wilkes, however, named Lopez Chauncy's Island after Capt. Isaac Chauncey, who commanded victorious ships on Lake Ontario in the War of 1812.

Local Knowledge
Our guru of "local knowledge" on Lopez is Ron Meng, owner of Islands Marine Center. He's lived on Lopez since the early 1970s, and given us good advice about various anchorages around Lopez, as well as historical information.

Naming Islands off Lopez

Geese Islets was the name originally given by the Wilkes Expedition to a group of islands which include Long Island, Buck Island, Mummy Rocks and Whale Rocks.

Pass Between Charles & Lopez

We went through the pass again in the fall of 1997 with John and Louise Dustrude of Friday Harbor in their 23 foot Sea Sport. It was SO narrow, rocky and shallow, that Jo couldn't believe she'd had the nerve to take **Sea Witch**, *4.5 foot draft, through the pass 15 years earlier.*

Carl first sailed through in **Condor,** *then later in* **Winsome** *with a 9 foot draft, using a hand leadline and caution.*

We recently went through in **Scheherazade,** *5.5 foot draft, with an electronic fathometer, still using caution.*

➡ **NOTE:** *Canadian Current Atlas* gives graphic images of current speed and direction in the passages off southwest Lopez Island.

Ron Meng, whose family owned Richardson Store in the early 1970s:
"Originally, Richardson was going to be the county seat when it was built in the late 1800s. The whole area was very commercial, with three canneries, barber shops, hotels, huge berry and truck farms, before there were refrigerated trucks and irrigation in eastern Washington. They could go back and forth to the islands and haul fruit, fish and other cargo by boat, which was easier than getting to eastern Washington."

The only float at Richardson was a small one Ron put in for a while, but the waters were too rough for it to last, he said. (Courtesy of the Supplement to the *San Juan Islander 1901,* Islander Ron Meng, and other sources)

⚓**UNDERWAY AGAIN,** we continue west from Richardson.

Charles Island is about 200 yards south of Lopez. It is about 450 yards wide and 800 yards long, east to west. An unmarked charted shoal extends off the east coast for about 500 yards, plus numerous other rocks surround Charles.

A channel between Charles and Lopez has a least width of about 25 yards between the 3 fathom depth curves. A tiny islet between Charles and Lopez is charted on the south side of the channel's east entrance. We favor the Lopez side in here.

Cable area charted at the east entrance may have replaced the charted overpower and telegraph cables between the islands which are no longer here.

[RW Bn] or **[RW]** red and white daybeacons, describes two identical daybeacons which are at two locations along the channel but not shown on all charts. Each daybeacon has a dayboard with two horizontal white diamond sectors, two vertical red diamond sectors and a white reflective border.

Richardson Daybeacon [RW Bn] or **[RW]** is on the south shore of Lopez midway through the channel. It is on a white box near a stairway and is described and named in the *1998 Light List,* #19545. Chart 18400 indicates a flashing light which has been replaced by the Richardson Daybeacon.

Twin Rocks Daybeacon [RW Bn] or **[RW]** is at the channel's west entrance. It is about 200 yards east of the charted 3 foot shoal, on an iron spindle between two charted but unnamed rocks. This dayboard, described and named in the *1998 Light List* as #19550. Charts 18434 and 18400 do not show the Twin Rocks Daybeacon.

The *Coast Pilot* notes, "(this) small passage should not be attempted without local knowledge."

Mummy Rocks

➡ **NOTE:** Chart 18423 states **CAUTION:** Currents of 5 knots or more with severe rips and eddies occur in San Juan Channel between Goose Island (off San Juan Island) and Deadman Island (off Lopez Island).

Secar Rock, Hall and Long islands area is well charted on larger scale charts, but we need to use caution and pay attention to currents and weather. Many of the rocks here are National Wildlife Refuges.

Mummy Rocks, NWR, are 0.75 mile northwest of Charles, and 0.3 mile north of Long Island. They don't look like mummies to us, but we don't go close enough to inspect. This is another nasty looking bunch of rocks, but gulls, seals and other sea life seem to think they're great.

Whale Rocks are slightly north and west of Long Island, and our preferred passage is in deeper water west of them in San Juan Channel. There's no problem with water depth passing either side of Mummy or Whale rocks.

Davis Bay on Lopez, north of Mummy Rocks, faces south and is open to the full fury of the Strait. It's mostly high bank, with cluttered rocks and tiny islets on both east and west shores. There's a fair amount of development in the bay, with a couple of private piers and buoys, but no real anchorage.

Buck Island, NWR, is in the southeast part of the bay.

Davis Point has charted rocks and kelp about 300 yards offshore. The sometimes treacherous current spills over the shoals with large tide rips, and could easily send the unwary mariner into **Deadman Island,** northwest of the point. The island is a National Wildlife Refuge, 3.5 acres of rocks less than 100 yards off Lopez.

It's possible to go between Lopez and Deadman in a small, fast boat. The current rips through here, as do short, steep waves, and it's pretty narrow. When we went through in a small boat there were substantial waves four to five feet high. Seals on Deadman rocks watched nonplused as we ran with a 5 knot current. "Mummy, Deadman," these names are rather unnerving, especially when thrashing around this area in rough weather.

The Lopez shore along here is made up of fractured, overhanging rocky cliffs.

Kings Point is about 0.4 mile north of Deadman. A nasty charted rock is 200 yards offshore and south of the forested rocky point.

Shark Reef DNR Day Use Park is between Kings Point and Deadman Island, and can be reached by experienced mariners in beachable boats, weather permitting. It is a peaceful, fragile and gentle 40 acres enjoyed by those who appreciate wilderness. A quarter-mile trail through the evergreen forest from the county road to the rocky shore is not always the easiest, sometimes slippery underfoot with tree roots clogging the way. If you tour the island by car or bicycle, visit the park and see for yourself. When you step out of the forest onto the wave-splashed rocks and look across San Juan Channel to San Juan Island, you feel the peace and beauty of this remarkable spot.

We continue cruising north along the Lopez shore with Turtleback Mountain off in the distance on Orcas Island.

White Cliffs on Lopez aren't really white, but are light colored sandy bluffs. Large erratic rocks are charted and visible along this shore.

Shark Reef, NWR, is 0.6 mile north of Kings Point and 0.1 mile offshore. This jagged mess of rocks looks surreal, as if floating on the surface, with kelp off the southwest side. Guarded by seals and cormorants, the reef is hard to see after dark. Bluffs 100 feet high stand above the Lopez shoreline.

Big Rock at **Rock Point** is our next landmark, about 1.3 miles north of Shark Reef. We've used the "white house" about 500 yards north of the rock as a reference landmark, but since there's always the chance that someone might paint the house, we now use Big Rock, a very visible huge rock not likely to move or burn down.

The semi-Victorian white house with its red roof stands out from the other nearby homes. A drying lagoon behind a long spit is charted just north of the white house at the southwest end of Fisherman Bay.

Otis Perkins Day Park straddles a road at the head of Fisherman Bay and is on both San Juan Channel and the bay. Named for the beloved, long-time Lopez Islander Otis Perkins, the park

Traditionally Deadman

It's been called Deadman Island for as long as anyone knows, but we're not sure why. A woman won the entire island in a contest in 1948, but it has since become a National Wildlife Refuge.

Shark Reef

Public Lands
Tidelands, unless otherwise noted, are state-owned. Some are leased and posted for aquaculture or private use. When going ashore take the Washington State Public Lands Quad Map of San Juan County. Public tidelands surround much of Lopez Island, many in inaccessible areas. Most of them extend from the mean high tide line to extreme low tide.

White house & Big Rock

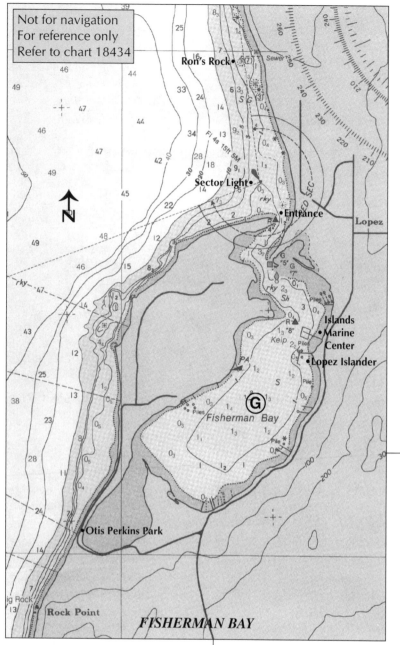

Not for navigation
For reference only
Refer to chart 18434

FISHERMAN BAY

is great for beachcombing, for landing kayaks and a neat place to picnic. Perkins was active in the community, starting the fire department, and later becoming chief. The park is a Lopez Wetland.

Approaching Fisherman Bay entrance is simple. We can choose virtually any course which keeps us outside the 10 fathom depth curves off Lopez and it's peninsula, avoiding charted rocks and shoals enroute.

Continuing north along this shore, after rounding the peninsula we pass an intriguing driftwood fence. Lopez Village now comes into view beyond the Fisherman Bay Entrance Sector Light. Although the village is on the waterfront, there is no moorage or anchorage, but there is inside Fisherman Bay, and that's where we're going.

Fisherman Bay Sector Light [Fl 4s 15ft 5M] flashing 4 second 15 foot high light visible 5 miles, is on a red and white diamond-shaped dayboard mounted on a pile structure. Charted near the 1 fathom depth curve, it is about 300 yards north of the sandspit at the west side of the entrance to Fisherman Bay.

We must keep this mark to starboard when entering Fisherman Bay.

Hard Aground!

A different island's yacht club planned a cruise to Fisherman Bay some years ago. The cruise chairman, a knowledgeable skipper, organized the cruise carefully, but in the crunch of duties somehow forgot to check the tides.

His was the lead boat as the flotilla crossed San Juan Channel and cut between Fisherman Bay Light and the spit. It was a falling tide, and before he knew it he was aground, as were a half-dozen other boats who had followed him. Others in the club took the "correct" route, keeping the red marks to starboard and went on into Fisherman Bay.

Several hours later the "groundees" floated free and slunk into the bay, cheered appropriately by fellow club members. There has never been a repeat of that grounding incident by that yacht club—that we've heard of.

➥ **NOTE:** Fisherman Bay Sector Light dashed line discrepancy charted on 18400 (1994) and 18434 (1996) shows Lopez Rocks in the white sector with the sector line bearing 170°T toward the light.

Light List (1999) #19560 indicates the red sector bearing as 166°T, which is as charted on 18400 (1997), 18421 (1998) and 18430 (1996), showing Lopez Rocks in the red sector.

(See p. 10 for sector line discrepancy at 5 foot rock shoal in Griffin Bay.)

Once we cross the 10 fathom depth curve charted about 300 yards northwest of the sector light, we use the courses suggested by Ron Meng.

Channel shape and depths as charted are subject to silting changes caused by currents and possibly by storms at the entrance.

Charted rock, awash, height unknown, near the 1 fathom depth curve is on the east side of the channel about 100 yards offshore and 100 yards northeast of R "4" red triangular daybeacon.

FISHERMAN BAY

The shallow, zigzagging channel makes some mariners understandably nervous. It's not really that difficult, but we still use care and try not to enter on a falling tide if it is predicted to be really low.

It helps to study the charts, *Tide Tables*, *Light List* and the following remarks, especially on the first trip through the channel.

Once inside, the anchorages, facilities, amenities and friendly villagers make the trip worthwhile.

Fisherman Bay entrance
(Photo courtesy IMC)

Entering Fisherman Bay

Ron Meng probably knows Fisherman Bay and the entrance better than just about anyone else around, and we share his advice about entering. (Statements in parentheses refer to the *Light List* and our comments.) There are no guarantees, but Ron's way works for us and many others:

"Properly navigated, there's actually about 6 feet of water in the shallowest part. Everyone says its 4.5 to 5 feet at low tide, but there's more than that. My rule of thumb, quickest way to explain, is keep in straight lines."

"Stay very close to the red and white diamond-shaped dayboard, keep it to the right, to starboard, stay within 20 to 30 feet. This marks the edge of a 3 foot shoal off the entrance. It's shoal all the way from the light to the sandspit. This is the most common grounding spot in the whole area.

"Go straight to R "4," red triangular entrance daybeacon on a pile at the northeast point of the spit. Stay close to it. Don't make an arc toward the beach on the other side, which the current will try to make you do.

"Past R '4,' stay in the middle of the channel, don't let the current sweep you around. Keep going straight down the middle and take both green marks real wide to port."

• (G "5," square green channel daybeacon on a pile off the east shore about 375 yards south of R "4")

• (G "7," green can channel buoy, about 150 yards south of G "5")

"A sand bar is building between the two green marks and it's never been dredged, so don't cut too close.

"Head straight to R '8,' red nun channel buoy. (It is charted about 200 yards off the west shore where it marks the edge of a 4 foot shoal. R "8" is about 350 yards south and a bit east of G "7".)

"Keep that red buoy to starboard and once past that, you're home free."

Best way to remember:
"Stay in straight lines, stay close to the red markers on your starboard and take all green markers very wide on your port."

Currents in the channel approach or exceed 3 knots on extreme tides. There are no current predictions for the channel or Fisherman Bay, but they are somewhat consistent with the currents in San Juan Channel.

Winds may blow in over the spit separating San Juan Channel and Fisherman Bay, with an accompanying mild chop.

Wave, You're on Lopez

The Lopez Wave is a well-established art form. Local drivers raise one finger, two if they're energetic, but no full hand, "parade queen" waves.

When walking, it's okay to raise your hand high enough to signal a real wave, and that you're not just picking blackberries along the roadside. Sometimes nodding your head and smiling will accomplish the same thing, especially if your arms are full of groceries.

Unusual Way into the Bay

Jo didn't always like knowing how shallow the water was under her 4.5 foot draft sailboat, Sea Witch.

After she sailed into Fisherman Bay several times and knew the channel, she'd turn off the fathometer and sail in, usually on an incoming tide, tacking back and forth in the channel. She seldom touched bottom.

"It was a lot less stressful that way," she claims.

Reefnet boats at Fisherman Bay entrance

Reefnet Fish Boats

Entering Fisherman Bay you will see remarkable looking reefnet boats on the sandy spit inshore from red triangle "4."

These vessels are historic fish boats from the past. They were originally used by Indian fishermen, and later fished by non-Indians who preferred the historical fishing method.

Farmers' Market

Wetlands Walk

When walking through Lopez Village there is a delightful, quiet wetlands stroll off Weeks Road on the shores of Fisherman Bay. Tromp around on trails with readerboards explaining the flora and fauna in the wetlands.

All buoys are private.

⚓ **Anchoring** in sand bottom with charted depths to 1 fathom, 4 foot max at MLLW is okay in Fisherman Bay.

Ⓖ The whole bay is a great **gunkhole,** a fine place to sail the dinghy or row. You might want to set your crab pot as crabbing may be okay here.

〰 **Public tidelands** in the bay are limited, refer to the quad map for locations.

Islands Marine Center is past red buoy "8," is the first stop in the bay. Lopez Islander Resort is immediately south of IMC. Both marinas have guest moorage and stress they don't compete, but complement each other.

IMC offers boat haulouts and repairs and Lopez Islander carries marine fuel and has a restaurant and lounge. IMC and Lopez Islander plan combined nature trails, children's playground and pet walk.

Tidal currents flow through both marinas, so be aware of the direction the current is setting when approaching or tying up.

Islands Marine Center has been owned and run by Ron and Jennifer Meng since 1972. The business started from the trunk of their car the year they were married. Now, more than 25 years later, their marriage and their business have endured and grown, along with their delightful daughter, Tina.

Islands Marine Center Facilities

➤ Guest moorage capacity 1,200 feet of dock space, reservations encouraged
➤ Daily moorage rates approximately 55¢ foot
➤ Shore power $3 day, water
➤ Pumpout & porta-potti dump, $5 fee
➤ Restrooms with hot showers
➤ Marine supplies, chandlery, propane cannisters, kerosene, fishing gear, bait
➤ Largest marine repair facility in San Juans with 20+ technicians, 15 ton travel lift, engine repair, emergency boat repairs
➤ High tide, single-lane launch ramp, $5 round trip
➤ Marine fuel next door at Lopez Islander
➤ Picnic area, barbecue
➤ Nearby services & activities, see below
➤ Monitors VHF Channel 69
➤ Contact: Ron Meng
➤ Tel.: 360-468-3377, FAX: 360-468-2283, e-mail: imc@rockisland.com
➤ Address: P.O. Box 88, Fisherman Bay, Lopez, WA 98261
➤ Philosophy: "We're on Lopez, 40 minutes from America, so we know we have to do a better job at a better price."

Activities in Fisherman Bay

➤ Visit Lopez Village, fish, scuba dive, crab, gunkhole, bicycle, walk, golf, kids' play area & tennis (soon), taxi service, spectacular sunsets

---

Lopez Islander Resort was bought by the Diller family of Seattle in 1997, with Bill Diller as manager. They are enthusiastic about the Islander and have new ideas, including yacht club rendezvous facilities and tent platforms for campers who may arrive by small boats or bicycles.

Lopez Islander Marina Facilities

➤ Guest moorage capacity, 52 boats, accepts reservations
➤ Rates: Memorial Day-Labor Day, 92¢ foot; off-season, 49¢ foot
➤ 30-50 amp shore power, water, included in fee
➤ Marine fuel: gas & diesel
➤ Restrooms, showers, laundry
➤ Basic store on dock, ice, fishing gear, bait
➤ Restaurant, lounge, lattes, gift shop
➤ Motel, hot tub, swimming pool
➤ Monitors VHF Channel 78
➤ Marina manager: Bill Diller
➤ Phone: 360-468-2233, FAX: 360-468-3382
➤ Address: P.O. Box 459, Lopez, WA 98261

Diller Hotel

The new owners of the Islander Lopez have been in the area a long time. The family built the Diller Hotel on First and University in Seattle in the late 1800s, which is now across the street from the Seattle Art Museum and Benaroya Symphony Hall.

Lopez Village and Fisherman Bay

Two restaurants are in Fisherman Bay. The first is at the Lopez Islander and the second is the Galley Restaurant about 0.25 mile south of the Islander. A sign wel-comes customers to tie up at the float just below the Galley, or walk there along Fisherman Bay Road.

Walking the less than one mile into **Lopez Village** from the bay is easy, with no hills, not much traffic, and it gives you a chance to practice the "Lopez Wave." You may also find succulent blackberries to graze on in late summer. You'll pass the red library building on the right side of the road. Built about 1894 as the Lopez School, it was one of four regional schools until 1941. Turn left to the Village at the library. In a couple of blocks you'll find basically all the major services on the island, including a wonderful grocery store.

Lopez Village from inside Fisherman Bay

Lopez Park, across from the store, had restrooms, showers, picnic areas, telephones, and a farmers market on summer weekends. Concerts are held at the nearby Village Performance Pavilion in the summer.

Lopez Historical Museum is a must-see. It's light, airy and you can see and touch the exhibits, including wonderful turn-of-the-century items, plus an annex with old farm machinery. The Museum offers a great Historic Landmark Tour pamphlet of old homes, including Sears homes, and historical sites. If you have a chance to tour the island by bicycle or car, or even walk a bit, it's an interesting tour. *(Museum hours are July-Aug.: Wed.-Sun., noon-4 p.m.; May, June & Sept.: Fri.-Sun., noon-4 p.m. Tel.: 360-468-2049)*

Lopez Library

Old-Time Towers

The Weeks Family Water Towers, 1914-1916, are in the heart of Lopez Village. Built by a family who homesteaded much of what is now Lopez Village, they were the first to settle this part of the island in about 1850. Water was pumped from wells to wooden water tanks atop the buildings by a gasoline engine.

Boats at Lopez Museum

✺**UNDERWAY AGAIN,** continuing our circumnavigation of Lopez, we head north from Fisherman Bay to Upright Channel. Keeping the Fisherman

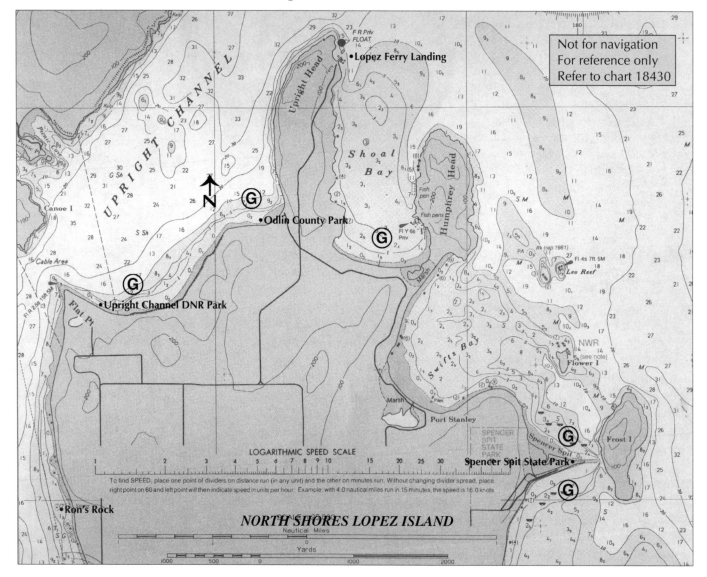

Not for navigation
For reference only
Refer to chart 18430

NORTH SHORES LOPEZ ISLAND

LOGARITHMIC SPEED SCALE

To find SPEED, place one point of dividers on distance run (in any unit) and the other on minutes run. Without changing divider spread, place right point on 60 and left point will then indicate speed in units per hour. Example: with 4.0 nautical miles run in 15 minutes, the speed is 16.0 knots.

Nautical Miles

Yards

"Ron's Rock"

The rock received the name because after boaters hit it they called for Ron Meng to help tow and repair their boats.

"Tepee Rock" was another name for the rock when a beautiful white tepee stood on the bluff above it for many years.

Fish at Flat Point

Salmon fishing is reported to be good off Flat Point during flood tides say our fisher friends.

Bay Sector Light to port we head west until reaching the 10 fathom depth curve about 500 yards offshore, and continue north along this shore of Lopez Island.

Staying outside the 10 fathom curve will also keep us off the erratic rocks along shore, including "Ron's Rock," a huge boulder charted about 200 yards offshore and approximately 0.65 mile north of Fisherman Bay. One way to locate the rock is to find the big log house with a blue metal roof that is atop the nearly 100 foot high bluff. The rock is almost directly below the house, and is visible at a 7 foot tide.

Flat Point is about 1.5 miles north of the entrance to Fisherman Bay. The point is at the southwest end of **Upright Channel**. At 400 yards wide, it's the narrowest part of the channel. The no-bank spit at the point has a number of waterfront homes.

Flat Point Light [Fl R 2.5s 15ft 5M] flashing red 2.5 second light 15 feet high visible for 5 miles, is on a triangular red dayboard on a pile offshore of the point.

Cable areas on either side of Flat Point cross to Canoe and Shaw Islands.

Upright Channel is about three miles long and from 400 yards to one mile wide separates Lopez and Shaw islands. Ferries serving Friday Harbor on San Juan Island ply the channel.

Current predictions for Flat Point or Upright Channel are not listed in the *Tidal Current Tables.* We have encountered currents in the Flat Point area which at times appeared much greater than the 0.25 to 0.5 knot currents flowing northeast and 0.25 knots or less flowing southwest indicated in the *Canadian Current Atlas.* Perhaps they relate more to the general channel current than to the Flat Point area.

Longtime friend and Lopez fisher Peter Roloff speaks of maximum ebbs of 3 to 4 knots and flood currents of 2 to 3 knots. He also confirms a big back eddy from Flat Point south to Ron's Rock.

If confronted with adverse currents when approaching either side of Flat Point, using backeddies can be a big help, at least in reaching the point.

UPRIGHT CHANNEL DNR PARK

About 500 yards east of the Flat Point Light is a Department of Natural Resources park with public beach access, a delightful new addition on Lopez for recreational mariners, and also for those arriving by cars and bicycles. Except for the mooring buoys, the park is day-use only. The park's three buoys are pale yellow, distinguishing them from nearby private buoys.

⚓ **Anchoring** is possible here in less than 5 fathoms. Watch for nearby cable crossing signs.

Ⓖ This is a **good gunkhole.**

Two of the picnic areas are in high beach grass. Others on the hill above are reached by gentle stairs and trails. A readerboard describes the park and a beach walk to Odlin County Park.

Upright Channel DNR Park

Upright Channel DNR Park
➤ Three mooring buoys, no fees
➤ Four picnic areas & firepits
➤ Three miles of public tidelands
➤ Water, restrooms
➤ Activities: beachcomb, swim, gunkhole, dig clams, picnic

🌿 This park really utilizes DNR public tidelands. It's an easy walk along the beach below the high tide line from about 300 yards west of Flat Point, and around the point to Odlin Park, 1.2 miles away. The firm sandy beach makes great walking. Dogs, kids and everyone must stay below the high tide line.

✺ **UNDERWAY AGAIN,** and we have an easy cruise about 300 yards off this lovely forested shoreline until we reach **Odlin County Park**. The park is at a "bend" where the shore turns north to the bluffs of Upright Head. It's easy to spot the park with its broad, sandy beach, no-bank waterfront, ball field, picnic area and campsites. An old beached rowboat makes a great pirate ship for kids.

The park is about one mile from the Lopez Ferry Landing, has a launch ramp, and is an ideal base for exploring the islands as it's in the middle of favorite cruising, kayaking and fishing grounds. A wide 1 fathom shelf extends over 100 yards off the marvelous, shallow sandy beach and low tidelands at the park's south end.

⚓ **Anchoring** is possible in 3 to 5 fathoms, sandy bottom. Boat traffic in Upright Channel passes less than 0.5 mile from the park, so wakes may roll your anchored boat.

Ⓖ Odlin is a favorite spot for families. It's a **great gunkhole**.

The dock at the north end of the park is near precipitous sandy cliffs nearly 100 feet high. The slippery slopes are signed, "Danger, do not climb," in several places. The dock is a stop for the foot ferry *Redhead,* which serves a number of islands from Bellingham to Victoria, with the schedule posted at the dock.

Odlin Park old cannon

Odlin County Park ramp & pier

Naming Swifts Bay

The bay was named for Charles A. Swift, who moved to Lopez in 1862.

Kelp Harvesting

Puget Sound Potash and Kelp Fertilizer Co. was established on the south shore of Swifts Bay during World War I. Kelp was harvested by the vessel "Harvester King," and potash was extracted for explosives.

A cement fuel tank and deteriorated cook house on the hill above the bay are all that remain of the three-story complex.

➥ **NOTE:** For those using **Chart 18434,** we're about to slip off it, so it's time to switch to **Chart 18429** Rosario Strait, Southern Part, covering all the rest of Lopez Island. (**Chart 18430,** Rosario Strait, Northern Part, covers a small portion of this area.)

⚓ **UNDERWAY AGAIN**, we leave Odlin Park and head northeast.

Upright Head, 200 feet high, is at the north tip of Lopez, less than one mile north of Odlin Park. These cliffs are quite stupendous, rising straight up out of the water, with a few homes atop the forested bluffs. Several resident eagles fish from lofty perches, swooping down on outstretched wings to scoop their next meal from the sea.

Lopez Ferry Landing is east around the point. We give it wide berth when ferries are in the vicinity. There is no float or landing here for recreational mariners.

Upright Head Ferry Landing Light [FR Priv Float] fixed red light 15 feet high on a black float, is a private aid at the ferry pier.

Shoal Bay is between Upright Head on the west and Humphrey Head on the east. Homes surround the bay. A private moorage owned by the legendary Seattle boat builder Anchor Jensen is on the east side below 100 foot bluffs.

Mussel and clam farms are in the south and east portions of Shoal Bay.

[Fl Y 6s] flashing yellow 6 second light, is a private aid marking the aquaculture facility on the east shore.

⚓ **Anchoring** is possible in the south part of the bay. Depths range about 3 to 4 fathoms and it's reasonably good holding ground, but watch for crab pot buoys. Local boaters tell us the worst winds are southeasterlies, which come across the isthmus at the bay's south end, making it hard to row out to an anchored boat.

Ⓖ We'd call it a **marginal gunkhole.**

There are no public facilities in the bay and only a small part of the west shore has public tidelands. A rock quarry on the east shore has towering rock cliffs reaching 200 feet high in places, often with eagles waiting eagerly for dinner to swim by.

Humphrey Head, where cliffs drop sharply and water is 15 to 19 fathoms deep within 50 yards of shore, is a mostly residential area. We round the head and go south towards Swifts Bay and Spencer Spit.

Leo Reef is less than 0.5 mile off the southeast part of Humphrey Head, a rock stew which seems to crop up out of nowhere. Avid fishers head towards Leo Reef as the steep rocky ledges and plateaus around here are what bottom fish love.

Leo Reef Light [Fl 4s 7ft 5 M] flashing 4 second light 7 feet high visible for 5 miles, is on a diamond-shaped dayboard with black and white sectors on a pyramidal base. The reef is charted, marked and uncovers, but nearby charted rocks, visible at a 2 foot tide, still manage to snag the unwary. A sign on the reef reads: "submerged **DANGER** rocks." Seals and sea lions often haul out on Leo Reef.

In 1981, a rock covered at 3 feet was reported about 350 yards west northwest of the light, and is charted PA, "position approximate."

Swifts Bay is off the northeast shores; a semi-circular, shallow, sandy bay stretching from Humphrey Head to Spencer Spit. Many recreational mariners pass through the outer portion of the bay on their way to Spencer Spit State Park. The bay is inside the 10 fathom curve, and in places it's just over 1 fathom deep.

⚓ **Anchoring** is possible in Swifts Bay, 2 to 3 fathoms, sand bottom.

Ⓖ It's a **reasonably good gunkhole** in reasonably good weather.

🌿 **Public access** in the bay is a 60 foot wide beach at a roadend near the charted marsh. Crabbing is good here, so be aware of crab pot and private mooring buoys.

Port Stanley is the community in Swifts Bay and homes line the shores. There are no facilities here, although it was once a booming town. The north end of Swifts Bay has forested shoreline gradually sloping down to no-bank waterfront. The cleared hill to the south is still farmed.

Lopez Ferry Landing

Port Stanley

In June of 1892, Port Stanley Townsite Development Co. started a Christian community in Swifts Bay. Frank Baum, an idealistic, opportunistic, moralistic attorney was appointed postmaster. He built a combination store, post office, home and newspaper office to publish the *San Juan Graphic*. Economic conditions put the new company out of business before it hardly started.

A two-story community hall was built at Port Stanley in 1889, used for community meetings and church services. Later it supposedly served as a "house of ill repute."

The *San Juan Islander* blamed the lack of growth of the east side community on "good roads leading to Lopez (Village) and other parts of the island," but not to Port Stanley. "Surrounding Port Stanley is fine grazing and fruit-raising country, which only awaits the proper people to make it prosperous and thrifty … a wharf is needed and a trading post to facilitate the development of natural resources which are so very abundant here …"

Where's Livingston?
Port Stanley was named for Sir Henry Stanley, a 19th century English explorer who presumably met Dr. Livingston in Africa.

Flower Island, **NWR,** is off the east side of Swifts Bay and is about 0.4 mile south of Leo Reef. This 4.6 acre island is important to mariners because of the many rocks 200 yards off the north end. Depths northwest of the island are 1 to 3 fathoms for about 400 yards. Nesting birds, seals and sea lions may be seen on Flower Island, but humans aren't allowed within 200 yards of NWR land. This isn't a problem around Flower, given the surrounding rocks, and we're inclined to stay farther off than that.

SPENCER SPIT STATE PARK

The long, curving, triangular sandspit at the park almost seems to touch Frost Island, about 75 yards away at low tide. The spit is the centerpiece of inviting Spencer Spit State Park, the only marine state park in the San Juans on salt waterfront which is easily accessible by both land and sea.

Lopez's First Settler …
This was William Humphrey who settled in the far north end of Lopez. He arrived in the late 1870s, farmed 166 acres, raised wheat, hay and chickens, and had a 500-tree orchard of apples and plums.

Spencer Spit State Park

Charts don't indicate water depth between the spit and Frost Island, but we've been through there many times. It's deeper close to Frost. Back in the "good old days," ferries and steamers occasionally passed through the channel.

Spencer Spit is one of the most popular of the marine state parks in the San Juans. It's not as far out in open water as the Sucia group, it's close to amenities and is quite protected. The half-mile long sandy beach is a good place for kids to play and swim, with plenty of driftwood to build forts, a rebuilt pioneer cabin to explore on the spit's end, bunnies in the meadows and deer in the evenings.

⚓ **Anchoring** is possible either side of the spit in 3 to 5 fathoms, mud bottom.

Ⓖ This is a **great gunkhole, another** favorite.

☛ **CAUTION:** Water at Spencer Spit is high in nitrites. Taps and faucets are posted that nitrites may be harmful to infants, children and pregnant women.

Theodore Spencer built a cabin from driftwood logs on the end of Spencer Spit before 1930.

The weather-worn, decaying cabin was replaced in 1978 with the present structure. As with the original building, driftwood logs and material from the spit were used, and the same design and notching techniques were used to rebuild the cabin.

Log cabin on the spit

Spencer Spit State Park Facilities
➤ 129 acres with 1.5 miles of shoreline
➤ 16 buoys, eight on each side of spit, plus anchoring space
➤ Buoy fees $5 night
➤ 46 campsites, including 8 beach sites, reservations May 15-Sept. 15; Tel.: 1-800-451-5687
➤ Washington Water Trails campsite
➤ Outdoor showers
➤ Picnic tables, beach fire rings
➤ Forest trails
➤ Restrooms, water (*sidebar*), telephone, no power
➤ Activities: gunkhole, beachcomb, fish, dig clams, crab, swim, scuba dive, birdwatch, camp, picnic, relax
➤ Tel.: 360-468-2251
➤ Address: Spencer Spit State Park, Rt 2, Box 3600, Lopez, WA 98261

The marvelous lagoon in the center of the spit is a wildlife preserve with herons, gulls, plus all kinds of other birds, sea grass, sea lettuce and a variety of flora. It's a fascinating birdwatching area, and a tidal stream runs in and out the north side of the lagoon. We hike out to the end of ever-changing Spencer Spit each time we're here. The park land access is closed from October through March, but the buoys and beaches are usable year-round by boaters.

A reader board informs:

"The sandspit was created by action of waves eroding sand from cliffs to the north and south and transporting sand along the shoreline to the spit. It gets its asymmetrical shape because sand is carried in nearly equal amounts from north and south. The very tip of the spit migrates seasonally with changes in direction of prevailing winds. Winter winds from the north force the tip to the south; summer winds from the south force the tip to the north. Will the tip ever reach Frost Island? Probably not. As the spit gets longer currents flow faster through the narrow channel. Sand is not deposited in this area and some may be carried away from the tip. Presently the channel and spit are in equilibrium."

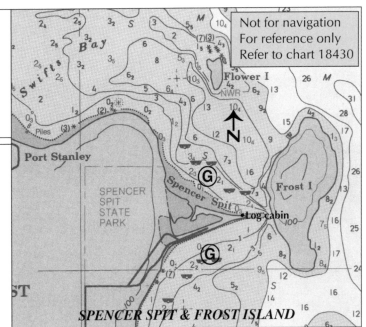

Not for navigation
For reference only
Refer to chart 18430

SPENCER SPIT & FROST ISLAND

Spencer Spit History

The spit has had visitors for thousands of years. The area was used by Salish Indians about 1000 B.C. as a temporary camp. Each spring, while living in mat and pole shelters, they gathered shellfish and herring, preserving them for the winter.

In the 1880s, the Spencer and Troxell families homesteaded and the families exchanged the land several times. In 1891, Troxell received a land grant under the Homestead Act. He built a home which stood until 1979. The nearby storage shed is all that remains of the house. State parks acquired the spit and uplands in 1967.

Frost Island off the tip of Spencer Spit is 200 feet high, with steep, rocky cliffs almost all the way around, topped by forests, except at the low southern end. There are no charted hazards offshore except for one rock near the northwest end of the island. Frost is private with several houses peeking out from the rocks and trees. On the east side is a small cove for property owners use.

Public tidelands are below the high tide line, but the island is so steep there is practically no beach access.

UNDERWAY AGAIN, we leave Spencer Spit and meander south.

Our cruising plan is to head through Lopez Sound along the west shore, looking into Hunter and Mud bays, then up the east side, past the "Triple R" islands (Rim, Ram, Rum), and Lopez Pass. After that we'll continue between Center and Decatur islands, go around the north end of Decatur, and slip over to James Island Marine State Park.

We'll complete our circumnavigation of Lopez by going south along the east shore, poking into bays along the south shores until we again reach Iceberg Point.

LOPEZ SOUND

This is a five mile long delightful, sheltered sound bordered by Lopez Island on the west, south and southeast, and Decatur Island on the east. The uncrowded Sound, often passed by cruisers heading for more well-known destinations, has good sailing, anchorages and crabbing. For cruising mariners who enjoy anchoring away from the "madding crowds," Lopez Sound is a real treat.

Depths in much of the sound are under 10 fathoms, although it is considerably deeper in the southern portion west of Center, Rim, Ram and Cayou islands. Most charted hazards are marked. There are several other islands in the Sound and some smaller bays, including Jasper, Hunter, Mud, Reads and Brigantine.

Lopez Pass, leading to Rosario Strait, is on the east side of Lopez Sound, between Decatur and Lopez islands.

As we leave Spencer Spit, we keep outside the 3 fathom depth curve because of shallow water and occasional erratic rocks near the beach. Forested bluffs rise to 100 feet above the shore, with a few homes along here.

Frost Island
It was named by the Wilkes Expedition for John Frost, a boatswain in the expedition, not because they were cold.

Oops ...
When walking along Spencer Spit one time we found a Washington State Parks mooring buoy mixed in with driftwood at the high tide line. Chain was sticking out of the top. It was disconcerting to find it here, especially since we depend on these buoys to stay where we usually find them, out in deep water. We don't think this happens often.

➡ **NOTE**: Much of the shore-line in Lopez Sound is public tideland below mean high tide. Refer to the DNR Quad map of San Juan County for details.

⚓ **Anchoring** is possible in the large bight about two miles south of Spencer Spit. There's good protection in a westerly here, and just about anywhere along this west shore of the Sound.

Ⓖ We like this bight, another **good gunkhole.**

Small Island, **NWR,** about 2.3 miles south of Spencer Spit and 0.1 mile off Lopez Island, is populated by birds and an occasional seal. Although it's possible to pass inside of the island in a small boat, it's still necessary to stay 200 yards off the island because of wildlife refuge regulations.

Cable area south of Small Island means anchoring should be avoided here. South of the cable area are several pocket-size coves. However, most of them have homes with private floats and private mooring buoys, leaving little room for an "outsider" to anchor.

The deepest portion of Lopez Sound is in the area southwest of Center Island and south of the cable area to Jasper Bay. Also note that depths along the shore here may be somewhat tricky, ranging from 2 to 17 fathoms within 100 yards.

Jasper Bay, one of the few small bays named on the east side of Lopez Island, is at the end of a road with several private homes. It is small and steep-sided, but offers a glorious view to the east of Mount Baker.

Hunter Bay and Mud Bay, both in the south end of Lopez Sound, are bisected by a forested peninsula. Three National Wildlife Refuge islands are located in these bays.

Hunter Bay is one of the most inviting anchorages in the islands, with its uniform depth of about 2 fathoms at low tide. Forested hills offer good protection from all but northerlies. A few homes are on shore and tidelands are private.

A charted aquaculture float is about 250 yards offshore of two yellow aquaculture buoys at the northwest edge of Hunter Bay.

Hunter Bay Aquaculture [(2) Fl Y 6s] two flashing yellow 6 second lights on yellow can buoys, are privately maintained.

⚓ **Anchoring** is possible near the head of Hunter Bay in 2 fathoms, mud bottom.

Our fisher Peter Roloff who knows Lopez Sound well, advises, "If there's a westerly, tuck right up near the southwest end, otherwise you could drag. The bay is not a good anchorage in a northerly."

Ⓖ This is a **good gunkhole**, with the above exception.

🐚 **County launch ramp and dock** are on the peninsula on the southeast shore of Hunter Bay. This means it's possible to anchor out and row ashore for public access, or tie up

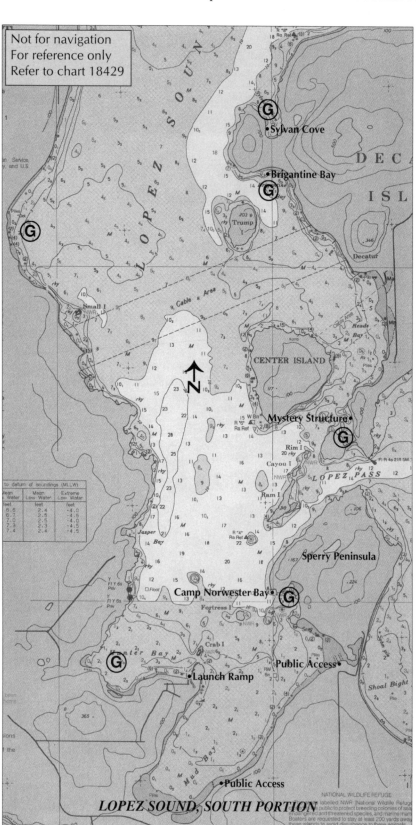

LOPEZ SOUND, SOUTH PORTION

for a short time at the float for loading and unloading. The dock and ramp are used by small boats and by residents of Center Island. There are no facilities here, except a parking area. It's several miles to the nearest store.

Crab Island, NWR, is about 100 yards off the southeast tip of Hunter Bay. It's about a half acre of grass-covered flat rock, a favorite spot with seabirds and occasional seals lounging on warm rocks.

Mud Bay is appropriately named, with a muddy bottom and shallow waters extending along a meadow at the bay's south end. **☙ Public DNR tidelands** are at the southwest head of the bay and along the eastern shore. Piles, dead-heads and several charted rocks are in the bay.

Launch ramp in Hunter Bay

Mud Bay Daybeacon [RW Bn] a diamond-shaped red and white dayboard on a spindle, marks a reef in the northeast portion of Mud Bay.

Sperry Peninsula, immediately south of Lopez Pass, is the large, forested knob connected to the northeast end of Lopez Island by a 1,500 foot long tombolo. The peninsula is a combination of high and low bluffs, with heights in the center exceeding 200 feet. It is charted but not named. The tombolo has long been used by Lopez residents for walking, sunset and sunrise watching and stargazing. According to local newspapers, peninsula owner Paul Allen has applied for a county open space designation on the tombolo which would again allow limited public use.

☙ Two small, unmarked public accesses are on Mud Bay. One is next to the tombolo leading to Sperry Peninsula. The other is at the end of a road next to homes less than 0.5 mile north and east of the charted slough at the head of the bay. They are used for hand-carried boat launches with limited parking at both accesses.

Fortress and **Skull Islands, NWR,** are west of Sperry Peninsula. Fortress is 3.21 acres and tiny Skull is unnamed on charts. The usual array of seabirds and sunning seals can be found on both islands.

Camp Nor'wester Bay, newly named**,** is a small bay on the southwest shore of Sperry Peninsula which was called Girls' Bay when Sperry Peninsula was the site of the former Camp Nor'wester, now located on Johns Island. *(See Ch. 5)*

⚓ **Anchoring** is possible in this bay in 1 to 4 fathoms, mud bottom.

Ⓖ It's a **small gunkhole,** a snug anchorage in a northerly blow.

Lopez Pass, often with swift-flowing currents, is between Lopez and Decatur islands, and opens east into Rosario Strait. It is about 0.4 mile long, 200 to 300 yards wide and 9 to 12 fathoms deep. There are no charted hazards in the pass.

Currents are based on Rosario Strait predictions. **Flood currents** flow west at 275° True and velocities may reach up to 4 knots. **Ebb currents** run east at 085° True and may also reach up to 4 knots. On a strong ebb the current shoots through Lopez Pass, straight across Lopez Sound where it splits and flows north and south, part of it right into Hunter Bay.

Lopez Pass Light [Fl R 4s 21ft 5M "2"] flashing red 4 second light 21 feet high visible 5 miles, is on a triangular red dayboard on a house at the northeast point of the pass.

Rim, Ram and Rum (Cayou) islands are in Lopez

Sperry Peninsula

Paul Allen of Seattle, multi-billionaire co-founder of Microsoft, bought 387 acre Sperry Peninsula for $8 million in 1996. It will be used as a family compound.

The peninsula formerly was the home of Camp Norwester, a youth summer camp for 51 years. The camp has relocated to Johns Island. (See Chap. 5)

Cayou/Rum Island

Rum Island was renamed **Cayou** by the State Geographic Board in the 1980s after Henry Cayou, a well-known islands' pioneer who lived to the ripe old age of 90.

Gunkholing in Lopez Sound

Mystery Structure

A fascinating concrete structure is on the tiny islet at the south end of Decatur.

Dan Crookes, who runs Island Transporter out of Flounder Bay in Anacortes, said it was once a kelp processing plant.

"I understand it was brick-lined and they heated kelp to extract iodine for the war effort during World War II," he said.

Decatur Beach

This tiny beach at the south end of Decatur Island, called Decatur Beach by residents, has been used in the past as a gathering spot each June for a community solstice celebration.

Record Flight

A Guinness Book of Records entry was set in the 1980s when a local mail plane pilot made the shortest flight between two mail stops, 44 seconds, from Center to Decatur Island. Jo made the same flight with the same pilot several months later, but it took 46 seconds.

Sound west of Lopez Pass. Rim and Cayou are designated as National Wildlife Refuges.

Rim, the most northerly, is the smallest of the three. It is rocky, covered with low bushes and shrubs, and there is a shoal off the north shore. We pass easily between Rim and Cayou in a 6 fathom channel.

Cayou (Rum), the middle island, is about two acres of shrubs and bushes, with shallows along the east shore and a shoal off the northern tip. The earlier name Rum made the islands the lyrical "Three R's." *(See sidebar)*

Ram Island, the southernmost, is the largest of the three at 8.8 acres, a beauty. The forested island has trails leading across the rocks and into the trees, with the highest spot a towering 98 feet. Ram is privately owned, but the last we heard the owners had generously designated it as open space and the public is permitted ashore, using care not to damage the flora and fauna. We found the pebbled beach near the south end the easiest place to land a small boat. A large shoal is charted off the island's east shore, and the bottom rises from 10 to zero fathoms in less than 100 feet. We found no good anchorage here.

Ram Island Rock Daybeacon [R "4"] triangular red daybeacon on a tower, is 300 yards southwest of Ram Island. The pass between the island and the daybeacon is 14 fathoms.

Inside the north shore of Lopez Pass at Decatur is a delightful beach on a spit. The isthmus and forested headland to the west are private, owned by San Juan Preservation Trust, accessible with permission only. An oval-shaped islet is in the tiny bay north of the isthmus. It dries at low tide between this islet and the spit.

⚓ **Anchoring** is possible in about 2 fathoms between the islet and Decatur's 100 foot bluffs, where some of the trees seem to be hanging on for dear life.

Ⓖ It's a neat little **gunkhole.**

Center Island, 178 private acres, is 0.2 miles northwest of this tiny bay. The island has a substantial number of summer homes, with piers and floats, and residents reach the island by airplane or boat. Erratic rocks surround much of Center, particularly on the north and west sides. A rocky shoal is off the northeast shore with 5 foot shallows extending nearly 300 yards off the island. The county quad map shows that island beaches below high tide are public, but before going on the beach we suggest consulting the map and watch for local postings.

Center Island Reef Daybeacon 6 [R "6" Ra Ref] triangular red daybeacon on a pile 100 yards off the southwest shore of Center, marking a mess of rocks.

Center Island Reef Daybeacon [W Bn] diamond-shaped white dayboard with black letters **"Danger Rock,"** is on a pile next to Daybeacon 6. Both daybeacons have radar reflectors and the same charted latitude and longitude according to the *Light List.*

DECATUR ISLAND

Decatur is the seventh largest island in the San Juans, and one of the most private, with 60 residents. Many of the beaches are DNR lands, but the only public access to the island is a launch ramp in the northeast bay near Decatur Head.

The 2,294 acre island hems in the waters between it and Lopez Island to form much of Lopez Sound. A private ferry serves the island. Basic facilities on Decatur are an airstrip, a post office the "size of two outhouses," a little red schoolhouse with a half-dozen students, administered by Lopez Island School District, a private dock signed "Decatur Shore Members Only," a shipyard which has been running since 1895, and a small store.

Reads Bay, off the west shore between Center and Decatur islands, is the core of Decatur. The private dock, island airstrip and shipyard are here.

We make a rather slow run between Center and Decatur because of the shallows in this passage at the southern part of Reads Bay. Midway between the tiny oval island in Decatur's hook and Center Island is a charted 1 fathom shoal, with nearby waters ranging from 3 to 7 fathoms. The portion of the bay between the northeastern bulge off Center and the shores of Decatur is charted 1 fathom, with a rock shown at 5 feet below the surface about midway between the two islands. It can

Reads Shipyard on Decatur

be tricky in here and we prefer to make the passage during a comfortable high tide, or at least on a rising tide.

Reads Shipyard is in the southeast corner of the bay. It's a full-service yard from September 1 through May 31, with some work done in the summer. Tel.: 360-375-6007. At the north end of Reads Bay is the dock for islanders only. The 1 fathom depth curve is 300 yards offshore for much of Reads Bay. Marshy tideflats line the beach between the shipyard and the private dock. Private mooring buoys are here, as well as private piers reaching into deeper water. Continuing north past Reads Bay we have 4 to 8 fathoms, with erratic rocks along the Decatur shoreline.

Cable areas run between Decatur and Center, and between Decatur and Lopez.

Trump Island, 19 private acres, is off the west side of Decatur, north of Center Island. It's over 200 feet high, with extremely steep cliffs on the east shore and rocky shoals along the north, south and west shores.

🐚 **Public tidelands** at Trump are below the high tide line, refer to the quad map.

Brigantine Bay is in a crook of Decatur Island northeast of Trump Island.

⚓ **Anchoring** is pleasant here, well protected in most weather. We anchor fairly close to Decatur in about 6 fathoms, mud bottom.

Ⓖ This is a **dandy gunkhole**.

There are several attractive homes along the shore and tidelands are private, for members of the Decatur Northwest community.

Sylvan Cove is north and east around a 200 foot headland in the northwest part of Decatur. "Sylvan" means "relating to, or characteristic of the woods or forest." Forests are along the shores, and a stately home at the head of the cove is surrounded by grassy fields and other homes. This lovely, gentle bay was once the site of a promising small resort called San Elmo. The bay is private, with a sign on a pier noting it is the community of "Decatur Northwest."

⚓ **Anchoring** is good in 2 to 3 fathoms in a beautiful setting.

Ⓖ This is a **good gunkhole,** if there's enough room. There are private mooring and crab pot buoys in here. Tidelands are private.

Undertakers Reef Daybeacon [R "8" Ra Ref] red triangular daymark with a radar reflector on a spindle, is less than 0.5 mile north of Sylvan Cove, on the northwest corner of Decatur Island. There are various bizarre reasons for the name of this reef, but we're not sure which is correct. The daybeacon is about 100 yards

Reads Shipyard

The yard was founded in 1895 by the Read Brothers. In 1903 the name changed to Reed and Cayou when they went into business with their brother-in-law, Henry Cayou. That might explain the change of name of Rum Island to Cayou.

Charted spelling is "Reads" while some references show it as "Reeds."

Shore at Brigantine Bay

Party island

Early Decatur settlers held barn dances and people would row over from Lopez to dance on Saturday nights.

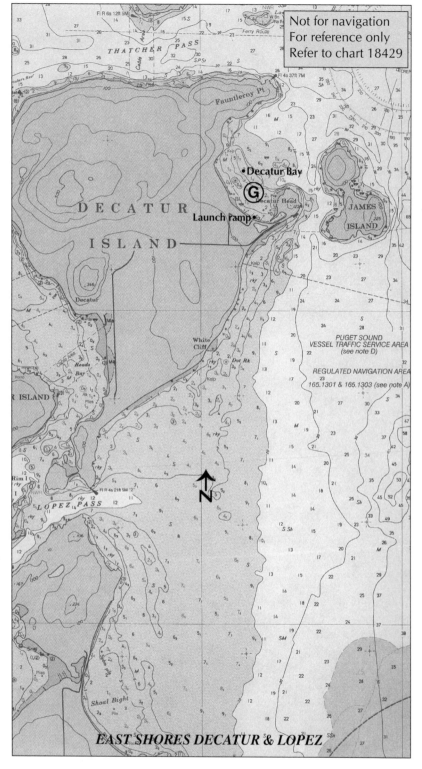

Not for navigation
For reference only
Refer to chart 18429

EAST SHORES DECATUR & LOPEZ

offshore on a mess of rocks, with a 100 foot high forested bluff above.

Thatcher Pass is the main ferry route between the San Juans and the mainland. This channel between Decatur and Blakely islands is one mile long, 0.5 mile wide at the narrowest point and 32 fathoms deep.

Currents in Thatcher Pass are based on Rosario Strait predictions. The **flood flows** slightly northwest at 300° True and velocities are usually less than 2 knots. The **ebb current** is nearly east at 075° True and may reach over 2 knots.

Cable area is midway along the pass.

Fauntleroy Point is the northeast point of Decatur at the east end of Thatcher Pass.

Fauntleroy Point Light [Fl 4s 37 ft 7M] flashing 4 second light 37 feet high visible 7 miles on a diamond-shaped dayboard in black and white sectors, is on a skeleton tower. We pass south around this point outside the 10 fathom curve, avoiding rocks off the east end.

Decatur Bay, our name, unnamed on charts, is a lovely, crescent bay between Fauntleroy Point and Decatur Head. It's about 0.5 mile across with depths from 16 fathoms at the eastern or outer edge, to 1.5 fathoms near the western shore. Some large rocks are in this part of the bay, plus a keel-banger at 3 feet below the surface. We watch the depth sounder carefully here. This picturesque bay has a small community of attractive homes and cottages at the south end, lining a curving sandy beach.

Decatur Head is a dramatic 123 foot promontory connected by a spit to the island.

❀ **County launch ramp** in the southeast corner of the bay at the road end provides public access. You can anchor, row in and walk the county roads on Decatur Island. It's a pleasant experience, and Decatur Islanders are nice folks, lucky enough to live on such a beautiful island.

⚓ **Anchoring** is possible in 7 fathoms or less, sandy bottom. Private buoys are in the bay.

Ⓖ This is another **pleasant gunkhole**. You might be more comfortable here than anchoring at James Island Marine State Park, about 500 yards east across the channel, although a southerly can whistle over the spit here.

Naming Decatur

Decatur Island was named by the Wilkes Expedition for Stephen Decatur, an officer in the U.S. Navy who served heroically in the War of 1812 and other conflicts.

Decatur Island School and the *U.S.S. Decatur*

Can't leave Decatur Island without this story.

Comm. Mike Knollman, skipper of the new destroyer *Decatur*, discovered Decatur School on the internet and made friends with the six students through e-mail correspondence. He and his crew "adopted" the school, named for the first *Decatur*. The kids wrote to the crew, sent them stories and pictures about their Decatur, under tutelage of their dynamite teacher,

Karen Lamb. In return, the excited students learned about the vessel, its duties and crew, plus some geography and history along the way.

In April 1999 the 527 foot destroyer *Decatur*, fresh after a trip up the coast from California, anchored near Bird Rocks in Rosario Strait. The skipper sent several large Zodiacs to Decatur to pick up the kids—and all interested islanders—to go aboard. Some 60 islanders went on what woman called an "awesome" cruise for everyone. Afterwards the islanders hosted the crew with snacks, conversation and pick-up basketball for the young crewmen, some barely out of school themselves. A wonderful time was had by everyone. Great things happen on Decatur.

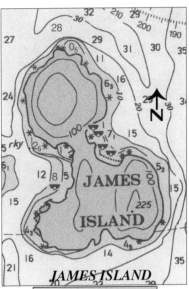

Not for navigation
For reference only
Refer to chart 18429

JAMES ISLAND MARINE STATE PARK

This island park east of Decatur Island looks on charts as though the island is a jigsaw puzzle piece that was pulled right off Decatur Head.

The beautiful 114 acre island has all the right stuff to make it a gorgeous marine park: two forested hills over 200 feet high with a low saddle in the center between two beautiful coves; hiking trails, deer, raccoons, birds and marine life.

Currents which boil past the **west cove,** and wash in and out of it in enormous back eddies, are the major drawback to this idyllic place. We've dragged anchor here several times and watched others also drag in the west cove. An uncharted rock in the southern part of the cove snagged a friend's boat for several hours. They escaped unscathed but unnerved. Best choice is to grab the one buoy or tie to the float in the west cove.

⚓ The **east cove** is a bit more comfortable and **anchoring** is possible in about 5 fathoms, rocky bottom. Four mooring buoys are in the cove. It's a refuge after a perhaps stormy crossing of Rosario Strait, although it is open to the wash from ferries and large ships, plus Rosario's currents. The mega-tankers in the Strait bound for Cherry Point do roll us a bit. For these reasons we hesitate to call James Island a gunkhole, although it is a pleasant place if you secure to a buoy, tie at the float, or anchor without dragging.

The small beaches are steep, gravelly and covered with driftwood, while the shore is lined with high, rocky cliffs. Trails criss-cross the forested island randomly from low spots to high bluffs where we see deer, sometimes atop cliffs. It's easy to circumnavigate the island keeping along the 10 fathom depth curve, as the rocks are close to shore.

Naming James

James Island was named by the Wilkes Expedition in 1841 for Reuben James, an American sailor who saved the life of Stephen Decatur in the Tripoli Campaign in Africa.

James Island Marine Park Facilities

➤ 113.65 acres with 12,335 feet of shoreline on Rosario Strait
➤ Four mooring buoys east side of island, one buoy on west side, $5 night
➤ 45' moorage float in west cove; boats under 26' $8 night; over 26' $11 night
➤ Moorage limited to three consecutive nights
➤ No power or water
➤ 13 primitive campsites, picnic shelters, fire grates
➤ Vault & pit toilets
➤ Pay station & bulletin board
➤ Designated Washington Water Trails campsite at south end of west bay
➤ Activities: camp, picnic, hike, beachcomb, fish, scuba dive

James' west shore float

Naming Kellett Ledge

Kellett Ledge was named in honor of Capt. Henry Kellett of the British Navy who was on a surveying expedition of the San Juans in 1846.

Cell Phones—Changed Lives

Telegraph Bay was supposed to be the first underwater point of what was going to be a Pacific underwater cable. It was an idea which never happened, and with cellular phones, it probably never will.

Early Chadwick Settler

Chadwick Hill was named for Sampson Chadwick who homesteaded the southeast area of Lopez in 1873. Only 11 other non-Natives were on Lopez at the time.

Watmough Bay beach & cliff

⚓ **UNDERWAY AGAIN,** we're in Rosario Strait heading south from James.

We continue along the east coast of Decatur, and then south along Lopez Island. The 10 fathom depth curve along the two islands is almost a straight line south of Decatur Head to Kellett Ledge, about 3.5 miles away, and as much as 1.1 miles offshore in places. Cliffs 100 feet high line Decatur's east shore south of the head.

🔱 **Public tidelands** are along most of Decatur and Lopez islands' east shores.

Cable area is south of Decatur Head across Rosario Strait to Fidalgo Head.

White Cliff on Decatur, 100 feet high, really is white, visible from a long distance. Tiny **Dot Rock** is about 300 yards offshore of the cliff.

Belle Rock, with two flashing lights, is about 1.7 miles east of White Cliff in the middle of Rosario Strait. It bares at extreme low tides and covers 3.67 acres.

Belle Rock Sector Light [Fl 2.5s 22ft 5M, Fl R 2.5s 20ft 9 M] diamond-shaped dayboard with white and black sectors is on a black cylindrical base. It has two flashing 2.5 second lights, white over red, marking a 42 foot shoal. The higher intensity white beam is 22 feet high with 5 miles visibility and shows up and down channel. The red sector light is 20 feet high with 9 miles visibility and is red from 173° to 177° True.

Bird Rocks, NWR, is about 0.5 mile southwest of Belle Rock. Three rocks close together, they total 3.75 acres, a nesting site to many seabirds and home to marine mammals. The southernmost and largest rock is 37 feet high. There are no navigation aids on the rocks.

The 10 fathom depth curve is about 1.1 miles offshore as we pass Lopez Pass.

Shoal Bight southeast of Sperry Peninsula is not recommended as an anchorage because of wave action and weather off Rosario Strait. Charted submerged piles are in the less than 5 fathom bight, along with a mix of rocks, logs, drift and snags.

Cape St. Mary juts out into the Strait and the shoreline rises to 100 foot bluffs with a few visible houses.

Kellett Ledge Buoy 3 [G C "3"] a green can buoy, marks a nasty bunch of rocks 800 yards east of Cape St. Mary. The ledge is marked by kelp and uncovers at the lowest tides. There's room to pass between the ledge and cape in 9 fathoms.

Telegraph Bay is scarcely a bay at all, just a bight, and very exposed to southeasterlies. It was once the site of summer solstice gatherings on Lopez, until a new owner declined to let anyone cross the property to the beach or to hike the trails to nearby high cliffs.

Watmough Bay is sometimes a good anchorage, depending on wind and weather. This is a spectacular spot, with towering black cliffs reaching to 470 foot high **Chadwick Hill** on the north shore.

Watmough Head, 242 feet high, is the south shore of the bay and wraps around into Rosario, with several homes above the beaches. Some mariners who arrive at Watmough after a lumpy crossing of Rosario or the Strait of Juan de Fuca consider it a haven. It is also an anchorage for those waiting for favorable weather to go south. It's a protected spot from sudden summer westerly squalls. Some local fishers like it as an anchorage, others don't, the *Coast Pilot* recommends it.

⚓ **Anchor** carefully, as Watmough is known for its rocky bottom. If the anchor isn't set well it could skid

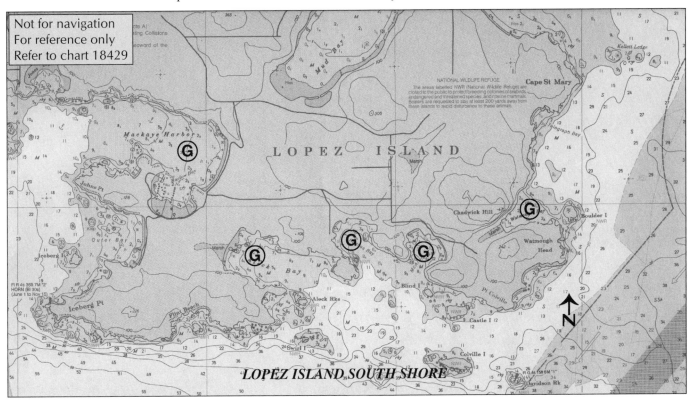

Not for navigation
For reference only
Refer to chart 18429

LOPEZ ISLAND SOUTH SHORE

across the bottom or it might get hung up on the rocks. Depths range from 2 to 6 fathoms.

Ⓖ Although we like the place, we consider it only a **marginal gunkhole** because of the bottom.

Historical Tidbits

The Spanish vessels, *Sutil* and *Mexicana,* anchored near Cape St. Mary and Watmough Head on June 10, 1792. "The chief object in making this anchorage was to observe an emersion (sic) of the first satellite of Jupiter."

Observing from a telescope on land, the precise accuracy of longitude could be calculated, using tables computed in Paris, as the first satellite emerged from behind the planet.

Captain George Vancouver reportedly anchored east of Watmough Bay in about 28 fathoms on June 7, 1792, during his brief time in the San Juans.

A beautiful, driftwood-strewn beach and marsh at the head of Watmough Bay is a Conservation Easement to protect wetlands. Donated by the Oles family to San Juan County Land Bank in 1993, there is public access for those who anchor and row ashore. This is a well-used, well-loved, well-cared for beach with dramatic sunrises. A short trail from the

Wilkes Names Watmough

Watmough Head, 240 feet high, was named in 1841 by the Wilkes Expedition. The Indians had called it Noo-chaad-kwun.

Oops!

*Veteran sailors and long-time friends from Olympia, George and Betty Hansen, anchored their 26 foot sailboat **Trina,** in Watmough Bay very carefully many years ago. Deciding the anchor was set, they went to bed.*

In the middle of the night they woke up to a howling wind and found themselves out in Rosario Strait. Their anchor had slid off the rocky bottom and away they went. The crab pot stayed behind in Watmough, and no doubt contributed its contents to a great dinner for someone.

Looking east to Rosario Strait from Point Colville bluffs

Well-known Hughes Bay Folks
*Hughes Bay has had some famous residents over the years. Remember Seattle TV's kids' favorite, Wunda Wunda? She was Hughes Bay resident **Ruth Prins.***

*   **Charlotte Paul Reese,** well known writer, and her husband **Robert Reese,** former under secretary of the treasury and Lopez Island pundit, lived in their home overlooking the bay for many years.*

*   All three died in recent years.*

South shore of Lopez on left, Castle Island on right

beach leads to restrooms and parking.

Boulder Island, NWR, is at the east end of Watmough Bay, 100 yards off Watmough Head. It is seven acres of barren, dome-shaped rock with a few scrub trees. The pass between Boulder Island and Watmough Head is charted somewhere between 1 and 3 fathoms deep and is less than 50 yards wide. Outside the bay, where Watmough Head juts into Rosario, it's windswept and rugged. A tepee is near the tree-line as it's been for about 40 years, say locals.

We are now running along the south shore of Lopez and in the Strait of Juan de Fuca. Given gentle summer breezes and reasonable tides and currents, this can be an incredibly beautiful cruising area. It can also be horrendous in a storm. Rocks and shoals, barren islands and several bays indent this southern shore which extends about four miles between Watmough Head and Iceberg Point. In a small, fast boat it can be traveled in about a half hour. In a slow boat it may take several hours. If this is an area you want to explore at your leisure, use caution and be aware of shifts in weather so you can escape without getting into problems. We have friends who spent a glorious week gunkholing this shore in their sailboat one summer.

❀ **Public tidelands** are along almost all of the south shores of Lopez Island. Refer to the DNR Quad map.

Point Colville is a spectacular place with beautiful pebbled and sandy beaches from Boulder Island to the point, but it is difficult to reach them because of steep rock cliffs, although they are public lands.

We hiked several miles along various upland trails on BLM land at Point Colville in what we would call "rain-forest type vegetation." It's absolutely beautiful. We ended up on cliffs nearly 100 feet above the beaches. Views are incredible, with tide rips and whitecaps, Castle and Colville islands, Davidson Rock, and you can even see out to Smith Island and the Olympics.

Davidson Rock is 0.5 mile south of Point Colville. The southbound lane of the **Vessel Separation System** is immediately southeast of Davidson Rock.

Davidson Rock Light 1 [Fl G 4s 15ft 6M "1"] flashing green 4 second light 15 feet high visible 6 miles, is a square green dayboard on a piling platform. A high intensity beam is directed toward Burrows Island Light. Davidson Rock is a welcome sight for those in the Strait, particularly after a foggy passage.

Colville Island, 0.3 mile west of Davidson Rock, is 11.5 acres of mostly barren rock, 64 feet high. It's a National Wildlife Refuge and nesting site for seabirds, including gulls and cormorants. The north shore's sheer cliffs drop straight into the sea, while rocks and shoals extend along the south and west shores. Heavy kelp is west of the island.

Castle Island is 500 yards north of Colville Island and 100 yards off Lopez at Point Colville, a wildlife refuge and seabird nesting site. This large, dramatic island is surrounded by five small rocky is-

lets, totalling over nine acres. It rises abruptly with a rounded southern edge. The very impressive north face drops to 20 feet of rock at the island's edge. The pass between Castle and Lopez islands is 6 to 7 fathoms deep and views of the cliffs on Lopez are spectacular.

Blind Island, NWR, is a two acre rock northwest of Castle and 100 yards off Lopez. It is sheer rock with a few trees on top, and kelp streaming in close to the island. A tiny unnamed isle between Blind and Castle islands has bare and gnarled trees.

McArdle Bay is the first bay encountered about 0.7 mile west from Colville Point. The crescent-shaped bay, often full of crab traps, has steep, barefaced bluffs on the east side. The east beach is about 500 feet long with rock outcroppings and little beaches.

⚓ **Anchoring** is possible in the southeast corner of the bay in about 2 fathoms, mud bottom.

Ⓖ This is a **pleasant gunkhole** in calm weather.

Hughes Bay is about 0.5 mile west of McArdle, out and around a 100 foot bluff. This beautiful little bay also has public access. The high bluff between Hughes and McArdle drops almost straight down into the bay, with a flock of erratic rocks, including a mess at 1 fathom, 1 foot, grazing at the southeast entrance. Beaches all around the bay are strewn with rocks.

🐚 **Tidelands** below high tide are public DNR lands.

A number of homes line the bay on medium to high bank waterfront, with several private piers and a number of private mooring buoys, as well as crab pots. Near the southwest shore is an unnamed NWR rock.

Brady Memorial Beach

Blackie Brady Memorial Beach is in the southeast corner of Hughes Bay. It's recognizable by a wooden stairway with a zigzag at the bottom leading to the delightful public pocket beach below a high bluff. The 75 foot wide beach is sand and gravel with driftwood-sitting logs.

⚓ **Anchoring** is all right if no southerly winds are blowing and the Strait is calm, in 2 to 4 fathoms, rocky bottom.

Ⓖ It's another good weather **gunkhole**.

Smugglers' Haunts

Peter Roloff, who's also quite a storyteller, told us of an old smugglers' stash in a cave "near here," when he was talking about the south end of Lopez, somewhere near Hughes and Aleck bays.

"You pass it and look back, there's a rock covering the entrance. It's a low water cave and you can only get in at low tide, but it was dry inside, and the booze stayed dry."

We undoubtedly did pass it because we looked back at every little nook and cranny we saw, and some seemed to match his description perfectly. We never did figure out just exactly which little cave he had in mind, however. To confound matters, he later said there were several other smugglers' caches along this shore, so we undoubtedly saw them.

Aleck Bay is about 500 yards west of Hughes Bay, after going out and around a headland. It is larger than the first two bays, lying east to west. It is 0.6 mile long and 0.25 mile wide. The conservative *Coast Pilot* speaks well of Aleck Bay: "The west and largest of three small bays on the south shore of Lopez Island, affords good anchorage except in heavy SE winds for small vessels in 4 to 7 fathoms, mud

Blackie Brady, Local Hero

Blackie Brady Memorial Beach in Hughes Bay was named in honor of Floyd "Blackie" Brady, whose dedicated research and tenacious spirit resulted in public access to this beautiful beach, dedicated by the Lopez Island Lions Club, May 1989.

Border Crossing on Lopez?

Several years ago Islandale Market in Lopez's south end declared itself an unofficial "border crossing." Those who wished to cross Lopez from north to south, or vice versa, were to stop at the store and sign in. All in good fun, of course. Part of the humor that binds islanders together.

Fond of Fauntleroy

Fauntleroy Point on Decatur Island was named by George Davidson, a topographer with James Alden in 1853. He was aboard the survey vessel **Fauntleroy***, but more significantly, he was in love with a young woman in Illinois whose last name was Fauntleroy.*

Longtime Monument

A U.S. Boundary Reference Monument was erected at Iceberg Point in 1909.

Naming Iceberg Point

It was named by George Davidon of the U.S.Coast Survey in 1854 for the "remarkable deep and smooth marks of glacial action."

bottom. Rocks, awash and covered, and reefs abound in these waters and caution is essential."

The bay shoals from about 10 fathoms at the entrance to 1 fathom at the head. There are 100 foot bluffs along the south shore and some of the north shore, with medium bank at the head of the bay, where there is a beach.

⚓ **Anchoring** near the head of the bay in less than 5 fathoms is good, especially in west winds.

Ⓖ This is a **gunkhole**, weather permitting.

Aleck Bay Inn is an attractive waterfront bed and breakfast at the head of the bay. Kayaks are stacked on the beach in front of the inn, next to the beach stairs. The inn offers a spa, fireplaces, bikes, private baths and meals. Tel.: 360-468-3535

The Neslunds

The Aleck Bay Inn was once owned by Rolf and Ruth Neslund. The inn was also their home. Although sometimes considered charming hosts, the couple had a long history of reportedly intoxicated brawls, often over Rolf's interest in other women.

They garnered their share of infamy in 1983 when Ruth was convicted by a jury of first-degree murder in the grizzly death of her husband Rolf, a Puget Sound Pilot who had been missing for months before her arrest. His body was never found. There was speculation that he was burned in a barrel at the home, but no evidence supported the idea.

After her conviction in a well-publicized trial in Friday Harbor, Ruth was interned at the Women's Prison in Purdy and has since died.

There is still no trace of Rolf, and some persons wonder if he just disappeared and may still be alive somewhere. Perhaps no one will ever know for sure what became of Rolf.

Several small bays and charted rocks are in Aleck Bay. A number of homes line the bluffs above the shoreline, several at the head of the bay. Some residents of Aleck Bay have a spectacular view out into the Strait, and in good weather they can see the Cascades and Mount Rainier.

Aleck Rocks, NWR, two rocks of 3.25 acres, guard the southwest entrance of Aleck Bay. They are totally bare, about 20 feet high, no beaches, rocky shoals around them, and kelp off the south side. In a small boat we went between the rocks and the peninsula to the west, something we wouldn't do in our sailboat.

Swirl Islands, NWR, five islets, are about 500 yards south of Aleck Rocks. Again, barren rocks, shoals and maybe a few seals lounging on the rocks.

Chart 18429 shows the area clearly and we keep it close at hand in here.

Storyteller & More ...

Peter Roloff, storyteller, fisherman, scuba diver and mussel grower (Shoal Bay Shellfish Co., Lopez Island Mussels), reefnetted off Swirl Rocks for many years. He said Robert Reese who lived in Hughes Bay (*sidebar p. 68*) was never "skunked" in summers when he sport-fished in the Strait.

"Robert would row out and fish. If he didn't catch anything, he'd buy fish from us, we'd toss it to him and tell people he'd 'caught' it."

As for Peter, he and his wife Anamo are long time friends of Carl's. They lived aboard their fishing vessel *Sonja* at Carl's place in Portage Bay in Seattle before moving to Lopez.

We continue along this open, rocky shore from Aleck Bay to Iceberg Point. It is so remarkable ... a primitive coastline of jumbled cliffs and rocks, windswept and primeval. Rock bluffs from 100 to 226 feet overlook the Strait.

Seals and sea lions pose on rocks along Lopez Island's south shore *(Photo courtesy of the late Robert Reese)*

We spotted a cave on the beach which looked like it might be a place where smugglers would have hidden booze. The beach and bay seemed wonderfully wild and unsettled, just the place for an artist or writer.

Flint Beach is a beautiful little bay with a small barren island in the center which is a Natural Wildlife Refuge. The bay is surrounded by medium to high bank bluffs. A tiny island, Flint Island, is inshore of the larger unnamed island. The house above a driftwood-piled beach belonged to Margaret Fitzgerald, an artist who lived there for over 40 years.

Cruising west, we pass more rocks, an unnamed NWR islet, kelp beds and rocky bluffs 100 feet above the shore. Even on a calm day the restless Strait sends large waves crashing against rocks at the base of cliffs along this bleak, fascinating, untamed coast.

Keeping about 0.2 mile offshore because of the rugged coastline with its offshore rocks, we reach Iceberg Point just a little over one mile west of Flint Beach.

We're back to where we started our circumnavigation of wild and wonderful Lopez.

In **Chapter 3,** we explore Shaw Island, the geographic center of the San Juan Islands, Wasp Passage and the Wasp Islands.

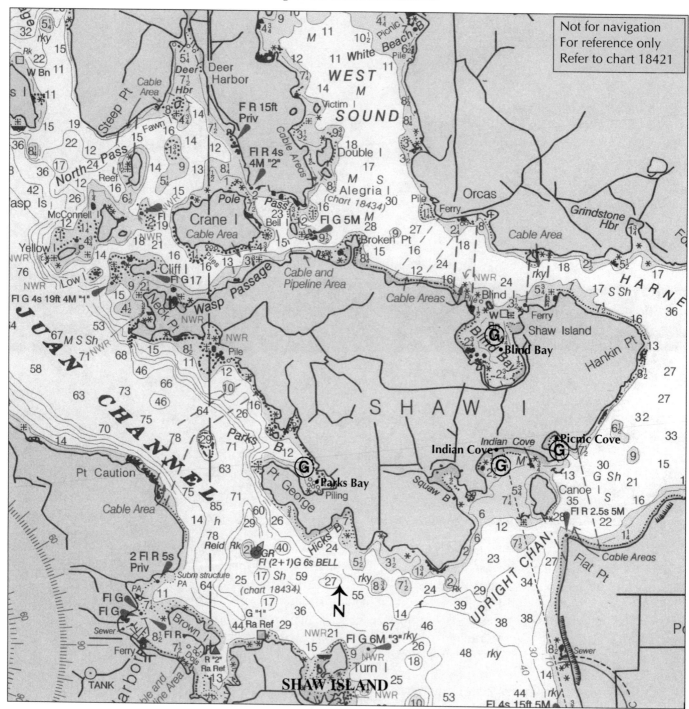

Chapter 3
SHAW ISLAND
Wasp Passage, Wasp Islands & Pole Pass

Charts & Publications for this Chapter

Chart	Date	Title	Scale	Soundings
U.S. 18421	03/21/98	Strait of Juan de Fuca to Strait of Georgia	1:80,000	Fathoms
U.S. 18423 SC	06/18/94	Strip Chart Bellingham to Everett, incl. San Juan Islands		
		Pages C & D	1:80,000	Fathoms
		Page C, inset 6	1:40,000	Fathoms
☆ U.S. 18434	04/27/96	San Juan Channel	1:25,000	Fathoms
CAN.LC3462	10/23/98	Juan de Fuca Strait to Strait of Georgia	1:80,000	Meters
🐚		Washington State DNR Quad Map—San Juan County	1:100,000	

Compare your chart dates with those above. There may be discrepancies between chart editions.
☆ = Preferred chart for this chapter 🐚 = DNR & other public tideland information

OVERVIEW OF SHAW ISLAND

Shaw Island, the smallest of the four ferry-served islands, is the geographic center of the San Juans. It is a delightful island of 4,936 acres with a permanent population of about 160 persons, which doubles or triples in the summer.

Two waterfront parks make Shaw a favorite stop for mariners: Blind Bay Marine State Park in Blind Bay on the north shore and San Juan County Park on the south shore.

Facilities on the island are the Little Portion Store and Marina run by Franciscan nuns who also are the ferry agents; a post office, library, historical museum, school, community center and two private airstrips. There are no resorts or restaurants, and for years Shaw was only a flag-stop for ferries.

There is an activity for non-islanders who are sailors: the fun, famous and frustrating Round Shaw Island Race, either direction, every August, sponsored by the San Juan Island Yacht Club. Adventurous sailors should check it out. Currents and flukey winds make it a real challenge.

Cyclists enjoy Shaw because of the "roads less traveled," not too many hills, rural beauty and the county park with its lovely, sandy beach and camping facilities.

Shaw's one-room red schoolhouse, K-8, is on the National Historic Register. The school now has a second room for computers. The log cabin Historical Museum, across the road from the school, is the rebuilt original post office. The library next to it has an old reefnet boat out in front.

➡ **NOTE: No marine fuel** is available on Shaw Island. The closest fuel docks are at Orcas Landing, Lopez Islander and Friday Harbor.

Shaw Island School

Shaw Historical Museum

National Wildlife Refuges

Some rocks and small islands off Shaw Island are part of the San Juan Islands National Wildlife Refuge and Wilderness Area (NWR).

Mariners must stay 200 yards away from these rocks and islands. All NWR islands are closed to public access except Matia and Turn islands.

Naming Shaw Island

The island was named by the Wilkes Expedition in 1841 for U.S.N. Captain John Shaw and his service in the war against Algiers in 1815.

Schooners Adventuress & Zodiac in Parks Bay

Cottage industries abound in various "cottages" on the island. A community center just south of Blind Bay is the scene of island activities and meetings. Our Lady of the Rock, a Benedictine Monastery, is in the center of the island where the nuns have a beautiful working farm, chapel and retreat facility.

A Bit of Shaw Island History

The first Shaw visitors were Native Americans who had been visiting the island for eons. They called the island "Somemana." It was the traditional place to gather mussels, clams and oysters.

By the 1700s, before settlers arrived, there were nearly 750 Indians on Shaw, with over 300 at Blind Bay. A second village with about the same population, was on south beach, near the present county park, according to a local historian. Some of the Indians married settlers, stayed on and established homesteads and families.

One of the island's earliest settlers around 1859 was Julien Lawrence, a French Canadian. He was hunting on Shaw when he met a young Indian woman named Thelma. The couple settled on a farm at beautiful Blind Bay. Current owners of the farm, Al and Lotte Wilding, bought the property in 1957. They love the intriguing history of their island home, including a friendly "haunt" who visits occasionally.

Another early island arrival was Hughie Parks, who settled in the 1880s in what is now Parks Bay. His neighbors literally drove the mild-mannered farmer insane with their constant harassment because he was a much harder worker than they. When he could stand it no longer he shot one of them, then another and another. Before lawmen could arrest him he shot himself. A sad story for such a lovely place.

⚓ **UNDERWAY,** we'll circumnavigate Shaw Island clockwise, starting at Point George on the west shore, and go clockwise around Shaw Island. We'll take a detour through the Wasp Islands, Wasp Passage and Pole Pass, and then we'll return to Shaw at Broken Point and continue our circumnavigation. *(Chart 18434 is helpful.)*

Point George is less than 1.5 miles northeast of Friday Harbor across San Juan Channel. The shoreline is rocky with forested bluffs reaching 164 feet above the point. After rounding the point and heading south into Parks Bay, we find the serenity of a beautiful bay.

Parks Bay is about 0.5 mile long and 0.2 mile wide, a secluded spot, the waters reflecting the deep green of surrounding trees. This is a place where yours might be the only boat at anchor. Mariners in Parks Bay tend to be quiet, picking up the tranquil mood of the bay. Several tiny shallow coves filled with submerged piles and old deadheads are fun to gunkhole by small boat.

⚓ This is a favorite **anchorage** among local boaters who prefer a small, quiet bay to a crowded harbor. The best anchorage is the south end of the bay, in 3 to 8 fathoms. There's good protection here, with a mostly mud bottom. Although northwesterlies may blow in, most of the time it's pretty calm. There's room for perhaps a dozen boats, but we've never seen that many.

Ⓖ It is a **delightful gunkhole.**

Herons stand for hours on long stick legs on the rocky shores of Parks Bay, waiting for snacks to swim past, darting their long beaks into the water for an instant meal. Eagles soar on huge outstretched wings high above.

There are no public tidelands in the bay and the entire shore is posted *"Scientific Research Area, positively no trespassing on tidelands or uplands and no dogs."* This is a University of Washington Biological Preserve on about 1,000 acres. The land was donated by the Ellis family: brothers Henry and Bob, both deceased, and Fred, who lives on Shaw. A pier near the head of the bay on the east side belongs to the U.W. Friday Harbor Labs. It has a shed, a float and an occasional small boat tied alongside.

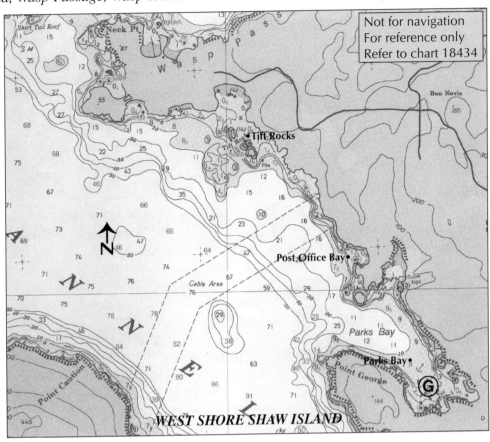

Not for navigation
For reference only
Refer to chart 18434

WEST SHORE SHAW ISLAND

The north end of the bay has a notch in the corner, east of a small peninsula, where we've also anchored in about 6 fathoms. It's more exposed to wind and waves from San Juan Channel, and there's room for just one boat in here. Sunsets and moonrises from this little cove are stupendous.

⚓ **UNDERWAY AGAIN,** we head north from Parks Bay along Shaw's west shore.

A tombolo, underwater at high tide, leads to an island on the end of the small peninsula at the north end of the bay. North of the peninsula is the all private Post Office Bay with several small piers, floats and mooring buoys. The name isn't charted, but there was once a post office here.

Cable area is about 0.4 mile north of Parks Bay.

Tift Rocks, NWR, are 1 mile northwest of the Parks Bay entrance, and blend in against the shores of Shaw, making them scarcely noticeable if you're cruising in San Juan Channel. The rocks are low, with scrub brush and grass growing from small nooks, surrounded by kelp-covered shoals. The north rock still contains the remains of a tiny, abandoned trapper's cabin. With care and a good depth sounder it's possible to go between the rocks and Shaw, staying 200 yards from the rocks. They teem with families of sunning seals who slip quietly into the water, swim out and take a curious look as you cruise by.

North of the rocks is a shoal bay with a large home and pier. As we cruise west to Neck Point we see more homes on rocky banks above shoal bights.

Tift Rocks

These fascinating rocks off Shaw's west shore were named for Bert Tift, the first postmaster on Shaw who homesteaded in 1883.

Tift Rocks

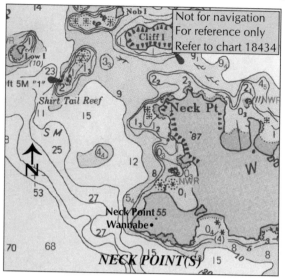

Not for navigation
For reference only
Refer to chart 18434

NECK POINT(S)

➡ *NOAA Chart No. 1, Nautical Chart Symbols Abbreviation and Terms* booklet is useful to explain sometimes obscure chart details.

Glossary of marine navigation in *Bowditch's American Practical Navigator* also helps clarify definitions of misused and misunderstood chart details.

Nob Island

From the Coast Pilot, "Local vessels bound from Friday Harbor to Deer Harbor use a clear deep channel about 70 yards wide through the rocks and shoals between Cliff and Low Island."

It did not specifically say the Nob-Cliff Channel appears to be the only channel which might have a restricted 70 foot width. Other channels are wider.

Kayakers in the Wasp Islands

Neck Point looks like a jigsaw puzzle piece that can't find a place to fit. There are actually two necks: the unnamed west one is a narrow, 55 foot headland jutting west into San Juan Channel. Carl calls it the "wannabe" Neck Point. Between the two necks is a tiny bay and charted, unnamed rock, part of the National Wildlife Refuge. The charted Neck Point projecting north into Wasp Passage has a much fatter neck and is 87 feet high.

We start at Shirt Tail Reef in San Juan Channel and take a close look at the Wasp Islands north of Shaw Island and through Wasp and Pole passages.

THE WASP ISLANDS

The Wasp Islands are a cluster of eight islands with messy rocks and reefs all grouped together in a 2.8 square mile area between Shaw and Orcas islands. They include Bird Rock, Cliff, Coon, Crane, Low, McConnell, Nob, Shirt Tail Reef and Yellow islands. The area can be a challenge as islands and rocks in the Wasp group are much closer together than they may appear on the charts. Visiting mariners sometimes are disoriented in this area and caution is needed. However, there are many and varied ways to cruise through these intriguing islands.

We suggest having chart 18434 handy while reading this description, hopefully before getting into the "Wasps' nest," as it best details the area at a 1:25,000 scale. Chart 18423 has an inset of the area at 1:40,000 scale. *(A magnifying glass helps.)*

Wasp Islands, Reefs, Rocks and Navigation Aids

Shirt Tail Reef, about 0.3 mile west of Neck Point on Shaw, is our starting place, at the west entrance to Wasp Passage. The reef rears its ugly rocks, some of them awash and visible at low tide, for nearly 300 yards northeast of the reef's green flashing light.

Wasp Passage Light 1 [Fl G 4s 19ft 5M "1"] flashing green 4 second light 19 feet high visible 5 miles, is mounted on a square green dayboard on a pyramidal structure at the southwest end of Shirt Tail Reef.

Low Island, NWR, 200 yards west of Shirt Tail Reef, is a tiny, 10 foot high island covered mainly with grass. A channel of 23 fathoms is between Low Island and Shirt Tail. A charted ledge, awash at low tides, extends about 50 yards southwest of the island, and a 1 fathom ledge extends 75 yards off the northeast shore.

Cliff Island, appropriately named, is a little less than 200 yards east of Shirt Tail Reef and about 250 yards north of Neck Point on Shaw across Wasp Passage. There's less than 10 fathoms in the channel between Cliff and Shaw, and Cliff and Shirt Tail. Cliff Island is 16 forested, rocky acres with cottages and cabins above steep, rocky banks that reach to 72 feet. Several private mooring buoys are in its tiny bights.

Cliff Island Light 3 [Fl G 6s 15ft 5M "3"] flashing green 6 second light 15 feet high visible 5 miles, is mounted on a square green dayboard on a square house midway along the south shore of Cliff.

Nob Island, NWR, is less than 100 yards northwest of Cliff Island and 100 yards north of Shirt Tail Reef. Nob is tiny, perhaps only 70 yards long, a bit less wide and 40 feet high. A cluster of charted rocks which are awash at low tides extends about 300 yards west of Nob. There is considerable nastiness around Nob and

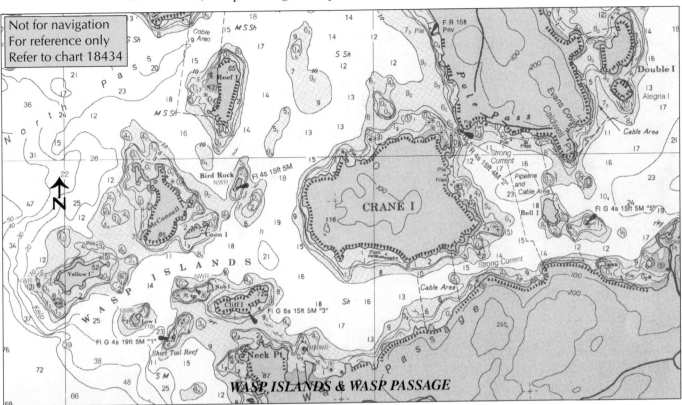

Not for navigation
For reference only
Refer to chart 18434

WASP ISLANDS & WASP PASSAGE

Cliff islands. Even those in small, maneuverable boats need to be watchful among these rocks. A narrow pass of about 70 yards approximately 5 fathoms is charted between Nob and Cliff.

Yellow Island, the westernmost of the Wasps, is also surrounded by shoals, but somehow we've navigated them more easily. The island needs to be approached with care. Spits extend from both the east and west points, and shoals are off the north shore, with a rock off the northeast baring at a 5 foot tide. It's also foul with kelp and rocks for 300 yards off the southwestern side, with a wildlife refuge rock that bares at a 3 foot tide, a real keel-catcher. *(See p. 78)*

McConnell Island, 32 forested acres, all private, is about 400 yards northeast of Yellow. It is surrounded by rocks and shoals on all but the south side, where it's 2 fathoms deep below 85 foot cliffs. A small island off the northwest point is joined by a tombolo, and it's shoal for about 200 yards around the point. A 100 yard long reef extends off a point on the east side.

Public tidelands of about 2,000 feet, mostly inaccessible, are below the high tide line along McConnell's steep southern shore. It's possible to pass between Mc-Connell and Yellow islands in depths of 5 to 10 fathoms, although there are several charted shoals and at least one rock awash.

Coon Island is 100 yards southeast of McConnell. The beautiful, 2.7 acre private island is heavily forested. A 2 fathom pass is between McConnell and Coon.

Public tidelands around the island are public below high tide.

Bird Rock, NWR, is about 400 yards east of McConnell Island. The reef extends north of a light for nearly 200 yards and is hidden at all but lowest tides. Surrounded by kelp, it catches its share of unwary boaters.

Bird Rock Light [Fl 4s 15ft 5M] flashing 4 second light 15 feet high visible 5 miles, is on a dayboard with black and white sectors mounted on a pile structure.

Reef Island, well named, is about 400 yards north of Bird Rock. The west shore is particularly shoal for 300 yards off the island, and shoals are also off the north and south ends. Only the high-bluff east side is relatively hazard free. The island is all private.

Public tidelands are below the high tide line.

Wasp Passage & Wasp Islands
They weren't named for the pesky insects at all.

They were named by Wilkes for the **Wasp,** an American ship commanded by Commodore Jacob Jones, which captured the **Frolic** during the War of 1812.

Bird Rock Light

Jo's Sea Witch at Yellow Island

Aground!

Lopez friends Jim & Miki Straughan ran aground in their 20 foot, deep draft, cat sailboat on rocks off Yellow's west side. Jim climbed into waist deep water, pushed the boat free, but lost his hold as the boat slipped away. Miki couldn't get the engine started. The boat drifted off, leaving Jim alone in the cold, strong current.

He called instructions across the water to Miki who then started the recalcitrant machine. She carefully manuevered the boat back to Jim. The shivering skipper gratefully climbed aboard. Miki was proclaimed an heroic mariner and they live happily ever after.

Dodd cabin on Yellow Island

Crane Island at nearly 222 acres is the largest of the Wasps. The south shore lies along Wasp Passage, while the northeast corner forms Pole Pass between Crane and Orcas islands. The north shore is foul below rocky cliffs, with covered rocks and shoals extending for 250 yards off this shore. The island has a high point of 116 feet on the southwest side. About a dozen residents live on Crane, which has a private marina at the northeast tip and a private landing strip.

Bell Island is the most easterly of the islands in Wasp Passage. It is 500 yards east of Crane and almost that far off the north shore of Shaw. It is shoal and foul nearly 200 yards southeast of Bell for over 500 yards.

Wasp Passage Light [Fl G 4s 15ft 5M "5"] flashing green 4 second light 15 feet high visible 5 miles, is on a square green dayboard on a pyramid structure surrounded by kelp. The light marks a shoal almost 400 yards east of Bell Island and 300 yards north of Shaw Island. The waters between the light and Bell Island are filled with rocks.

Yellow Island

Now we digress a bit and go back to visit the most delightful island in the Wasps, glorious Yellow Island.

This lovely 10 acre island was purchased from the Dodd family by The Nature Conservancy in April 1980. Brilliant red Indian paint brush, blue camas and spectacular yellow buttercups for which the island was named cover the meadows in wild disarray at the peak of their spring blooming. Hummingbirds dart among flowers to get their share of sweet nectar.

Now a nature preserve, the island is open to the public on a limited basis: stay on trails, no pets, picnicking, camping, no collecting plants or animals, and prior permission required for six or more visitors at one time. Visitors may wander the many trails interlacing the island, but are asked not to stray from the paths as the fragile island shows every footprint.

⚓ **Anchoring** is best along the south side in about 2 fathoms where we've had good holding ground for a short visit, but we wouldn't plan an overnight stay here. The island has no dock or public mooring buoys.

Lew & Tib Dodd

The couple bought Yellow Island in 1946 and lived a halcyon life in the cabin they built from driftwood, which still nestles between beach and forest on the island's south side, overlooking San Juan Channel. The heavy-beamed, low-ceilinged cottage was furnished from tide-given lumber and other treasures; the cedar shake roof hand-hewn from driftwood cedar. A guest house and primitive sauna, now gone, were on the west shore.

Lew never left the island except for short trips to Deer Harbor or Friday Harbor for mail and groceries, and never overnight. He died in 1960 in the cabin; his ashes are buried at his favorite island spot, Hummingbird Hill.

Tib lived alone on Yellow for six months each year until 1978. She rowed or ran a small outboard to Deer Harbor for mail and groceries until she was in her late 70s. The driftwood home they built is now the caretaker's cabin.

WASP PASSAGE

Wasp Passage runs between San Juan Channel and West Sound, and separates Cliff, Crane and Bell islands from the north shore of Shaw. The pass is about two miles long, with ferries and strong currents encountered anywhere along the way.

Currents in Wasp Passage flood northwest at 288° True and ebb southeast at 075° True. **Flood currents** may reach over 2.6 knots; **ebb currents** may be about 2 knots. Currents are based on San Juan Channel current predictions. Currents in the pass can be a trial or a joy to sailors in the annual "Round Shaw Race."

West entrance to the pass is between Neck Point on Shaw and Shirt Tail Reef, marked by Wasp Passage flashing green light "1."

Cliff Island is on the north side of the pass across from Neck Point. Ferries go cautiously through this narrow part of the pass, fairly close to Cliff Island flashing green light "3," where currents eddy just off the rocks. The waters off Neck Point on the south side are less than 5 fathoms deep until 0.3 mile east of the point. A shallow cove with a dock for Neck Point residents is here. The dock extends 200 yards into the cove near an unnamed NWR rock. It's all private and the uplands are posted.

Wasp Passage widens and deepens to 13 to 18 fathoms from Cliff Island Light to the east end of Crane Island.

The shore of Shaw along the passage has tiny bays and rocky forested bluffs that reach more than 100 feet. Shoals extend into the passage in rather surprising spurts, so we tend to stay in the center of the channel. Homes, several small piers and some mooring buoys line this shore.

Wasp Passage narrows again near the east end of Crane to less than 100 yards wide between the 5 fathom depth curves, with depths over 15 fathoms in the channel center. An exception is a charted 3 fathom, 5 foot shoal about 150 yards off Shaw. "Strong Current" is charted here for good reason.

Cable area between Crane and Shaw is near the east end of Crane Island.

It's shoal for about 200 yards off the southeast shore off Crane, and then the passage opens to the north once past the island. We see Pole Pass between Crane and Orcas as we approach the south side of Bell Island.

Pipeline and cable areas are from Shaw past both sides of Bell across to Orcas.

We stay in 12 fathoms south of Bell Island and give plenty of room to the Wasp Passage green light "5" marking the shoal. The Shaw shore along here has more high bluffs and virtually no beaches. In the bay west of Broken Point are two small islands, one joined to Shaw by a tombolo. Rocks and shoals surround them with small cabins planted on each.

Broken Point on Shaw Island marks the eastern end of Wasp Passage. Ferries pass close by its rocky cliffs which plunge nearly straight into the channel.

Now that we've successfully navigated the Wasp Islands and Wasp Passage, let's take a look at Pole Pass before we continue around Shaw Island.

Pole Pass is the narrow pass between Crane and Orcas islands north of Shaw. It is about 75 yards wide in its narrowest part, and less than that between the 3 fathom depth curves.

Charted depths in the pass are 6 fathoms. Low, rocky shores form the east side of Pole Pass. Rocks enclosing the marina on Crane form the west side.

McConnell Island

It was named for the first settlers who arrived on the island in the 1880s.

Son Victor, who lived with his widowed, well-respected blind mother and five siblings was "asked" by his family to leave the island when they discovered he was smuggling just about everything from apples to sugar, shoes, whiskey and wool.

➡ **NOTE: Bell Island** is a Marine Reserve area in the Voluntary bottomfish "No Take" zone program. The "No-Take" zone is on the east side of the island to about 300 yards north of the reef. All zones extend seaward 400 yards from the shoreline.

Logical name for Pole Pass

It was named for 40 foot high poles placed on both sides of the pass from which Native Americans suspended nets so they could snag ducks.

In the evening the Indians would climb the poles and put up the nets made of cedar bark strips. The ducks flew into them and fell into the water, stunned by the impact. Indians paddled out and retrieved them.

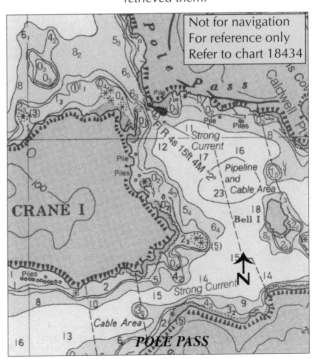

Pole Pass Light

It was officially established in 1887 when the government hung a 10 candle-power lantern that could be seen for 4 miles 18 feet above the water.

A Mr. Cadwell hung a lantern on his property each night many years before that to aid vessels running the pass in the dark.

Formerly Fox Island

In the late 1800s a squatter named Fox lived on Blind Island, building a small cabin, storage sheds, rock cistern and garden plot. With a bit of fishing, he sustained himself for many years. It was called Fox Island and he lived there with a wife and son.

In 1905, she left him while he and their son were fishing in Alaska, sold the house and moved away. The house was moved off Blind Island onto Shaw that year.

The father and son lived on Fox for many years. After the son died around 1960, the state took the island and changed the name back to Blind Island.

Pole Pass Light [Fl R 4s 15ft 4M "2"] flashing red 4 second light 15 feet high visible 4 miles, is on a triangular red dayboard on a tower on the Orcas side of the pass.

Currents in Pole Pass **flood northwest** and **ebb southeast**, and sometimes we shoot through under sail with the right wind and current. There is no reference station listed in the *Tidal Current Tables* for Pole

Sailing through Pole Pass

Pass, although currents would be similar to those in Wasp Passage, we suspect.

In years past, ferry captains piloting smaller vessels, like the old *Vashon,* would occasionally nudge the ferries through Pole Pass on the way to Friday Harbor. It was a tight squeeze and surprised many passengers who saw trees as they looked out the ferry's windows. As far as we know, no ferries ever grounded in Pole Pass. With the advent of larger vessels and stricter rules, skippers no longer make such "side trips."

We've reached Broken Point again at the east end of Wasp Passage and are ready to continue around Shaw …

Broken Point is high, sheer rock with little beach and houses tucked back in the trees. The bay on the east side of the point has low-bank waterfront with several houses and boats on buoys. About 1 mile east of the point are charted rocks which extend nearly 300 yards into the channel approaching Shaw's Blind Bay.

BLIND BAY & BLIND ISLAND MARINE STATE PARK

Blind Bay is immediately west of the Shaw Ferry Landing and indents the north shore of Shaw Island for about 0.5 mile. The bay is about 0.5 mile wide east to west, and depths are mostly 2 to 3 fathoms throughout, except for 4 to 6 fathoms south of the island.

Blind Island Marine State Park is a 3 acre jewel in the middle of the bay's entrance. This has long been one of our favorite destinations. The island feels like we're at one of the "Outer Islands" because it's such a wonderfully primitive place, even though it's just 500 yards from the Shaw Ferry landing and 0.8 mile from Orcas Landing across Harney Channel. The bustling vessel traffic in the channel makes us realize we're still very close to "civilization."

Blind Island's 1,280 feet of rocky shores have pocket beaches on the east and west sides where a small boat can land. You can fish from the north bluff. It's a great spot for kids to play hide and seek as there are so many neat places to hide. You can scuba dive or even swim here if you don't mind chilly water. One large madrona tree is on the western ridge, and elsewhere there are blackberries, waist high grass and stubby evergreens. A huge composting toilet has replaced an old-fashioned outhouse.

A wonderful variety of views from the island look across Harney Channel to Orcas and West Sound, east to Mount Baker and south into Blind Bay.

There was a time when we could tie our boat to a buoy at Blind Island and send the kids ashore with sleeping bags so they could spend the night safely camping out "in the wilds." No more. The Washington Water Trails sites at Blind Island means that only those arriving in human-powered boats are allowed to camp overnight on the island. Kids rowing to shore in the dinghy from the

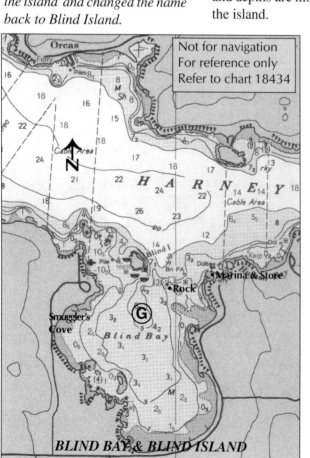

BLIND BAY & BLIND ISLAND

family boat don't qualify.

Blind Bay is great for small boat gunkholing along the low-bank waterfront. A road from the ferry landing is visible as it follows the south and east shores of the bay. The upland is lined with meadows, orchards and a few homes. Reefnet boats are often pulled up on the beaches.

🐚 **Public tidelands** in several parcels are around the bay, refer to the DNR Quad map before going ashore.

⚓ **Anchoring** is possible just about anywhere in the bay in 2 to 6 fathoms, mud bottom.

Ⓖ This is a **terrific gunkhole.**

Blind Island, Orcas Landing in background

Blind Bay Park Facilities
➤ Three acres with 1,280 feet of shoreline on Blind Bay & Harney Channel
➤ Four mooring buoys & room to anchor off the south shore of island
➤ Buoy fees $5 night
➤ Three consecutive nights maximum
➤ No power, no potable water
➤ Picnic tables, fire grates, composting toilet
➤ Four Wash. Water Trails campsites; annual permit or $7 person/night
➤ Activities: gunkhole, camp, walk, picnic, fish, scuba dive, swim, beachcomb

Boats can enter Blind Bay on either the east or west side of Blind Island with caution as both sides are rock-strewn.

Entering Blind Bay east of Blind Island, keeping west of the charted mid-channel rock marked with a navigation aid, is the easier entrance.

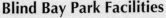

Looking south past Scheherazade in Blind Bay

Blind Bay Rock Daybeacon [W Bn PA] is a white diamond-shaped dayboard with a **"DANGER ROCK,"** pole-mounted on the rock, position approximate. The nasty rock, which dries at 3 foot tides, is about 150 yards east of Blind Island. This unlighted private aid is named and numbered 19665 in the *Light List.*

The charted 5 fathom depth curves of this channel favor the Blind Island side when entering the bay. The area between Blind Bay Rock (our name) and Shaw Island to the east is a mess of rocky shoals. Local residents use the west side of Blind Island with apparent ease, but we've seen boats aground in the barnacle-encrusted jungle.

Enterprising Blind Bay

A fish cannery, commercial orchards of prunes and apples, and a three-story prune dryer all were located on Blind Bay shores during the turn-of-the-century.

➡ **NOTE: Chart 18434** shows the Shaw shore west of Blind Island as having two 10 fathom, 3 foot holes inside the 1 fathom depth curve. This didn't seem right to us, so Cap'n Jack Culver, our Orcas sailing friend, verified our doubts when he took his ketch *Kahagon* over the area in doubt. Sure enough, he agreed with us.

"I stuck *Kahagon's* nose everywhere, and the depth never exceeded 12 feet. It varies from 0.5 fathom to 2 fathoms, no more. The charted piling doesn't exist," he said.

Thanks Jack.

A small nub of an island, an oyster-catcher rookery, is along the south shore of Blind Bay. The rock is state-owned and posted "no trespassing." A heron rookery is also in the south end of the bay, and a Native American midden is reported along the south shore.

Smuggler's Cove, a small cove on the west shore, is unnamed on charts. During Prohibition the smuggler's fast boats would race through the rock-infested channel between Blind and Shaw at speeds up to 35 mph to elude the Revenuers.

⚓**UNDERWAY AGAIN,** we leave lovely Blind Bay and make a quick trip to Shaw Landing, visiting the marina and store immediately east of the ferry landing. The landing is like no other in the islands …

Franciscan nuns in their brown habits are the ferry agents, and also manage the store and marina. They raise and lower the ferry ramp, joke with ferry employees, speak to everyone on the island as they come and go, and enjoy what they're doing.

Mother Kerper Chapel is on the pier, named after one the first Franciscan Sisters here. Mass is held every Sunday at 8 a.m. A Coast Guard bell dated 1964 hangs in a bell tower at the chapel, which is open to visitors.

The marina floats are east of the ferry dock. A few steps up a ramp and we're at the Little Portion Store and Shaw Post Office.

Nun at Shaw Landing

"We have no marine fuel, or any other kind, and there is no longer a laundromat on Shaw," said one of the nuns. There are restrooms and a telephone. (The 1997 *Coast Pilot* erroneously states that "gasoline, diesel, water and ice are available.") They do have ice.

Little Portion Marina Facilities
➤ Room for two to three guest boats, maximum size 25 ft.
➤ Fee: 35¢ foot
➤ Accepts reservations
➤ Nearby toilets
➤ No power, water, fuel or launch ramp
➤ Nearby facilities are store, post office
➤ Manager: Sister Dorothy Hood
➤ Phone: 360-468-2288, FAX: 360-468-3766
➤ Address: Box 455, Shaw Is., WA 98268

The Little Portion Store is great. There's been a store on Shaw for many years, and the Franciscans have been running it for over two decades with a staff of four

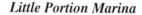

Little Portion Marina

nuns. Little Portion Store was named after an Italian church, Portuncula, "little portion of earth," which was the favorite spot of Saint Francis of Assisi.

There are wines, beers, cards, gifts, provisions including dairy products, fresh produce and seasonal local fruits and vegetables. It's a fully stocked grocery store.

The hardware selection is befitting an island's only store: extension cords, screws, bolts, fix-a-flat, batteries, small propane cannisters, solder fittings, electrical devices and magnets. Boaters will feel at home with the skeleton of a small island-built craft suspended from rafters.

Sister Kateri designs indigenous T-shirts.

Benedictine Sisters from Our Lady of the Rock make herb seasonings, mustards and vinegars, there are other island products and pottery from Bellingham.

Store hours are 9:15 a.m. to 5 p.m., always closed on Sunday. During winter months the store closes at 2:30 p.m. on Tuesday and Thursdays.

Little Portion Store

Shaw Landing Ferry Stories

Shaw ferry service started in the early 1930s when the islands' ferry stopped at a floating dock if someone flagged it down.

Once the float tipped up on one side as a Friday Harbor grocer attempted to board the ferry with a truckload of cattle and pigs. Truck and livestock landed in 10 feet of saltchuck, and the owner and critters swam to shore. Shortly after, a new landing was built at Shaw. When islanders wanted to board the ferry, they still flagged it down. In the late 1960s, the flag system was replaced with scheduled ferry service.

A true Shaw ferry story: The last late-night ferry left Anacortes for the islands (early 1980s), where it would spend the night in Friday Harbor, its last stop. Four young men on board were "feeling no pain" as they discussed going to Friday Harbor where there was bound to be plenty of "action."

"You want action?" queried a local islander overhearing them in the ferry cafeteria. "Hey, go to Shaw. That's where the action **really** is."

The four "happy" men trundled off the ferry at Shaw Landing in their pickup truck. They realized as they drove past the dark store and down the dark road, there would be no "action" on Shaw. In despair they watched the ferry pull out of the slip for the last time that night, bound for Friday Harbor.

We understand that after departing Shaw on the first ferry next morning they never returned to the islands.

⚓ **UNDERWAY AGAIN,** we leave Shaw Landing and continue clockwise around the island. East of the landing is a derelict boat still on the rocks as it's been for many years. Locals regard it with as much interest as they do seagulls on the ferry pilings. A heron rookery is on forested headland east of the ferry landing.

Harney Channel runs about one mile between Shaw and Orcas east of Shaw Landing. Currents in the channel may help or hinder mariners a bit along the wooded, uninhabited north shore of Shaw. **Currents** in Harney Channel flood westerly at 250° True, and ebb southeasterly at 120° True, at generally less than 1.4 knots.

Hudson Bay is a bight east of Shaw Landing, past a heavily timbered area. A private dock, an older home and a warehouse are in the bight. There are rumors that a private marina may be built in the bay. The 10 fathom curve is about 300 yards offshore from the ferry landing until about 0.3 mile east of Point Hudson, where it slips to about 100 yards off Shaw.

Cable area crosses through Hudson Bay and over to Orcas Island.

Point Hudson is at the east end of the bay of the same name. Forested bluffs of 100 feet or more mark the point and the area to the east.

Hankin Point at Shaw's northeast end one mile from the landing, is a scarcely-defined point. We round its rocky, forested shores and enter Upright Channel.

Upright Channel, between Shaw and Lopez, is about three miles long. It ranges from about 0.8 mile wide to less than 500 yards wide in the narrowest spot between Flat Point on Lopez and Canoe Island off Shaw's southeast shore. (*Ch. 2, p. 54-55*)

The 1.2 miles from Hankin Point to Picnic Cove on Shaw follows mostly uninhabited, steep, forested, rocky shores with few pocket beaches. Eagles soar above

Boat Near Shaw Landing

We met a man in the San Juan County Courthouse who told us the history of the old boat beached near Shaw Landing.

It was apparently built out of steel from plans calling for plywood by a man named Lee Thomason many years ago. It had an old Ford V-8 engine that didn't run well. When it got into trouble somebody apparently backed it into the cove sometime in the 1960s, where it still remains.

Naming Upright Channel

The channel was named Frolic Strait by the Wilkes Expedition in 1841. The Frolic was a British brigantine captured by the Wasp during the War of 1812.

When the U.S.C.S. chart, "Washington Sound and Approaches" was produced in 1866 the waterway name was changed to Upright Channel.

The name had been directly taken from an 1859 British Admiralty chart.

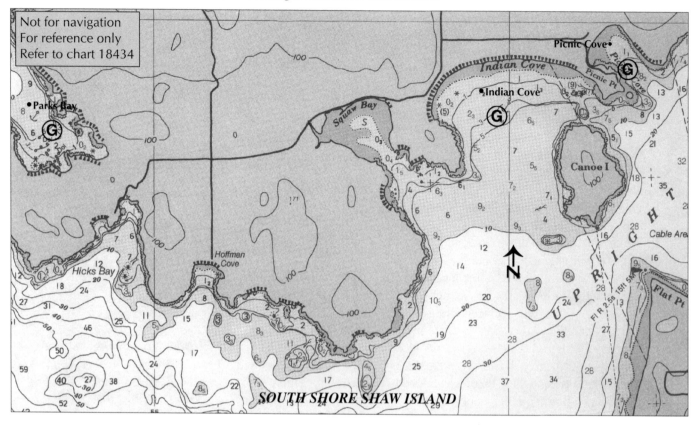

Not for navigation
For reference only
Refer to chart 18434

SOUTH SHORE SHAW ISLAND

Public Tidelands
🐚*Unless otherwise noted, public tidelands are state-owned. Some may be leased and posted for aquaculture or other private use. When going ashore take the Washington State Public Lands Quadrangle Map of San Juan County.*

Many of the tidelands on Shaw Island are Department of Natural Resource (DNR) lands, with the exception of posted shorelines in Blind Bay, Indian Cove and Parks Bay. We feature accessible tidelands throughout the chapter.

the shore in their never-ending quest for a meal.

🐚**Tidelands** are public below the high tide line.

Picnic Cove is a delightful, sheltered bay indenting Shaw Island for about 500 yards, with **Picnic Point** on the southwest shore. A tiny tombolo is off the end of the point, which is posted private. A field slopes up from the head of the low bank shoreline of the cove with several homes above sandy beaches. Private mooring buoys are in the bay, as well as crab pot buoys in season. There is no public access in the bay, although tidelands are public below high tide along the east shore.

⚓ **Anchoring** is possible near the head of the bay with protection from almost all prevailing winds.

Ⓖ This is a pleasant **gunkhole**.

Canoe Island is just a stone's throw south of Shaw. This nearly 50 acre, all private island is home to French Camp where teenagers are immersed in French language and culture. The youngsters learn French folk dancing and sometimes take part in summer parades and festivals in the islands, showing off their dancing talents. They also learn archery, boating skills, tennis, swimming (in a heated pool) and hiking. You may see these youngsters sailing, rowing or canoeing in the islands.

It's possible to pass between Canoe and Shaw islands. A kelp bed leads north from Canoe and a kelp-covered reef stretches south from Shaw, but the two do not meet. We stay fairly close to Canoe, out of the kelp, keep our depth sounder on and find we have about 35 feet beneath us, even at low tide.

Many mariners choose to stay in Upright Channel on the outside of Canoe Island as they are usually on their way to somewhere besides Indian Cove. The narrowest part of the channel, 500 yards, is off the rocky, south point of Canoe Island.

Charted rock shoal, awash at MLLW, is about 200 yards off the southwest shore of Canoe Island. It is sometimes, but not always, covered with kelp.

Cable area crosses between Shaw, Canoe and Lopez islands.

We suggest an enjoyable stop at the County Park at Shaw Island.

Beach at Shaw Island County Park

Wetlands at Indian Cove

Two protected wetland sites are Indian Cove Salt Marsh on the cove's east shore and Intertidal Mudflat at the county park, a narrow, rocky intertidal mudflat.

Pickleweed is at the lowest elevation of the marsh where salt concentrations are highest. As the marsh rises in elevation, saltgrass is dominant, and changes to Baltic rush, Lyngby sedge and slough sedge.

The transition zone between the salt marsh and upland contains alder, pine, spruce and red elderberry, maple, Douglas fir, salmonberry, oceanspray, snowberry, swamp rose and bracken fern.

INDIAN COVE & SHAW ISLAND COUNTY PARK

Indian Cove is the delightful, half-mile long, crescent-shaped cove on the south shores of Shaw, the site of **Shaw Island County Park.** This 64 acre park is a favorite spot for islanders and visitors alike, covering the western half of the cove and continuing around the forested peninsula.

The easiest way to locate the park is to look for a small red house with white-trimmed windows just above the beach, about half-way along the cove. A one lane launch ramp is immediately west of the house. Kayaks, canoes, rowing boats and small runabouts can be launched here. The ramp is the east boundary of the park. The park's sandy beach is one of the best in the islands, with a long tide run-out that can produce reasonably warm swimming on a hot, sunny day. Drift logs are tossed about at the high-tide line, making for great beachcombing and fort building for kids, big and little, who love to play on the beach and in the water.

⚓ This is an excellent anchorage with considerable space for boats. While it offers protection from northerlies, it's exposed to southerlies.

Ⓖ It's a great **gunkhole** except in a strong southerly.

Erratic rocks are scattered along the park beach with one wonderful, huge rock about 300 feet west of the launch ramp.

Shaw Island County Park Facilities
- ➤ 64 acres with 3,250 feet shoreline
- ➤ Anchor only, no moorage facilities
- ➤ 12 campsites, fees for camping & parking
- ➤ Picnic tables and shelter, fireplaces, drinking water, no beach fires
- ➤ Launch ramp, no fee
- ➤ Pit toilets
- ➤ Activities: picnic, beachcomb, dig clams, swim, crab, fish, camp, hike, play

---

Squaw Bay is just around the wooded, small peninsula from Indian Cove. It's an easy hike overland, but not a good anchorage as it is shallow.

Squaw Bay Salt Marsh is an interesting place to view from a small boat. It is a tidal wetland system of mudflats surrounded by low, salt marsh, with pickleweed,

Naming Hoffman Cove

The cove was named for the Hoffman family, early settlers on Shaw, some of whom still live on the island.

seaside arrowgrass and Baltic rush near the drift line.

⎈ **UNDERWAY AGAIN,** and we cruise past the unnamed point at the south tip of Shaw. This is the area where reefnet boats are most likely to be anchored off Shaw. They are also seen off Lopez and Stuart islands and the west shore of Lummi Island.

Reefnet boats off Shaw's south shores

Note the 2 to 4 fathom shoal off the point near the 20 fathom depth curve. West of this shoal, it's foul along the south shore until we reach Hoffman Cove.

Hoffman Cove has room for perhaps one or two boats to anchor, but offers no protection from wind and waves that travel up San Juan Channel from the south. A pretty little cove, it has a low-bank gravel beach, evergreens to the tideline and large erratic rocks on either side of the beach. A house and boathouse are in the cove, and part of the shoreline is owned by the University of Washington, as is much of the forested upland on the southwest side of Shaw. It is off-limits to visitors and maintained as a wildlife preserve by the U.W.

Hicks Bay, around a small projection from Hoffman Cove, has some beautiful beaches, also posted "no trespassing" by the U.W. A rocky shoal extends about 100 yards off the eastern shore at the entrance to the tree-lined bay. The rocks are a seal rookery, and as we go slowly past we watch the young pups with their moms and dads. A small, private dock is here and a house is on the eastern shore. Although there is room for several boats, there is no protection from southerly channel winds and waves.

We head out of Hicks Bay in a northwesterly direction and we have once again reached Point George, successfully circumnavigating Shaw Island!

Protect Squaw Bay

A pretty, handpainted sign at Squaw Bay notes:

"Passersby: Squaw Bay's beach, spit and lagoon are rich feeding, nesting, & resting areas for birds. Many species from bald eagles to sanderlings are often here.

Please do not go out on the spit or remove driftwood. Beach, spit and tidelands are privately owned. Please enjoy the view, and help us to preserve the beauty that brings us all here. Thank you, the owners and great blue herons, cormorants, grebes, yellow legs, killdeer, osprey, herring gulls, bonapartes, green wing teal, widgeons, scopes, mallards, kingfishers and more."

> In **Chapter 4** we circumnavigate Orcas, the largest island in the San Juans, with all its coves, bays and villages, and include Blakely, Doe, Jones and Obstruction islands.

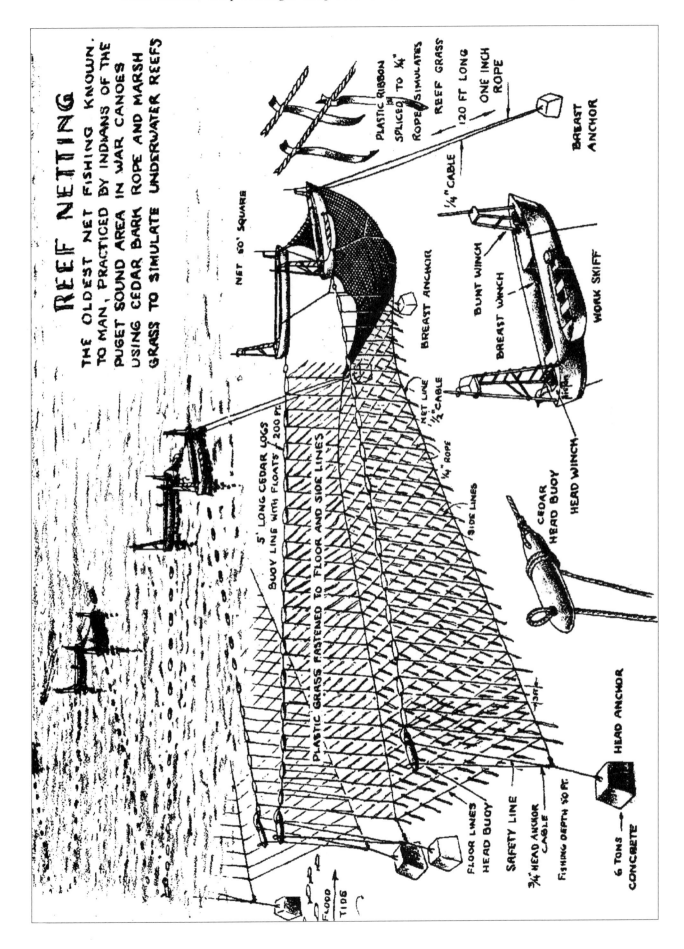

REEF NETTING

THE OLDEST NET FISHING KNOWN. TO MAN, PRACTICED BY INDIANS OF THE PUGET SOUND AREA IN WAR CANOES USING CEDAR BARK ROPE AND MARSH GRASS TO SIMULATE UNDERWATER REEFS

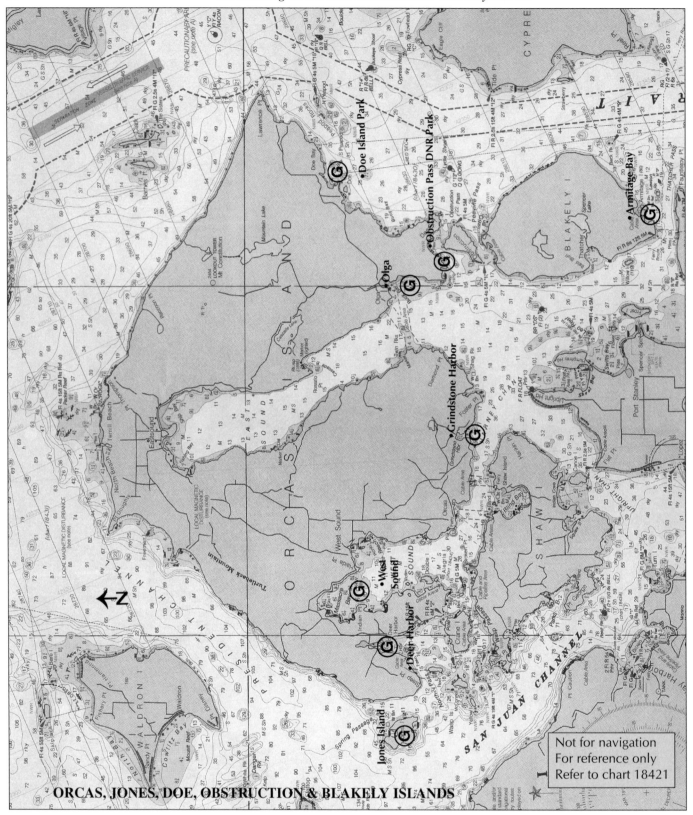

ORCAS, JONES, DOE, OBSTRUCTION & BLAKELY ISLANDS

Not for navigation
For reference only
Refer to chart 18421

CHAPTER 4
ORCAS ISLAND
Jones, Doe, Obstruction & Blakely Islands

Charts & Publications for this Chapter

Chart	Date	Title	Scale	Soundings
U.S. 18421	03/21/98	Strait of Juan de Fuca to Strait of Georgia	1:80,000	Fathoms
U.S. 18423	06/18/94	Strip Chart Bellingham to Everett, inc. San Juan Islands		
		Pages A, C	1:80,000	Fathoms
		Page C, inset 6	1:40,000	Fathoms
☆ U.S. 18430	11/02/96	Rosario Strait, Northern Part	1:25,000	Fathoms
U.S. 18431	10/05/96	Rosario Strait to Cherry Point	1:25,000	Fathoms
☆ U.S. 18432	08/15/92	Boundary Pass	1:25,000	Fathoms
☆ U.S. 18434	10/05/96	San Juan Channel	1:25,000	Fathoms
CAN. 3313	07/28/95	Gulf Islands & Adjacent Waterways		
		Pages 6, 24	1:40,000	Meters
CAN. 3441	12/06/96	Haro Strait, Boundary Pass & Satellite Channel	1:40,000	Meters
	🐚	Wash. State DNR Quad Map—San Juan County	1:100,000	

Compare your chart dates with those above. There may be discrepancies between chart editions.
☆ = Preferred chart for this chapter   🐚 = DNR & other public tideland information

ORCAS ISLAND OVERVIEW

Orcas Island is an energetic mix of several unique communities separated by geographic differences, yet allied by all being on the same "rock." The 36,432 acre island is divided into unequal thirds by three bays which deeply indent the island from the south, East Sound, West Sound and Deer Harbor. Stretches of uninhabited and densely forested coastline surround the island. Steep cliffs along northern shores add to unpredictable thermal winds and equally confusing currents that can carry mariners far off course. Tiny bays, some pristine, seemingly untouched, and some cantankerous expanses of saltwater encircle Orcas.

A number of small, state owned islands are within its bays, as well as two Department of Natural Resources marine parks, four county launch ramps and several private marinas and resorts.

A public day-use dock with floats is at Eastsound village so mariners who wish to sail the six miles up East Sound can easily access shopping, restaurants and other village amenities. Other communities accessible by water on East Sound are Rosario Resort and Marina, and a community dock at Olga. Obstruction Pass Campground and a county dock and launch ramp are at Obstruction Pass.

Undeveloped state park islands, West Sound Marina, and a county dock are in West Sound. Deer Harbor has two marinas, one with guest moorage, the other for permanent moorage only. Jones Island State Marine Park is a scant 0.5 mile from Orcas' west shore.

On the "outside" north shore of Orcas island are West Beach Resort and Bartwood Lodge. Doe Bay community and Doe Island State Marine

➡ **NOTE: Marine gas and diesel** are available at four places year-round on Orcas:
• **Orcas Landing**
• **West Sound Marina**
• **Deer Harbor Marina**
• **Rosario Resort**
Gas only, seasonally:
• **West Beach**

West Sound

Orcas Landing

Park are on the east side along Rosario Strait. There are other private resorts we mention later.

Some things are "bigger" on Orcas, compared to other San Juan islands: Orcas has the tallest mountain, Mount Constitution, the longest shoreline at 125 miles, the most communities, the largest state park (inland), the most tourists and the largest resort. It's so spread out it can take an hour or more to drive from one end of the island to the other.

Orcas has important Native American history and there are traces of prehistoric people. When settlers first arrived in 1851, the Indians of the Flat Head tribe inhabited the land. Many tales were told by old timers of bloody encounters with the Stickeens, a warlike tribe from British Columbia.

West Sound was the scene of violent fighting by marauding Indians, whose battles left names like Massacre Bay, Victim and Skull islands. Stone relics, particularly tools, have been uncovered here. Implements of bone and flint, arrows and spearheads have been found, mainly at East and West sounds.

Early settlers farmed, logged, fished and worked in the limestone quarries. At one time fruit orchards were a prime industry on Orcas, with apples, pears and prunes the leading crops. With the completion of Grand Coulee Dam in the 1930s and the irrigation of formerly dry lands in Eastern Washington, commercial fruit operations ceased on the island as island farmers could not compete with those on the mainland. Thousands of fruit trees on Orcas still produce fruit for local use.

The ferry to Orcas stops at Orcas Landing on the south shore. From there it's a 10 mile drive to the village of Eastsound, the heart of the island, the "metropolis" at the head of East Sound. Schools, banks, medical and dental services, book stores, restaurants, real estate offices, a library, historical museum, shopping center, performing arts center, sheriff's office, drug store, liquor store and a post office are all located here.

Tourism has always been a major industry on the island, nicknamed the "Tourist Island." For centuries, Native Americans arrived for the wealth of berries, fishing and clamming. In the early 1900s, visiting vacationers from the young state camped on beaches and hillsides or stayed in newly-built beach cottages.

Through the 1980s and 90s, tourism flourished and with it came many related jobs. There are about 40 resorts, bed and breakfasts, lodgings, restaurants and gift shops on the island, along with sailing, kayak and whale watching charters. Over 150 campsites are at Moran State Park inland, plus more sites at DNR parks and private resorts.

Telecommuting enables professionals to live and work on the island, and cottage industries flourish. Construction grew with the demand for vacation and retirement homes, and real estate is big business. As with other islands in the San Juans, education and net-worth levels of residents are above state averages.

Ferry service has grown along with the population, but always seems to lag behind needs, say islanders. Almost all have tales of long ferry lines, either at Anacortes or Orcas, especially during the heavily traveled summer months.

✸**UNDERWAY,** we start our circumnavigation of Orcas at Orcas Landing in Harney Channel on the south shores, going clockwise around this diverse island.

ORCAS VILLAGE AT ORCAS LANDING

Orcas Village is easy to spot from the water, with the white Victorian Orcas Hotel rising above five large fuel tanks at the ferry landing and the public moorage. When the ferry stops here, wide-eyed, first time visitors step off into the magic that is the San Juan Islands. Orcas Landing is the vital connection to the mainland for islanders.

Orcas public moorage float and fuel dock are immediately west of the ferry landing. The long float parallels the shore, with the fuel dock at the east end. Larger boats tie up on the outside of the float, while shallow draft, small boats can moor on the shore side. This fuel dock and temporary moorage has no protection on the outside of the floats, leaving them open to a thrashing from southerly winds and wakes.

Orcas Hotel

⚓ **Anchoring** is possible between the east of the ferry dock and some boats do anchor here. Caution is advised because of a cable area, exposure and traffic.

Facilities at Orcas Moorage at Orcas Landing
➤ Moorage 30 min. free; over 30 min. $5; overnight 50¢ foot
➤ Fuel: diesel & gas, no propane, kerosene or pumpout
➤ Water & ice
➤ Kayak launch $10 round trip
➤ Nearby market & restaurants
➤ This is the only kayak launch at a ferry terminal in the islands

---

Elegant Orcas Hotel overlooking the ferry landing is on the National Historic Register. Built in the early 1900s, the 12 room inn has a restaurant, fireside lounge, espresso cafe with terrific soup, and a bakery with equally terrific pastries.

Russell's Landing is a unique combination boutique, liquor store and wonderful latte stop. Orcas Village also has restaurants, sandwich shops, Mamie's Famous Fudge, kayak and bicycle rentals, a post office, gift shops, real estate offices, car rentals and whale watching tours—a blend that is truly Orcas.

Cable areas surround the landing.

Bayhead Marina is east of the landing in a small bay—it's private with no transient moorage.

⊛ **UNDERWAY AGAIN,** we leave Orcas Village, heading west around the unnamed point with its many waterfront homes and then enter West Sound.

WEST SOUND

Delightful West Sound, the middle of the three bays indenting Orcas' south shore, is one of several favorite anchorages. The three mile long sound ranges from 0.5 mile to nearly one mile wide in places, with several small islands and coves. It is known for quiet bays and moorages, but southwesterlies can blow hard in here.

Turtleback Mountain, over 1,500 feet high, towers above the northeast end of the Sound. The turtle's head is Orcas Knob, height 1,005 feet. *(Charted discrepancies in the heights are noted on page 101.)*

Oak Island is about 0.7 mile north of the entrance to West Sound, a tiny, picturesque island with a few trees just offshore of a 200 foot bluff. The channel between the island and Orcas is only 3 feet deep at low tide. For the next mile or so we cruise along the rugged eastern shore with homes nestled among the trees on the bluffs, an occasional private pier out in front and boats moored offshore.

White Beach Bay has several tiny coves, Picnic Island and the West Sound community. The southern cove includes charted log booms and dolphins. The mid-

Russell's Landing
    The landing is at the ferry dock, run by Margaret Russell and daughter Mary, it's a shop like no other. The main floor is a boutique with gifts, clothing, jewelry, cards, candles and lattes. The lower level is a homey state liquor store, but of a different type ... Windows have views of Harney Channel and the ferry landing, there are wall hangings, books on display, and finally, shelves with wines and liquor.
    It's a charming and unusual liquor store.

Orcas Village: No New Marina
    A proposal for a marina for about 100 megayachts was withdrawn in September 1999 by developers.
    Orcas Islanders who fought the proposal said they plan to purchase the property so that it will remain natural and never be allowed to become a marina.

Naming West Sound

The sound was named **Guerriere Bay** *by the Wilkes expedition in 1841.* **Guerriere** *was a British warship sunk by the American* **Constitution** *in the War of 1812.*

The British deliberately changed the name on their charts to neutral West Sound, also changing other names they considered equally offensive. British charts were published before the American charts.

Carnage

One of the most bitter and deadly encounters between raiding Indians and Lummi Indians was in 1858 in West Sound.

The Stickeen Indians from British Columbia paddled stealthily in canoes and in the night attacked their unsuspecting prey and slaughtered about 100. Every one who resisted was killed. Many women and children were carried away as prisoners.

White Beach Bay

According to the 1861 Coast Pilot, White Beach Bay was ..."so named from the quantities of white clam shells, the remains of native feasts, lying on its shores ..."

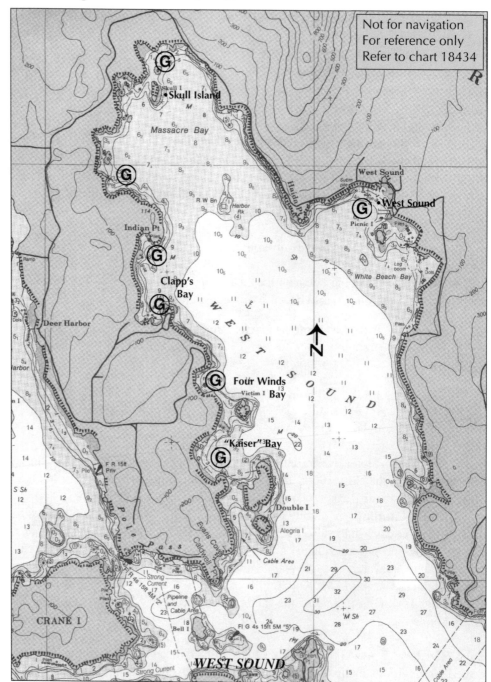

portion of the bay has a gravel launch ramp with a five dollar fee. There's also a small private moorage here.

Entering West Sound

Picnic Island (alias **Sheep Island**) fronts the middle cove with a shoal 100 yards off the south end of the private two acre island. A tiny tombolo is off the northeast shore.

West Sound Marina, a landmark in West Sound for nearly 50 years, is past the north side of Picnic Island.

The Wareham family, Mike, Peg, their son Ian and daughter Betsy, have run the marina since the mid-1970s. It has expanded both in size and services and has a fine reputation. The marina is protected from all but westerlies, which usually aren't too bad in West Sound. The marina dog, Mercury, has perfected the art of boat begging to such a fine degree that practically everyone who ties up here thinks they have just found a new pet.

When entering the marina, keep west of Picnic Island. The 250 foot long guest float is along the south side of the marina.

Ian Wareham helps tie up a boat at West Sound Marina

West Sound Marina Facilities
➤ Guest moorage for about six boats
➤ Moorage rates: 60¢ foot per day
➤ 20/30 amp power, $2 day, water
➤ Restrooms with showers
➤ Fuel: gas, diesel, propane, kerosene, pumpout, $10
➤ 30 ton hoist, hull and engine repair
➤ Scheduled Kenmore Air flights
➤ Reservation policy, 24 hours advance notice
➤ Summer hrs.: M-F 8-4:45; Sat. 9-4; Sun. 10-3.
➤ Winter hrs.: M-F 8-4:45; Sat. 10-3, closed Sunday
➤ Nearby activities: West Sound Cafe, B & Bs, taxi, bus service in summer, walk, fish, scuba dive, gunkhole
➤ Monitors VHF channel 16 for 24-hour emergencies
➤ Marina manager: Betsy Wareham
➤ Tel: 360-376-2314/FAX: 360-376-4634
➤ Address: P.O. Box 19, Orcas, WA 98280

West Sound Marina

The marina was started by Ray VanMoorham near the present small moorage south of the marina. He worked at a lime quarry at the site and piled the lime tailings into a little spit. A boat shed was at the marina's present site, where he worked on boats and eventually created his marina.

West Sound community is located at the north end of White Beach Bay. This quiet hamlet includes two docks, a store, cafe and a bed and breakfast.

Orcas Island Yacht Club dock, the easternmost dock, offers moorage to members of reciprocal yacht clubs. A clubhouse and picnic area are upland of the dock.

West Sound county dock has a 50 foot long float for daytime tie-up. Stairs at the head of the dock provide beach access.

⚓ **There is ample anchorage** in the bay in 3 to 5 fathoms, mud bottom, although it is exposed to south winds.

Ⓖ It's a **good gunkhole** in good weather.

West Sound Store and Cafe is west of the two docks. The store has groceries, gourmet foods and a restaurant, with great breakfasts and lunches. Kingfish Inn Bed & Breakfast is adjacent to the store.

Haida Point is next as we leave White Beach Bay and continue north into Massacre Bay where hills rise to 100 feet close above the shoreline.

Harbor Rock Daybeacon, [R W Bn] is a diamond-shaped red and white dayboard on a spindle marking a rock that is charted baring at a 4 foot tide which is 0.3 mile west of Haida Point. (*Light List #19680 indicates it bares at 6 feet.*)

A shoal runs about 100 yards north and east of the mark. Passage is easy on either side of the rock in 9 to 10 fathoms.

Early West Sound

The historic West Sound Store was built in October 1891, and the post office was established in June 1892.

West Sound county dock

***Beachcombing at Skull
Island***

Anchors Away

*Jo anchored north of Skull
Island once a while back, but
left when large rocks began
appearing all around the Sea
Witch as the tide was falling.*

"Cap'n" Jack & Nan Culver

MASSACRE BAY

The bay encompasses the northwestern third of West Sound, north of Harbor Rock. It's less than 10 fathoms deep throughout—a really beautiful place. On the eastern shore hills rise steeply to 900 foot high Ship Peak, with a mix of forests, grassy fields and rocks watching over the sound. The north and west shores are forested and homes line the rocky beaches or are tucked back in the woods. A small cove on the east shore with a charted rock in the center and several private piers is not suitable for anchoring.

SKULL ISLAND MARINE STATE PARK

This is a little treasure of state-owned land in the northwest corner of Massacre Bay, an "unimproved marine park." It's in a natural, pristine state with no water, toilets or campsites, a perfect little island. A small, crushed-shell beach is on the east shore, providing an easy place to land the skiff, go ashore and do a bit of beach and tide pool exploring.

About three acres in size, it's really not much more than a rock covered with a little bit of soil in which juniper trees grow—they're not too demanding about water. They join wild rose thickets and bracken. Magnificent Ship Peak and Turtleback Mountain to the northeast are yours to view from this delightful spot as eagles perch on skeleton trees above the rocky shoreline. We found they also fly away when we get too close for their comfort.

We circumnavigated Skull Island in our sailboat, *Scheherazade*, 5.5 foot draft, with Jack and Nan Culver, well-known, active sailors who live on the shores of West Sound and sail their Mariner 31 ketch, *Kahagon*.

We started at the southeast tip going clockwise and even though there are shoals, we found ourselves in 25 feet of water about 30 feet off the island. Along the rocky west shore we had 15 to 20 feet. Around the north end we had about 15 feet of water about 20 feet offshore. Then it dropped to 10 feet and slowly went back up to 20 feet, as we finished going around the island. Waters around the northwest part of Skull, between the little island and Orcas, are charted at less than 3 fathoms.

The charted rock and shoal surrounding the island are about 75 yards off the north end. A small cave at the northeast end of Skull goes in a short way, and with a bit of imagination we think of it as a stash location for contraband. Immediately over the cave is a juniper skeleton. More shoals are off the east shore.

"There are only two places in West Sound to 'hide' in really bad weather, and behind Skull Island is one," Jack said. The other is in unnamed Clapp's Bay.

"The place that's decent to anchor is just north of Skull Island, between the island and the charted rock," he said. "We can always tell when the Canadians come in here. They'll put a stern anchor out and put the bowline up on a rock, or tie to a tree, and sit pretty. It can blow hard in here and the boat's back there just rocking gently because they're in the lee of the island. It's a good place, the only hidey-hole off the northwest tip of Skull Island."

⚓ **Anchoring** is good north of Skull in about 3 fathoms, mud bottom.

Ⓖ It's a **great gunkhole,** quiet and peaceful.

The Orcas shore west of Skull has a private pier and a small bay littered with rocks. As we head south along this side of West Sound, we find shoals, rocks and pocket beaches lining much of the shore.

Indian Point has a rocky shoreline and although there are many intricate indentations we found no pocket beaches. It is reasonably protected in several places, except in an easterly. There are homes in here, almost all of the beaches are private, and it's beautiful. There is fairly low bank waterfront with private buoys and some piers.

⚓ **Anchoring** is possible in a large bight northwest of Indian Point in 2 to 6 fathoms, mud bottom.

Ⓖ This is a **good gunkhole,** weather permitting.

Clapp's Bay, south of the point, is about 600 yards wide, named for a property owner. This bight is the second anchorage that Jack Culver referred to as being a good place to tuck in during bad weather.

Skull Island

🐚 Some of the tidelands in this bay below the government meander line are public, but check the county quad map before going ashore.

⚓ **Anchoring** is good in the bay at either end. Depths range from 4 to 9 fathoms, mud bottom.

Ⓖ This is another **good gunkhole**.

Continuing south along the west shore of Orcas another 0.5 mile, we round a point into an unnamed bay. Camp Four Winds is an uncharted local name of the 0.1 mile wide cove. A private camp for youngsters is on the north shore and kids from the camp sail around in small boats and enjoy many activities. The camp has a 60 foot yawl, *Carlyn,* which is available for charter.

⚓ **Anchoring** is possible in about 3 to 5 fathoms, mud bottom, in this bay, which offers good protection in most winds.

Ⓖ It's a **reasonable gunkhole**.

VICTIM ISLAND MARINE STATE PARK

🐚 This tiny island is about 125 yards off the west shore of Orcas, another "unimproved" state park. It is beautiful and relatively untouched. It's not easy to climb the island's rock face to the top, and if you do, there's not much of anywhere to go. Kids love it, since parents will probably just wait on the beach while they explore, unless the parents are fit, agile and good sports. The logical place to anchor is in Four Winds Bay and then dinghy to the island.

Charted rocks off Orcas extend about 150 yards offshore at the south end of the channel between Victim and Orcas. An unnamed bight west of Victim and Double Island to the south is about 400 yards wide. An estate here was once owned by the Henry Kaiser family of automobile fame, and the bay is locally called Kaiser Bay.

⚓ **A reasonable anchorage** in good weather is in the bay in 3 to 9 fathoms, mud bottom, no public tidelands.

Ⓖ It's another West Sound **gunkhole.**

Double Island is offshore of Kaiser Bay. On the northeast end of Double is a small private uncharted marker on a rock, a tower with four legs to alert boaters of the shoal at the island's end. There is also a cairn of white painted rocks. A rock about 50 yards off the island's northwest end bares at 2 feet.

Between Double and Orcas a rocky ledge and shoal covers and uncovers. Local advice is "don't go between Double and Orcas."

Alegria Island is joined by a tombolo to Double at low tides. The island is often referred to as "Little Double" by locals. The two islands, privately owned by one

West Sound Reminders

The names of **Massacre Bay, Skull and Victim islands,** are traced to the battles between peace-loving local Native Americans of the Lummi tribe and invasions by tribes from British Columbia and southeast Alaska.

The goal of the invaders was to capture Lummis to use as slave workers.

Haida Point was named for the Haida Indians from B.C. who marauded and captured the gentle Lummi Indians for use as slaves. Indian remains were found at Haida Point around 1900.

➡ **NOTE:** A charted depth discrepancy is in the shoal between Victim and Orcas islands.

Chart 18434 shows 1 fathom, chart 18423 shows 3 feet in the same area.

These soundings are at MLLW.

A Wee Bit Shallow

We slipped between Victim and Orcas islands in the Sea Witch once, and once was enough, as the bottom was too easily seen. We went through at high water, fortunately.

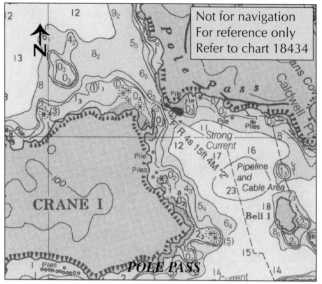

Not for navigation
For reference only
Refer to chart 18434

Four Post Offices on Orcas

Orcas has post offices at Eastsound, Deer Harbor, Orcas Village and Olga, all with different zip codes.

Gold Coast?

The west shore of Deer Harbor has been locally nicknamed the "Gold Coast" because of the plethora of wealthy off-islanders' vacation homes.

Deer Harbor Marina

family, are beautifully forested with evergreens and madronas, and together cover nearly 26 acres.

Cable area in an unusual configuration runs from the south tip of Orcas at Caldwell Point to Alegria and Double islands and back to Orcas at Kaiser Bay.

The bay between Orcas and Alegria is about 200 yards wide and interesting, but the cable area discourages anchoring without extraordinary local knowledge.

Evans Cove is an open bight at the southwest entrance to West Sound, not a suggested anchorage.

Caldwell Point extends south into Wasp Passage. Two shoal areas of 1 to 3 fathoms charted about 250 yards southeast and southwest of the point are good places to avoid.

Pole Pass is the 75 yard wide pass between Orcas and Crane islands marked by a flashing red light on Orcas. Currents can be strong in the pass, with the flood flowing northwest and the ebb flowing southeast. Water depths are adequate even at low tides, but we stay pretty much in the center, slightly closer to Orcas.

Pole Pass Light [Fl R 4s 15ft 4M "2"] flashing red 4 second light 15 feet high visible 4 miles, is on a triangular red dayboard on a tower on the Orcas shore.

DEER HARBOR

This is the most western and smallest of the three harbors that indent Orcas' south side. The harbor runs from Crane Island north about 1.25 miles and is about 0.8 mile wide from Reef Island to Orcas, tapering to 0.2 mile wide in the north end. A 3 foot shoal extends 0.2 mile off the north shore of Crane Island. The forested shores of Deer Harbor are slowly filling with new homes. About 0.4 miles north of Pole Pass is a pier and estate once owned by the Isaacson family, formerly of Isaacson Iron Works in Seattle.

Deer Harbor Pier Light [F R 15ft] fixed red light 15 feet high, is the private aid at the Isaacson pier, the largest privately owned pier in the islands. The bight north of the pier is muddy, shoal and not suitable as an anchorage. In fact, the east shore is shoal for 200 yards offshore from the bight to Deer Harbor Marina.

Deer Harbor community includes Deer Harbor Marina, Resort at Deer Harbor, Cayou Quay Marina, a post office, restaurants and a gift shop.

Deer Harbor Marina is about 1.1 miles north of Pole Pass. Enter the marina near the fuel dock on the west side of the floats.

Deer Harbor Marina Facilities
➤ Guest moorage for 90 boats, reservations recommended
➤ Rates: $1 foot, 30 amp shore power, limited water
  ➤ Fuel: gas, diesel, pumpout $5; no porta-potty dump
  ➤ Restrooms, showers, laundry, ice
  ➤ Basic store with deli & lattes, beer, wine
  ➤ Nearby: restaurants, post office, picnic, sandy beach
  ➤ Guests may use pool at Deer Harbor Resort
  ➤ Kayak & small boat rentals, whale watching wildlife cruises, shuttle van & rental cars, island bus & taxi
  ➤ Activities: scuba dive, fish, swim, beachcomb, picnic
  ➤ Mike Douglas, manager, monitors VHF Ch. 78A
  ➤ Tel.: 360-376-3037/FAX: 360-376-6091
  ➤ e-mail: deerharbor@rockisland.com; http:// www.@boatnet.com
  ➤ Address: 210 Deer Harbor Rd., P.O. Box 344, Deer Harbor, WA 98243

⚓ **Anchoring** is possible in Deer Harbor in 5 to 7 fathoms, mud bottom.

Ⓖ This is a **good gunkhole** in good weather.

Resort at Deer Harbor across the road from the marina has accommodations with private decks overlooking the marina, including a restaurant, heated pool and hot tubs. Tel.: 360-376-4420

Cayou Quay Marina in northwest Deer Harbor has permanent moorage but no guest spaces. It was named after the family of one of the first four settlers in Deer Harbor, men who came to hunt deer for the Hudson's Bay Company in 1852.

Deer Harbor Boatworks is on the east side of Deer Harbor, north of the marina and just south of a bridge which blocks boat access to marshland. The channel to the boatworks from Cayou Key Marina is narrow, winding and requires local knowledge. Boatworks manager is Debi Yerly, Tel.: 360-376-4056 or 360-376-6477.

Deer Harbor Inn, built in 1915, is north of the marina on a knoll overlooking the harbor. They have a wonderful restaurant and accommodations in cottages with fireplaces. They pick up customers at the Deer Harbor dock and drive them to the inn in a 1969 baby blue Cadillac limo that used to belong to Henry Kaiser. The phone number, 360-376-4110, and menu are posted on the dock by the pay telephone.

Frank Richardson Wildlife Preserve, less than two miles from Deer Harbor Marina, is a great place for those who want to get off the boat, stretch their legs and do some birdwatching. This large marshland caters to a diverse mixture of waterfowl and other birds all year. You can stroll the road armed with binoculars and cameras and feast on birdwatching. There's a plaque on a large rock noting the "San Juan Preservation Trust Frank Richardson Wildfowl Preserve. Dedicated in loving memory to Dr. Richardson … this preserve is for the benefit of all, 1994." Dr. Richardson, a zoology professor at the University of Washington, lived on Orcas until his death in 1985.

To reach the preserve, walk north along Deer Harbor Road, go left at the intersection with Sunset Channel Road, cross a bridge over a slough at the far north end of Deer Harbor, and follow the road about one mile.

Deer Harbor Inn

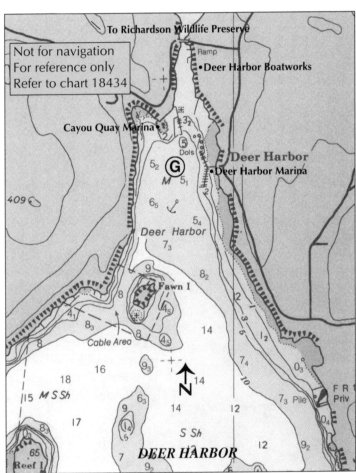

Early Post Office

Deer Harbor's first post office was established in 1893 by J. T. Stroud, postmaster and operator of a general "merchandising business." In 1901, his store carried a "fine line of dry goods, notions, general household and useful articles, boots, shoes, glassware, groceries, provisions, flour, feed, canned and bottled goods.

"He also provides entertainment for the traveling public. He has a fine garden and orchard of 14 acres. He married Miss Mary A. Cobble of Tennessee and has a family of four charming girls." *(San Juan Islander)*

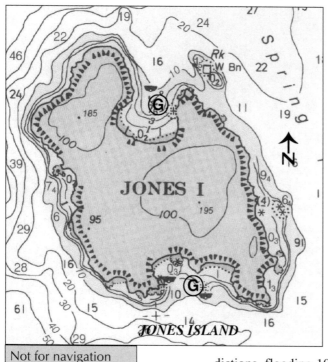

Not for navigation
For reference only
Refer to chart 18434

Jones Chapel

While wandering on Jones in the 1980s, we came upon a small outdoor chapel in the woods.

A rough-hewn altar and log benches were obviously well-used, although not a soul was about. As far as we know, it still stands.

Jones' north cove anchorage

⚓ **UNDERWAY AGAIN,** we leave Deer Harbor and head southwest towards Steep Point and then west to Jones Island.

Fawn Island, all private, is about 150 yards east of Orcas as we leave Deer Harbor. A rocky shoal is charted off the south end, but there's no problem passing between Fawn and Orcas as the channel is 8 fathoms deep.

Cable area surrounds Fawn Island.

Steep Point, steep and rocky with several homes atop cliffs soaring to 425 feet, is at Orcas' southwest tip.

North Pass, between Steep Point and the Wasp Islands, runs from San Juan Channel to Deer Harbor, about 1.2 miles.

Reef Island, which we visit in the section on the Wasp Islands, is 0.2 mile off the south end of Orcas.

Spring Passage is between Orcas and Jones islands, about 0.25 mile wide in the narrowest spot. Jones Island is on the west side of the passage. The passage is from 11 to 50 fathoms deep, south to north. A 5 to 9 fathom reef rises in the north end, making a notable bottom fishing spot. Some beach cabins are nestled on the shores of Orcas on Spring Passage.

Currents in the pass are based on San Juan Channel predictions, flooding 10° True and ebbing 150° True. Currents can run over 2.5 knots, with strong winds increasing them.

"Along the western cliffs (of Orcas) … are feldspar deposits which reach 60 feet thick and 300 feet deep. Feldspar is used in glazing pottery and manufacturing glass, but the demand has not justified development at this point." (Edmond Meany, *History of the State of Washington*)

JONES ISLAND MARINE STATE PARK

This is another of our favorite island parks, with two excellent moorages, several pocket beaches where beachable boats can land, and nearly five miles of forested shoreline. Jones is a favorite destination for paddlers as well as other recreational mariners, and is easy to reach from both Orcas and San Juan. It's less than two miles west of Deer Harbor, and less than six miles north of Friday Harbor up San Juan Channel.

We circumnavigate Jones going clockwise, starting at the south cove. The cove is surrounded by rocky shores and a gravel beach, and is divided into two bights by a rocky promontory. One park mooring buoy is in the east bight and two park buoys are in the west. Along the cove's west shore are some wonderful tide pools perfect for exploring little marine critters. Swimming is chilly, despite the great-looking beach.

⚓ **Anchoring** is possible in the cove in 10 fathoms or less. This is not the most comfortable moorage in a southerly blow as the long fetch up San Juan Channel causes boats to bounce about, in which case we suggest moving to the north cove.

Ⓖ It's a **good gunkhole,** weather permitting.

Rounding the southwest tip of Jones, we travel along the 10 fathom curve, close to small pocket beaches and rocky cliffs topped with evergreens and madronas. The Washington Water Trail Site is on the southwest shore. Whales sometimes swim along this shore as eagles soar overhead, always hunting for the next meal.

We continue north for less than one mile and swing into Jones' north cove, with bluffs on the east and west sides and a fairly low bank at the head of the bay. Four park mooring buoys, a dock and moorage float are in the cove. Floats are removed in the winter.

⚓ **Anchoring** in the north cove is good in 3 to 10 fathoms if it's not too crowded. The bottom is rocky and the anchor needs to be well set, perhaps even with a stern line to shore.

Ⓖ This is another **good gunkhole.**

The northwest bluff of the cove is a steep cliff rising to 185 feet with a signed slide area. A trail crosses a sandy, eroding cliff and often disappears underfoot. Flailing hikers attempting mini-Everest ascents are sometimes "rescued" by boaters who climb above them and lower their extra boat lines to the stranded souls.

The head of the cove is a gravel beach with driftwood below a low rock face. It's an easy place to land a dinghy and gives the kids a place to run. The northeast bluff above the cove is rocky and forested with camping and picnic areas, a favorite with youngsters. Water and vault toilets are on shore near the dock.

"Island of Bambis"
Scarcely able to contain her excitement at being so close to a deer, that's the name given to Jones Island by a delighted four-year-old. She stood eye to eye with one of the friendly deer on the south side of the island.

Jones Island Marine State Park Facilities
➤ 188 acres with 25,000 feet of shoreline
➤ 7 mooring buoys: 4 in north cove, 3 in south cove, $5/night
➤ Dock and floats with 128 feet of moorage in north cove
➤ Three consecutive nights max
➤ Moorage rates at floats: boats under 26' $8 night; boats over 26' $11 night
➤ Limited potable water, 21 primitive camping & picnic sites
➤ Reservation group camp area, vault & pit toilets
➤ Many hiking trails
➤ One Washington Water Trail campsite on southwest beach
➤ Activities: hike, camp, fish, scuba dive, swim, beachcomb, relax

Jones Island Rock Daybeacon [W Bn] white diamond-shaped daybeacon worded **"Danger Rocks,"** marks a charted rocky shoal about 150 yards off the northeast tip of the island. A charted reef off the east side of Jones about 0.4 mile south of the daybeacon, extends 200 yards offshore. We pass around the tip of the island and find ourselves back in the south cove.

Now that we've completed our circumnavigation of Jones Island, let's go ashore and discover more about this wonderful island park. The short walk across the island through towering evergreen trees is delightful, although the tree configuration has changed since the 1990 windstorm. From the north cove, the trail winds gently uphill past the water tanks in the island's center, then just as gently down through an old orchard to the south cove where we're greeted by friendly deer. The orchard is near the site of an early homesteader's cabin. The deer are accomplished scroungers and are often hand fed. Visitors are thrilled taking photos of their kids feeding the fawns. The clearing above the south beach has water, campsites, toilets, a reader-board and trails leading around the bluffs. Dogs must be leashed on the island.

Along the south shore of the island are tide pools and rocky shores for exploration at low tide. Tiny fish, snails, crabs, barnacles, clams, urchins, starfish and a host of other marine life are fascinating. Live species may not be removed from any of the San Juans as they are part of a vast wildlife preserve.

Early Settlers
The south side of Jones was homesteaded in the late 1800s by a settler named Kittles and his Indian wife. They raised a family and made a living by trapping and also selling fresh produce in Friday Harbor.

A newspaper article in 1899 noted that "Robert Kittles Sr., one of the oldest settlers in the county, died on Jones Island, age 73, and was buried there."

Jones Island was formerly a lighthouse reservation and has also been a wildlife reserve.

Jones Island

It was named by the Wilkes Expedition in 1841 in honor of Capt. Jacob Jones, U.S.N.

*While Master Commandant of the sloop-of-war **Wasp,** he captured the British brig **Frolic** on October 18, 1812.*

National Wildlife Refuges

Many rocks and small islands off Orcas Island are part of the San Juan Islands National Wildlife Refuge and Wilderness Area (NWR).

Mariners must stay 200 yards away from these rocks and islands. All National Wildlife Refuge islands are closed to public access except Matia and Turn islands.

Jo stands before a tree uprooted by the storm of 1990

➡ **NOTE:** If using chart **18434** while running northeast along Orcas Island, change to chart **18432** about two miles north of Steep Point.

Tread Lightly at Jones

The readerboard asks visitors to "enjoy the marine wildlife habitat, observe and appreciate its fragility, and tread lightly so the marine environment remains for generations ... "Puget Sound and other habitats are part of a complex system in which all species serve vital functions. The largest octopuses in the world live in these waters and also the largest and fastest sea stars. The waters harbor diverse species ranging from over 200 kinds of fish, rare and unusual crabs, sea slugs, harbor seals, diving birds and killer whales.

"Marine life in any location is dependent on a subtidal zone habitat. Waters in the Pacific Northwest are generally cold, 45° to 50° F., and turbulent. Twice daily a vast quantity of water is moved back and forth by tides."

The Winter Storm of 1990

Rocky, forested, hilly Jones Island was hit by a devastating nor'easter in December 1990. The fierce wind blew down and damaged thousands of trees, forcing temporary closure of the island park. Concerned agencies considered how best to handle the damage. A decision was made to remove no logs, but to remove flammable forest debris from a buffer zone, construct perimeter fire trails and let most logs recycle nutrients back into a new forest. The decision and cleanup was a cooperative effort of the Swinomish Tribe, Recreational Boaters Association of Washington (RBAW), state parks staff and others who spent much of April and May 1992 cleaning up the island.

A readerboard at the north harbor urges visitors to: "Look on top of upturned roots and decomposing wood and in sunny openings for new plants taking advantage of the changes. Watch for deer feeding on this lush new growth. Look for beetles boring into logs for feed and to lay eggs. Mosquitoes may hatch from water in the root ball depressions. Tree-nesting birds have temporarily lost some habitat, but birds that rely on insects for food may benefit from the change. Logs and big limbs lying on the forest floor may slowly decompose and release nutrients back into the system. If all woody debris had been removed, much of the nutrients accumulated in the forest for centuries would have been removed also."

Jones is slowly rejuvenating itself in its own natural way.

⚓ **UNDERWAY AGAIN,** we leave lovely Jones to continue our circumnavigation of Orcas Island, heading along the northwest coast.

For the next four miles there is breathtaking, beautiful, mostly uninhabited forested coastline which rises abruptly from the sea. The mountains on this side of Orcas range from 425 to 1,500 feet high, plunging almost straight down into the sea, producing tempestuous thermals challenging mariners.

PRESIDENT CHANNEL

We are now in five mile long President Channel between Orcas and Waldron islands. Channel depths reach 109 fathoms. The shallows along Orcas are close to shore until we approach West Beach.

Tidal currents can run from 2 to 5 knots here. The current floods northeasterly and ebbs southwesterly. Predictions are based on Boundary Pass currents at a station north-northeast of Skipjack Island. *(Refer to Tidal Current Tables)*

Cormorant Bay is a small charted but unnamed bay about two miles north of Steep Point which used to belong to the Girl Scouts and is now privately owned. A dolphin and two charted rocks, baring at a 3 foot tide, are in the bay.

Public access at a charted county road-end is about 0.3 mile north of Cormorant Bay. *(Chart 18434)* The uplands on either side of the access area are privately owned. There is no anchorage here, so this is of interest for those with small boats.

Many of the tidelands along these bluffs are DNR lands, but there are no beaches as the shore is often rocky cliffs diving straight into the sea.

Turtleback Mountain is two miles north of Cormorant Bay. Orcas Knob, the "head" of the turtle of is 0.8 mile west of the turtle's "shell." The mountain reputedly has an immense stone anchor. We haven't hiked up to see it, so we quote from the James Francis Tulloch diary of early Orcas Island.

Orcas' rugged north shore

> **Tulloch writes:**
>
> "While prospecting on Turtleback Mountain I ran across the anchor of which I had heard the old settlers speak so often. It was on a bare piece of rock some hundred feet in extent at the very summit of the mountain overlooking the Gulf of Georgia and its magnificent group of islands.
>
> (The anchor) consists largely of a number of small rocks laid in the form of an immense anchor and a short piece of cable. The first settlers found the rocks … just as moss covered and ancient looking as when I saw it … Most probably it was put there by early explorers of these islands who would naturally climb to this mountain peak for the view, and being sailors, would be apt to leave an anchor as a memento."

Turtleback Mountain's Height

We note discrepancies in the charts: the "shell" height is charted as 1,497 feet on chart 18423, and is 1,519 feet on chart 18432. The "head" is charted at 1,060 feet on 18423, and at 1,005 feet on 18432.

Construction of new homes is gradually encroaching the bluffs above President Channel, with houses tucked among the trees along the high bank. We've seen remains of old, abandoned lime kilns along this shore over the years as we've cruised past. They're much harder to find now as they've receded back to nature and greenery covers them. By staying fairly close to shore southwest of Orcas Knob you may catch a glimpse of them.

Lovers Cove

Lovers Cove is about four miles northeast of Steep Point, less than two miles southwest of Madrona Point, below Turtleback Mountain. It's a beautiful spot with several large charted rocks in this tiny bay. We never found the reason for the fanciful name. When we cruised by recently, we knew we were obviously at Lovers Cove as the painted "Lovers" is still faint on the outside rock, as it has been for years. Now there's a dock and several houses so there's no more privacy for lovers in the cove. The area has long been a favorite with scuba divers, as well as lovers.

As we continue along the shore the vertical bluffs are now more moderate, drop-

Working in the Lime Mines

This was big business on the west coast of Orcas in the very early 1900s. The Orcas mines employed 15 men. They were second in production to the Roche Harbor Lime and Cement Company on San Juan.

ping to about 25 feet. Trees have been logged and vegetation cut away as we approach an area of considerable development. A long, gently curving beach with low bank shoreline unfolds, leading to West Beach and Madrona Point.

West Beach is a delightful change after the steep cliffs of this coast, with its low bank, crescent bay and shallow beaches. The 3 fathom depth curve is 0.2 mile offshore. Private homes are along the southwest shores. Shops at West Beach include the Naked Lamb antique shop and Orcas Island Pottery.

Public access county road-end, often used as a kayak launch, is next to West Beach Resort.

West Beach Resort is easy to spot with its long dock extending into President Channel, about 1.4 miles southwest of Point Doughty. The sign on the end of the pier identifies it, and a Texaco service station sign is visible. There's been a resort with cabins here since the late 1930s. In 1981, Steve and Bernardine Hance bought the resort. They moved to the island after being inspired by a book written by adventurer and environmentalist Floyd Schmoe, who at one time owned Flower Island off Swifts Bay on Lopez.

West Beach Resort

Steve said prevailing summer winds are fairly calm and the resort is sheltered from southeasterlies. "People kayak along the cliffs and it's dead calm about a half mile from shore. Then thermal winds just spill over the top of the mountains and create a horizontal backeddy."

Kayakers camp overnight at the resort, where showers and laundry are available for guests. Almost all the resort floats are pulled out during winter and stored on shore because of storms.

Enter the marina at the outer fuel float.

West Beach Resort Facilities
➤ Short time moorage for customers who buy gas or groceries
➤ Mooring buoys and/or moorage at floats for resort guests only
➤ Marine gas, propane
➤ **WARNING**: there's 4 feet of water at the end of gas float at a zero tide
➤ Grocery store, ice, lattes, scuba air, bait & tackle
➤ Launch ramp, kayak rentals & guided tours, 17 cabins, 60 campsites
➤ Summer hours: 8 a.m. to 7 p.m.
➤ Activities: fish, crab, scuba dive, kayak, camp, beachcomb, swim
➤ Owners: Steve, Bernardine, Tim & Liz Hance
➤ Tel.: 360-376-2240, toll free: 877-937-8224
➤ 190 Waterfront Way, Eastsound, WA 98245
➤ e-mail: vacation@westbeachresort.com., www.westbeachresort.com

➥ **NOTE:** Not all names are on all charts:

Lovers Cove is named on chart 18432, but not on strip chart 18423.

Madrona Point, immediately north of West Beach and 1.4 miles south of Point Doughty, is named on strip chart 18423, but not on chart 18432.

Cormorant Bay isn't named on any chart.

History of West Beach

History of this area goes back hundreds of years, and resort owner Steve Hance enjoys talking about it.

"This was a logical place for early people to come because of abundant fresh water, clams, crabbing, fishing and shelter from storms. There was once a Lummi Indian longhouse right here where the store is. A whale skeleton was found under the longhouse. An article in the 1946 *Island Sounder* told of carnage that took place here many years ago when Haida Indians came down and massacred the Lummis.

(continued on page 104)

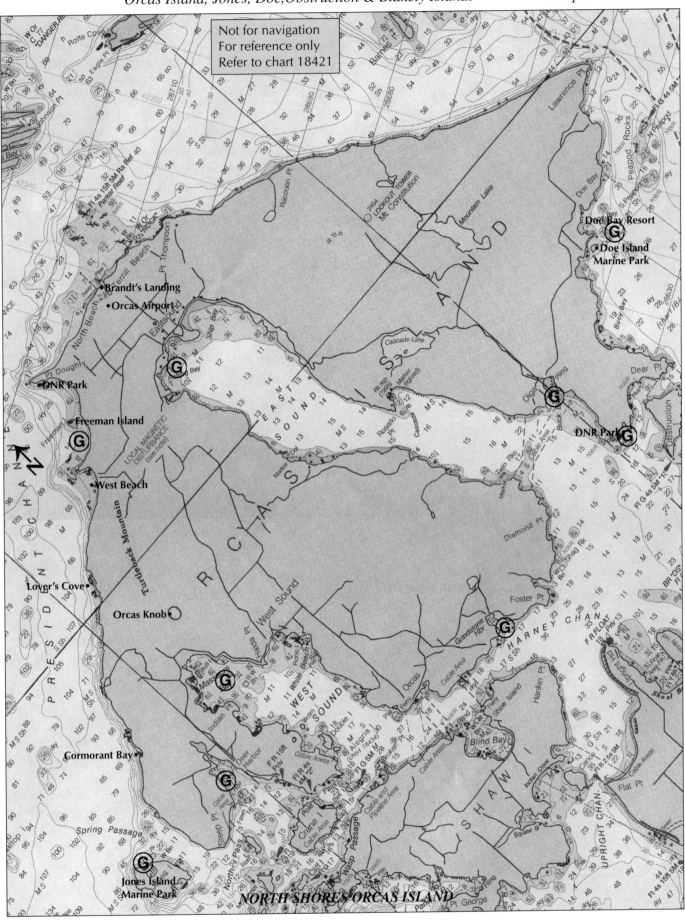

Not for navigation
For reference only
Refer to chart 18421

Doe Bay Resort
G
Doe Island
Marine Park

Brandt's Landing
Orcas Airport

G

DNR Park

Freeman Island
G

West Beach

DNR Park
G

Lover's Cove

Orcas Knob

Foster Pt
G

Cormorant Bay

G

G

G

Blind Bay

G
Jones Island
Marine Park

Public tidelands

Unless otherwise noted, public tidelands are state-owned. Some may be leased and posted for aquaculture or other private use. When going ashore take the quad map of San Juan County.

Many tidelands surrounding Orcas Island are Department of Natural Resource (DNR) lands, many inaccessible. We will feature accessible tidelands in the chapter.

Naming Freeman Island

The island was named for S.D. Freeman, a sailmaker with the Wilkes Expedition.

Freeman Island

Point Doughty

The point was named for John Doughty, an officer with the Wilkes Expedition.

> "There was a brick factory at West Beach and pilings were put on the beach for salmon fishtraps in the early 1900s. The marina was once reconfigured and the creosoted pilings cut down. They were like absolute iron and burned up three chain saw blades. Pilings were put back in the early 1930s and had old insulators in them as they used to have lights on them."

UNDERWAY AGAIN, we head around Madrona Point to Orcas' north shore.

Madrona Point north of West Beach, has a charted 3 fathom, 3 foot shoal 400 yards off the point. A second shoal, similar to that above, extends 200 yards out beyond the first.

Northeast of the point is a crescent-shaped bay nearly 1.5 miles long extending to Point Doughty. Beach Haven, a private resort with cabins, is charted in the south portion of the bay. All facilities, including mooring buoys, are for resort guests only.

Freeman Island State Park

This tiny state-owned island is midway along this shore, less than 300 yards off Orcas. A skiff can land on the rocky beaches. It's a challenge to find a way up the rocks to the well-worn paths along the island's narrow spine. Madrona, firs, cedars and underbrush cover the island. It's charming, with a knoll on the western end offering spectacular views toward Sucia, Patos, Waldron, the Strait of Georgia and Canadian Gulf Islands. A benchmark is atop the knoll. Most of the island's shores are black rock with tide pools and a sandy beach on the eastern side. The island is often visited in small boats by kids from nearby Camp Orkila or by guests from Beach Haven.

Anchoring is possible in calm weather between Freeman and Orcas Islands in 3 to 7 fathoms, mud bottom.

(G) A fair weather **gunkhole**.

Camp Orkila is a large YMCA co-ed summer camp in the north portion of this bay. The camp, for youngsters ages 8 to 17, was established in 1906. About 3,000 youngsters camp, fish, sail, canoe, and swim here yearly. Orkila also hosts family weekends, a community day camp, pool.

Point Doughty is a formidable point jutting nearly 0.4 mile into President Channel where the Orcas shoreline turns from west to north. The nearly barren, rocky point is not a destination for larger boats. Because of offshore rocks, strong swirling currents, kelp and waves, it is virtually inaccessible to any except those with hand-carried boats. The point is DNR land and is a favorite stop for kayakers. Guided kayak trips as well as independent kayakers use Point Doughty with its free campsites. Steps from a pocket beach on the south side of the point allow access to grassy uplands. Youngsters from Camp Orkila sometimes hike to the point on their trail.

Point Doughty DNR Park Facilities
➤ 60 acre park with 1.5 miles of shoreline
➤ Inaccessible to most boats except kayaks
➤ Washington Water Trails campsite, no fees
➤ Three camp sites, picnic tables & fire rings, no water, toilets
➤ Activities: camp, scuba dive, beachcomb, fish

North Beach and Terrill Beach stretch about three miles east from Point Doughty to Point Thompson along the north shore of Orcas. This low bank area has several resorts, homes, one beach access and eagles soaring on the wind currents.

North Beach runs from Point Doughty to the North Beach Road end, about 1.7 miles. From west to east are the waterfront resorts of Glenwood Inn and North Beach Inn, whose waterfront facilities are open to registered guests only.

The 10 fathom curve is less than 100 yards offshore near Point Doughty to 0.7 mile offshore near Parker Reef. Anchoring along the north shore is not encouraged because of exposure to open water and unexpected winds.

Orcas Airport is uncharted but located inshore from North Beach. It is west of the "ditch" between North Beach and East Sound, and accounts for the frequent small planes overhead.

Brandt's Landing, charted but unnamed, is locally known as "the ditch." It's a dredged, private moorage between North and Terrill beaches. About 400 yards long and 100 to 150 feet wide, the channel entrance is marked by four pilings. It is an all private boat moorage with no transient moorage. A state park workboat moors here.

Smuggler's Villa Resort on the north shore has customer moorage at the east side of the ditch for boaters who spend the night in the resort. Reservations are recommended. Resort facilities include a hot tub, sauna, swimming pool, children's playground, tennis and basketball courts, and laundry privileges. Tel.: 800-488-2097; e-mail: smuggler@pacificrim.net

⚜ Public access at North Beach Road end is immediately east of Smuggler's Villa. The sand and gravel beach is the only public access on the north shore and is used as a launch for kayaks and other hand-carry boats. Beaches on either side of the narrow road end are private and there is no overnight parking or camping here.

Not a Gunkhole

DNR personnel told us about access to Point Doughty and agreed with information compiled on the DNR Recreation Guide: Strong currents and submerged rocks make landing difficult and sometimes dangerous; skiffs or kayaks are best for landing. This is most definitely not a gunkhole.

North Shore "Ditch" with Orcas Airport in back (right) and Smuggler's Villa (left)

Terrill Beach runs east of the roadend to Point Thompson, about 1.3 miles.

Parker Reef, NWR, a mess of rocks and shoals, is about 0.7 mile north of Terrill Beach off Orcas' north shore, and is marked by a light. The reef is visible on a 9 foot tide and extends 110 yards in all directions from the light, except on the east side where it extends about 160 yards from the light. Kelp covers the reef and the area to shore. There are several shallow spots west and southwest inside the 10 fathom curve although it is possible to go between the reef and the island with care in 5 to 8 fathoms.

Parker Reef Light [FL 4s 15ft 5M Ra Ref] flashing 4 second light 15 feet high, visible 5 miles with a radar reflector, is mounted on a diamond-shaped dayboard with red and white sectors, on a pile structure.

Orcas Island North Shore Daybeacon and **Orcas Island North Shore Buoy** mark an unnamed reef extends 0.1 mile off Terrill Beach south of Parker Reef. This reef runs about 0.2 mile east to west, is charted and marked.

Daybeacon [W Bn] on a diamond-shaped white dayboard on a pile marks the reef, with a warning sign, **"Danger Submerged Rocks."** The daybeacon is maintained from March 15 to Oct. 15.

Buoy [W Or] is a white can buoy with orange bands and an orange diamond warning, "Rock." The buoy is about 300 yards east of the daybeacon.

➥ NOTE: Once again we must change charts. If using **18432**, change to **18430** at North Beach going from west to east. If going from east to west, reverse the chart order.

Lawrence Point

It was named by Wilkes for Capt. James Lawrence who pleaded to his men as he lay dying in the War of 1812, "Don't give up the ship."

His men gave up anyway.

Three Names to Choose From
Rosario Strait was called **Canal de Fidalgo** by Eliza in 1791, and **Ringgold's Pass Channel** by the Wilkes Expedition in 1841.

However, the English Admiralty chart of 1847 showed it as **Rosario Strait**, a name by which it has always been known.

Schooner Adventuress—often seen in the islands

➡ **NOTE: Lawrence Point** is a Marine Reserve area in the Voluntary Bottomfish "No Take" Zone Program.

On the east side of Orcas Island, it runs from the point northwesterly for 1,500 yards. All zones extend seaward 0.25 mile from the shoreline.

Peapod Light, Since 1903

A navigation stake light was installed on Peapod Rocks in 1903. The light was tended by a man who rowed out from Doe Bay.

The Navy cruiser **Boston**, enroute to Boundary Bay for target practice, grounded on the rocks briefly in 1906.

Bartwood Lodge, formerly Bartell's Resort, is inshore of Parker Reef, about 0.3 miles west of Point Thompson. Trailerable and small boats can launch here. For years this was a favorite gas stop for those cruising the islands, but the fuel facility closed down permanently in 1998 and tanks were removed.

Marine Facilities at Bartwood
➤ Private launch ramp west of dock
➤ Launch fees round trip: boats $10, kayaks $6
➤ 16 room inn, Tel.: 360-376-2242; Rt. 2, Box 1040, Eastsound, WA 98245
➤ Sean Paul's Restaurant Tel.: 360-376-7030

From Point Thompson southeast to **Raccoon Point** and on to **Lawrence Point** Orcas again becomes steep and forested, tumbling from the mountains to the sea with no bays, bights, coves, beaches or good anchorages. There are no roads to this impressive northeast coast, it is virtually uninhabited.

Orcas Island's tall mountains all loom above this shore: **Buck Mountain**, 1,472 feet, **Mount Constitution**, 2,407 feet, and **Mount Pickett**, 1,700 feet.

ROSARIO STRAIT

We have reached the northwest side of 20 mile long Rosario Strait, which runs north and south between the Strait of Juan de Fuca and the Strait of Georgia. Ranging from 1.5 to 5 miles wide, it's the easternmost of the three main channels between the two straits and is in constant use by large commercial vessels and recreational craft between Bellingham, Cherry Point, Anacortes and the San Juans.

Currents in Rosario run more than 3.5 knots on the southerly ebb at 175° True, and often more than 2.5 knots on the northwesterly flood at 335° True. On a strong ebb against a south wind, tide rips may be challenging to small craft. *(See predictions in Tidal Current Tables)*

Lawrence Point is the easternmost point of Orcas Island, infamous for turbulent waters and good fishing. Rocks surround the point which tapers from 500 feet high to its tip at the water's edge where it juts into Rosario.

Point Lawrence Lodge was built by a long-time island family in a cove about a 0.8 mile southwest of the point. Sea Acres Resort is near the site of the old lodge. When the resort closed down, the cabins were sold off and there is now residential development in this eastern part of the island.

"Flotsam" Lodge

Carroll Culver graduated from the University of Washington with a journalism degree and came to Orcas Island in the early 1920s where he built Point Lawrence Lodge, a fishing retreat. He built the cabins from lumber that floated by. He'd sit in the lodge living room (the old building is still there), drinking coffee, watching the ebbing tide for drifting logs.

He had an outboard all gassed up and ready to go, and if he saw a log he'd start the engine, go roaring out to it, drive a "dog" in it, put a line through the dog and tow the log back to the beach. If it had a brand on it he'd cut it off with his chain saw. If it was cedar he made it into shakes. If it was fir, after he got three or four, he'd tow them over to cousin Willis' sawmill, turn them into lumber and take them home to use in building his own house, which came almost entirely off the beach. All he had to buy was glass, he said it didn't come floating by. He died in 1996 at age 92. *(Thanks to Jack Culver of West Sound who filled us in on Culver family history. He's a third cousin once removed of long-time Orcas resident Carroll Culver.)*

Peapod Rocks, about one mile southwest of Point Lawrence, are no longer a State Parks Underwater Recreation Area. The four acres of rock islets stretch nearly one mile northeast to southwest, and are now part of the National Wildlife Refuge. Seals and sea lions haul out on the rocks, with seabirds and occasionally bald eagles visiting them. Boats are not allowed to land on the low rocks and must keep 200 yards away. Scuba divers often explore the area from Peapod Rocks to Doe Bay with its diverse underwater topography and varying degrees of diving difficulty, from the capricious currents near the rocks to the protected waters of the bay.

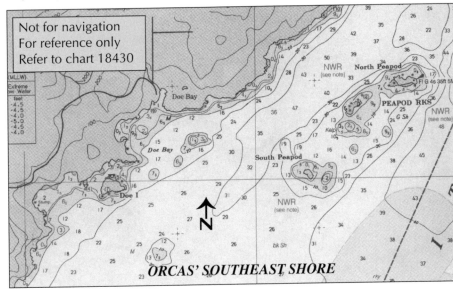

Not for navigation
For reference only
Refer to chart 18430

ORCAS' SOUTHEAST SHORE

Peapod Rocks Light [Fl G 4sec 35ft 5M "15"] flashing green 4 second light 35 feet high visible 5 miles, is on a square green dayboard on a white octagonal house on the northeast end of North Peapod Rock.

Doe Bay, a beautiful little bay facing Rosario Strait is west of the Peapods. This is the site of Doe Bay Resort. The gray resort buildings, the road leading to it and brightly colored kayaks on the beach makes it easy to spot from the water.

Doe Bay was a small, thriving community in the early 1900s, with a post office and general store, both now on the National Register of Historic Buildings. The village had a tavern, dancehall, restaurant, community building and steamer dock. The steamer dock is long gone, and some of the old buildings have been incorporated into the resort.

⚓ **Anchoring** is possible in about 3 fathoms, mud bottom, providing the weather is calm.

Ⓖ Doe Bay is a possible **gunkhole** under calm conditions.

Doe Bay Resort Facilities
➤ No moorage, anchor in 3 fathoms, weather permitting
➤ 60 acres with hiking trails
➤ Cafe & small store, two hot tubs & sauna
➤ Washington Water Trails campsite
➤ Cabins, yurts, RV hookups & campsites
➤ Activities: camp, picnic, beachcomb, volleyball, hike, hot tub, meditate
➤ Tel.: 360-376-2291, e-mail: doebay@pacificrim.net
➤ Address: P.O. Box 437, Olga, WA 98279

A Touch of Doe Bay History
Doe Bay has been a resort and retreat center for many years. Native Americans used it as a sanctuary. At various times it has been an artist colony, health spa and a human potential center.

In the early 1900s the community had a post office and general store serving the east end of Orcas. The steamer *Osage* would make regular stops at the Doe Bay wharf for island freight and passengers. In the 1970s, it was the site of the Polarity Institute, a private, new-age

(continued on next page)

No More Phones

Years ago we noticed a weather-beaten old "Cable Crossing" sign on the point. At one time a telephone cable came underwater from Lummi Island and rose out of the water at Lawrence Point, but no more.

Peapod Rocks

They were named by someone in the Wilkes Expedition with a rather creative idea of peapods.

Looking east from Doe Bay to Lummi Island

Steamer Osage

*The **Osage** used to dock at the old docks at Doe Bay and Olga until the 1950s, when the vessel lost the mail contract.*

The docks in both communities, now gone, were sturdy enough that trucks could be driven on them, said an old timer who worked on the steamer one summer long-ago.

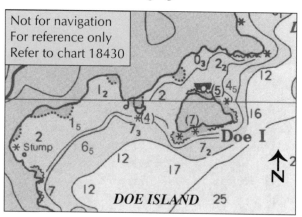

experiment in communal living, with meditation groups, among other "communal" activities. In 1982, when the institute fell on financial hard times it moved to California. The property at Doe Bay was sold and it became a resort.

The resort still retains some of the commune flavor of Polarity, with a trail to "Contemplation Point" and "swimsuits optional" signs at the two hot tubs.

☸**UNDERWAY AGAIN,** we head in a slightly southwest direction to another marine state park.

DOE ISLAND MARINE STATE PARK

Southwest of Doe Bay less than a half-mile from the resort is a charming, six acre state park where you feel like you could stay forever. Doe Island is magical, tall evergreens, madronas, unspoiled beaches, and a romantic quality in the peace and quiet of the woods and shores. Trails crisscross the island, leading to beaches filled with driftwood treasures. Every direction offers picture perfect scenery, especially north and east across Rosario Pass. Doe Island is as good as it gets.

The recommended approach to the Doe Island float at the north side of the island is from the east. Waves and swells from Rosario Strait can make tying at the float a bit rolly at times. Nevertheless, Doe Island is a great stopover, giving kids and dogs a place to run off steam while adults relax with an easy island hike. All buoys in the area are private.

The south shore's undercut bluffs lead to an intriguing cave formation caused by strong wave action. Perhaps the caves were used by smugglers during their heyday. A Native American "canoe pullout" site and an archeological site are on the north shore.

⚓ **Anchoring** is possible in the bay north of Doe Island in 2 to 4 fathoms, but park rangers and Orcas islanders don't recommend it. The bay is exposed to easterlies and notheasterlies; the bottom has kelp, eelgrass and old cables left over from the early logging days. They suggest tying to the float if possible, or anchoring for only a short time.

Treasures from island shores

A fascinating home, built almost completely from beachcombing treasures, is inside a little hook on the Orcas shore behind Doe Island.

Moorage at Doe Island

Doe Island Marine State Park Facilities

➤ Six acres with 2,049 feet of shoreline
➤ Guest moorage dock on north shore with 32 feet each side
➤ Fees: May-Sept. boats under 26' $8 night; boats over 26' $11 night, floats removed October thru April
➤ Five campsites; three in forest, two in clearings
➤ Picnic tables, no water, vault toilet near float
➤ Loop trail on bluffs above the beach
➤ Activities: hike, camp, picnic, fish, beachcomb, gunkhole

Strong currents flow through the 2 fathom channel between Doe and Orcas islands. An alternative anchorage is a charted 2 fathom bay off Orcas shores west of Doe.

☸**UNDERWAY AGAIN,** and we head to Obstruction Pass.

Buoy Bay, a long indentation that runs south of Doe Island to Deer Point, is flanked by reefs. The bay's north end has steep, rock banks with very little beach. Houses are scattered among the trees in the fields above the beach along the south shores of the bay.

Although there are DNR tidelands along this shore, it would be a less than satisfactory anchorage because of offshore rocks and exposure to waves from Rosario.

Deer Point, with steep, high banks, separates Rosario Strait from Obstruction Pass. It has several coves and bights with tiny beaches. The point as charted looks like jigsaw puzzle pieces.

Cable area along the south Orcas shore goes to Obstruction and Blakely islands.

OBSTRUCTION & PEAVINE PASSES, OBSTRUCTION ISLAND

Obstruction Pass, an upside down U-shape, separates Orcas and Obstruction islands, leading from Rosario Strait to the inner passages and sounds of the San Juans. The pass is just over one mile long with a width of 350 yards at its narrowest.

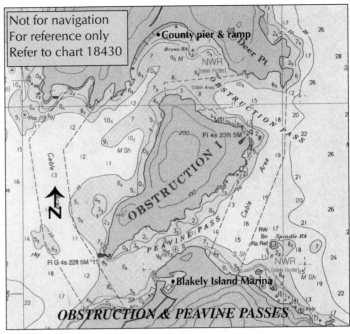

Not for navigation
For reference only
Refer to chart 18430

OBSTRUCTION & PEAVINE PASSES

Obstruction Island sits squarely between Orcas and Blakely islands, 200 feet high with 217 acres, creating Obstruction and Peavine passes, around the north and south sides of the island.

Flood currents flows southeast at 100° True. Ebb currents flow west at 270° True, with heavy tide rips east of Obstruction Island. Currents may race through the pass at up to 5.5 to 6.5 knots according to the *Coast Pilot.* Currents in both passes are based on Rosario Strait predictions. *(Refer to Tidal Current Tables)*

Obstruction Pass Light [Fl 4sec 23ft 5M] flashing 4 second light 23 feet high visible 5 miles, is on a diamond-shaped dayboard with red and white diamond sectors on a white house at the northeast tip of Obstruction Island.

Obstruction's shores are rocky and several houses perch on high banks with stairs or ladders leading to pocket beaches. The island is all private with no public access. Two private community docks and several private mooring buoys are around the island, which has over a dozen homes with several full-time residents.

Peavine Pass, about 0.5 mile long, separates Obstruction and Blakely islands, south of Obstruction Island. This pass is considered safer and straighter than Obstruction Pass, according to the *Coast Pilot.* It's a little over 200 yards wide at its narrowest part. The least depth in mid-channel is 6 fathoms. In 1973, two submerged rocks were reported in the pass about 0.4 mile east of Peavine Pass Light, as charted on 18430 and noted in the *Coast Pilot.*

Obstruction Island

The island was named by the Wilkes Expedition, maybe because they felt it got in their way?

Peavine Pass Light

Currents may reach from 5.5 to 6.5 knots in the pass, according to the *Coast Pilot.* Flood current in Peavine flows northeasterly, 55° True, and the ebb current flows westerly at 265° True.

Peavine Pass Light [Fl G 4sec 22ft 5M "1"] flashing green 4 second light 22 feet high visible 5 miles, is mounted on a square green dayboard on a tower on the southwest point of Obstruction Island.

Ferries occasionally use Peavine Pass when there are heavy seas on Rosario Strait, although they regularly use Thatcher Pass south of Blakely. Peavine is also an alternate entry into the San Juans for recreational mariners if they get into strong winds on Rosario Strait.

Blakely Island Marina

BLAKELY ISLAND

Sometimes called the "flying island," Blakely forms the south side of Peavine Pass. This 1,042 foot high heavily forested island has a 2,500 foot long private airstrip, which accounts for the nickname. The island is all private, except for a marina with transient moorage near the west end of Peavine Pass. There is also one fairly good anchorage at the south end of the island.

There are no county roads on Blakely and only property owners and guests have access to the lakes, miles of hiking trails and private roads. San Juan County records show a population of 36 permanent residents. Children on Blakely go to Orcas by "school boat" to attend classes.

Seattle Pacific University has a 900 acre campus on the island where marine biology and island flora and fauna are studied. Facilities include a laboratory, library, dining hall and dormitory. There are several preservation and conservation easements on Blakely to preserve parts of the island from any future development.

Blakely Island Marina, open almost year-round, has concrete floats and manicured lawns. As the island is all private, only the marina facilities and the store are open to visiting cruisers. The well-marked fuel dock is outside the marina, south of the entrance. Boats can either tie at the fuel dock and then check in at the store for slip assignments, or enter the marina.

The 100 foot wide marina entrance passes by a breakwater into the nearly landlocked harbor, which is 7.5 feet deep at zero tide. Marina managers advise that boats stay in center channel and suggest not cutting it too close as a sandbar extends off the northeast point of the entrance. The marina hosts various yacht club rendezvous.

Public Access
🐚 *Almost all of the tidelands surrounding Blakely Island are public access DNR lands below mean high tide. To avoid trespassing, it is recommended that mariners refer to the quad map which shows ownership of tidelands before going ashore.*

Facilities at Blakely Island General Store & Marina
➤ Guest moorage for approximately 35 boats, reservations accepted
➤ Fees based on length, example: 22'-$18; 30'-$25; 35'-$29; 40'-$38; 45'-$42
➤ Complimentary power & water
➤ Fuel dock: gas & diesel
➤ Heated restrooms, showers, laundry, garbage, no pump out
➤ Well-stocked general store, groceries, gifts, clothing, fishing gear, post office
➤ Beautiful lawns, pet area for the pups
➤ Large sheltered area for barbecues & picnics
➤ Marina managers: Richard & Norma Reed
➤ Tel.: 360-375-6121/FAX: 360-375-6141
➤ Address: Blakely Island General Store & Marina, Blakely Is., WA 98222

Original Chinook name
*Blakely was known to Native Americans as "**Hum-Hum-Ilch**" in Chinook jargon, which was related to the smell of tule reeds growing near the island's two lakes. Indians used the fibrous reed in weaving baskets.*

A Bit of Blakely Island History
The 4,436 acre island wasn't always private. That happened in 1954 when Ola and Floyd Johnson bought it as a private airpark for fellow pilots.

Although no permanent Indian settlements were on the island, there is evidence of Indian visits. Middens are on a beach at the northern end. The area offered camas, seaweed, fish and shellfish. Large parties of raiding northern Indians stopped at the west beach near Thatcher Bay for years.

The first non-Native settlers arrived on the island in the 1850s. Theodore Spencer moved from Lopez to homestead in 1889 and three years later purchased a sawmill and box factory on Thatcher Pass, which the family ran until 1945. A log cabin schoolhouse built in the 1880s still stands in Thatcher and now serves as the island museum. It was reportedly the oldest continuously used log school in the state, with classes from 1890 to 1950.

Teacher Richard H. Straub shot and killed school board member Leon Lanterman on August 30, 1895, the only murder ever on Blakely. Straub was convicted after a trial and hung on April 23, 1897, in Friday Harbor, the only recorded hanging in San Juan County. Tickets were sold to about 20 people who attended the hanging. Straub may have been the only condemned man in history who had to show the executioner how to tie the knot.

Gold mining was tried around 1900, but it never panned out.

Blakely Island

*The island was named by the Wilkes Expedition for Johnston Blakely, an Irish born naval officer in the U.S. Navy. He won a congressional gold medal for capturing and burning the British brig **Reindeer**.*

*He was commander of the **Wasp** when the ship sunk in a gale on Oct. 9, 1841.*

Blakely Marina entrance

⚓**UNDERWAY AGAIN,** leaving Blakely Marina we head east through Peavine Pass to circumnavigate Blakely, keeping clear of the shoal outside the north side of the marina. A rock is reported near the island's north end, about 400 yards east of the marina entrance.

Spindle Rock, NWR, is off the northeast shore.

Peavine Pass Rocks Daybeacon [RW Bn Ra Ref] is a diamond-shaped dayboard with white and red sectors and a radar reflector marking Spindle Rock. It's possible to pass between Spindle Rock and Blakely in about 6 fathoms, but a number of offshore rocks and tiny islands in the channel make it a challenge.

The east side of Blakely all the way south to Armitage Island is steep and forested. We stay fairly close to the island along the 10 fathom depth curve.

Black Rock [Fl G 4s 10ft 4M "9"] flashing green 4 second light 10 feet high visible 4 miles, is on a square green dayboard on a skeleton tower 0.4 mile off the east shore in Rosario Strait about three miles southeast of Spindle Rock. It is a National Wildlife Refuge.

Pointer Island, NWR, 0.7 mile southwest of Black Rock, is 500 yards off Blakely.

THATCHER PASS

This east-west pass between Blakely and Decatur islands is less than one mile long and about 0.5 mile wide. Washington State Ferries use the heavily traveled pass as access to the San Juans.

Currents in the pass can exceed 2 knots. The flood current is northwesterly at 300° True, and ebb current flows easterly at 75° True. Currents in the pass are based on Rosario Strait predictions.

Lawson Rock, NWR, is the only charted danger in the pass, nearly mid-channel, 700 yards southeast of Armitage Island and 700 yards north of Fauntleroy Point.

Lawson Rock [R N "2"] red nun buoy is about 200 yards east of Lawson Rock.

Lawson Rock Danger Daybeacon [W Bn Ra Ref] diamond-shaped white dayboard is on the rock about 250 yards west of the red buoy, with a **"DANGER ROCK"** sign, and radar reflector.

Not for navigation
For reference only
Refer to chart 18430

BLAKELY ISLAND

Bay at Armitage Island

Once a steamer stop

A long wharf served as a steamer landing at Obstruction Pass around the turn of the 19th century.

Moorage in Obstruction Pass

Armitage Island off the southeast end of Blakely is all private. Owners of docks and facilities on the seven acre island have access to Blakely. All buoys are private.

🐚 Some **public tidelands** are in the bay. Check the quad map before going ashore.

⚓ **Anchoring** is possible in the bay inside of Armitage Ⓖ This is a **pleasant gunkhole.**

Blakely Island Light [Fl R 6s 12ft 5M] flashing red 6 second light 12 feet high visible 5 miles on a triangular red mark on a pile, marks Blakely's south tip.

Cable area from Blakely to Decatur is near the light. We head northwest and pass a wonderful log cabin on the beach, as well as several other homes.

Willow Island, NWR, is 300 yards off Blakely's southwest shore. State ferries sometimes pass between Blakely and the 9.6 acre island for a change of scenery.

Thatcher Bay, about one mile north of Blakely Island Light, is the site of an old sawmill where a stream comes down from Spencer Lake. The shallow bay, 1 to 2 fathoms deep, still has many old piles left over from the mill.

⚓ **Anchoring** may be possible in a mud bottom in calm weather, although we have not done it. There are submerged logs in here which make it tricky.

Bald Bluff, on the northwest side of the bay, was the site of a gold mining operation in the early part of the century. The shoreline north of here is steep, but it's shoal offshore with rocks and piles. At times the 10 fathom curve extends as far as 0.2 mile from the island.

Blakely Island Shoal Lighted Buoy [BR "DS" Fl (2) W] flashing white light on a black and red horizontal striped buoy marks a 1 fathom, 5 foot shoal about 0.5 mile west of Blakely. "DS" means isolated danger. From here, planes flying into and out of Blakely airfield are easily seen.

Cable area is from the northwest shore of Blakely to the southern tip of Orcas.

OBSTRUCTION PASS "REVISITED," we're back ...

The community at Obstruction Pass has several dozen homes, a resort with a small store and piers, county dock and launch ramp.

Brown Rock, NWR, is in the eastern third of the pass, 200 yards off Orcas.

Spring Bay Inn, a waterfront bed and breakfast catering to kayakers and offering kayak tours, is also in the east portion. Facilities include a hot tub and brunch. Tel.: 360-376-5531

Obstruction Pass County Dock is the east dock, used for loading and unloading, with no overnight moorage. The county ramp adjacent to the dock is used by fishermen and kayakers, many who launch and head to Obstruction Pass Campground DNR park 0.5 mile west.

Lieberhaven Marina Resort, inside the white picket fence, is west of the ramp. Several boats moor at the resort pier, along with the sailboat *Lieberschwan*. The resort's small store carries basic groceries, snacks, drinks, ice, toys, fishing gear and gifts. Signs at the store door list the clever "Rules of the Tavern." The resort has furnished cabins and apartments, kayak tours, boat rentals, fishing and sailing charters, and welcomes children. Tel.: 360-376-2472. The passenger ferry *Redhead* runs from Bellingham through the San Juans in summer, stopping at Lieberhaven.

⚓ **UNDERWAY AGAIN,** and we're off to Obstruction Pass DNR Park and then to East Sound. On the way west we pass two small bays with homes and pocket beaches. A black and pink sculpture gyrates on a point between the bays.

Cable area crosses to Blakely Island here.

OBSTRUCTION PASS DNR PARK

🌿 We've arrived at the great DNR Park at the west end of the pass, accessible only by boat or a walking trail. We've been here several different times by boat and by foot. Sailing in and picking up a mooring buoy is far easier than the hike. The beautiful trail feels five times as long as the mere 0.5 mile it's reputed to be from the trailhead at the parking area. It winds through "miles" of deep forest and along the edge of a cliff overlooking East Sound. If you tie to a buoy, plan to row ashore and hike the trail. It's worth it.

⚓ **Anchoring** is possible near the three mooring buoys in 2 to 5 fathoms, being aware of the cable area. The anchorage is exposed to southerlies.

Ⓖ It's a pretty good **gunkhole.**

The campground is on a bluff with two sets of stairs to the shore. The gently sloping beach is pea gravel and sand, topped with driftwood at the high tide line. This is a great place for beachcombing, wading and swimming (if you're part polar bear), and just relaxing. Marvelous trees lean out over the beach. It's a beautiful site, well used and well-maintained. The park is a favorite destination for kayakers, and is used occasionally as a survival training camp for Scouts. A private home on the point just west of the park can be reached only by boat.

> **Obstruction Pass DNR Park Facilities**
> ➤ 400 feet of public tidelands, 80 acres of uplands
> ➤ Three mooring buoys, no fees, no water
> ➤ 12 campsites, picnic tables, fire rings, 3 latrines
> ➤ Washington Water Trails camp site
> ➤ Activities: camp, hike, picnic, beachcomb, swim, enjoy

> **Unique Pacific Madrone**
>
> The tree with the reddish trunk and large old leaves is called Pacific Madrone or arbutus. It is characterized by a twisting trunk and heavy irregular branches. The loose peeling on the trunk isn't the bark, but bark scales. The lighter smooth material underneath the scales is the bark. The tree is a good indicator of rocky or hard subsoil beneath the surface. The Pacific Madrone has little commercial value except as an ornamental tree.

⚓ **UNDERWAY AGAIN,** we round the point at the west end of Obstruction Pass, giving it a wide berth because of a reported rock and a tiny NWR island, venturing into East Sound.

DNR park beaches overused

Obstruction Pass DNR Park is one of the two most heavily impacted by kayakers in the San Juan Islands area. The other DNR park is Pelican Beach on Cypress Island.

Mount Constitution

It's a terrific place, even in the fog. The tower at Mount Constitution was built in 1936 by the Civilian Conservation Corps with sandstone blocks from island rock quarries.

Many of the trails and campgrounds at Moran Park were also built by the CCC.

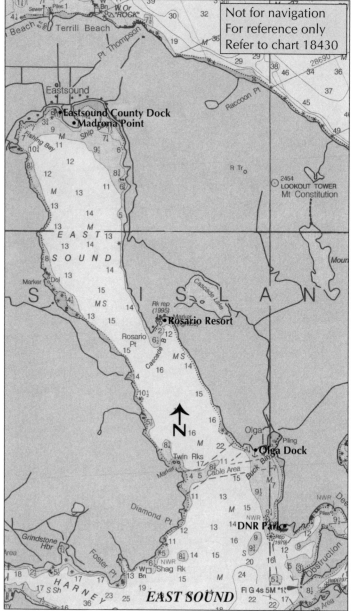

Not for navigation
For reference only
Refer to chart 18430

EAST SOUND

This schizophrenic, six mile long body of water can be glassy calm or blowing a veritable gale within minutes of each other. Winds tend to blow straight up and down this fjord-like sound with steep, forested sides. The waves build up and it is exciting sailing even though it may be calm elsewhere in the islands.

The communities of Olga, Rosario Resort and the village of Eastsound are located on East Sound—note the differences in spelling.

Mount Constitution dominates East Sound, as it does almost every place on Orcas. It's an incredible mountain, one of three along the northeast arm of Orcas. The mountain is within Moran State Park, and the road to the summit from the main county highway in the park is approximately six winding miles. Many trails in the park make it possible to hike to the top. We highly recommend a visit to the mountain if possible.

The 2,407 foot high peak rises almost straight up out of the sea, less than one mile from Orcas' northeast shore. Mount Pickett is southeast of Constitution and Buck Mountain is northwest.

Olga and **Buck Bay** are just over one mile north of the entrance to East Sound. Olga is the community west of Buck Bay which wraps around the bay, a tideflat and old log booming ground.

Olga Dock at the charted road end offers a public moorage float maintained and operated by the Olga Community Club. The moorage is exposed to southerly winds and waves. The float is removed in late September and returned in May. Several private buoys are near the dock.

⚓ **Anchoring** is possible near the Olga dock in 4 to 5 fathoms, mud bottom.

Ⓖ In good weather it qualifies as a **gunkhole**.

Olga Dock

Facilities at Olga Dock
➤ Moorage float
➤ Fee: 25¢ foot
➤ Three night maximum stay

The old Olga General Store is on the road end at the head of the dock. The store is open only in summer as the owners are off-island schoolteachers and run it during their vacation. They carry grocery and deli items, and gas is no longer sold, although the old pumps are still there. The Olga Post Office is across the street from the store. In the "old days" it was in a corner of the store.

Cafe Olga & Orcas Island Artworks are 400 yards from the head of the dock in a wonderful old building built in 1938 for "barreling" island strawberries. This is a top notch cafe with outstanding meals, homemade pies are a specialty, and even locals love to eat here. The first thing that assails your senses when you open the door is the aroma of home baked bread, but you don't see the restaurant yet, it's in the back. What you see is an array of beautiful island-made crafts: yarns, woolen fabrics, hand-knit sweaters, paintings, jewelry, pottery, woodworking, clothing and much more. The people you deal with are the creators of these crafts and they love to talk about their work and listen to your ideas. A bookstore is upstairs. Cafe Olga & Orcas Island Artworks, a co-op formed in 1982 and in the same building, are open daily from 10 a.m. to 6 p.m., and closed in January and February. Cafe Olga was founded by skilled chef Marcy Lund. This is truly a warm and unique place to get a feel for Orcas Island life.

Olga General Store

⚓**UNDERWAY AGAIN,** we continue north, now nearly under the 1,200 foot peak of Entrance Mountain which rises virtually straight up from East Sound. There are no charted hazards along the rocky shore outside the 10 fathom depth curve, which is less than 100 yards offshore. In two miles we reach the largest resort in the San Juans.

Rosario Resort is in the magnificent, historic, white 54 room Moran Mansion, built in Cascade Bay in the early 1900s as a private residence by Robert Moran, former Seattle mayor and shipping magnate. It dominates the East Sound shoreline and can be seen for miles, even from ferries in Harney Channel. It is in an incredible landscaped setting on a rocky point at the foot of steep, forested hills. Many mariners find the luxury resort a haven, enjoying the swimming pools, jacuzzis, pipe organ concerts and dress-up nights of dinner and dancing.

Ironsides Inlet

That was the name given to East Sound by the Wilkes Expedition.

"Old Ironsides" was the nickname of the Constitution, a famous American frigate of the War of 1812.

The name was changed to East Sound later by the British and appeared as such on their 1866 charts.

Eastsound Public Tidelands

🐚 *Public tidelands of several miles are in separate parcels on the east and west shores of East Sound.*

Refer to DNR Quad map for locations.

Rosario & the Moran Mansion

The Moran Mansion is impressive, inside and out. Completed in 1909 by Robert Moran, it was built as elegantly as an ocean liner of the period: 12 inch walls paneled with mahogany, more than 100 doors, six tons of copper sheeting on the roof and 6,000 square feet of teak parquet floor.

The centerpiece of the home is the music room with a 1,972 pipe Aeolian organ built in 1913. This is the largest pipe organ installed in a private home in the U.S., according to a Rosario spokesman. An antique Steinway grand piano is also featured.

A maritime museum contains a fascinating look into Seattle's early shipbuilding. Moran's shipyard was located in what was the south parking lot of the Kingdome, and is now the Seattle Mariners Safeco Field.

The Morans were philanthropists, and gave 3,600 acres of forest and lakes to the state for the wonderful park on Orcas that bears their name. Moran developed water systems, built roads and contributed to the island's economy during the Depression in the 1930s by furnishing jobs to islanders. He sold Rosario in 1938 after his wife died. It became a resort in 1960 when it was purchased by Gil Geiser, ex-mayor of Mountlake Terrace, and has changed hands several times since. *(see next page)*

Moran Mansion

Figurehead

*The figurehead from the Clipper ship **America** is at Rosario. Carved from a solid white pine log, it was donated to Robert Moran in 1916. The ship was built in 1874 in Massachusetts and wrecked on San Juan Island in 1914. She sailed from New York to San Francisco in 89 days; from San Francisco to Liverpool in 102.*

In 1979, the original buildings were named on the National Register of Historic Places. In October 1998, the National Trust for Historic Preservation named Rosario in its Historic Hotels of America program.

For those who stay in Rosario Marina, benefits include four spa passes daily, unlimited use of swimming pools and tennis courts, and use of a courtesy van.

The DNR mooring buoys in Cascade Bay outside the marina breakwater are in 5 to 10 fathoms, and are exposed to southerly winds. Mariners may tie free to the buoys, but must check in with the Rosario harbormaster. Those on buoys can dinghy into Rosario, go to the restaurants and tour the grounds. If they pay Rosario a 15 dollar per day landing fee they will receive four day-passes, which include unlimited use of resort swimming pools, spas, tennis courts, showers and courtesy van. Winter landing fee at the buoys is 10 dollars.

The marina is protected by a rock breakwater and outer floats. Enter the marina between the lighted breakwater and fuel float. In the summer, staff will assign a slip and assist with docking.

Rosario Resort Marina Facilities
➤ Guest moorage for 30+ boats in marina
➤ 30 DNR mooring buoys outside marina, first come, first served
➤ Marine fuel: gas & diesel
➤ Moorage fee: $1.25 foot, includes 30 amp power, water, showers
➤ Staff on floats assists with docking
➤ Launch ramp
➤ Restrooms, showers, laundry, pumpout, pools
➤ Three restaurants, Mansion Museum, Deli, sundries & provisions
➤ Moorage reservations recommended & necessary for July, Aug. & Sept.
➤ Scheduled Kenmore Air flights & stop for Victoria *Clipper* passenger vessel
➤ Activities: hike, visit historical land marks, fish, swim, tennis
➤ Monitors VHF Channel 78A
➤ Harbormaster: Nelson Moulton
➤ Tel.: 800-562-8820, 360-376-2222, Ext. 700
➤ Address: 1400 Rosario Rd., East sound, WA 98245; www.rosarioresort.com

Rosario Marina

⚓ **UNDERWAY AGAIN,** we leave Rosario and go around Rosario Point north toward the head of East Sound, three miles away. This stretch along the east shore is similar to that between Olga and Rosario—fjord-like steep, forested slopes with no moorages.

A small bay with a 5 fathom shoal offshore about 1.8 miles north of Rosario Point was the site of an early lime kiln and cooper shop. It was also known to the Lummis as the place where the first deer was created. The bay is less than 0.5 mile south of Giffin Rocks.

Giffin Rocks, one mile south of Crescent Beach, are just north of a small bay which offers a little protection from winds. These rocks were a "burying" ground for Indian tribes. Custom was not to bury the dead, but to put them in canoes and place them among the branches of scrub juniper trees on the rocks. A log that lay on the point had its limbs cut short and each was decorated with a human skull. More than 20 skulls were seen there. *(From Tulloch Diary)*

Coon Hollow is a geographical pockmark north of Giffin Rocks. It is shallow and offers little protection for anything, except perhaps raccoons.

We've now reached the head of East Sound which is split into two bays at the village of Eastsound. Ship and Fishing bays are on either side of south-pointing Madrona Point peninsula.

Ship Bay, which is too shallow for any vessel except a kayak, is the east bay, at Crescent Beach. At low tide the bay is a vast expanse of beautiful sandy beach. This was a favorite camp site with early vacationers; tourist tents and cottages lined the no-bank shore. It is now a privately-owned oyster farm, and the beach is no longer open to the public. A county road runs above the driftwood beach. A few old beach cabins remain on the inland side of the road.

A kayak rental firm has a marked channel between buoys near the center of the beach allowing kayak access. Windsurfers must be careful of not to get too near the oyster growing area as they might get impaled by the spiky poles in the oyster beds. The one fathom depth curve is as much as 600 yards offshore in places.

Madrona Point peninsula, a public park, is between Ship and Fishing bays at the head of East Sound. It is absolutely beautiful and offers a wonderful hiking area, a favorite spot for islanders and visitors alike. There are easy trails above the rocky shores among madrona trees and evergreens, with squirrels running around. It's day-use only, with no vehicles or bicycles allowed.

Fishing Bay at Eastsound is quite different from Ship Bay, and there is no aquaculture.

East Sound County Dock and float are on the northeast shore of Fishing Bay at a road end on Madrona Point. At long last there's public moorage in East Sound. A sign on the dock reads: "Attention boaters! Sensitive eel grass habitat exists shoreward of an imaginary line extending in a northwesterly direction from this point to the rock island (Indian Island). Please anchor your craft seaward of this line. The half acre grass-covered island is about 0.25 mile away."

⚓ **Anchoring** is possible in about 3 fathoms, sand and mud bottom. Set the hook well as you never know when a southerly will blow up East Sound.

Ⓖ A marginal **gunkhole.**

Facilities at East Sound County Dock
➤ 50 foot long float, boats moor either side, no fee
➤ Rafting on outside of float, not on shore side
➤ Day use only, easy walk into Eastsound Village

Eastsound Village
🐚 A day-use park is in Eastsound Village near the west end of Fishing Bay and provides beach access for those anchoring out who wish to dinghy ashore. There are picnic tables, grass, and a view south to all of East Sound.

Several businesses in Eastsound line the water's edge. Outlook Inn, which has been providing meals and overnight accommodation since 1883, is across the road from the park. Emmanuel Episcopal Church, a beautiful, small white church above the beach, has been caring for islanders since 1886.

Indian Island is the half-acre rock island less than 200 yards offshore, at high tide. Some Japanese

---

No Condos at Madrona

In 1989, developers planned to transform forested Madrona Point from wilderness to condominiums.

However, Lummi Indians consider it a sacred, historic burial ground, and fought the developers with a great deal of public support.

They lobbied for and received federal funds to buy and preserve the land, just before the earth movers were slated to move in and forever change Madrona Point.

Early Docks at Eastsound

In the early 1900s Templin's Dock extended to Indian Island where steamers loaded and unloaded passengers and freight.

The present county dock at Madrona Point is the site of the old Standard Oil dock. Before it was named the Standard Oil dock it was called Harrison's Dock in the early 1900s.

Eastsound waterfront park, county dock in left background, Indian Island on right

Orcas Historical Museum

Quick Getaway

The Orcas Island Airport is scarcely one mile from the East Sound County Dock, for those mariners who find they need to leave Orcas, or perhaps wish to pick up or drop off guest crew.

What's the World Coming To?

In Summer 1998 two adventurous Orcas boys, 11 and 12 years old, built a three-story dream fort of driftwood, scrapwood and plastic tarps on Crescent Beach—a fort to be envied, better than any that had been built there by other enterprising kids since 1949.

Someone, who had never been a kid, found the fort offensive and complained.

"San Juan County Code 16.40.517 does not allow such structures on the beach," stated a county official. The enforcement officer advised that the structure must be removed.

It's hard to believe that two kids in the San Juans were to lose an annual rite of passage by a cold-hearted code. If you can't build a driftwood fort in the San Juans, where can you build it, for heaven's sake?

The happy ending is that the county relented and the kids kept their fort!

were held on the island for a brief time after the start of World War II. Before that it was known as Little Island. At extreme low tides it's possible to walk out to the island from Eastsound beach.

Eastsound is not a very water-oriented village even though it's on the water. Mariners need to visit West Sound or Deer Harbor for their boating needs. Eastsound has been the heart of Orcas since the 1880s, when it catered to early settlers, and it still caters to islanders' needs. Just about everything is here: restaurants, inns, grocery stores, medical and dental offices, real estate offices, bookstores, banks, library, liquor store, pharmacy, hardware store, boutiques, galleries, historical museum and much more. Moped, bike, kayak and car rentals are available.

The charming museum was built from six original pioneer log cabins which were moved to Eastsound. It's full of impressive displays of early pioneers, their crafting tools and early island photographs. One room shows the old island resorts at Bartell's, Pole Pass and White Beach.

The Ethan Allen collection of hundreds of San Juan Islands artifacts is housed in the museum. As school superintendent, "Old Ethan" rowed more than 10,000 miles in his homemade boat, keeping in touch with his schools from his home on Waldron. He was called the "Sage of the San Juans." *(More in Chap. 5)*

⚓ **UNDERWAY AGAIN,** we head south in East Sound along the west shore.

Judd Bay is a small bay with a booming ground and log skid. Local boats are sometimes anchored here, and there's room for a couple of extras in a pinch.

⚓ **Anchoring** is possible in about 5 fathoms, sandy/mud bottom, but be aware of piles and submerged logs. This is not a recommended anchorage.

Continuing south, a fair number of homes are along this west shore and development is spreading. Prevailing northerlies or southerlies sweep into any of the minor indentations and there are no good anchorages along this shore.

Dolphin Bay, just under four miles south of Eastsound, is the next named bay, with charted offshore rocks and pilings just north of the bay. It isn't considered a good anchorage and apparently gets its name not from playful marine mammals but from several log dolphins near shore, indicating that it was a log dump at one time.

Twin Rocks, about 1.2 miles south of Dolphin Bay, are two similar small islets belonging to U.S. Wildlife Service, and cover a combined 1.14 acres. They have no trees or shrubs, just grasses and bracken.

Twin Rocks daybeacon is a diamond-shaped dayboard with red and white sectors on a spindle marking the rocks which are just over 100 yards offshore.

White Beach south of Twin Rocks has a long shoal covered by 4 to 8 fathoms extending 0.4 mile offshore. It poses no problem for most recreational mariners.

Cable area runs from White Beach across to Olga.

South from White Beach, Orcas has several tiny coves with homes tucked in along forested bluffs. There are few offshore rocks, but we prefer to stay out along the 10 fathom curve as we round Diamond Point, which has no apparent diamonds and nothing marking it as a point.

HARNEY CHANNEL

The channel runs about four miles from East Sound to West Sound between Orcas and Shaw islands. Depths are from 9 to 35 fathoms. We've seen orca whales in here.

Currents in Harney Channel are based on San Juan Channel predictions. They

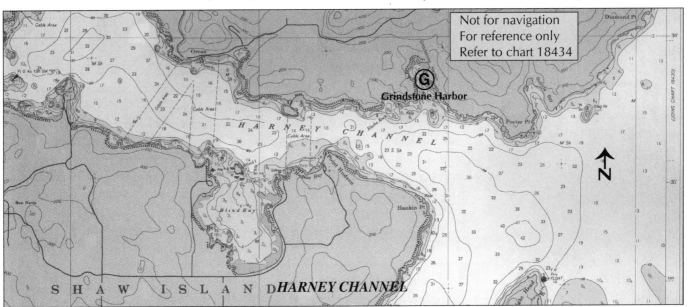

flood westerly at 250° True, and **ebb** southeasterly, 120° True, at generally less than 1.4 knots.

🐚 **Public tidelands** are along much of Orcas south shore. See DNR Quad map.

Shag Rock, NWR, is about 200 yards off Orcas in Harney Channel, near the southwest entrance to East Sound. Depths are from 6 to 9 fathoms between Shag Rock and Orcas. The rock, visible at a 3 foot tide, is sometimes used as the start for Orcas Island Yacht Club races.

Shag Rock [W Bn Daybeacon] diamond-shaped white dayboard is on a spindle with an orange reflective border and black letters stating **"Danger Rocks."**

Guthrie Bay is a beautiful little bay with a rocky shoreline, some pocket beaches, a tiny island at the north end and private buoys. It looks like it would be a great anchorage in about 4 fathoms, except it is very exposed to southerlies. Our Orcas friend Jack Culver said, "It can be rougher than a cob in there."

➡ **Note:** Between Diamond Point and Grindstone Harbor, we need to change charts again—this time from Chart **18430** back to Chart **18434**, the one we started with at the beginning of this chapter.

Harney Channel, Blakely Island on right, Orcas on left

Naming Grindstone Harbor

The harbor was the home of Paul Hubbs (we met him earlier on Blakely Island), who built the first store on Orcas. He had the only grindstone in the area, hence the name of the harbor. It became a popular place to sharpen knives.

Foster Point, with rocks about 100 yards offshore, forms the west shore of Guthrie Bay. We continue about 150 yards offshore to keep along the 10 fathom depth curve. A number of homes line the fairly steep bank.

Grindstone Harbor—the infamous Grindstone Harbor. It will be etched in the historic annals of Orcas Island as the place where the ferry *Elwha* ran aground in 1983. We'll tell you about that in a moment.

Grindstone is a shallow cove less than 3 fathoms deep, about 500 yards long and more than 100 yards wide, with two major rocks. The outer submerged rock is outside the harbor entrance and is surrounded by kelp. The inner rock, visible at a 7 foot tide, is just inside the entrance. The cove is rimmed by private homes and is considered a good anchorage by some, once you get inside. We enter the harbor, hugging the west shore, keeping west of the inner rock.

⚓ **Anchoring** is possible in Grindstone Harbor in under 2 fathoms, mud bottom.

Ⓖ It's a reasonable **gunkhole,** but not for ferry boats.

"Elwha on the Rocks"

It wasn't even a dark and stormy night that Sunday evening, October 2, 1983, when the ferry *Elwha* was returning islanders, including the Friday Harbor High School football team, back to their homes on Orcas and San Juan from the mainland.

The skipper, who is no longer with the ferry system, had as a guest in the wheelhouse an Orcas female passenger who lived in Grindstone Harbor. He decided to let her see her home from the ferry—not the wisest decision he ever made. She protested, and was horrified to discover that he really was going to gunkhole in there with a 382 foot long ferryboat.

Studying the chart, it seems barely possible to get a vessel with a 73 foot beam through the narrow passage between the inner and outer rock. We understand it had been done at least once before. But this skipper tried to do it at more than 15 knots, making a tight turn inside the outer submerged rock to avoid the 15 foot shoal off the point. The *Elwha* draws more than 17 feet.

It hit the rock.

A gentleman who lived just above newly-charted "Elwha Rock," watched the whole scenario from his living room window.

"Here came the *Elwha* full bore! It got about a third or half of the way in the harbor, went right between those rocks and then headed directly across the harbor … I wouldn't dream of cutting inside that kelp bed in my outboard. The ferry went about 300 yards and then hit the reef with a terrible crunching noise. It sounded like thunder … it raised that boat about two feet out of the water." (From the weekly *Friday Harbor Journal* of Oct. 5, 1983)

A long gash ripped the *Elwha's* hull, and she began taking on water. The skipper took the ferry immediately to Orcas Landing. Terrified disembarking passengers told of the horrendous, scary jolt when the *Elwha* went on the rocks. Divers were called and quickly installed temporary patches to the hull. The ferry went under her own power to Seattle's Todd Shipyard where she was hauled out, repaired and later returned to service.

A hit tune by the Island City Jazz Band of San Juan Island appeared in the San Juans soon after the grounding, titled, "*Elwha* on the Rocks."

Harney Channel

It was named for Brigadier General William Selby Harney, stationed in the San Juans during the Pig War era.

A former Tennessee Indian fighter, he also served in the Mexican War and later was sent to command the forces in the Northwest.

He was relieved of his command in the San Juans when he became too aggressive towards the British.

Elwha on the Rocks
Same ferry, different rocks. This photo of the Elwha was taken by Jo when it went aground in Anacortes, sometime after the Grindstone Harbor grounding.

⊕ **UNDERWAY AGAIN,** leaving Grindstone Harbor, we cruise about 1.2 miles west along this lovely shore of Orcas with its rocky beaches, forests and homes, past a small island attached by a small isthmus to Orcas and around a point.

We're back at Orcas Landing where we first started this 125 mile circumnavigation of Orcas Island.

In **Chapter 5**, we begin our exploration of the "Outer Islands" of the San Juans, including Stuart, Johns, Spieden and Waldron islands, and neighboring smaller rocks and islands.

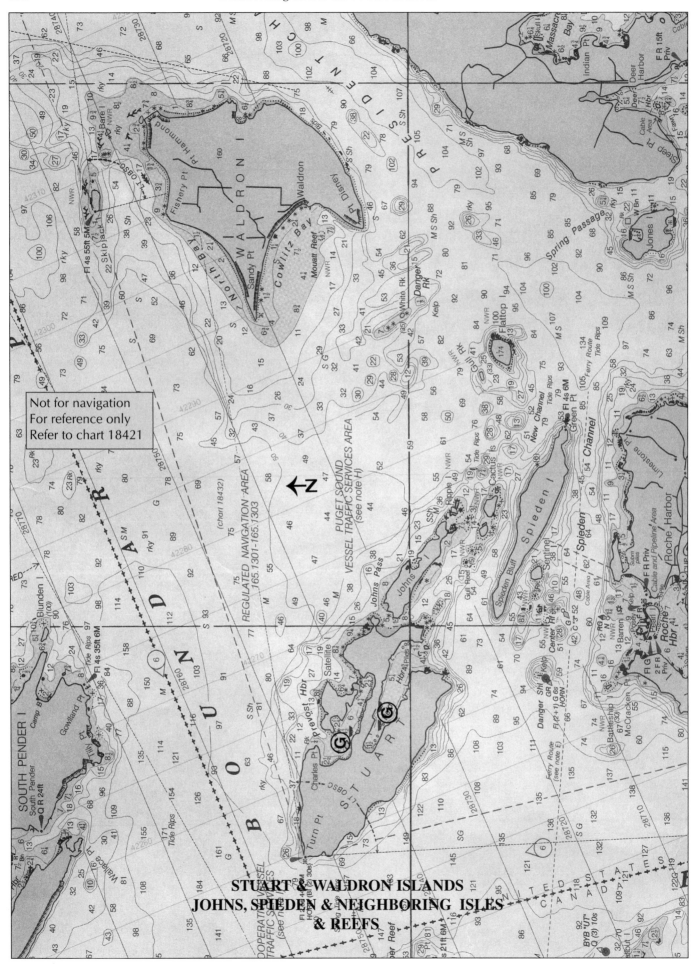

Not for navigation
For reference only
Refer to chart 18421

**STUART & WALDRON ISLANDS
JOHNS, SPIEDEN & NEIGHBORING ISLES
& REEFS**

CHAPTER 5
STUART & WALDRON ISLANDS
Johns, Spieden & Other Islands

Charts & Publications for this Chapter

Chart	Date	Title	Scale	Soundings
U.S. 18421	03/21/98	Strait of Juan de Fuca to Strait of Georgia	1:80,000	Fathoms
U.S. 18423	06/18/94	Strip Chart Bellingham to Everett, inc. San Juan Islands Page C	1:80,000	Fathoms
U.S. 18431	10/05/96	Rosario Strait to Cherry Point	1:25,000	Fathoms
☆ U.S. 18432	08/15/92	Boundary Pass	1:25,000	Fathoms
☆ U.S. 18433	04/20/91	Haro Strait—Mid-Bank to Stuart Island	1:25,000	Fathoms
CAN. 3313	07/28/95	Gulf Islands & Adjacent Waterways Pages 23, 24	1:40,000	Meters
CAN. 3441	12/06/96	Haro Strait, Boundary Pass & Satellite Channel	1:40,000	Meters
CAN. L/C 3462	10/23/98	Juan de Fuca Strait to Strait of Georgia	1:80,000	Meters
🐚		Washington State DNR Quad Map—San Juan County	1:100,000	

Compare your chart dates with those above. There may be discrepancies between chart editions.
☆ = Preferred chart for this chapter 🐚 = DNR & other public tideland information

---

OVERVIEW of STUART, WALDRON, ADJACENT ISLES &CHANNELS

In this chapter we'd like to cruise with you to Stuart, Waldron, surrounding islands and adjacent channels, noting challenging currents in this northwest part of the San Juans.

Beautiful Stuart is at the northwest tip of the San Juans, an arrow-shaped island with the tip at Turn Point Light pointed toward the angled U.S. and B.C. boundary, only three miles from Canadian islands. This junction of Haro Strait and Boundary Pass is the vicinity of sometimes horrendous turbulence caused when powerful tidal currents are coupled with strong winds.

Turn Point, with a lighthouse atop rocky cliffs, is a major turning point of huge ocean ships, commercial and recreational vessels, passing between the Pacific Ocean and Vancouver or Alaska.

This is a sparsely populated area compared to the four ferry-served islands of San Juan, Lopez, Shaw and Orcas we visited

➡ **NOTE: No marine fuel** is available at the islands visited in this chapter. Fuel is available at Roche Harbor on San Juan.

Turn Point Light on Stuart

(See p. 19 for currents and other information on Spieden Channel)

Natural Wildlife Refuges

Small islands and rocks are part of the San Juan Islands National Wildlife Refuge and Wilderness area (NWR). Mariners must stay 200 yards away from these rocks and islands, but wildlife may be observed with binoculars.

All refuge islands except Matia and Turn are closed to the public.

in the first four chapters. Stuart, Waldron, Johns and Spieden have a combined population of less than 200 permanent residents, although the number soars in the summer. Stuart Island has a marine state park with two of the most popular sheltered harbors in the islands, Reid and Prevost.

Neighboring islands and rocks are unoccupied by humans, but well inhabited by seals, sea lions and a wide variety of marine birds.

Near Stuart are Cemetery and Gossip islands at the entrance to Reid Harbor. Satellite Island is at the entrance to Prevost Harbor; southeast of Johns Island are Ripple Island, Gull Reef and the two Cactus Islands.

Southwest of Spieden are Sentinel Island, Sentinel Rock, Danger Shoal and Center Reef. Southwest of Waldron are Flattop Island, Gull, Danger and White rocks; north of Waldron are Bare and Skipjack islands.

We'll cruise in interesting waters on the way to these landfalls, including Spieden and New channels, Haro Strait, Boundary and Johns passes, often encountering strong currents along the way.

⚓ **UNDERWAY TO STUART ISLAND,** we approach the island from various directions. It's about three miles north of Roche Harbor, four miles south of Bedwell, seven miles east of Sidney, B.C., 11 miles northwest of Friday Harbor, 12 miles southwest of Sucia Island, 14 miles northeast of Victoria at Cadboro Bay. Significant currents are encountered from all of these locations and it is prudent to plan ahead by checking *Tidal Current Tables.*

From San Juan Channel we reach Stuart by passing either side of Spieden Island, through Spieden Channel on the south side or New Channel on the north.

Spieden Channel, about three miles long and over 0.6 mile wide, runs between Spieden and San Juan islands. The east end meets San Juan Channel and the west end is at Haro Strait. Spieden Channel is deep, from 12 to 90 fathoms, except for three shallow areas in the west end. There are strong currents, heavy tide rips and eddies. *(See p. 19 for currents and other information on Spieden Channel)*

Sailing along Spieden Island's south shore

Spieden Island (pronounced Spy-den), lying southeast and northwest, is about three miles long and less than 0.5 mile across at the widest spot. A nearly 400 foot high ridge runs lengthwise along the top of the island. The most distinguishing features of this 480 acre island are nearly barren rock and grass bluffs on the south side and densely forested, rocky bluffs on the north side. There are no natural harbors. A small breakwater was built to provide moorage for small private boats along the southeast corner near Green Point at the barren southeast tip.

Alternate Route

Ferries occasionally pass between Sentinel and Spieden and their way between the San Juans and Sidney, B.C.

Green Point Light [Fl 4s 20ft 5M] flashing 4 second light 20 feet high visible 5 miles, is on a diamond-shaped dayboard with black and white diamond sectors on a skeleton tower. It is the only navigation aid on Spieden.

Sentinel Island is the tiny neighbor south of Spieden near the west end. Cliff-sided, no beaches, with trees on the north shore and rocks on the south, it's 15 acres of solitude and eagles. *(More on Spieden & Sentinel islands, pages 138-140)*

Shoal with a depth of 3 feet is between Sentinel Island and Sentinel Rock.

Sentinel Rock, **NWR,** often covered with seals and sea lions, is 400 yards west of Sentinel Island.

Center Reef, NWR, is in Spieden Channel, 0.7 mile south of Spieden. It bares at low tides and once in a while a boat unexpectedly grounds on it.

Center Reef [G C "3"] green can buoy, marks the reef which actually extends about 0.2 mile northeast of the buoy.

Danger Shoal Buoy [Fl (2+1) G 6s Horn] group flashing green 6 second light plus a horn on a red and green banded buoy is about one mile west of Center Reef. The buoy is on the edge of a 1 fathom shoal which extends north 0.15 mile.

It's possible to pass either side of these two buoys, but there may be strong currents setting east or west. Kelp is often in the area, but don't rely on it.

We continue on past the west end of Spieden then head to the northwest and in one mile we're at the entrance to Reid Harbor.

From New Channel, which is between the forested north side of Spieden Island and the south shores of Cactus Islands and Gull Reef, we head for the southeast tip of Stuart and the entrance to Reid Harbor. The channel is about two miles long, 400 to 800 yards wide, with depths of 13 to 69 fathoms.

Currents here are often radically different in speed and direction from currents in Spieden Channel and adjacent waters. *(See Canadian Current Atlas)*

From Haro Strait either harbor on Stuart Island is a handy overnight stop for mariners crossing to Victoria or Sidney, or those going north from the Strait of Juan de Fuca. Haro is 16 miles long between Boundary Pass and the Strait of Juan de Fuca, separating San Juan and Vancouver islands. It is six miles wide at the south end and two miles wide at Turn Point at the north end. *(See p. 22)*

From Boundary Pass, Prevost Harbor is the closer of Stuart's two harbors. The pass is 11 miles long and 2.5 to 3.5 mile wide. It separates the U.S. and Canada, from Turn Point to the Strait of Georgia east of Patos Island. Prevost is a favorite stop for U.S. mariners before crossing into B.C to clear customs at Bedwell Harbour on South Pender Island, a short four miles away.

Currents in Boundary Pass as predicted at Turn Point Station #2246 may reach or exceed 1.5 knots on a flood at 080°T. and 2.6 knots on an ebb at 260°T. *(136,142)*

At 1.5 miles northwest of Skipjack Island the predicted flood currents may reach or exceed 1.56 knots at 035° True and 2.25 knots on an ebb at 290° True.

STUART ISLAND

We've now reached the island with all its delights, including the two lovely harbors. It is a little over three miles long southeast to northwest and 1.4 miles wide. Seven hills, from 300 to 640 feet high make the island easy to identify from the water. An 1,850 yard long isthmus, 200 yards wide, separates Prevost and Reid harbors and the high northwest uplands from the lower northeast end. Stuart is the eighth largest in the San Juans with 1,786 acres.

The approximately 40 island residents are retirees, young families searching for a gentler place to raise their youngsters, dreamers who yearn for a lifestyle that allows them to return to the land, high-tech workers who can telecommute to their city jobs, and families whose members have lived on the island for generations. There are none of the "amenities" associated with city living: no electricity, telephones, cable TV, running water or other so-called luxuries. Islanders have adapted with solar panels, generators and batteries if they want electricity, propane and kerosene if they don't. However, with cell

> ➡ **NOTE:** Customs regulations state that U.S. mariners on the way to B.C. may not anchor at any Canadian islands before clearing B.C. Customs at Bedwell, Sidney or Victoria.
>
> When returning from Canada, U.S. boaters must clear customs (Roche or Friday Harbors or by radio or telephone) before landing or anchoring at any U.S. islands.

Naming Stuart Island

The island was named in 1841 by Lt. Charles Wilkes for Fredrick D. Stuart, captain's clerk.

Local Island?

Folks in the San Juans often consider Stuart as "their" island, but sometimes avoid it until after Labor Day when local cruisers can once again find space to anchor or catch a mooring buoy.

Reefnet boats off Reid Harbor

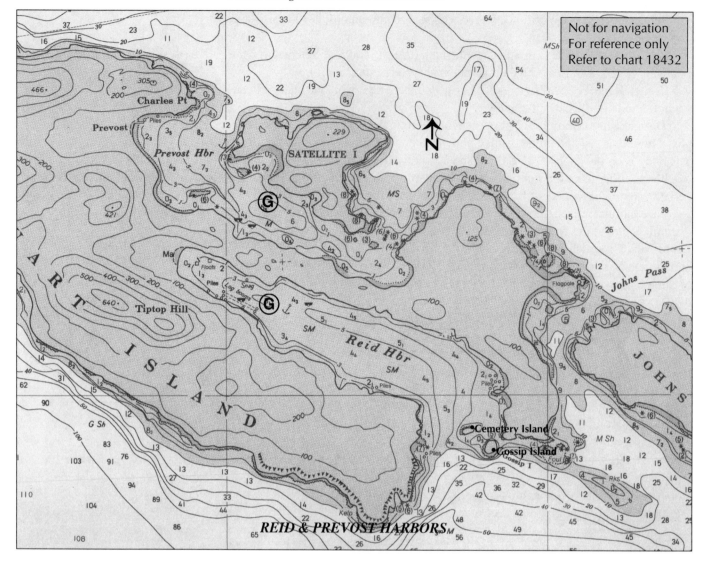

Not for navigation
For reference only
Refer to chart 18432

REID & PREVOST HARBORS

phones, TV dishes and other modern high-tech devices they are easily in communication with the world beyond Stuart.

Most jobs on the island center around the one-room schoolhouse, but fishing, farming, logging and construction also provide work for islanders, as it has for generations.

There is no store on Stuart and no ferry service. There is a private airport at the east end of the island used by islanders and also for mail delivery. A number of island residents have boats so they can reach San Juan or other islands when they want to go off island.

Stuart Island Marine State Park encompasses nearly 148 acres and over 4,000 feet of shoreline for fascinating gunkholing, beachcombing and reasonably warm swimming. It's one of our favorites.

The two harbors in the park are excellent anchorages. Both have docks with floats and mooring buoys, are equally beautiful but quite different. Both harbors run southeast-northwest, with Reid opening to the south and Prevost opening to the north. Reid is long, slender and almost totally enclosed by land. Prevost, the smaller of the two is enclosed by Satellite Island forming the north shore. From either harbor it's a short walk across the isthmus that separates them. Information boards, campgrounds, picnic areas, toilets and water are accessible at both. State park lands can be explored from Reid and Prevost by hiking the many park trails, including the ridge trail across the top of the island offering spectacular views through the trees down into Reid from high cliffs. *(More about hiking, pages 131-134)*

Shellfishing in Reid Harbor

🐚 *It's possible to gather shellfish again, after previous closures due to pollution. Let's hope there are still clams left on the beach.*

The pumpout station in Reid has helped clean the waters, otherwise we wouldn't recommend either swimming or clam digging.

Do check the readerboard for up-to-date info that would indicate a shellfish closure.

Stuart Island Marine State Park Facilities

➤ 148 acres with 4,000 feet of shoreline
➤ 25 mooring buoys: 18 in Reid Harbor, 7 in Prevost, fees $5 night
➤ Docks with floats in Reid & Prevost harbors, two extra floats in Reid
➤ Moorage fees at floats: boats under 26' $8 night; boats over 26' $11 night;
  3 night limit
➤ Pumpout & porta-potty dump on a separate float in Reid Harbor
➤ Water on isthmus between harbors, in campgrounds at head of Reid
➤ 19 campsites, picnic sites, toilets
➤ Hiking trails throughout park
➤ Four Washington Water Trail campsites, fees $7 person/night
➤ Activities: hike, camp, picnic, shellfish, beachcomb, swim, gunkhole

Reefnet Fishing at Reid Harbor

Mariners may find that during fishing season reefnet fish boats are anchored off the east end of Stuart at the entrance to Reid as they have been for generations. The distinctive boats with their ladders and high platforms work in pairs. A net is spread deep in the water between the boats. A spotter on the platform watches for salmon swimming over the reef below. As the salmon approach the reef, the two boats are pulled together by the crew, and the salmon are caught in the net and gathered into a hold on one of the boats. *(Diagram p. 87)*

Night to Remember …

Years ago we climbed to the bluff above Reid Harbor and spent the night under the full moon and stars in mid-October. A treat we've never forgotten.

Reid Harbor

Reid is snugged in behind 640 foot Tiptop Hill to the south and behind Stuart's rugged, hilly terrain to the northwest. Reid is about 1.3 miles long and 300 yards wide at the northwest end to 650 yards wide near the southeast end where it bends and opens to the south.

Two small islands, Gossip and Cemetery, are at the east side of the entrance to Reid Harbor. Both islands are charted but Cemetery is unnamed. *(p. 129)*

Enter Reid Harbor from the south through a channel between Stuart and Cemetery islands. The channel is about 200 yards wide between the 3 fathom depth curves. The depth curves widen to about 500 yards as we turn northwest past a small, local uncharted buoy. The width of the curves gradually narrows to 200 yards and join about 300 yards from the head of the harbor.

Depths are between 2 and 5 fathoms in most of the harbor with its sand and mud bottom. It offers good protection from all but the strongest southeasterlies.

Moorages in Reid Harbor

⚓ **Anchoring** is possible anywhere in the harbor—it could hardly be better.
Ⓖ This is a wonderful **gunkhole,** another favorite, but it gets crowded, especially in summer.

The southeast bay has a mix of rocky shores, homes, piers, a small marine railway, reefnet boats and gillnetters. It's the working part of the island. Along the northeast shore is a break in the trees, and a road from the beach leads past where Littlewolf's house once stood. *(pages 134-135)* A private pier west of the road has triangular red daybeacons, not to be mistaken for the state park dock which is about

Heron awaiting dinner at Reid

one mile farther into the harbor. More homes line this lightly forested shore with southern exposure. Across the bay on the south shore of the harbor are several homes, some with piers, tucked into tiny forested bights.

A large Coast Guard buoy in the harbor is used by visiting CG vessels.

The first of the 18 state mooring buoys is near the park's east boundary. The pumpout float is just east of the park dock and moorage float. Two other tie-up floats are between the dock and the head of the harbor, providing a large amount of moorage space, especially nice for small rendezvous.

Trails from the park dock lead to restrooms and water, across the narrow isthmus to Prevost Harbor, the ridge trail and more.

Reid Harbor terminates in a gently sloping beach at the northwest end where there's a county road end and a launch ramp used by islanders. This sandy, pebbled beach is great for beachcombing, sunning or shellfishing, and the water is reasonably warm for swimming, one of the few places in the San Juans with tolerable water temperature. It's a good place for bird and people watching. Several campsites with water and toilets are in this low area, including four Washington Water Trail sites on the north side. A marsh is inland.

Gunkhole in the dinghy a bit, run out to Gossip or Cemetery islands, or explore the shady south shore covered with evergreens, and the north shore's cliffs. The sun crosses the cliffs, the rocks absorb heat, and it's remarkably warm along this shore. Herons gracefully stalk their prey along here searching for snacks.

Sometimes on a quiet evening in Reid Harbor, we remember old Stuart Island friends, Littlewolf and Gladys, who spent many years on her boat, the *All Right*, anchored in Reid Harbor. The two added so much character to the island.

Gladys & the *All Right*

Gladys Prince was a grand "old lady of the sea" with a lifetime of boating experience. She lived alone aboard her old 36 foot cruiser *All Right* for many years in the San Juans, spending long periods of time at Stuart Island. She was affectionately cared for by boaters and islanders.

Gladys spent her last years in West Sound Marina on Orcas where the Wareham family kept a watchful eye on her. *(Ch. 4)*

When she was 76, Gladys suffered from an illness that blocked her normal navigating sense while she was cruising. She was caught in a storm in Georgia Strait, and after a long, disoriented voyage, ran the boat aground on rocks off Lasqueti Island. She ended up in a Nanaimo hospital for days.

Her son later towed Gladys and her boat to West Sound where the Warehams repaired the *All Right* and made sure she was cared for with home-cooked food and warm clothing.

Gladys anchored near the marina, but never really recovered from the disorientation. Several times she took off alone on cruises, grounding her boat twice. She ran onto the rocks in Blind Bay at Shaw on Memorial Day 1982, saying, "I should have known where the rocks were." Betsy and Ian Wareham helped free the boat and towed it back to the marina.

Gladys and the All Right

In early July 1982, thinking she was heading northwest back to Reid Harbor, she ended up south, across the Strait of Juan de Fuca on the rocks at Protection Island. A friend helped her take her boat back to West Sound.

A short time later, on July 18, Gladys apparently slipped into the water while boarding her dinghy from the *All Right*. Peg Wareham saw the dinghy bouncing on the beach that Sunday afternoon—not tied up as usual. Gladys was found floating in the water near her boat.

Jo spent many hours visiting with the remarkable Gladys on the *All Right* at Stuart Island. Gladys loved to tell stories of her early days and fascinating cruising experiences. She said she was born on the beach near Browns Point in Tacoma, and that once a boat she owned had been sunk by a tugboat while she and her son were fishing off Point Defiance.

Gladys, who never wanted to trouble anyone, repeated to Jo not too long before she died something she had been saying for years: "Well, my dear, someday I'll just wrap this old anchor chain around my neck and slip over the side."

It almost happened that way. We like to think that Gladys, who never wanted to trouble anyone, is forever *"all right."*

Public Tidelands

❀ *Unless otherwise noted, public tidelands are state-owned; some may be leased and posted for aquaculture or other private use. When going ashore we recommend taking the Washington State Public Lands Quadrangle Map of San Juan County.*

Some of Stuart Island shores are designated as public ownership on the 1984 DNR map. However, some environmentally sensitive beaches or privately leased beaches are not open for public use. Check the DNR Quad Map and local postings before using these beaches, to avoid trespassing.

Cemetery & Gossip Islands

These two tiny delightful islands at the entrance to Reid Harbor are day-use only state park lands. They are to be used only for walking, observing, enjoying and no picnicking. Walkers are urged to be careful because there are cactus and unique wild flowers that are on the sensitive list, according to Bill Hoppe, assistant park manager for Stuart Island Marine State Park.

Cemetery is the smaller, west islet, and we found no signs of burials. It is tiny, with clumps of small bushes on its rocky shores and yellowish vegetation on the south side. In 1874, government surveyors reported Cemetery Island had been used by Indians as a burial site. Native Americans did not bury their dead, but usually placed them in canoes in trees.

Gossip Island, 100 yards southeast of Cemetery is a treasure, all 1.75 acres of it. We beached the skiff on a white shell beach on the north shore, the best landing place. From there we scrambled across the rocks and walked the short trail to the south shore. We could see a ferry in Spieden Channel, a container ship in Haro Strait and reefnetters off Stuart. A sign cautioned "No Fires." We walked gently past tiny plants, pale green mosses, the gnarled, silvered remains of an old tree and admired cactus-like plants. We wandered back down the fissured rocks to our skiff, passing a tiny rock pool filled to the brim with thick green water, too high above the beach to be a tide pool.

Small boats often run the narrow, shallow pass between Gossip and Stuart.

From Gossip we watched boats at the south end of Johns Pass between Stuart and Johns islands, where huge kelp beds cover rocks and shoals.

Gossip Island

Gossip—a "Puget Prairie"

In September 1997, an island newspaper reported that local biologist Terry Domico discovered examples of the disappearing Puget Prairie on Gossip Island, containing a rare plant called Lance-Leafed Stone. This occurred just as Gossip was about to become a designated Washington Water Trail campsite for kayakers.   *(Continued on next page)*

***St. Speeder, with seal
congregation***

Puget Prairies are made up of native grasses and wildflowers, remnants of a prairie climate in the region 2,000 years ago.

As a result of Domico's discovery, the island has been reclassified as natural and will remain day-use only. The state will close it down if visitors threaten the native eco-system.

Saint Speeder

The remains of old *St. Speeder,* a 70 foot long, 10 foot wide former passenger ferry, are barely visible above the water's surface in Reid Harbor, off a pier on the south shore. In WW II she was on the Bainbridge Island-Seattle run. Earlier, she ran between San Juans ports, reportedly the first gas engine boat in the islands. In the 1950s, she moved to Reid Harbor, a derelict awaiting restoration.

The Rev. Ted Leche, former Episcopal vicar in Friday Harbor, used *Speeder* as a chapel for Stuart Island services in the early 1980s. After Sunday morning services in town, Father Ted cruised to Stuart in his own boat, the *Archangel.* Stuart families rowed out to *Speeder* and built a fire in its rusty old stove awaiting his arrival.

Father Ted celebrated communion on an old wooden crate. His half-dozen parishioners sat on stools during the service. He recalled with a smile that the boat was usually damp and musty smelling, but that didn't deter the tiny congregation, which affectionately dubbed the vessel, *Saint Speeder.*

Several years later services moved to the island home of one of Stuart's faithful. *Speeder* settled deeper in the water.

PREVOST HARBOR & SATELLITE ISLAND

Now that we've been to Reid Harbor it's time to visit Prevost Harbor off Boundary Pass on the north side of Stuart Island. The harbor is about 1.2 miles long and 0.3 mile wide.

The state park is along 1,000 feet of the south shore, on both sides of the state park dock and float.

Prevost nestles inside **Satellite Island** which forms the north shore. The island is just over 0.6 mile long and less than 0.5 mile wide. The 106 acre, mostly forested island has a 227 foot hill near its north shore. A small 2 fathom, 2 foot cove on the southwest shore faces the state park dock.

Depths in Prevost are more erratic than in Reid Harbor. As charted, they range from 8 fathoms in the entrance to the shallow southeast end with its rocks and reefs, where depths are 2 fathoms, 4 feet.

Shoals and rocks of Prevost are well-defined but unnamed on chart 18432. We identify them here by location before entering the harbor.

Charles Point on Stuart at the west entrance to the harbor has a 2 foot shoal extending 200 yards northeast.

Satellite Cove Shoal and Rocks has a rock that bares at 3 feet about 75 yards off the southwest tip of Satellite Island. The shoal then curls southeast about 300 yards, back towards Satellite's cove to another rock baring at 4 feet.

Southwest Harbor Shoal baring at 6 feet is about 100 yards off the Stuart shore 300 yards southwest of Satellite Cove shoal. The shoal is in front of a white house. A charted rock is awash about 100 yards southeast of the shoal, or about 300 yards northwest of the state park dock.

Satellite Southeast Shoal is within the 1 fathom depth curve with reefs and rocks baring up to 6 feet as it extends 200 yards south and east of the island.

Prevost Harbor

This harbor on Stuart Island was named for Capt. James Charles Prevost, the British Skipper of H.M.S. Satellite.

Charles Point on Stuart, and little Satellite island in Prevost Harbor (previously called James) all honored this one man.

Enter Prevost Harbor from the north through the channel between Satellite Island and Charles Point on Stuart. High and rocky, the point is on the northwest shore of the entrance from Boundary Pass. A 2 foot charted shoal extends 200 yards northeast of the point, extremely close to the 3 and 5 fathom depth curves along this shore. We find ourselves staying outside the 5 fathom curve. We usually stay slightly closer to the rocky bluffs of Satellite as we enter until reaching its southwest rocky tip.

On entering we look almost due south to a barn, pasture and bluffs, with Tiptop Hill visible beyond, the highest point on the island.

Prevost Harbor moorage, Satellite Island & Cove in background

Inside Charles Point on the west shore is a county dock where islanders' vessels are sometimes moored. Although the dock is public and at a county road end, there is no float for dinghies or other small boats, so cruising boats must tie at the marine park floats or buoys. There are a few houses and fields in the area beyond the dock. A log dump along the north shore awaits a new harvest.

The state park dock and floats are on the Stuart shore about 300 yards east of the Southwest Harbor Shoal. Seven mooring buoys are spread through the harbor.

🌿 **Tidelands** in Prevost Harbor and around Satellite Island are public, so it is possible to walk the beach, gently, to keep from crunching red rock or Dungeness crabs that enjoy hunkering down in eelgrass. Satellite is owned by the YMCA, which doesn't encourage boaters to go ashore. *(See Public Tidelands in Appendix)*

To us, the island's charted shape looks like a duck in a puddle.

⚓ **Anchoring** in Prevost is possible just about anywhere within 3 to 6 fathoms, mostly mud bottom. The south-facing cove at Satellite is an excellent anchorage for a couple of boats. Enter the cove from the southeast side, avoiding the shoal.

Ⓖ Prevost Harbor is a **great gunkhole.**

We encourage gunkholing about the harbor, rowing or with a small outboard, to get a closer view of the shoreline with its rocky beaches and wooded hills behind. The only uplands that are public are those in the park.

Wedding Atop Tiptop

Jo once attended a wedding on Tiptop. A glorious sunset event, with the bride arriving barefoot and breathless after hiking to the hilltop in a lovely gown. Vows were exchanged, with views so spectacular they almost, but not quite, overshadowed the charming ceremony.

"False" East Entrance

Although it appears Prevost Harbor can be entered on either side of Satellite Island, the only entrance for boats larger than skiffs and kayaks is at the west end of Satellite, except those whose skippers have local knowledge. The harbor's east end has many rocks, shoals and kelp, but is interesting to gunkhole by small boat.

We know a couple who ran their 36 foot sailboat aground on the rocks here when they saw the east "entrance" and ran in at six knots, forgetting to check their chart first. He suffered a concussion and she broke her arm in the ensuing melee.

Stuart—a Walking Island

Stuart is a special island. It combines 148 acres of state park land and private land, county roads and private roads. All orchards and gardens are private. There is

➥ **NOTE:** Hikers must stay within signed park boundaries or on county roads.

Students Sell Postcards

A selection of original art postcards bu island students is for sale at the old white school to help raise money to fund the "Littlewolf Memorial Account."

The funds are for student activities and scholarships and honor the legendary islander, Littlewolf.

Check at the old schoolhouse when you hike to the school.

Stuart Island School

The kids set personal goals at Stuart School. They can study oceanography with the lab just 0.7 miles away; or study local history with pioneers on the island with tales to tell, or study birds in the surrounding wilds. One boy plans a "Small School Olympics."

They take field trips as a whole school, including parents, and sometimes join with the students of Waldron and Shaw island schools.

nothing commercial on the island, no place to buy even an ice cream cone—or anything else. Visitors may walk all the trails within the park and on county roads, including the three mile road out to Turn Point Lighthouse, a hike well worth taking, visiting Stuart Island School and the island cemetery along the way. Carry your own snacks and pack out any garbage.

Tiptop Hill, private property which was once open to the public, is now off-limits and is signed as private.

To reach the county road leading to the schoolhouse and lighthouse from the head of Reid Harbor, we take the road which starts at the ramp at the southwest corner of the harbor. There's an array of skiffs on the beach, and a "Keep Out" sign notes everything south of the road is private, with state park land north of the road.

Hike to the School

From the beach the road angles west, uphill beneath arching deciduous and evergreen trees, past fairly dense underbrush and old stumps leftover from logging, with delicate sword ferns lining the roadsides. A trail intersects the road with a charming sign made by Stuart school kids which notes:

"School 0.7 miles," and "Lighthouse 2.4 miles." Several more of these signs are along the way, decorated with fish or whales. The smell of wood smoke means we're nearing the school, heated by wood stoves. It seems farther than 0.7 mile, maybe it's because it's uphill all the way. A tiny, old log schoolhouse, long gone, once stood in the nearby brush. Youngsters rowed to this school from Spieden and Johns islands in early times.

Stuart Island School, grades K-8, is the heart of the island community. We find unexpected treasures at the school, including the octagonal shake one-room schoolhouse with the red metal roof. The building won architectural awards for its design when built in 1981. Despite the fact the island has no electricity or phone service, the school has computers, TVs and a VCR. The fan-shaped building has hardwood floors, a stage, library and many windows looking across playfields and forests. An outhouse is across the field.

Any or all of the eight or nine students may be sprinting about the school grounds in an active soccer game or perhaps some are practicing flutes or violins outdoors if the weather is good, serenading passersby. The small white building nearby, built in 1902, was the second schoolhouse, used between the time of the old log building and the present school.

Kids walk to school or arrive by boat. One family at the far east end of the island commutes to the county dock in Prevost with mom running the family boat. From there, they drive along Stuart's roads in the old family Citroen.

Stuart students study music

Hike to Stuart Island Cemetery

It's a short walk along the county road beyond the school to the island cemetery. A right turn at "the tree," then left down a little-used, unmarked road and we're there.

The cemetery is a virtual "Who was Who" of early islanders. Step inside between cement guard lions atop brick columns. This is the resting place of Littlewolf, whose headstone is decorated with his trademark copper bracelet. Gary Vesoja, the islander who designed the headstone, is buried nearby. He died several years ago when struck by a falling tree.

A readerboard reveals land for the small cemetery was donated by Chris Cook who paid one dollar for it. The area was chosen because of its central location, beauty, solitude, and indeed it is a lovely spot. His mother, Maria, was the first person buried here in 1904. The second was a Civil War soldier named Douglass.

In a quirk of fate when the cemetery deed was recorded in 1918, no one knew the legal description was wrong. It described a spot 200 feet deep in Haro Strait.

In 1980, islanders discovered they didn't own the cemetery when the owners wanted it closed, so residents formed a tax district. In 1989, the Cemetery District purchased the 480 square foot site, "donated" for $500 by Hope Barnes, a young woman who died shortly after in a climbing accident in the Cascades.

Stuart Island Cemetery

Hike to Turn Point Lighthouse

Looking east to Prevost Harbor entrance, Satellite Island in background

Back on the county road, we continue in a northerly direction, passing a house or two, some cows, and in about 0.5 mile we intersect the road to Prevost Harbor. The county dock is down a short road off to the east. But the school kids' sign points us west to reach the lighthouse, so west we go.

It's a 1.5 mile hike that takes us uphill and downhill, over a rocky, dusty road, seldom used by cars. The private, grassy airstrip, Stuart West, is along the south side of the road. After that it's rocks, trees, peace and quiet, except for occasional other friendly hikers. We see an old rusted car body far down a ravine, overgrown with trees and brush. Continuing on, sun glints off the distant sea which we glimpse occasionally through the trees. Then the road takes us down a long, rocky stretch.

"Turn Point Light Station, property of the U. S. Department of the Interior," the sign announces. We're here. The readerboard explains land for this lighthouse was reserved in 1875, and that the light, lightkeeper's quarters and barn were completed in 1893. The light was equipped with a lens lantern and a steam-operated Daboll trumpet. Early lighthouse keepers had to deal with itinerant smugglers and shipwrecked vessels.

The Light House Service ran Turn Point Light from 1893 to 1939 when the Coast Guard took over, and they ran it until 1974 when it was automated. The fog signal and building reverted to BLM (Bureau of Land Management), and this national and cultural resource was saved.

View from Turn Point Lighthouse grounds

The 300° view out across Haro Strait and Boundary Pass is spectacular. Forested Canadian islands are south, west and north; huge container ships and other vessels pass in an almost continuous parade about 0.5 mile off the point. Uncounted whales swim by, and small boats fight major currents near the point. Kelp swirls around the base of the steep cliffs in gigantic back eddies, 44 feet below the light.

Sloping lawns, large rocks and giant trees surround the now vacant, two-story, red-roofed white house which was once home to lighthouse keepers who lived on this

Turn Point Light

Schoolteacher Sees the Light

The Stuart teacher lived in the charming caretaker's house at Turn Point Light in 1983, walking the three mile road daily on his "commute" to work.

View is Gone …

The wonderful old outhouse perched on the north side of Turn Point Light property commanded an incredible bird's-eye view of Boundary Pass and the Gulf Islands for the user.

It's gone now, replaced by a Clivus composting toilet near the readerboard—no more view.

Tragedy at Sea …

In 1961 the Stuart teacher and his children, who were also students, capsized in their boat while crossing stormy Spieden Channel. All but the baby drowned.

The school closed down and didn't reopen until 1977 when there were enough kids on the island to have a local teacher again instead of sending students to San Juan Island.

remote headland for 81 years. A concrete walkway leads to the fog signal building from the house. The grounds are a favorite picnic and resting spot for those who are here to enjoy the view.

Bits of Stuart Island History & Trivia

Like all the others in this area of scattered islands, Stuart is a mountain top protruding up from the sea, left after the last glacier slid through. Tiptop Hill, along the southwest side of the island, is the highest peak at 640 feet. Other hills reach 523 feet and 466 feet farther north and west. All these hills are private and are not accessible to the public.

An Indian village was on Stuart when it was surveyed in 1874, and the island was declared "worthless except for stock range." However, high quality sandstone was found on dramatic cliffs on the west side and was quarried in the early 1900s. Some of Seattle's streets were paved with it.

Bernard Mordhorst from Germany was the first person to apply for a claim on Stuart in 1876. Part of the park in Reid Harbor is on the old Mordhorst place.

Early settlers were fishermen, farmers and loggers, including generations of families with names familiar throughout the San Juans, especially the Ericksons, Chevaliers, Lofgrens, Littlewolf and Gladys. The island was logged at the turn of the century to provide firewood for Roche Harbor Lime Kilns, and again in the 1950s. Visitors to Stuart over the years included smugglers and rum runners.

About 35 to 45 people call Stuart Island home year round, but numbers vary as some people may live here three or four days a week, commuting by plane or boat to wherever their job is for the rest of the week. In the summer, the population may swell to 200 or more. In winter time, it's a snug island.

Stuart Island residents ask that the 15,000 visitors who arrive by boat each year—because they also enjoy the island's beauty and remoteness—help maintain the peaceful life islanders value by respecting posted private property, staying on public lands and leashing their dogs, as many animals share the island.

Legendary Littlewolf

There was once a cabin, silvered with age, at the east end of Reid Harbor in a small bight on the north shore. Alongside the cabin a flagpole with a high flying pennant displayed a design of a wolf's head. This was the home, now gone, of legendary Littlewolf, who lived here until his death in May 1984.

Littlewolf's life story is a melding of fact and fantasy, a wondrously naive mix of Romulus and Remus, Hansel and Gretel. He told his story with such warmth and sincerity that visitors willingly put aside their disbelief. He was short, slight, wiry and his birth date was vaguely "about 1908."

He said he'd been a fisherman, a rumrunner and dabbled a bit in smuggling. He claimed he learned rum-running in Chicago during the time he worked for Al Capone at the height of Prohibition. Not all the booze he handled got delivered he admitted, with a twinkle in his eye.

When he was a small boy, he explained, he and his sister were rescued from the wilds by wolves who cared for them after they had been kidnapped and abandoned in the wilderness by an evil baby-sitter. He told of leaving a trail of bread crumbs on the path as he and his sister were kidnapped. It is unlikely that Littlewolf had read Grimm's Fairy Tales, not being the bookish sort, but who are we to question his stories.

After an undetermined time as human pups, the children were found by hunters who returned them to civilization. They lived in an orphanage until the sister was adopted and Littlewolf ran away at the tender age of 18, off into a life of adventure. Sometimes, with a quick grin, he told of a brief period in which the two were exhibited in circus cages as "wolf children."

After he moved to Stuart Island, his forays into Friday Harbor were legendary, even back in the days when it was a hard-drinkers' town. Many a time the sheriff would escort Glen Chester (his other name) to the dock, put him in his boat and tell him not to come back.

A few weeks later, the beloved little hell-raiser would be back in town, swapping outrageous stories with his fishermen friends. During the evening's fracas the sheriff would be called and Littlewolf would once again be ushered out of town. After all, you don't arrest a legend.

Lighthouse Keepers

They often had large families, and Ed Durgin was no exception with his eight children.

His daughter, Helene Glidden later wrote a best-selling book about the family's hardships and adventures, **The Light on the Island.** *It's a story of life on Patos Island, where the family moved to be lighthouse keepers after leaving Stuart. It's a good read.*

Littlewolf

He was most famous, at least in the islands, for his "Littlewolf Bracelet," a circlet of heavy copper wire to help ward off arthritis. He never kept count of his production, but he figured he made "about three million."

His most illustrious client, he said, was former first lady Betty Ford.

Does the bracelet work its medical charm? Hundreds of San Juan Islanders still wear them and swear by them. There may be something magic about the fact that the material, #6 gauge solid copper wire, had been purloined from OPALCO, the islands' power company. The bracelets were free to all. Nobody who arrived at Littlewolf's cabin was ever turned away or charged for a bracelet. A goodwill offering was always accepted, however, especially if it was a staple he highly favored—a fifth of McNaughton's.

Deepest Water

A 1927 report states the deepest water in this area is 1,356 feet or 220 fathoms, at one mile north of Turn Point.

Fish Story

Carl was fishing from Condor in the 1940s near the vertical cliff at Turn Point in 112 fathoms (672 feet) during slack water, when he hauled up a fish.

Its eyes popped out, caused by lack of pressure, as it rose to the surface and was brought aboard.

Carl's eyes nearly popped out, too, when he saw the fish.

Boundary Marker

The boundary between the U.S. and Canada was triangulated from a monument erected at Turn Point in 1909, after the Treaty of 1908.

Settling Johns

Settlers have been on Johns Island since 1874, when John Todd kept sheep here.

Paul Hubbs, whom we met earlier on both Blakely and Orcas islands, completed a homestead patent and later had a house on the northwest end of Johns.

⚓ **Underway again,** we circumnavigate Stuart Island clockwise, starting at Reid Harbor and continue west along Stuart's southwest shore toward Turn Point. A tepee perches near the southeast end of the island, and several homes appear, some with solar panels to benefit from the southern exposure. Rocky shores from the southeast gradually rise to brownish bluffs. The island here is similar to Spieden's south shore.

There are no charted hazards along this flank of Stuart, although we stay outside the 10 fathom curve. During fishing season purse seiners may set nets along here. Just south of Turn Point is a tiny bight which a small boat might enter. Friends say there's good fishing just off the bight.

Turn Point's sheer rocky cliffs rise ahead a little more than three miles after leaving Reid Harbor. Madrona trees cling to rocks high above turbulent waters while undulating kelp extends out several hundred feet. Cliffs are chalky white in some places, other places they're yellowish brown.

Turn Point Light [Fl 2.5 sec 44ft 8M, Horn (Gp Bl (2) 30sec] flashing 2.5 second light 44 feet high visible 8 miles with a horn which operates continuously with two blasts every 30 seconds, is on a white concrete tower. The light is obscured from 260°30' to 357°. The automated lighthouse keeps its vigil on a steep grassy point in front of the boarded-up former lighthouse keeper's residence.

Predicted currents at Turn Point may reach 1.5 knot floods and 2.6 knot ebbs at NOAA's Turn Point-Boundary Pass current station. But currents at Turn Point may actually reach or exceed 6 knots, based on our own and other's observations. There may be overfalls if the wind is blowing really hard. Strong backeddies off Turn Point can be very useful if bucking the mainstream flow, otherwise we avoid them like the plague. But the whole area gets nasty when wind is against the current.

We "turn the corner" and head east into Boundary Pass along Stuart's north shore where the U.S. and Canadian boundary is only 0.75 mile away, and the Pender Islands are just 2.5 miles north. Sheer cliffs topped with trees climb 100 to 300 feet above Stuart's unapproachable north shore.

About halfway between Turn and Charles points the 10 fathom depth curve bulges briefly seaward about 160 yards. Inshore, within the 5 fathom curve, a rock bares at 2 feet and a ledge awash is charted extending about 50 yards off the abrupt cliffs. As we skirt Stuart almost at Charles Point we pass another rockpile baring at 4 feet. At Charles Point we note the charted 2 foot ledge that extends nearly 200 yards offshore and its close proximity to the 3 and 5 fathom depth curves.

Prevost Harbor entrance is between rocky Charles Point and the west end of Satellite Island.

Continuing on, we pass the charted channel at the east end of Satellite, advised only for small boats. The north shore of Stuart has a bight filled with rocky shoals and homes upland. At the northeast point of Stuart is a charted flagpole with a three-part house behind it. We're now at Johns Pass and Johns Island.

Johns Island, Johns Pass & Ripple Island

Johns Island is about 1.3 miles long and about 0.3 mile wide. It rises to 100 feet near the northwest end. Two small bays are along the north shore, both with a few homes. The shores along most of the north side are rocky banks with few beaches, exposed to wind, waves and boat traffic in Boundary Pass. A 113 foot hill dominates the bluffs at the island's east end. Johns' southeast shore is rocky bluffs with shallows and rocks. The southwest shore has gentle beaches.

Johns Pass is the "fast passage," separating Stuart from Johns Island. It is used as a short-cut between Boundary Pass and Spieden Channel.

The crescent-shaped pass is about 1,000 yards long. Shore to shore at the north entrance the pass is about 250 yards wide and 225 yards wide at the south entrance.

Channel width between the islands at both ends is about 100 yards between the

5 fathom depth curves. The channel widens to 225 yards midway, with depths of 5 to 11 fathoms.

Johns Pass Currents

Strong currents can be a hazard to the unsuspecting cruiser as water sometimes races through the narrow pass. *Tidal Current Tables* give no predictions for the pass, and there appears to be discrepancies in current speed and direction between what has been observed by local mariners and what is shown in the *Canadian Current Atlas* charts.

Although we've been through the pass a number of times, we talked with local observers who travel the pass much more often. They tell us currents can run well over 2 knots, possibly 4 knots or even faster in extreme tides. One told us the pass sometimes "runs like a river."

Strongest currents, they told us, are about midway to three-quarters through a tidal current cycle. Currents generally run north on the flood and south on the ebb. Currents push hard both ways over reefs at the south end of the pass off Stuart.

On the Stuart side of Johns Pass is a large shallow bay with several shoals inside the 3 fathom curve between the points at either end of the pass. The land is low in here and the windsock from the Stuart East private airstrip can be seen. The south end of the pass has high, rocky, overhanging bluffs.

On the Johns Island side of the pass are several small bays, while rocks and shoals lurk offshore.

Camp Nor'wester, formerly at Sperry Peninsula on Lopez Island, has purchased over 100 acres on the pass on Johns Island for its new youth camp. A dock and camp buildings are planned, and the first sessions will be in the year 2000 with a modified season for 170 youngsters ages 9 to 16. The camp site is the former Nell Robinson Ranch on the pass, and her white house is visible from Spieden Channel. Paul Henriksen and his wife Christa Campbell are camp directors.

Kelp-covered shoals and rocks about 500 yards south of Johns Pass bare at 4 to 7 feet and extend about 300 yards southeast of Stuart. A rocky shoal with a depth of 2 feet is charted about 700 yards southeast of Stuart. It is surrounded by 1 and 5 fathom depth curves.

Gull Reef, NWR, is two separate reefs separated by a 100 yard wide, 9 fathom channel about 0.8 mile southeast of Johns Pass, and 300 yards south of Johns Island. The southeast rock bares at 7 feet and the northwest rock bares at 5 feet.

Cactus Islands are 300 yards southeast of Gull Reef. Cactus (Cacti?) have sculptured sandstone bluffs off the south shores.

Rock, NWR, and adjoining

"White house" on Johns Island

This house on the large west point of Johns jutting into the pass was home to early islander Nell Robinson for many years until her death in spring 1997. The island comes down in a gradual slope to the narrow part of the passage at the house.

*We're not sure when she moved to the island from Mercer Island, but June Burn mentions her in **100 Days in the San Juans,** originally written in 1946.*

Fish traps were built near this part of Johns Pass many years ago, and four reef net sites were nearby.

Nell's place is now the new site of Camp Nor'wester, and her white house will be preserved by the camp, said Paul Henriksen, camp director.

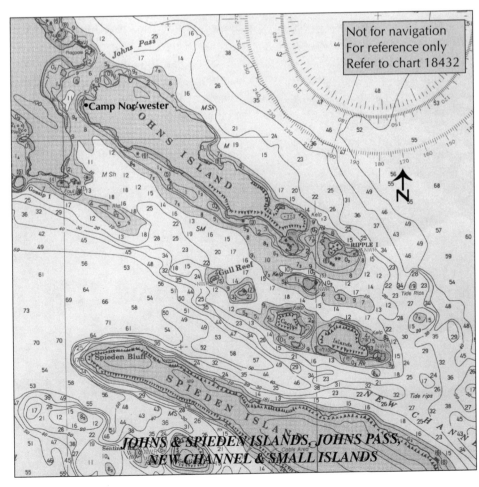

Not for navigation
For reference only
Refer to chart 18432

*JOHNS & SPIEDEN ISLANDS, JOHNS PASS,
NEW CHANNEL & SMALL ISLANDS*

Beautiful Underwater

An island friend tells us that diving is "exquisite" in this area along the southeast shores of Johns Island, especially along Gull Reef, and he says the whole area is tremendous cod fishing.

Spieden Style "Round-up"

In the early 1980s, Spieden caretakers decided to save some of the 300 animals imported when the island was a game pre-serve. They flew 100 volunteers (including Jo), to Spieden from San Juan Island to help in a "round-up."

The animals rebelled, and by the time the volunteers had "swept" the entire three mile length of the island by a human, hand-held chain, only one deer was in the corral. He looked in dismay at his hundred captors. With a mighty leap he plunged into the strong currents of Spieden Channel off Green Point.

The island caretaker went after the deer in his outboard, pulled him over the side of the boat and took him back to the island. So much for the "Spieden Round-up."

Spieden Island south shores

reef, are about 250 yards north of the Cacti. Kelp-covered, the reef is awash at MLLW and the rock bares at 5 feet. Charted, unnamed but locally called **Shag**, the shoal can be passed on either side.

Ripple Island, **NWR,** off the southeast end of Johns, is a tiny island about 150 yards across, with sparse trees. Because of wild roses and other bushes it often appears greener than some other small islands. A nearly 300 yard long reef extends off its east end. Large rocks bare at 6 feet off the south end of the island.

With extraordinary local knowledge and a bit of courage, it's possible to pass in the kelpy soup between Ripple and Johns in a fairly large sailboat. A friend has done it, but we didn't.

These islands and reefs line the north side of New Channel between Johns and Spieden, closer to Johns. The small channels north of Spieden Island can be navigated with care.

SPIEDEN ISLAND

Spieden Island is an anomaly, with it's dry barren south shore and the steep forested north shore. An airstrip runs east and west across a ridge on the western third of the island, and from a boat in Spieden Channel you may see the windsock.

Spieden Bluff is the 200 foot cliff which drops straight into the sea at the narrow west end of Spieden. Spieden has no public access or harbors. A private small boat moorage is inside the small breakwater on the southeast shore near Green Point. All tidelands around the island are publicly owned. *(Refer to DNR Quad Maps)*

Look for exotic animals grazing as you cruise past the south shore, left over from the island's earlier days as a private game preserve. Local legend says there may even be a Sasquatch on Spieden.

Spieden History

The island has a patchwork history that includes among its early settlers the well-known and loved Ed and Mary Chevalier, called "Dad" and "Ma" by most islanders. Mary's father was Robert Smith, a British soldier who served on San Juan Island in the Pig War. He later married a Native Ameri-can woman and moved to Spieden where he lived with her, their daughter Mary and his mother-in-law. He died while Mary was still a girl. The grand-mother and Mary stayed on Spieden, working Robert's sheep farm after Mary's mother remarried and moved to Stuart.

Young Ed Chevalier from Stuart Island was attracted to beautiful, black-haired Mary. They married in 1894, raising five children. They farmed Spieden Island with 200 turkeys, 200 sheep, horses, and milk cows; grew all their own food, including a fruit orchard, and logged. "Dad," who also fished commercially, was known as "the King of Spieden Island." Most important was Dad and Ma's unfail-ing hospitality to friends and strang-ers who arrived at the island.

After 45 years on Spieden Island the Chevaliers moved to Johns Island, then to Stuart and then to Friday Har-bor, where they lived out the rest of their lives, surrounded by a large lov-ing family and wonderful memories.

The Jonas Brothers, Seattle taxidermists, bought Spieden in 1970. They renamed it "Safari Island," imported exotic animals, such as Barbary sheep, Corsican mouflon, Indian blackbuck, Axis deer, Japanese Sika deer, European fallow deer and Spanish goats. Placid Spieden became a game preserve for wealthy trophy hunters, who drove around the island in Jeeps, sipping martinis and shooting sheep and deer.

By 1973, wildlife advocates, environmentalists and San Juan Islanders decried the enterprise and the operation closed down. Many animals stayed on Spieden. As their numbers grew some migrated to nearby islands, swimming across narrow channels.

Alaska Airlines bought the island for use as a rest and recreation facility for its employees a few years later. As of 1999, Spieden island was back under private ownership.

Naming Sentinel Island & Rock
The island was named by the Wilkes Expedition, but we're not quite sure why.

SENTINEL ISLAND

Sentinel is the tiny neighbor south of Spieden. Cliff-sided, no beaches or drinking water, trees on the north shore, rocks on the south, it's 15 acres of solitude and eagles. In 1919, the island became home to those late, lovable adventurers, June and Farrar Burn. It was the last island in the San Juans available for homesteading.

In 1979, The Nature Conservancy bought Sentinel from their son North Burn to protect the island's eagles. The "green gumdrop" is surrounded by deep water except for the 1 fathom shoal off the northwest corner.

Spieden Island, left, & Sentinel Island

Homesteading Sentinel

June and Farrar Burn first saw their homestead on Sentinel Island from a Bellingham mailboat. As the boat neared the island, June wrote in her autobiography, *Living High:* "Across another channel, seagulls screaming. Around the immense hip of Spieden, and there was Sentinel Island, like a green gumdrop, fir trees lifting their beautiful crowns into the sky, sedum-covered bluffs sheering straight down into the rich, green-blue water."

They moved onto the island a short time later, settling into a two dollar a month tent they rented from Roche Harbor where Farrar rowed daily to his part-time job. They built a cabin on their 100 foot high island by tearing down an unused shack on Johns Island, floating it to Spieden and rebuilding it. They loved their life. Best of all, Ed and Mary Chevalier of Spieden took them under their wings and became their close friends and mentors.

The Burns later lived at Fishery Point on Waldron Island. Their two sons, North and Bob (South), were Waldron Islanders all their lives, although education and careers often took them away from their island.

In 1946, June published *100 Days in the San Juans*, based on articles she had written for the Seattle P.I. The delightful book details the experiences she and Farrar had while sailing around the islands in a surplus Coast Guard lifeboat they bought for five dollars. They truly were an incredible pair.

Marooned!
In March of 1906, two sons of John Kertula of Waldron were marooned on Flattop for three days and nights with no food or water. They were able to kill two rabbits and a goose which they cooked over a driftwood fire. Icicles provided drinking water.

*A distress signal they raised was spotted by sharp eyes at the Island Lime Works on Orcas. The steamer **Buckeye** made a run to Flattop after unloading barrel staves at the Lime Works where they heard about the boys and rescued the brothers.*

⚓ **UNDERWAY AGAIN,** we're on our way to Waldron Island, and we pass several groups of rocky islands as we go.

Greatest depth recorded within the San Juans Islands is 134 fathoms in a hole about an equal distance between Jones, Spieden and Flattop islands.

Flattop Island and **Gull Rock** are about 1.5 miles east of Cactus Island or about two miles slightly northwest of Jones Island.

Flattop Island, NWR, nearly 50 acres, is 174 feet high near the center, where there are dark scrub trees. Bare rocky bluffs face south and the east side's sculptured, sandstone caves are home to glaucus-winged and red-footed Bonaparte's gulls. A rocky, kelpy shoal is off the northeast corner where there are also strong tide rips. The island was once a lighthouse reservation.

Gull Rock, NWR, a 1.3 acre, 33 foot high barren rock inhabited by gulls, is 0.3 mile northwest of Flattop. A seagull nursery is visited occasionally by biology students who are studying the marine birds. The island's charted outline suggests a gull's shape, with a bit of imagination.

White Rock and **Danger Rock** are midway between Flattop and Waldron. Both rocks are good places to avoid, and are charted but have no navigation aids.

White Rock, NWR, is 35 feet high and about 1.5 acres. The reef at White Rock, sometimes marked by kelp, extends nearly 0.3 mile to the northwest.

Danger Rock, 0.3 mile southeast of White Rock, is 3 feet below MLLW, and is usually marked by kelp, but we never trust kelp, as it can be a great help in marking a reef, sometimes it isn't there when we need it.

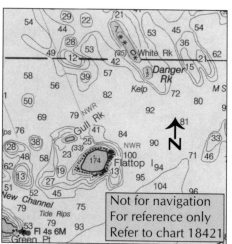

FLATTOP ISLAND, GULL, WHITE & DANGER ROCKS

Not for navigation
For reference only
Refer to chart 18421

WALDRON ISLAND

Waldron is less than 1.5 miles off the northwest shore of Orcas across President Channel, about 2.5 miles northeast of Flattop Island, and a little over three miles north of Jones Island.

The island is the sixth largest island in the San Juan archipelago, with 2,936 acres. It's about three miles long and as much as two miles wide with an irregular shape. Waldron is almost all private land and Waldronites value their privacy and long history of independence. Some do not respond cordially to uninvited visitors.

"Visitors on public roads are likely to be questioned as to whom they are visiting on the island. They want to know who is responsible for the behavior of strangers and loose, undisciplined strangers are watched very closely. I certainly was in 1981 when I first visited," said a friend who moved to the island. He can chuckle about the experience now.

We believe Waldron folks are extremely lucky to live on their beautiful, peaceful island, where spectacular stars in the night sky aren't overwhelmed by city lights, and the air is clean and pure. We understand if they don't immediately take to strangers on their island.

The public places on the island are the county dock, roads, gravel pit, cemetery, school, Nature Conservancy biological preserve on Cowlitz Bay (which is not a recreational area) and the U.S. Post Office, where mail is delivered three times a week. There are no parks on Waldron so all land off the public roads is private. There is also a private landing strip on the island. Like Stuart Island, Waldron has no stores, electricity or telephone service.

Waldron has a year-round population of about 90 people. More than 200 families own land and the summer population is much larger. About 14 children are in the school, grades K-8. These students receive individual instruction and independent study, occasionally taking field trips and having combined activities with Stuart and Shaw youngsters. High school students go to school on the mainland.

There have been no stores on Waldron since 1942. We understand that a yacht rental service gives their clients a brochure which urges them to stop at the "general store" for a cold drink.

Much of the island is fairly low with marshes along the north shores of Cowlitz Bay and lowlands along much of the northwest side of the island. The island rises

Naming Flattop Island
The island was named by the Wilkes Expedition in 1841 to depict the obvious topographical shape of the island.

➡ **NOTE: Gull Rock** is a Marine Reserve area in the Voluntary bottomfish "No Take" zone program. The "No-Take" zone encompasses the entire shoreline of the rock. All zones extend seaward 0.25 miles or 400 yards from the shoreline.

Naming Point Disney
The rugged 400 foot high Point was named in 1841 by the Wilkes Expedition after sail maker Solomon Disney who served aboard Wilkes' ship.

abruptly to heights of over 600 feet in the south end.

We circumnavigate Waldron clockwise, starting at the southeast end. The east side of the island, facing President Channel, has steep, rocky cliffs. Spectacular **Point Disney** (no relation to Walt) with a peak 405 feet above sea level, is at the south tip. The highest hill on Waldron is 612 feet, and is about 0.75 mile north and east of Point Disney.

Cowlitz Bay is a broad, open bight at the southwest side of the island. Depths are 1 to 10 fathoms as far as 0.75 mile offshore. The county dock and float are in the southeast niche of the bay for public use. Boats may "load/unload only," as signed on the float. Persons wishing to go ashore are not permitted to moor their boats at the float. Instead, they should anchor out and dinghy to the float. Mooring a large boat to the float while meandering the island could result in later finding the boat perhaps at the end of its bow line, bumping against pilings.

⚓ **Anchoring** in the bay is possible in mild weather in 2 fathoms, mud bottom. All buoys are private. We don't really consider this a gunkhole.

Mouatt Reef, NWR, in the south portion of Cowlitz Bay is about 600 yards off the Point Disney shore, and is covered by kelp and 3 feet of water at low tide.

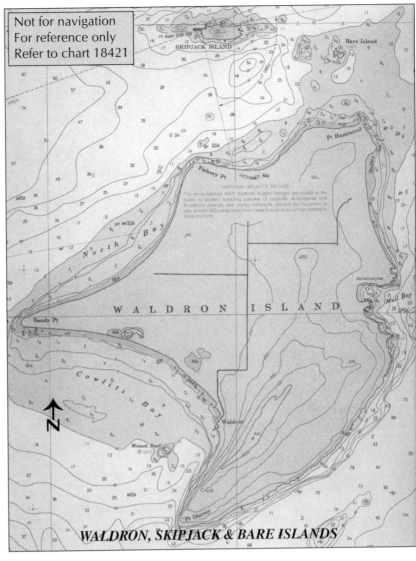

WALDRON, SKIPJACK & BARE ISLANDS

Waldron Island Preserve belonging to The Nature Conservancy is 273 acres of beach, meadow and marshland on 4,000 feet of shoreline in Cowlitz Bay. Island residents supported the purchase by the environmentally conscious group to keep the land from development. It is stressed that this area is a biological preserve and is used only for studying and viewing the vast assortment of birds, including migratory birds resting on long flights. This is not a recreational area.

Sandy Point is the island's far western tip, with a long sandspit, shoals and rocks extending nearly 300 yards offshore.

BOUNDARY PASS

As we go northeast around Sandy Point we again enter 11 mile long Boundary Pass.

North Bay is the large, slightly crescent-shaped bay stretching 1.5 miles between Sandy Point and Fishery Point on Waldron, washed by the waters of Boundary Pass. It's almost all low bank along here with homes tucked back in the trees, and even a windmill near Sandy Point. This is a beautiful shoreline, all private, with a few buoys offshore.

Waldron's Point Disney

Christmas Time in the Islands

The Santa Ship from British Columbia arrives at Waldron Island county dock in Cowlitz Bay where it's greeted by smiles, waves and balloons.

B.C. sailors bring presents to youngsters throughout the San Juans.

Fishery Point

This was the site of early Native American fish traps. Later, settlers installed their fish traps at the point, where, it is said, millions of herring were caught.

Farrar and June Burn, modern island legends, lived at the point in log cabins they built with sons North and South (Bob) on their 44 acres in the 1930s and 1940s. Bob was the musician who invented the wonderful, unusual "bazoo," which we first heard on the Bob Hope radio show in the 1940s.

Naming Point Hammond

The point was named after Henry Hammond, a quartermaster with the Wilkes Expedition.

Early Discovery

Waldron Island was discovered by Spaniard Juan Pantoja in June 1791.

⚓ **Anchoring** off this beach in 2 to 5 fathoms with its muddy, sandy bottom is possible for short periods. It's easy to drag anchor because of strong currents which generally run parallel to the shore.

Ebb currents in this area usually flow southwest and may reach or exceed 3 knots. **Flood currents** flow northeast and may reach or exceed 2.5 knots. Currents here seem consistent with NOAA predictions and charts in the *Canadian Current Atlas.*

From Fishery Point around Point Hammond almost to Mail Bay there are rocks baring up to 6 feet, foul ground, shoals and boulders charted at various locations, waiting to skewer reckless vessels (an oxymoron with the term *wreckless*?). Most are indicated inshore of the charted 5 fathom depth curve, except for a 1 fathom 5 foot shoal 0.6 mile west of the tip of Point Hammond.

Generally, we keep outside the 5 fathom depth curve.

Fishery Point scarcely feels like a point when cruising past. The ebb current can be very vigorous at times, and very loud, according to local residents. The point is actually made up of five distinct rock fingers which reach for the sea. One of these, the rock finger immediately south of the main, recognizable point, seldom touches the water, except during winter high tides and storms. Waldron humorists named it **Moot Point.**

Severson's Bay, unnamed on charts, is between Fishery Point and Point Hammond. The large bight has a fairly low bank with a sandy beach.

Point Hammond, the northeast point of Waldron, is bluffy and rocky, with a tombolo off the point. Tide rips sometimes boil off Point Hammond.

Mail Bay, with numerous old pilings in the north section and rocks around the south part, is not the best anchorage. We've never anchored in here, but friends who have were not impressed. They said there are better anchorages around. Remains of piles, snags and cables are in the bay, which once was the mail boat stop.

Running past the three shoal projections south of the bay, we can pass fairly close to steep bluffs, with the 10 fathom depth curve fairly consistent at about yards offshore. We've now reached the area where the rock quarrying operation at Point Disney began shortly after the turn of the century. Almost all signs of the quarry are gone now, except for a couple of "coyote holes," 26 iron bars, hooked at the ends projecting from the rock wall on which the wooden walkway was suspended above the water. There are some tailings left along the steep bluffs.

Waldron Island History

For centuries, Waldron was a summer campground of Native Americans, who called the island "Schishuney," meaning "place to fish with a pole." They arrived from other islands and from the Skagit and Whatcom county areas. They were members of the Lummis, Saanich, Songish and Samish tribes, an easy-going, convivial group of peoples. They went by canoe to Schishuney in the spring, summer and fall, camping on the beaches, fishing and gathering shellfish. Occasionally they hunted deer, elk and rabbits, while the fields provided camas and varieties of berries.

Life would have been idyllic for these relaxed foragers, except for visits by two tribes from the north, the warlike Kwakiutl and Haidas, who came to abduct slaves. For centuries, the peaceful locals coped with the raiders, sometimes hiding in the heavy forest and towering rocky crags. Legends say they fought and won some pitched battles with the invaders.

The northern Indians had traded hides to Russian traders for muzzle-loaders. Devastating guns made the contests unequal during the early part of the 19th century. They would descend on the island in 50 man canoes, killing resisting males, kidnapping others, including women and children. Like other predators, the warlike northerners took care to never completely destroy the tribes—they were too good a source of loot and manpower.

Near the end of the 19th century the settlers appeared, and contact with the strange pale humans became almost as devastating as the Haida raids. When the new interlopers discovered the beauty and natural resources of the island, they staked out claims. Visiting Indians came no more. The new settlers even changed the island's name to Waldron from the lyrical Schishuney. *(From a Monograph by Charles H. Ludwig, 1959)*

One of Waldron's first non-Native settlers was Frederick Marks who lived on Waldron as early as 1863. He and his daughter were murdered by Indians on Saturna Island as they moved to the Gulf Islands in British Columbia several years later. Another early settler was James Cowan, homesteading in a small shack at Cowlitz Bay. In March 1868, friends from adjoining islands sensed something was amiss with Cowan. He had not been seen for some time, no smoke arose from his chimney. He was found murdered, shot in the back, his body buried under some brush. The killer was never found, although some speculated it might have been notorious old "Skookum Tom," a renegade Indian accused of a number of murders in the islands.

By 1870, four families were living on Waldron, including two bachelors, Benjamin Hunt and John Brown. Brown decided to drain a marshland and convert it to a planting field. He imported a crew of Chinese and Indian laborers, whom he paid the munificent sum of 25 cents per day to dig ditches, some of them 40 feet deep. When the land dried it began to sprout weeds so he burned the area to get rid of them—and also burned all of the peat moss—leaving the land virtually worthless.

Rock quarrying began at Point Disney to gather stones to pave Yesler Way in Seattle in the early 1900s. The quarrying operations, run by Tacomans George Savage and George Scofield, imported about 150 laborers, tough and skilled men earning the mind-boggling sum of $1.50 per hour. They worked as powdermen, coyote hole drillers, donkey engine operators, cablemen, cooks, storekeepers and quarrymen. They lived in a bunkhouse about 1.5 miles from the stone face, and had to climb to work along narrow footpaths and wooden walkways which clung to the side of the cliff above the sea.

At the beginning of each operation the drillers would hang like spiders from ropes tied to trees at the cliff top. When they drilled 60 feet into the rock they would shift to one side and drill another hole at a right angle to the first. This second hole was the "coyote hole." After it was completed, the men would pad their shoes with gunnysacks to avoid sparks and form a human chain of powderbag handlers.

The coyote hole was filled with gun powder, the cap was placed, wires strung and everyone would take cover. The generator handle was plunged and the face of the cliff would blow off and avalanche down. Then the cutting crew would shape the broken rock into 6x6x12 inch rectangular blocks which were loaded onto a barge and shipped to Seattle. We understand some of these blocks are still on the Queen Anne Counterbalance.

In 1906, Seattle pavers discovered that concrete was superior to paving stones and the Waldron contract was cancelled. When the Waldron boss heard
(See next page)

Public Tidelands

🐚 *Unless otherwise noted, public tidelands are state-owned; some may be leased and posted for aquaculture or other private use.*

Some of Waldron Island shores are designated as public ownership on the 1984 DNR map. However, some environmentally sensitive beaches or privately leased beaches are not open for public use. Check the DNR Quad Map of San Juan County and local posting before using these beaches.

Mail, the important link

Mail is now delivered three times weekly to Waldron Island. For many years it was delivered six days a week by a large boat starting from Anacortes or Bellingham and stopping at all the post offices in the islands until it reached Friday Harbor, where it stayed overnight. It made the same stops on the way back the next day.

In the "olden days" many of the San Juan Island's post offices were at docks.

Schooner Rainbird sails the San Juans

of the cancellation he left with the payroll funds, and also stole the company food. The next morning when workers showed up they found they'd been had. Some stayed on trying to cut and sell stones, while a few settled on the island to homestead.

Ethan Allen and his wife, Sadie, migrated to Waldron in 1895 and homesteaded a claim just south of Mail Bay. They both taught school and in 1898 he became superintendent of schools for all of San Juan County. He rowed more than 10,000 miles in his homemade rowboat from island to island to check on 27 schools, most of them one-room schoolhouses. He became legendary during his term of office.

Allen was a major collector of Indian artifacts and his collection is on display in the "Ethan Allen Room" in the Orcas Island Historical Museum. The collection contains artifacts gathered over a lifetime, with more than 3,000 items, including arrowheads, spearheads, Indian baskets, pottery, stone dishes, grinding implements, paint pots, ornaments and ceremonial pieces.

Allen was also an extremely generous man. We remember reading an anecdote years ago in a book by Orcas writer Beatrice Cook. She had rowed to Waldron's shores and was about to cook freshly-caught salmon over a beach fire. Allen came along and offered a fresh lemon to go with the fish. She protested, claiming it was so difficult to get lemons on Waldron he shouldn't give it away. "But precious things are so much better when they're shared," he replied.

Waldron's post office first opened on January 6, 1880, in the center of the island, with George Dingmans as the first postmaster. He rowed weekly to West Beach on Orcas where he left his boat and walked into Eastsound to pick up the mail.

Whulj or Whulge

Either term means about the same thing, "that big stretch of salt water," or "the salt water we know."

"Whulj" was the name for inland waters given by local Indians, the original inhabitants of this entire area.

"Whulj" was renamed as Puget Sound by Captain George Vancouver. Admiralty Inlet and other waterways were all named by early explorers, who ignored the original Native American names, and left us with bland seconds.

Writer Bryce Wood points out that Capt. Vancouver was criticized for ignoring Indian names of geographic places.

"In the naivety of his own cultural background, he reported his voyage as a discovery," Wood wrote. He named that big stretch of salt water "Puget's Sound," instead of calling it "xwaltc"—"Whulge," a term the Native Americans also used for the Pacific Ocean.

We applaud author and outdoorsman Harvey Manning's continued use of "Whulj" (or Whulge) on the salt waters we know, and wish it would once again be the name of choice for the area.

⚓ **UNDERWAY AGAIN,** we're off to Skipjack & Bare islands.

These islands, less than one mile off Waldron's north shore, are National Wildlife Refuges. Landing on them is prohibited and boats must stay 200 yards offshore. The islands are rookeries for many seabirds, including black oystercatchers, pigeon guillemots, glaucous winged gulls and auklets. Intruding upon these rookeries scares nesting birds away, leaving their nests and babes open to predators.

Skipjack is about 0.8 mile north of Fishery Point. It is 0.3 mile long east to west, 19 acres and is 120 feet high in the center, with small trees, wildflowers and nesting seabirds on rocky bluffs. Reefs around the island are covered with marine life, including anemones, starfish, limpets, chitons, barnacles and many others. The island at one time was a popular destination for small boats because of good fishing and scuba diving off the reefs. For many years it was a favorite spot for Waldronites to swim and picnic. A tiny unnamed islet is about 150 yards due east of Skipjack.

Skipjack Island Light [Fl 4 sec 55 ft 5M light] flashing 4 second light 55 feet high visible 5 miles, on a diamond-shaped dayboard with black and white sectors on a steel tower at the west end of Skipjack, is obscured from 261° to 347°.

Bare Island, you guessed it, a bare rock barely 150 yards across, is about 50 feet high with beaches heaped with driftwood, is 0.65 mile off the east end of Skipjack. It's a habitat for puffins and cormorants. A group of rocks awash at a 2 foot tide are midway between the two islands. These charted rocks sometimes are hit by unwary mariners not reading their charts, according to the Coast Guard.

Carl, the *Condor* and Skipjack Island

After sailing and being carried by current with the engine not working, *Condor* went northeast toward a large kelp bed between Skipjack and Bare islands off Waldron. The wind vanished, the currents turned adverse and I tied off to a bundle of kelp. From the skiff my leadline proved the bottom and rock depths were not a problem for *Condor's* 3 foot draft, even at low tide. The earlier drop in barometric pressure was a concern.

With sails lowered and stopped it was reassuring that in strong winds the choice of hoisting the fors'l, or only the main and jib on the little schooner, would provide a balanced rig, saving the time and need to reef. Totally exposed in a bad "anchorage" the best idea was to chow down and turn in "all standing" (dressed).

Hours later, wakened by wind in the rigging and a bright moon traveling across the open hatch, *Condor* swung on both a rising favorable wind and flood current. An hour and four nautical miles later, under jib and main, with the moon now behind clouds in the black of night, lead line again in hand, I eyed Sucia Island's changing black topographic contours. *Condor* cautiously sounded her first entrance into Shallow Bay at Sucia Island. *(More adventures of Carl and Condor in Ch. 6)*

Condor under sail

WASHINGTON SOUND

It's not charted on today's navigation charts, but the term most often refers to the waters of the San Juan Islands, according to Richard Vanderway of the Whatcom Museum of History and Art in Bellingham's Gallery District.

"Washington Sound" is not on any recent map or chart. Individual waterways are named, but there is no overall name for waterways in the northwest area of the state north of the Strait of Juan de Fuca except for "San Juan Islands." Surveyors may have discussed Washington Sound earlier, but its first appearance was only as an appendix to the annual report of the United States Coast Survey.

Washington Sound first appeared on a sketch of navigation Chart K in 1856, where it is written in an arc with the "W" in Washington south of Smith Island. The name follows San Juan Channel between San Juan and Lopez Island, across President Channel, passes west of Waldron Island and the "d" in "sound" is between East Point on Saturna and Patos Island.

Washington Sound was on the charts from 1868 to 1935, and it was removed, partially because of protests by a towing company in 1930, according to author Bryce Wood. It was suggested that the name be replaced with "San Juan Archipelago."

That was changed to "San Juan Islands" by a decision of the U.S. Board of Geographic Names on January 14, 1964.

NOAA Chart 18400 carried "San Juan Islands" as the name in 1976.

A formal "Proposal of Name for an Unnamed Domestic Feature," was made in 1977 to the Washington State Board on Geographic Names to return Washington Sound to the charts, but it was not approved.

Finally, in 1979 the board agreed that the term "sound" did not apply to the waters within San Juan County, and that no new name was needed for the waterways as they were individually named. The board also received a proposal that the term San Juan Islands should include Cypress, Guemes, Sinclair and other islands east of Rosario Strait.

Some San Juans Islanders, lead by Jack Culver of Orcas, would love to restore "Washington Sound" as the name of the waters surrounding the San Juans. More power to you, Jack, we support your great idea.

Naming Bare & Skipjack

Ship Jack Islands (Bare and Skipjack) were named by Wilkes, possibly for fish, of which several species are commonly called "shipjack,"a fish that breaches from time to time.

The original spelling eventually evolved to Skipjack.

➡ **NOTE: Bare Island** is a Marine Reserve area in the Voluntary bottomfish "No Take" zone program. The "No-Take" zone covers the entire shoreline of the island. All zones extend seaward 0.25 miles, 400 yards, from the shoreline.

Excellent Swimmers

Deer are magnificent athletes and strong swimmers. Occasionally those cruising in the San Juans may spot deer swimming between islands. Observations show they can sustain a water speed of 10 mph.

Does will sometimes swim to small islands to give birth in a tranquil setting.

We've finished the trip around Waldron, the nearby rocks and islets and now it's time to move on.

⛭ **UNDERWAY** again, and we're on the way to the outer islands of Patos, Sucia, Matia and Clark, but first let's stop at Gordon and Adolphus Islands on the way.

Gordon & Adolphus?

Adolphus Island was charted one mile north of Orcas Island and one mile west of Parker Reef in 1841 by "someone" in the Wilkes Expedition.

Gordon Island was charted 0.25 miles farther west of Adolphus at the same time. Both were plotted in waters 70 to 90 fathoms deep.

Is this a joke?

Perhaps not so much a joke as "The Midshipmen's Revenge," aimed at Lt. Charles Wilkes who led the first American survey and mapping of the San Juan Islands in July 1841. Some of his midshipmen were not overly fond of him. One theory is that several young officers in the expedition developed disagreements with Wilkes. He filed two court-martial charges against Passed Midshipman William May for "Insubordination and Mutinous Conduct" and "Disrespect of his Superior ..."

Perhaps May decided charting the two non-existent islands would in some way discredit Wilkes's cartography, his revenge for the court-martial. Or, it may be that charting the two false islands was an honest mistake made by an officer assisting in the survey due to fog or a mirage the night they were hastily charted when the expedition was cut short.

Wilkes was in the San Juans a remarkable three short days in 1841, from July 26, 27 and 28, three days less than he thought he needed. During this time he visited and named an enormous number of islands, channels, bays and landmarks.

He had to return as quickly as possible to the Columbia River where one of his vessels, *Peacock*, had foundered on the Columbia bar, luckily without loss of life.

The chart of the "Archipelago of Arro, Gulf of Georgia, Ringgolds' Channel and Straits of Fuca, Oregon Territory, by the U.S. Exploring Expedition, 1841," which showed Gordon and Adolphus, wasn't published until 1848. Some authorities doubt that Wilkes was even aware of the addition of the two bogus islands to his map-making.

Charting the non-existent islands was discovered in 1853 by George Davidson, a young assistant in the U.S. Coast Survey. He wrote, "on some recent maps two islands, called Adolphus and (Gordon) are laid down close to the Skipjacks, but in 1853 we examined the vicinity and satisfied ourselves that they did not then exist."

Despite this error and other deficiencies, Wilkes' exploration and charting of the San Juans and the Pacific Northwest was praised in 1901 by historian W.D. Lyman as having had a "profound influence on government officials in bringing about a realization that 'Puget Sound was an inherent and integral part of Oregon ... essential to the proper development of American commerce upon the Pacific'."

(Compiled from **San Juan Island—Coastal Place Names** *by Bryce Wood, & information from Dr. Lloyd Keith, professor at Shoreline Community College in Seattle)*

Look-alike Wilkes' vessel leaving the area

Midshipmen's Revenge

When we first heard about Adolphus and Gordon islands we tried to place them on shallow West Bank, west of Sucia, just in case they were really supposed to be a joke.

But that didn't work—they had been charted where the water is just too deep at 70 to 90 fathoms, to make our idea work.

So we'll just have to wonder whether "Midshipmen's Revenge" is an honest mistake or real revenge, against Wilkes.

Although Adolphus and Gordon islands were named by the Wilkes Expediton, we never discovered the source of the names. Maybe we weren't supposed to.

In **Chapter 6,** we visit the most popular islands in all of the San Juans, the group we call the "Outer Islands." This includes Patos, Sucia, Matia and Clark islands, all Washington State Marine Park islands.

Not for navigation
For reference only

Patos Island

Sucia Islands

O

GORDON
ISLAND

Skipjack Island

ADOLPHUS
ISLAND

R

R

Waldron
Island

Orcas Island

A

Stuart Island

HULLS ISLAND

E

Jones Island

D

Shaw Island

HODGER

San Juan Island

ISLAND

CHAUNCYS

Lopez Island

ARCHIPELAGO
OF
ARRO
GULF OF GEORGIA
RINGGOLDS CHANNEL
AND
STRAITS OF FUCA
OREGON TERRITORY
BY THE
U.S. Ex. Ex.
1841

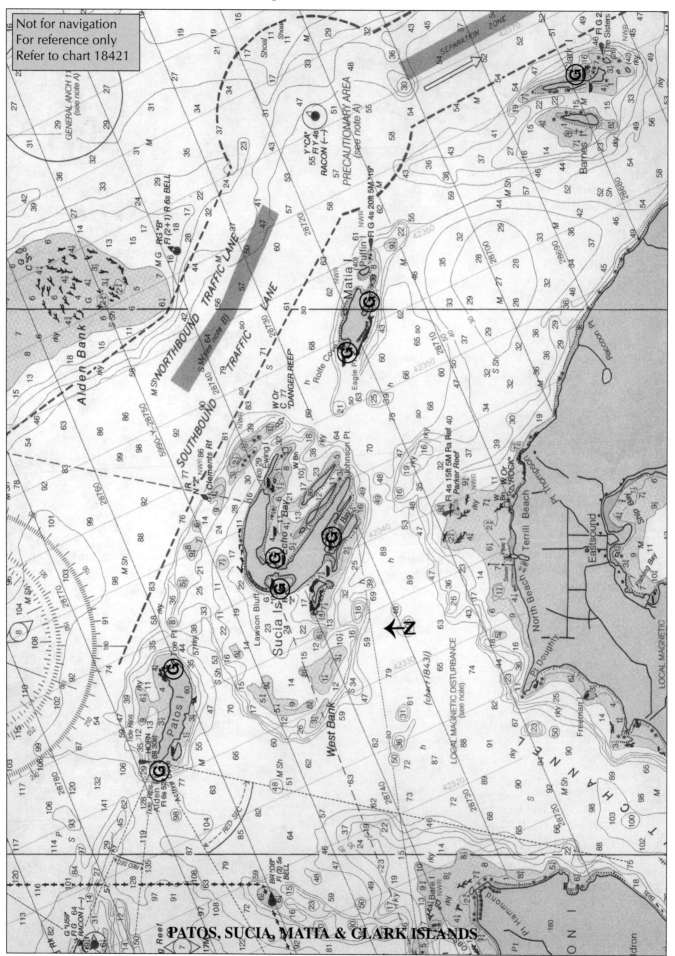

PATOS, SUCIA, MATIA & CLARK ISLANDS

Chapter 6
THE "OUTER ISLANDS"
Patos, Sucia, Matia & Clark

OVERVIEW OF THE "OUTER ISLANDS"

Just saying the words rings of excitement—of exotic, far away islands yet to be discovered. Perhaps we'll be the first ever to step foot on a white sandy beach …

Afraid not. In the San Juans many of the "outer islands" were home long ago to Native Americans, later settled by pioneers, and now many have become marine state parks. They have definitely been "discovered." These are the islands that thousands of northwest boaters surge to every summer to enjoy outstanding cruising and the amenities state parks offer.

In this chapter we'd like to take you with us on a sweep of these glorious islands, including Patos, Sucia, Matia and Clark, and several smaller private islands. These include Barnes, Puffin and Sisters, which have little or no public access. We take a quick look at them as we cruise by.

These scenic islands seemingly float on the waters of the Strait of Georgia. East of the boundary between the U.S. and Canada, and north and east of Orcas, they are the favorite islands of thousands of recreational mariners throughout the Northwest. Their unique geology features sandstone shorelines eroded by wind and waves into incredible and sometimes grotesque shapes.

The island groups of Patos, Sucia and Matia include a couple of dozen small islands and rocky reefs. They are state park lands, except for Finger Islands in Echo Bay on Su-

➡ **NOTE: No marine fuel** is available in the islands visited in this chapter. Closest fuel is gas at West Beach Resort, 5 miles, or diesel and gas at Deer Harbor Resort, 12 miles, both on Orcas Island.

Sandstone bluffs in the Sucia group

Patos = Ducks

Patos means "ducks" in Spanish, and was named by the Spanish Expedition of 1791.

Francisco Eliza sent the schooner Santa Saturnina into the region, commanded by Juan Pantoja y Arriaga, and they dropped anchor off the southeast end of Patos.

The Wilkes Expedition renamed it Gourd Island in 1841.

Capt. Henry Kellett restored the original name to the British Admiralty chart in 1874.

Alden Point

This west point of Patos Island was named for Lt. James Alden, chosen to head the U.S. surveying teams beginning in 1853.

He'd been on the whole voyage of the Exploring Expedition with Wilkes and had frequently been at odds with him. Perhaps that accounts for the remote location that bears his name?

> ➥ **NOTE:** Extreme currents are in waters near Patos Island.
>
> Currents may reach or exceed 3.9 knots on a 045°T. flood and 2.9 knots on a 270°T. ebb 0.5 mile south of Toe Pt.
>
> Currents may reach or exceed 2.5 knots on a 025°T. flood and 4 knots on a 185°T. ebb 2 miles south of Alden Pt.
>
> Currents may reach or exceed 2.24 knots on a 065° flood and 3.6 knots on a 180° ebb 1.4 miles west of Patos Light.

Patos Island Light

cia, and Patos which is owned and managed by the U.S. Bureau of Land Management (BLM) through a cooperative agreement. Washington State Parks manages the island for use by boaters.

STATE PARKS INFORMATION

Parks Ranger David Castor suggests we pass on the following information to mariners who plan to visit these islands. Brochures are available with more information.

♦ Don't cruise in the islands without good charts; know how to use them.

♦ When navigating around these islands realize the geology of the islands is unique–long narrow fingers of submerged rocks and reefs are often between bays. The park staff is knowledgeable and helpful.

♦ When you think you've gone far enough to miss a reef, go farther.

♦ Rangers have seen 'amazing maneuvers' of anchoring, where boats have anchored too close to shore and crews wake up in the morning surprised to find they are surrounded by beach.

♦ 'Pack it out' has really improved the parks. Rangers used to take 100 bags of garbage off Sucia daily in the summer. Now that people take such good care, they off-load only 10 bags annually.

♦ There are definite fire hazards on the islands during the driest part of the year, July, August and September. Use caution and firepits.

♦ No camping is allowed except in designated campsites.

♦ Kayakers have the most impact on flora and fauna as they can easily access any shore. Kayakers are asked to be careful when beaching their craft and when going ashore.

♦ Tourist season is also breeding season for many sea mammals and birds. Mariners are asked to be extremely sensitive, keeping clear of wildlife refuges and other breeding and nesting areas.

⚓**UNDERWAY AGAIN,** it's off to Patos, the outermost of the "Outer Islands."

Patos is the most northerly island in the Pacific Northwest, about four miles north of Waldron, five miles north of Orcas, and 2.5 miles from Shallow Bay on Sucia. Patos has an isolated feeling that we find different from any other island. Perhaps it's the power of nature, man has not yet really tamed his environment. While this is a terrific spot, it sometimes feels eerie because it's just us and the elements—winds, waves and currents, and sometimes feels incredibly free.

Patos is at the junction of Boundary Pass and the Strait of Georgia, a lump in the midst of swirling currents, exposed to winter's gales. It's 1.3 miles east to west, and 0.25 mile north to south. There are several spots on the island where the land rises to 100 feet, the rest of it is gentle hills.

Patos Island Light [Fl W 6 sec, 52ft 6M Horn] flashing white 6 second light 52 feet high visible 6 miles, is on a lighthouse at **Alden Point** at the northwest tip of Patos. It has two red sectors: (1) red from 011.5° to 059.5° which covers a 6 fathom shoal, (2) red from 097° to 114° which covers Rosenfeld Rock off Tumbo Island in B.C. The horn operates every 30 seconds continuously. The automated lighthouse is visible from both the U.S. and Canada.

From Alden Point the views are stunning of the Canadian islands, U.S.

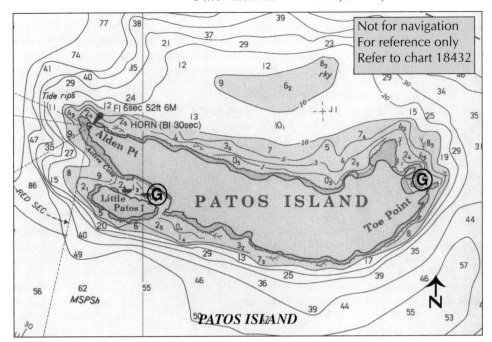

Not for navigation
For reference only
Refer to chart 18432

➡ **CAUTION:** State parks suggests boaters tie to a buoy and avoid anchoring in Active Cove if a high pressure system is building, as it causes strong westerly winds to howl down the Strait of Georgia and into the cove.

Island Stories

*Patos has some wonderful tales to tell, best memorialized in Helene Glidden's book, **Light on the Island**. She grew up on both Patos and Stuart islands where her father was lighthouse keeper at the turn of the century.*

She tells a personal account of her large family's life on the remote island with smugglers, shipwrecks, storms, and tragedies.

President Teddy Roosevelt went near enough to Patos on his ship to dip the colors to his old friend, Helene's father, manning the lighthouse at Alden Point.

Experience Counts

We visited with a lone camper who had kayaked the 2.5 miles to Patos from Sucia Island. It was a lonely trip to this remote island, but he had carefully checked weather, charts and currents before leaving Sucia. This is not a trip for a novice kayaker.

Moorage at Active Cove

mainland shores, mountains, and almost constant commercial and recreational vessels in the surrounding waters. Saturna Island in B.C. is west, Point Roberts is north, Birch Bay is northeast, Cherry Point with its tall stacks and steam from oil off-loading facilities is east, Lummi Island is to the south.

Active Cove is at the west end of Patos, immediately southeast of Alden Point. It's a small cove that goes dry at the far east end, with Little Patos Island as its boundary on the south side. What looks like a channel through the cove at the east end of Little Patos is **not,** at least not for anything larger than a beachable boat, as the "channel" is extremely shallow. The ranger said, "Never go between Patos and Little Patos except in a small boat."

⚓ Patos is okay as a short term anchorage, but rangers don't recommend it as a good overnight anchorage because of the rocky bottom, eelgrass, strong currents and swells from passing tankers or storms which wash into the cove and can cause anchors to drag. **Depths** are 2 fathoms, 4 feet at the entrance and rise to less than 1 fathom in less than 200 yards.

Ⓖ If you can nab one of the two state park buoys in Active Cove, it is a wonderful spot, the favorite of many boaters—an ideal **gunkhole**.

Patos Island Marine Park Facilities

- ➤ 207.5 acres with nearly four miles of shoreline
- ➤ Two mooring buoys, $5 night, May 1-Sept. 30
- ➤ Seven campsites with tables, fire-pits, toilets
- ➤ 1.5 mile loop trail
- ➤ No water
- ➤ Bulletin board
- ➤ Activities: camp, picnic, fish, hike, dig clams, beach-comb, swim, gunkhole

Above the beach at the east end of the cove is a grassy spit with three campsites and toilets. Two additional campsites are in the woods and two more are on the trail to the lighthouse. There's a beautiful loop trail around

Patos Lighthouse, with Sonja and Eric Hazelton
(Rich Hazelton photo)

Active Cove

The cove was named in honor of the U.S. steamer, Active, which was active in survey duties in the Northwest in the 1850s and 1860s.

Patos Lighthouse

It was built in 1893, and the old triplex dwelling is enclosed by a fence on a low, rocky bluff. The old pier is in a state of disrepair, unusable and dangerous, and is considered a hazard area. The automated light is still bright and the horn blasts to help mariners on their way through sometimes challenging weather conditions.

the western half of the island, from the head of the cove along the bluffs, plunging into forests and emerging onto the spectacular north shore. A branch of the trail leads west to the lighthouse. Wildflowers are especially lovely in April and May. Rangers ask that hikers keep off the eastern half of the island. It's being evaluated in a flora and fauna survey and may be made into a protected natural area because of unique plants. Your best chance in the islands for a beautiful anchorage, peace and quiet, and a private cold swimming beach, just may be here at Patos.

⚓ **UNDERWAY AGAIN,** we circumnavigate Patos Island counter-clockwise, starting at Active Cove. For almost 200 yards offshore it is less than 2 fathoms deep slightly east of the channel between Patos and Little Patos islands.

Midway along the south side, the 10 fathom curve is less than 100 yards offshore, with kelp in places. This is typical San Juans with few beaches, heavily forested bluffs covered with madronas and evergreens, low to medium banks with large indentations and rock sculptures. Cave-like holes appear as we round the southeast shore where wave-strewn driftwood is heaped on the beach.

Toe Point, so named because the point and its reef sticks out like a big toe, is at the east end of Patos. It slopes northeast into the Strait of Georgia for nearly 0.1 mile. Inside the tip of the toe is a 2 fathom cove.

⚓ **Anchoring** is possible in the right weather. The ranger confirmed this bay is a good place for one or two boats to anchor because there's good holding ground and it's a reasonably sheltered anchorage.

Ⓖ All of the above makes it a **good gunkhole.**
"Even in a southeasterly wind there is some protection in there. It's a good gunkhole," he said. " It's the only safe anchorage on Patos in high pressure—a true cove with no currents. Camping or fires are not allowed on the beach." We've talked with several mariners who have spent the night anchored in the bay, one who hung in there when it was too foggy to move, and another who overnighted there as a new spot and loved it.

On the north side of Toe Point bay is another bit of low land that juts out nearly 150 yards into the strait. Currents and back-eddies swirl around this point. It's a bird watchers delight, with perhaps a few seals included. West of the point is a long, drying reef that extends at least 0.1 mile beyond the shore, a shoal of conglomerate rock, shells, gravel and sandstone.

⚓ West along the north shore are several possibilities of temporary anchoring, weather permitting. There are currents here, so the anchor needs to be carefully set. The bottom is no doubt rocky.

Beaches along Patos' north forested side are covered with silvered driftwood. An enormous bleached stump stands upright on the beach—it must have been quite a tree when it was alive. East of the stump is a sheer rock which shows the horizontal line of rock strata. It's a wonderful area in here. A bit farther and we've reached Alden Point again. We keep about 200 yards offshore, encountering strong tide rips, and now we're ready to leave fascinating Patos.

⚓ **UNDERWAY AGAIN,** we cruise 2.5 miles southeast to Sucia Island, the number one cruising destination for over 100,000 boaters each year, which keeps getting more popular all the time. The sculptured sandstone cliffs above sandy beaches lure the first-time boater, as well as those who keep coming back year after year. Sucia is practically our second home after visiting it for over 60 years.

There are 10 islands officially in the Sucia Islands group owned by State Parks: Sucia, Little Sucia, Ewing, Justice, a sprinkling of islets called Cluster Islands, not designated on the charts, and several smaller, unnamed islands. Land area of all these islands is about 749 acres, with shorelines of more than 14.5 miles, six major anchorage areas and 10 miles of trails and roads.

Sucia in Spanish means foul. Even a quick look at our charts gives an indication of why Spanish explorers decided the rocks and reefs surrounding the Sucia Islands were "foul." They're well charted now, but too late for those early arrivals

Shoals include: Clements Reef off the northeast, Danger Reef at the southeast, reefs in Ewing Cove, Wiggins Rock in Echo Bay, extended reefs off Little Sucia, West Bank only 0.5 mile west, and reefs off Ev Henry Point at the entrance to Fossil Bay. Many of these shoals are "discovered" anew each year by first-time visitors to the islands who leave bottom paint, if not the boat, on the rocks.

Eagles Still Soaring

In the early 1980s, state parks personnel said they did not plan to establish overnight camp sites on Patos because they didn't want to disturb the island's eagles.

There are now eight camp-sites and eagles are still on the island. State parks still doesn't want to disturb them, but apparently we're all learning to live together. Please be particularly careful not to bother them.

Ken Lloyd

Sucia Island State Park

The island was acquired by the state in five parcels. The first was in 1952, another with the 1960 Interclub donation, and the last in 1974, for the unbelievably low cost of $6,818.67.

Plaque at Sucia

Birth of a Marine State Park

The wonderful thing about Sucia is that not only does the entire park belong to the public, it was bought in part by the public, the recreational boaters of Puget Sound, who gave it to Washington State Parks to be used by boaters forever.

In 1946, Mr. and Mrs. Wilbur H. Johnston of Orcas bought land on Sucia and had a summer camp between Echo and Shallow bays. Among their friends were many boating families who arrived at the island each year. They had a chance to sell the island to a wealthy Californian who planned to turn it into a private estate, but they didn't want that to happen, so they contacted Interclub, representing 36 northwest boating organizations. Ev Henry, a founder of Interclub, initiated a high-powered fund drive among Puget Sound yacht clubs to buy the island paradise for the asking price of $25,000. Money was raised by pledges of two to five dollars from members.

On April 29, 1960, Puget Sound Interclub Association placed Sucia Island in trust of the state. This was in the days when the average family "yacht" was 20 to 30 feet long, well before the megayacht era.

It was a memorable moment on Memorial Day weekend in 1960 when the island was dedicated as Sucia Marine State Park. Ev Henry and Seattle Power Squadron Commander Ken Lloyd, now of Lopez Island, were instrumental in arranging the island's purchase.

A large carved map of Sucia is at the head of the dock in Fossil Bay. On it are names of all the clubs involved in the gift to the parks and to the public. The boating public owes these clubs a great thanks for preserving this remarkable island sanctuary. It also notes that "Ev Henry Point was named for Everett George Henry, 1910-1972, a tireless and devoted worker toward the development of recreational boating ... with the major effort in the Pacific Northwest ... Sucia Island was acquired through the efforts of state's boaters and turned over in perpetuity to the state ... a fitting tribute to him that the point be named in his honor and memory by recreational mariners."

Ev Henry Hike

Among the trails on Sucia is a beautiful hike out Ev Henry Finger to the memorial to the man who was the driving force

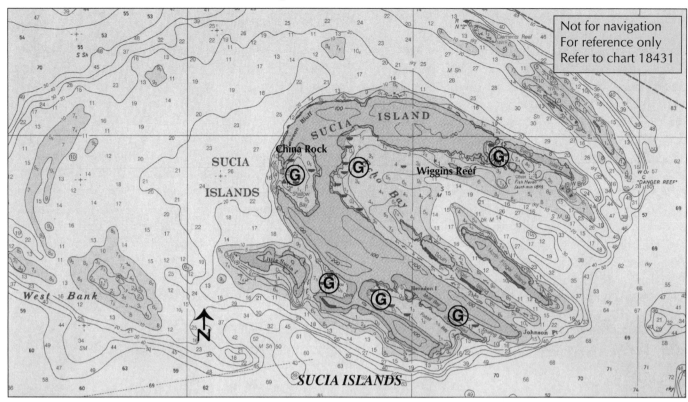

Not for navigation
For reference only
Refer to chart 18431

Fossil Bay Fossils

In the 1960s, Jo and her kids found small fossils when sifting through the sand and gravel on the beach at Fossil Bay.

Search as we may, we've not found any others in the 30 years since.

Sleepy Caretaker

The first park caretaker on Sucia was John Congdon. It was John's habit to row from Fossil Bay to the adjacent bay for an afternoon nap.

One day park officials found him asleep in his dinghy and named the cove "Snoring Bay"— or so the story goes.

Smuggler's caves at Sucia

in making Sucia accessible to the public. The trail varies in degrees of difficulty, but if we made it, anyone can. Just watch your footing. Dramatic views of Orcas Island and sometimes of surf crashing on rocks below are rewards for the hike.

Now let's look at the rest of this plum of the islands! Whenever we return to Sucia we feel like we've come home, it's that kind of place. Doesn't matter how many people are here, we always find our favorite spots away from the crowds, and how lovely it is. There's something very special about this island with its many bays, coves, beaches, forest walks and incredible beauty that keeps us returning, and causes first time visitors to be unabashedly enthusiastic about it.

Ⓖ ⚓ We consider all of the bays around Sucia as wonderful **gunkholes** and good **anchorages**. We encourage mariners to discover their own favorite spots.

Sucia Islands Marine State Park Facilities

➤ 564 acres with 77,700 feet of shoreline
➤ 48 mooring buoys:
  Fossil Bay 16; Snoring Bay 2; Echo Bay 14;
  Ewing Cove 4; Shallow Bay 8; Fox Cove 4
➤ Buoy moorage fee $5 night
➤ Two docks in Fossil Bay with mooring floats; boats under 26' $8 night; boats over 26' $11 night
➤ All buoy & moorage fees are from May 1-Sept. 30
➤ Moorage limited to 3 consecutive nights
➤ Underwater marine park in Ewing Cove
➤ Information board at Fossil Bay with maps & information about the island
➤ 55 campsites & two reservation group camps
➤ Picnic shelters, water, fireplaces, composting and pit toilets
➤ No pumpout, no power
➤ 10 miles of trails & roads, most open to hiking & bicycling
➤ Activities: camp, picnic, swim, fish, scuba dive, gunkhole, crab, dig clams, beachcomb, birdwatch, relax, enjoy

---

Our circumnavigation of Sucia begins at Fossil Bay, the hub of the park, near the ranger's station and docks. We go counter-clockwise around the island.

Fossil Bay is about 0.5 mile long and 250 yards wide, between 100 foot high, steep-sided Ev Henry Point on the west and Wiggins Head on the east. Both have charted shoals off the points, but the shoals off Ev Henry seem to test more skippers who cut too close. The bay ranges from 3 fathoms near the entrance to 1 fathom near the head.

⚓ **Anchoring** is generally good in Fossil Bay, but it is susceptible to southeasterlies. In the summer, the buoys are usually filled and boaters anchor wherever possible. In the off-season you can snag a buoy or tie at the dock. In the winter you may be, as we have been, the only boat in the bay. That's awesome!

Dock One, the east dock, is the main park dock, just below the map and information about the island. From the head of the dock, trails fan out around the island. It's a short walk to restrooms and water. Drying **Mud Bay** is east of the dock, and the head of the bay is the site of the ranger station.

Dock Two, the west dock, is near the head of Fossil Bay, and the state park boat ties up here. A concrete launch ramp next to the dock is used by park boats which load and unload on the beach. The picturesque abandoned rock quarry is near this dock. We think of it as a Greek amphitheater with sunlight and shadows creating constantly changing patterns in the hewn rock. Sinuous and flesh-colored madrona trees are everywhere, looking like a tableau in ballet.

Between the head of Fossil Bay and Fox Cove is a low grassy isthmus with picnic tables and camping areas, toilets and water faucets. Beaches are great for wading, beachcombing and brave souls to take a dip.

Snoring Bay is east of Fossil Bay, around **Wiggins Head**. There are two mooring buoys in here and a group reservation camp area is at the head of the bay.

We round **Johnson Point** with its shoals and we're about to explore big **Echo Bay,** another favorite place. Let's face it, though, they're all favorites!

Echo Bay can be entered three ways: through two narrow passages, along either side of South Finger Island, or through the wide eastern channel between North Finger Island, Ewing and Sucia islands.

The skinny route between South Finger and Sucia is picturesque because it's so narrow, about 100 yards wide at most. Depths are 2 to 7 fathoms west of South Finger.

It's a spectacular trip between **North** and **South Finger islands,** with 11 to 17 fathoms along North Finger. Both islands, privately owned, have sandstone sculptured cliffs.

Justice Island, all two acres, is off the northwest end of South Finger Island. While the west half is private, the east half of the island became part of state parks in the 1990s as a

East dock in Fossil Bay, looking southeast to Orcas

Trails from Fossil Bay

From the head of the bay, trails and roads spread over much of Sucia Island.

Follow well-marked trails to Ev Henry Finger, Johnson Point, Echo Bay, Shallow Bay, Lawson Bluff and Ewing Cove.

Wander through deep forests and along spectacular cliffs. We guarantee the 10 miles of trails on the island are marvelous.

West dock in Fossil Bay, looking northwest to Fox Cove

Enjoying the beach at Sucia

"gift." A Florida couple had purchased most of the island in the winter, unaware it was the heart of the most popular marine park in the state. The island was planned as a drug drop site, and the Coast Guard and the San Juan County Sheriff had the island under surveillance. A large amount of baled marijuana was seized when a fishing boat near the island was boarded by Coast Guard and federal drug agents. Part of the island was seized and turned over to state parks as a wildlife area with no camping. The west half of the island is still privately owned.

Wiggins Reef, charted but unnamed, is along the northern rim of Echo Bay, about 500 yards west of Ewing Cove and about 100 yards offshore, all within the 3 fathom depth curve. Watch for the submerged rock at its east end. The cliffs along here are spectacular with fascinating rock formations.

⚓ We sometimes anchor in the shelter of the Finger Islands if we can't get one of the 14 buoys in Echo, and hope for fair weather. In a southeaster, and they spring up suddenly, even in summer, there is a 25 mile fetch, and wind and waves can be pretty impressive. It's fairly common to drag in here. The chart shows a mud bottom, but we're not sure about that, given the way we've slid across it.

Old Lighthouse Reserve monument along Echo Bay

There is a reef just offshore at the head of the bay which is mostly covered at all but low tides, and then it is great place for beachcombing. The head of Echo Bay is lovely, with driftwood at the high tide line above a fairly steep gravelly beach that is tempting, and cold, to swimmers, but a good place to land skiffs.

A narrow isthmus separates Echo and Shallow bays, and it's a brief walk between the two. Restrooms, information boards, picnic tables and campgrounds are on the isthmus, serving both bays. Trails radiate south to Fossil Bay and Fox Cove, southeast to Johnson Point, east to Ewing Cove and northwest to Lawson Bluff.

A terrific hike is to Ewing Cove from the head of Echo Bay. The trail follows bluffs along the bay, up and down, along somewhat precipitous shoreline, with madronas barely managing toe-holds. Views are breathtaking to Wiggins Reef and to windswept trees on Finger Islands.

We found an old 1895 U.S. Light House Reserve monument on a bluff above the beach, just off the trail. The trail then wanders through remains of an old apple orchard. Was it the Wiggins family, or the Herndons who planted the trees, or perhaps one of the quarry workers who wanted fresh fruit?

Ewing Cove is another treat. The cove is off the east side of Echo Bay, formed where Ewing Island and Sucia create a small bay amidst the rocks. Although there's

Ewing Cove

limited space, it's a choice spot, unless it's blowing a southeaster. There are four mooring buoys in the cove. This is also an **underwater park** for scuba diving, with a sunken vessel providing an underwater reef for fish habitat.

⚓ **Anchoring** is possible with care, but we prefer to tie to a buoy here because of strong currents racing into the cove through a slot between Ewing and Sucia islands.

Underwater Park at Ewing

In the mid-1970s, state parks planned to sink the 45 foot classic yacht, *M.V. Governor John Rogers,* a former state fisheries patrol boat, to provide a fish habitat at Ewing Cove. Brothers David and Jim Dickinson of Lummi Island decided the old boat, which they knew as kids, was too good to destroy and convinced the state to trade it to them for two other vessels they would sink. They found the old 40 foot troller *Lady Alyce* in Bellingham, kept afloat by a sump pump, while serving as a home for some counter-culture folks. They traded an old gillnetter for her and set out for Sucia with *Lady* on a towline alongside. An extension cord fastened to a gas-powered generator on the deck of their boat, *Noah,* lead to a sump pump on *Lady.*

Small boats at Ewing Cove

They stopped at Lummi Island and hauled some large rocks onto *Lady Alyce,* which promptly began to sink, but was saved by the sump pump. With the pump running full tilt, *Noah* and tow arrived at Sucia, both still afloat. They shut down the generator, removed the pump and as planned, she began to fill, but all the junk wood in the boat floated up into the bow and kept her afloat. The next day the boat sank and the trunk cabin washed up on the beach, along with lots of other wood and junk.

When you dive down to explore, give thanks to the *Lady* resting serenely on the bottom, providing nice dark corners and crannies for fish to enjoy.

Ewing Island Reef Daybeacon [W Bn] diamond-shaped white dayboard on a pile worded **"Danger Reef,"** is about 250 yards off the southeast shore of Ewing Island. An underwater rocky reef extends from the daymarker west toward the Cluster Islands. Many boats have contributed bottom paint to it.

Cluster Islands are an intriguing string of islets, form the southern boundary of this cove. A great place to roam the beach, especially on a low tide. It's good for kids, with interesting tide pools and beachcombing.

Ewing Island forms the northeast side of the cove, and a wide indent on Sucia edges the west. There's a good beach here, campsites, picnic tables and restrooms, plus trails back to the head of Echo Bay.

Entering Ewing Cove, according to our friendly park ranger:

From the east, enter the cove keeping Ewing Island 50 feet to starboard.

From the south, enter from Echo Bay, keeping the last rock of the Cluster Islands 75 feet off the port side. Head for the eastern buoy. Go slowly, watching the depth sounder.

Between Ewing and Sucia is a narrow pass out into Georgia Strait. We went through the pass with the ranger in his fast, shallow-draft park boat.

"I'd advise you NOT to go through here in your sailboat!" he cautioned us. "The pass is narrow, current swift, and waves come from all directions, particularly in a northerly." He suggested the pass be used by small boats during slack water.

⚓ **UNDERWAY AGAIN,** we continue circumnavigating Sucia, going out past Ewing Island Daybeacon and head northwest outside of Ewing Island.

Danger Reef [W Or C buoy] white with orange bands and worded **"Danger Reef,"** is 0.3 mile east of Ewing Island. It marks the southeast end of **Clements Reef** and unnamed charted rocks southeast of Clements.

The *Coast Pilot* describes Clements Reef as "... 0.5 mile north of Sucia

Naming Sucia

Choo-sa-nung was the original Indian name for Sucia.

Spanish Captain Eliza named it "Isla Sucia" when he explored the area in 1791. Sucia in Spanish means "dirty" or in a nautical sense, "foul." The shore around Sucia was considered unclean and full of reefs.

Wilkes changed the name to the Percival Group in 1841 to honor John Percival, a distinguished captain in the U.S. Navy.

The name was changed back to the original Sucia, probably in 1853-54 when George Davidson and James Alden changed some geographic names back to "old" Spanish names.

Correctly pronounced, the name would be Su-CEE-ah, but common usage is Su-shah. Perhaps they should have stayed with Choo-sa-nung.

Shallow Bay swimming hole

Shallow Bay windsurfing

Foggy Crowd in Shallow Bay

There's an amazing amount of room in Shallow Bay—in fact during the intense fog on Labor Day weekend in 1997 we counted over 50 boats! They were pretty much cheek-by-jowl, and it was much too crowded, but somehow it all worked, mainly because everyone was having a good time.

The fog was so thick that even those with radar stayed. We hiked over to Echo Bay in the fog and quit counting anchored boats after we reached 100.

Carl with Miki & Jim Straughan of Lopez check out China Rock

Islands … two miles long and 0.3 mile wide." The entire reef is National Wildlife Reserve. Don't disturb the area, which is a breeding and nesting ground.

Clements Reef [R N "2"] red nun buoy, marks the reef's northwest end. Between **Clements Reef** and the north side of Sucia depths go to 30 fathoms, so there's no problem going between the reef and the island, but somehow it always feels like a lonely spot. Fishing is good out near the reef, we've even caught fish here, and that makes the trip more interesting.

We continue past forbidding 160 foot high forested bluffs with steep cliffs and no beaches, then on to Lawson Bluff. In less than 2.5 miles from Echo Bay, we've arrived at another favorite spot on Sucia, crabshell-shaped Shallow Bay.

Shallow Bay entrance is marked by two daybeacons and we enter between them, staying 30 feet inside the daymarkers.

Sucia Island Daybeacon [G "1"] square green dayboard on a pile is on the sculptured rocks on the north side of the channel, just off **Lawson Bluff.**

Sucia Island Daybeacon [R "2"] triangular red dayboard on a pile, marking a submerged rock is on the south side of the entrance.

We slip between the markers and we're in this marvelous west-facing bay. The sunsets are magnificent out across Boundary Pass. Swimming is warm, comparatively, and hiking and beachcombing are easy. The scenery is beautiful. This is a good place to gunkhole in the skiff, sail the dinghy, and do a little windsurfing. Eight buoys are in Shallow Bay.

Depths in the bay are a maximum of 1 fathom, 4 feet. Check the fathometer before tying to a buoy or anchoring, especially on low or minus tides.

Shallow Bay is amazing. It may have the best protection of any of the bays in the Sucia group, and is exposed only from southwest to northwest, which is not the prevailing wind direction. Because of the tight entrance, there's little fetch for waves.

⚓ **Anchoring** is possible in just about any part of the bay.

There are three easy beach accesses in Shallow Bay. One is the north access near China Rock or Dragon Head, where there are camping areas, picnic shelters, water, restrooms and trails. As far as we're concerned, this delightful sandy beach is the best beach for kids to play and swim.

A second beach access is the gravelly cove at the Echo-Shallow bays isthmus, where there are restrooms, a pay station, picnic shelter, bulletin board and 12 campsites. At low tide it's possible to walk between these two beaches along sculptured sandstone shores, past China Rock.

The third access is at the south side, where ghostly, silvered, dead trees stand beyond a marsh. At first glance, it looks like an inland moorage with hundreds of white masts.

The marsh is a favorite with amateur biologists. Two campsites are here and trails lead to other parts of the island.

Enormous China Rock looms against the northeastern shore, an eroded sandstone giant. Shadows engulf the huge rock as it spreads back into the woods. A dragon-like sandstone sculpture guards the rock as it might the entrance of an ancient Chinese temple. One theory for the name is that smuggled Asian laborers were hidden in the holes in the rock to escape detection from the customs and immigration authorities in the mid-1800s.

Dead trees at Shallow Bay

Smuggling & China Rock

The San Juans have a long, colorful and seamy history of smuggling. There are untold numbers of tiny coves, bights, bays and caves where smugglers could hide out. With so many islands, overhanging trees, notched-out hideaways and even large rocks, smugglers found plenty of places to conceal their fast boats. Most of these boats were faster than the government cutters used to chase them.

Smuggling was well underway with illegal booze when Americans and British troops set up camps on San Juan Island during the Pig War in the mid-1800s. That product reached its smuggling peak during Prohibition, from 1919 until it was repealed in 1933. We hear we may still find bottles of "white lightning" on the sea bottom, where they were hastily dumped before a revenuer caught the smuggling vessel.

Liquor wasn't the only commodity that was smuggled. There was also Canadian wool. There are stories of San Juan Island sheep farmers whose winning rams would "grow" several hundred pounds of wool each year when it was being declared (including that from Canadian counterparts), as opposed to the normal amount of 10 pounds of fleece or less per sheep.

China Rock "dragon"

The San Juans still have their share of smuggling. Now it's illegal drugs crossing the border, a major concern of customs officials of the U.S. and Canada.

The most heinous of all smuggling was of human beings – Chinese laborers in the late 1800s. Large numbers of Chinese had entered the country legally to work as laborers in unskilled jobs for railroads or canneries. After 300,000 Chinese were here, Congress passed the Chinese Exclusion Act of 1882 making smuggling Asians illegal and creating a profitable black market business for those who did it.

Still, there were many Chinese who wanted to enter the country to be with relatives. After they reached Canada they were willing to pay the one hundred dollars or more it cost to be put ashore in the U.S.

One of the islands' most famous smugglers, "Kelly," smuggled whenever he was out of jail, according to the diary of Orcas Islander James Frances Tulloch. "It was claimed by his friends that on one of his trips with a load of Chinese, he was being overhauled by a revenue cutter and he killed the Chinese and threw them overboard, then let himself

(Continued on next page)

Checking out hiding possibilities!

Sunset at Shallow Bay

be overhauled and examined." (*See Ch. 10 for more on Kelly*)

All this is to introduce China Rock in Shallow Bay. This sandstone giant sits on the edge of the beach and extends at least 100 feet back in the woods. There are ledges, caves and holes that snake all through the rock, which is about 40 feet high. In the water immediately in front is a dragon-like sandstone sculpture. The trees are tangled and the shadowy woods make many of the shallow caves difficult to see in the dim light. What a great place to hide contraband!

It's easy to imagine the scene: a fast little sloop maneuvers into Shallow Bay, ducks in behind the point off Lawson Bluff, and in the dark with everyone speaking in hushed tones, the Chinese are rushed onto the shallow beach. They run along the edge of the water, the smuggling skipper knowing that their footprints will be erased by the incoming tide later that night. They reach the comparative safety of the enormous rock. The smuggler urges the Chinese farther back into the forest and caves where they won't be seen and can wait to be picked up and safely taken to Seattle or other ports in the area to find jobs.

It makes for fascinating fantasies as you stand there surveying the rock. Possibly there is some semblance of truth. How else did this labyrinthine sandstone rock get its name?

Carl and the *Condor*

I reached Shallow Bay on Sucia in the middle of the night after leaving the kelp-bed mooring east of Skipjack Island, and I turned in. With her old-fashioned kedge anchor set securely in mud we had safe swinging scope for the 24 foot schooner near a small sailboat with a kerosene anchor light. There are times when presence of another vessel is reassuring.

The next morning I rowed over and met the owner of the neighboring sailboat, Fred Elsethehagen, of KVOS-TV in Bellingham. We visited for a while and then I went ashore to explore the island. This was in the early 1940s, long before Sucia became a state park. I walked across the isthmus to Echo Bay, wandering far along its north side when darkness fell. Without a flashlight I stumbled along the forested, poorly defined path back to Shallow Bay, blundering into bushes, branches and holes scarcely noticed in daylight.

I thought of a friend in a similar situation, hands outstretched, coming in contact with a huge warm, fur-bearing, heavy-breathing creature. Terror gripped his very being as he thought of bears and cougars. The creature burst forth with a thundering exclamation, MOOOO!!!—and walked away.

That didn't happen to me. I emerged from the forest, unscathed, and dinghied out to the safety of *Condor*. The next day I left Sucia and headed to

Chuckanut Bay. In fresh, broad-reaching, fisherman-stays'l weather, a predicted strong southeasterly current along the northeast shore of Orcas was just too much to pass up. I took a tempting close look at the west and east bays of Matia Island. My pending wartime enlistment (WWII) made me seriously wonder if I'd ever again set eyes on these enticing islands. Some of my friends did not.

Except for seafood, my supplies and

fresh water were getting scarce. Bellingham beckoned to me as a solution and new adventure. The passage to the south end of Lummi was memorable, with lee rail awash and a more leisurely approach to the sheltered north corner of Chuckanut Bay, a total of about 21 nautical miles as the gull flies. *(Carl & Fred were reacquainted 55 years later while researching this book. More on Fred in Ch.12. More of Condor in Ch. 11.)*

⎈ **UNDERWAY AGAIN,** we're headed out through Shallow Bay and around the bend to Fox Cove.

Fox Cove's two sides are steep cliffs over 100 feet high. The head of the cove is a sandy and muddy beach. The tide runs far out, but despite empty clam shells we didn't find any clams when we dug. Four mooring buoys are well offshore, and shallow draft boats can anchor inside the buoys, but skippers should keep an eye on low tides and the depth sounder.

We gunkholed about in Fox Cove in our skiff, watching nearby seals swimming and splashing loudly. Perplexed, we first thought it might be a way to get attention, perhaps a mating ritual. Our commercial fishing friends suggested the thrashing seals might be using their basic instinct for herding fish into their lairs for food.

Mushroom Rock

Kids love to climb the fabulous giant "mushroom" or "toadstool" rock picture below in Fox Cove. It still retains a symbol carved in its top in 1892 to mark the southwest corner of the Edith Warner stone claim.

Turns out it's more likely to be mating behavior, or perhaps both.

The south head of the cove is the same grassy isthmus which bounds the north side of Fossil Bay, formed by sediment left from the receding glacier, similar to the isthmus between Echo and Shallow bays. One U.S. Lighthouse Reserve monuments was set here in 1895 during the second of three government land surveys on the islands when surveyors laid out two reserves for lighthouses on Sucia. The Sucia group was surveyed in 1892, 1895 and 1925.

Little Sucia Island is the west boundary of Fox Cove. It is beautiful, and wooded, isolated and primitive, with driftwood covered shores, and no man-made trails. It is a wildlife refuge with eagles and no public access from January 1 to August 15 of each year. When allowed to visit the island, there are good beaches to land a small boat. No camping or fires are allowed.

There is a navigable 100 yard wide pass, 2 fathoms deep at low tide, between Sucia and Little Sucia. Charted shoals and kelp extend from both sides of the pass. Except at slack water, currents can run through the pass at a fairly good rate.

Dad & son enjoy the quiet isthmus between Fox & Fossil

Rocky shoal extends about 500 yards off the west shore of Little Sucia and occasionally traps boaters who cut too close. Continuing around the island, we can either go through the pass from Fox Cove or around the west end of Little Sucia. We cruise along Ev Henry Finger, passing the high bluffs at the southwest end the and then tuck back into Fossil Bay. We've completed the circumnavigation of delightful Sucia.

West Bank Shoal, charted but unmarked, is one mile west of Little Sucia. It is 0.6 mile long by 0.3 mile wide with only 1 fathom, 2 feet below the surface at MLLW. Boats frequently run aground here on extreme low tides, according to the Coast Guard.

Ev Henry Point

They made it for all

Clubs whose members supported Sucia becoming a state marine park are:

Anacortes Yacht Club
Anchor Bell Yacht Club
Bellingham Boat Owners Ass.
Bellingham Y.C.
Bellingham Wheel and Keel
Bremerton Boating Club
Bremerton Power Squadron
Bremerton Y.C.
Corinthian Y.C.
Day Island Y.C.
Everett Y.C.
Holiday Sailors
International Y.C.
L. & K. Cruise Club
Meydenbauer Y.C.
Olympia Outboard Ass'n.
Olympia Y.C.
Orcas Island Y.C.
Port Angeles Y.C.
Port Orchard Y.C.
Port Townsend Y.C.
Poulsbo Y.C.
Puget Sound O.B.C.C.
Quartermaster Y.C.
Queen City Y.C.
Rainier Y.C.
Sand Point Y.C.
Sea Scouts
Seattle Power Squadron
Seattle Y.C.
Shelton Y.C.
Tacoma Outboard Ass.
Tacoma Power Squadron
Tacoma Y.C.
Totem Y.C.
Tyee Y.C.
Vagabond O.B. Boating Club
Viking Yacht Club
Wave Toppers
Whidbey-Dec. Boat Club

History of the Sucia Group

The isolated coves and bays of Sucia once served the Lummi Indians in their seal hunting days. They later provided excellent hideouts in the 1800s for smugglers of illegal Chinese laborers, as well as for hiding illegally imported wool and opium. Still later, the islands played a large role in rum-running during liquor prohibition of the 1920s and 1930s, and in recent years they have figured in drug-trafficking. The smuggling goes on and on.

The first Sucia homesteader was Henry Wiggins, for whom a reef is named in Echo Bay. He moved to the Mud Bay area in 1860. The Wiggins' family raised cows, fox and sheep, as well as farming fruit trees and other crops.

A plaque along the beach between Fox Cove and Fossil Bay details fascinating information for history-hungry cruisers. A U.S. Lighthouse Reserve monument was set at this spot in 1895, when surveyors laid out two reserves for lighthouses. A second monument is at Echo Bay near Ewing Cove, a third is in the forest midway between Ewing Cove and the head of Echo Bay, and a fourth is at Johnson Point.

In 1925, surveyors extended the survey system to Sucia Island by triangulating from the north shore of Orcas Island. The surveyors' marks can be found along the bluffs, bays and small islands of Sucia. Sucia Island sandstone claims covered ridges between Fossil and Echo Bays.

From 1900 to 1909, a rock quarry operated at Fossil Bay. Large barracks and cookhouses were built on the hill above Mud Bay, where there was a dock. The quarry shut down when sandstone rock, used to pave Seattle streets, was found too soft for paving.

The Herndon family (Harnden) moved to deserted Mud Bay in 1920 to live in the old quarry workhouse. Herndon built his famous boat, the *Tulip King*, which ran excursions among the islands. In 1929, the family returned from vacation to find all their buildings had burned down, and devastated, they left the island. A stone water cistern is all that remains of their farm.

Others schemed of ways to get rich on Sucia. Someone staked a placer gold claim on the island; in 1924 a coal claim was filed, and another dreamer attempted to raise foxes. Private logging operations existed on the island sporadically from the late 1800s until 1955. Numerous tree stumps are found along the old logging roads, which today are trails and park roads.

In the early 1950s, skipper Chris Wilkinson lived on Herndon Island and renamed it "Christmas Island." (The actual name is Wilkinson Island although the name shown on navigational charts is Herndon Island.) Wilkinson took visitors out on his 50 foot ketch, the *Orcas Belle*, for romantic cruises of the San Juans. We last saw the ketch at Dockton on Vashon Island in the late 1990s.

⚓ **UNDERWAY AGAIN** to the southeast, we slip across two miles to yet another jewel on Georgia Strait, Matia Island.

MATIA ISLAND MARINE STATE PARK

Matia is 145 acres of beautiful island, a lovely gem in the outer island chain, with typical sculptured sandstone shores and pocket beaches. The island is about one mile long and 0.3 mile wide, with three coves somewhat suitable for limited anchoring. Matia is set apart as both a marine state park and part of the San Juan Islands National Wildlife Refuge.

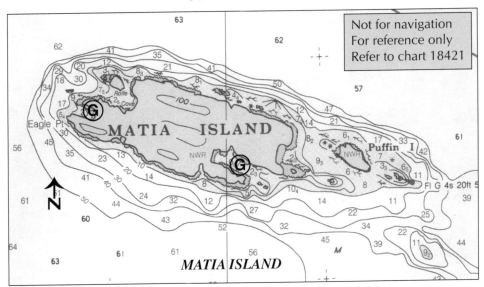

Not for navigation
For reference only
Refer to chart 18421

MATIA ISLAND

National Wildlife Refuge

The U.S. Fish and Wildlife Service, managing the refuge and wilderness areas, allows limited use of Matia with the idea that public use and wildlife preservation can be mutually beneficial. Although such use will end if animals and birds are threatened by humans, who are asked to observe all regulations.

Five acres of the island are marine state park and the rest of the island is national wildlife refuge and wilderness area. There is about one mile of hiking trails through the wilderness area. The small area on Rolfe Cove, managed by state parks, includes a 45 foot long moorage float, camping and picnic sites.

Regulations include that visitors at Matia may moor only at the docks and buoys provided, camp and picnic in the marine park, hike only the wilderness trail and be aware that no pets are allowed on the island.

We do a quick circumnavigation of Matia going clockwise, starting just outside of Rolfe Cove at the northwest end. This north shore is fraught with reefs off the steep-sided bluffs. The shoals are inside the 10 fathom depth curve which at times extends nearly 200 yards offshore. At the east end of the island the waters are also somewhat rocky and the 10 fathom depth curve extends over 0.5 mile off the east shore.

Puffin Island, a National Wildlife Refuge, is about 300 yards east of Matia. There are some tiny pocket beaches along Puffin's south shore, but as with all refuge islands going ashore is prohibited. However, watching seals, sea lions and seabirds with binoculars is encouraged.

An 8 fathom channel about 100 yards wide is charted between Matia and rocks off Puffin's west shore.

A charted shoal which bares at MLLW is off the southeast side of Matia. A charted rock is about 200 yards east of the shoal and about 200 yards south of Puffin Island.

A shallow cove, about 300 yards long is at the southeast shore. This cove must be entered with care because of rocks about 200 yards off the point along the south side of the entrance.

We continue west along the south shore which is relatively free of charted problems.

Matia Wildlife Refuge

Matia Island is one of only two islands in the San Juans which are both a marine state park and a U.S. Fish and Wildlife Service National Wildlife Refuge. (The other is Turn Island State Park near Friday Harbor.) All other refuge islands are closed to the public.

When visiting Matia and Turn islands visitors may:
* *Camp and picnic in the Marine State Parks area*
* *Hike the designated wilderness trails*
* *Moor only at the docks and buoys provided*
* *Bring binoculars and cameras to observe wildlife*

Rolfe Cove

Rolfe Cove moorage, Little Matia Island at left

Naming Matia

Matia was named "Isle de Mata" by Spaniard Francisco Eliza in his discovery cruise in 1791. Matia has several meanings in Spanish having to do with lush plant growth. It also means "no protection."

Matia is correctly pronounced Ma-TEE-ah, but is more often called May-shahh.

Kayak Safety

We kayaked from Shallow Bay around the north side of Sucia to Ewing Cove once. It was a spooky trip along the "outside" of the island, especially as the wind and waves intensified, knowing there were no good places to put in if need be.

Shortly after that we took a very instructive kayaking class on how to handle emergencies, something we should have done BEFORE that trip.

The 10 fathom depth curve is less than 100 yards offshore and two tiny bays are along here. We call the western bay Hermit's Cove.

Eagle Point is at the southwest end of the island. After rounding the point there is a 2 fathom, rocky-cliffed bay about 100 yards wide and 100 yards long. Around the next point is the main cove on Matia.

Rolfe Cove, between Matia and Little Matia Island is at the northwest corner of Matia. The state park dock and two mooring buoys are in the cove. A narrow pass of about 100 feet is between the two islands, and a strong current often runs through it.

We've anchored in Rolfe Cove briefly, but we don't consider it as a good overnight anchorage because of winds, strong currents and a rocky bottom. The beach at the head of the cove is fairly steep gravel.

There are two other bays besides Rolfe Cove where anchoring is more suitable.

⚓ **Anchoring** is possible for one boat in the tiny bay southwest of Rolfe Cove, inside Eagle Point. The boat should be stern-tied to shore for a secure anchorage.

Ⓖ This is a **delightful gunkhole.**

⚓ **Anchoring** is also possible in the bay at the southeast end of the island. Depths are also about 2 fathoms here.

Ⓖ This is a **pleasant gunkhole,** if there's no southeaster blowing.

Matia Island Marine State Park Facilities

➤ Matia is 145 acres, but the state park is only 5 acres around Rolfe Cove with 680 feet of public waterfront
➤ Two mooring buoys, $5 night
➤ One dock in Rolfe Cove with 12 foot x 60 foot mooring float
➤ Fee at floats: boats under 26' $8 night, boats over 26' $11 night
➤ Moorage limited to 3 consecutive nights; fees from May 1 through Sept. 30
➤ Bulletin board with information about the island
➤ 6 campsites, no water, composting toilet
➤ Pets must be leashed
➤ One mile trail from campground across Matia to south end cove. Trail loops back on southwest side—hikers must stay on trail
➤ Activities: camp, picnic, swim, fish, hike, gunkhole

Both Matia and it's tiny rock satellite, Little Matia, have intriguing sandstone rock formations, carved by Strait of Georgia waves which have pounded against the soft rock for centuries. The hike around Matia is enchanting. The trail leads through towering cedars, magnificent ferns and brilliant greens. Some places have no underbrush, in others it's impenetrable.

Matia Island History

The last, full-time settler on Matia was Civil War veteran Elvin Smith. He fell in love with the island and moved here in 1892 to spend the rest of his life. He built a small cabin on a tiny bay along the south shore facing Orcas. This nearly land-locked bay about 500 yards east of Eagle Point was Smith's treasure. The crescent-shaped pebble beach, flanked by rocks at the opening, provided nearly total protection and was hard to see from outside the cove. A glorious spot for a small boat.

He cleared a five acre plot inland for a garden and orchard, and stocked the island with sheep, chickens and rabbits, even though he was a vegetarian. Seafood was easy to come by, so he netted fish and cod to his heart's content.

Although called the "hermit of Matty's," he was anything but a recluse. Every Saturday he rowed his skiff 2.5 miles to Orcas Island. There he socialized with his many friends, collected his mail and did his weekly shopping. Eventually, Smith abandoned his oars for an outboard motor, although as he reached into his 80s, his trips to the mainland became less frequent.

Occasionally, old Civil War buddies would be his guests for extended periods of time.

In the stormy winter of 1920, Smith's friends on Orcas became alarmed when they hadn't seen the old man for over two months. They sent a party to the island to check on him and were shocked when they found him gaunt and haggard. The stranded old man was near starvation after the hardships of the winter. His vegetables and fruits were gone, store food depleted, and he wasn't gathering seafood. His only skiff had smashed on the rocks during a storm.

He agreed to have an old buddy stay on Matia with him for the rest of the winter of 1920 to satisfy his friends' concern. On a calm February afternoon, Smith and George Carrier loaded Smith's new boat with supplies from Orcas. They climbed aboard the heavily-laden, flat-bottom skiff, pulled the starting rope on the 2.5 horsepower outboard, and chugged out on the glassy-surfaced sea toward Matia. *(Continued on next page)*

Skookum Tom

Once upon a time a B.C. Indian named Skookum Tom hid out on Matia. He was suspected of murders in both B.C. and the U.S., and Matia made a perfect hideout. He could see when waterborne police from either country were approaching by looking towards the Strait of Georgia to the north and Rosario Strait and the shores of Orcas to the east and south. He would then head into the forest in the opposite direction from whichever group tried to track him down.

Tom eventually vanished into the shadows of history.

Hermit's Cove on Matia

Lush Matia forest

Puget Sound Interclub Assoc.

This group has been re-named "RBAW," Recreational Boaters Association of Washington, dedicated to safe boating. Boaters are encouraged to join RBAW, either as individuals or through a yacht club or marine organization, but membership in a club is not necessary.

A friend on shore watched as the small boat bobbed across gentle swells heading toward the indistinct line of a tide rip. Soon he could see nothing in the growing dusk. The putt-putt of the outboard was lost in the sounds of growing winds and waves. Worried about the two elderly men in the small open boat, the Orcas friend tried to make sure they'd arrived safely. He couldn't reach the Coast Guard, but he did contact Capt. William Herndon of Sucia, who went to Matia and searched the island and surrounding waters to no avail. There was no sign of the boat or the two men.

It wasn't until spring that Indians found part of the wrecked boat in the sand at Gray's Point near the Canadian border. Smith's outboard motor was still attached.

In the 1980s, while wandering about Matia, we found the remains of old planking, mellow with moss and decay. Nearby was a tiny orchard of cherry and pear-apple trees. We walked through chest-high China berries and bamboo, and suddenly burst out on the shores of one of the most glorious diminutive coves we had ever seen—Smith's treasure.

Puffin Island is the third island in the Matia group, about 0.2 mile off the southeast end of Matia. It's mostly steep rock about 40 feet high, with just a bit of trees and grass on top. We haven't heard of any puffins here, but there are seabirds, seals and sea lions, and it's all off-limits as it's part of the National Wildlife Refuge.

It's possible to cruise between Puffin and Matia in 8 fathoms, being aware of rocks and kelp surrounding Puffin. During this cruise binoculars bring wildlife into close view. Many seabirds, such as murres, auklets, gulls, of course, and pigeon guillemots are on Puffin. These birds lay eggs in the rocks and tend them until the chicks fly. Vessels must stay at least 200 yards away so baby birds and eggs aren't crushed or trampled when adult birds leave the nest in terror. When disturbed, bald eagles may abandon their nests, and baby seals may be drowned or crushed when adults stampede if the rock is invaded by thoughtless humans.

Puffin Island Shoal Light [Fl G 4s 20ft 5 M "19"] flashing green 4 second light 20 feet high visible 5 miles is on a square green dayboard on a house on a cylindrical structure about 300 yards east of the island. It marks the reef and kelpy shoals extending east of the island.

⎈**UNDERWAY AGAIN,** we head southeast for Clark, Barnes and the Sisters islands.

These are a cluster of islands and rocks in Georgia Strait a little over three miles southeast of Matia, about 1.3 miles off the northeast coast of Orcas and less than two miles west of Lummi Island. They appear as one island until the 0.3 mile wide channel separating them begins to open up and we can see them as individual islands.

Barnes Island is privately owned and all of Clark Island is a marine state park. The four tiny, rocky Sisters Islands southeast of Clark are part of the National Wildlife Refuge area.

Barnes Island, with 36 forested acres, is a little over 0.5 mile long and about 0.1 mile wide. A 95 foot hill is midway along the island.

Rocky shoals surround all but the south end of Barnes. Rocks and a submerged structure are charted up to 300 yards off the west shore. More rocks extend about 200 yards off the north end and also off the northeast side. In some instances the hazards are inside the 3 and 5 fathom depth curves.

Several houses are on the beautiful low bank near the north end, which is exposed to northerlies. All uplands on the island are private.

❀ **Tidelands** from extreme low tide to mean high tide are public DNR land. However, as pointed out on the quad maps, some beaches are privately leased, environmentally sensitive or otherwise not appropriate for public use.

A channel between Clark and Barnes is less than one mile long and 11 to 22 fathoms deep. It's about 0.15 to 0.2 mile wide between the 10 fathom depth curves which may be 300 yards off the islands.

CLARK ISLAND MARINE PARK

At 55 acres and almost one mile long, this skinny island is nearly twice the size of Barnes, with a hill in the center which reaches 100 feet.

This island has had the most intense use of any state marine park in recent years, according to rangers. Two DNR parks, Pelican Beach on Cypress and Obstruction Pass on Orcas, have the same problems. Clark's popularity is attributed to its proximity to Whatcom County.

Experienced kayakers from Lummi Island, Sandy Point and Ferndale, or from other islands in the San Juans often paddle to Clark to enjoy exploring and camping the island.

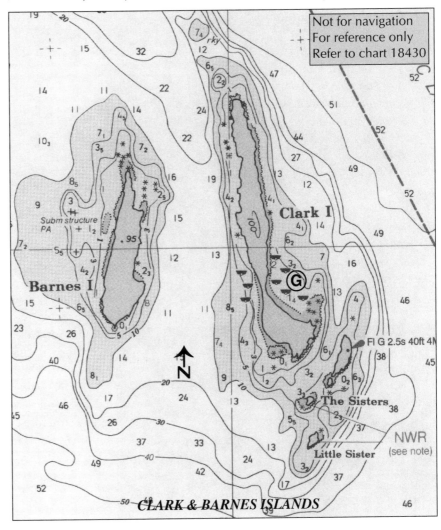

We'll circumnavigate Clark and then explore the island. We begin at the north end where tree-covered, jagged bluffs stretch around the tip and then slope down the east side forming several tiny driftwood covered pocket beaches. This shore is relatively free of hazards until near the south end. About two-thirds of the way down island, the shore angles southeast, creating a crescent-shaped cove with some of the park's mooring buoys. The shore continues southeast about 0.2 mile farther. At its tip, jagged rocks hook north about 200 yards and are visible at a 5 to 7 foot tide. A charted rocky underwater ledge and a rock barely awash at high tide extend another 200 yards. This whole reef poses a real hazard, and in rough water it's hard to see.

Sisters Islands group is less than 200 yards east of the southeast tip of Clark.

The islands cover about 8.27 acres and their main duty is to provide good nesting places for glaucous-winged gulls, cormorants and other pelagic birds. The two south islands are National Wildlife Refuges.

Sisters Island, the big sister, is pretty much barren brown rock with dry

Clark and Barnes Islands

The two islands were discovered by Juan Pantoja of the Eliza expedition in 1791.

Clark was named by the 1841 Wilkes Expedition honoring John Clark, a midshipman killed in Perry's Battle of Lake Erie.

The Sisters Islands off Clark, looking northeast

Clark Island's west shore

Rough Channel

Tying **Sea Witch** *to a mooring buoy on the west side of Clark one time, Jo rowed ashore, and a storm came in.*

From the beach, Jo watched her sailboat leap and roll with much of the keel coming out of the water, until she couldn't stand it. She rowed the dinghy through the seas out to the **Witch** *and climbed aboard to be with her.*

They were, after all, very dear friends for 30 years.

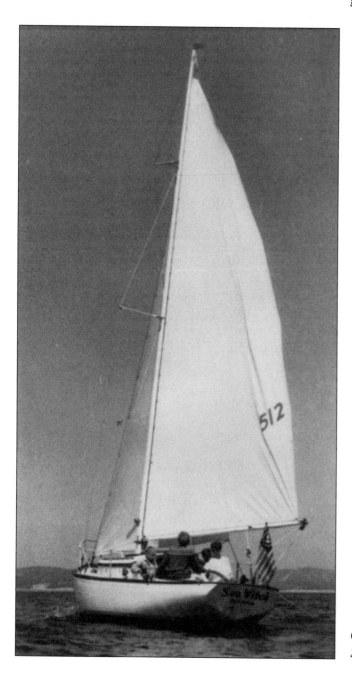

grass. There was once a single pine tree on the island, and it was promptly named Lone Tree Island. Over the years the tree faded from sight and the islet now is populated by nesting birds. A charted rock is over 100 yards north of the island, inside the 5 fathom curve.

The Sisters Light [Fl G 2.5 sec 40ft "17"] flashing green 2.5 second light 40 feet high is on a square green dayboard on a structure on the northeast tip of the largest island.

We don't try to dodge between The Sisters themselves, but it certainly can be done in a kayak or small boat.

We approach the channel between Clark and The Sisters from the north along the outside edge of Clark's 10 fathom depth curve, which ends just before we reach the islands. We continue through the 5 fathom curves while they last, and then we're in the 3 fathom curves for about 300 yards, now favoring the Sisters side. Once we're into 5 fathoms again we skirt the shallows extending about 250 yards off Clark's southwest tip.

After passing Clark's rocky southwest shore we reach the three mooring buoys at the lovely western bight, about 0.5 mile north. Clark's west shore 10 fathom depth curves are charted about 75 yards offshore at the north and south points, but as much as at 500 yards offshore near the mooring buoys.

Several charted rocks are just south of the north end of the island, inside the 5 fathom curve. We've just finished going around Clark and it's time to explore.

We head back to the east side anchorage and pick up one of the six buoys.

⚓ **Anchoring** is possible here, although it is exposed to northerlies.

Ⓖ This is a **good gunkhole** in calm weather.

Cap'n Jo & Her Loyal
Sea Witch Crew 1965

Clark Island Marine State Park Facilities

➤ 55 acres with approximately 11,292 feet of shoreline on Strait of Georgia
➤ Nine mooring buoys; six on east side, three on west side, fee $5 night
➤ Moorage limited to three consecutive nights
➤ Moorage charges May 1-Sept. 30, self-registration pay station
➤ Eight campsites on east side, two picnic sites on west side
➤ No water, two toilets
➤ Trails across the island connect east & west beaches & campsites
➤ Hiking restrictions to protect nesting wildlife
➤ Activities: beachcomb, hike, camp, picnic, birdwatch, scuba dive, swim

Clark Island's east shore

We landed our skiff, *Zade's Emir,* on the east shore's pebbled beach and walked a trail where campsites were nestled above the beach. We crossed the island to the fabulous west side, which has one of the most beautiful sandy beaches around, but swimming is still icicle cold. The sky seems incredibly blue here, with madrona trees overhanging the beaches. It is glorious. Two paths cross the island from east to west, the most southern has 12 steps to the west beach and the northern one has 23 steps, for those with access concerns.

Sitting on driftlogs, sunsets from this western shore are a spectacular treat. With the exception of these trails across the 300 yard wide island, most of Clark is heavily overgrown and the brush is almost impenetrable.

Back on the boat, tied to an east side buoy, a tide rip is offshore, boiling along, well beyond the buoys. Looking across Rosario Strait, we see Village Point and Point Migley on Lummi Island, when our boat suddenly begins a roll of about 15 degrees each way as huge waves from a passing ship reached us. This beautiful spot is less than 0.5 mile from VTS lanes in Rosario Strait, and yet feels so isolated.

At night we saw the flashing yellow 4 second light of the Vessel Traffic System buoy "C" a little over one mile southeast of Clark, and the flashing yellow 4 second light of Traffic Lane Separation Lighted Buoy CA 1.5 miles to the north.

Morning at Clark brought a brilliant pink sunrise, "Red in the morning, sailors take warning." We heard an owl hoot and saw two seals frolicking nearby. Our resident spider was still busily spinning a web inside the dodger, an Alaska ferry was heading south in Rosario on the way to Bellingham at a good clip, and a tanker was in view. Clark is not as isolated as it might seem.

Not only that, we've completed our grand arc of the "Outer Islands!"

In **Chapter 7** we explore the **Deception Pass** area and the **"Secret Seven"** islands at the north end of Skagit Bay.

We'll be on the east side of **Rosario Strait** for the rest of the book, Chapters 7 through 12, which includes Swinomish Channel, Anacortes, Guemes, Cypress, Lummi, other small islands; Bellingham, Blaine and Point Roberts— a whole new cruising experience.

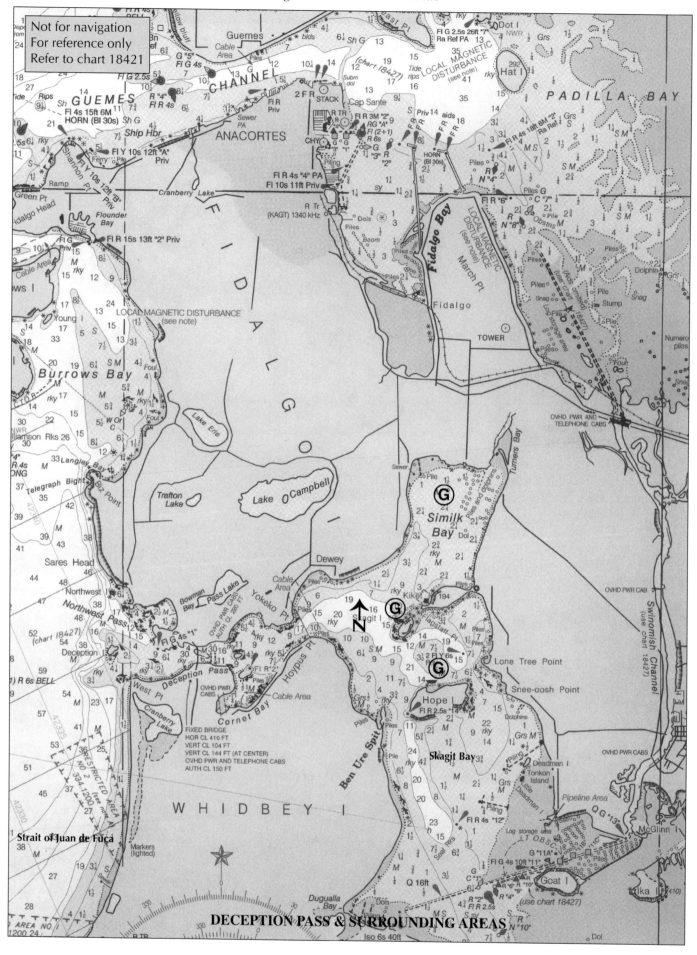

Not for navigation
For reference only
Refer to chart 18421

DECEPTION PASS & SURROUNDING AREAS

Chapter 7
INSIDE DECEPTION PASS
Including the "Secret Seven" Islands

Charts & Publications for this Chapter

Chart	Date	Title	Scale	Soundings
U.S. 18421	03/21/98	Strait of Juan de Fuca-Strait of Georgia	1:80,000	Fathoms
U.S. 18423	06/18/94	Strip Chart Bellingham to Everett inc. San Juan Islands		
		Page A	1:80,000	Fathoms
		Page B, Inset 3	1:40,000	Fathoms
		Page B, Inset 4	1:25,000	Fathoms
☆ U.S. 18427	02/21/98	Anacortes to Skagit Bay	1:25,000	Fathoms
CAN. LC 3461	12/07/94	Juan de Fuca Strait, Eastern Portion	1:80,000	Meters
CAN. LC 3462	10/23/98	Juan de Fuca Strait-Strait of Georgia	1:80,000	Meters
🐚		Wash. State DNR Quad Map—Port Townsend	1:100,000	

➥ *Compare your chart dates with those above. There may be discrepancies between chart editions.*

☆ *= Preferred chart for this chapter* 🐚 *= DNR & other public tideland information*

Deception Pass Bridge

OVERVIEW OF THE DECEPTION PASS AREA

The San Juan Islands are to the west, and we are on the east side of Rosario Strait in a marvelous scenic cruising area. Awesome Deception Pass is one of the outstanding passages in the Pacific Northwest. Immediately east of Rosario Strait, it is a two mile long, swift-running narrow pass separating the steep forested cliffs of Whidbey and Fidalgo islands at the north end of Skagit Bay.

The region is rich in history which parallels that of the San Juan Islands in many ways, and although it's not politically "in" the islands, some topography and geography are similar.

The centerpiece is a two lane bridge towering 182 feet over the canyon-like pass, with a navigable width of barely 150 feet.

Our plan is to cruise from the north end of Skagit Bay past Goat Island to Similk Bay, including the "Secret Seven Islands" in Skagit Bay. We then scout out the north end of Whidbey Island and the south end of Fidalgo Island, visit huge Deception Pass State Park which encompasses several islands in Skagit, Cornet and Bowman bays and run through daunting Deception Pass. We include facilities, historical bits, plus other information and stories as we go.

Mariners traveling north from Puget Sound through Saratoga Passage and Skagit Bay approach Deception Pass from the east side of Whidbey Island. Others coming from the north and west approach through Swinomish Channel or Rosario Strait.

Much of the area we cover in this chapter, including several islands, is part Deception Pass Park. We start with the park facili-

Deception Pass Bridge from North Beach on Whidbey, looking east

➥ **NOTE: Marine gas and diesel are available at:**
• **Deception Pass Marina** in Cornet Bay.

Public Tidelands
🐚 *Unless otherwise noted, they are state-owned. Some may be leased and posted for aquaculture or other private use. When going ashore take the Washington State Public Lands Quad Map of the Port Townsend area.*

Public tidelands in this chapter surround all the parks, and line much of Whidbey's east coast, from Polnell Point north to Ben Ure Spit.

ties, especially those of interest to mariners. Then we'll cruise to Skagit Bay and visit Skagit and Hope islands which are satellites of the park, and whose facilities are included in the following list.

Deception Pass Park Facilities
➤ 4,128 acres with 78,300 feet of saltwater shoreline
➤ 11 buoys: Bowman Bay 5, Hope Is. 4, Skagit Is. 2
➤ Buoy fees: $5 night
➤ Moorage floats, one dock each in Cornet & Bowman bays, Sharpe Cove, one fishing pier in Bowman
➤ Moorage rates: boats under 26' $8 night, over 26' $11, 3 night max
➤ Five saltwater launch ramps, Cornet Bay (4), Bowman Bay (1)
➤ Pumpout at Cornet Bay, no fee
➤ Restrooms, some with showers
➤ About 35 miles of hiking trails, 1.5 miles of interpretive trails
➤ Day-use areas at West Beach, North Beach, Cranberry Lake, Cornet Bay, Rosario, Bowman Bay (Heart Lake and Pass Lake inland), with 306 picnic sites, kitchens, picnic shelters
➤ 251 campsites, includes 5 primitive bike/walk-in sites, 3 group camp facilities for 65 persons; stoves, fireplaces
➤ 300 feet of unguarded swimming beach at Cranberry Lake
➤ Environmental Learning Center at Cornet Bay, CCC Interpretive Center at Bowman Bay, amphitheater & underwater park at Rosario Beach; state parks marine construction and maintenance headquarters at Cornet Bay
➤ Activities: fish, gunkhole, scuba dive, swim, hike, bird watch, bicycle, explore tidepools, sight-see
➤ Island Transit serves the park from Oak Harbor—call for pick up at dock
➤ Ranger: Bill Overby, 41229 State Route 20, Oak Harbor, WA 98277
➤ Tel.: 360-675-2417; toll-free line, 800-562-0990; FAX: 360-675-8991

SKAGIT BAY
☸ **We're underway** to Deception Pass from the south. We've come north through Saratoga Passage between Whidbey and Camano islands and into shoal Skagit Bay through a well-marked channel bound for Deception Pass. We are about to pass the Swinomish Channels entrance buoys to starboard. At that moment to port the two Swinomish Channel range lights in Dugualla Bay will line up to port. The next chapter is about Swinomish Channel, and we discuss these aids in more detail.

Swinomish Channel Lighted Buoy 2 [R "2" Fl R 2.5s] flashing red 2.5 second light on a red nun buoy, is at the southwest side of the channel entrance.

Swinomish Channel Buoy 1 [G C "1"] green can buoy, is at the northwest side of the entrance. We keep this buoy to starboard and continue north.

Hope Island is about 2.2 miles ahead. This part of Skagit Bay is two miles wide and shoal to the east.

Seal Rocks is a group of rocks at the edge of Skagit Bay shoals which bare at 8 feet. It's about 0.75 mile north of the channel entrance. Boats do go aground here.

Seal Rocks [Fl R 4s 20ft "12"] flashing red 4 second light 20 feet high, is on a triangular red dayboard on a tower marking the rocks.

🐚 The two tiny **Tonkon Islands** in eastern Skagit Bay are about 1.2 miles northeast of Seal Rocks, across water that ranges from 1 fathom to 0.25 fathoms deep at MLLW. They are unimproved state parks with no facilities, which means their tidelands are public. Visiting the Tonkons is best done by shallow draft boats, kayaks and canoes. We didn't visit there ourselves but friends tell us they are delightful.

They are also known as **Deadman's Island** and **Little Deadman Islands,** because Native Americans held their traditional last rites for deceased tribal members here.

While much of Skagit Bay has depths of 0.25 to 5 fathoms with a mud bottom, a surprising 6 to 22 fathom "hole," about 0.5 mile wide by .08 mile long, with a rocky bottom is off the southeast side of Hope Island.

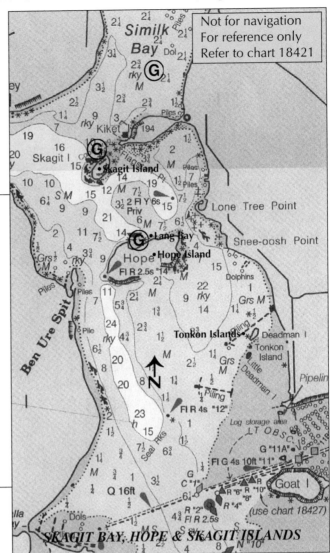

Not for navigation
For reference only
Refer to chart 18421

SKAGIT BAY, HOPE & SKAGIT ISLANDS

The Secret Seven Islands in Skagit Bay

These islands are the "best kept secrets" of the Deception Pass area. They are also considered "San Juan Islands" because the geology is the same, like glacial leftovers.

"The seven islands, starting with the two tiny Tonkon Islands midway between Goat and Hope islands, include Hope, Skagit, Kiket, Ben Ure and Strawberry islands, but not Fidalgo," according to John Aydelotte.

John, who's lived in Cornet Bay for over 20 years, is our local authority for some of the information and tales in this chapter. John and his family have explored virtually every place there is to explore in the pass area and he's a great storyteller to boot. He assures us there have been pirates and smugglers all through the region, and that there are many places to explore that most of us haven't even heard about, but soon will.

Hope Island is less than 1.5 miles north of Seal Rocks near the north end of Skagit Bay.

Hope Island Light 14 [Fl R 2.5s 4M "14"] flashing red 2.5 second light 23 feet high visible 4 miles, is on a triangular red dayboard on a tower on the west point of the island.

HOPE ISLAND MARINE STATE PARK

This delightful island park has trails, rocky bluffs, beaches and is heavily forested, reminiscent of early days before the islands were logged with cross-cut saws to provide firewood for the steamboats connecting early waterfront communities.

State park buoys and picnic areas are located along the north shore at Lang Bay, unnamed on charts, also known locally as Smuggler's Cove, like so many other places in the region. The northwest tip of the island gives the bay, actually a bight, some protection from unruly west winds blowing past the island. Mariners have discovered Hope Island, and the buoys may already be taken when you arrive.

⚓ **Anchoring** is possible east of the buoys along the north shore, or along the south shore in about 2 to 5 fathoms, mud bottom.

Ⓖ Hope Island is a good **gunkhole**—absolutely.

➡ **CAUTION:** The chart notes: "Shifting channels of one to two foot depths at mean lower low water exist across the mud flats from Skagit Bay to North Fork Skagit River."

Swing at Hope Island

Hope Island Park Facilities
➤ 166 acres with about two miles of shoreline
➤ Four mooring buoys, $5 night, 3 night max
➤ Picnic tables, campsites & fireplaces
➤ Trails across the island
➤ No water, pit toilet
➤ Activities: gunkhole, beachcomb, hike, swim, fish, crab

East shore of Hope Island

Just as we were leaving *Scherherazade* tied to a buoy so we could gunkhole around Hope Island in our skiff, *Zade's Emir,* an otter swam to the beach, snatched his breakfast and swam back out. A heron watched him as we watched them both. And then we took off going east.

Lone Tree Point—also known as **Tosi Point**—is on the east shore of Kiket Bay about 0.2 mile north of the east tip of Hope Island. It is the site of a Thousand Trails private campground. Offshore of the point is an aquaculture facility marked by flashing yellow lights.

Hope Island Fish Pen Lights [FL Y 6s A & C Priv] two flashing yellow 6 second lights, are private aids at the facility.

On a flood tide we headed south through the channel between Hope Island and the mainland. The water runs fairly fast as the tide rises quickly in shallow Skagit Bay. The channel is over 5 fathoms deep and about 50 yards wide between the 5 fathom depth curves.

We'd heard there were fossils on the east shore beaches of Hope but didn't find any. We saw a pair of eagles circling gracefully above us. Near the tombolo off the southeast end of Hope drift logs lie at 90 degree angles to the beach, which is lovely sand and gravel. We tried digging clams, but didn't find enough to bother with, so we just enjoyed the peaceful beauty of the island. The shore surrounding the rest of the island has low rocky bluffs, and the island hills reach about 154 feet in the eastern third. The roar of jet fighter planes on training flights from Whidbey Island Naval Air Station occasionally interrupts the quiet of Skagit Bay.

Pointing the way on a Hope Island trail

The hike across the island from north to south reveals wondrous things, such as gloves on sticks which point the way on scarcely distinguishable trails. Lush and verdant forests with huge cedars and firs makes us feel as if we'd arrived a century earlier. Past and present mingle in the silence of the cedar-scented shadows. Ferns, salals, blown-down trees and patches of sunlight make the hike spectacular. From the forest on the south bluff are fabulous views of Skagit Bay to Seal Rocks, Dugualla Bay, Goat Island and the two tiny Tonkons.

⎈ **UNDERWAY AGAIN,** in Skagit Bay, we take a look at **Snee-oosh Point,** about 0.5 mile east of Hope Island. The point is the site of legendary Hope Island Inn. Outstanding meals are served amid antiques, artifacts, books and other collector items, of which many are for sale. Grant Lucas has owned the inn since 1989, making major renovations over the years. Cruisers are welcome, but they need to make reservations, Tel.: 360-466-3221. The inn has two mooring buoys.

South shore of Hope Island

Hope Island Inn

This inn on the east shore of Skagit Bay facing Hope Island was built in 1939 by Fred and Vivian Fahlen. In the 1940s, **Gourmet Magazine** wrote the inn has "perhaps the finest smorgasbord in the Pacific Northwest." The restaurant provides spectacular sunsets and the scent of pure salt breezes.

Among the more than one million diners who have visited the inn are such celebrities as John Wayne, Bing Crosby, Duncan Hines, Bob Hope, Eddie Bauer and Bill Cosby.

With a good chart and depth sounder, getting to the inn is possible by going around the north end of Hope Island and through the narrow channel to Snee-oosh Point. Alternatively, tie to a buoy at Hope Island and go by skiff, or moor at the marina in LaConner and take the Rainbow Van to the inn.

A small launch ramp and public access are along the beach south of the inn.

SKAGIT ISLAND MARINE STATE PARK

Skagit Island, about 0.7 mile north of Hope Island across Kiket Bay, is a delightful tiny version of Hope, with animal trails through deep forests. The island is often used as a layover for those waiting to go through Deception Pass. Kayakers also enjoy the island, and on the north tip is a wonderful small boat camp with a sandy beach—and porcupines. A hiking trail is around the perimeter of the island.

⚓ **Anchoring** is possible off Skagit Island in 5 to 10 fathoms, mud bottom, but be aware of currents and westerly winds.

Ⓖ This beautiful little island is a good **gunkhole**, especially if you can get one of the two buoys off the northwest shore. The western buoy looks very close to the rocks, but we found there's still plenty of room.

Skagit Island Marine State Park Facilities
- ➤ 21 acres, about one mile of shoreline
- ➤ Two mooring buoys, $5 per night, 3 night max
- ➤ Picnic tables, two campsites, no water
- ➤ Hiking trails
- ➤ Activities: picnic, camp, hike, fish, scuba dive, swim, crab, dig clams, beachcomb, gunkhole

Bits of Skagit Island History

The island was the site of a shoot-out in October 1901, when Henry Ferguson, known as the "Flying Dutchman," was cornered and captured at his hideout on the island. This briefly interrupted his smuggling, piracy and burglary career.

Ferguson had been a member of Butch Cassidy's "Hole in the Wall" gang. He was hung for murder on August 28, 1913. Rumors are that the infamous Ben Ures had encampments on Skagit Island where he buried his loot. From the island the outlaw could see into both Deception Pass and Skagit Bay; it was not easy for revenuers to surprise him.

John Aydelotte, who knows the area well, said he has done metal detector searches and scans on Skagit Island.

"I like rumors and like to propagate them. I've seen ivory, opium, silver and jade from Ben Ures' stash, trinkets left by him, stuff smuggled in. These guys' stories die with them if they don't get out—this is historical."

⚙ **UNDERWAY AGAIN,** we leave Skagit Island for a quick look around Kiket Island and Similk Bay.

Kiket Island east of Skagit Island is private, part of the Swinomish Indian Reservation. The rock-infested channel between Skagit and Kiket is known as "propeller killer country," and should be left to paddle boats.

Similk Bay is the large shallow bay immediately north of Kiket Island, stretching about 1.5 miles north, less than one mile across and depths range from 1.25 to 3.75 fathoms. The north portion is filled with old piles and snags, the bay is sometimes used for log storage and there is no public access.

Old growth forests are on Skagit Bay islands

"Snee-oosh" Point

"Snee-oosh" is an Indian term meaning looking westward over the water.

Tosi Point

Lone Tree Point was called "Tosi Point" by nearby Indians. Tosi is an Indian word meaning "single tree standing."

Similk Bay

Similk, the Indian name for the bay north of Skagit and Kiket islands, means "salmon."

Kayakers in Skagit Bay

⚓ **Anchoring** is possible on the east side with a mud bottom, and on the west side, sandy and rocky bottom. Mariners should be aware of prevailing westerly winds and a plethora of crab pots in the bay. While anchoring is feasible, it somehow doesn't quite feel like a gunkhole, a subjective choice on our part.

Ben Ure Spit is 0.2 mile west of Hope Island across the channel on Whidbey. It's shoal around the spit, and the bay west of it has only 0.5 fathom of water at MLLW. The spit was formerly known as Ala or Troxell Spit until the county officially changed the name. There was once a cannery in the bay.

🐚 **Public tidelands** are along the east side of the spit, as well as along most of the eastern shore of Whidbey as far as the south shores of Dugualla Bay.

Naming Deception Pass

The survey parties of sailing explorers Peter Puget & Joseph Whidbey camped at the entrance to Deception Pass on June 8, 1792.

They had just completed their incredible seven day survey of Puget Sound. The next day they found the passage from Rosario Strait into Skagit Bay.

On June 10, Vancouver named the pass between Fidalgo and Whidbey islands Deception Pass.

The Inland Sea of Skagit Bay

This huge area of saltwater mudflats and river channels has been well explored by John Aydelotte, charismatic Cornet Bay character and his family, who also run the Vessel Assist program in the Deception Pass area. Besides saving boats and lives, John and his family have explored just about every place there is to explore in the pass area and he's a great storyteller.

His favorite stories are often about the "secret seven" islands. *(Page 173)* The myriad of marshy islands, forks and passageways of the Skagit River are fascinating, and John has explored almost all of them.

"The Skagit River puts more water into Puget Sound than any other river as it filters through sand islands, even more than the Nisqually River in South Sound. All this is accessible to small boats, canoes, kayaks and shoal draft boats. You could spend much time exploring Fir Island, and Ika Island is spectacular to circumnavigate. Plan for tides, there's not much current, but do it in a small boat. You have to pay attention to tides and depths, and there are miscellaneous pilings and snags in some places. All these little-bitty dot islands are great for canoe or kayak trips."

John talks about treasures in this area and he doesn't mean smuggler's treasures. "I would say if you're going to find treasure here you'll find quiet coves, without the hustle and bustle of Friday Harbor. So many people run by here to get to the fabulous San Juans and miss this little paradise. They go on by because of world famous Spencer Spit, Sucia, Roche Harbor, Rosario. If you're looking for three-ring activity and you want to take city living with you, go to one of those places.

John & Trish Aydelotte

"This is inland sea, it's sheltered, it's got a humungous river to gunkhole in shoal draft boats, good fishing, great crabbing. You can literally run around these islands in an hour or spend three days anchoring in the lee as the wind moves you around. You can go out any day, any weather and get some slop outside in Rosario Strait, but you can come to any one of these islands and anchor in a peaceful, calm space and have a special day—that's the treasure. There aren't a lot of people out here."

John told us another little-known secret about Skagit Bay: "Go into the bay in a kayak on a hot day and ground out on a minus tide. All of these little sand ripples that are filled with fresh or brackish water turn

into hot tubs. You can see these kayakers—can't tell their gender, but you can tell they don't have clothes on—dancing around in the hot sunlight where a minus tide has turned the tideflats into a whole series of hot tubs.

"One of the joys of my life is that I live here. Rescue responsibilities keep me close-by seven days a week, so I recreate right here. Don't be afraid to be in little boats here, because there are so many places you can't go with keel boats. Anchor your big boat in deep water and get in the small boats to see everything. Just take care and know your small boat survival skills."

DECEPTION PASS

This awesome two mile long pass offers a challenging route from the north end of Skagit Bay to Rosario Strait. It's used by mariners going between Puget Sound and the San Juan Islands, Bellingham or other points north. Our plan is to go through Deception Pass east to west, with a look at Cornet Bay on the way. Once past the bridge, we go into Bowman Bay, outside the pass.

The east entrance to the pass is between Hoypus Point on Whidbey Island and **Yokeko Point** on Fidalgo. A large, unnamed bight is west of Yokeko.

Strawberry Island is in the center of the pass, 0.5 mile east of the bridge. It is a three acre state park island, accessible only by small boat. We can go either side of Strawberry, being aware of shoals about 125 yards off the south shore. The flood current around the island sets northeast.

Ben Ure Island is 300 yards south and slightly east of Strawberry Island.

Ben Ure Island Light 2 [Fl R 4s 25ft "2"] flashing red 4 second light 25 feet high is on a triangular red dayboard on the north side of Ben Ure Island, the only navigation aid in the pass.

CORNET BAY

The bay is the site of Cornet Bay Park, part of Deception Pass State Park. Cornet Bay's north side is formed by Ben Ure Island and Goose Rock headland, and it ends in mudflats at the west.

Hoypus Point and forest at the east end of the bay are a Natural Forest Area adjacent to Cornet Bay Park. A two-lane road enters the forest east of Cornet Bay launch ramp and follows the waterfront for about one mile, the only vehicle access to the forest. The road ends at a concrete foundation for a former ferry dock where a sandy beach faces Skagit and Kiket islands, Similk and Skagit bays. It's a great place to walk, especially at low tide. A trail on the upland side leads into the beautiful old-growth forest and to 395 foot high Hoypus Hill.

The park along the south shore of Deception Pass is a favorite place for mariners to lay over while waiting for slack water through Deception Pass, or

Deception Pass ferry

Ferry service in the pass began in 1913 when Fred Finson's launch pushed or towed a barge between Yokeko and Hoypus Points. In 1920, Mrs. Berte Olson won a bid to operate a regular ferry service. Her husband Aug used his fishing boat as a launch.

*In 1922, the ferry **Deception Pass** was built, a 64 foot long, 24 foot wide, open-deck ferry which could carry cars. Ferry fare was 50 cents for cars and 10 cents for passengers. The Olsons operated the ferry until the Deception Pass Bridge was completed in 1935.*

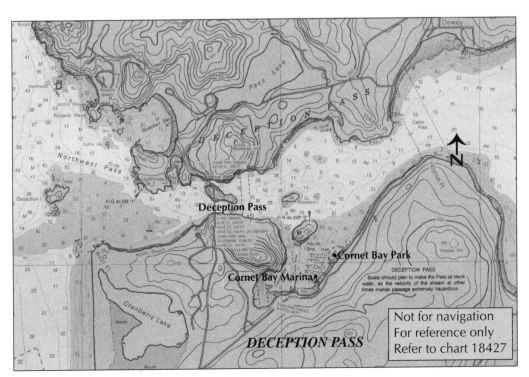

Not for navigation
For reference only
Refer to chart 18427

DECEPTION PASS

Cory Michaud and Pepper cruise Cornet Bay after sailing from Alaska with dad Tod

a place to settle in for a night or two. Except for moorage, the park is day-use only, heavily used by locals and visitors. Deception Pass Park campgrounds are in the West Point and Cranberry Lake areas on the west side of State Route 20 on Whidbey, and at Bowman Bay on Fidalgo.

Launch ramp at Cornet Bay is popular for trailered boats cruising in Skagit Bay, fishing or heading to the San Juans.

Cornet Bay's main float is an extremely popular crab fishing spot. The float swarms with those tossing out crab rings and bringing them up, filled with flailing-legged crabs who would prefer to remain in the depths. We did note several crabbers were caught by Fish and Wildlife and State Park personnel when they failed to show proper licenses or had undersize crabs. Boats have first rights to tie to floats and crabbers and fishers are to move aside for those wanting moorage, say rangers Signs are posted on pilings.

Except for those with local knowledge, mariners are discouraged from using the pass between Ben Ure and Goose Rock because of a 3 foot shoal.

⚓ **Anchoring** is possible in Cornet Bay between park floats and Ben Ure Island, or east of the floats. There is heavy boat traffic near ramps, floats and underwater utilities to Ben Ures Island.

Ⓖ This is a reasonable **gunkhole**.

Cornet Bay Park Facilities
➤ Dock with main float with 96 feet of moorage on each side
➤ Two anchored mooring floats, 96 feet of moorage each side
➤ Fees: boats under 26' $8 night, over 26' $11 night, 3 nights max
➤ Launch ramp with 4 lanes, 2 floats
➤ Launch fee $4; overnight parking $5; parking for about 70 vehicles
➤ Hand pumpout & porta-potty dump on separate float, no fee
➤ Restrooms with showers, water, picnic sites w/tables, barbecues
➤ Day use only, no camping, nearby store, children's play area

---

Community at Cornet Bay

Cornet Bay's south shore is private for about 0.6 mile from west of Cornet Bay park to the head of the bay. The area between sections of Deception Pass Park has several businesses of interest to mariners, a marina, store, boatyard, gift shop, fly fishing shop, boat service and sales.

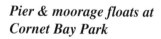

Pier & moorage floats at Cornet Bay Park

Deception Pass Marina (formerly Cornet Bay Marina) offers the only marine fuel in the area, as well as a grocery store. Dundee Woods has managed the store and marina since 1994. A marina has been here since 1963.

"Yes, we love having guests here!" said Dundee. "As you enter the marina stay in the well-marked channel and follow the markers. It's easy enough to do. The depth at zero tide is 6 feet, and that keeps some sailboaters away. We're dredged, but at a (minus) -2.45 tide some boats sit in a bit of mud," he said.

We took *Scheherazade* with her 5.5

foot draft through the channel at a low tide with no problems.

"We complement the state park, and they complement us. We've got the power, they've got the pump-outs. We've got the store, they've got showers. We have Texaco fuel, they have launch ramps," Dundee said.

Deception Pass Marina Facilities
➤ Guest moorage capacity varies, drop-ins welcome, reservations a good idea
➤ Moorage rates 70¢ foot May-Sept., 50¢ foot Oct.-April
➤ 30 amp shore power, no fee; water; check-in at store
➤ Marine fuel: diesel, gas, propane, kerosene
➤ Hours: 8 a.m.-5 p.m., longer hours in summer, open year-round
➤ Restrooms
➤ Marine supplies & chandlery, fishing gear, bait
➤ Basic store, well stocked, including ice cream, beer, wine, ice
➤ Activities & attractions: restaurant, lounge, tavern, gift shop nearby, taxi service, hike, bicycle, fish, crab, scuba dive, shellfish, gunkhole
➤ Nearby haulout, up to 36 feet; nearby boat & engine repair
➤ Showers & pumpout at state park
➤ Monitors VHF Ch. 16; CB Ch. 10; Manager, Dundee Woods, Tel.: 360-675-5411
➤ Address: 200 North Cornet Bay Rd., Oak Harbor, WA 98277

Entrance channel into Deception Pass Marina

Marine Services & Assist Boatyard, the Aydelotte family businesses for over two decades, are across the road from the marina and store. They have haulout facilities, do boat and engine repair, towing, diving and salvage, plus Vessel Assist. John and Trish are at 221 W. Cornet Bay Road, Deception Pass, WA 98277, Tel: 360-675-7900 FAX: 360-675-8896, captn@Whidbey.net.

Kathy Kranig started **E.Q. Harbor, Service & Sales** in Cornet Bay in 1985 in a building built by Clyde Willie, a classic wooden boat builder. Two men repair Honda motors full time. The business handles boats to 32 feet or 20,000 pounds maximum. Phone/FAX: 360-679-4783.

Cornet Bay Shoppe includes two business in the same handsome building, owned by Joanne and Arnie Deckwa. **Gallery & Gifts**, Joanne's shop, carries work by local artists, Cornet Bay Coffees, hand-made chocolates, northwest gourmet foods, local cookbooks, field guides, and specialty gifts. Arnie sells hand-tied flies, fishing rods, is an authorized fishing gear dealer, and tells stories in his **Fly Fishing** shop.

Growing up in Cornet Bay

Arnie's told us stories about life around Deception Pass as a kid. He grew up on Cornet Bay, moved away to seek his fortune as a country western singer and is now delighted to be "back home."

His parents ran the Cornet Bay Marina back in the 1960s, and his dad and Bill Lang were the first to net fish off West Beach. He was raised on working boats and learned at an early age how to pilot a boat safely through Deception Pass and how to fish commercially.

He said when he was young he and his friends would row over and tell sailboaters not to anchor in the shallows off Ben Ures Island. "Since we were just kids they didn't pay much attention. Next thing you knew, they'd lay over high and dry, and try to get themselves under control."

Lunch at the Island Grill

We discovered the Island Grill on State Highway 10. It's a fairly easy walk to the restaurant from Cornet Bay, about a mile or so, and worth it. They opened in 1994, serve breakfast, lunch and dinner; snacks of clams, mussels, nachos, sandwiches, fish and chips; seafood, chicken and beef dinners, beer and wine. Desserts include whiskey bread pudding and key lime pie, all with a discount for seniors.

Beautiful white deer are occasionallly seen along Cornet Bay Road *(John Aydelotte photo)*

An Island County day-use only dock is near the bayhead, with permanent moorage for small boats only, as it dries at low tide. A sign on the dock notes "No liveaboards and No night fishing." Contact Bud Rodgers, 360-675-0590.

After passing the county dock we're once again in Deception Pass Park and it continues from here west to Rosario Strait. State Highway 20 bisects the park as it runs north and south along Whidbey Island.

Goose Rock at 490 feet towers over Cornet Bay, and has several miles of well-marked, often criss-crossing trails which we hiked. Trails start north of the Environmental Learning Center, go around the perimeter of the rock and to the summit. They can also be accessed from the park's North Beach. ELC camp facilities are used by environmental and educational groups, available by reservation. We heard coyotes howl at night from Goose Rock when we were in Cornet Bay.

On the west side of Highway 20 are park offices, trails, an amphitheater, large camping area and Cranberry Lake, with a swimming beach and launch ramp on the east shore for kayaks, canoes, small sailboats and boats with electric motors, no combustion engines allowed. This part of the park is not easily accessible for mariners, although if you tie up in Cornet Bay and want to do some walking or have bicycles on board, it's a great place to visit. Views of the bridge stretching from one rock wall to another are fabulous from the North Beach area.

Popular Place

West Beach was popular with liquor smugglers during Prohibition. They would unload their boats on the beach and the liquor was loaded into trucks that were hidden in a building.

Under the cover of darkness, trucks went to the east side of the island and the liquor was again loaded onto boats for delivery to the final destination, often Seattle.

More Deception Pass History

Native Americans were the first in the area, displaced by settlers and smugglers in the mid-to late 1800s. Cornet Bay was named for a lone early settler, John Cornet. Goose Rock apparently got its name because it was a nesting place for geese.

Smugglers are the ones who made the news here. Most infamous were "Pirate" James Kelly, who gained a reputation as a renowned Puget Sound smuggler, and Ben Ures, who dabbled in "importing and exporting." Ben Ures, a Scotsman, farmed on Whidbey until his cattle were stolen by rustlers about 1860. He turned up on San Juan Island during the Pig War, running a small boat into Canadian waters, and furnishing rum to both American and British troops. He lost real estate investments in Anacortes in the panic of 1893, and then sailed his small sloop to "his" island in Deception Pass.

Ben Ure's island was transformed into a night spot, with a dance hall and saloon where rowdy partying went on nightly. Tugs, fishing boats and assorted other vessels tied up to the small island dock at night, only to be gone in the morning. Revenuers suspected illegal activities by Ben Ures, but failed to get evidence against him. After the Chinese Exclusion Act in 1882, authorities presumed he was using his fast sloop to smuggle Chinese workers from Canada into the U.S.

His Indian wife spent a great deal of time on Strawberry Island, just north of Ben Ure's Island, where she had a view of Deception Pass to east and west. When he was "away on business," the rather large woman would keep a fire going on the island. "She sits behind the fire when the patrol boats are around, and in front of the fire when it is safe to come in through the pass," as she could block the fire with her bulk, he reportedly said. This, of course, was before the days of radios or

North Beach fun

radar. We understand the firepit is still on Strawberry Island.

A Seattle newspaper ran this story on May 29, 1902:

"White-haired Benjy Ure, accused of harboring smugglers and pirates, is under arrest, formally charged with receiving stolen goods." Cases of contraband cigars, whiskey and opium were found stashed on his island. He spent five days in jail, and then lived quietly on his island where remnants of the foundation logs of his buildings remain. He died Nov. 15, 1908, on his island. At present the island is private, but we understand state parks is interested in buying part of it.

Booze smuggling during Prohibition was big business. In July 1921, Island County Sheriff William Gookins and deputies captured two rum-runners with 900 quarts of whiskey worth $9,000.

Johnny Schnarr was another well-known smuggler in the 1920s and 30s, according to John Aydelotte. In mahogany runabouts, Schnarr used Whidbey and Ship Harbor in Anacortes as drop-off points. He used big motors and light boats to outrun the revenuers.

"They'd pack whiskey in boxes wrapped in burlap in a 'daisy chain' so it wouldn't break. They'd throw a bottle out of the boat—whoops—the whole clip would empty," Aydelotte said. "They could discharge the goods when they were in the chase mode, so when revenuers caught up with them they didn't have anything. Those bottles are laying in a row on the sea bottom somewhere, filled with old, cold Scotch. So if you see this funny row of something on the bottom, go wiggle it. If the cork's good, you found some."

Looking east from Deception Pass Bridge to Strawberry Island & beyond, Pass Island in left foreground

⎈ **UNDERWAY AGAIN,** and we're about to go under the Deception Pass Bridge.

CAUTION: Tumultuous **currents** can churn through the deep pass at more than 8.5 knots on the ebb and 7.3 knots on the flood, causing whirlpools and strong eddies along the shores. Flood current flows easterly, 090°, and ebb current flows westerly, 270°.

There are direct daily predictions on Deception Pass in the *Tidal Current Tables*. Since the current velocity in the pass at times makes it prohibitive for some craft, the *Coast Pilot* and the *Tidal Current Tables* both advise negotiating the pass at slack water, which lasts approximately 20 minutes.

Park rangers suggest not proceeding through if the current is over 3.5 knots, although some fast boats run the pass in any currents. Mariners with local knowledge, experience and fast boats are often seen bucking the adverse currents while slower boats are seen running with the currents.

Westerly winds, huge swells and tide rips can make the passage dangerous to small craft. It's not unusual to have wind gusts through the pass at 45 to 50 knots during storms.

Naming Fidalgo

The island on the north side of Deception Pass was named Fidalgo in 1791 by Don Francisco Eliza for the Spanish explorer Lt. Salvador Fidalgo.

Deception Pass Bridge

The bridge has 410 feet of horizontal clearance, with actual navigable width of

Here's that bridge again

about 150 feet. Vertical clearance is 104 feet, with 144 feet at the center, high enough for even the *Lady Washington* to pass under. It is spectacular, high above us, between canyon-like rock cliffs. As the kids say, it's "totally awesome." The longer section of the span crosses from Whidbey Island to Pass Island. A shorter span reaches from Pass Island to Fidalgo over Canoe Pass.

Running Under the Bridge

Our run through the pass begins between Yokeko Point and Hoypus Point. There is no recommended anchorage along the north shore of the pass. In just 0.7 mile we reach and pass Strawberry Island.

The pass narrows and 0.3 mile ahead on the north shore is Pass Island. The bridge, often filled with tourists watching boats in the currents, is just ahead. The intricate steel girders securing the bridge to concrete pillars and Pass Island loom high above us as we head through the channel between Pass and Whidbey islands. Those in fast boats may choose the dog-leg of narrow Canoe Pass on the north side of Pass Island.

And then we're under the bridge.

Running through the pass at near slack water, it is relatively calm with only small waves. We are amazed at the stunning beauty and energy in this chasm. In less time than it takes to tell, we're through the pass and on our way out towards Rosario Strait.

Going on, **Lottie Bay**, a half-drying bay, on the north shore 0.3 mile west of the bridge, is shoal and charted with piles.

Lighthouse Point is 0.5 mile west of the bridge on the north shore, and we can pass fairly close as it's 9 fathoms deep near the cliffs.

Lighthouse Point Light 1 [Fl G 4s 6M "1"] flashing green 4 second light 60 feet high, is on a square green dayboard on a white house on a skeleton tower.

Deception Island at the west end of Deception Pass is about one mile from the bridge and 0.4 mile northwest of **West Point** on Whidbey. It is a 78 foot high rock, part of the state park, and small boats may land there with care, although currents can be strong.

Foul shallows of 2.5 to 5 fathoms are off the south and east shores of the small island. The *Coast Pilot* advises that vessels should not attempt to pass between Deception and Whidbey islands and should always stay in Northwest Pass. Shoals of less than 2 fathoms extend nearly 200 yards north of the island. Off the west side the water depth drops quickly to 16 fathoms from the offshore rocks. Some of the shoals may be marked by kelp, but we wouldn't count on it.

Northwest Pass north of **Deception Island** is the recommended channel. Least depth in the channel is 6.25 fathoms.

We can now continue northwest into Rosario Strait past Rosario Head towards the San Juans, or we can turn into Bowman Bay by passing through the channel between Reservation Head and Coffin Rock.

On the Bridge at Deception Pass

It's dramatic to stand on Deception Pass bridge and look down at the whirlpools, currents and boats going through this fantastic rock canyon.

Tugs, Kayaks & Divers

Tugs with tows often use Deception Pass to avoid rough weather west of Whidbey Island.

Some experienced kayakers practice running the pass. Experienced scuba divers find the marine life in the pass fascinating. Hazardous currents makes diving here only for extremely proficient divers.

A large carved board at the bridge tells of early Deception Pass: "To the north of this narrow passage is Fidalgo Island, so named for the Spanish explorer, Lt. Salvador Fidalgo. To the south is Whidbey Island, second largest island in the contiguous 48 states, which Vancouver, while exploring the region in 1792, at first thought to be a peninsula. Further exploration conducted by him disclosed the existence of this intricate channel. Upon the realization that he had been deceived as to the character of the large island, Vancouver gave this channel the name of Deception Passage, and in naming the island he gave it his trusted officer, Joseph Whidbey."

Megan & Robin Bailey run the little "Winsome" under Deception Pass Bridge in the 1960s

Carl and *Winsome* in Deception Pass

Single-handed aboard *Winsome*, sailing from the San Juans in the 1950s with 15-25 knot westerlies, I was in Rosario Strait approaching Northwest Pass enroute to Deception Pass. It was a bit lumpy and too late, the ebb was flowing west out of the pass.

Built in 1908, *Winsome's* 12-15, 2-cylinder Sterling engine combined with her working jib, stays'l and main storm tri'-s'l, had broad reached to, and was crossing a line drawn between Reservation Head and Deception Island. Her taffrail log recorded she had been charging along at sustained speeds of 10 knots when her engine slowed and stopped. It should be downwind all the way. The wind funneling between Deception's 300 foot pass may be enough to sail against the ever-increasing ebb. If the wind died, this 50 foot yawl, about 70 feet from bowsprit to mizzzen boom, would be dead in the water and totally without steerage to deal with the turbulent predicted 7 knot ebb current, whirlpools and back eddies in the pass.

Her 9 foot draft always demanded attention and a 2 fathom depth is charted along the Whidbey shore south of the east end of Pass Island. I used only a hand leadline. A closer look east through the pass showed it was just too iffy under these conditions to attempt sailing through without the engine. I had to find out why the engine stopped, which meant spending time below. *Winsome* would have to be self-tending, which she did very well. Anchoring in the lee of Deception Island was an option, but wind, sea condition and rocky bottom holding ground was questionable. If the engine would start and continue to run, proceeding through Deception into Cornet Bay seemed to be another option.

If I dumped the tri-s'l to reduce speed under sail, I could check out the engine. In confined sea room that would still leave the rig balanced and give greatest sail leveraging capacity along with the rudder, to deal with currents and back eddies.

Sailing before the westerly just south of Lottie Bay headed east in the pass, I lowered *Winsome's* main tris'l, changed course, and began short, close-hauled tacks to weather. Chop created by the current flowing against the wind did ineed reduce *Winsome's* speed.

Below, quickly disconnecting the gravity-fed gas line at the carburetor indicated the line was plugged. I turned off the adjacent upstream valve, ran topside and put *Winsome* about just south and east of a kelpy 2 fathom shoal on a course west of Reservation Head peninsula.

Below again, opening hatches, portlights and skylights, I opened the drain cock on the bottom of the gas tank filter. In spite of gas treatment and filter cleaning after the tank was last filled, a small amount of rusty water and gas drained into a large can—and stopped. Normally that would be followed by a brisk flow of gas.

(Continued on next page)

Deception Pass Bridge

Fantastic Deception Pass Bridge, with the highway 182 feet above the churning waters of the pass, connects the north and south rocky cliffs of the park.

It is actually two bridges: the 976 foot southern span over the pass between Whidbey Island and Pass Island, and the northern bridge, 511 foot Canoe Pass arch over Canoe Pass, between Fidalgo and Pass islands.

Construction of the 1,487 foot long bridge took just one year. It was dedicated on July 31, 1935, when more than 12,000 people watched the ribbon-cutting ceremony in the center of the bridge. More than 700 cars passed over the span in the first hour.

The bridge was built by Puget Construction Company and the Civilian Conservation Corps at a cost of $482,000. It now costs more to paint the bridge than it cost to build it.

Carl's Yawl Winsome

Topside, I saw *Winsome's* heading was not going to clear the peninsula. Again she came about and sailed toward Whidbey's West Point.

Below, the worst imagined and most dangerous fear was realized: the pipe between the valve and the tank was plugged. The valve must be unscrewed from the pipe to clear the obstruction. The valve bonnet reinstalled, the valve turned off, it was topside again to check *Winsome's* course and to plug the topside gas tank vent to help reduce the flow, should further unexpected conditions develop. Still some distance from North Beach on Whidbey's shore, there was time to shut down all electrical systems to avoid accidental electrical arcs.

About once again, we were headed for Coffin Rock. Below, when the gas tank valve was unscrewed and removed, only a few drops dripped from the 1/2-inch pipe. Flakes and debris, disturbed by days of rough sailing, easily would have passed thru a gate valve into the fuel filter bowl, but had plugged the globe valve, ultimately stopping the engine. Right now it's most important to not end it all on Coffin Rock. Taking a deep breath inside a towel curtain, wire in one hand and valve in the other, I poked the wire into the pipe and it dislodged the obstruction, followed by about a gallon of gas, mostly into the can.

I tightened the valve amidst overpowering gasoline fumes and quickly went topside into fresh air. *Winsome's* course changed again, avoiding Coffin Rock. With the plug removed from the topside gas tank vent, this problem seemed at least under control.

Winsome's course through the pass under sail and travail

Again below, the air was better, and in a few minutes the filter and its bowl were reinstalled on the valve, the gas line to the carburetor was purged of air, reconnected and checked for leaks. *Winsome* still had some sea room.

Since the radio equipment on board had not detected any ignition arcs, right or wrong, there seemed less risk to hand crank the engine with the flywheel jacking bar than using the combination generator/starter. With a little gas in the priming cup and the gravity fuel supply, the engine lit off immediately, much to my surprise.

Meanwhile, a small crowd of onlookers had gathered on the bridge above. Several shouted down to me and asked if they could help. An interesting idea.

Topside, and with the main tris'l hoisted once again, sailing be-

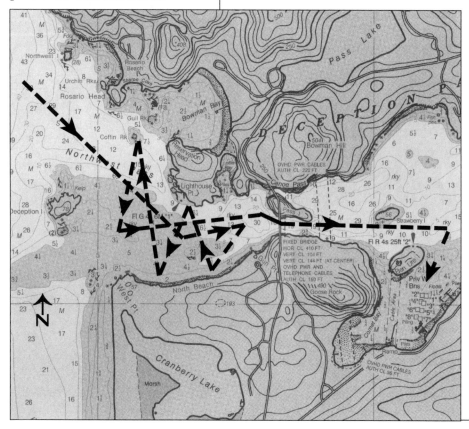

> fore the wind with engine running, *Winsome* made her way slowly through Deception's turbulence a bit before max ebb, to the cheers from those on bridge above, and we anchored in Cornet Bay.

Entering Bowman Bay, we keep outside the 5 fathom curve about 100 yards offshore, go around Reservation Head and past the charted kelp between the head and Coffin Rocks.

Coffin Rocks (such a dreadful name) shoal is just over 0.1 mile west of Reservation Head, a nasty pile of rocks.

Bowman Bay is nearly circular, about 400 yards across, with depths ranging from 1.25 to 2.5 fathoms. Campsites and picnic areas, forests, hiking trails and lovely beaches are all in this part of Deception Pass Park. The CCC (Civilian Conservation Corps) Interpretive Center depicts their work at the park in the 1930s. In the past there was a fish hatchery at Bowman Bay.

⚓ **Anchoring** is possible in Bowman Bay, mud bottom. The southeast part of the cove has the most protection from westerlies and is the shallowest.

Ⓖ Bowman Bay is a **good gunkhole**—if the weather is good.

Sharpe Cove with a dock and float, is a small bight at the northwest corner of Bowman Bay. Rocky shoals are off the north shore between the cove and bay.

Gull Rock is south of the shoals and about 100 yards northeast of Coffin Rock, and there is no navigable passage through the rocks. There is a 5.25 fathom channel about 100 yards wide between Gull and Coffin rocks. Sharpe Cove is not recommended as an anchorage because waves off Rosario Strait and these nearby rocks.

Postman
    Some scenes in the movie, "The Postman," with Kevin Costner were filmed at Rosario Beach in July 1997.

Facilities at Bowman Bay & Sharpe Cove

➤ 5 moor. buoys in Bowman Bay, fees: $5 night, 3 night max
➤ Two mooring floats southwest of pier with 96 feet of moorage
➤ Dock with floats in Sharpe Cove; floats removed in winter
➤ Fees at floats: boats under 26' $8 night, over 26' $11 night
➤ Single lane launch ramp & fishing pier in Bowman Bay
➤ Restrooms at both sites, showers
➤ Washington Water Trail camp for human-powered craft
➤ 16 campsites, kitchens, picnic shelters, water, fireplaces
➤ Children's playground
➤ Activities: gunkhole, fish, swim, dive, hike, tidepools, camp, sports fields
➤ Underwater park at Rosario Beach

Dock & floats at Sharpe Cove, looking east past rocks into Bowman Bay

Hikes and Walks

It's an easy walk along Bowman Bay Trail between Sharpe Cove and the beach at Bowman Bay. The rocks between the bay and cove are quite obvious, especially at low tide. Hiking trails along the east side of Bowman Bay lead to Lighthouse Point on Reservation Head and Canoe Pass Vista Trail overlooking Deception Pass.

A trail from **Rosario Head** goes to **Vista Point** and **Rosario Beach** with terrific views southwest of the Strait of Juan de Fuca. The south half of the beach is state park, the rest is private. A designated underwater park is here with fabulous underwater flora and fauna, and it's well used by both neophytes and experienced snorkelers and divers. The bay is small and too exposed to Rosario Strait to be recommended

Urchin Rocks
    They're off the west end of Rosario Beach and were named for the resident sea urchins on the rocks.

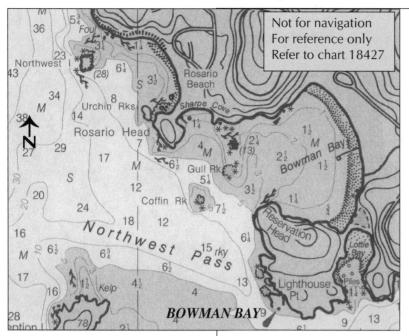

BOWMAN BAY

for overnight anchoring, although short-time anchoring in calm weather is good.

Northwest Island, park land about 0.2 mile northwest of Rosario Beach, is enjoyed by divers for its sea life. Currents are strong and divers are advised to go to the island by boat rather than swim out to it.

A Bit More Deception Pass History

For centuries Swinomish and Samish tribes camped peacefully during summer in the pass area where they fished and hunted.

Spanish explorer Don Francisco Eliza first charted the pass in 1791. Capt. George Vancouver led an exploration of the area by sea in 1792, including Puget Sound, the San Juan Islands, U.S. coastal mainland, Canada and the Strait of Georgia. He first thought Deception Pass was an inlet, but when Sailing Master Joseph Whidbey and his crew rowed and sailed their longboat through the passage, they discovered it was more than an inlet and that the land to the south was an island.

"In consequence of Mr. Whidbey's circumnavigation, I distinguished by the name of Whidbey's Island, and this northern pass, leading into Port Gardner, Deception Pass," Vancouver wrote.

In the early 1800s, the Hudson Bay Company built a trading post cabin on the north shore of Pass Lake, within the park. The Wilkes Expedition further explored the area in 1841. Later President Andrew Johnson set aside part of the region as a military reservation. Settlers "discovered" the area in the mid-1800s and moved in to farm, fish, log and build mills, as they did in most of the islands and lands around Puget Sound.

In the 1890s, the notorious and mysterious Ben Ure settled on the island of the same name in the pass, smuggling and running a dance hall and saloon.

Deception Pass Bridge was a gleam in the eyes of Whidbey Islanders long before it was built, when it first was envisioned in the 1880s by Capt. George Morse. A miniature model of the proposed bridge was exhibited at the Alaska Exposition in Seattle in 1909.

Also in 1909, a contract was let for the installation of the "Fidalgo crusher" rock quarry on the north side of Deception Pass. Rock from the quarry was used for road building. Convicts from Walla Walla Penitentiary operated the quarry from 1910 to 1914 at the Fidalgo Prison Camp.

The quarry shaft was located about 200 feet above the water. After the rock was crushed, it was sized and delivered by gravity into bins at the

Neither Vancouver nor Wilkes ship, but same era

Rosario Beach, chilly water, but lots of fun

water's edge, about 600 tons daily. Electric current was transmitted 2,000 feet from a powerhouse near a wharf on the pass to the crusher.

Using a scow loader, rock was discharged from any one of 10 discharge spouts onto scows anchored in the pass about 50 feet from the side of the bunkers. The quarry was dismantled in 1924. A large cave and a fall of rock debris are still visible north of the east end of Pass Island.

The 1,487 foot long Deception Pass Bridge was built in one year and dedicated on July 31, 1935. It is estimated now that over two million vehicles annually drive over the bridge. It was declared a National Historical Monument in 1982.

Land for Deception Pass Park was acquired in 16 acres, the first in 1925 and the last in 1992. Total cost was $7,497,628.71. A Congressional land grant in 1925 gave Washington state 1,744 acres for public park purposes. In 1933 the Civilian Conservation Corps (CCC) started development of the park.

Ko-Kwal-Alwoot, the Maiden of Deception Pass

A whimsical legend of a Samish princess is depicted on the double-sided story pole on the peninsula between Sharpe Cove and Rosario Beach. Ko-Kwal-Alwoot holds a salmon high above her head. One side of the cedar pole shows her as an Indian maiden, while the other side shows her with long flowing hair turned into kelp from her life undersea.

According to legend, as she reached into the icy waters of Deception Pass to retrieve a fallen shellfish, the hand of the Water Spirit grasped her. He assured her he wanted to enjoy her beauty, and each time they met he told her of wonderful things in the sea.

Eventually, he went to her father's house to ask to marry her. The father refused, certain his daughter would die if she lived underwater. The spirit said all seafood would disappear from the tribe unless she married him. When the seafood disappeared, Ko-Kwal-Alwoot's father finally agreed to let her marry if she would be allowed to return and visit her tribe yearly.

The tribe prospered and seafood was again plentiful. Each time she returned her people saw she was unhappy, growing barnacles on her arms and face, and they agreed to let her go to the sea forever. The waters filled with fish and the people had plenty.

Today, the guiding spirit of Ko-Kwal-Alwoot is a legacy for those who live on her shores. As currents run through Deception Pass sometimes her hair can be seen gently drifting on the water's surface— the legend lives on.

We have now reached Rosario Strait which we can cross to the San Juan Islands, or we can head north to Bellingham or beyond. We tell more about the Strait in Chapters 9, 10, and 12.

In Chapter 8, we follow the Swinomish Channel into La Conner, Padilla Bay, and reach Anacortes, which we cover in Chapter 9.

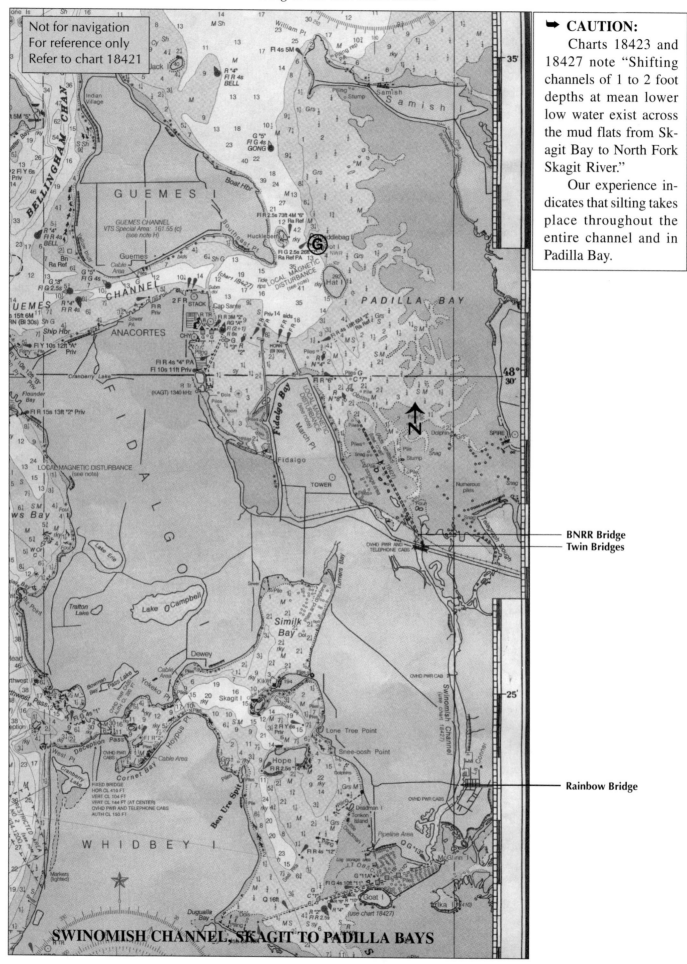

Not for navigation
For reference only
Refer to chart 18421

➡ **CAUTION:**
Charts 18423 and 18427 note "Shifting channels of 1 to 2 foot depths at mean lower low water exist across the mud flats from Skagit Bay to North Fork Skagit River."

Our experience indicates that silting takes place throughout the entire channel and in Padilla Bay.

BNRR Bridge
Twin Bridges

Rainbow Bridge

SWINOMISH CHANNEL, SKAGIT TO PADILLA BAYS

Chapter 8
SWINOMISH CHANNEL
Including La Conner & Samish Island

Charts & Publications for this Chapter

Chart	Date	Title	Scale	Soundings
U.S. 18421	03/21/98	Strait of Juan de Fuca to Strait of Georgia	1:80,000	Fathoms
U.S. 18423	06/18/94	Strip Chart Bellingham to Everett, inc. San Juan Islands		
		Page A,	1:80,000	Fathoms
		Page B, inset 3	1:40,000	Fathoms
U.S. 18424	07/12/97	Bellingham Bay	1:40,000	Fathoms
☆ U.S. 18427	02/21/98	Anacortes to Skagit Bay	1:25,000	Fathoms
	🐚	Wash. State DNR Quad Map—Bellingham	1:100,000	
	🐚	Wash. State DNR Quad Map—Port Townsend	1:100,000	

➡ *Compare your chart dates with those above. There may be discrepancies between chart editions.*
☆ *= Preferred chart for this chapter* 🐚 *= DNR & other public tideland information*

SWINOMISH CHANNEL OVERVIEW

In this chapter let's cruise north through nearly 12 mile long Swinomish Channel, visit the town of La Conner, find out about shoal Padilla Bay, take a quick look at March Point's oil refineries and huge docks, and reach Anacortes, which we explore in Chapter 9.

Many mariners going between Puget Sound and Bellingham or the San Juans prefer the calmer and scenic channel to potentially turbulent Strait of Juan de Fuca, Deception Pass or Rosario Strait. The channel is also used extensively by tugs with tows. We enter the Swinomish Channel South Entrance in Skagit Bay. Strong currents are often encountered in the channel.

The channel heads east-north-east from Skagit Bay, past Goat Island, through Hole in the Wall, makes a couple of bends to the north and passes under the Rainbow Bridge before arriving at the charming waterfront town of La Conner. This fishing village, tourist destination, writer and artist colony with a population of nearly 800, is snugged between Swinomish Channel and the quilted fields of brilliant tulips and daffodils in the Skagit Valley.

"Red Right Returning" applies to both ends of this channel. *(See page 202)*

Most of Fidalgo Island west of the channel and south of twin bridges at State Highway 20 is Swinomish Indian Reservation.

Mudflats cover a massive portion of Padilla Bay's south and east areas, extending north to Samish Island, an incredibly magnificent estuary.

➡ **NOTE: Marine gas & diesel** is available at **La Conner Landing Marine Services,** diesel & gas, at La Conner Marina.

Swinomish Channel at low tide

"The million dollar mile"
(Photo courtesy John Aydelotte)

Trish & John Aydelotte

The turn at Hole in the Wall

Advice for Cruising the Swinomish Channel

Before we head into the Swinomish Channel we'd like to share some advice we've had from John Aydelotte of Vessel Assist about cruising here. He calls the Swinomish Channel south entrance "my million dollar mile," where he rescues boaters who stray "just a tiny bit" out of the channel.

"It's fraught with reefs. Stay in the channel, it's 12 or 15 feet deep. Watch the depth sounder all the time," is John's advice.

Many of his rescue horror stories involve boats in the channel, or slightly out of it. We've strayed ever so slightly from the channel once or twice and quickly found ourselves in water too shallow for comfort—almost dusty. While thousands of boaters transit the channel each year with no problems, the few who aren't paying strict attention occasionally end up needing a rescue.

John has a reputation throughout the Skagit Bay, Swinomish Channel, Deception Pass and Rosario Strait areas for responding very quickly to a boat in distress. Newspaper articles carry prominent "saves" he's made, usually when someone's life was in danger. Several times he's saved persons who have fallen off a cliff into the frigid, turbulent waters of Deception Pass. He's made a commitment to help people, and does it with flair and humor.

"Big John" is a big guy with a beard, long braid and an infectious laugh. His wife, Trish, is tiny beside his bulk, her hair also in a long braid, a hat that says "Woman in Command," and an equally infectious laugh. They are a hard-working, intense couple. He has a mix of many rescue stories.

"I show up in my

Vessel Assist boat with lights and I'm commercial-looking. I've been talking to a boat by radio for maybe 10 to 40 minutes,easing their fears while I'm getting there. When I arrive I usually lean out the hatch and say, 'You the guys who ordered the pizza?' —sets the tone. When boats crash, a guy's ego is wounded, somebody's scared, and you've got to deal with that as much as with a crashed boat.

"I've had some women get right in my rescue boat because they just wanted to get off their own blankety-blank boat. If you look at the husband and their boat and then look at me what would you rationally do?" John erupts with laughter. "She's in a cabin with me and her husband is 300 feet back on the end of a string on their boat? I don't think so, but that's what wives do. They're **off** their boat. Of course, you've got to see me to understand the humor. Call us, we'll even tell you where to get the best pizza. The benefits of Vessel Assist far outweigh the costs."

"Bad boats, bad judgment, bad navigation, bad weather, and good whiskey, that's what crashes boats," John says.

Vessel Assist

Vessel Assist is similar to AAA on the water. It costs $70 a year to join, but if you need a tow you'll be glad you have it, as towing is $130 an hour without VA.

John Aydelotte, VA in Cornet Bay, said they deliver parts, diesel, etc., free—boaters pay only actual costs, no delivery charge.

The Aydelottes keep a 24 hour radio watch. Hail them as "Vessel Assist Whidbey," on VHF channel 16, CB channel 9 or 10, phone 360-675-7900.

⊕ UNDERWAY AGAIN, and we're heading into Swinomish Channel.

We've come north into Skagit Bay along the east side of Whidbey Island or east from Deception Pass. From either we approach Swinomish Channel's South Entrance east of Dugualla Bay. This is a dredged channel, and waters outside the channel are extremely shallow, mud flats at low tides, making it essential to stay in the channel. Distance from the entrance buoys to Hole in the Wall is about two miles. Even small boats need good navigation charts when transiting this channel.

Currents for the channel are not predicted in *Tidal Current Tables,* but we have information about them from local experts on page 193. All navigation aids for the channel are listed separately as Swinomish Channel South Entrance or North Entrance aids in the *Light List.*

South Entrance Channel Navigation Aids, starting at Dugualla Bay.
Two range lights:
Range Front Light [Q 17ft] quick white light 17 feet high is on a red dayboard with a white central stripe on a skeleton tower. It is visible all around, with a higher intensity light on the rangeline.

Range Rear Light [Iso 6s 41ft] 6 second isophase light (equal durations of light and dark) is on a red dayboard with a white central stripe, visible 4° each side of the rangeline on a 41 foot high skeleton tower. It's 1,100 yards and 252° (west) of the front range light.

Swinomish Channel buoys:
Buoy 1 [G C "1"] green can buoy is at the north side, west end of the entrance.

Lighted Buoy 2 [R "2" Fl R 2.5s] flashing red 2.5 second lighted buoy is at the south side, west end of the entrance.

South entrance red navigation aids are on the channel's south [right] side.

[R N, "4"] red nun buoy, and daybeacons **[R "6"]**, **[R "8"]** and

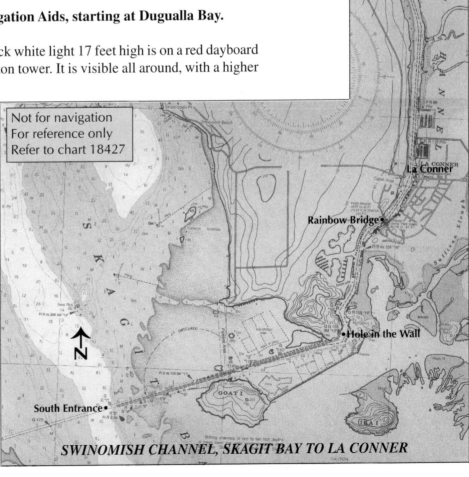

Not for navigation
For reference only
Refer to chart 18427

SWINOMISH CHANNEL, SKAGIT BAY TO LA CONNER

➡ **NOTE: "No-wake for the next three miles"** sign advises of this restriction in the Swinomish Channel through La Conner.

Port and Starboard Aids

When we transit channels such as the Swinomish we pass from one nav aid to the next, checking them off on the chart as we reach them.

However, instead of ratcheting back and forth from side to side in the book, we list the aids by port (green) and starboard (red) channel sides for ease of reading.

Apparently not all boaters are aware of the no-wake signs in the channel

Slough Adventures

Kayakers or shoal draft vessels may provide an interesting way to investigate hidden sloughs along either side of the Swinomish Channel.

Swinomish Channel

The channel was named for the Swinomish Indian Tribe.

Until 1954 it was called Swinomish Slough.

[R "10"] which are red triangle markers on piles. All three red daybeacons are 60 feet outside the channel limit, according to the *Light List*.

South entrance green navigation aids are on the channel's north [left] side.

Light 11 [Fl G 4s] flashing green 4 second light is on a square green dayboard 10 feet high on a white platform on a dolphin. It is obscured from 072° to 255°.

Green daybeacons ["11A"], ["11B"] and **["11C"]** are all square green dayboards on piles east of Goat Island.

Goat Island, part of the Skagit Wildlife Recreation Area, is about midway along this portion of the channel. This is not the time to stop and visit the island without local knowledge, but at another time in a small boat it could be an interesting trip.

From here east there are dolphins, log booms, and a 1,000 yard long rock jetty off the south side of the channel, built to help keep water and debris from Skagit River's north fork from flowing in, silting and obstructing Swinomish Channel.

[Q G 15ft 3M "13"] quick green light 15 feet high on a square green dayboard, marks the northwest side of the entrance to the dog-leg at Hole in the Wall.

Hole in the Wall, a wonderfully descriptive name for this 90° turn in the channel, is charted about 0.5 mile east of the last green daybeacon. The turn here is between beautiful, rugged, 100 foot high rocks on both sides of the channel. The bluff to the northwest is 415 feet high.

McGlinn Island is east, connected to the mainland by a dike.

Light 14 [Q R 15ft "14"] a quick red light 15 feet high on a triangular red daybeacon, is on the east shore.

North of this marker is a small channel leading to **Skagit Bay Boatyard** which does boat repair and construction, specializing in wood and aluminum, and has a 100 ton haulout and storage facility. Bob Coe, owner, phone: 360-466-4905.

[G "15"] a square green dayboard on a pile, is in a small bight on the west shore, across from the channel leading to the boatyard.

Shelter Bay is a residential development atop former marshlands along the west side of the channel. It has a large, private marina, wall-to-wall homes along the channel and a man-made bay. The entrance is about 0.4 mile north of G "15."

[Fl R 4s 15ft "16"] flashing red 4 second light 15 feet high, is on a triangular red dayboard on a dolphin on the east shore of the channel. It's just at the curve where the bright orange **Rainbow Bridge** comes into full view, framing La Conner and Mount Baker.

Vertical clearance of the bridge is 75 feet for the central 310 feet as charted.

Overhead power cables are 91 feet high.

We continue into La Conner after detailing helpful conversations with tugboat skippers, all of whom are familiar with the pitfalls in this area.

Advice From The Pros—Tugboat Skippers

We talked with several tugboat skippers from Dunlap Towing in La Conner, men who know the channel and surrounding areas extremely well. We share their information and advice—great local knowledge.

Southeast End of Swinomish Channel

"This end of the channel used to be log storage. Recently, about half the pilings were knocked out as required by the state. But those pilings were always a marker for the south side of the channel because the river delta is out there. Now at high water people see only the jetty, which basically separates the (Skagit) river from the bay, and there are no markers. When boats are headed east there are no channel markers on the south side, and just before the 90 degree turn into Hole in the Wall they get too far over toward the river. We showed the Coast Guard and they said they would put in daymarkers. Almost every summer day there's somebody stuck there on the mud," said one skipper.

Swinomish Channel Currents

Currents not predicted in *Tidal Current Tables.* One tug skipper said he could figure currents within an hour using the Berentson Bridges over the channel's north end.

Tug Swinomish in Swinomish Channel at La Conner

"There are many variables at work in the channel. It's easy to figure currents on the big tides with 12 foot high water because it's consistent. Working with it all the time you don't really think about it.

"Up until three hours after high tide the current will run to the north. Then it will turn and run toward the south through low water until about three hours after low tide on major highs and lows. That equation will work on anything from a 12 foot high tide to 3 foot plus tides to minus tides.

"As soon as we get 6 foot low tides and high tides that aren't too high, currents run real close together and will run longer one direction than the other. We call those 'north floods,' where the water's still raising but the tide's running out.

"When we start talking about high, low and north floods, that's a whole different time of year, and currents will run one direction all the way through sometimes because of rain, river water or flooding."

Dunlap Towing has a float in the central part of La Conner Marina, between "F" and "G" floats. The tugs work channel and the northwest, including Alaska. Their headquarters have always been in the slough since they started business with a couple of small tugs on the Skagit River years ago.

Tugs & Tows: Leave them plenty of room

Mariners need to be aware that tugs are towing in the vicinity. Some boaters just don't understand that tugs may be towing barges or logs, and think they can cross towlines and cables between tugs and tows. They just don't understand the two are connected.

Towlines can be as much as 1,500 feet long between the tug and tows, and tows may be several hundred feet long. Boaters should know the rules of the road and not go between a tug and its tow.

We keep a pretty good eye on what's happening. If it looks like someone's going to cross between the tug and tow we throttle back and let the towline sink down and then they cross. It can be pretty dicey. A safety line hangs off the stern, or behind or alongside the barge, just in case."

A pleasure boat ran between a tug and tow in Canada in the summer of 1999, the boat turned over and two persons were killed.

Their advice: "Whenever you see a tug, look to see if it has a tow, and don't go between them."

"A Seafarer's Guide to Swinomish Channel Marine Services" is a *pamphlet is put out by La Conner Chamber of Commerce.*

In addition to essential information they add these words:

"CAUTION: Be aware during docking that while Swinomish Channel waters may appear deceivingly calm, tricky tidal currents may still be running at several knots, presenting a challenge while maneuvering."

➡ **CAUTION: Anchoring is not recommended in the Swinomish Channel because of swift currents and lack of space.**

La Conner's Rainbow Bridge
(Photo by Sally Cox Bryan)

LA CONNER

La Conner is a boater-friendly town. The waterfront village features a National Register Historic District, including museums, antique shops, art galleries, restaurants and pubs, all within walking distance of the marina.

Pioneer City Park is located on both sides of Rainbow Bridge along the southeast shore. The forested park has an amphitheater which looks out over the channel, a covered picnic area and restrooms. Trails wind from the park to the bridge, where you can walk out and have fabulous views of the channel, the village and its surroundings, including Mount Baker, on clear days.

One-lane concrete launch ramp with a float, is at the park just north of the bridge. There is parking for about a dozen vehicles.

The west side of the bridge leads to the Swinomish Indian Reservation on Fidalgo Island where the Swinomish Tribe honors its traditions and customs. Moorage for the Swinomish Tribe fish boats is here.

La Conner, once the hub for fishing and farming, now relies heavily on tourism. The restaurants, boutiques and galleries are in charming, renovated buildings on piers and pilings along the east waterfront. It can take a day or two just to browse through the museums and galleries in La Conner, and sample the food in the many great eateries.

One of several public moorages in La Conner

Moorage is available at three public floats, at several private floats where signs indicate moorage, and at La Conner Marina near the north end of town where there is overnight moorage.

La Conner Marina has 2,400 feet of transient moorage on the outside of floats "F" (south) and "G" (north) basins of the marina. If planning to stay overnight, the best bet is to moor at the port so you can fully explore the town.

La Conner Marina South Basin Light [Fl R

11ft Priv] flashing red private light 11 feet high.

La Conner Marina North Basin Light [F R 8ft Priv] a fixed red private light 8 feet high.

Facilities at La Conner Marina, Port of Skagit County

➤ Guest moorage is at "F" & "G" floats, 2,400 feet of moorage space
➤ Moorage rates 60¢ foot
➤ Shore power, 30 amps, $2 night, water
➤ Marine fuel: diesel, gas available at La Conner Landing Marine Services at float north of "F" guest float; marine supplies, ice, pop, beer, snacks, tackle, bait, Tel.: 360-466-4478
➤ Pumpout at fuel float $5; porta-potty dump free
➤ Restrooms, showers, laundry, telephones
➤ Port office between north and south basins
➤ Monorail boat launch, two lanes, 7,500 lb. capacity, $10 each way
➤ Boater's Discount Center float, north of fuel float: propane, NOAA charts, marine supplies, hardware, books, clothing, beer, wine, pop, ice, bike & boat rentals, Tel.: 800-488-0245 or 360-466-3540
➤ 50 ton travel lift
➤ Marine canvas shop
➤ Nearby: boat & engine repair, restaurants, pubs, gift shops, book stores, post office, liquor store, bed & breakfasts, markets, bus & taxis
➤ Activities & attractions: explore town, museums, picnic areas, play areas, bicycle, Skagit Valley daffodil & tulip festival each spring
➤ Marina monitors VHF Ch. 68
➤ Marina manager: Russ Johnson
➤ Tel.: 360-466-3118/FAX 360-466-3119
➤ Address: 1120, 613 N. 2nd St., La Conner, WA 98257

➤ **NOTE: In April 1993 the midchannel controlling depth** in Swinomish Channel was 10 feet, from Skagit Bay to deep water in Padilla Bay, except for shoaling to 8 feet across the channel just south of the twin fixed Berentson highway bridges near the north end. (From *U.S. Coast Pilot*)

La Conner Marina

After facing the challenge of channel currents we're securely moored at the marina and ready to explore. But first, a bit of history to make the exploring more fun.

A Touch of Swinomish Channel History

Earliest residents of the area were Native Americans, but by early 1830s many Pacific Northwest tribes were greatly reduced by diseases early white traders and explorers introduced, and to which the Indians had no resistance.

Before settlers arrived, Indians lived along the salt water, building their permanent houses near larger creeks. They were often built of split cedar boards, constructed without nails. They had an endless supply of seafood, clams, oysters, crabs and salmon. The Swinomish fished for sustenance and there is still a tribally owned fish company on the channel.

They were excellent basket weavers, making various shapes and designs for many purposes, including backpacking, carrying water, clams or berries, for cooking and many other tasks.

In the Point Elliott Treaty of 1855, which literally forced Indians into signing away their lands for a variety of concessions 7,000 acres of land on Fidalgo Island were reserved for the Swinomish, Samish and Lower Skagit people. The Lower Skagits were from the Skagit Delta and central Whidbey; the Swinomish were from nearby small islands and northern Whidbey, and

Fidalgo Island

The island was named in 1791 by Don Francisco Eliza when he explored a group of islands he called "Isla y Archipielago (sic) de San Juan."

However, in 1841, the name was changed to Perry's Island by the Wilkes Expedition, named for Oliver Hazard Perry, a commodore in the U.S. Navy who was victorious in the Battle of Lake Erie during the War of 1812.

The name reverted to Fidalgo when Capt. Henry Kellet restored as many Spanish names to the islands as he could.

Magnus Anderson's log cabin

How La Conner was named

In Pioneer Park we found the plaque honoring Louisa Ann Conner, an educated newcomer who arrived in 1869 with her husband, John, and a wagon full of children.

He bought the post office and trading post and named the town for his 27-year-old wife, the first non-Indian woman in the area. He took her first two initials and her last name to form the town's name of La Conner.

the Samish were from Samish, Fidalgo and Guemes islands. They moved to the Swinomish Reservation on the channel's west side.

The reservation was served by Catholic priests who had been in the area since the late 1830s. Swinomish Indians built a "brush" church on the site where Saint Paul's Mission Church was built in 1867 on Reservation Road facing the channel. The church has a rare print of one of the original Catholic Ladders, used for religious instruction, called the "soul stick" by Indians.

The Skagit Flats were a maze of marshlands and shallow sloughs until after the Civil War when Michael Sullivan and Alex Underwood undertook the huge job of diking the flats to reclaim them from twice daily high tides and annual floods. The two men, along with nearby farmers, worked at low tides with hand tools and horse teams, slowly diking the area, turning it into fertile farmland over the years.

The main channel of the Swinomish Slough was originally Telegraph Slough, east of the present channel at the north end. When Swinomish was dredged and straightened, Telegraph was no longer used and blocked off.

In 1869, John Conner arrived, bought a newly established trading post and changed the name of the town from Swinomish to La Conner.

In 1873, brothers George and James Gaches purchased the store from the Conners and began shipments of hay and grains from the Swinomish flats. George and his wife Louise built the Gaches Mansion on Second Street in 1891, an elegant building that survived a 1973 fire and has changed hands several times. The restored mansion is on the National Historic Register and now houses the La Conner Quilt Museum.

La Conner Civic Garden Club across from the mansion was built about 1875 as a grange hall. At various times it served as the first federal court north of Seattle, district court for Whatcom County, first courthouse for Skagit County, a schoolhouse, church, lodge room and community center. Tillinghast Seed Company, began as a mail order firm in 1882, moved to La Conner in 1890, and is the oldest continuous business in the county.

La Conner was a hub for steamboats carrying passengers and freight from Seattle. In 1900, La Conner's population was larger than it is now, with 1,000 residents. Floods, slowdowns in the fishing industry and the Depression in the 1930s saw many leaving town in search of work. About mid-century the town became a quiet artists' and writers' colony. The waterfront village now is a popular tourist destination for those arriving by land and sea.

Today, many of La Conner's historic buildings have plaques defining their long existence which earned them a place on the National Historic Register. Explore the numerous antique shops, galleries, specialty shops and restaurants, and we'd like to share a few places we particularly enjoyed.

A huge tree section, measuring 8 to 9 feet across, is near the public restrooms on First, called One More Outhouse. Across from the tree is an old wood telephone booth.

Carl checks the rings on La Conner's gigantic tree section

Totem Pole Site is on First Street and Commercial in front of Maple Hall. The original pole, restored in 1993 by Swinomish carver Kevin Paul, depicts eagle, whale and octopus symbols.

Magnus Anderson's log cabin, one of the towns earliest buildings, is next to Town Hall. He built the cabin in 1869.

A shovel-nosed Skagit River Indian canoe, 24 feet long, is suspended in a shelter around the corner from the log cabin. These canoes were sometimes up to 50 feet long and 5 feet wide. A readerboard gives the history of canoe building and different styles of canoes, along with tales of canoe adventures, both tragic and humorous, when canoes were the only form of transportation in this region.

Firehouse Museum on First Street is not to be missed, especially if you have youngsters or delight in looking at wonderfully maintained old fire engines. Two retired engines, built in 1850 and 1930, and an 1850 horse-drawn hose cart are in the museum which is on the National Register of Historic Places. The 1850 pumper came around Cape Horn in 1861 on its way to San Francisco, before it ended up in La Conner.

Shovel-nosed river canoe

The **Quilt Museum** is in the lovely restored, 22 room **Gaches Mansion** on South Second Street. Displays include quilts from around the world, and celebrates talented northwest quilters and quilting heritage. The first floor retains its turn-of- the-century decor, exhibit space and retail gallery are on the second floor, as is a gift shop with almost everything created by local artisans. The third floor has display space and quilt frames set up for local quilters. Hours are Wed.- Sun.,11 a.m. to 5 p.m. A fee is charged, with children under 12 admitted free. Tel.: 360-466-4288

The Skagit County Historical Museum, atop the hill on Fourth Street, is another favorite with history buffs. There are permanent and changing displays of pioneer life in Skagit Valley, plus a research library. In addition, the view from the museum over fields to the east is quite dramatic.

La Conner waterfront

The north wing of the concrete block building features displays of early domestic life, including a doll collection, spinning wheels, tools, a kitchen with a Majestic wood cook stove, sewing machines, coins, glass, crystal, china, school desks, baby cribs, washtubs, hand-cranked washing machines and wringers.

There is a wonderful display of beautiful Indian artifacts which illustrates the many ways they utilized the environment without using it up. Old photos show ships cruising through the slough, fish traps near Anacortes, women in white gowns at elegant parties, men logging fir trees with an average height of 250 feet. A great look at northwest history. Tel.: 360-466-3365

Museum of Northwest Art on First Street has a goal to preserve and perpetuate "Northwest Tradition" in art, and to encourage and develop an awareness of regionalism in the arts. Known as MoNA, the museum is a reminder of the importance of art in the community. Some of the region's finest artists, including J. L. Hansen, Guy Anderson and Morris Graves are exhibited.

Skagit Valley tulip fields

Two bookstores in La Conner provide reading material for long summer evenings. O'Leary's Books and Other Comforts is at 609 First; The Next Chapter is at 721 First. The latter building, on the National Historic Register, was at various times the Nevada Saloon in 1890, a post office, Chinese laundry, tobacco shop, confectionery, real estate office, and town clothier.

If you have bicycles on board or rent them in town, you can tour miles of level roads through farmlands. Should you be lucky enough to be there during the Skagit Valley Tulip Festival each spring, you'll have a magnificent ride past glorious fields of tulips and daffodils. We're told that usually daffodils bloom in March, tulips bloom the first two weeks of April, and iris bloom during May, if Mother

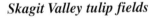

Nature cooperates.

St. Paul's Parish, a Roman Catholic Church built in 1867 on the Swinomish Indian Reservation on Fidalgo Island, is a charming white church facing the Swinomish Channel. There we met Ivan Willup Sr., his wife Agnes and son Ivan Jr. The elder Willup has worked in the tribal government senate for over a quarter century. There are about 600 members of the Swinomish Tribe, about 250 of them over 21 years of age, he said. Willup and his wife were both raised by their grandparents, and their families are here. He and his wife were baptized as Catholics and their backgrounds included some Shaker religion. Each family has a land allotment.

We were enchanted by the beauty of a circular stained glass window in the parish hall symbolizing land, sea and air around a large cross. From outside, a raven is in the upper right section, an eagle in the upper left; a deer is in the lower right, and a killer whale in the lower left, all surrounding the upper portion of the cross. Feathers run along the length of the cross. As we admired the striking colors and beautiful sections, we learned that Ivan Jr., a graduate of the Santa Fe, N.M., Art School, designed and executed the lovely glass art.

Ivan Sr. took us on a tour of the church, small and beautifully restored, with carvings by local carver Kevin Paul in the sanctuary. He showed photos and explained the church's history. He said that early parish priests slept in a lean-to at the back of the church.

A drawing of the "Sahale Stick," or Catholic Ladder, is in the church. It was created by Father Blanchet who arrived in 1855, and was used as a schematic presentation to help Indians understand Christianity.

There are many photos in the parish hall, including one in 1907 of Indian children attending a government school. As in all the government schools, the children were not allowed to speak their own language or observe any of their tribal customs. Now the youngsters in the Swinomish Tribe attend schools in La Conner. Tribal members are working to restore the cultural beliefs and language which were denied them for many years.

Willup said in 1936 a reorganization act slowly brought services of health, housing and education to tribes in the area.

"We had a government nurse and the clinic was outside the church. They took us to Tulalip for births and health problems, or we went to Cushman Hospital in Tacoma for tonsils and other operations," he said.

Willup told how the Kateri ministry, headquartered in Spokane, helped local tribes continue church services without a priest, including the Lummis, Upper Skagit, Swinomish, Tulalip, and those in Seattle and Tacoma. St. Paul's was without a permanent priest for four years. Willup praised "Father Pat" Twohy who has been at the church since 1986, helping with many projects. A beautifully carved and painted canoe, given to the priest, is suspended in the parish hall.

Fishing was once a good way to make a living, he said, but it's not too good recently, "With the help of tribal biologists it may get better." The vessel *Boxer* brings fish from Cypress Island fish farms several times weekly, using the fish processing plant leased from the

Commercial fishing docks on west Swinomish shore

tribe. He discussed annual canoe races, such as the Paddle to Seattle race. "They paddle for four hours, rest and eat, and continue," he said, usually travelling with two boats so the crews can change places.

Carver Kevin Paul

Swinomish Carver Kevin Paul

Just south of the church on the same street is the home and studio of Indian carver Kevin Paul, the progeny of several generations of talented carvers. Paul started carving in 1986, and his works are beautiful. The place smells of sweet cedar.

"My uncle was a totem carver and I would just sit and watch him and learn the meanings of what he carved. I was always knocking on his door. He gave me a knife, and I found out from other carvers it takes lots of studying." He learned about the Coast Salish style from the University of British Columbia Museum in Vancouver, from visiting villages and reserves in Canada, and studying totems.

Paul mainly works with masks, wall plaques and totems, and does commissioned work. He has taught woodcarving at La Conner High School, in the same room where he had been a student.

⚓ **UNDERWAY AGAIN,** leaving La Conner Swinomish Channel continues north then angles a bit west.

A huge log storage lot is on the channel's west side. A sandy slope along the east shore has driftwood, fields with clumps of trees, and surprisingly, no development, yet. A blocked-off channel winds northeast.

About 1.2 miles north of La Conner Marina the channel angles north.

Pipeline area crosses the channel on either side of the next two buoys.

Buoy 20 [R N "20"] red nun, is to starboard on the east side.

Buoy 19 [G C "19"] green can, is on the west side near a rock.

Overhead power cables are charted just north of GC 19, authorized 96 foot clearance at MHW. Poplar trees are near the power lines, and so is the first house since leaving La Conner. Houses now appear on both sides of the channel, more on the east shore than the west.

Light 21 [Fl G 4s 27ft "21"] flashing green 4 second light 27 feet high, is on a square green dayboard on a dolphin along the west shore, about 0.2 mile north of G19.

Buoy 22 [R N "22"] red nun buoy on the channel's east side, is the last or northernmost of the South Entrance aids, less than two miles south of the twin highway bridges. The red and green lateral navigation aids reverse sides of the channel at R N "30," 0.4 mile north of the twin State Route 20 bridges. The change is consistent with the "Red Right Returning" (from seaward) conventions because both channels open seaward.

Several houses are on the east side of the channel, and there is a small channel leading inland and a private launch ramp. Sloughs on either side of the channel are not easily visible from pleasure boats. As the east shore gains more houses the west shore has unoccupied lowlands. The channel jogs slightly northwest and the twin Berentson Bridges loom into view, about 1.1 miles north.

Overhead telephone and power cables cross the channel near the bridges. The three sets of cables are north and south of the twin and the BNRR bridges. The lowest charted authorized vertical clearance is 72 feet.

Pipeline area is charted under the channel for 400 yards south of the bridges.

Private marina on the west shore is next to the twin bridges.

Fixed twin Berentson Bridges have vertical clearances of 75 feet and horizontal clearances of 160 feet.

Channel nun buoy "20"

National Wildlife Refuge lands

Some rocks and small islands in this region are part of the National Wildlife Refuge and Wilderness Area (NWR). They are closed to the public to protect breeding colonies of seabirds, endangered and threatened species and marine mammals.

Boaters are requested to stay at least 200 yards away from these islands to avoid disturbing these animals.

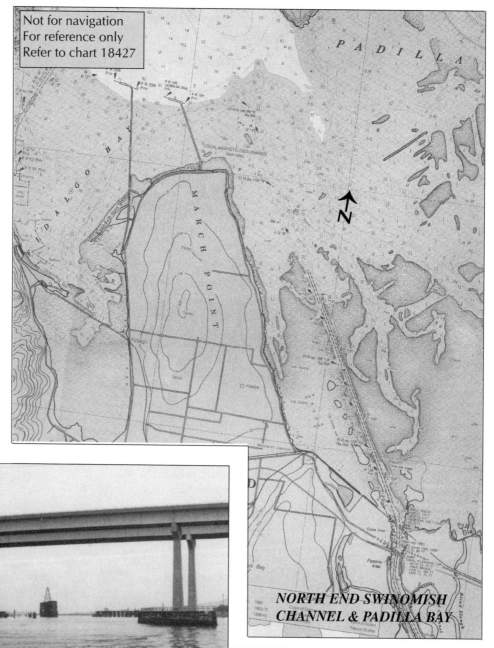

Not for navigation
For reference only
Refer to chart 18427

NORTH END SWINOMISH CHANNEL & PADILLA BAY

Looking north through Berentson Bridges over the Swinomish Channel, DNRR swing bridge is open, Padilla Bay is beyond

Before the Berentson Bridges

Before the fixed twin bridges of Highway 20 were completed in the early 1980s, vehicles and vessels were subjected to the vagaries of a lift bridge with only 14 feet of vertical clearance. Vessels, some struggling with tows or against wind or currents, would jog in the narrow confines of the channel waiting for the bridge to lift. Drivers trying to make the ferry in Anacortes or go east to Mount Vernon on the old two-lane bridge were all delayed by bridge openings

After the first of the two new bridges was completed, half the drivers had a chance to reach their destinations quickly, while boaters still had to jog in the channel waiting for the bridge. Then the second bridge was finished and all travellers now pass without delays.

Swinomish Channel Launch Ramp under the bridges is impressive, and a good place to launch a small boat.

Swinomish Channel Launch Ramp Facilities
➤ Two concrete lanes
➤ Floats and wing walls keep ramps protected from wakes
➤ Parking area for trailers and cars
➤ Handicap access
➤ Picnic tables
➤ Portable toilets
➤ No fees, but voluntary donation of at least $2 is requested
➤ Ramps are courtesy of Skagit County Parks and Recreation

Channel launch ramp under the bridges

Obstruction is charted 50 yards north of the twin bridges as "reported in 1983." Army Corps of Engineers said the obstruction was an old bridge pier remnant that was removed in 1991.

Bingo! Northwest of the bridges is the large Swinomish Tribe casino. A large marina near the casino is planned for completion "within several years," according to a tribal member.

(BNRR) Burlington Northern Railroad swing bridge is about 0.2 mile north of the twin bridges at the south edge of Padilla Bay.

Mariners should not rely solely on the following information and need to verify it because of changing conditions. They should make themselves familiar with "Draw Bridge Operation Regulations" part 117 in Ch. 1 of U.S. Coast Pilot 7 and NOAA chart #18427.

Vertical closed bridge clearance is 5 feet at MHW.

Channel is between the east and center bridge piers and has a horizontal clearance of 100 feet.

Normally open, this bridge closes twice daily Monday through Saturday for train traffic to the March Point oil refineries.

When closing or closed, vessel traffic needs to be prepared to deal with other waiting vessels, possibly tugs with tows, winds and north or south flowing currents.

Railroad swing bridge, looking south to Berentson Bridges

Bridge closing or closed signal is normally 5 short blasts which should be similarly acknowledged by vessel traffic.

Opening signal as requested or acknowledged between vessel and this bridge is one long and one short if the bridge can be opened or is opening.

Red traffic signal lights on the bridge indicate it is closing or closed. Green traffic signal lights indicate the bridge is in its normally open position.

VHF radio channel 13 contact is usually possible with this BNRR bridge tender except during its normally open period.

On opening, this bridge swings counter clockwise and clockwise when closing.

BNRR Bridge

The railroad bridge over the Swinomish Channel was put in place in 1953. It was built in Seattle and brought up on a barge through Deception Pass and the channel before it arrived in its present location.

The bridge is operated from a remote location on the east shore. He may be reached on VHF Ch. 13 if he is there.

The bridge has been damaged four times in 10 years, usually by log tows or barges which have been out of control.

Navigation Aid Change
Swinomish Channel Navigation Aids from 0.4 mile north of the BNRR Bridge change sides. The red aids are on the west (left) and the green aids are on the east (right) side of the channel.

[R N "30"] red nun buoy, the first buoy north of the BNRR bridge is the first red right returning buoy from here to the north end of the Swinomish Channel at Fidalgo Bay, a distance of 2.5 miles .

Padilla Bay is now in view on the east side. We're no longer in the canal-like channel between land masses. Instead we're in a marked channel through Padilla Bay's huge tide flats, with almost nothing but water or drying mudflats to the east.

March Point peninsula is off to the west between Padilla and Fidalgo bays,

Bay View

This was the home of Pat-Teh-Us, a Noo-Wha-Ah Indian Chief, and a signer of the Point Elliott Treaty in 1855.

The Bay View State Park site was formerly a baseball field, race track and local picnic site. Park property was aquired between 1925 and 1968. It was named for the waterfront community of Bay View.

Naming Padilla Bay

The bay was named by Narvaez and Pantojo, members of the 1791 Eliza Expedition of Spanish explorers who discovered the bay on the northeast side of Fidalgo Island.

Eliza named it for the viceroy of Mexico whose name was Senor Don Juan Vicente de Guemes Pacheco y Padilla Orcasitees y Aquayo, Conde de Revilla Gigendo.

*The bay was called **Penguin Harbor** by the Wilkes Expedition in 1841. It was named for the **Penguin**, a British ship captured by Capt. James Lawrence and the **Hornet** during the War of 1812.*

Padilla Bay was the name recognized on British Admiralty Charts of the 1850s.

Bayview boat launch, looking west across Padilla Bay to March Point

with its with tank farms and two giant oil refineries. Their stacks, frequently belching flames, steam and fumes skyward, dominate our western view on the north part of the channel. Between the channel and the point are log booms, snags, piles and sandbars, including remains of a few small wrecked boats.

Continuing north, we now list the navigation aids in the Swinomish Channel North Entrance by west (red) side and east (green) side, as we did at the South Entrance. In going through any channel we check off each aid as we pass it.

Swinomish Channel North Entrance 12 red navigation aids on the west side in order going north:

[R N "30"] [R N "28"] red nun buoys.

[Fl R 4s 15ft "26" Ra Ref] flashing red 4 second light 15 feet high is on a triangular red daymark on a pile with a radar reflector.

[R N "22"] [R N "20"] red nun buoys.

[Fl R 4s 18ft "18" Ra Ref] flashing red 4 second light 18 feet high on a triangular red dayboard on a dolphin with a radar reflector is next.

Wreck symbol is charted between "20" and "18" on the west side of the channel but we didn't find it.

[R N "14"], [R N "12"], [R N "8"] red nun buoys.

[Fl R 6s 15 ft "6"] flashing red 6 second light 15 feet high on a triangular red dayboard on a dolphin, is almost opposite the north end of March Point. Once we are north of "6" we can escape to the east a bit for deeper water off March Point.

[R N "4"] red nun buoy.

[Fl R 4s 18ft 6M "2" Ra Ref] flashing red 4 second light 18 feet high visible 6 miles with a radar reflector, is on a triangular red dayboard on a dolphin, the last marker. Or the first channel marker for mariners heading south.

Swinomish Channel North Entrance 4 green navigation aids on the east side in order going north:

[G C "29"], [G C "23"], ["17"], ["13"], ["7"] green can buoys. We note that "7" is on the edge of the 1 fathom curve and marks the location of two charted obstructions to the east.

Lo and behold, we're at the north end of the channel and ready to head west or north. But first, let's explore Padilla Bay a bit …

Padilla Bay National Estuarine Sanctuary

We pass Padilla Bay every time we go through the Swinomish Channel, regarding it as a place to avoid. It's way too shallow for our boat, it's muddy and it's nothing we want to deal with. We pass by, happy we haven't hit the bay's bottom accidentally by veering out of the channel. We don't want to leave keel tracks in Padilla Bay.

The bay is, however, a remarkable 14,000 acre National Estuarine Sanctuary from the south end north to Samish Island. The bay is over six miles long and almost three miles wide. It's a huge shallow shelf, with depths seldom over one fathom. It includes Saddlebag Island State Park, Dot Island, NWR, and nearby Hat Island which is a Natural Resources Conservation Area.

When freshwater rivers enter salt water an estuary is created, resulting in natural nurseries for fish, crabs and clams, as well as resting areas for migratory ducks and sea birds.

The Breazeale Padilla Bay Interpretive Center north of Bay View was established in 1982 for estuarine education and research when a grand 87-year-old lady, Edna Breazeale, donated the 64 acre family farm on the bay to research. She had lived there since 1901. The center has permanent displays, lectures and walks, an observation deck and beach access where it's possible to view migratory waterfowl and hundreds of other birds and wildlife.

The interpretive center prevented some ridiculous ideas of private exploitation of the "useless" bay, including building a nuclear plant, a log export complex, magnesium smelter, concrete plant, oyster-ranching, more oil refineries and a "Venice" community with 90 miles of artificial peninsulas where 30,000 souls could live with their boats tied up by their front doors.

Padilla's eelgrass beds are vital to wintering black brants, seals, herons, a large variety of seashore plants and animal life. An unmarked charted channel less than 2.5 fathoms deep angles southeast through mud flats to Bay View from the north part of Swinomish Channel. Piles are in the channel and the rest of the bay.

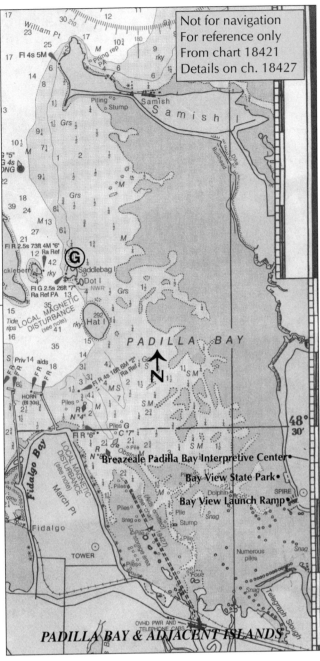

Bay View is a small community about two miles north of Highway 20 along the southeast shore of Padilla Bay. A charted spire is the town's church, and the only business in town is the **Rozema Boat Works**, which has been here since 1955. They do aluminum and stainless boat design and fabrication. Clarence Rozema, CEO, Tel.: 360-757-6004

Bay View Boat Launch, a high-tide only, single lane ramp, is adjacent to the boat works. This Department of Fish and Wildlife ramp into shallow Padilla Bay is used by small, shallow draft boats. Some boats use the unmarked channel out of the bay as mentioned.

Upland trails and the 2.5 mile long Padilla Bay Trail for hiking or biking along the southeast shore from Bay View to Little Indian Slough provides more interesting vistas. The trail has interpretive signs, natural history, benches and picnic tables. Parking is in Bay View.

BAY VIEW STATE PARK

The park is of particular interest to those who camp, hike the shoreline, visit the interpretive center or launch kayaks at high tide to paddle in Padilla Bay and the sloughs to the south. The park is about 0.5 mile north of Bay View launch ramp.

The low bank park shoreline is gravel and sand, except at the north border which is large rocks. While there may be good clamming in the bay, it is occasionally posted for contaminated shellfish. The picnic area along the shore is almost treeless and flat. Campsites are inland from the beach on the east side of the road in the forest.

Picnicking at Bay View Park

Facilities at Bay View State Park
➤ 25 acres with 1,285 feet of shoreline
➤ No moorage or facilities; hand launch kayaks, canoes at high tide
➤ Picnic sites, 67 campsites, trailer hookups
➤ One comfort station, five vault toilets
➤ Activities & attractions: Padilla Bay Interpretive Center 0.5 mile north of park, kayak, swim, camp, hike, bicycle

Saddlebag Island
The island was originally identified as one of the "Porpoise Rocks" by the Wilkes Expedition in 1841. The U.S. Coast and Geodetic Survey shows the present name possibly derived from the island's shape.

SADDLEBAG, DOT, HAT & HUCKLEBERRY ISLANDS

These state-owned islands off the west shore of Padilla Bay seem to sit in a watery never-never land. Saddlebag, Dot and Hat are about two miles northeast of Anacortes and just over 0.6 mile east of Guemes Island. Huckleberry Island is nearby, less than 0.2 mile east of Guemes.

The eastern shores of Saddlebag, Dot and Hat sit precariously on the edge of Padilla Bay's extremely shoal waters while their western shorelines are near or on the bay's 5 fathom depth curve. Within short distances depths plunge sharply to 14 or 15 fathoms off the west shores of Hat and Saddlebag, with only 1 to 5 feet off the east side.

There are spots east of the islands with unexpected depths. Dot Island has charted depths of 3.5 fathoms on the edge of its south shore, with intermittent depths of 1 to 3 fathoms extending about 1,400 yards east. All this is constricted by a 0.5 fathom shoal just south of Dot, a challenging area. These shoal eastern waters can be explored in a kayak or other shoal draft boat.

Saddlebag Island State Park Recreation Area includes adjacent Dot Rock, and the two almost meet at extreme low tides. Tiny Dot, about 200 yards all around, is a National Wildlife Refuge, a bird nesting area and animal refuge. Visitors may not go ashore and boats must stay 200 yards off.

The outline of Saddlebag is almost like a miniature of Jones Island in the San Juans, with bays indenting the north and south sides, a low saddle across the center and a bit more height on the rocky headlands of the east and west sides. A 77 foot hill is above the southwest shore. The island is about 0.2 mile long by 0.2 mile wide. in places.

Saddlebag, left, & Dot islands
(Photo by Sally Cox Bryan)

When stopping at Saddlebag, enter either the north or south cove from the west. The east is too shallow to even consider, except in a shoal draft boat or kayak.

Rock awash charted off Saddlebag's southeast shore impares passage between Dot and Saddlebag, except for small craft.

⚓ **Anchoring at Saddlebag** is necessary as there are no buoys, but there is good mud holding ground. The shelf at the north cove is the most popular anchorage, in 1.5 to 2.5 fathoms. Anchoring is all right in the shallower south cove, however the eelgrass bottom is slippery for some anchors and the hook needs to be well set. Be aware of winds and currents.

Ⓖ A good **gunkhole** in fair weather.

Facilities at Saddlebag Island Marine State Park

➤ 23.7 acres, including adjacent Dot Rock, with 6,750 feet of waterfront
➤ Anchor in north or south coves, no buoys or floats
➤ Five campsites with picnic tables & fire pits
➤ No water, vault toilet
➤ One mile of island trails
➤ Two Washington Water Trails campsites
➤ Activities: camp, hike, picnic, fish, crab, swim, scuba dive, gunkhole, peace & quiet

➡ **NOTE:** It's time to change charts from 18427 to 18424 as we head north fromSaddlebag Island.

Saddlebag Island Light 7 [Fl G 2.5s 26ft Ra Ref PA] flashing green 2.5 second light 26 feet high with a radar reflector, is on a square green dayboard on a platform on the west rocky headland of the island. The chart shows the light is in an "approximate position."

Hat Island, about 0.5 mile long and 0.35 mile wide, with a 292 foot hill near the center, is a Natural Conservation area. There are no facilities, and visitors are discouraged from going ashore because of wildlife protection. Almost the entire shore along the east side has less than 0.5 fathom of water at low tide.

Hat Island

Huckleberry Island Marine State Park is an undeveloped, 10 acre jewel with 2,900 feet of shoreline on Padilla Bay. The island is 0.3 mile west of Saddlebag and 0.2 mile east of Guemes. Because the shoreline is so steep, getting ashore is difficult, except at a shelf on the southwest side. This is a good place for kayaks and small boats, scuba divers enjoy it, but rocks make it a challenging place for larger boats to anchor.

Huckleberry Island
(Photo by Sally Cox Bryan)

Huckleberry Island Light 6 [Fl R 2.5s 73ft 4M "6" Ra Ref] flashing red 2.5 second light 73 feet high with a 4 mile range and a radar reflector, is on a triangular red dayboard on a platform on the rocky east headland of the island.

SAMISH ISLAND & SAMISH BAY

Samish Island is the north boundary of Padilla Bay and its estuarine sanctuary. It is joined to the mainland by an isthmus. We arrived by car as we figured it might be hard to find a place to anchor *Scheherazade* offshore and be able to land onshore.

It's fairly shallow all along the south shore and even off the northeast side, so the island is of interest mainly to kayakers and other small boaters. The north shore near the west end for about 0.1 mile offshore has 4 to 6 fathoms, mud bottom, and anchoring might be possible.

🐚 Samish Bay, between the island the mainland, is about four miles across by six miles long. Depths are less than 2 fathoms from the narrow isthmus in the middle of Samish Island in an arc northeast to Wildcat Cove at Larrabee State Park *(Ch. 11)*. Local boaters tell us the bay is not a good gunkhole because of the shallows. The Samish River and Edison Slough empty into the south end of the bay forming a natural channel. The bay's south end is home to oysters, clams and crabs.

Public tidelands

🐚 *Unless otherwise noted, public tidelands are state-owned. Some may be leased and posted for aquaculture or other private use. When going ashore in this area take the Washington State Public Lands Quadrangle Map of Port Townsend.*

The public tidelands in the area covered in this chapter are at Goat Island, the south end of McGlinn Island, along the eastern shore of March Point, and on Samish Island.

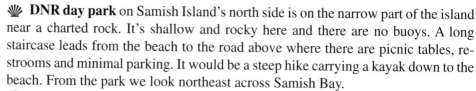

Skunk on Samish

Peter Puget of Capt. George Vancouver's survey party wrote that while the group camped at William Point on Samish Island on June 10, 1792, "An animal called a Skunk was run down by one of the Marines after Dark.

"The stench it created absolutely awakened us in the tent. The smell is so bad for a description ... The Man's cloaths (sic) were afterwards so offensive that notwithstanding boiling, they still retained the stench of the animal & in the next expedition others were given him on condition that those that retained the smell should be thrown away & happy he was to comply with it."

Scatchet/Skagit Indians

"The Scatchet Indians are fine looking ... they go about quite naked except for a blanket about their shoulders ... they use little cloaks made of feathers or hair. The bay in which they reside is a handsome place," said John Work, when he met with Skagit Indians in December 1824 in Padilla Bay.

He later became Chief Factor at Hudson Bay Company's Fort Nisqually near present-day Olympia.

Samish River moorage, looking northwest

🐚 **DNR day park** on Samish Island's north side is on the narrow part of the island near a charted rock. It's shallow and rocky here and there are no buoys. A long staircase leads from the beach to the road above where there are picnic tables, restrooms and minimal parking. It would be a steep hike carrying a kayak down to the beach. From the park we look northeast across Samish Bay.

🐚 **DNR tidelands** are also off the east end of Samish Island at Scotts Point and Fish Point. The bay here ends up as mud flats, and uplands are private. More DNR tide lands are east of the island in Samish Bay between the Samish River and Edison Slough and south of Blanchard.

The Smiths, who build beautiful 8 foot El Toro sailing dinghies, have their shop on Samish Island. (Jo raced her home-built El Toro against Smith boats and respects their beauty, sail ability and speed.) They also build Pelicans, a larger version of the El Toro. Both boats, especially if built by Smiths, have great reputations.

Snippets Of Samish Island History

Samish Island, a quiet treasure, has a rather remarkable history. A great many Native Americans lived on the island and many more camped here to catch salmon, dogfish and dig clams in earlier days. At the time of the Point Elliott Treaty in 1855, Samish Tribal members lived on Guemes, Samish, Cypress, Lopez and the western half of Fidalgo Islands although they occupied only Guemes and Samish islands permanently. Two longhouses were on Samish: the one on the southeast part of the island was 1,250 feet long, and that on the west side was 999 feet.

The Samish were master craftsmen who excelled in carving totems, building large cedar plank houses and canoes.

Among the first settlers on the island was Daniel Dingwall who had a store at Fish Point. William Dean joined him as a partner, and established a post office there on June 16, 1871. Dingwall also built small hotel at the site.

Steamers were the major connection between Samish Island and the outside world as water was the only highway in the last half of the 19th century.

In 1873, Dean located his own store on the north shore at the narrowest part of the island where there was a deep-water wharf, building a small hotel called Dean's Inn. Steamers stopped several times a week with supplies and mail. Loggers arriving by boat usually stayed overnight at Dean's Inn before heading inland to work. Dean's brother George built a sawmill on the island.

In 1888, the ***Mary F. Perley***, the largest sternwheeler constructed in the county, was designed and built by J.F.T. Mitchell for the Dean brothers and Captain Perley on Samish Island. The lumber for her was logged and sawn on the island; she was 101 feet long and 184 tons.

In 1883, the island was platted for two towns, Samish at the west end, and Atlanta near the east end. George Washington Lafayette Allen, a Confederate veteran, platted Atlanta on June 12, 1883, to be a "refuge and sanctuary for persecuted Confederates and other sympathizers. He also built the Atlanta Home Hotel on the north shore.

George Dean, platted Samish three days later on June 15, 1883, and the fracas began. Allen built a dock to corner the steamship trade

for Atlanta. William Dean lengthened his dock. Allen extended his. Dean put a post office on his dock. Allen established a saloon.

Competition arose on the docks between the crews who were to load cordwood for the steamers serving the island. By 1895, an armed battle broke out and one man was killed.

The upshot was that neither townsite sold enough lots to incorporate, the cordwood business declined, and the railroad from Seattle terminated at Bellingham instead of Anacortes. That was the end of the commercial importance of little Samish Island. On September 10, 1920, the Samish post office closed down and mail was transferred to Edison.

We stopped at a little bridge over the **Samish River** near **Edison** and found a small moorage where a catamaran, an old fish boat and a couple of other small boats were moored. They access the river at high tide knowing their way across Samish Bay flats. It is a pretty neat place.

We retrace our wake back to where we took the diversion at the north end of Swinomish Channel and look at March Point and the entrance waters to Anacortes.

Two deepwater wharves at the north end of March Point have long approach trestles extending over shoal waters leading to berthing space for tankers arriving at the refineries.

Tesoro Northwest Company Wharf is the eastern of the two, with a 3,466 foot trestle and a deck height of 22 feet. Two private navigation aids are at the east and west ends of the 820 foot ship-berthing space.

[F R 18ft] fixed red light 18 feet high marks the east end of the wharf.

[F R 16ft Horn (Bl 30s] fixed red light 16 feet high and a horn with a 2 second blast every 30 seconds marks the west end.

Texaco Oil Company Wharf is west, with a 7,150 foot approach trestle and a deck height of 22 feet.

Texaco Oil Company Wharf Lights [F R 25ft] (2) are two fixed red lights 25 feet high at the east and west ends of the wharf. At the land end, the trestle crosses Crandall Spit on the west side of March Point.

Fidalgo Bay is between March Point and Anacortes on Fidalgo Island. The bay is less than 3 fathoms deep southwest of the oil refinery piers. It is mudflats south of a 0.7 mile railroad trestle from Fidalgo on March Point to Weaverly Spit on the west shore of Anacortes.

From the Texaco wharf it's about 0.6 mile west to Cap Sante Waterway which leads into Cap Sante Marina in Anacortes. A dredged channel to the southwest leads to private moorages.

In **Chapter 9** we explore Anacortes and its moorages, Guemes Channel, Flounder Bay, Burrows and Allan islands.

In **Chapter 9** we explore Anacortes and its moorages, Guemes Channel, Flounder Bay, Burrows and Allan islands.

Recent Refinery Accidents

In November 1998, a major accident at the refineries killed six workers. Another explosion in March 1999 and an accident in April 1999 injured 10 more.

Looking east from Cap Sante toward March Point refinery piers with tankers, Padilla Bay in the background

Fidalgo Bay

The bay was known to Native Americans as the "Protected Place Where There is Calm Water."

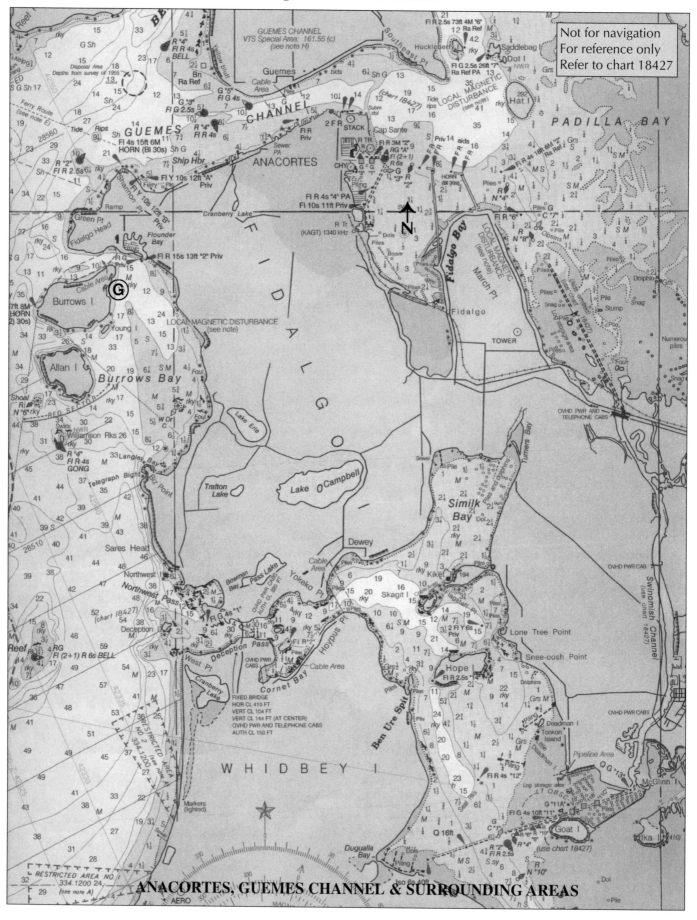

ANACORTES, GUEMES CHANNEL & SURROUNDING AREAS

Chapter 9
ANACORTES & GUEMES CHANNEL
Burrows & Allan Islands

Charts & Publications for this Chapter

Chart	Date	Title	Scale	Soundings
U.S. 18421	03/21/98	Strait of Juan de Fuca to Strait of Georgia	1:80,000	Fathoms
U.S. 18423	06/18/94	Strip Chart Bellingham to Everett, inc. San Juan Islands		
		Page A	1:80,000	Fathoms
		Page B, Inset 2	1:40,000	Fathoms
★ U.S.18427	02/21/98	Anacortes to Skagit Bay	1:25,000	Fathoms
CAN. LC3462	10/23/98	Juan de Fuca Strait to Strait of Georgia	1:80,000	Meters
CAN. 3313	1995	Gulf Islands Chart Book, Page 1	1:200,000	Meters
🐚		Wash. State DNR Quad Map—Bellingham	1:100,000	
🐚		Wash. State DNR Quad Map—Port Townsend	1:100,000	

➡ *Compare your chart dates with those above. There may be discrepancies between chart editions.*
★ *= Preferred chart for this chapter*   🐚 *= DNR & other public tideland information*

ANACORTES: "GATEWAY TO THE SAN JUANS"

In this chapter we explore the delightful city of Anacortes, the self-proclaimed "Gateway to the San Juans." With its natural deep harbor, Anacortes sprawls across the east, north and west portion of north Fidalgo Island, bounded by water on three sides. The chapter will include Guemes Channel, Flounder and Burrows Bays, and Allan and Burrows islands.

Mariners using the "inside passage" through Swinomish Channel often visit this city of about 13,500 people. It is a welcome stop when heading north on vacation, or returning from the north. It's also the terminal for state ferries serving the San Juans and British Columbia, and the Guemes Island ferry. Anacortes has some of the islands' charms, without the frustration of waiting hours for the ferries.

Two major marinas in Anacortes offer overnight moorage: Cap Sante Boat Haven, with guest moorage for approximately 300 boats in downtown Anacortes, and Skyline Marina in Flounder Bay on the southeast side of Fidalgo Head, with guest moorage for about 45 boats.

For those cruising the Swinomish Channel, Cap Sante may be the choice, as it's close to the north end of the channel and tucked inside a protected bay at the south end of the 200 foot high rocky promontory of Cap Sante. Skyline Marina may be better for those mariners using Deception Pass, the Strait of Juan de Fuca, or who simply want to be out of downtown.

Anacortes has some great places to visit within walking distance of downtown. Wandering around town with its wide streets and refurbished store fronts provides a slice of Anacortes life. There are restaurants galore, delis, pizza shops, gift and antique shops, clothing and book stores, a post office, liquor store, and a supermarket right across the street from the marina.

➡ **NOTE: Marine gas & diesel** are available at:
- **Cap Sante Boat Haven** at Port of Anacortes
- **Skyline Marina/Penmar Marine** at Flounder Bay

Seafarers' Memorial

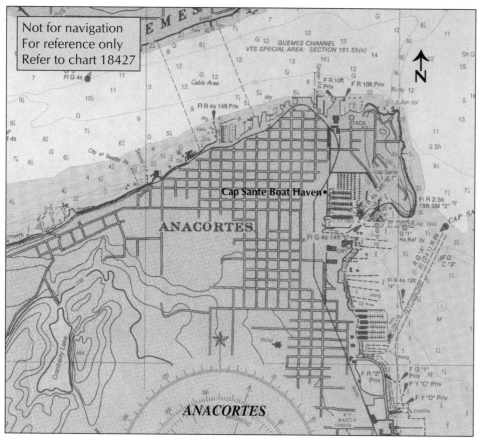

Not for navigation
For reference only
Refer to chart 18427

Anacortes offers unique outdoor, life-size, cut-out murals, based on early photographs of Anacortes. They are all over town, and include mayors, bartenders, gold miners, railway conductors, priests, boxers, musicians, storekeepers, and judges, as well as various modes of transportation, including bicycles. Wonderful turn-of-the-century restored houses are within walking distance of the marina.

Entering Cap Sante Boat Haven

Those boats coming north from Swinomish Channel will have passed the Tesoro and Texaco piers off March Point, as described near the end of the previous chapter. If arriving from Guemes Channel, boats will go south around the east end of the bluffs of Cap Sante. Either way, boats end up at **Cap Sante Waterway.**

Anacortes Harbor Junction Lighted Buoy [RG "A," Fl (2+1) R 6s] flashing red 6 second light on a red and green banded buoy, is at the junction of Cap Sante Waterway and the marked channel leading southwest to Anacortes Marina. Cap Sante Boat Haven is west of the junction buoy, through the marked channel. Anacortes Marina, behind a piling breakwater, is all permanent moorage and offers no guest moorage.

Enter Cap Sante Boat Haven through a dredged channel, red right returning. The "No-wake zone, 5 mph," starts at the entrance and extends through the entire channel approaching the breakwater.

Cap Sante Waterway navigation aids are:

Daybeacon 1 [G "1," Ra Ref] square green daybeacon with a radar reflector on a pile on the channel's south side, is 15 feet outside the channel limit.

Light 2 [Fl R 2.5s 15ft 3M "2"] flashing red 2.5 second light 15 feet high on a triangular red daybeacon on a dolphin on the channel's north side, is 15 feet outside the channel limit.

Daybeacon 3 [G "3"] square green daybeacon on a pile on the channel's south side, is 15 feet outside the channel limit.

Daybeacon 4 [R "4"] triangular red daybeacon on a dolphin on the channel's north side, is outside of the rock jetty.

Light 5 [Fl G 4s 14ft "5"] flashing green 4 second light 14 feet high is on a square green daybeacon on a dolphin, is on the channel's south side.

Light 6 [Fl R 4s 14ft "6"] flashing red 4 second light 14 feet high, is on a triangular red daybeacon on a dolphin on the channel's north side is at the entrance to the marina, which has two piling breakwaters.

Commercial docks "A" and "B" are almost straight ahead when entering the marina. We make a jog to starboard after entering, keeping the fishermen's net float to starboard, and head to the outer end of "C" dock, the check-in float. After tying there, we walk to the head of the dock, turn north along the pedestrian walkway and we're at the harbor office, an attractive building on the west side of the street. They

➡ **CAUTION:** Mariners are advised when entering Cap Sante Boat Haven to stay in the channel and not go inside the rock jetty.

Anacortes Marina

They have 466 permanent moorage slips, liveaboards on every dock, and tenants do their own sub-leasing. During the winter storms of 1996-97, they lost 60 slips, but have since rebuilt.

assign moorage and provide a detailed map of the marina.

Cap Sante Boat Haven has moorage for more than 1,100 vessels, and is also home port for the 130 vessel Anacortes fishing fleet.

Facilities at Cap Sante Boat Haven

➤ Guest moorage for approximately 300 boats, accepts reservations
➤ Moorage rates 75¢ foot in summer; 60¢ foot in winter
➤ Shore power, 20-30 amps $3 day; water
➤ Fuel dock: gas, diesel and propane
➤ Free pumpouts and porta-potty dumps, three locations
➤ Restrooms with showers, laundry, garbage disposal
➤ Chandlery: marine supplies, charts, books, clothing, fishing gear, bait, ice
➤ 35 ton boat haulout, boat and engine repair
➤ Woodworking & fiberglass repair, canvas work
➤ Sling launch ramp, used oil disposal, recycling services
➤ Picnic areas, barbecue at nearby Rotary Park
➤ Customs port-of-entry by phone: 360-293-2331
➤ Anacortes & Fidalgo Yacht Clubs have reciprocal moorage at "D" dock, check-in at harbor office
➤ Nearby: supermarkets, restaurants, delis with lattes, gift shops, post office, liquor store, hardware store, swimming pool, taxi, free bus service in Skagit County
➤ Activities: play area, museum, art galleries, parks, movies, tennis, walk,
➤ Monitors: VHF Channel 66A
➤ Call for slip assignment: 360-293-0694 or VHF Channel 66A
➤ Harbormaster: Dale Fowler
➤ Tel.: 360-293-0694; Security: 360-929-0900: FAX: 360-299-0998
➤ Address: P.O. Box 297, Anacortes, WA 98221

A number of intriguing places are near the marina. Along the eastern shore below Cap Sante is the Rotary Park Walkway to a park and picnic area above the marina's rock jetty, a scenic and easy walk, with benches and picnic tables along the way. Take a trail from the park up to the rocky top of Cap Sante where spectacular nearly 360° views of the sparkling surrounding waters await. Vistas include the entrance into the marina, Guemes Channel, Saddlebag and Hat islands, snow-tipped Mount Baker and the Cascades, March Point and its refineries, and the city. Although the path isn't much more than 0.25 mile long, the elevation gain is about 200 feet.

Cap Sante

This is the prominent rocky headland at the northeast corner of Fidalgo Island in Anacortes.

There are two stories as to its name origin. One is that it is the corruption of a Spanish name given it by an unknown explorer.

*Another is based on an article in the March 19, 1925, issue of the **Anacortes American** which reports it was first called Bowman's Hill after Amos Bowman, the founder of Anacortes.*

Later, the property was acquired by Melville Curtis and was called Cap Sante because it resembled Cap Rouge on the St. Lawrence River where Curtis had lived.

A Coast and Geodetic Survey marker was placed at the Cap Sante viewpoint in 1990. See if you can find it when you hike up there.

Anacortes, Cap Sante Boat Haven & March Point beyond

An alternate route for those who would rather stroll than climb, is the slightly less than one mile long walk along a twisting roadway to the top, through forests, past some homes, and then to the summit for the stunning view. We've seen joggers on this road, so for those in the mood for an early morning "challenging" run, this might be it.

The *W.T. Preston* is a retired sternwheel snagboat, once operated by the Army Corps of Engineers to clear snags from Puget Sound waters. The 163 foot paddle-

W. T. Preston, old sternwheel snagboat

Seafarer's Memorial

🐚 *Public tidelands, unless otherwise noted, are state-owned. Some may be leased and posted for aquaculture or other private use. When going ashore take the Washington State Public Lands Quadrangle Maps of Bellingham and Port Townsend to avoid trespassing.*

The public tidelands in the area covered in this chapter are along Burrows Bay and around Burrows and Allan islands.

wheel vessel, now on land at the northwest edge of the boat haven, is on the National Register of Historic Places. The *Preston* was built in 1929, the third of three self-propelled snagboats to remove navigation hazards from the Sound. She is open for tours during summer or by special arrangement.

Tommy Thompson's narrow-gauge steam train in Anacortes was a summertime delight for 13 years, carrying railroad buffs and tourists in its miniature, detailed passenger cars. After Thompson's death in January 1999, the family said the tiny but elegant train would no longer run on the 14 block track through downtown Anacortes.

Seafarer's Memorial monument is in South Harbor Park in the boat haven, where lawns sweep to the shore. It is dedicated to the memories of local seafarers who lost their lives at sea following their profession, and to the families and friends who wait for them. The statue of the Lady of the Sea was part of the American Bicentennial Project, as suggested by Ray Separovich, mariner, father and public servant. The artist who designed and sculpted the lady in 1994 was Deborah Copenhaves.

Marine Supply and Hardware between Second and Third streets on Commercial is another "must-see." Founded as the Junk Store by Mike Demopoulos in 1910, it became Marine Supply and Hardware in 1913. Mike's son Theo and grandson Steve formed a partnership after Mike's death in 1981 to keep the store in the family. Steve now owns the store, which covers an entire city block.

"We're the oldest marine store you'll step foot in on the West Coast," Steve says. "We carry everything from anchors to zincs, except groceries." "Everything" includes being a unique supplier of wood, steel and fiberglass to industry, commercial and pleasure boats. The store has gift items such as clocks, barometers, brass items, antiques, as well as practical things like boots and raingear.

"We specialize in a lot of stuff. We have red brass pipe fittings, hardware that's hard to find, crab rings and pots. Everything that comes in is sold, it doesn't see the light of day, just rotates through," said Steve. It's hard to get out of the store without buying something you just discovered you can't live without.

"If Marine Supply and Hardware doesn't have it you don't need it," Steve adds. The extroverted company cat will pose for its photo or play with the kids while you visit.

On the building's exterior are several of the life-size murals of old-times scenes around town, including Steve's grandfather's junk wagon.

Flounder Bay Lumber Company on Third Street and O Avenue, is another must-visit, especially if you're into boat woods. Erica and Bob Pickett started the business in 1972 in a grand old building that was once Schwartz Iron Works.

Their specialty is helping the builder get the right material for building the boat. They carry quality western softwoods and specialty hardwoods for boat building, handmade carving and woodworking tools, custom milling and offer expert advice. We used to own wood sailboats and this place fascinates us.

They carry boat kits: a nearly 8 foot skiff and a 13 foot canoe. Both fit together like jigsaw puzzles and turn into handsome, seaworthy craft. This is a terrific lumber company, with a company cat named Lunker.

Handsome old Victorian homes are in the north end of town. In 1889, there were 40 people in town, by 1890 there were thousands. No houses predate that time, with many built between 1890 and 1891.

On Eighth Street at M and N Avenues are a couple of treats: Causland Memorial Park with its stunning rock work and the Anacortes Historic Museum. Both the memorial and the museum are on the National Register of Historic Places.

Causland Memorial Park, a one-block-square park with shade trees, picnic tables and a band shell, is dedicated to the memory of men from Fidalgo, Guemes, Decatur and Cypress islands who died between 1917 and 1919 in World War I. There are plaques dedicated to veterans of World War II, the Korean War and the Viet Nam War. The band pavilion memorial plaque was named for veteran Leon Causland. Unusual white quartz and red argillite rock work on a background of brown and gray sandstone at the pavilion was constructed by John Baptiste LePage, a French Canadian artist and architect who designed the park and supervised its building.

Anacortes Historic Museum is across the street from the park, at 1305 8th St., and it's a treasure, housed in the 1909 Carnegie Library building. A drinking fountain used by horses, dogs and humans is now in the entry. It was commissioned by the Women's Christian Temperance Union.

The museum features books, exhibits and public programs about the history of Fidalgo and Guemes islands. Photos of old Anacortes, which was both a fishing and mill town, include logging and sawmill operations, fish boats, canneries, farms, dairies, early railways, homes, stores, Native Americans, schools and churches, all depicting how early settlers lived and worked.

Unusual rock work at the park

Anacortes Mural Project and Historical Tour

This is the creation of Bill Mitchell, lifelong Anacortes resident and local historian with a warm sense of humor. He came up with the idea of the murals, which is now past the mid-point in his goal to create 100 murals representing 100 years of Anacortes history. The Newcomers' & Visitors' Guide to Anacortes lists locations of both the Mural Project and Historical Tour. This is an amazing "not to be missed" part of Anacortes.

Mural at Marine Supply & Hardware

A Brief History of Anacortes

Settlers built the city on north Fidalgo Island in the mid-1800s, displacing Native Americans who had lived in the forested area for thousands of years. Settlers called it the "City of Necessity" and the "Magic City."

"It passed from insignificance to prominence and from one extreme to another with singular rapidity within a span of a few colorful years." (*Anacortes American*)

The city was groomed to become a railroad town after Amos Bowman arrived in 1876, certain that the Canadian Pacific Railroad would establish its western terminus on Fidalgo Island. He and his wife bought 186 acres, built a wharf and store, and started a newspaper in "Ship Harbor," the original name.

When Bowman established a post office in 1877, Ship Harbor became Anacortes, the name he created from the maiden name of his beloved wife Anna Curtis Bowman.

He published a map of Puget Sound and the area around Anacortes in 1882, predicting its future as a railroad terminus and major seaport. The map earned him the title of "Father of Anacortes."

Bowman thought the city would be the foremost Pacific Coast link with the Orient.

(Continued on next page)

Naming Guemes Channel

The channel was named "Isla de Guemes" by members of the 1791 Eliza Expedition of Spanish explorers, to honor the viceroy of Mexico, Senor Don Juan Vicente de Guemes Pacheco y Padilla Orcasitees & Aquayo, Conde de Revilla Gigendo.

*In 1841, the Wilkes Expedition renamed the channel **Hornets Harbor** for the American warship **Hornet,** active in the War of 1812.*

In 1847, the name was restored to Guemes Channel by Captain Kellett.

Fish Processing

This was a major industry in Anacortes, where about 400 Chinese worked in the six salmon canneries from 1895 to 1925.

Most of the laborers lived in a "China House" at each cannery. Many were smuggled into the country without papers to work in the U.S.

Unfortunately, some of the smugglers lacked consciences, and would dump their human contraband overboard if they were in danger of being caught by authorities.

Railroads would be the most important and necessary key to the future.

From 1889 to 1890, the boom in Anacortes peaked, boosting population from 40 to 3,000. The crash came just as suddenly with the news that Tacoma was chosen as the terminus. While Bowman's railroad dream didn't materialize, his desire to create a special community was fulfilled.

Native Americans in the area regarded fishing as their right and fished constantly. When they had more fish than they could use, they would sell or barter them. Non-Indians entered the commercial fishing industry and built fish-processing plants in the 1890s, fishing with both boats and fish traps.

By 1914, Anacortes was a major hub of water transportation and ferry traffic for the region. Steamers made daily runs to Seattle, Bellingham and the San Juans. Fishing, logging, lumber and shipping formed the economy.

The forests are long gone, victims of over-logging; the fishing industry is waning, victim of over-fishing. Today's economy is fueled by shipyards, seafood processing facilities, oil refineries, tourism, the Port of Anacortes, marinas and retirement. Anacortes is the second largest city in Skagit County and is the county's top industrial and shipping center.

There were a dozen mills and canneries in Anacortes in the early days, Terry Slotemaker, museum curator said. "Most of the mills in Anacortes were located along Fidalgo Bay; two were on Guemes Channel near Cap Sante, and one was where Skyline Marina is today." The canneries were along Guemes Channel. Two landmarks still remain from the early mill days: the Morrison Mill smokestack on 17th Street, and the 600 foot long kiln-drying shed from the E.K. Wood Mill at Skyline Marina, now used for boat repair. The Anacortes Lumber and Box Company's tall, white-painted smokestack near Boomers Restaurant was imploded in early 1999. This was a longtime landmark, with "Welcome" spelled out on the stack with signal flags. There is no longer a dock here for customers.

✺ **UNDERWAY AGAIN,** we head west in Guemes Channel to Flounder Bay and Skyline Marina, staying nearer the south shore.

Guemes Channel is the three mile long channel between Fidalgo Island on the south and Guemes Island on the north which leads east from Rosario Strait to Padilla Bay. It's about 0.5 mile wide at its narrowest spot with depths of 8 to 18 fathoms. Lighted buoys mark the channel at the west end. We address the north side of the channel and lighted buoys "3," "4" and "5" in the next chapter.

We pass the northeast tip of Cap Sante unnamed on some charts, locally called Tide Point. Port of Anacortes' commercial docks are along the north shore near Cap Sante.

Anacortes Dock Lights [(2) F R 10ft] two fixed red lights 10 feet high are private aids on dock.

This is all industrial, big ship stuff, with a shipyard, floating drydock, big cranes, and tugs moored outside the main pier.

Anchor Cove Marina, a condo moorage is next, with a large piling breakwater across its face. This is all permanent moorage with no transient moorage.

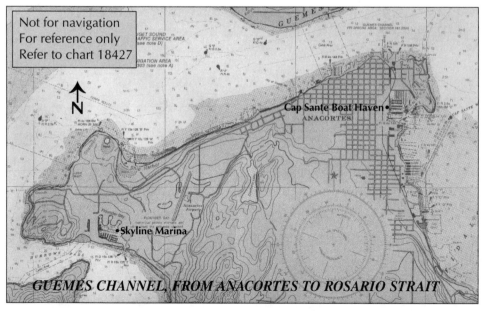

Not for navigation
For reference only
Refer to chart 18427

GUEMES CHANNEL, FROM ANACORTES TO ROSARIO STRAIT

Guemes-Anacortes Ferry Landing is west of the marina.

This is a great little ferry, making the run across Guemes Channel in about five minutes many times daily, and it's a fun ride. Bicyclists especially enjoy the short trip and the ride around Guemes Island. The ferry is operated by the Skagit County Department of Public Works. *(Guemes, Ch. 10)*

Anacortes Ferry Breakwater Light [Fl R 4s 14ft Priv] flashing red 4 second light 14 feet high is on the Anacortes-Guemes Island ferry landing.

City of Seattle Rock is about 0.4 mile west of the ferry landing about 200 yards offshore and is covered at 1.75 fathoms. There's also a residential area and a fish company pier with massive pilings along this shore.

Lovric's Sea-Craft Marina is next, about 0.4 mile west of Seattle Rock, identifiable from the east by a couple of large vertical tanks and a sloping, flat-roofed building. A pile breakwater runs across the front with a variety of fishing and commercial vessels inside. Tony Lovric has run the shipyard since 1965.

The yard does custom designing, new construction, repair service, repowering for wood, fiberglass, aluminum and steel boats. Marine railway capacity is 200, 400, and 2,000 tons, and there is a 160 ton lift. There is mostly permanent moorage and occasionally temporary moorage at the marina, said Mrs. Lovric. Some expansion is planned in the future, which will provide some guest moorage.

From the west, the yard is easily recognized by the huge ship on the breakwater, *La Merced,* a former four-masted schooner turned floating cannery in Bristol Bay in the 1940s. Before that, the vessel shipped lumber from Alaska. When decommissioned, everything was taken out of it and scrapped, and she was at St. Vincent de Paul's dock on Lake Union in Seattle. The Lovric's bought the vessel in 1966 to use as a breakwater at the marina. They also have a section of the old Lake Washington Floating Bridge in the breakwater.

Washington State Ferry Terminal is in Ship Harbor, about 1.2 miles west of Lovric's. Thousands of cars and passengers board ferries daily for the San Juans and Sidney, B.C. Mariners need to be aware that ferries run almost 24 hours a day in the summer, and to keep boats well away from the piers. There is no float at the ferry terminal to land a recreational vessel, making it difficult to pick up passengers here, except by anchoring and rowing ashore.

Anacortes Ferry Terminal Light [Fl Y 10s 12ft "A"] flashing yellow 10 second light 12 feet high is on the east dolphin at the ferry landing.

Anacortes Ferry Terminal Light [Fl Y 10s 12ft "B"] is an identical flashing yellow 10 second light 12 feet high on the west dolphin at the ferry landing.

A long road leads to the ferry landing from the main road. Parking is both near the terminal and on the hill above. Many old pilings still stand in the harbor east of the ferry dock, where there was once a cannery and pier. There have been proposals for years to build a private marina here east of the terminal, with homes and condos on the hill above the harbor, but development has not yet begun.

Codfish Plant to Marina

The only surviving codfish processing plant building in Anacortes is the large Robinson's Fisheries Building at Lovric's Marina on Guemes Channel.

Robinson Fisheries grew into one of the largest codfish processing plants in Puget Sound in the first few decades of the 1900s, providing year-round employment for several hundred persons.

West of Robinson's was a glue factory which made carpenter's glue, wool sizing, fish oils and fertilizer from fish wastes in the early 1900s.

Breakwater with old schooner at Lovric's Marina

Atop old pilings in Ship Harbor, an intrepid ferry rider awaits his ferry

On the Rocks

The ferry Elwha, arriving from the San Juans, ran aground on the rocks on the east side of Shannon Point in the early 1980s.

Although no one was hurt, it took several hours to remove passengers, who then had to wait several hours more for the ferry to float free so they could retrieve their vehicles after the ferry finally was docked.

It was what San Juan Islanders call, "just another ordinary day in the islands."

Totem at Washington Park

Puget & Whidbey at Fidalgo

Peter Puget and Joseph Whidbey, sailing with explorer Capt. George Vancouver, landed their men and camped for the night at Green Point near Fidalgo Head on June 9, 1792.

They were "... tormented by Musquitos (sic) & Sand Flies which however was in some measure forgot in the Morning by a large Supply of Strawberries and Wild Onion ... growing ... close to the Tents."

⚓ **Anchoring** is possible in fairly well protected waters east of the ferry terminal within the 5 fathom curve, mud bottom, except during winds from northeast or northwest.

Shannon Point is a rocky point about 500 yards west of the ferry terminal with a shoal extending 200 yards east, north and west of the point.

Shannon Point Light [Fl 4s 15ft 6M Horn (Bl 30s)] flashing white 4 second light 15 feet high with a horn, is on a diamond-shaped dayboard with black and white sectors on a dolphin. The horn operates continuously, and there is also a radar reflector. The light is about 75 yards offshore and 500 yards west of the ferry terminal.

Guemes Channel Lighted Buoy 2 [Fl R, 2.5s R "2"] flashing red 2.5 second light on a buoy, is about 0.6 mile west of Shannon Point Light in Rosario Strait.

Washington Park is southwest of Shannon Point on Fidalgo Head. This lovely 220 acre Anacortes waterfront park and campground at the western edge of the city has four miles of wrap around forested shores from Guemes Channel to Rosario Strait and into Burrows Pass.

Views from the park are fabulous from the southwest rocky bluffs above Rosario Strait across to Burrows' forested, craggy hills, and include tugs with tows, pleasure craft and fishing boats in the pass. Summer sunsets are magnificent, when shades of pink, lavender and purple meld into unbelievable hues over the evergreens of the San Juans to the west.

Launch ramp with two lanes is at Sunset Beach in the park.

⚓ **Anchoring** near the ramp is possible in calm weather in about 1.25 to 3 fathoms, mud bottom, but it is exposed to currents off Rosario Strait.

The park roadway and picnic areas are easily seen above the shoreline while cruising out into Rosario Strait around the park.

Facilities at Washington Park

➤ 220 acres, four miles of shoreline on Rosario Strait
➤ Two-lane launch ramp with float, trailer parking
➤ No overnight moorage
➤ 48 campsites, picnic tables, fireplaces, restrooms, showers, drinking water
➤ Miles of hiking & biking trails
➤ Activities: scuba diving, fishing, gunkholing, picnicking, camping

Green Point, virtually a non-point, faces Rosario Strait about 0.4 mile west of Sunset Beach.

Fidalgo Head's rocky bluffs rise 255 feet above the Strait, about 0.5 mile south of Green Point, and still within Washington Park. This is a precipitous head with trees way back on its forehead, and sloping tops indicating prevailing wind direction. Trails lead down the bluff, but there are no beaches here.

Burrows Pass is between Fidalgo and Burrows islands, and we head east into the pass.

Strong tidal currents run through the pass, with the flood flowing west at 270° and the ebb flowing east at 090°. Currents are based on predictions of those in Rosario Strait. The flood is 1.6 times that in the Strait and can reach or exceed 4.25 knots. The ebb is half that in the Strait and can reach or exceed 2 knots. The pass is a nasty, choppy spot when a fast-flowing flood meets a westerly wind.

Flounder Bay, a well-sheltered basin and popular yacht harbor with a marked entry channel, is about one mile east of Fidalgo Head, past steep rocky bluffs,

Skyline Marina Light 1 [Fl G 15s 13ft "1"] flashing green 15 second light 13 feet high, is on a dolphin on the west side of the entrance channel into the bay.

Skyline Marina Light 2 [Fl R 15s 13ft "2"] flashing red 15 second light 13 feet high is on a pile on the east side of the entrance channel.

The narrow channel is about 200 yards long.

Controlling depth at the entrance at zero tide is 6.5 feet. Controlling depth inside the bay is 12 feet, according to Dick Britton, operator of Skyline Marina.

Enter Flounder Bay between the markers, going pretty much straight in toward a "No Wake" sign. We turn to port and go to the main fuel dock with its UNOCAL sign. That's where moorage assignments are given. Those who come in after hours can take a spot on the fuel dock and register in the morning. This is a busy harbor with much boat traffic.

Skyline is a designated seaplane base, but not a regular seaplane stop, and is used by float planes only in summer. Space for planes is at the end of the outer fuel dock. They land outside the bay and taxi in through the channel. Dick is the airport manager.

Just about everything boaters need is here at Penmar Marine, a family-run operation owned by Dick and Penny Britton who took over in 1991 from Skyline Marina, Inc. Son Alex runs the shop, daughter-in-law Julie runs the office, and daughter Bethany runs the harbor. Dick and Penny are licensed skippers and airplane pilots. Dick says Anacortes is the "absolute mecca for bareboat charters in the northwest."

Washington Park launch ramp

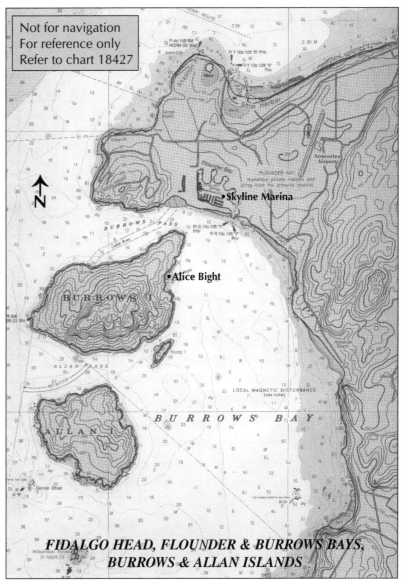

Not for navigation
For reference only
Refer to chart 18427

FIDALGO HEAD, FLOUNDER & BURROWS BAYS,
BURROWS & ALLAN ISLANDS

Winds and currents

Weather in this Anacortes area is 180 degrees different from what is forecast 50 miles south in Seattle because of the convergence zone in central Puget Sound, according to Dick Britton, operator of Skyline Marina, who has kept extensive weather records.

Prevailing winds in this area are southwesterly, with westerlies generally shifting to southwesterlies, he said.

Currents flood around both sides of Burrows and Allan islands almost 90 percent of the time, he said.

Facilities at Skyline Marina
➤ Guest moorage
➤ Fees: 80¢ foot May-Sept.; 65¢ foot Oct.-April
➤ 20, 30 & 50 amp shore power, $3; water
➤ Fuel: gas, diesel, propane, kerosene, CNG
➤ Restrooms, showers, laundry, picnic area
➤ Used oil disposal $1 per gallon, garbage & recycling services
➤ Pumpout $5
➤ Accepts reservations with VISA/MC
➤ Chandlery & basic store with marine supplies, charts, bait, ice, deli, lattes
➤ 55 ton haulout, boat & engine repair
➤ Monorail boat launch, 5 ton capacity, $1 foot round trip
➤ Penmar Yacht Charters, sail and power, 25 to 65 feet, 1-800-828-7337
➤ Customs port-of-entry by phone, 360-293-2331
➤ Nearby: restaurant with lounge, gift shop, market, free bus service into Anacortes & throughout Skagit County; taxi service
➤ Activities: hiking trails near marina & Washington Park, fish, bicycle, picnic, play area, walk to Washington State Ferries
➤ Monitors: VHF Ch.16
➤ Marina manager Alex Britton, Harbormaster Bethany Britton
➤ Tel. 1-888-9-Penmar, 360-293-5134; FAX: 360-293-2427
➤ Address: 2011 Skyline Way, Anacortes, WA 98221

Flounder Bay & Skyline Marina, looking southeast

Bit Of Flounder Bay History

Originally Flounder Bay was part of a log pond used by tugboats with log rafts for the E.K. Wood Mill. The mill began production in 1923, specializing in cutting large beams from logs, and it ceased operation in the 1950s. The 600 foot long kiln drying shed at the site was built of wood and is now used for boat repair and storage by the marina.

An airport was beside the shed for a time, but for safety's sake the Anacortes Airport was moved to the hill east of Flounder Bay, less than a five minute drive from the marina. The shed was used for airplane storage, and contrary to rumors, was never used as a dirigible hangar.

Old drying shed at Flounder Bay—NOT a dirigible hangar

Flounder Bay became the first condominiumized marina in the U.S. in the 1960s when Harry Davidson developed the hillside subdivision surrounding the bay and dredged the cays, planning a dock for each lot.

The Myth of the Drying Shed

"Was the drying shed a zeppelin or dirigible hangar during World War II as we've heard?" we asked Dick Britton.

"No way!" he laughed. "It's a natural assumption that because there was an airport here back then that airplanes had been stored in there, but there were NEVER dirigibles or blimps in the shed. There was nowhere to land them. With the winds here, you need to have a wide open field." Not only that, the blimps would have been too big to fit in the shed.

The old drying shed is now used for boat work and boat storage.

Old Salts Market and Deli, with a lighthouse and an "old salt" standing at it, is the only market at Skyline, and is handy for visiting mariners. Owner Alex Kim keeps the store open from 7 a.m to 10 p.m. in summer, closing at 9 p.m. in winter. He carries deli foods, soft drinks, beer, wine, ice, fresh apples, ice cream, lattes, movie rentals, maps, books, daily newspapers, sweatshirts, and other items.

Alex said, "I sell the most ice cream in a convenience store in Skagit County, the most ice in a convenience store in the county, the most wine in a convenience store in the county; but not the most beer, because this is a neighborhood of retired folks who drink more wine than beer."

Flounder Bay Cafe is on the bay shore at Skyline. The restaurant specializes in local seafoods, mussels, clams, salmon, oysters and whatever is available. It was formerly Slocum's.

ABC Yacht Charters, Inc., Gene Jordeth, owner, is at Skyline. In addition to chartering yachts they have a friendly store with boating goods, gifts, books and other items. ABC is located at 1905 Skyline Way, Tel.: 800-426-2313.

Two other businesses at Skyline operate as chartered, privately-owned freight and passenger vessels.

Paraclete Ferries, run by Skip Heeter, serves non-ferry-served islands in the San Juans. Heeter is also groundskeeper and caretaker at Allan Island.

Island Transport Ferry Service, Inc., owned by Dan Crookes and a partner, has served various islands since 1992 with both a landing craft freight service and a high-speed catamaran passenger water taxi.

Dan Crookes of Island Transport

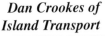

⚓ **UNDERWAY AGAIN,** we head south in Burrows Bay toward Deception Pass, and then we circumnavigate Burrows and Allan islands.

Burrows Bay runs about four miles southeast of

Burrows Pass from Washington Park, Lopez Island in right background

Public Tidelands

🐚 *About 14,000 feet of public tidelands are along some of the shores of Burrows Bay, with the longest section of about 6,000 feet north from Edith Point.*

Tidelands are also public around Biz Point and south of the point for about 8,000 feet until they meet with the public tidelands of Deception Pass Park.

Channel between Young, left, and Burrows islands

Flounder Bay.

Biz Point with its rocks and bluffs marks the end of the bay. Along the bay's east shore, hills rise above beaches, with homes replacing forests.

Shallow Anaco Beach covers the first 0.7 miles south of Flounder Bay. A non-point separates it from shoal Alexander Beach covering the next .07 mile.

Depths are less than 6 fathoms as much as 0.4 mile offshore for 1.5 miles from the south end of Anaco Beach to Edith Point.

⚓ **Anchoring** is possible along the beaches in calm weather. Britton said several 85 foot boats occasionally anchor outside of Flounder Bay in about 70 feet. here is good holding ground outside the 2 fathom depth curve along the beaches to the south, he said. Anaco Beach has a sand and mud bottom, while Alexander Beach has a rocky bottom.

Rocky shoals extend more than 200 yards offshore for about 0.4 mile north of Edith Point in Burrows Bay.

Burrows Bay Danger Rock Buoy [W Or C] white can buoy with orange bands worded **"Danger Rocks,"** is about 0.3 mile northwest of Edith Point. It marks submerged rocks which are "Uncovered (at) extreme low tides." *(Chart 18427)* A kelp-covered 1.5 fathom shoal is 450 yards east of the Danger Rock buoy.

Langley Bay, about 0.8 mile long, is between Edith Point and Biz Point. Charted rocks are off the northwest point of the crescent-shaped bay which is less than 3 fathoms deep for 500 yards offshore. The bay might offer temporary shelter.

A rock that bares at 5 feet is about 0.3 miles northeast of Biz Point on the edge of the erratically shaped 5 and 10 fathom depth curves. A shoal that dries at 2 feet is 400 yards offshore in the south end of the bay.

Telegraph Bight is the tiny bay south of Biz Point, almost directly across Rosario Strait from Telegraph Bay on Lopez Island. *(p. 66)* The coast has high rocky shores to the south.

Sares Head is 1.1 miles south of Biz Point and one mile north of Deception Island. It's cliffs are steep and rocky. Heights range from 250 to 512 feet.

We're once again at Rosario Head and the entrance to Deception Pass, which we left in Chapter 7, so now we head back to Burrows & Allan islands.

BURROWS & ALLAN ISLANDS

These two are a pair of great-looking, forested, rugged, hilly islands south of Fidalgo Head, with their east sides facing Burrows Bay, the west shores on Rosario Strait, and with the Strait of Juan de Fuca to the south.

🐚 Almost all the **tidelands** around both islands are DNR lands and open to the public below the high tide line.

Burrows Island, the larger of the two, has 329 acres of undeveloped state park land at the site of Burrows Island Lighthouse on the west shore. The hilly island has a 635 foot high peak above the southwest shore.

Alice Bight is on the island's east

Burrows Island Lighthouse
on the west side of the island

shore. Although pilings are charted they have been eaten away. The bight is out of almost all weather, except southerlies. Southwesterlies are the prevailing winds. It's all forested in here and a good place to explore by small boat or tromping along the beach. This bight on Burrows' east shore is a favorite anchorage with several persons who charter boats out of Skyline Marina, said Dick Britton.

"We have customers that charter boats from us and all they want is peace and quiet. So they take a boat, possibly a 40 footer, and go over to Alice Bight, a half-mile away and anchor. They'll stay there all week, it's amazing.

"At the end of the charter they tell us they've just had a wonderful time relaxing on the boat and hiking around the island on the animal trails," he said.

⚓ **Anchoring** is possible in Alice Bight inside the 5 fathom depth curve, rocky bottom. This would be a great spot for the state to put in mooring buoys since all the tidelands are state-owned.

Ⓖ It's a lovely **gunkhole**, weather permitting.

Continuing south along Burrows' east side, it's well over 10 fathoms deep just offshore. There are a couple of private, rustic-looking cabins on the island.

Young Island, all private, is off the southeast shore of Burrows. The channel between Burrows and tiny Young has 9 to 10 fathoms in the center. Kelp is on a charted ledge off Young Island. We saw a boat tied in a little bight on the north end of Young Island and people wandering the beach.

Peartree Bay is on the southeast corner of Burrows, opposite Young, with some signs of summer habitation. The south shore of Burrows is steep and rocky, with 6 to 17 fathom depths less than 100 yards offshore, except for a rock covered at 3.5 fathoms midway along the south shore.

Naming Burrows & Allan islands

These islands were named *"Las dos Islas Morros,"* or *"Islands of the Forts,"* by Spanish explorers in 1791.

Naming Burrows Island & Bay

Both were named by the Wilkes Expedition in 1841 after William Burrows. He was a lieutenant in the U.S. Navy who served in the War of 1812 and was killed in the capture of the vessel **Boxer** during the war.

Fog causes crash

    A small float plane crashed on the northwest shore of Allan Island in a heavy fog in August 1998, killing a passenger and injuring the pilot.

Private bay on Allan Island's east shore

Naming Allan Island

    *The island was named by the Wilkes Expedition for William Henry Allen, a captain in the U.S. Navy who was killed in the battle between the **Argus** and the **Pelican** during the War of 1812.*

Burrows Island Light [Fl 6s 57ft 8M Horn] is a flashing 6 second light 57 feet high with a 10 mile range, and a red sector light with an 8 mile range which covers Allan Island and Dennis Shoal. The horn has 2 blasts every 30 seconds. The light is mounted on a short white hexagon tower on a square building on the west side of the island, *Light List #19350.*

After the Coast Guard automated its light stations, the state acquired the property at Burrows Island Light, as well as some adjoining property. There are 329 acres of undeveloped state park land with 8,670 feet of shoreline on Rosario Strait. As yet, no plans for its use have been finalized, but the park land is open to the public, although there is no drinking water. Possible use of the land may be as a Washington Water Trail site for kayakers or as a marine park.

Kayakers paddle around Burrows and stop at the small bay north of the lighthouse. The former lighthouse residence is shuttered, the red roof faded. Beyond the lighthouse is a red-roofed white shed with mast and boom rigged on the beach, which was apparently used to service the facility. There are few other beaches on the island, except for **Short Bay** along the north shore, where kayakers sometimes land.

Cable area runs from Short Bay north to the marsh on Fidalgo Island west of Flounder Bay.

 Allan Island is due south of Burrows, but about half the size, with several small bights and hills reaching over 250 feet high. Billionaire Paul Allen, co-founder of Microsoft, paid 7.4 million dollars for the 280 acre island in 1992. It remains undeveloped. Before Allen bought the island it had an airstrip and had been subdivided into 50 acre lots.

Allen offered the island to Camp Nor'wester, the youth camp formerly on Lopez, after he bought Sperry Peninsula on Lopez where the camp had been located for 51 years. It was determined unsuitable by the camp board.

Camp Nor'wester bought over 100 acres on Johns Pass on Johns Island. First sessions for the new camp are planned for 2000. *(Ch. 5)*

Along the east shore of Allan a private dock is inside a floating breakwater in a bight. It is signed no anchoring within 300 feet to avoid fouling on breakwater anchors. A home is on shore above the bay.

We continue along the island's southeast shore with its windblown trees, driftwood clinging to the beach, vertical cliffs and rocks. Much of the island seems to be vertical, with only an occasional tiny beach. The terrain is abrupt and rocky, with brownish grass, stubby trees and barren rock. We carry a bit of current and move out from shore, following the shoreline. We're going really fast now, we have a flood current. A white sign on the beach proclaims "Private Property, No Trespassing," as we speed past, which means we're maybe going 6 or 7 knots.

Williamson Rocks, National Wildlife Reserve, is a group of small, grass-covered islets and rocks 0.5 mile south of Allan.

Williamson Rock Lighted Gong Buoy 4 [Fl R 4s Gong, R "4"] flashing red 4 second light on a buoy, marks the rocks northwest of Williamson Rocks.

Dennis Shoal is 500 yards southwest of Allan Island, a tiny islet with kelp and

Seals and sea lions lounge on Allan Island's northwest point

a rock awash at MLLW about 50 yards north.

Dennis Shoal Buoy [R N "6"] a red nun buoy, is off the west side of the shoal.

Continuing north along the west shore of Allan, we're an area totally exposed to the whims of Rosario Strait's winds and currents, with no good places to take shelter. Allan's shores look as though big hunks of bluffs have calved off and left overhanging ledges. We see a tiny beach with driftwood and the remains of a small aluminum skiff, pretty well smashed up.

Seals and sea lions laze about on rocks off the northwest end of Allan. In reasonably quiet weather we enjoy skirting close to the shorelines of Allan and Burrows islands with their steep rocky cliffs plunging straight down to depths of 10 to 14 fathoms.

And that's about it for Anacortes and Burrows and Allan islands.

Dennis Shoal
These rocks were named for an unidentified crew member of the Wilkes Expedition of 1841.

In **Chapter 10** we visit some fascinating, often overlooked, islands north of Guemes Channel: Guemes, Cypress, Strawberry Sinclair and Vendovi islands.

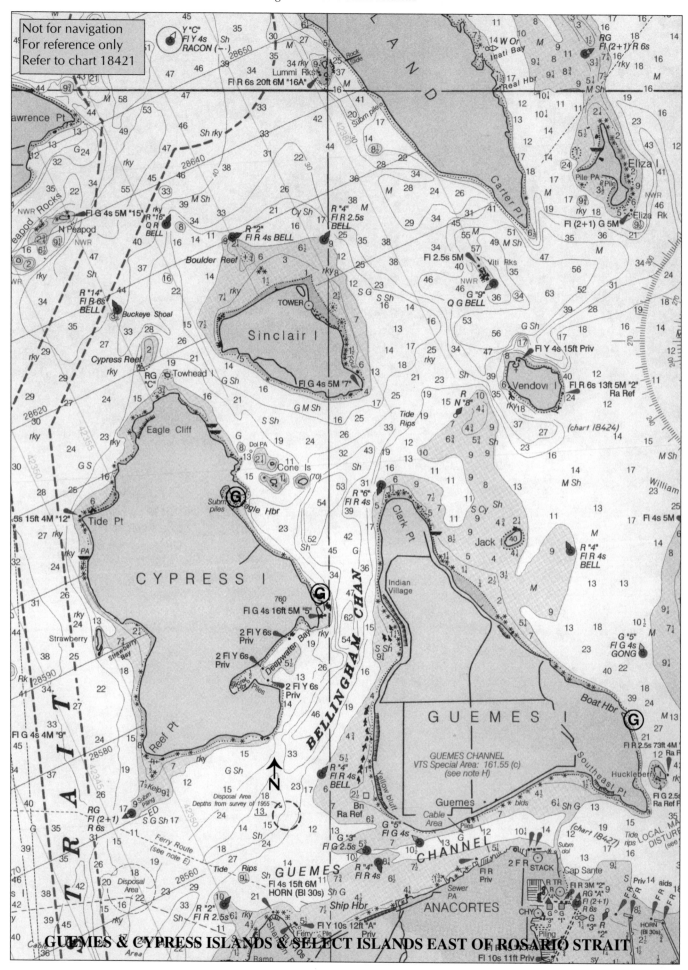

GUEMES & CYPRESS ISLANDS & SELECT ISLANDS EAST OF ROSARIO STRAIT

Chapter 10
GUEMES & CYPRESS ISLANDS
SELECT ISLANDS EAST OF ROSARIO STRAIT

Charts & Publications Useful for this Chapter

Chart	Date	Title	Scale	Soundings
U.S. 18421	03/21/98	Strait of Juan de Fuca to Strait of Georgia	1:80,000	Fathoms
U.S. 18423	06/18/94	Strip Chart Bellingham to Everett, inc. San Juan Islands		
		Page A	1:80,000	Fathoms
☆ U.S. 18424	07/12/97	Bellingham Bay	1:40,000	Fathoms
☆ U.S. 18427	02/21/98	Anacortes to Skagit Bay	1:25,000	Fathoms
☆ U.S. 18429	03/16/96	Rosario Strait, Southern Part (partial)		
☆ U.S. 18430	11/02/96	Rosario Strait, Northern Part	1:25,000	Fathoms
CAN. LC3462	10/23/98	Juan de Fuca Strait to Strait of Georgia	1:80,000	Meters
CAN. 3313	1995	Gulf Islands Chart Book, Page 1	1:200,000	Meters
🐚		Wash. State DNR Quad Map—Bellingham	1:100,000	
🐚		Wash. State DNR Quad Map—Port Townsend	1:100,000	

➡ *Compare your chart dates with those above. There may be discrepancies between chart editions.*
☆ *= Preferred chart for this chapter* 🐚 *= Indicates DNR & other public tideland information*

OVERVIEW OF GUEMES, CYPRESS & ISLANDS EAST OF ROSARIO

We're venturing off into islands that are "not the San Juans" politically, even though they are part of the San Juan archipelago geologically and geographically.

The San Juans Islands are regarded geo-politically as only the islands within San Juan County. These islands we're about to explore in Skagit County are east of Rosario Strait. They are rural, not heavily populated nor as well known as those west of the Strait, and offer few facilities for boaters, which makes them intriguing. We'll be cruising through Guemes Channel, Bellingham Channel and Rosario Strait as we explore these islands.

Guemes is a lovely forested rural island, with islanders served by a county ferry. It has one small county park, several public beach accesses and one good anchorage.

Cypress Island is ruggedly dramatic, with forested mountains, few residents and is about 80 percent Department of Natural Resources land, with several DNR parks and anchorages. State-owned Cone Islands and Strawberry Island nearby are managed by DNR.

Sinclair is private, served by passenger-only *Redhead* in summer. It has a county dock and several parcels of DNR tidelands, but no recommended anchorages. Vendovi Island is all private with no anchorages. It is almost totally surrounded by DNR beaches below the high-tide level, except in the private northwest bay.

GUEMES CHANNEL

The channel, which leads from Rosario Strait to Padilla Bay is about 0.5 mile wide and three miles long. It separates Anacortes

➡ **NOTE: Marine fuel** is **not** available in the areas covered in this chapter. Nearest fuel is in Anacortes or Bellingham.

Anchorage at Cypress Head

Guemes Name

Guemes Island and Guemes Channel were discovered in 1791 by Spanish explorers Don Jose Narvaez and Pantoja, members of the Eliza Expedition.

Eliza named the island, "Isla de Guemes," in honor of the Viceroy of Mexico under whose order he was sailing. His full name was Senor Don Juan Vicente de Guemes Pacheco de Padilla Horcasitas y Aquayo, Conde de Revillagigedo.

In 1841, the Wilkes Expedition tried to change the name to Lawrence Island for James Lawrence, a U.S. Navy captain who died in the battle of the Chesapeake and Shannon in the War of 1812.

In 1847, the names Guemes Island and Channel were restored by Captain Kellet.

Early settlers often called the island Dog Island because the Native Americans had a large population of dogs. They raised white, long-haired dogs with thick fur, almost like sheep's wool, which they wove into blankets and clothing.

Explorers noted that the dogs reminded them of Russian sled dogs. They were seen in the villages and canoes of the Indians of Guemes Island.

on Fidalgo Island on the south side from Guemes Island on the north.

Currents in Guemes Channel are predicted on Rosario Strait and can be quite challenging, particularly on the ebb. If opposing winds are blowing during strong currents, a very heavy chop is likely, with short steep waves. If winds are with the currents, the currents tend to be greater than predicted.

Ebb currents flow slightly southwest at 255°, and can reach or exceed 4 knots or more. The ebb current is predicted at 1.1 times the ebb in the Strait.

Flood currents flow east at 095°, and can reach or exceed 2 knots. The flood current is predicted at 0.8 of the flood in the Strait.

GUEMES ISLAND

Roughly triangular in shape, the island is bounded on the west by Bellingham Channel, on the east by Padilla Bay, with Guemes Channel along the south.

Pastoral, quiet, and forested, Guemes is a five minute ferry ride and a world away from the bustling city of Anacortes. About 500 people live on the island year-round, and the population surges in the summertime when city folk return to their island hideaways. The island's interior is beautiful with forests of tall evergreens turning roads into tunnels of green.

Facilities on the island include a community hall near the ferry landing, and a launch ramp west of the landing. A highly visible lighthouse structure near the ferry dock was supposed to be part of a development which hasn't yet happened. In the summer of 1998, a store with a gas pump opened near the ferry landing. It's a welcome addition to the island, with a deli and basic groceries.

Guemes Island Playground is five acres with ball fields, basketball and volleyball courts, soccer field, tennis courts, nature area, picnic tables, playground and no water. The Skagit County-Guemes Island schoolhouse and playground is near the center of the island on the southeast corner of Eden and Guemes Island roads. Guemes Island Fire Station is on the northwest corner of the intersection. North of the station is Edens Memorial Cemetery.

Cruisers who are moored in Anacortes and have bicycles on board often find that taking the ferry to Guemes Island and riding on reasonably level roads with reasonable traffic is a great diversion. Carry your own food and water. *(The Guemes Ferry Terminal is near downtown Anacortes at Sixth and I streets.)*

Young's Skagit County Day-Use Park is on the northeast shore adjacent to **Guemes Island Resort**. The resort has a launch ramp and a small store.

Ferry arrives at Guemes

⎈ **UNDERWAY AGAIN,** we go counter-clockwise around Guemes Island, starting near the ferry landing where currents are swift. We experienced this first hand from both our boat and the ferry, and were impressed with the way the crew handled the current and landed the vessel perfectly. They are pros with years of experience. The ferry landing is at the eastern edge of a **cable area**. This is not a place for anchoring because of strong currents.

🌿 **DNR tidelands** run along the beach for about 0.8 mile east from the ferry landing.

Continuing east, we pass **Deadmans Bay,** a small bight, with some boats on permanent moorages. Submerged piles and rocks are along the shore.

⚓ Possible short-term **anchorage** in the bay is in about 1.5 fathoms, rock bottom.

Cooks Cove is next, at the end of a county

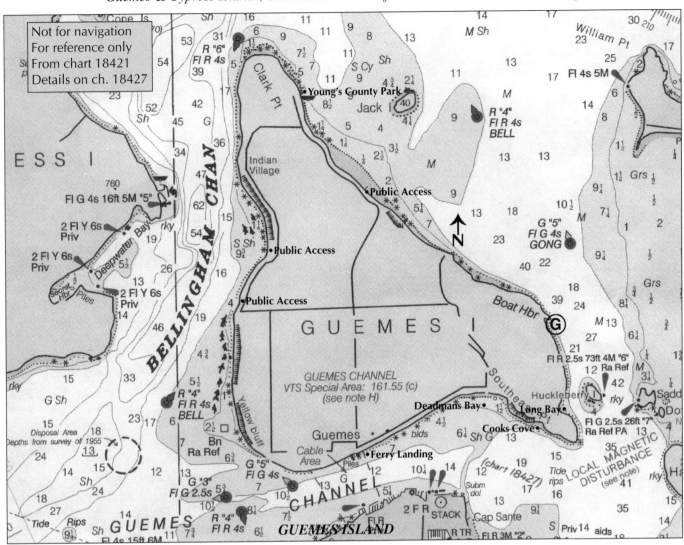

Not for navigation
For reference only
From chart 18421
Details on ch. 18427

road with a private boat launch and several small boats scattered around on the beach above. It's a lovely little beach with a small lagoon about 0.25 fathom deep. It's quite beautiful, but not a very good anchorage.

Southeast Point is high and forested, with 7 fathoms of water just offshore. We turn to the north and head along the eastern shores of the island.

Long Bay is a bight off the southeast side of the island, facing Huckleberry Island.

Public tidelands run from the southeast coast of Guemes at Long Bay to about 1.4 miles north, with no upland access. The east shore is very steep with depths of six fathoms close to rocky cliffs.

Huckleberry Island Marine State Park is less than 0.2 mile east of Guemes' southeast shore. It is an undeveloped, 10 acre park with 2,900 feet of shoreline on Padilla Bay. Because the shoreline is so steep, getting ashore is difficult, except at a small shelf area on the southwest shore. This is a good place for kayaks and small boats, and scuba divers enjoy it, but large submerged rocks make it an unpredictable anchorage for larger boats. *(Ch. 8)*

Huckleberry Island Light 6 [Fl R 2.5s 73ft 4M "6" Ra Ref] flashing red 2.5 second light 73 feet high on a triangular red dayboard on a platform with a radar reflector is on the southeast tip of Huckleberry Island.

Boat Harbor, sometimes called **Square Harbor,** is about 0.8 mile north of Long Bay. This beautiful, steep, forested bay, 100 yards wide, is the only bay with sheltered anchorage on Guemes. It is exposed to the southeast, however. There's 1 fathom in the inner part of the harbor, with rocky bluffs all around. The northern

Public Lands Quad Map

 Public tidelands, unless otherwise noted, are state-owned. Some may be leased and posted for aquaculture or other private use. When going ashore take the Washington State Public Lands Quadrangle Map of Bellingham to avoid trespassing.

The public tidelands in the areas covered in this chapter are plentiful, surrounding nearly all the islands visited.

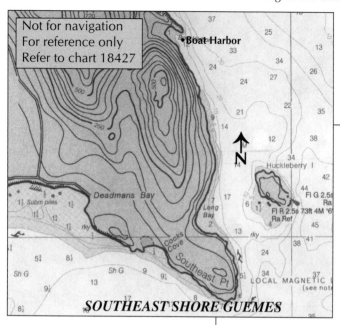

Not for navigation
For reference only
Refer to chart 18427

SOUTHEAST SHORE GUEMES

➡ **NOTE: Change charts again**. When we reach Boat Harbor going north we need to switch charts from **#18427 to #18424**.

Smuggling Stories

Larry Kelly's legacy lives on in stories, and one told about him takes place in Square Bay on Guemes …

It seems an old resident said he saw Kelly's sloop anchored in the harbor. He visited with Kelly and then Kelly suddenly yelled, "Come out, John, he's okay."

At that, Chinese appeared from behind nearly every bush around the bay where they had been hiding. They were part of the human cargo he smuggled into the country from Canada, illegal immigrants anxious to work in the U.S.

cliff is nearly 100 feet high, sheer rock. Public tidelands surround the bay with is no upland access.

⚓ **Anchoring** is possible in quiet, lovely Boat Harbor. There's enough swinging room for one boat. We might stern tie or anchor if another boat were sharing the harbor.

Ⓖ It's a **small gunkhole.**

Guemes Historical Tidbits

Spanish explorers aboard the schooners *Sutil* and *Mexicana* entered Guemes Channel on June 11, 1792. As they explored the northern shore of the channel they noted, "… A beach at the entrance, saw a village close to the northwest point and upon examining it with the telescope found it to consist of two large houses. Several Indians ran down to the beach, got into a canoe and steered for the schooners, pursuing them with as much skill as the most experienced sailor could do. In it an old man and four young ones of pleasant appearance came boldly alongside and gave us bramble-berries. With a shell of 3 to 4 inches in diameter they took some of the quantity they brought and tried to hide those they did not offer. We gave each a metal button and they repeated their gifts in small portions to obtain something else in exchange, seeing that we gave them a string of beads or piece of ship's biscuit for each present. They also gave us dried shellfish of the sort sailors call verdigones (a species of green molluscs, similar to clams), threaded on a cord of bark, and others of different kind on skewers. We accepted a sufficient quantity of them, and also obtained from them a blanket of dog's hair, quilted with feathers, and a tanned deerskin."

Chechaco was the Chinook term for newcomer and early pioneers, who began arriving on the island in the mid-1800s. Chechacos eventually displaced the Native Americans.

The J.J. Edens family was among the first of the Chechacos who landed on Guemes about 1870. The family homesteaded a large farm that included an orchard of fruit trees surrounding their house. Edens held many prominent positions in the island community and Mrs. Edens taught school on Guemes.

H.P. O'Bryant settled on the south side of Guemes and planted an orchard of 400 apple trees and 225 prune trees. Settler Cephas Parker Woodcock raised hay. Other farmers raised cattle, potatoes and onions. Large strawberries were a major crop on Guemes in the 19th century, but getting them to market was difficult. A post office was opened on Guemes on April 2, 1873. It closed in 1958 and mail was then rerouted to Anacortes.

Regular ferry service to Guemes Island began in 1917 with the *Guemes,* but the company soon went bankrupt. Bill Bessner was hired in 1920 to run the ferry, bought it the following year and ran it until 1948 when he sold it. The ferry was beached permanently in 1959.

The new *Guemes* was launched in 1978 and makes at least 17 round trips daily, with extra sailings on Fridays. With careful loading, the ferry can hold 23 vehicles, but will return for others if it's over capacity. The ferry is run by the Skagit County Department of Public Works.

Guemes Island's most well-known character is probably smuggler Lawrence Kelly, the "Scourge of the Sound." *(See p. 231)*

⚓ **UNDERWAY AGAIN,** and we continue northwesterly around Guemes.

Padilla Bay Lighted Gong Buoy [G "5" Fl G 4s] flashing green 4 second light on a green gong buoy is about 0.7 mile north of Boat Harbor along the western edge of the 10 fathom curve of Padilla Bay. The bay shoals to less than 1 fathom about 0.5 mile east of the buoy.

From Boat Harbor, the shoreline trends northwest and steep bluffs eventually drop down to low to no-bank waterfront. Rocky shores give way to long, sandy North Beach, which is south and slightly west of privately owned Jack Island.

🌿 A 40 foot wide **public access road,** Department of Fish and Wildlife, off North Beach Road makes it possible to reach nearly 3,000 feet of sandy tidelands from the mean tide line to extreme low tide at North Beach. Hand-carried boats can be launched here. For those driving to the island for this purpose, go north from the ferry on Guemes Island Road for about 1.5 miles past the intersection of Edens Road. The access road is south of many bramble bushes and a house at 427 Guemes Island Road. The access is buried in a development of wall-to-wall summer cottages and is hard to see from the water.

Low tide on North Beach, Jack Island in background

Young's Park, a Skagit County day-use only park, and Guemes Island Resort are next to each other about due west of the north end of Jack Island. A charted mooring buoy shows the approximate location of the park and resort. Young's is the only public waterfront park on the island, and is about 4.5 miles from the ferry landing at Guemes Island Road end. Hand-carried boats are launched here. In fact, as we sat on the delightful beach enjoying lunch we met a group with five double kayaks preparing for an expedition to Lummi Island.

⚓ **Anchoring** is possible here in 5 to 8 fathoms in calm weather, but it is quite exposed. Bottom is charted as sand and clay.

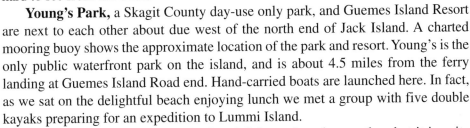

> **Facilities at Young's Park**
> ➤ 11 acres with 500 feet of no bank waterfront and lovely beach
> ➤ Hand carried boats may be launched across logs
> ➤ Picnic tables, fire grates
> ➤ Toilet
> ➤ Spectacular views

Guemes Island Resort is a well-kept secret. An attractive, old style resort with a quiet family atmosphere, there are six cabins and a beach-front home, a seasonal swimming pool and boat rentals, including double kayaks. Meals are not served, but all accommodations have kitchens with the added luxury of no TV, telephones or radios. There's a lending library, lawn checkers, horseshoe court and many places for swimming, boating, beachcombing, kite flying and relaxing. Mooring buoys are for resort guests only.

Launch ramp is available for both guests and non-guests of the resort. The country store at the resort carries a little bit of everything, including beverages, ice cream, groceries, sundries, ice, bait, fishing tackle, fishing and shellfish licenses. Guemes Island Resort Tel.: 800-965-6643; e-mail: guemesresort@juno.com

Guemes Island Resort Totem

⊕ **UNDERWAY AGAIN,** we continue around Guemes Island.

Jack Island, all private, is about 40 feet high and forested. It's in Padilla Bay about 0.7 mile east of the resort and Young's Park. Jack has rocky bluffs on the east shore tapering to low bank on the west.

Padilla Bay Lighted Bell Buoy 4 [R "4" Fl R 4s Bell] flashing red 4 second light with a bell on a red bell buoy, is 0.6 mile east of Jack Island. It marks an area

Low tide at Guemes

Naming Jack Island
Jack Island was named by the Wilkes Expedition in 1841, probably for "jack," a common name for a sailor.

of less than 10 fathoms east and south of the island.

Clark Point at the north end of Guemes is a steep, forested bluff. A rocky reef extends 300 yards north from the point.

Public tidelands of about 4,000 feet surround the point.

Bellingham Channel Lighted Buoy 6 [R "6" Fl R 4s] flashing red 4 second light on a red buoy, is about 300 yards off the northwest tip of Clark Point, marking the shoal. In July 1983 this buoy was reported submerged during by strong currents.

Public tidelands of 0.25 miles surround Clark Point, with great beachcombing, plus spectacular views of Mt. Baker, Vendovi, Lummi, Sinclair, Cypress and Cone islands. Some persons walk around the point heading north from the resort, but incoming high tides or heavy waves can block access, as bluffs above the shoreline are steep and there is no inland access.

Bellingham Channel, as much as 62 fathoms deep and six miles long, runs between Guemes and Cypress islands. It is the most direct route to Bellingham Bay from the south.

Tidal currents in the channel may be strong. Predictions are based on Rosario Strait currents and referenced off Cypress Island Light.

Flood currents flow northeast at 045° at 1.1 times those in Rosario and may reach or exceed 3 knots.

Ebb currents flow south at 185° and are 1.2 times those in Rosario and may reach or exceed 4.3 knots.

Indian Village is charted on the west shore of Guemes about 1.1 miles south of Clark Point on the west shore of Guemes. This is apparently the site of a "village close to the northwest point" observed by Spanish explorers in 1792.

South of the village is a rock and kelp filled bight about 0.75 mile wide. The rocks are awash at MLLW. The shore rises abruptly to bluffs 120 feet high for about 0.5 mile along the north part of the bight. The south end, where the shore descends, it is locally called Potlatch Beach.

Depths north and south of the bight plunge to 10 fathoms near shore, but within the bight the 10 fathom curve extends 700 yards, while the 3 fathom curve is 300 yards offshore.

Public tidelands of less than three miles in four separate parcels are along the west shore of Guemes from Potlatch Beach to Kellys Point. We suggest referring to the DNR Quad Map.

Beachwalking at Kellys Point

Access by road to these tidelands is possible from two public road ends which allow kayak launching and fabulous views across Bellingham Channel to mountainous Cypress Island. Private homes are on either side of both road ends.

Chart 18424 shows the south road end, just west of the intersection of West Shore Road and Edens Road.

Lervick Road beach access is 0.7 mile north off West Shore Road.

Yellow Bluff is the impressive southwest bluff of Guemes Island, 150 feet high, barren and towering above a beachcomber's "dream beach"—**public tidelands** of about 1.2 miles. Rockhounds search for treasures here. Climbing the bluff's bank is frowned upon as it is subject to slides.

Yellow Bluff Reef, less than 5 fathoms deep, extends 0.4 mile west of the bluff and runs about 0.5 mile along shore.

Yellow Bluff Reef Obstruction Daybeacon [W Bn Ra Ref] diamond-shaped white dayboard on a dolphin worded **"DANGER REEF"** with a radar reflector, is about 300 yards offshore marking the reef.

Kellys Point is about 0.3 mile south of Yellow Bluff, named for Larry "Smuggler" Kelly, who lived on the island.

➡**NOTE: Change charts again.** If using chart **#18424,** it's now time to switch back to **#18427** just north of Yellow Bluff.

"King Of The Smugglers," Larry Kelly

Kelly, whose smuggling and sailing reputation was legendary throughout the northwest, was born about 1839 in Europe. He was a deep water sailor, joined the Confederate Army in the Civil War, and arrived in the Pacific Northwest aboard a ship in 1865.

He married an Indian woman named Lizzie Kotz and built a cabin on Guemes in 1872 where he lived until 1878. Hidden in the woods, the cabin was only a short walk to the bluff at the point where he watched for revenue cutters in Rosario Strait, Guemes and Bellingham channels. He supported his family by hauling contraband around the waters in an ordinary fishing sloop. He could easily outrun the slower revenue boats because of his extraordinary boat-handling skills.

Kelly smuggled wine, opium and occasionally Chinese during his 35 year "career." He did so well that he later bought 320 acres on Sinclair Island, nearly one-third of the island, which was then called Cottonwood. There he was elected to the school board and was thought to be an outstanding citizen, even though his profession was not a secret. From Sinclair he could see Rosario Strait, Bellingham Channel, north to Georgia Strait and Canada, and any customs vessels that might be patrolling the area.

One story is that he specialized in importing opium from one of 14 licensed refineries in Victoria. He buried packets of it on his farm or along the beach on Sinclair. Later he would sell it to an agent in Port Townsend or Seattle for 12 dollars per pound.

Kelly frequented jails in King County, Victoria, Tacoma, and McNeil Island at the federal penitentiary. After he was released from jail he was in his seventies and moved to a Confederate soldiers' home in Louisiana. Stories about Larry Kelly abound in island lore publications.

Naming Kelly's Point
Kelly's Point on southwest Guemes was named for Lawrence Kelly, reknowned smuggler of opium, alcohol and Chinese.

His smuggling career, which began in the 1870s, lasted about 35 years.

Larry Kelly's cabin?

Guemes Channel Lighted Buoy 5 [Fl G 4s "5"] flashing green 4 second light on a green buoy, is 0.3 mile southeast of Kellys Point along the 10 fathom curve.

Guemes Channel Lighted Buoy 3 [G "3" Fl G 2.5s] flashing green 2.5 second light on a green buoy, is 0.5 mile southwest of Kellys Point

[Lighted Buoy 4 R "4" Fl R 4s] flashing red 4 second light on a red buoy, is 400 yards southeast of buoy "3," 0.55 mile southwest of Kellys Point.

From Kellys Point to Guemes Ferry Landing is about 0.85 mile. The beach is gravel and 1 to 2 fathoms deep for about 100 yards offshore all along this south end. The shore is constantly beaten by surf from Guemes Channel.

Launch ramp is west of the ferry dock, single lane, and used by small boats and kayaks.

We've completed our circumnavigation of Guemes Island and now we're off to visit mountainous, sparsely inhabited Cypress Island.

Potlatch on Guemes' west shore
Native American potlatches were held at a longhouse on West Beach, possibly 900 feet long, before settlers arrived at Guemes Island.

Guests arrived by canoe from many miles away for these traditional celebrations where all guests received gifts.

CYPRESS ISLAND

This is an absolutely fascinating island, with a nearly 1,500 foot high forested

No Development

In the late 1970s, a developer had plans to build 170 homes, 190 condominiums, a 100 slip marina and an 18 hole golf course on Cypress. Of the 3,000 acres he owned, 747 were proposed for develpoment.

A few vocal, concerned citizens stopped the project and the state purchased the island, which is now preserved in its natural state.

Cypress Island trees

peaks, clear, shallow bays, magnificent cliffs and over 25 miles of hiking trails. It is the largest relatively undeveloped island in the entire San Juans region, where extensive areas of undeveloped shoreline and uplands are becoming a rarity. The state owns over 80 percent of the island, most of it Department of Natural Resources land. Eagle Harbor, Cypress Head and Pelican Beach are the three anchorages.

Cypress contains "unusual geological characteristics, outstanding examples of native biological communities, critical habitat for federally protected species, and significant marine and cultural resources," according to the Department of Natural Resources. Seven prehistoric sites are on the island, several of which are eroding by natural processes.

This is an exceptional island that needs to be studied and protected, and for these reasons and others, 4,660 acres on Cypress were selected to be a Natural Resources Conservation Area. Private lands encompass 840 acres, for a total of 5,500 acres on Cypress.

Public tidelands surround all but about two miles of Cypress and all of Strawberry and Cone island.

Coastal Salish Indians had seasonal camps on Cypress that were centers for hunting, fishing, gathering and ceremonies. However, there are no indications of permanent villages, and after early homesteaders arrived in the mid-1800s, Indian use slowly died out.

Early settlers did extensive logging, fishing and sporadic mining of chromite and olivine. Try as they might, homesteaders found that the difficult access, rugged topography and poor soils made building roads, schools and community services on the mountainous island extremely difficult. Eventually, most homesteads were abandoned. A post office on Cypress served hard-working islanders for 15 years, from July 1, 1880 to February 28, 1905.

Recent proposals for residential developments have not worked out, and in view of the designation of Cypress as a Natural Resources Conservation Area "homesteading" will probably not be developed.

For a time, a large portion of the island had a single owner who built some roads and an air field. Presently, the roads are used as hiking trails as no motorized vehicles, except those belonging to the state, are permitted on the island.

The challenging Eagle Cliff Trail is closed annually from February 1 through July 15 because it traverses an endangered species breeding habitat.

The air field near mid-island, closer to the east side, is used for emergencies, such as fire fighting. Mountain biking and pack animals are prohibited. Pets are allowed on leash in designated areas, and hunting is allowed as determined by local tribes and the State Department of Fish and Wildlife.

An environmental group camp is at Reed Lake. If groups want to come to the island for research or to volunteer for trail clean-up they can stay at the camp. There are two public camp sites on Cypress, at Cypress Head and Pelican Beach. Camping is also allowed on Strawberry Island off the west shore.

Cypress has 11 lakes and ponds ranging from one to 15 acres; one stream, Strawberry Bay Creek, and 33 springs. About 33 inches of rain falls on Cypress annually. There are still some stands of old-growth fir trees which are five feet in diameter.

Black-tailed deer, red fox, river otters, raccoons, and small rodents live on the island, but wolf, mink, elk, moose and black bear are no longer here. Over half of the 120 bird species on

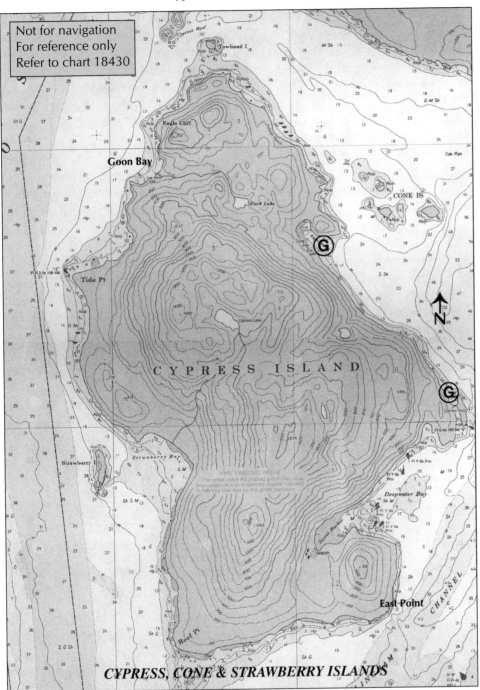

Not for navigation
For reference only
Refer to chart 18430

CYPRESS, CONE & STRAWBERRY ISLANDS

Hide from Haidas

The peaceful Coast Salish Indians led a fairly quiet lifestyle, with easy access to clams, crab, fish and berries.

They had seasonal camps on Cypress for hunting, fishing, gathering and ceremonies. But even here the warlike northern Haidas would occasionally descend.

The story we heard was that if the Indians saw a Haida canoe come around Lawrence Point on Orcas, they would climb Eagle Cliff and hide in the caves.

Our friend said someone claimed to have found baskets in the caves where food had been stored for supplies the next time the Haidas appeared.

Cypress are marine birds, including herons, pigeon guillemots, gulls, grebes, loons, scoters, buffleheads and the endangered marbled murrelet.

⊗ **UNDERWAY,** we start our circumnavigation of Cypress Island at the junction buoy off **Reef Point** at the southwest corner of the island and go counter-clockwise. We've learned much about the island thanks to the wealth of information we received from Department of Natural Resources personnel and other helpful folks.

Reef Point Junction Lighted Buoy [R G Fl (2+1) R 6s] flashing red 6 second light on a red and green banded buoy, marks the under 10 fathom shallows extending nearly 0.7 mile southwest of Cypress. The shallows lead north and east towards the island so that at the island's unnamed southeast point the 10 fathom depth curve is less than 50 yards offshore. Bluffs rise 100 feet above the shore and climb to a mountainous 1,243 foot peak in less than 0.8 mile.

East Point is the local name for the hill at the southeast point of Cypress. The eastern portion around the head where hills reach nearly 600 feet is private land.

Cypress Peak

*The 1,500 foot peak near the center of Cypress was called "**She-ungtlh"** by the Lummis. It was the home of the Great Thunder Bird.*

Whoops!

There's a story about a mine on a cliff above one of the fish pens in Secret Harbor:

During the Depression in the 1930s, some folks decided to mine chromium for ball bearings. They dug the mine, built a hopper and pulled a barge in.

In the first barge load, the hopper got loose with a load on it, went thru the barge and sank. The workers all went home. The barge frames are still there.

Between Reef Point and East Point are remnants of old olivine mining operations. Olivine was used in making cement. Olivine found on the surface of the island is uncommon because this dense mineral is usually overridden by lighter rocks. A road comes down near the point to a long beach where there were once open mines, and it's visible from the water. Pilings are still at an old barge landing.

Deepwater Bay is around East Point. At the head of the bay is **Secret Harbor** where there's a private boys' school. Lawns and several school buildings are set around the harbor, which is backed by steep Cypress hills. A cobbled rock beach with a high bank slopes back into the trees.

There are several fish farm pens in Secret Harbor and Deepwater Bay.

Secret Harbor Fish Pen Lights [2 Fl Y 6s Priv maintd] two flashing yellow 6 second lights, privately maintained, are on three pairs of fish pen buoys on the steel salmon pens. One set of pens is along the south shore of Deepwater Bay, one is at the north end of Secret Harbor and the third is along the north shore of the bay. The fish farms have a dozen or more large round floats marking them.

Anchoring is not advised in the harbor because it's difficult to find a good place to drop the hook due to the fish pens; generators from the school often run all night long, disturbing the peace, and currents, which are fine for salmon farming, are not ideal for anchoring. A shoal of 5 to 10 fathoms is in the center of the bay.

Privately owned buoys are along the north shore of the bay. A dock is in a small, shallow cove at the north east corner. A second cove between Cypress Head and the island is about 400 yards long. It is not recommended as an anchorage because it is rocky and as shallow as 2 feet at MLLW for much of the bay.

🐚 **DNR public tidelands** run from Deepwater Bay north around the top of the island and along the west shore to about one mile north of Tide Point.

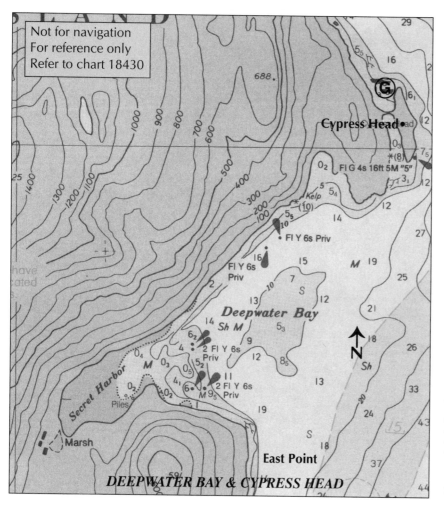

Not for navigation
For reference only
Refer to chart 18430

DEEPWATER BAY & CYPRESS HEAD

CYPRESS HEAD DNR PARK

We've now reached Cypress Head, an "almost" island off the east side of Cypress, connected by a tombolo.

Bellingham Channel Light 5 [Fl G 4s 16ft 5M "5"] flashing green 4 second light 16 feet high with 5 mile visibility is mounted on a square green dayboard on the southeast end of Cypress Head. The *Light List* shows there is a higher intensity beam up and down the channel.

Cypress Head is a fairly high, 500 yards long, narrow forested islet joined to the east shore of Cypress by a low isthmus.

The beaches on the north and south sides of the isthmus are beautiful, with driftwood, cobblestones, sand and shells. Picnic areas and campgrounds, with varnished picnic tables, firepits and plenty of room to set up tents, are on this low stretch of land. From here a trail heading west connects to old island roads leading to the airstrip and Reed Lake. DNR has a compound at the lake with an office and living quarters for the island steward and volunteers.

We go around the "hammerhead" that is Cypress Head and into the north cove, one of those treasures that turn up now and then. It is lovely, quiet and all the things we hope to find when we're out cruising, including five mooring buoys, set rather close together. More campgrounds are on Cypress Head, and trails wander all around it. Steep stairs have been cut into the rocky bank leading to the head from the low land.

Views from here are unique. Open to the north and northeast, we can see Mount Baker, Bellingham Channel, Lummi, Sinclair and Cone islands, and east across the channel to Guemes.

Currents in Bellingham Channel during the ebb hook into the cove and causes a strong easterly set. The large back eddy downstream of Cypress Head during the flood also causes an easterly set. The combination of wind and current often turns boats crossways to the current causing them ride up on the buoys. We occasionally pull the chain up through the buoy and secure it so the chain hangs straight down.

⚓ **Anchoring** in this cove near the buoys is something we do not recommend, based on our experience with the currents. However, some boats manage to anchor

Ⓖ This is a **lovely gunkhole,** but be aware of strong currents.

Facilities at Cypress Head DNR Park

➤ 5 mooring buoys, no fee
➤ 11 campsites, no fee
➤ Vault toilets
➤ No water
➤ Washington Water Trails campsite
➤ Activities: hike, gunkhole, fish, scuba dive, swim, relax

Naming Cypress Island

The common explanation is that Capt. George Vancouver named Cypress Island after a tree which doesn't grow on the island. But cypress and fir trees look fairly similar from a distance, and firs are numerous on the island.

However, we understand that biologists and botanists in Olympia feel that this common explanation of the mistaken tree identity seems unlikely, according to Kathryn Gunther with the Department of Natural Resources.

"Vancouver's botanist, Archibald Menzies, was too intelligent to make such an error. They believe that he did in fact notice the Rocky Mountain Junipers (not the firs) and since junipers are members of the larger Cypress family— Cypressus—named the island Cypress. Perhaps in that time period they even referred to junipers as cypress."

**Moorage at Cypress Head,
Zade in the center**

➡NOTE: Change charts again. Chart #18427 is all right for the southern shore of Cypress, but for the rest of the island **chart #18424** is needed.

A Night at Cypress Head

One weekend at Cypress Head five boats on the five buoys, plus another six boats either anchored or side-tied to the moored boats. The 11 boats in the bay ranged from 21 to 40 feet, including several San Juan 21 foot sailboats and the "mother ship," a San Juan 34.

We had "one of those nights" at Cypress Head, when we stayed dressed and sat in the cockpit wrapped in blankets ready to take action as the boats careened restlessly around the moorage.

During the night a strong southerly blew across the isthmus into the cove, maybe 20-25 knots, and boats swung around. We encountered each other as the current carried boats closer together, and part of the time they were spread wide apart. When "things went bump in the night," we fended off. In fact, our neighbors were all friendly folks and we visited a fair amount during the rest of the night as we all tried to avoid contact.

Lovely bay at Cypress Head

The next day DNR ranger Sean Hewitt swung by in the park boat.

"This is one of those weird spots where currents are different and boats don't all lay the same way. Perhaps some day we'll shift the buoys. When the main blocks, saddle blocks and chains were replaced, the dive time was during big tides so perhaps the blocks didn't get placed quite where they should have," he said.

The buoys are secured by 2,000 pound blocks of concrete, each with a 500 pound satellite concrete block anchor, and generally they hold even 50 footers. With a strong current or wind a heavy boat could "wind up elsewhere, even though there's strong suction of mud holding the concrete blocks," he said. "Prevailing winds tend to be south and southeast, they slot around the islands, usually are light in morning, build all day, and lay down at night. We get 'williwaws' (strong, gusty winds) here when high pressure builds up."

Sean said Eagle Harbor is considered the best anchorage on Cypress and sometime in the near future DNR buoys may be put in. He said he wouldn't trust anchorages at Pelican Beach and Cypress Head during strong currents, as he'd seen boats drag at both places.

Conversely, our editor, Sally Cox Bryan and her husband Bob tied to a buoy at Cypress Head in their 50 foot classic cruiser, *Corsair II,* when they were lucky enough to be the only boat there. They had a calm time, with no swinging or bumping other buoys, although they could see impressive rips and waves from currents in Bellingham Channel running off the head.

Trails on Cypress Head are beautiful. The hike across the ridge to the south is on an irregular trail along the west side, with only a few steep places and fallen trees, some clearly left over from that 100 mph northeast storm that struck the whole area in 1990. We're glad we weren't in the little cove during that storm.

We had a picnic lunch sitting amidst the sun-dappled trees and rocks on the south end of the Head, overlooking the channel light, watching currents in the channel near shore, and boats farther out as they cruised through the waters.

From the light there's a trail along the east side above the channel. There isn't

➡ NOTE: An information board at Cypress Head informs about the Natural Resources Conservation Area and urges visitors to: "camp and build fires in designated areas only, stay on marked trails, keep pets on leash, leave cultural artifacts undisturbed, pack it in, pack it out, tread lightly and leave no trace."

much of a beach below, but scenery is spectacular and the trail is easy.

At the north end of Cypress Head were currents and rips like those which had misbehaved so during the night. The backeddy was hanging on the corner as the current ran around the shoal at the north end of the Head.

A fascinating old snag full of holes in the late stages of decay is in the north end camping area. There are also marvelous old evergreen and madronas trees, many birds, picnic tables, fire rings, toilets and a readerboard detailing the geology of the San Juan archipelago. The last major ice event ended 10,000 years ago when the Vashon glacier retreated back to Canada. It also explains tombolos, marine habitats, tidepools and just about everything else. We suggest reading this before hiking around Cypress Head. It's full of great information.

⚓ **UNDERWAY AGAIN,** we move on to Eagle Harbor.

We slip the buoy at Cypress and sail north to Eagle Harbor, 1.5 miles away. This east side of Cypress is deep green, forested, steep and precipitous, with scarcely any shoreline, just an abrupt drop to the sea from 500 foot hills. The 10 fathom depth curve is usually about 150 yards offshore, but there are a couple of errant shallow spots. The chart clearly shows that most of **Eagle Harbor** is less than 5 fathoms deep. A 1 foot shoal is off the west side near the charted piles.

We anchor in soft, oozy mud, about 150 feet from the steep eastern bluffs, in about 20 feet. Soon we're swinging from 20 to 40 foot depths, with about 80 to 100 feet of anchor line out. Several other boats had anchored before we arrived, including a 40 foot sailboat in the center harbor. This seems like a good anchorage, but there's a lot of eel grass and some boats have problems anchoring. The wind is from north to northwest down the gully at the head of the bay.

Jo rows the skiff to the head of the bay for a swim, finding trails that lead off to Duck Lake and Eagle Cliff, as well as an interpretive site. While she's ashore, Carl watches a power boat come in and anchor between us and the sailboat in the center. The boat anchors, backing down toward us, but doesn't hold. They **throw** the anchor over, run up on it, back down, run forward again, on top of their line. When the anchor finally hooks, the crew almost falls overboard. They appear to be set for the night.

After a great swim in reasonably warm water, Jo rows out, picks Carl up and goes to the charted area of "submerged piles and log booms" along the west shore, where a ramp leads to more trails connecting with the head of the bay, Pelican Beach, Duck Lake and Eagle Cliff. Pilings and ruins of old logging operations, logged-off trees, no log booms, and another interpretive reader board are here. The loading ramp is used by DNR for landing supplies, people and equipment.

Because we're uneasy about leaving the boat too long in a new anchorage with gusty winds and neighbors who might drag, we don't walk very far on those trails. We hear so many good things about hiking on Cypress we vow to go back.

By dusk there's 11 boats in the harbor, a lovely calm evening and the northerly "laid down" as predicted. We were ready for a good night's sleep after the previous night's vigil.

More About Eagle Harbor, according to Ranger Sean Hewitt:

The wind here compresses and shotguns right through the harbor. Problems arise if boats anchor and set back into the harbor, and then winds and currents tug at them and they slide off the shelf.

The bottom is eel grass in places and bare in others. If you can get a good set in the bare parts you're okay. If not, and you set the anchor in eel grass you're likely to slide off. The best anchor to use in Eagle Harbor is a plow type, CQR or Bruce.

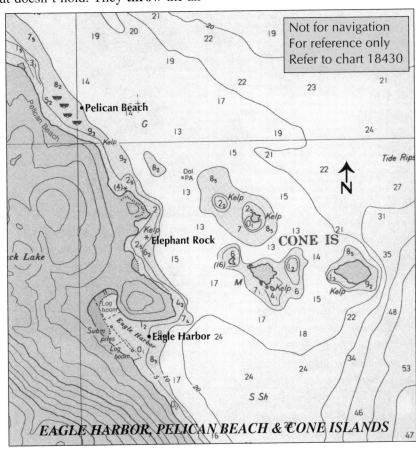

Not for navigation
For reference only
Refer to chart 18430

EAGLE HARBOR, PELICAN BEACH & CONE ISLANDS

Plans for Eagle Harbor

DNR has tentative plans to designate Eagle Harbor as a main entrance to parklands on Cypress, according to their management plan.

They are in the process of planning for buoys in the harbor, and then limiting anchorage to minimize the impacts on eelgrass and kelp beds.

Night in Eagle Harbor

2130: We began getting current which swung us around. The wind picked up again, coming down over the top of the high, steep banks and through the draw at the head of the bay, gusting 20 to 25 knots. We were swinging all around our anchor, as was everyone else.

2200: We crawled into bed as the wind quieted down, and woke up soon after, rolling considerably. Gusts seemed to be coming from every direction. They would hit from the east, then come down off the steep north point where we were anchored, then down off the west side of the bay. The "williwaw" had arrived. Currents eddied around, a heavy chop from seas bounced back from the steep rock bluffs. The powerboat nearest us was getting closer, and even watching the radar we weren't sure who was dragging, us or them. We later found out we weren't the dragger. Good old Danforth.

Beautiful Eagle Harbor looking southeast to Guemes

Arrive Early

Several days after our Eagle Harbor experience, we met the couple on the first sailboat we had seen anchored in the harbor. By then we were both anchored in Chuckanut Bay.

They were from Bellingham and said Eagle Harbor was their favorite anchorage as they loved to hike the island.

They usually arrived early in the day, anchored securely in the center of the harbor, and spent the afternoons hiking the trails.

"If we get one good night at Cypress without strong winds we're lucky, but we've never dragged there," they said.

0130: We watched as a sailboat began circling around close to us, with no lights, apparently hunting for another spot to anchor. We had some concern about it hitting our anchor line as it passed close to our bow. The boat made several passes and dropped the hook to the north of us in a position to be threatening to a small anchored sailboat. The smaller boat shined a light on the vertical bluff behind to show how close to shore they were.

0315: Stars were brilliant against a black sky. We could see no lights from anything except anchored boats. As we swung near each other in the dark, windy dance, skippers would shine flashlights to make certain others saw them. It was difficult to tell where the water ended and shore began.

0500: We finally turned in as dark slowly turned to gray daylight. We checked our position once or twice after that, using the radar to determine if we were dragging, luckily we weren't.

While Eagle Harbor is considered the best anchorage on the island, in company of other boats there is a concern about currents, winds, dragging anchor or being too close to others. Cypress Island had given us two restless nights in a row, but we learned that most boats did not drag during those windy nights.

We left Eagle Harbor in the morning as squalls gusting up to 25 knots were increasing inside the bay, but outside it didn't look that bad. A very large, rather strange looking vessel entered the bay just before we raised our anchor. Those on board seemed to be observing both the shore and us, then put the vessel in forward, aimed straight at us and suddenly anchored less than 100 feet away. Definitely time to move on.

⚓ **Anchoring** is possible here, being aware of crowds, possible williwaws—and remember to set the hook very carefully.

Ⓖ This can be a **delightful gunkhole.**

⚓ **UNDERWAY AGAIN**—it's time to finish circumnavigating Cypress Island.

Northward, around the steep bluff at Eagle Harbor and about 500 yards beyond are two small bays with beautiful beaches and no real protection. They can be an option to drop a "lunch hook," or for kayakers to beach their craft for a break.

Elephant Rock, a small island with a hole through it, is between the two bays. If this place looks somewhat familiar, it may be that you've seen the movie "Free Willy." The opening scenes were filmed here when the camera panned around large rocks and then the whole scene explodes at you with the rock in the foreground. Filming was done on the east side of Cypress for about two weeks, with huge barges, mechanical whales and with Guemes Island sometimes in the background.

🐚 **Cone Islands State Park,** less than 0.4 mile northeast of Cypress, is five rocky islets surrounded by kelp and shoals. The undeveloped state park is nearly 10 acres in size with about 2,500 feet of shoreline. Going ashore is difficult because of steep cliffs and no beaches on the islets. They are most often enjoyed by boaters cruising past, kayakers and occasionally by scuba divers.

Cone Islands

PELICAN BEACH DNR RECREATION SITE

This is a beautiful spot, forested with evergreens and madronas, about one mile north of Eagle Harbor on the northeast side of Cypress. There's a great beach and some facilities, but the reason many visitors choose this site is to hike through deep forests, especially on the Eagle Cliff Trail.

> **Facilities at Pelican Beach DNR Recreation Site**
> ➤ Six mooring buoys, no fees
> ➤ Seven campsites, no fees
> ➤ Three picnic tables
> ➤ Two restrooms
> ➤ No water
> ➤ Washington Water Trails campsite
> ➤ Activities: hike, beachcomb, swim, wade, picnic, camp

As lovely as Pelican Beach is, the northerlies blow down Rosario Strait right onto the beach. This made us a bit uneasy, especially after the last two nights. Even though winds weren't too strong when we arrived good-sized breakers were rolling onto the beach. The buoys were all taken, the beach was covered with tents and kayaks, and the crowds made this remote island site look more crowded than Sucia. This didn't seem to be a good place to anchor in these conditions.

For the adventurous, it's possible to walk the beach around the north end of Cypress, but hikers should check the tides so as not be caught between the sea and the high bank on incoming tides.

Everything Hangs On

We felt a sort of empathy between our windy nights hanging on the hook and the constant struggle that evergreens and madrona trees have in hanging on to their rock faces and bluffs.

It's a pretty tenuous survival situation for them. There's enough earth, nutrients and water for them to grow and cling to steeply sloped, barren rock faces, just as our anchor allowed us to cling to the bottom in Eagle Harbor.

Beaches Overused

Pelican Beach is the park most impacted by kayakers' use in the parks managed by DNR in the greater San Juan area.

Second most impacted is Obstruction Pass DNR Park on Orcas Island.

Eagle Cliff on Cypress, center right, Lummi in background

How high the cliff?

Take your choice about the height of Eagle Cliff. Chart 18430 shows the height at 752 feet. Chart 18424 lists it as 840 feet.

Strawberry Island

Towhead Island, privately owned is about 200 yards off the north end of Cypress. There's a dock, but no house. Depths mid-channel between the Towhead and Cypress are about 6 to 8 fathoms.

Cypress Reef is about 600 yards west of Towhead.

Cypress Reef Daybeacon [R G "C"] dayboard on a pile bearing horizontal bands of red and green, red band topmost, marks the reef. A 2 fathom shoal about 500 yards long is 100 yards north and slightly east of the reef.

Buckeye Shoal is 0.6 mile northwest of Cypress Reef and 1.2 miles west of Sinclair Island, with a least depth of 3.5 fathoms.

Buckeye Shoal Lighted Bell Buoy [Fl R 6s Bell R "14"] flashing red 6 second light with a bell, marks the shoal.

We're now heading along the rugged, steep northwest end of Cypress Island, where stunning **Eagle Cliff** soars 752 feet above the water. Sheer, partially forested cliffs drop straight down to Rosario Strait. There is no good anchorage in the bights below the cliff because of the rocky bottom, kelp and strong currents. However, we met a man who said he had spent a lot of time at Tide Point as a kid, and that he considered locally named "Goon Bay" just north of the point a good anchorage. We didn't try it.

Tide Point, rocky and fairly low for Cypress, juts out into Rosario Strait off the west side of the island. There is no public tideland around the point. Friends tell us fishing is good between the north end of the island, called Eagle Bluff locally, and Tide Point. South of the point are charted mooring buoy symbols, but DNR rangers told us there are no secure anchorages on the west side of Cypress.

Tide Point Light [Fl R 2.5s 15ft 4 M "12"] flashing red 2.5 second light, 15 feet high visible 4 miles on triangular red dayboard on a pile.

❀ **DNR public tidelands** run south along the west shore of Cypress for about three miles, starting about 0.5 mile south of Tide Point.

Strawberry Island is about 1.3 miles south of Tide Point, 300 yards offshore in **Strawberry Bay,** a DNR campsite off the southwest side of Cypress.

Trees crown the island, with high bluffs on the northwest side, and it tapers to abrupt bare rock at the south end. Strawberry is an island where only small boats can land because of deep water and strong currents.

DNR warns, "Danger: Strong currents and submerged rocks make landing difficult; skiff or kayak best for landing." Best place to land is on the southwest shore of Strawberry, at the cove between the small knob and the rest of the island, said DNR staff.

As a friend said, "Strawberry Island is a horrible anchorage, but good for beachable boats, mostly kayaks, with a high tide landing."

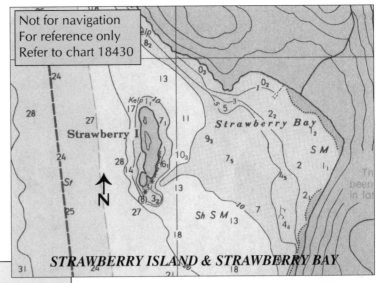

Not for navigation
For reference only
Refer to chart 18430

STRAWBERRY ISLAND & STRAWBERRY BAY

Facilities at Strawberry Island DNR Site
➤ 11 acres with 4,000 feet of shoreline on Rosario Strait & Strawberry Bay
➤ Three campsites with picnic tables & fire grates
➤ No fees
➤ No water, vault toilets
➤ Short trail
➤ Washington Water Trails campsite
➤ Activities: short walks, beachcomb, scuba dive, paddle

⚓ Anchoring in Strawberry Bay might be a good short term in 2 fathoms, sand and mud bottom, but it is exposed to wind and currents.

About a half-dozen private cabins are along the shores, although tidelands are public. An unimproved trail head with a trail map is on the beach at Strawberry Bay, south of the private property line near the eastern indent of the shore. Strawberry Creek drains into the northern third of the bay.

Bit of Strawberry Bay History
Capt. George Vancouver arrived in Strawberry Bay on June 8, 1792.

"With a tolerably good breeze from the north … and with a flood tide, we turned up into Strawberry Bay where we anchored in 16 fathoms, fine sandy bottom. This bay is situated on the west side of an island, which, producing an abundance of upright cypress, obtained the name of Cypress Island. The bay is of small extent and not very deep … a small islet, forming nearly the north point of the bay … and the bottom of the bay east, at the distance of about three quarters of a mile. This situation, though very commodious in respect to the shore, is greatly exposed to winds and sea in a south-southeast direction."

It's just 1.1 miles from Strawberry Bay south to Reef Point along steep shores.

We started and ended our circumnavigation of the island at the point, and now we cruise north and east of Cypress Island to visit two more islands.

SINCLAIR & VENDOVI ISLANDS
These islands east of Cypress are private and not particularly good anchorages. They are simply interesting looking islands we pass as we cruise in the area.

Naming Strawberry Island
Strawberry Bay was named by Capt. Vancouver in his 1792 Voyage of Discovery.

*Lt. William Broughton anchored the brig **Chatham** here during the Vancouver Expedition and found wild strawberries on shore.*

When Vancouver arrived a short time later the strawberries were gone, to his disappointment.

The island was called "Hautboy Island" by Lt. Wilkes in his 1841 Expedition.

Hautboy was was the common name for a species of strawberry, "Fragaria elatior."

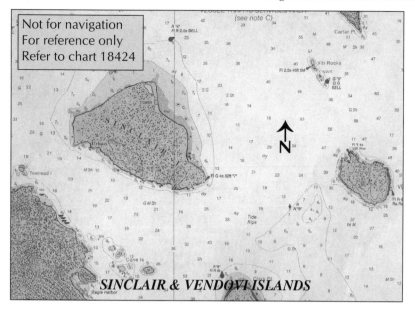

Not for navigation
For reference only
Refer to chart 18424

SINCLAIR & VENDOVI ISLANDS

Sinclair Island, on the northeast edge of Bellingham Channel, is the larger of the two, less than one mile northeast of Cypress.

Boulder Reef extends 0.8 mile off Sinclair's north shore. Portions of it uncover at half tide, and kelp marking the reef is often drawn under by the current. A 7 fathom channel passes through the reef with dangerous rocks on both sides.

Boulder Reef Lighted Bell Buoy [R "2" Fl R 4s Bell] flashing red 4 second light with a bell, marks the outermost end of this reef.

Sinclair Island Lighted Bell Buoy [R "4" Fl R 2.5s Bell] flashing red 2.5 second light with a bell is about 0.6 mile off the north end of Sinclair, and about 1.1 miles east of the Boulder Reef buoy and also marks the 10 fathom depth curve.

Sinclair is fairly low and forested, with only a couple of hills over 100 feet high on the south shore. A fair number of cabins and homes line the beach on the south side. The shoreline becomes steep and precipitous near the eastern end.

꧁ **Public tidelands** are at Mary Leach Natural Area at the southeast side of Sinclair, as well as surrounding much of the island. Check the DNR Quad Map before going ashore.

The village of **Urban** is at the southwest end of the island where there is a piling breakwater at a short county pier. There is no overnight moorage. It is a stop for the seasonal passenger ferry *Redhead*.

⚓ **Anchoring** may be possible in the small coves on either side of the dock, but it looks exposed to us. Currents that race through Bellingham Channel might make this an uncomfortable anchorage.

Bellingham Channel Light 7 [Fl G 4s 32ft "7"] flashing green 4 second light 32 feet high on a square green dayboard, is on Sinclair's southeast tip.

Bellingham Channel Buoy 8 [R N "8"] is a red nun buoy between Sinclair and Vendovi islands, marking an area less than 10 fathoms deep with 4 fathom depths east of the buoy.

Vendovi Island, all private, is about 1.6 miles east of Sinclair. Heavily forested, the island rises to 330 feet in the center. Shores are steep, rocky and there are no anchorages around the island. Vendovi has a small cove at the north end with a large dock and a man-made jetty protecting it. The island is owned by the Fluke family; the late John Fluke Sr. is the inventor of the volt-ohm-meter, among other things. He was a well-known Pacific Northwest entrepreneur. Family members have yachts which moor in the cove. A caretaker manages the island.

Vendovi Cove Light [Fl Y 4s 15ft Priv] flashing yellow 4 second light 15 feet high on a steel tower, private, marks the north side of the entrance into the cove.

Vendovi Island Light 2 [Fl R 6s 13ft 5M "2" Ra Ref PA] flashing red 6 second light 13 feet high, visible 5 miles with a radar reflector, is on a triangular red dayboard on a platform, position approximate. It is on the east (Padilla Bay) side of the island.

Dangerous Boulder Reef

We have heard distress calls on the radio several times from boats which have run aground on the reef.

Naming Sinclair Island

*The island was named by the Wilkes Expedition for Arthur Sinclair Sr., a captain in the U.S. Navy who commanded the **Argus** during the War of 1812.*

It's Wonderful!

There's more to Vendovi than meets the eye.

A fox farm was on the island in the 1920s.

Evangelist Father Divine had a small community on the island in the 1930s. The handful of full-time residents embraced positive thinking and faith healing while shunning sex, liquor and tobacco.

It was a meditation center and provided R & R for other workers in the movement, who's motto was "It's wonderful!"

Our friends Lee and Pearl Callaway considered buying Vendovi for about $3,000 in the 1950s, but rowing their three daughters to Anacortes to school helped changed their minds.

Vendovi Adventure

We were sailing past the north end of Vendovi heading northeast to Chuckanut Bay on a lovely August day with a strong ebb current. Winds were northerly, about 30 knots, holding steady down Rosario Strait past Lummi Island. Glancing over the side through clear surface water, we saw what looked like brown rocks below.

We were on a lee shore, with Vendovi a little too close for comfort off our starboard side as we hit nearly six knots under sail—very fast for us.

Our depth sounder was reading 20 fathoms.

Winds picked up, steep, dirty brown waves picked up, and the white tops of the brown waves surrounding us looked like waves crashing on rocks. We pointed up as high as we could, and after a few gut-wrenching minutes we sailed past the north end of the island. It was then we realized we were in an extremely dense algae bloom. What we thought had been white-topped brown rocks were really white-capped brown waves.

Viti Rocks are less than one mile north of Vendovi and 0.6 mile from the south tip of Lummi Island. The most northern rock is about 35 feet high and 200 yards long. The rocks are a National Wildlife Reserve marked by two navigation aids.

Viti Rocks Light [Fl 2.5s 45ft 5M] flashing white 2.5 second light is 45 feet high, visible 5 miles, on a diamond-shaped dayboard with black and white sectors on a steel tower on the large north rock.

Viti Rocks Lighted Bell Buoy 9 [Q G Bell G "9"] quick green light with a bell marks a shoal extending from the southernmost rock.

And we leave off here to sail over to Chuckanut Bay and other fascinating spots.

In **Chapter 11** we explore the mainland shore from south of Chuckanut Bay north to Bellingham and Gooseberry Point.

Fiji Connection

Vendovi Island and Viti Rocks were named by the Wilkes Expedition in 1841.

Vendovi Island *was named for Vendovi, a chief from the Fiji Islands who was taken prisoner by Wilkes and then accompanied the explorers during their travels.*

Erskine, a member of Wilkes' Expedition, wrote that "... It was indeed amusing to observe the contempt that our prisoner, the Fiji Chief Vendovi, entertained for these local Indians. He would hardly deign to look at them."

Vendovi became ill and died in New York.

Viti Rocks *were named for the Viti or Fiji Islands, home of the prisoner Vendovi.*

Murky waters off Vendovi Island's north shore

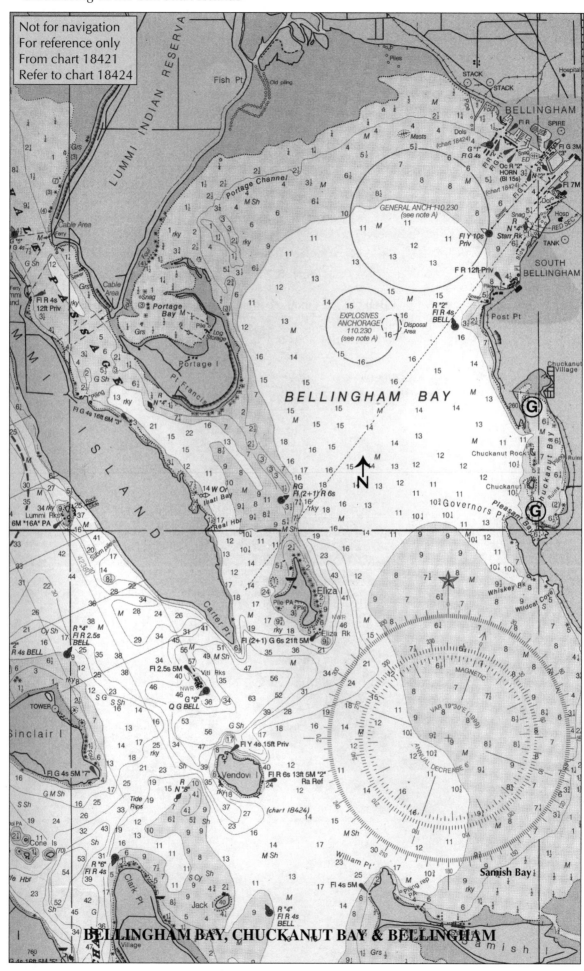

BELLINGHAM BAY, CHUCKANUT BAY & BELLINGHAM

Chapter 11
BELLINGHAM BAY
INCLUDING BELLINGHAM & CHUCKANUT BAY

Charts & Publications for this Chapter

Chart	Date	Title	Scale	Sounding
U.S. 18421	03/21/98	Strait of Juan de Fuca to Strait of Georgia	1:80,000	Fathoms
U.S. 18423	06/18/94	Strip Chart Bellingham to Everett, inc. San Juan Islands		
		Page A	1:80,000	Fathoms
		Page B, Inset 1	1:40,000	Fathoms
☆ U.S. 18424	07/12/97	Bellingham Bay	1:40,000	Fathoms
		Bellingham Harbor Inset	1:20,000	Fathoms
CAN. LC3462	10/23/98	Juan de Fuca Strait to Strait of Georgia	1:80,000	Meters
CAN. 3313	1995	Gulf Islands Chart Book, Page 1	1:200,000	Meters
	🐚	Wash. State DNR Quad Map—Bellingham	1:100,000	

Compare your chart dates with those above. There may be discrepancies between chart editions.
☆ = Preferred chart for this chapter 🐚= DNR & other public tideland information

OVERVIEW OF BELLINGHAM BAY, BELLINGHAM & CHUCKANUT

Bellingham Bay has a reputation for remarkable cruising, intriguing anchorages and moorages, and occasional blustery weather. The bay is 12 miles long and about five miles wide, bounded by mainland shores on the south and east and by the Lummi Indian Reservation peninsula on the northwest.

Bellingham Bay, which opens to the southwest, is surrounded by mainland shores for about 70 percent of its perimeter. It lies, more or less, within the arms of Williams Point on Samish Island to the south and Point Francis on Portage Island nearly seven miles to the north.

Although there doesn't seem to be an exact western side to Bellingham Bay, we decided for this book that part of its western boundary is along the shores of mountainous Lummi Island. Little Eliza Island is caught in between.

Samish Island is connected to the eastern mainland shores at the south end of Samish Bay, while Portage Island is joined by a tombolo to the Lummi Indian Reservation Peninsula at the northwestern end.

Bellingham Bay is approached from Padilla Bay, Bellingham Channel or Rosario Strait from the south or southwest, and from Hale Passage on the northwest.

The energetic city of Bellingham is firmly planted along the northeast shores of Bellingham Bay. The city, the result of a merger of four communities in 1903, has a charming traditional "old town," with 100 year old brick buildings, specialty shops, cafes, newly planted trees, food and flower vendors and a seasonal Farmers' Market.

Beautiful narrow Chuckanut Bay, with its back against small

> ➡ **NOTE: Marine fuel** is available at two places in Bellingham:
> - **Port of Bellingham** fuel dock in Squalicum Harbor
> - **Hilton Harbor Marina** east side of I & J Waterway, Tel.: 360-733-1110

Historic "Natural Drydock"
(Photo by Fred Elsethehagen)

Local Knowledge

Past commodores of Bellingham Yacht Club, Steve and Meredith Ross, shared some local knowledge with us when we visited them in Bellingham:

Weather comes from west and southwest, and Bellingham Bay can stack up quickly, sometimes with 10 foot waves. It can be pretty bad if a southeaster is blowing across Padilla and Skagit Bays. The worst winds, though, are from the north.

Chuckanut Bay is a favorite cruise, with warm swimming, but watch for charted rocks.

Inati Bay on the east side of Lummi Island is the favorite overnight place. Stern tie so you don't swing into other boats.

Reil Harbor, DNR, south of Inati, is good for kayaks and camping, with one mooring buoy.

Lummi Rocks, west side, is a neat place to watch sunsets, but there's no place to overnight there.

San Juan Islands are always a great place to go, and close for Bellingham boaters.

Sucia in the San Juans

➥ **NOTE: Larrabee State Park** is named on strip chart 18243, but not on chart 18424.

mountains, is about two miles long, midway along the east side of Bellingham Bay, with a couple of great anchorages. Larrabee State Park is south of Chuckanut.

We find the whole area fascinating. The Port of Bellingham runs the fine Squalicum Harbor marina, a working harbor that is home port to more than 1,800 commercial and pleasure boats. The port also has public moorage at the historic Fairhaven District, also known as South Bellingham.

Early Explorations in Bellingham Bay

Early settling of the area began when ancestors of Lummi, Nooksack and Semiahmoo tribes settled along the bay, part of the great migration from Asia to North America, more than 10,000 years before white men arrived.

The Spanish explorer, Don Francisco Eliza, was the first of the early European explorers to find Bellingham Bay. He entered it in 1791 and named it the Gulf of Gaston. Two Spanish vessels, the *Sutil* and the *Mexicana* actually grounded in Bellingham Bay when they anchored in about 4 fathoms and were then blown into shallower water.

On June 11, 1792, Sailing Master Joseph Whidbey, an officer with Capt. George Vancouver, discovered, explored and charted the bay while Vancouver was on an expedition to Texada Island in what is now British Columbia. Vancouver named the bay for Sir William Bellingham, the man who checked over his supplies and accounts as he was leaving England on his famous "Voyage of Discovery," which included exploring our Pacific Northwest.

The Spaniards later sought to restore the name to Bahia de Gaston, but widely-used British Admiralty charts had been published before Spanish charts, in the 1800s, and the name Bellingham prevailed.

⚓ **UNDERWAY**, we're at the south end of Bellingham Bay where it nudges up against Samish Bay. We're over two miles out from the mainland shore as we follow the 5 fathom depth curve heading north to the Wildcat Cove area.

Our cruising plan is to visit Larrabee State Park, spend some time gunkholing about in long-time favorite Chuckanut Bay, then on to explore Fairhaven, and Squalicum Harbor in burgeoning Bellingham.

Depths in Samish Bay are extremely shoal until about 1.2 miles south of Governors Point where the five fathom curve is generally less than 300 yards offshore.

The mainland shore is steep and forested, backed up against the westward side of nearly 2,000 foot high Chuckanut Mountain. It's a beautiful area to cruise or paddle, but be aware of shallow waters.

LARRABEE STATE PARK

This is not a marine park in the true sense, but it is an important park for those with trailerable and paddle boats as it offers a launch ramp, camp sites and other facilities. Larrabee Park shoreline runs south from Wildcat Cove for about 8,100 feet, although the beach is not accessible from the uplands because of steep bluffs. The best way to explore the shore is by walking at low tide or by small, beachable boats. This is a popular park, with more than 700,000 visitors annually. By land it is reached by beautiful, winding, two lane Chuckanut Bay Drive.

Wildcat Cove is a pretty little bay with a pebble beach suitable for a swim. Sheer bluffs are on the south side, and a ragged, abrupt shoreline with pocket beaches is on the north side.

⚓ The cove could be an anchorage in 2 fathoms, sand bottom, but it's exposed from the southeast to the northwest. It's small and there's not much room for large boats to swing, not a gunkhole.

A two lane paved ramp at the head of the cove is fairly steep but accommodates the launching of many trailerable boats.

Campers at the many sites find they are between Chuckanut Drive and the railroad tracks, a fair distance above the beach, but close enough to hear those comforting train whistles at night.

Hiking trails through the park's quiet old forests are well worth the time.

Larrabee launch ramp at Wildcat Cove

Larrabee State Park Facilities

➤ 2,765 acres with 8,100 feet of shoreline
➤ Two lane boat launch ramp at Wildcat Cove, fee $3, parking
➤ 51 campsites, 26 RV sites, 8 walk-in sites, three primitive sites, group camp
➤ Picnic sites & shelters, restrooms, showers
➤ 13.5 miles of hiking trails, 10 miles of road, three mountain lookout sites
➤ Activities: gunkhole by small boat, fish, clam, hike, camp, water ski, crab, beachcomb, swim, scuba dive
➤ Tel.: 360-676-2093
➤ Address: 245 Chuckanut Dr., Bellingham, WA 98226

The Interurban Trail, a wide, surfaced, reasonably level path begins near the park entrance and runs 5.5 miles north to Bellingham. It was built along the old interurban rail bed on the east side of Chuckanut Drive, and is a pleasant trip through the woods for walkers and bicyclists.

The Good Old Interurban

The electric Interurban train flourished between 1912 and 1929, serving passengers, carrying freight, and was the school "bus" for many youngsters during those years. Station stops were almost every mile along the line. The service was stopped when the train could no longer compete with cars, buses and trucks.

Larrabee State Park

This was the first park in the state park system. It began with the donation of 20 acres by C.X. Larrabee and Cyrus Gates in 1915. The last of 27 parcels in the 2,765 acre park was acquired by the state in 1993.

The new park was first a mine, but the coal in the Wildcat Cove area was of such poor quality it was mined for only a short time in the 1850s.

⚓ **UNDERWAY AGAIN,** we cruise north from Wildcat Cove to Chuckanut Bay.

Whiskey Rock is 0.3 mile north and 100 yards west of Wildcat Cove. Other charted offshore rocks are in the area, so we stay outside the 5 fathom depth curve.

CHUCKANUT BAY

The lovely bay is about two miles long, north to south, and 0.5 mile wide. It is inside the arms of Governors Point at the south end and charted but unnamed Clarks Point 1.2 miles north. The points encompass smaller, protected bays.

Chuckanut is open to the west, which allows phenomenal sunsets over Lummi Island. Chuckanut Island and Chuckanut Rock are in the center of the bay.

Although Chuckanut Bay shores are now almost totally residential, and homes abound along the bay, some near the shore and others climbing the hills. Railroad tracks skirt the bay as they have since 1896, above the beach and inland from some of the homes.

Depths throughout Chuckanut Bay are charted quite consistently between 4 to 8 fathoms. The 3 fathom depth curve rarely extends more than 200 yards offshore.

Rocks charted inside the bay are few and inside the 3 fathom curve.

🌿 **Public tidelands** in Chuckanut surround Chuckanut Rock and include about 4,000 feet of shoreline south from the charted "Piling Ruins." All tidelands are water access only.

⚓ **Anchoring** is good in many sections of the bay which has a fairly level bottom with depths mostly in the 6 to 8 fathom range.

Chuckanut is …

A Native American term meaning: "A small bay lying adjacent to a large bay with a steep hill or mountain rising from its shores."

➡ **NOTE: Chart 18424** details Chuckanut Bay more thoroughly than other charts.

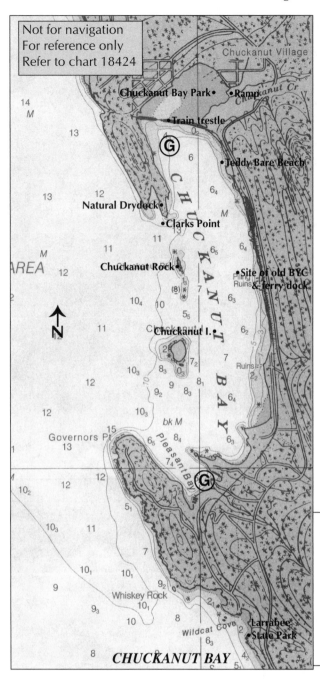

Not for navigation
For reference only
Refer to chart 18424

(On map): Chuckanut Village, Chuckanut Bay Park•, •Ramp, •Train trestle, (G), 6, •Teddy Bare Beach, Natural Drydock•, •Clarks Point, Chuckanut Rock•, •Site of old BYC, Piling Ruins & ferry dock, Chuckanut I.•, Ruins, Governors Pt•, Pleasant Bay, (G), Whiskey Rock, Wildcat Cove, Larrabee State Park•, CHUCKANUT BAY, N, AREA, CHUCKANUT BAY

(G) This whole bay is a delight. **It's prime for gunkholing** and exploring, especially in small paddle boats or dinghies.

Enter the bay at any of three distinct channels: the south end between Chuckanut Island and Governors Point in 8 to 9 fathoms, between the island and Chuckanut Rock in 5 fathoms, and between the rock and the north point in 11 to 13 fathoms.

We look first at Chuckanut Island and Chuckanut Rock in the center of the bay about 0.4 mile off the east shore and then explore the bay from south to north, finding some fascinating history and good anchorages.

Chuckanut Island, 0.5 miles north of Governors Point, is a five acre island belonging to The Nature Conservancy Wildlife Preserve. The island is covered with old-growth Douglas fir, madrona and western red cedar trees which somehow managed to escape being logged. Bald eagles nest on the island and many other birds are seen here.

Rocks and shoals extend about 200 yards off the south and west shores of the island. The northeast shore slopes gently, and kayakers often pull out here for a break to explore. The family of the late Cyrus Gates donated the island to The Nature Conservancy.

Chuckanut Rock, which is actually several rocks in a north-south line, lies about 0.2 mile north of the island and 0.2 mile south of Clarks Point. The rock is signed as a delicate nesting habitat—"do not disturb."

Rocks baring at an 8 foot tide extend 300 yards off the south end and a rock awash is 100 yards off the north end. Read on for what happens without charts.

Don't Forget the Charts!

While we were anchored in north Chuckanut Bay we saw a boat sink off Chuckanut Rock. Coast Guard Auxiliary boats were on the scene almost immediately and took passengers off the damaged 26 foot Tollycraft before it went under. It apparently drove right up on the rock and was holed. Fortunately, no one was hurt. The Coast Guard said later that apparently no charts were on board the vessel.

We explore Chuckanut Bay, using chart 18424, starting at the southwest end.

Governers Point is a steep, forested rock bluff about 200 feet high. The east side is sculptured sandstone, similar to that found in the San Juans.

Pleasant Bay around the east side of the point is about 0.3 mile long and nearly 0.2 mile wide. Depths are 6 to 7 fathoms. This is indeed a pleasant bay with beach cottages and homes tucked in amongst the trees, several piers, moored boats, private buoys, and usually crab pots. Beaches are all private.

⚓ **Anchoring is good** in Pleasant Bay, especially in southerlies, in about 6 fathoms, mud bottom.

(G) We find it a **good gunkhole.**

Continuing east is another cove

Kayakers at the north end of Chuckanut Island

with some private mooring buoys. It's a possible anchorage in calm weather. The beach along this shore was named Finn Beach after a number of Finnish loggers who lived here in the early part of the 20th century in cabins they built from beachcombed lumber.

Bellingham Yacht Club was built in 1928 where "Ruins" are charted east of Chuckanut Island. Black Ball Ferry Company started a ferry service from here to the San Juan Islands with the ferry *Mount Vernon.* The service lasted until 1941 when the vessel was condemned. During World War II from 1941 to 1945 when no ferries were built, there was no replacement for the vessel and the service ended.

Chuckanut Rock

Cruising north, there was once a fish cannery near "Piling Ruin." Near that was Chuckanut Shell, a dining and dancing establishment until it burned down in 1949. An old stone quarry was 500 yards north of the "ruins."

Brickyard Beach was the site of the last industrial establishment along the northeast part of the bay at a pretty little cove, renamed Old Brickyard Beach when the plant was torn down. For many years Old Brickyard Beach has been called "Teddy Bare Beach" and is well known in the area as a "nudie" beach.

Pleasant Bay

Families cruising with youngsters may find the best place to anchor is in the northwest corner of Chuckanut Bay, thereby avoiding embarrassing questions the kids might have about unusual antics on the bay's northeast beach.

A railroad trestle about 700 yards long crosses east to west at the north end of the bay. The trestle is built mostly on riprap rock, although the west section is on pilings. Spaces between the pilings allow small boats to glide under the tracks into narrow "Mud Bay" lagoon to the north, which dries almost completely at low tide. The bay was originally much deeper, but after construction of the trestle silt built up at the mouth of Chuckanut Creek which empties into the lagoon, and it became a mudflat. We gunkholed about in the shallow muddy bay in our skiff near low tide. It's full of sand dollars half-buried in the muck, but at high tide it's beautiful. The bay is the site of undeveloped Chuckanut Bay Park, part of Bellingham's park system.

Fred Elsthehagen of Chuckanut Bay and Carl meet again 50 years after their first meeting at Sucia Island (Ch. 6)

Hand launch ramp, usable at fairly high tides and good for paddle boats, is at the northeast corner of Mud Bay. Chuckanut Creek empties into the lagoon and Chuckanut Village is at the head of the bay. Many homes line the hills above.

⚓ **We anchored** in the northwest corner of Chuckanut Bay in about 4 to 6 fathoms, mud bottom, well protected by Clarks Point to the west. It was a quiet, comfortable anchorage.

Ⓖ This northwest corner of Chuckanut is a **lovely gunkhole.**

We found the nightly trains enjoyable and no hindrance to a good

Train on trestle at Chuckanut

Granddaughter Gaea Bailey enjoys warm Chuckanut Bay

night's sleep while anchored in the bay.

We were there in summer when there were calm nights with only gentle northerlies, and wonderful moonlit evenings. We never had a southerly while we were there on several occasions. We find it interesting that one of our favorite anchorages was at the edge of a city. Anchoring here was like being far away from the "real world," except for occasional haunting train whistles.

At Clarks Point we enjoy the sandstone shores, much like Sucia in the San Juans, and swim in the warm waters of the bay. We row our skiff around the point, watching deer quietly feeding, and admire the four homes on the point. That's all the homes there will ever be as this is part of the Whatcom Land Trust for Open Space Preservation. We explore the delightful little bay tucked into the south end of the point, once called "Natural Dry Dock." We think we found a fossilized palm tree left over from prehistoric days along the rocks.

Ashore, we walk trails in the park at the north end of Clarks Point. A wooden stairway at the head of the bay zig-zags through trees up the hill next to the train tunnel. A parking lot and information board are at the trail's top, and then it continues west down the slope. We arrive at a beautiful rocky, treed bluff looking west across Bellingham Bay toward Lummi Island. Train tracks emerge from the tunnel and head north along Bellingham Bay, reminding us we're still near "civilization."

Possible fossil at Chuckanut?

"Natural Dry Dock," circa 1940
(Fred Elsthehagen photo)

Tidbits of Chuckanut History

In prehistoric times the area was sub-tropical, and prehistoric animals roamed about. Fossilized tropical plants and leaves can be seen at some rock cuts on Chuckanut Drive and along the bay.

Pleasant Bay in the south has long been a good anchorage. In the early 1900s, a fleet of large sailing vessels owned by a salmon packing company moored each winter in the bay. Some old mooring rings may still be seen in the rocks, relics from the early sailing ships. In the late 1920s, Bellingham Tug & Barge used the bay for log storage and it was full of log booms.

Chuckanut Island, also called Dot Island, is thought to have been an early Indian burial place, as bones were found there. It was homesteaded in the 1870s by a man who had a chicken ranch and garden.

Two rock quarries were on the east side of Governors Point. One operated in 1878 by Sidell and Burfeind, was later abandoned, reopened in 1921 and was worked for a year by Pacific American Fisheries.

In 1931, the first Pacific International Yachting Association (P.I.Y.A.) Regatta was hosted by the Bellingham Yacht Club in Chuckanut Bay where they then had their yacht club building.

In 1934, the Port of Bellingham opened a quarry to get rock for the Squalicum breakwater. Quarry workers were WPA (Works Project Administration) workers who were ferried back and forth each day from the Bellingham Yacht Club dock.

A rock quarry at the northeast end of Chuckanut Bay provided stone for many early government buildings of Washington Territory, and later for state, county and city buildings.

The lovely bay at Clark Point's south end was called "Natural Dry Dock" in the early part of the 20th century. Promoters tried to interest shipbuilders in building a shipyard there with dry-docking facilities as they said the water was deep enough to accommodate the largest ships in the world at that time. All that was needed was to install pumps and flood gates to create the drydock.

A similar scheme was developed when the Navy planned to build a shipyard and drydock somewhere in Puget Sound. Developers hoped to build a breakwater across the reefs between Chuckanut Island and Chuckanut Rock, forming an all-weather, deep anchorage in the bay. In addition to the anchorage, they would also use Natural Dry Dock.

The Navy decided to build the shipyard in Bremerton.

During Prohibition, many of the streams in the Chuckanut Bay area had stills alongside to brew "moonshine." The furtive liquor industry flourished, although smugglers in fast "rum-runners" reportedly carried better and safer illicit spirits than those that moonshiners manufactured locally.

Jo swims in Natural Dry Dock
(Photo by Carl)

⚓**UNDERWAY AGAIN,** we leave Chuckanut Bay bound for Bellingham.

By the time we hauled up our anchor and washed off the gunk, we were the only boat in the north end of the bay, and this was in August. Remarkable. We passed between Clarks Point and Chuckanut Rock with about 80 feet of water under us. A small boat was tucked in the little bay, Natural Dry Dock, along with crab pot buoys. We would have loved to stay longer.

On the Bellingham Bay side of Clarks Point high, rocky bluffs plunge nearly straight down into the bay. We pass the park north of the point, and as we reach the west end of the train tunnel a train emerges—perfect timing.

Post Point is about 1.5 miles north of the entrance to Chuckanut Bay. Homes line the uplands, and the shoreline gradually becomes more industrial.

Post Point Lighted Bell Buoy 2 [Fl R 4s Bell, R "2"] flashing red 4 second buoy, marks a shoal that extends about 450 yards west of the point.

Rounding the point, 100 year old Western Washington University dominates the hill to the east. We've reached South Bellingham, also called the Fairhaven District. Large piers are on shore, including the impressive Alaska State Ferry Terminal, where the *Columbia* and *Matanuska* sail weekly to Alaska.

Ferry Pier Light [F R 12ft] fixed red light 12 feet high, is on a dolphin at the ferry pier.

The terminal is the hub of the Fairhaven Transportation Center, where there is also a pier for private ferries. The *Redhead*, a passenger-only vessel, serves the San Juans on a regular schedule during the summer season. The classic wood schooners *Zodiac* and *Adventuress,* offering seasonal charter and sail training cruises through the San Juans, moor here.

In addition, the Amtrak train station and Greyhound bus terminal are in Fairhaven.

We cruise east past the piers towards the southeast corner of the bay where there's a launch ramp and public moorage managed by the Port of Bellingham. The launch area is a bustling place in summer. Port mooring buoys and a linear buoy system are on a first-come, first-served basis. We scoop up a buoy and settle in for a couple of days. About a dozen boats are anchored semi-permanently in the bay.

A pier and float are in front of Padden Creek Marine immediately south of the mooring buoys. The west side of the float is for Padden Creek customers only.

The east side is Port of Bellingham reserved moorage with a three day limit. Signs on the float advise: "Rough seas may occur suddenly, do not leave boat unattended."

Padden Creek Marine, Inc., is a boat builder and large

R.R. Crossing

As we rowed out of Mud Bay back to our anchored **Scheherazade***, we noticed several young men fishing from the trestle. We asked how often trains came by. They said they didn't have a clue, and kept fishing.*

A couple of minutes later we heard the whistle of an oncoming train and they scattered like buckshot, several jumping off the trestle into the water.

The trains come by quite often, it appears, and we don't recommend hiking along the railroad tracks without an easy exit—like jumping into the bay.

Alaska ferry at Fairhaven

Zodiac & skipper at Fairhaven

repair facility with a travel lift for boats up to 55 feet. A complete marine service and repair business, they also build pleasure boats. Tel.: 800-479-3590

Fairhaven moorage, with buoys, launch ramp, linear tie-up & a train running past

Facilities at Fairhaven
➤ 10 mooring buoys
➤ 300 foot linear buoy system,
➤ Mooring fee 50¢ foot overnight, 72 hour limit
➤ Water, garbage for moorage patrons at Padden dock
➤ Two lane launch ramp with float & parking, fee $4
➤ Small store
➤ Haulouts for boats up to 27 feet, 7,500 pounds
➤ Nearby restrooms, portable pumpout
➤ Dry storage for approximately 100 small boats
➤ Activities: visit historical district, fish, gunkhole, enjoy, Fairhaven Farmers' Market nearby
➤ Rental sailboats, kayaks, rowboats
➤ Harbormaster: Char Byrns
➤ Phone: 360-647-2469
➤ Address: 501 Harris, Bellingham, WA 98225

➥ **NOTE:** A tip for cruisers in need of groceries: It's a shorter walk to a supermarket from Fairhaven moorage than it is to a super-market from Squalicum Harbor Marina in downtown Bellingham.

➥ **NOTE:** Chart 18424 shows Fairhaven bay filled with log booms. We saw none.

Fairhaven Moorage
Tip Johnson, former harbormaster at Fairhaven, was our source of "local knowledge." He said prevailing winds are southeast to southwest 90 percent of the time, but in summer they tend to be southwest to northwest. The harder it blows the shorter time it lasts. Northeast and northwest winds are arctic outflows. The marina was wrecked in 1947 and 1965 heavy winter storms.

He said Fairhaven is a good launch for boats up to 24 feet; boats larger than that should go to Squalicum. The port considers Fairhaven moorage as "seasonal visitor moorage."

Buoys in Fairhaven
A problem we had with the buoys in Fairhaven was that they had so much scope we had to tie to three of them to keep them from bumping into us as we swung around with the wind and current.

Scheherazade tied to three Fairhaven buoys

Fairhaven, a charming historic district where businesses have names like Dirty Dan Harris (restaurant), Mud in Your Eye Pottery, Village Books, and a sign stating "Tied dogs will be towed," is only a short walk from the moorage. A walking-tour map gives insight into the area's rich historic background.

You'll never go hungry or coffee-less in Fairhaven. Espresso bars seem to be everywhere. There are more than 10 restaurants, one even in Village Books, which has great food as well as great books. At a nearby supermarket you can easily stock up on groceries. This South Bellingham community has a laundromat, pharmacy, bank, post office, florists, gift shops and just about anything else.

There's a lagoon between the moorage and Fairhaven, and it's a pleasant diversion with walkways, benches, plantings and interpretive boards. A nice spot to sit and watch herons, geese, ducks and other birds a walk into Fairhaven.

Local Lore Lives on in Fairhaven
Fairhaven has many intriguing, unusual and sometimes bizarre plaques celebrating events and places along the sidewalks on several streets as well as on buildings.

Below are examples, look for others as you stroll.
- Location of Town Pillory—1890
- Benton's Bath Parlor and Tonsorial Palace—1890
- Cigar Factory—maker of Puro Cigars—1907
- Here is where Mathew was cut in two by a streetcar—1891
- Site of drowning pool—dogs only—1891
- Policeman Phil Defries shot at 23 times, 1899-1905
- Jailhouse here—giving prisoners whiskey meant 25 days on chain gang—1890
- City garbage dumpsite, "Smells like breath of an elephant"—1890
- U.S. President McKinley buggied past here—1901
- Huge freight wagon disappeared beneath quicksand here—1910
- Cleopatra's barge—lions and camels paraded here—1891

Brief History of Industrial South Bellingham

In the early 1900s, Bellingham was one of the world's leading processing centers for both canned salmon and western red cedar shingles. Pacific American Fisheries (P.A.F.) and Puget Sound Sawmill and Shingle Company stood on opposite sides of the Fairhaven lagoon. Located on the west shore, the P.A.F. plant was once the largest cannery in the world, able to pack up to 14,000 cases of salmon a day. The mill on the east shore used the lagoon to store raw timber and remove bark. As many as twenty-three red cedar shingle mills circled Bellingham Bay.

Cedar stands in Alger and Lake Samish areas were widely claimed to be the richest on the west coast. The logs were transported to Fairhaven via the Fairhaven and Southern Railroad, later the Great Northern Railway.

Now, the huge salmon runs and gigantic trees are gone, as are the giant mills and canneries, which are sometimes more easily remembered than the riches which they consumed. The world's largest salmon cannery now is in King Cove, Alaska, and the nearest cedar shingle plant is in Mission, B.C. Refrigeration and modern transport allow them to process harvests from much wider areas.

⚓ **UNDERWAY AGAIN,** from Fairhaven we head to Squalicum Harbor Marina in Bellingham. *(See "Squalicum Harbor Entrance Options" next two pages)*

The marina is less than two miles north of Fairhaven along the northeast shore of Bellingham Bay. Leaving Fairhaven we pass two navigation aids.

Starr Rock Buoy [R N "4"] red nun buoy, is about 35 yards west of the rock which is covered by 1 fathom of water at low tide. The buoy, the first aid we encounter, is about 0.75 mile north of Fairhaven and about 200 yards offshore. Log booms are sometimes stored inshore of Starr Rock.

Georgia Pacific Outfall Lighted Buoy [Fl Y 10s Priv] flashing yellow 10 second light is on a buoy with white and orange bands. It is a private aid about 0.5 mile west of Starr Rock Buoy.

Squalicum Harbor Marina with its forest of masts behind the large riprap breakwater is about one mile northeast of the buoy. The marina covers nearly one mile of waterfront in two separate harbors, both of which have moorage for commercial, pleasure and guest boats. More than 1,800 boats of all sizes and types are moored in this modern marina.

"Dirty Dan" Harris

Fairhaven was first developed about 1883 by "Dirty Dan" Harris, a colorful local character known for wearing a plug hat and shabby coat over a red undershirt, heavy socks and boots.

Many tales have been told about Dirty Dan, who arrived in the 1860s. He started a hotel and had a deepwater dock, important for development. Bellingham Bay was deep at the south end and shallow at the north because of the Nooksack River delta.

Whatcom Creek Tragedy

Whatcom Creek empties into Whatcom Creek Waterway, the waterway at the northeast corner of Bellingham Bay. The creek was the scene of a horrific tragedy in June 1999.

A rupture in the Olympic Gas Pipeline which runs under the creek resulted in a devastating 277,000-gallon gas spill.

The gas erupted into a huge fireball in a city park along the waterway and caused the deaths of two 10-year old boys and a young man.

It also ravaged part of the creek and surroundings, killing thousands of young fish. The pipeline was shut down for some time.

When this book went to press the spill was still under investigation.

South/Outer Harbor Entrance

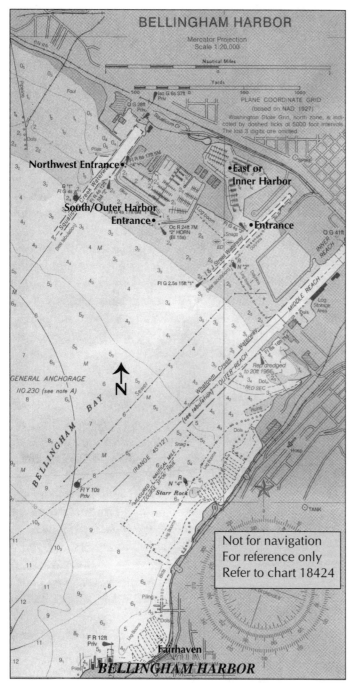

Not for navigation
For reference only
Refer to chart 18424

Spectacular Mount Baker is the backdrop for the city which rises beyond the marina. As we approach from Bellingham Bay we see historical landmarks, including spires from churches and remodeled old buildings in the downtown area. Handsome old homes line the northeast bluff, as well as charted stacks and radio towers.

Bellingham Bay Waterways

It's sometimes a bit confusing to find the marina entrance for the first-time. We'll try to explain it as simply as possible. Chart 18424 with its 1:20,000 insert of Bellingham Harbor, is great for reference.

Three industrial dredged waterways are in Bellingham Harbor:

• **Whatcom Creek Waterway** is at the farthest east and longest of the three dredged channels at the northeast end of Bellingham Harbor.

• **I & J Street Waterway** is the second waterway, about 700 yards northwest of Whatcom Creek, and about 1,300 yards from Squalicum Creek Waterway.

• **Squalicum Creek Waterway** is the third waterway. It is at the northwest edge of Squalicum Harbor Marina.

The marina is between I & J Street Waterway and Squalicum Creek Waterway.

Squalicum Harbor & Navigation Aids:

East or Inner Harbor Entrance is on the west side in I & J St. Waterway.

I & J Waterway Light 1 [FL G 2.5s, 15ft "1"] flashing green 2.5 second light 15 feet high on a square green dayboard on a pile, marks the southwest end.

Keep the light to port, proceed northeast about 250 yards to the red nun buoy which is to starboard.

I & J Waterway Buoy 2 [R N "2"] is a red nun buoy.

Continue about 300 yards past the buoy to breakwater entrance on the port side.

I & J Waterway Light 3 [Fl G 4s "3"] flashing green 4 second light on a square green dayboard 16 feet high, is on the rock breakwater.

Turn to port and enter the Inner Harbor. Day moorage float is at Zuanich Point Park, to port. Make a jog to starboard and it's about 300 yards to the visitor floats, called Gate 12, on the starboard side. Tie up where indicated. Commercial fishing vessels moor farther in at floats along the port side at Gates 6 & 7.

South or Outer Harbor Entrance is midway between I & J and Squalicum Creek Waterways. Locate the outer end of the breakwater, 0.3 mile northwest of the entrance to I & J Waterway. Lights are on both sides of the entrance.

Bellingham Breakwater Entrance Light 1 [Fl G 4s 17ft 6M "1"] flashing green 4 second light 17 feet high visible 6 miles, is on a square green dayboard on a pile at the end of the breakwater on the port side of the entrance.

Bellingham Breakwater Entrance Light 2 [OC R 4s, 24ft 7 M "2" horn] an occulting red 4 second light 24 feet high, visible 7 miles with a horn, is on a triangular red dayboard on a steel tower marking the starboard side of the entrance.

Enter by going east between the two markers, then turn northeast and head straight

Algae Bloom

As we sailed past Post Point in summer 1997 we found ourselves in the midst of a huge mess of brown, foamy, thick algae bloom. This was the same ugly stuff we had seen off Vendovi Island several days earlier.

We understand that this particular algae bloom lasted about a week. We did not see it in Chuckanut Bay.

to the visitor float 300 yards away at the head of Gate 3 channel and tie up. Commercial vessels moor on the starboard side and may be in the channel any time.

Northwest Entrance is in Squalicum Creek Waterway on the east side, and also leads into the Outer Harbor.

Squalicum Creek Entrance Lighted Buoy 1 [Fl G 4s G "1"] flashing green 4 second light on a buoy is on the port side of the

East/Inner Harbor Entrance

waterway. Proceed northeast 300 yards to the red marker on the starboard side.

Squalicum Creek Entrance Light "2" [Fl R 4s 12ft 5M "2"] flashing red 4 second light 12 feet high visible 5 miles, is on a triangular red dayboard on a post near the breakwater and about 100 yards southwest of the entrance.

Breakwater North Entrance Light 4 [Fl R 6s 17ft 5M "4"] flashing red 6 second light 17 feet high visible 5 miles, is on triangular red dayboard on a pile. Turn to starboard, east, and proceed to the fuel float, which is 300 yards ahead on the north shore.

After arriving at either the Inner or Outer Harbors, all skippers are required to register by completing an envelope and depositing it in a drop box, or at the Harbor Office at Gate 3. That's where a good map of the marina is available.

We are here! We can now take advantage of the great marina facilities and enjoy the city of Bellingham. Wide, level walking paths surround the sprawling harbor complex, connect inner and outer harbors and lead out to lovely Zuanich Park Point overlooking Bellingham Bay. It's a popular place for a brisk morning run or walk. Walkers (or runners) can view the large commercial fishing fleet area, which includes three working piers, gillnet loading berths and web houses for gear storage, as they stroll the paths around the marina. A large bronze statue, "Safe Return," by Dr. Eugene Fairbanks is planned for the park, honoring fishermen lost at sea from 1943 to 1975.

Yacht Club Moves

In the early 1900s, three and four masted sailing ships were built on the beach at Camp Perfection, near the site of the old Bellingham Yacht Club in Chuckanut Bay.

In 1946, the yacht club moved from Chuckanut Bay into the city, the old clubhouse was removed and the dock torn down. Today, nothing remains to mark the site.

BYC now has its clubhouse in Squalicum Harbor, near the harbor office.

Facilities at Squalicum Harbor Marina
➤ Moorage for approximately 50 guest boats
➤ No reservations, first-come, first-served, moorage rates, 50¢ foot night
➤ 30 amp power, water included, restrooms with showers, laundry
➤ Fuel float near the NW entrance, gas, diesel, propane, Tel.: 360-734-1710
➤ Pumpouts and porta-potty dumps at several locations, no charge
➤ 30 ton haulout, boat and engine repair
➤ Marine supplies, fishing gear, bait, ice at shop by launch ramp
➤ Four-lane launch ramp, fee $4 or $60 annual, parking
➤ Restaurants, lounge, lattes
➤ Coast Guard Station
➤ Customs port-of-entry, Tel: 360-734-5463; after hours: 800-562-5943
➤ Home port for Bellingham & Squalicum Yacht Clubs; reciprocal moorage at Bellingham Yacht Club, Tel.: 360-733-7390
➤ Marine Life Center with live displays of local marine life in tanks
➤ Nearby: marine supply store, hardware store, post office, liquor store, small grocery store, movies, tennis, museums, parks, golf, restaurants, seasonal Farmers' Market
➤ Taxi and bus service
➤ Monitors VHF Channel 16
➤ Harbormaster: Reed Gillig
➤ Tel.: 360-676-2542/FAX: 360-671-6411:
➤ e-mail: reedg@portofbellingham.com
➤ website: http://www.portofbellingham.com
➤ Address: #22 Squalicum Mall, Bellingham, WA 98225

➥ **NOTE:** The enlarged inset in Chart 18424 (25th ed., 7/12/97) does not show the location of all the moorage floats in the harbors.

Marine Life Center

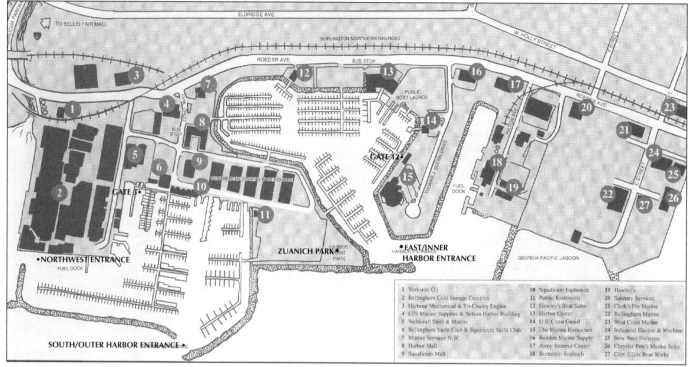

Squalicum Harbor map

Bellingham launch ramp

Bellingham Farmers' Market

The marina has a four-lane launch ramp in the northeast corner of the Inner Harbor with a large parking area and a washdown facility for boats.

Kids get a kick out of the Marine Life Center with live displays of local marine life in three large tanks in the marina along the northeast shore, not far from the launch ramp.

Marine history buffs enjoy exploring the Whatcom Maritime Museum south of the marina at 1000 C Street, behind Chrysler Pete's on the waterfront in nearby Old Town. The museum displays items associated with the historic fishing industry as well as other relics. We found old outboard motors, feathering props, a Sears and Roebuck Water Witch, a 112-year old steam engine over 10 feet high weighing several tons, and many other remarkable items. The intriguing museum is open Fridays and Saturdays, 10 a.m. to 4 p.m., free admission. For more on the historical society contact Steve Paus, president, 360-676-0084, or Paul Schneider, museum director, 360-384-3622.

Our favorite restaurant for breakfast or lunch is in Old Town, a short walk from the marina. Old Town Cafe at 316 West Holly Street serves breakfast all day in an old triangular corner building with a wonderful atmosphere—no slick modern eatery—just friendly and comfortable. It's won a number of local awards, including Bellingham's Best Restaurant, as well it should.

There's an exciting, busy Farmers' Market less than a one mile walk southeast of Squalicum Harbor each weekend in summer, filled with fresh produce, flowers, crafts, music and food.

"Bellingham—City of Subdued Excitement"

That's the marvelous sign on an old building next to the Whatcom Museum of History and Art. Indeed, the city does have a fascinating history. We gathered much of our historical information from a great source at the Museum, Richard Vanderway.

"Think what those early explorers saw when they

arrived here—a 200-foot palisade, and the bottom 50 feet was sandstone, with the top 150 feet all trees, so nothing really appeared to them except those trees," he said.

Henry Roeder and Russell Peabody, ex-49ers after failing in the gold rush, arrived in 1852 hunting for a waterfall to run a mill. They'd heard it was called "Whatcom," meaning "noisy water," by the Indians. Roeder and Peabody built an unsuccessful mill, and then they ran across coal. That was the industry that got them—and Bellingham—going.

The Point Elliott Treaty of January 22, 1855, ceded all tribal lands south of the 49th parallel and west of the Cascades to the U.S. Conflicts between natives and settlers were provoked.

In 1856 Capt. George Pickett arrived and Fort Bellingham was built. He later went to San Juan Island where he participated in the "Pig War." *(Ch. 1)*

In 1858, gold was discovered on the Fraser River in British Columbia. An old trail from Bellingham Bay into the Fraser River valley was a launch point to the gold fields. In Edward Eldridge's autobiography he writes of looking out over the bay and seeing seven steamers and a dozen square-rigged sailboats anchored, with passengers and crew on shore trying to hike up the trail to gold. On the shore in the middle of nowhere was a giant tent city.

"In February 1871, I arrived at Whatcom on Bellingham Bay. I came on the side-wheel tub of a steamer, *J.B. Libby,* the only boat on the route from Seattle to Bellingham. The trip was three days each way; the fare $7, meals 75 cents, berth $1, making the total cost of the round trip $14.75," Eldridge wrote. Arriving at Whatcom, the steamer anchored offshore and Native Americans came out in canoes to ferry the passengers to land, 25 cents apiece.

In the 1890s railroads reached Bellingham, but even after trains arrived boats were the preferred method of transportation. In 1903, the communities of Whatcom, Bellingham (Unionville), New Whatcom (Sehome) and Fairhaven merged under the name of Bellingham, with a population of 23,000.

"Bellingham is built upon an ideal townsite on the eastern shores of Bellingham Bay, famous for many generations as the most perfect large harbor on the Pacific Coast, it being 50 square miles in extent, practically landlocked, free from teredos, owing to the flow of fresh water streams into the bay, from 4 to 16 fathoms deep, and having a bottom of green mud, the best anchorage-holding ground in the world." (From the *Bellingham City Directory 1906)*

According to Vanderway, "Before 1912, when the Army Corps of Engineers began to dig out the three waterways that remain today, the towns had to have mile-long wharves out through the tide flats to deep water, especially important with competing towns. Before wharves were built, Indians and other burly fellows made a living carrying people ashore through the mudflats. Colony Mill, which started in the late 1880s, had a wharf which went one mile out into the bay. Originally, mile-long Citizens Dock had a steamer terminal at its far end. That dock was built in 1913, reportedly to take advantage of Panama Canal traffic. The builders felt once the Canal was opened traffic would come through and this dock would service that traffic. In fact, very little shipping came from the canal.

"There was beach and bayshore below the highly visible bluff around the bay, but now most of it is filled in. Everything from the Port of Bellingham north is built on fill, turning the shore into valuable industrial waterfront."

Local businessman Ken Speer said that 25 years ago Bellingham Bay "was so polluted you could virtually walk across it. You didn't have to paint a boat bottom as nothing could grow on it. We haven't cleaned up the bay, we just stopped polluting it."

Not really the J.B. Libby, just an imposter

Popular Place
Bellingham has had four national magazines feature it recently as the country's best small town. The city of about 58,000 people has been showcased on morning news shows.

Tidelands

🐚 *Public tidelands, unless otherwise noted, are state-owned. Some may be leased and posted for aquaculture or other private use. When going ashore take the Washington State Public Lands Quadrangle Map of Bellingham to avoid trespassing.*

There are about two miles of public tidelands in the area covered in this chapter, mainly in Chuckanut and Bellingham bays.

U.S. Coast Guard Station Bellingham

The Port of Bellingham Station's former Operations Officer Tom Larson (now in San Francisco) and Ann Melton of the Coast Guard Auxiliary gave us the following information.

Bellingham Bay is notorious as very rough with short, steep waves, and winds are sometimes clocked at more than 50 knots.

Coast Guard personnel are concerned that some boaters are not using navigation charts in the northwest, and there are many unseen dangers. "Navigation charts are a must for safe boating in the islands."

Three areas are the scenes of frequent groundings:

(1) Channel between **Bare and Skipjack islands** off Waldron Island where there are charted rocks. *(Ch. 5)*

(2) Charted but unmarked shoal of 1 fathom, 2 feet in **West Bank Shoal,** 1.15 miles west of Sucia Island. *(Ch. 6)*

(3) Rocks just off the southeast side of **Clark Island** that are exposed at low tide but cannot be seen at high tide. *(Ch. 6)*

The Coast Guard monitors all radio calls but can only launch a boat for urgent or immediate distress. They advise boaters out of gas or broken down to find a "good samaritan" or coordinate commercial assistance to provide help. All mariners should have a marine radio, all aboard should know how to use it. Check weather reports frequently while out on the water.

During an average year, station personnel handle over 200 search and rescues, conduct 150 boardings, assist about 150 people and save a dozen lives. They also have the unfortunate job of searching for and recovering bodies that have been lost at sea. Law enforcement interdictions have resulted in seizure of over 20 tons of marijuana and numerous vessels. The station works with federal, state or local agencies in law enforcement, pollution control and clean-up, and public education in boating safety.

Bellingham Coast Guard

Port Angeles Air Station has helicopters available for search and rescue, and they often work in conjunction with Station Bellingham.

Pleasure boating begins with a well-maintained boat that is safely equipped and a knowledgable skipper. They also suggest a "Float Plan:" Leave a written description of your boat, where you are going, and when you plan to return with a family member or friend. Booklets of regulations are available at Coast Guard Stations and at marine dealers. The C.G. Auxiliary conducts free safety examinations of pleasure boats and commercial fishing vessels.

Station Bellingham, under operational control of Coast Guard Group Seattle, has 21 personnel, augmented by reservists and auxiliary members, two 41 foot boats and one 25 foot Safeboat. The current boats are not heavy weather boats and are rated for winds no more than 30 knots and eight foot seas.

The station was moved from Squalicum Harbor to its location on the west side of I & J Waterway in able to accommodate a new 47 foot motor life boat, due at the station before 2001. The new heavy weather craft will be able to operate in 30 foot seas and 80 knot winds, greatly increasing search and rescue capability.

⚓ **UNDERWAY AGAIN,** we leave Squalicum Harbor Marina and cruise along the north shore of Bellingham Bay.

One mile of public beach lines this shore of the bay, beginning one mile west of Squalicum Creek. Drying tideflats from the Nooksack River extend 1.2 miles into the north end of Bellingham Bay. There are no navigation aids in this area.

The Lummi Indian Reservation peninsula begins at the east side of the Nooksack River, extends southwest around the entire peninsula, including Portage Island, and north past Lummi Bay to Neptune Beach, including the Sandy Point area. There are no public tidelands on the reservation.

Portage Island is attached by a tombolo at its northwest tip of Lummi Peninsula. At low tides tire tracks may be seen on the tombolo, as the island is accessed by tribal members. Portage Island is over 1.5 miles long and a little less than 1.5 miles wide. The lowland at the north end of the island eventually becomes bluffs of about 200 feet off the south end. Landing is not permitted on the island.

Portage Bay and Channel, north of the island, are shallow with charted rocks and foul bottom. Kayaks and paddle boats may go through the channel and cross over the tombolo at high tide.

Point Francis rocks and shoals abound as charted, about 500 yards offshore. Depths of 2 to 3 fathoms extend about 1.5 miles southeast to a 1 fathom, 3 foot kelpy rocky shoal with a lighted buoy. Cruisers in this area need to go south around Portage Island, past Point Francis.

Rocks Junction Lighted Buoy [Fl (2+1) R 6s] flashing red 6 second light on a buoy with red and green bands, marks the south edge of the shoal. The buoy is 0.9 miles north of Eliza Island.

Eliza Island, all private, is about 0.8 mile south of the Rocks Junction Buoy, one mile east of the south tip of Lummi Island, and 1.6 miles northeast of Viti Rocks. It is low, partially wooded with shoals surrounding most of it for as much as 0.2 mile offshore. The island has vacation cabins, an airstrip for residents and a pier on the west shore. It is a stop on the seasonal passenger ferry *Redhead* run. Boats sometimes anchor in bights on either of the large point extending west. There are no public tidelands on Eliza.

Eliza Rock, NWR, is 0.1 mile off the southeast shore of the island. This is a scuba diving area with a rocky bottom.

Eliza Rock Junction Light [Fl (2+1) G 21ft 5M] flashing green light 21 feet high visible 5 miles, is on a dayboard with horizontal bands of green and red, green band topmost, mounted on a house 0.1 mile off the southeast tip of the island.

Before we leave Bellingham Bay, Carl shares some experiences he had in the Bellingham area in his 24 foot schooner Condor in the early 1940s when he was still a teenager. It gives a bit of insight into cruising in the pre-WW II era.

Carl and the *Condor*

The anchor and chain rattled out and set in Chuckanut Bay mud after the trip from Sucia. While getting sail off, a lovely young mermaid swam out to visit *Condor* and me. Unfortunately, she returned to her friends ashore without boarding the schooner. Next day as the wind died *Condor* drifted to a mostly fishing vessel moorage in Fairhaven in South Bellingham where we tied up. The moorage was destroyed by severe northerly storms years later.

A 50-year-old guy on the float, we'll call him "Rough and Tumble," casually said he'd just sent a 20 pound gift-wrapped brick COD to his unfaithful divorced wife on their wedding anniversary. His comments indi-

---

Lummi Indian Historical Bits

Fish Point is the site of an old Lummi village site.

Portage Channel off the southeast shore of Lummi Indian Reservation peninsula led to the low-tide portage for Indian canoes between Portage Island and the southeast tip of the peninsula for hundreds of years.

Lummi Indians hunted seals along the rocky shoal south of Point Francis.

Naming Point Francis

Point Francis on Portage Island was probably named by Vancouver when he explored the area in 1792. However, this was not mentioned in his journal, and there is no mention of the person for whom the point was named.

Flour Power

During World War II, training planes from Whidbey Island Naval Air Station regularly "bombed" Eliza Island with bags of flour during their practice runs.

Naming Eliza Island

The island was named for Lt. Juan Francisco de Eliza, the Spaniard who was in charge of explorations in the area in 1790 and 1791.

Strong Arms Needed

Whatcom County originally included both Skagit and San Juan counties. The sheriff had to ROW to all these island areas to keep order—a huge job.

Maybe that's where the saying "Strong arm of the law" really comes from!

Moored fishing boats, similar to those moored 60 years ago in Fairhaven

What was "Preservo?"

Carl: These were the days of my mentor/peer group and Waumsutta canvas sail cloth— Bill Garden, John Adams, Rupert Broom, Jack Kutz, Heine Dole, Bob Schoen and Miles McCoy.

Liquid Preservo was the way these sailors prevented mildew from rotting their sails, and used by some for shirts, shorts, skivvies, socks and hats, though less than comfortable.

And Preservo was what I had on my tanbark sails.

cated he fished commercially and had flown small planes.

Queried about old rum-running days brought forth surprising tales. Fishing vessels from Canada loaded with booze would depart, often after dark, sometimes without lights, for secret rendezvous with other boats or to the San Juans, he said. Patrolling revenue vessels spotting suspicious craft would give chase, sometimes using search lights or sneaking up on unwary smugglers. Vigilant smugglers maneuvered their vessels to conceal dumping the booze overboard, then immediately began doing fishboat work as the revenuers approached. When boarded, nothing was found. Full cases of booze with added flotation would later rise to the surface after rock salt ballast, which had caused them to sink, was dissolved by sea water. Rock salt was a common item aboard certain fishing vessels. Allowing for the set of the current, smugglers' vessels would return to the vicinity to fish out the floating cases. Revenuers eventually caught on.

One story involved his early bi-plane, so heavily loaded with booze it could barely take off. He flew to the Duwamish flatlands south of Seattle where ground signals indicated the landing site. A truck and driver were ready, and the coast was clear. He would land, unload, take off again and the truck would leave. That became too risky when other lights and activities were seen. He set down at an alternate site, unloaded, abandoned the plane, evaded the revenuers, escaped with the booze and a truck, and decided to get a job in Bellingham. Some similarities with Rough and Tumble's smuggling accounts and those earlier escapades of Dirty Dan in Bellingham were fascinating.

Casting off from Fairhaven, fair wind and current permitted *Condor* to reach the Whatcom Creek city float, which was Bellingham's only usable waterway, I believe. I walked into the skid-road waterfront section of town, buildings not much different from today. I went through a dark door overhung by a sign, "Pawn Shop—no minors allowed."

Now in Bellingham my cash on hand was about six bits. I didn't want to phone and ask my working parents in Seattle for money while I played boat. I had gold pocket watch I didn't want to part with given to me by my uncle who I had lived and travelled with in Mexico several summers earlier—that was my only hope. I was tired of fish and clams and needed real food.

Referred to the pawn broker's office back in a dingy, smoke-filled room, I passed pool and card tables occupied by grim-faced men. Some were noisy, overdosed, jousting with macho vulgarities, arrogant, bottles in hand. I found the steely-eyed broker eyeing me suspiciously. Cross-examined about my uncle in Mexico, my parents, addresses and phone numbers, he completed a form in triplicate with several paragraphs in fine print. I had to sign, and he implied a copy went to the police.

Reluctantly he handed me $25, saying, "Get the hell out the back door, kid, and don't come back." I went to the nearest market for food and returned to the boat. Bellingham at that moment seemed unfriendly. I wanted most to leave, but I still needed water. It was flat calm with a rising tide, but after dark a light easterly rose and the ebb had started. Casting off, *Condor* sailed to a fuel float on the north side of the waterway where fresh water surely would be available.

Condor's Preservo'd tanbark red sails appeared to avoid detection when a police car spotlight swept the area from the street above the city float and drove off. I coasted to the darkened fuel float and found the water was turned off inside the locked main valve shed on the pier.

I found an open window through which I crawled. No sooner inside, footsteps approached, a night watchman making rounds. Or maybe it was police following up a routine lead from a suspicious pawn broker who had seen my boat leaving. A shadowy figure flashed a light in the closed window. Standing next to the wall I wasn't seen; footsteps faded down the ramp. From the window I watched as he shined his light in *Condor's* porthole without going aboard. He started back up the ramp.

Sounds of a padlock being unlocked became the more familiar sound of a watch station key actuating the watchman's recorder, and then departing footsteps. (I had worked as a night watchman and knew the sounds and routine.) My heart stopped pounding for the moment as I watched him disappear in the dark shadows in what then seemed a smuggler-riddled, gambling town to a teen-aged kid. Looking about, I found the shutoff valve, crawled out the window and strolled to the boat, as if for a casual walk on the pier. I turned on the water at the tap and filled the 15 gallon wooden keg, which I had possibly bought from Jo's mom who was working in the office at Western Cooperage on Lake Union in Seattle at this time.

Carl & the Condor before red Preservo'd sails

It seemed best to depart immediately with the ebb rather than moor till morning. With a favorable breeze, *Condor* had sailed several hundred yards away when a spotlight from the fuel pier swept the area without consequence.

We were underway once again.

In the next and last chapter, **Chapter 12,** we explore Hale Passage, Lummi Island and the mainland as we go north to Drayton Harbor, Blaine, Semiahmoo and Point Roberts.

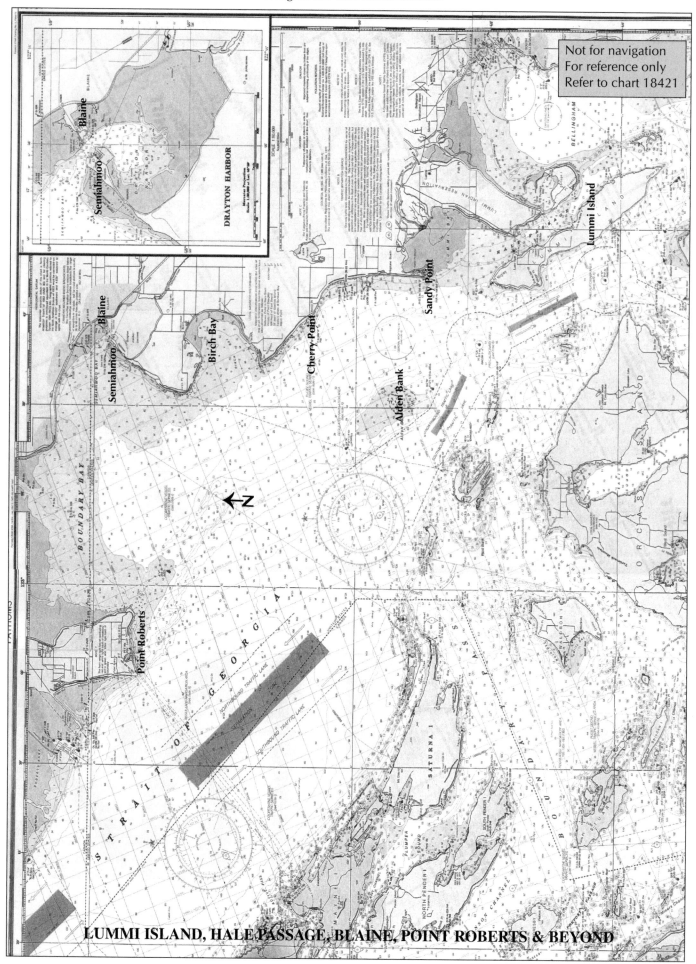

Not for navigation
For reference only
Refer to chart 18421

DRAYTON HARBOR

Blaine

Semiahmoo

Blaine

Semiahmoo

Birch Bay

Cherry Point

Sandy Point

Alden Bank

Lummi Island

BOUNDARY BAY

Point Roberts

STRAIT OF GEORGIA

SATURNA I

LUMMI ISLAND, HALE PASSAGE, BLAINE, POINT ROBERTS & BEYOND

Chapter 12
LUMMI ISLAND, HALE PASSAGE, BLAINE & POINT ROBERTS

Charts & Publications for this Chapter

Chart	Date	Title	Scale	Soundings
U.S. 18400	08/30/97	Strait of Georgia & Strait of Juan de Fuca	1:200,000	Fathoms
★ U.S. 18421	01/25/97	Strait of Juan de Fuca to Strait of Georgia	1:80,000	Fathoms
		Inset, Drayton Harbor	1:30,000	Fathoms
U.S.18423	06/18/94	Bellingham to Everett, inc. San Juan Islands,		
		Page A	1:80,000	Fathoms
		Page B, Inset Blaine	1:30,000	Fathoms
★ U.S. 18424	07/12/97	Bellingham Bay	1:40,000	Fathoms
★ U.S. 18431	10/05/96	Rosario Strait to Cherry Point	1:25,000	Fathoms
BR. ADM.79	08/05/94	Strait of Georgia, Southern Part	1:200,000	Meters
CAN. 3313	1995	Gulf Islands Chart Book, Chart 2	1:200,000	Meters
★ CAN. LC3462	10/23/98	Juan de Fuca Strait to Strait of Georgia	1:80,000	Meters
★ CAN. 3490	07/25/97	Fraser River	1:20,000	Meters
★ CAN. 3492	11/27/98	Roberts Bank	1:20,000	Meters
🐚		Wash. State DNR Quad Map, Bellingham	1:100,000	

➥ *Compare your chart dates with those above. There may be discrepancies between chart edition*
★ *= Preferred chart for this chapter* 🐚*= Indicates DNR & other public tideland information*

AN INTRODUCTORY NOTE

In this final chapter, we explore fascinating, mountainous Lummi Island, Hale Passage, the mainland shores from the Lummi Indian Reservation north to Blaine and Semiahmoo at Drayton Harbor and west along the Canadian Boundary to Point Roberts. Once north of Hale Passage and Lummi Island we will be in the Strait of Georgia as we cruise to the last destinations in this book.

The chapter chart gives a brief perspective of the magnitude of the not always user-friendly southern end of the Strait of Georgia, and a sense of the distance to places visited in previous chapters and to the Gulf Islands.

In case we inadvertently sail off the north edge of NOAA Chart 18421 due to adverse weather or other problems near Point Roberts we should have Canadian Charts 3462, 3490 and 3492 in the ship's chart inventory. We briefly look at the region north of the border near the end of the chapter.

Vastly different from the San Juans, British Columbia north of Point Roberts has its own beauty. Multitudes of mariners north or south bound through the San Juans choose courses through the protected Gulf Islands, while some opt for the Strait of Georgia on their way to Vancouver or perhaps Desolation Sound and beyond.

But that's another book—or two.

➥ **Note: Marine fuel** is available in five places in the areas covered in this chapter:
- **Blaine Harbor**
- **Crescent Beach Marina**
- **Gooseberry Point,** gas
- **Point Roberts Marina**
- **Semiahmoo Marina**

Tug in a hurry

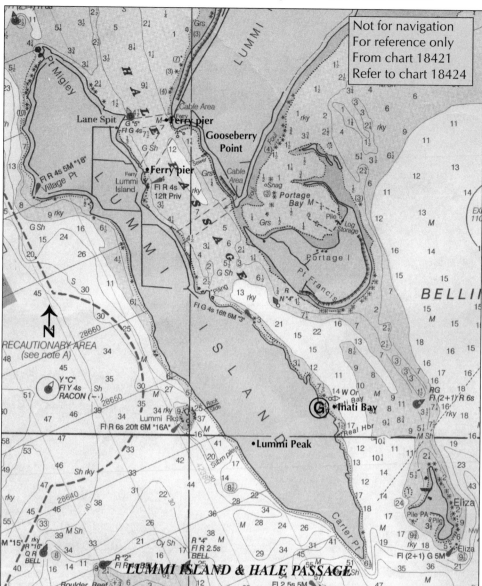

LUMMI ISLAND & HALE PASSAGE

CHAPTER OVERVIEW

We start our cruise through this chapter in Hale Passage between Lummi Island, Bellingham Bay and the mainland.

Then we circumnavigate high forested Lummi counterclockwise, starting from the south end at Carter Point, finding an anchorage or two.

We then enter Georgia Strait and continue north to shallow Birch Bay with a beautiful and popular state park, and then visit Semiahmoo Spit at Tongue Point, Drayton Harbor and Blaine, home of the International Peace Arch.

A quick detour takes us briefly into B.C., and then we cross Boundary Bay, ending up at Point Roberts, that most unlikely tiny part of the U.S. that must be reached—at least by land—by going through British Columbia.

And before we actually get underway we'll begin with a good look at Hale Passage and a bit about amazing Lummi Island.

HALE PASSAGE

Hale Passage separates forested Lummi Island on the west from the mainland Lummi Indian Reservation peninsula and Portage Island on the east. It is used by commercial, fishing and pleasure craft of various types and sizes.

The pass opens southeast to Bellingham Bay and northwest to Georgia Strait between Point Migley at the north tip of Lummi Island and Sandy Point on the mainland, about 2.3 miles north of Lummi.

Hale Passage is six miles long, and its least width shore to shore is 0.6 mile at Lane Spit near the north end and Lummi Light 3 near the south end. It is one mile wide at various places in the pass.

Winds tend to funnel through Hale Pass, sometimes causing 6 to 8 foot swells.

Controlling depths in the pass range from 2 fathoms, 2 feet at the north end to over 20 fathoms near the south end. Oddly, a narrow seabed shoal extends north from Lummi Point to Sandy Point. The shoal is from 100 yards to 300 yards wide, evidence of the ongoing battle between tidal currents, river silt, wind and seas. A single 3 fathom, 1 foot sounding is between the 3 fathom mainland curve and the far north end of the shoal.

Currents in Hale Pass are based on *Tidal Current Tables* predictions on Rosario Strait, with flood currents at the same speed as Rosario and ebb predictions half those in the Strait.

Flood currents run nearly north at 350° True and during extremes may reach or exceed 2.8 knots. Ebb currents run southeast at 145° and may reach or exceed 1.8

knots. Currents predictions are based on tidal current cycles and do not include river flood conditions. Local mariners say they have encountered currents of 4 knots or more.

If predicted currents are strong in Rosario Strait off the west side of Lummi, the weaker ebb in Hale may make this pass preferable to Rosario.

Lummi Bay is off the northeast side of Hale Pass, between Gooseberry Point and Sandy Point. The triangular-shaped bay extends about 2.2 miles north-northeast from the pass and is virtually all mudflats, except for a narrow western edge of about one fathom.

LUMMI ISLAND

Lummi Island is an unexpected treat—sometimes called "the forgotten island of the San Juans," or the "refuge of tranquility" by the Whatcom County Visitors Bureau. It's linked to the mainland by a short ferry ride across Hale Pass from Gooseberry Point. Although many of us have thought so, it is not part of the Lummi Indian Reservation.

The island is about eight miles long and from 0.5 mile to nearly 1.5 miles wide. The population of Lummi is about 615 persons, most of whom live in the northern portion of the island, with elevations from sea level to about 300 feet. The north end is nothing like the mountainous, virtually roadless, unpopulated south end. Deer and eagles reign supreme in this part of the island, where Lummi Peak reaches 1,625 feet.

There is one good anchorage at the island, several other possible anchorages in calm weather, and one DNR park.

Public tidelands surround much of the island, but are often inaccessible.

Lummi has about 18 miles of roads which cyclists enjoy riding as vehicle traffic is light. The island has several bed and breakfasts—the exact number appears to change occasionally. Numerous artist's studios and galleries represent the colony of accomplished island artisans.

A market, rental shop, library, post office, grade school, grange hall and a charming restaurant are on the east side of the island, all within walking distance of the ferry landing. The community church, cemetery and reefnet fishing boats are on the west shores at Legoe Bay.

Islander Market, south of the ferry landing, is a casual meeting place for the community. The market carries a full line of groceries, including freshly baked bread, has a gift shop, videos and many other items. The rental shop is next door and they rent bicycles, as well as necessities for island living. The library (part of Whatcom County Library system), post office and the cafe are all island meeting places.

Beach Store Cafe is one of the most charming restaurants we've seen—and is accessible to those arriving by boat. The restaurant has two mooring buoys out in front, just north of the ferry landing, that are deep enough for sailboats, they tell us. Some cruisers anchor off the cafe long enough to enjoy a meal, but be aware of the charted cable area here. A small Whatcom County Park is on shore in front of the cafe, with stairs leading to the beach below. The island ferry dock was originally located where the park is.

The cafe, in a lovely, restored building, is warm and friendly, with a potbellied stove and wonderful odors wafting out the door. It features fabulous soups—their clam chowder would make even Ivar

Lummi Island Library

Beach Store Cafe, center, public stairs on right

envious. They've won awards in an annual Soup Festival. Sandwiches, salads, snacks and desserts are equally mouth-watering. Tel.: 360-758-CAFE

Beach Store Cafe was built in 1901 as a store and is now on the Washington State Historical Register, an example of how the islands were settled. When pioneers arrived they would build a dock, then build a store at the head of the dock which became the community center and gathering place. This was where messages were left, and where the first post office and telephone were established. The store played a central role in any settlement.

The island grade school, just beyond the Beach Store Cafe, goes through sixth grade, with about 50 to 60 youngsters enrolled. Starting with seventh grade, students take the ferry and then are bused to mainland schools.

✺ **UNDERWAY,** let's begin our counter-clockwise cruise around Lummi.

Carter Point is the rocky south tip of Lummi. The island's east shore, densely covered with trees, rises as we head north. The shoreline is forbidding, no neat little pocket beaches and coves at this south end, just rocky bluffs that keep getting steeper.

❀ **Public tidelands** are along the entire south half of the island's east side. *(See DNR map)*

Reil Harbor is about 1.75 miles north of Carter Point, a Department of Natural Resources site. A large DNR sign visible from the water is a good way to identify this east-facing bay. Several small coves are in this site, connected by wooden steps and steep trails. The coves are surrounded by rock bluffs with tiny beaches, best suited to kayaks and other beachable boats.

⚓ There is possible anchorage here for a larger boat in calm weather. There is little protection.

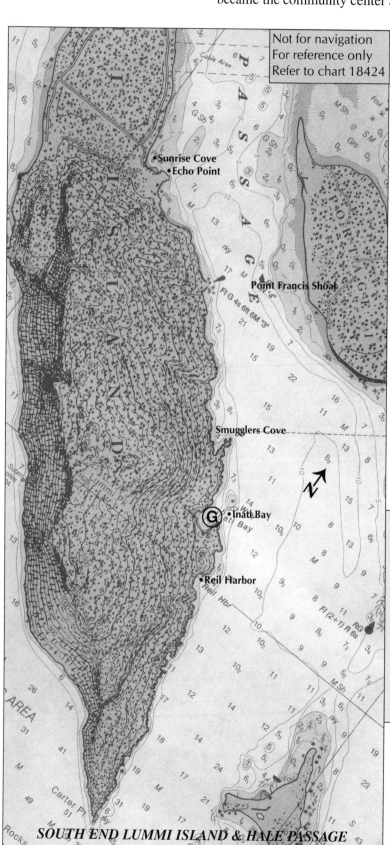

Not for navigation
For reference only
Refer to chart 18424

SOUTH END LUMMI ISLAND & HALE PASSAGE

Facilities at Reil Harbor
➤ 42 acres with 2,125 feet of shoreline, much of it steep, rocky bluffs
➤ Water access only
➤ One mooring buoy
➤ 5 campsites—with "the best tent pads in all the islands"
➤ Washington Water Trail campsite
➤ No water, no fees
➤ Fire rings, restrooms
➤ Hiking trails
➤ Activities: camp, fish, paddle, hike

Much of Lummi Island south of Reil Harbor is a DNR Conservation area.

We leave Reil Harbor and continue north along the rocky coast about 0.5 mile to the one recommended anchorage on Lummi.

Inati Bay is a favorite spot of Bellingham area recreational mariners. It is one of the most beautiful small bays we've seen, with rocky points and forested shores surrounding the bay, which is about 200 yards across. It opens to the northeast, and is well protected in south, southeast and northwest winds.

Inati Bay Reef Buoy [W Or] marks a rock near the north end of the entrance. The buoy, white with orange bands, is worded **DANGER ROCK**. The reef is about 200 yards east of Lummi's cliffs and about 500 yards northeast of the head of the bay.

Entrance to the bay is south of the buoy, not between the buoy and Lummi.

A gently-sloped sandy beach is at the head of the bay—good place to land the dinghy, do a bit of beachcombing, and is a great place for a swim. The water here is warm and pleasant. We tested it, naturally. A swath of lawn holds picnic tables and benches made from split logs. A lyrical waterfall is at the bay's west end.

Inati Bay

Inati Bay was once a log booming ground; an old logging skid is along the southeast shore. Abandoned logging roads nearby offer easy walking.

⚓ **Anchoring** is good here in 3 to 4 fathoms, mud bottom. Stern-tying is suggested to keep from swinging and to allow room for other boats.

Ⓖ **This is indeed a lovely gunkhole,** and chances are you'll be sharing the bay.

Facilities at Inati Bay
➤ Picnic tables, fireplaces
➤ Hiking trails
➤ No fees
➤ Anchorage for a dozen or more boats
➤ Activities: camp, picnic, fish, swim, walk, gunkhole, beachcomb

---

Inati Bay and Bellingham Yacht Club

Perhaps the most unusual aspect of Inati Bay is the generosity of the Bellingham Yacht Club which leases the land. A sign states: "Leased and maintained for all pleasure boaters by Bellingham Yacht Club. Please help by packing out all garbage and using the toilets only as intended."

Seldom have we heard of yacht clubs sharing their outstation properties with non-members. All of us who use Inati Bay owe Bellingham Yacht Club hearty thanks.

✹**UNDERWAY AGAIN,** we leave Inati Bay and continue north along rocky, forested Lummi shores.

Smugglers Cove is about 0.5 mile north of Inati Bay. A large gravel quarry is in the bay with roads zigzagging down to the shore, and it's constantly busy as gravel is barged from the quarry. The road through trees leading to the quarry has a sign posted, "Tree Farm."

⚓ **Anchoring** might be possible in the cove, which is well protected from south, southeast and west winds, but exposed to the north. We understand the quarry often operates late into the night. This could be a noisy, somewhat crowded anchorage, but it might work in a pinch.

Lummi Island Light 3 [Fl G 4s 6ft 6M "3"] a flashing green 4 second light 6

➥ **NOTE:** We recommend using Chart 18424 in Hale Passage and around Lummi Island because of its details.

Changing Times

The Rev. Lee Conrad, Lummi Island minister, said island life is changing with the arrival of city-oriented people, citing the new island condos we saw. He said much of the new home development is back in the trees.

"This island has always been rural and everybody looked after everybody. Now we're getting a high proportion of summer people who see this as a retreat, a place to get away from city pressures."

The same reason so many of us go cruising.

Fisherman Cove Marina

Whatcom Chief

Carl visited ferry skipper Mike Moye during our six minute trip across Hale Passage in the **Whatcom Chief**. *Mike's been on the Lummi Island run for 22 years. He said:*

"Weather seldom holds us up, we don't let it bother us, but it can bother some people.

"Basic prevailing winds are southeast pretty much year round. Highest winds ever were 114 mph out of the northeast.

"Northwest winds can give us 6 to 8 foot swells, and southeast winds can give us green water over the pilothouse.

"There's some protection off Lummi from southwest to northwest winds for pleasure boats along the east side: in Inati Bay, in three or four little coves, or the lee sides of Lane Spit."

End of conversation—the six minutes were up and the ferry was about to dock.

➥ Lummi Point/LaneSpit

"Lane Spit" is the name on some charts for the point 1.5 miles south of Point Migley and 1.0 mile north of the ferry landing on the east side of Lummi Island.

"Lummi Point" is the name used in the *Tidal Current Tables* and the *Light List.*

On Chart 18430 both names are used.

---

feet high visible 6 miles, is on a square green dayboard on a tower on Lummi about one mile north of the quarry.

Echo Point, unnamed on charts, is about 0.7 mile north of Lummi Island Light. Charted bays are on either side of the point. **Sunrise Cove,** also unnamed on charts, is the north bay. The bays might be used as anchorages in calm weather in 1 to 2 fathoms. There is no public beach access here, uplands are private.

Homes on moderate banks are above the shore as we proceed north. It's about 1.6 miles from here to the ferry landing and Lummi Island Village.

Along the East Shores of Hale Passage

Portage Island, part of the Lummi Indian Reservation, forms the southeast shore of Hale Passage. There are no public tidelands on reservation lands. *(Ch. 11)*

[R N "4"] red nun buoy marks a shoal with a depth of 2 feet extending 450 yards southwest into Hale Passage from Portage Island. The buoy is about 650 yards across the pass from Lummi Island Light 3. This is the narrowest part of Hale Pass.

This shoal, with depths of only 1 to 2 feet in places, runs from Point Francis to Gooseberry Point. It is named in the *Light List* as Point Francis Shoal Buoy 4, although that seems a bit confusing to us as Point Frances at the south end of the island is about one mile from this buoy.

Cable area is charted at the south tip of Lummi Indian Reservation about 1.3 miles north of the red nun buoy, across the pass to Lummi Island.

Gooseberry Point is at the southwest tip of Lummi Indian Reservation peninsula. It is the terminus for the *Whatcom Chief* ferry, which sails daily to Lummi Island from about 6 a.m. to midnight, making the crossing in about six minutes. Fishing vessels and other boats occasionally anchor in the shallow bight of Fisherman's Cove, just southeast of the ferry landing.

Cable area from Gooseberry Point splits into two sections, one to the southwest in the vicinity of the Lummi ferry dock and the Beach Store Cafe, and the other comes ashore about 150 yards south of Lummi Point. They should be avoided if anchoring nearby.

A "hole" of 11 to 16 fathoms is south of Gooseberry Point, the only deep spot in Hale Passage north of Portage Island.

Fisherman's Cove Marina is at a pier with a float immediately west of the ferry terminal.

Facilities at Fisherman's Cove Marina
➤ Gasoline
➤ Marine supplies
➤ Hull and engine repairs
➤ Double hoist launch for boats up to 4 tons
➤ Dry storage for boats under 30 feet
➤ Water, ice
➤ Nearby market

Fisherman's Cove Mini-Market near the ferry pier is a small grocery store that's been in operation more than 25 years, a friendly place.

The Lummi Casino at Gooseberry Point is no longer in operation.

Back to the west shores of Hale Passage along Lummi Island

We continue north in Hale Pass, reaching the Lummi Ferry landing.

Lummi Island Ferry Landing Light [Fl R 4s 12ft Priv] flashing red 4 second private light 12 feet high is on the ferry pier.

⚓ **Anchoring** temporarily is possible on either side of the ferry landing, depending on weather, tides, currents and being aware of the cable area.

Beach Store Cafe is just north of the ferry pier.

Lane Spit, less than one mile north of the ferry dock, extends about 0.2 mile out into Hale Pass from the otherwise fairly straight Lummi shore. There are a fair number of homes along here and all beaches are private.

Lummi Point Lighted Buoy 5 [Fl G 4s "5"] flashing green 4 second lighted buoy, is off the tip of Lummi Point/Lane Spit. *(See sidebar)*

⚓ **Anchoring** is possible in the shallow coves off either side of the spit, whichever is the lee side, depending on the weather.

Cable areas cross from the south side of the point to the mainland.

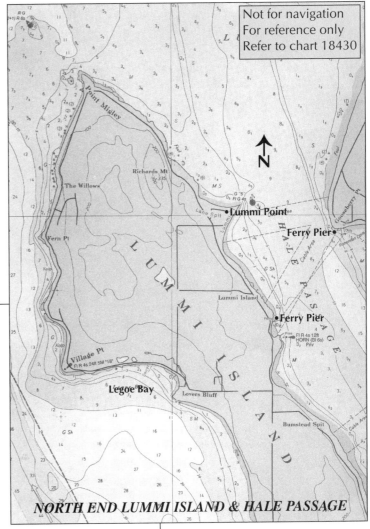

Not for navigation
For reference only
Refer to chart 18430

NORTH END LUMMI ISLAND & HALE PASSAGE

A Tale of Hale Passage

Longtime Chuckanut Bay resident and old friend of Carl's, Fred Elsethehagen, tells his harrowing sailing story that happened long ago (1940s):

I'd sailed to Inati Bay on the final leg of a single-handed, two-week cruise in the San Juans. My boat was *Topsy*, a Flattie (18 foot Geary design), the only Flattie in the world with a 4'x5'x5' high folding cuddy cabin. It was August, and I'd been out long enough. I wanted to get home and see my kids and wife, so I took off. Quite a little breeze blowing but I hadn't any trouble so far. I sailed out of 'Nati and into open water where a williwaw caught me—flipped the little Flattie completely over.

I finally got her turned on her side, and drifted with the wind and current. I ended up on the south face of Portage Island, on the cliff side. The boat's whole top for 8 to 10 feet was broken up and a plank had broken out. I anchored out as far as I could, walking and swimming a little to keep her off the bottom. I suddenly realized I was going to be in trouble as the tide was going out, the boat would be on the rocks soon, and I hadn't seen anybody all day.

So I decided, by gawd, I'll just have to take a chance and see if I can get around Portage and find a little lee somewhere. It's starting to get dark and I'm not seeing very much, but I moved the Flattie by sitting on her side and paddling. All of a sudden the seas start making up and water starts sloshing through the holes and she went over—again. It was pitch dark, the water was cold, the boat was on her side and I was sitting on the few inches that were out of the water.

I decided to stay with the boat, because at least it would float. By then we were drifting north through Hale Pass; it must have been about 10 o'clock.

Topsy

(See next page)

Village Point Light 18

When I got across from the populated end of Lummi, I started yelling in short sentences, so I wouldn't sound like some bird if I yelled, "Help, help!"

I saw headlights from a car driving on the island from one place to another. Turned out this was a fellow who'd heard me and was trying to find a friend to go out with him and pick me up.

He finally found a fisherman with a boat moored on Hale Pass. They reached me just as it was getting daylight and I was entering Georgia Strait. They put a hitch on the mast, pulled the boat upright, got enough water out so it was floating, and took me to shore on Lummi, with many thanks by me.

I called the Coast Guard in Bellingham, chagrined as hell with myself. I asked if they could come over and tow me back to Bellingham Boat Owners' Association on the south side of the bay (South Bellingham). I found a bunch of thin box wood and patched up the side of *Topsy* so she wasn't wide open.

They came and towed me across the bay and then my pride took over. I made them drop the tow just before we got to the boat basin. I grabbed a paddle and nonchalantly came paddling in, just as though the last 24 hours hadn't happened.

Legoe Bay reefnet boats

Lummi Community Church

Point Migley is the north extremity of Lummi Island. The full force of north and west winds hammer Migley, and heavy surf pounds the rocky shore. It's an area frequented by scuba divers in good weather. Point Migley's 3 fathom depth curve almost touches the shoreline on the northeast tip of Lummi, but immediately moves about 300 yards offshore as we round the point. On the west side of the point a rocky patch bares at MLLW within the kelp, and numerous ledges and rocks bare up to 3 feet as we head past bluffs down the south side of Lummi.

Point Migley Lighted Buoy [Fl (2+1) R 6s] flashing red 6 second light on a red and green banded buoy is about 0.5 mile northwest of the point. It marks a 2 fathom, 3 foot shoal surrounded by its own 3 and 5 fathom depth curves. There's 350 yards between the 5 fathom depth curves of the lighted buoy and the point.

Onshore, condominiums hike up the hillside, taking advantage of incredible views west across Rosario Strait to Clark, Barnes, Orcas and Sucia islands, with often breathtaking sunsets.

Much of the shoreline from north of Lane Spit and around Point Migley to around Village Point is DNR tideland. *(See Quad map)*

We are now back to keeping outside the 5 fathom curve until it disappears in shore and we shift to the 10 fathom curve for reference to keep clear of shoreline ledges and rocks.

Village Point juts west into Rosario Strait about two miles south of Point Migley. It's low bank, and the beach is piled with driftwood.

Village Point Light 18 [Fl R 4s 24ft 5M "18"] flashing red 4 second light 24 feet high visible 5 miles, is on a triangular red dayboard on a tower at the point. A higher intensity beam north towards Rosario Strait and Boundary Bay is obscured from 180° to 264°.

Legoe Bay indents the northwest shore of Lummi in the bight which hooks east and south from Village Point for about .75 miles to **Lovers Bluff**. This bay is pleasant in calm weather, but is exposed to south and west winds. It can provide relief from some north and east winds. Small houses line the shores along Legoe Bay.

Legoe Bay is fascinating as this is the location of a large number of reefnet fishing boats. During fishing season they anchor offshore where they catch fish by the old reefnetting method. The rest of the year the boats are hauled out on railways across the no-bank beach road at the bay.

Launch ramp is at a road end at the east side of the bay shortly before Lovers Bluff. A classic white New England style Community Church and cemetery, built in 1914, graces this side of the island, an important community institution.

Continuing south, Lummi Island's personality changes abruptly along this west shore as elevations jump from less than 100 feet to 900 feet and climbing. The shores get steep and rocky and beaches all but disappear. The 10 fathom depth curve is less than 250 yards offshore, close to a gaggle of charted rocks awash, so we move out to 15 fathoms. As we near Lummi Rocks the cliffs are almost straight up to over 1,600 feet.

Lummi Rocks are about midway between Legoe Bay and Carter Point. The rocks, about 0.2 mile offshore, are about 400 yards long and as much as 200 yards wide. Depths between the rocks and the island range from 5 to 37 fathoms.

Lummi Rocks Light 16A [Fl R 6s 20ft 6M "16A"] flashing red 6 second light 20 feet high visible 6 miles, is on the south end of the rocks, mounted on a triangular red dayboard on a tower.

Sunsets are beautiful from here, but a good nearby anchorage is hard to find.

Inshore of Lummi Rocks is a huge rock slide, and it's even charted, although not named. This is "Devil's Rock Slide," off the southwest side of Lummi Peak. Several rock climbers have reportedly died on this cliff.

❧ The rocks and all of Lummi's west shore south around Carter Point are DNR public tidelands. It's possible to go ashore if there's a place to land a beachable boat or set an anchor.

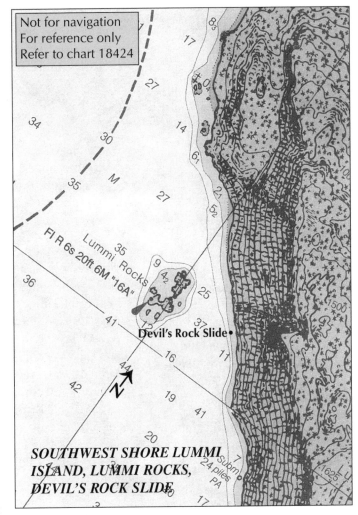

Not for navigation
For reference only
Refer to chart 18424

Devil's Rock Slide

SOUTHWEST SHORE LUMMI ISLAND, LUMMI ROCKS, DEVIL'S ROCK SLIDE

Bits Of Lummi Island History

Lummi tribal members were the original settlers on the island. The Indians once used the huge rockpile called Lummi Rocks as a favorite seal hunting spot. When a hunter sat on the rocks and stirred up the phosphorescence with his feet the seal's eyes could be seen as it neared the surface—and its demise. The Lummis used the entire animal: they ate it, used its fat for lights and the bladder was a buoy when hunting sea lions.

Some information points out that the Lummis fled the island near the end of the 1800s to avoid becoming slaves of Indians invading from the north. An old settler also said there was a time when Lummis were forced off the island at gunpoint by early settlers.

Early in the 20th century fishing and fish

Devil's Rock Slide

➡ **NOTE:** When we left the north end of Hale Passage we sailed off Chart **18424.**

Chart **18243** goes only as far north as Bellingham Bay. It does have a harbor chart of Drayton Harbor and Blaine, but doesn't show how to get there.

Chart **18431** goes only as far north as Cherry Point where there are piers for large ships.

So, we move on to Chart **18421,** Strait of Juan de Fuca to Strait of Georgia, 1:80,000, the only chart that gets us to Drayton Harbor & Pt. Roberts.

Lummi Villages

Several early Lummi village sites are on the Lummi Indian Reservation peninsula. The point at the southern tip was the possible site of a battle between a plundering tribe from Vancouver Island's north end.

A Clallam tribal woman, captured by the invaders, escaped near Village Point on Lummi's west side, crossed the island and warned Lummis fishing in Hale Passage of the impending invasion.

The Lummis won the battle.

packing were important on the island. Companies were building fishtraps and catching staggering numbers of fish near Legoe Bay. There were three fish canneries on the island: one by Lane Spit, one at Sunrise Cove farther south on the east side, and one in Legoe Bay near Village Point.

And, of course, rum runners dashed in and out in their fast boats, leaving their loot at Reil Harbor, Smuggler's Cove, and other bays.

The same spectacular scenery continues during the last three miles south: high, forested cliffs, not a home or person in sight, unchanged for eons. Under sail, or if a power boat engine is shut off, the silence is almost magical, just the wind, water and perhaps a few seabirds.

We've reached Carter Point and we've just circumnavigated Lummi Island.

⚓ **UNDERWAY AGAIN,** as if by magic, we're back at the north end of Hale Passage. As we leave the pass we cross the 2 fathom, 2 foot shoal running almost due north from Lummi for nearly two miles between Lummi Point and Sandy Point. This bar can be lumpy with adverse currents when the wind is up.

Massive Georgia Strait is now to our northwest.

Vessel Traffic System Buoy [Y "CA" Fl Y4s Racon (--)] a flashing 4 second yellow buoy is two miles west of the Point Migley Light, and we can see the buoy in the Strait as we travel north.

Sandy Point Shores with its bell-shaped dangling peninsula at the northwest corner of Lummi Bay is an extensive private development built along dredged channels on leased reservation land. Homes and private docks are along the inner basin.

Two navigation lights are at the entrance channel to Sandy Point.

Sandy Point Light 2 [Fl R 4s 16ft 5M "2"] flashing red 4 second light 16 feet high visible 5 miles, is on a triangular red dayboard on a pile, marking the south side of the entrance.

Sandy Point Light 3 [Fl G 2.5s "3"] a flashing green 2.5 second light 15 feet high visible 4 miles, is on a square green dayboard on a pile, at the north side of the entrance.

Obstruction is charted at 2-3/4 fathoms about 300 yards west of the entrance channel to Sandy Point. It bumps the 3 fathom depth curve to the west briefly.

Alden Bank, well marked by three buoys, is in the Strait of Georgia, four miles west of Sandy Point and three miles north of Matia Island. It is known for good fishing, and divers may be curious about it. The bank is about three miles long in a southeast direction, and about 1.5 miles wide.

Depths on the bank are less than 10 fathoms and there are two shallows of only 2-3/4 fathoms in the south end near others that are 3-1/4 to 4-1/4 fathoms. It is surrounded by its own 10, 20 and 30 fathom depth curves and kelp covers the bank as it sits on a seabed plateau.

From south to north the Alden Bank buoys are:

Alden Bank Buoy B [RG "B" Fl(2+1) R 6s Bell] buoy with red and green bands, flashing red 6 second light visible 5 miles with a bell. It is anchored off the southeast edge of the buoy in about 20 fathoms about 0.8 mile bearing 148° True from the two 2.75 fathom shoals.

Alden Bank Buoy 5 [GC "5"] green can buoy is on the east side of the bank about 1.2 miles bearing 28°True from the 2.75 fathom shoals. It's anchored in about 10 fathoms.

Alden Bank Lighted Gong Buoy A [R G "A" Fl (2+1) R 6s Gong] buoy with red and green bands, flashing red 6 second light visible 5 miles and equipped with a gong. It is anchored about 0.5 miles northwest of the 10 fathom depth curve in 16 to 19 fathoms about 2.8 miles bearing 328°True from the 2-3/4 fathom shoals at the south end of bank.

On a clear day a 10 mile line of sight bearing of 15°True from the west end of Matia to the west end of the cliffs of Point Whitehorn passes over Alden Bank's 2-3/4 shoals. The bank is three miles from Matia or six miles from Whitehorn.

As we continue north along the mainland shores Roberts we note charted hazards from two mile north of Sandy Point almost all the way to Point Roberts.

Rocks and shoals are charted inshore of the 3 fathom depth curve off the mainland, and are more common but not limited to shorelines backed by steep cliffs. They are obvious off Point Whitehorn, Birch Point and particularly off the southeast end of Point Roberts. These are erratic rocks left by earlier ice ages, a bit before our time.

Huge ships may be encountered from about 2.5 miles north of Sandy Point for the next nearly three miles to the large bight south of **Cherry Point** where there are three massive piers. These ships ply the waters of the Straits of Georgia and Juan de Fuca, Rosario or Haro straits and Boundary Pass to reach this destination.

The whole view of the Cherry Point complex is quite amazing, day or night, when the lights look like a small city. Somehow, we never expect to see this kind of industrial enterprise along a seemingly pristine coastline.

Two of the long wharves are oil refinery piers and the third is an aluminum smelter pier, all with privately maintained navigation aids.

The south pier is L-shaped, 1,800 feet long belonging to British Petroleum, about 2.4 miles north of Sandy Point.

Tosco Northwest North and South Lights [(2) F R 16ft Priv] two fixed red lights 16 feet high, are on diamond-shaped white dayboards with orange borders and black letters mounted on a dolphin. There is also a horn.

The middle pier is 950 foot long Intalco Aluminum Corporation Pier, 0.8 mile north of the B.P. pier.

Intalco North and South Lights [F R 24ft Priv] fixed red lights 24 feet high, are at the ends of the pier. There is also a horn.

The north pier is Atlantic Richfield Company Pier, with a 2,400 foot angular approach trestle, 4.5 miles northwest of Sandy Point.

Atlantic Richfield Lights ["A" and "B" F R 28ft Priv] are fixed red lights 28 feet high, on mooring dolphins.

We continue along to shallow Birch Bay.

Point Whitehorn, a conspicuous bold bluff 164 feet high with a steep cliff of white clay, it's 2.5 miles north of Cherry Point.

🐚 **Public tidelands** of four separate parcels totaling about 18,400 feet run from 2.9 miles north of Sandy Point to about 0.75 mile south of Point Whitehorn. All parcels are separated by private tidelands, particularly at the Cherry Point piers. Public tidelands in five parcels totaling 29,100 feet are around Point Whitehorn, including the south shore of Birch Bay, Birch Bay State Park, charted wreck symbol and portions of Birch Point Peninsula. Upland access is at Birch Bay State Park. (*See Quad Map*)

Naming Birch Bay

Birch Bay was named by Archibald Menzies in 1792, botanist with the Vancouver expedition.

"The black birch grew in such abundance it obtained the name of 'Birch Bay'," Capt. Vancouver wrote.

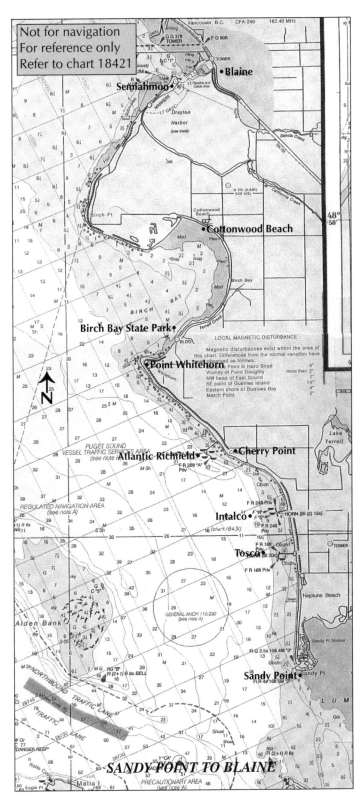

SANDY POINT TO BLAINE

Brrrrr...

For the hardy, we add a note about Birch Bay:

We understand there's an annual Birch Bay Polar Bear Swim. Tel.: 360-371-7800

BIRCH BAY

U-shaped Birch Bay opens to the northeast between Point Whitehorn at the south and Birch Point at the north. The bay is roughly 2.5 miles wide by 2.5 miles long. Depths are between 3 and 7 fathoms in the outer part, while in the inner mile depths are 3 fathoms to drying tideflats, including some charted snags. We poke around here to within about 0.5 mile of shore, where it gets less than 2 fathoms deep. The tideflats are great for wading, swimming or clam digging, and suit shoal draft craft. Kayakers and canoeists love it.

For the past 100 years or so, Birch Bay has been popular for the summer resorts and cottages lining its shores, with visitors enjoying the warm shallow waters. A road parallels the no-bank waterfront from Cottonwood Beach at the northeast corner of the bay to Birch Bay State Park along the south shore, the area of much activity, especially in summer. Along the north shore of the bay is Birch Bay Village, a private residential community about 1.5 miles from the head of the bay. A dredged boat basin is for residents only and there are no charted navigation aids.

⚓ **Anchoring** is possible in Birch Bay in good weather in 3 to 4 fathoms about 0.2 to 0.3 mile offshore, mud bottom.

Ⓖ This is possibly a gunkhole.

BIRCH BAY STATE PARK

Although this is not a marine park, there is plenty of spectacular waterfront.

Terrell Creek Marsh, which runs through the park, is one of the few remaining saltwater/freshwater estuaries in northern Puget Sound.

The park's northeast end is a natural game sanctuary where no development can occur. Bald eagles, great Blue Herons, and migratory waterfowl may be seen feeding along the creek banks. Interpretation boards at Terrell Creek Marsh point out the plants and animals inhabiting the area. Birch Bay is an official Audubon Sanctuary with family day-use and camping facilities.

Birch Bay beach boys at the park

Facilities at Birch Bay Park
➤ 193 acres, 8,255 feet of shoreline on Birch Bay
➤ 14,923 feet of shoreline on Terrell Creek
➤ 2.2 miles of trails
➤ 147 campsites with picnic tables & fireplaces, trailer hookups
➤ Restrooms with showers, bathhouse
➤ Designated places to hand-launch small boats across the road paralleling the shore, parking
➤ Activities: gunkhole about the large shallow bay, fish, beachcomb, dig clams, crab, swim, scuba dive, hike, camp, picnic, enjoy
➤ Phone: 360-371-2800
➤ Address: 5105 Helwig Road, Blaine, WA 98230

Birch Bay Beginnings
Birch Bay was inhabited by Semiahmoo, Lummi and Nooksack Indian tribes for many centuries. Their descendants have continued to carefully use the resources, still harvesting shellfish, waterfowl and salmon.

In June 1792, two of Capt. Vancouver's vessels, the *Discovery* and *Chatham*, anchored in Birch Bay in about 6 fathoms. While Capt. Vancouver and Lt. Peter Puget continued north in the pinnace and launch, others on the ships set up tents on shore for astronomical instruments, blacksmiths, brewers and ship's carpenters.

Botanist Archibald Menzies found an Indian village overgrown with nettles and bushes, and an old canoe suspended five or six feet above ground between two trees with decayed human bones wrapped in mats and covered with boards … "It would appear that this is the general mode of entombing their dead in this country." He also found grass and wild flowers and a "winding stream of fresh water…"

At the beginning of the 20th century huge fir trees in the area were logged with ox and horse teams. There are still some large stumps around with springboard marks on them.

> **NOTE:** Insets on Charts 18421 and 18423 show Drayton Harbor, including Blaine and Semiahmoo, in a 1:30,000 scale.

⚓ **UNDERWAY AGAIN**, on our way to Drayton Harbor, about three miles away.

We round Birch Point on a northeast course to Semiahmoo Bay and Drayton Harbor. The well-known and highly visible white Blaine Peace Arch is on the shore ahead, charted as "Monument." We are now almost in Canadian waters. The **International Boundary** between the U.S. and Canada is less than 0.5 mile from the entrance to Drayton Harbor.

International Boundary Range Lights

The **International Boundary** is marked by three sets of charted range lights on the boundary line where it crosses Semiahmoo and Boundary Bays.

All lights are named International Boundary Range lights.

One set is in the east part of Semiahmoo Bay, a second set is on the west side of Boundary Bay at Point Roberts, and the third set is on shore at the point. The lights are maintained by the International Boundary Commission, United States and Canada.

From east to west the lights are:

Range C Front Light [Q G 37ft] quick green light 37 feet high on a rectangular-shaped orange daymark on a gray skeleton tower, is in Semiahmoo Bay about 0.9 mile west of the Blaine shore. The light is visible 4° each side of the rangeline.

Range C Rear Light [F G 80ft] fixed green light 80 feet high on a rectangular-shaped orange daymark on a gray tower, is onshore at the Peace Arch Monument. The light is visible 14° each side of the rangeline.

Obstruction Light [Fl Y 4s 36ft] flashing yellow 4 second light 36 feet high on a rectangular block, is about 0.7 mile east of Point Roberts shoreline between Range C and Range B lights.

(See next page)

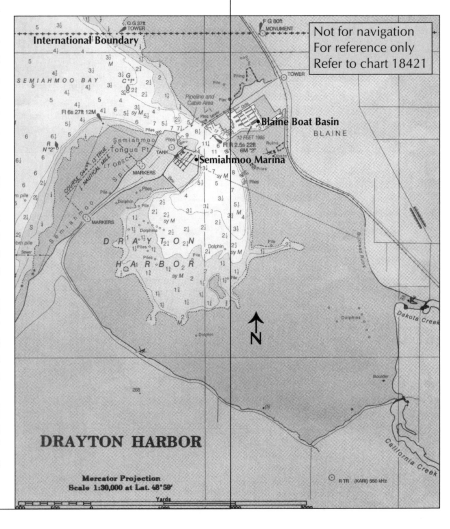

Not for navigation
For reference only
Refer to chart 18421

DRAYTON HARBOR

Mercator Projection
Scale 1:30,000 at Lat. 48°59′
Yards

➡ **NOTE: A measured nautical half-mile** is charted off Semiahmoo Spit with a course of 044° 13' True with markers at both ends.

Semiahmoo Spit Quandry

Ancient Lummi tribal remains removed from burial grounds at Semiahmoo Spit in 1999 put a city water-treatment plant for Blaine on hold.

Excavation for the new plant at the head of the spit revealed the ancient remains which were trucked seven miles, along with dirt and shells, to a private business. The Lummis want the remains reburied at the site. In the meantime more bones remain exposed at the construction site.

The 4,300 member Lummi tribe wants the new city plant relocated and the site designated a cemetery. Tribal authorities say it needs $7 million to restore the site and store the bones.

Authorities hadn't reached a decision on the stalemate when this book went to press.

Landmark water tower at Tongue Point

Range B Front Light [F G 65ft] fixed green light 65 feet high on a rectangular-shaped orange daymark on a gray skeleton tower, is on the east shore of Point Roberts near Maple Beach. The light is visible only on the rangeline.

Range B Rear Light [F G 258ft] fixed green light 258 feet high on a rectangular-shaped orange daymark on a gray pile, is slightly west of the center of Point Roberts. It is visible eastward. A fixed red aircraft warning light is on top of the tower.

Range A Rear Light [F W 258ft] fixed white light 258 feet high on a rectangular shaped orange daymark on a gray pile, is on the same structure as Range B rear light. The light is visible westward.

Range A Front Light [F W 180ft] fixed white light 180 feet high on a rectangular-shaped orange daymark, is on a gray skeleton tower. The light is visible on the rangeline only. Chart 18421, Note F, "The front range light has an oscillating red and white light south of the boundary, and an oscillating green and white light north of the boundary." It is lit all 24 hours.

Semiahmoo Spit, less than 100 yards wide and 1.5 miles long, separates Semiahmoo Bay and Drayton Harbor. Tideflats off the spit extend nearly 0.5 mile into Semiahmoo Bay and are marked by two charted navigation aids.

Semiahmoo Bay Buoy 2 [R N "2"] red nun buoy, is in 6 fathoms about 900 yards offshore and midway along the length of the spit.

Semiahmoo Bay Light [Fl 6s 27ft 12M] flashing 6 second light 27 feet high visible 12 miles, is at the northeast end of extensive sandy flats, about 700 yards offshore. It is on a diamond-shaped dayboard with black and white sectors on a tower, and is visible from 024° to 294°. The light is a helpful west side aid into the entrance channel to Drayton Harbor.

Semiahmoo Bay Buoy 1 [G C "1"] green can buoy, is about 500 yards northeast of the Semiahmoo Bay Light at the east side of the channel. The two lights are guides to the entrance into Drayton Harbor.

Near the northeast end of the spit and the entrance to Drayton Harbor we pass condominiums and the large, modern Inn at Semiahmoo, a resort hotel which covers the entire outer end of Semiahmoo Spit at Tongue Point.

Tongue Point is the northeast end of the spit. A charted landmark water tower, remnant of the old fish cannery at the point, is visible from afar. The faded green tower was built in 1944. It is charted as a "tank" on 18421.

Semiahmoo Marina is in Drayton Harbor on the northeast side of Semiahmoo spit.

Blaine Harbor Marina is east across the 350 yard channel from Tongue Point on the peninsula in Blaine.

We enter Drayton Harbor and then visit Blaine and Blaine Harbor. After that we cross the narrow channel into Semiahmoo Marina, and then we'll delve a bit into the extraordinary historical background of this area.

DRAYTON HARBOR

Drayton Harbor is about 2.3 miles long and less than two miles wide, much of it mudflats unsuitable for anchoring.

⚓ **Anchoring** is possible in an area about 1,000 yards wide and 1,000 yards long which is over 2 fathoms deep.

Ⓖ This is a possible **gunkhole.**

Entrance channel is 0.1 miles wide with a controlling depth of 21 feet between Tongue Point and the man-made fill at Blaine Harbor boat basin.

Currents in the channel average one knot. The flood sets southeast and the ebb sets northwest.

Blaine Small Boat Harbor

Entering Drayton Harbor, we pass about 300 yards north of the Semiahmoo Bay Light and stay in the center of the channel between Tongue Point and Blaine Harbor boat basin. After passing the tank and wharf on Semiahmoo Spit we favor the north side of the channel to avoid shallows southeast of Tongue Point.

Blaine is a city virtually on the edge of the United States—right at the International Boundary between the U.S. and Canada. The city is known for the dramatic Peace Arch monument 67 feet high, marking the boundary between the two countries. Flags of both countries fly from the monument and the phrase, "Children of a Common Mother," is engraved on it. The Arch is visible from Semiahmoo Bay when approaching Drayton Harbor and is an easy walk from Blaine Harbor Marina.

Blaine Small Boat Harbor, managed by the Port of Bellingham, is just 0.25 mile from the border. The harbor is at the southeast side of a man-made peninsula.

Blaine Small Boat Harbor Light 2 [Fl R 2.5s 22ft 6M "2"] flashing red 2.5 second light 22 feet high visible 6 miles, is on the breakwater marking the entrance into the boat basin. We keep the light to starboard, proceeding past moored fishing boats to the visitors' float in front of the harbor office.

Peace Arch at Blaine
The arch straddling the U.S.-Canadian border commemorating peace and good will between the two countries was dedicated on Sept. 6, 1921.

It was the gift of railroad-builder Samuel Hill who spent many years promoting world peace.

Facilities at Blaine Harbor

➤ Guest moorage for 20-30 boats, no reservations, first come, first served
➤ Moorage rate: 50¢ foot, limit 3 days
➤ 20 amp shore power & water included
➤ Fuel: gas, diesel, kerosene
➤ Restrooms, showers, laundry
➤ Pumpout & porta-potty dump, no fee
➤ Marine shipyard, travel-lift, engine and boat repairs
➤ Two-lane launch ramp, fees: $4 U.S./$5 Canadian
➤ Customs port-of-entry, phone: 1-800-562-5943
➤ Public fishing pier
➤ Two restaurants in harbor area
➤ International Yacht Club of B.C. & Blaine offers moorage to reciprocal yacht club members on guest float on first come basis, register with harbormaster
➤ Nearby: basic store, laundry, post office, liquor store, hardware store, park with picnic & play area, walking trails, golf
➤ Activities: fish, crab, explore Blaine, visit Peace Arch, gunkhole in Drayton Harbor, ride *Plover* to Semiahmoo
➤ Monitors: VHF channel 66A
➤ Marina harbormaster: Alan Birdsall
➤ Ph.: 360-332-8037/FAX: 360-332-1043
➤ e-mail: alanb@portofbellingham.com
➤ Mailing address: P.O. Box 1245, Blaine, WA 98231
➤ Street address: 275 Marine Dr., Blaine, WA 98230

Good crabbing at Blaine

Underwater Derelict

A sunken tug in Drayton Harbor has been underwater since about 1990. It was built at a Bellingham shipyard which closed down in the 1960s.

The tug was reportedly trying to sink at a dock and was moved out into the harbor for its final resting place. It is visible at extreme low tides.

Blaine Harbor recently underwent renovation, with dredging and new floats accommodating an additional 300 boats, bringing total moorage to over 700 boats, about half of them commercial. The visitors' float will stay the same in 1999 and will later move to a new pleasure boat center.

The harbor peninsula has several marine-related businesses, two restaurants, a fishing pier and a small park with tables, barbecues and a totem pole.

Public tidelands inside Drayton Harbor are in two parcels totaling 7,500 feet. Both are in mud flats, the larger parcel near the head of the bay and the smaller just south of Blaine

---

M.V. Plover

We rode the restored *M. V. Plover* across the channel from Semiahmoo Spit to Blaine Harbor round trip. It was short but memorable.

The 32 foot wooden vessel was built in 1944 for Alaska Packer's Association Cannery at Semiahmoo to ferry workers from Blaine across the channel to the cannery at Tongue Point. Listed on the National Register of Historic Places, the boat is now owned and operated by the Whatcom Maritime Historical Society of Bellingham. The *Plover* can carry 17 passengers and bicycles on a space available basis.

Michael Jacobsen "Jake" was our skipper. He particularly likes having kids on board, and "lets" them run the boat, they think. He then gives them an "Honorary Captain" certificate.

He cruised the *Plover* past the 150 or so resident seals on the south breakwater floats of Semiahmoo, telling the kids they were "lumps" on the floats. We slowed down and watched them as they lazed about, a few sliding off into the harbor.

He gave an interesting running commentary on the history of the harbor and took us past the historic sunken tug. We saw herons, turns, cormorants, gulls and he assured us bald eagles are also plentiful.

Jake swam in the "*Plover* Swim" from Blaine to Semiahmoo. About $3,500 was raised in pledges to benefit the vessel by those who did the 300 yard swim, in "warm" water, he said.

The ferry runs on weekends from a dock below the Blaine Harbormaster's office and the Wharf at the Inn at Semiahmoo. There is no charge, but donations are accepted.

M.V. Plover

UNDERWAY AGAIN, we cross the channel from Blaine and enter Semiahmoo, a great recreation area.

Semiahmoo County Park (Whatcom County) covers 322 acres of Semiahmoo spit, including 6,700 feet of shoreline on Semiahmoo Bay and Drayton Harbor. Walking and biking trails run the whole distance of the spit on either side of the road leading to Semiahmoo resort and marina at Tongue Point. There are picnic tables, restrooms, beach access and historical buildings, including a museum converted from cannery workers' bunkhouses.

Wave-tossed driftwood lies strewn along the west shore's sandy high tide line, with views across the Strait of Georgia, spectacular sunsets, and north into British Columbia. The protected harbor side of the spit has tidal mudflats and looks across to Blaine and the Cascade Mountains.

"Lumps" of seals on floats in Drayton Harbor, Semiahmoo Spit & condos in background

Small boats can be launched or landed on the beach on either side, although there's a possibility of being stuck in the mud on the east side during low tides. There's a good opportunity for swimming on either side. We prefer the west side where the beach is nicer and the water's not too cold, but the harbor side is best for clam digging. Crabs may be found on either side.

⚓ **Anchoring** is possible in the first 1,500 yards in the harbor in about 3 fathoms, mud bottom. The rest of the bay is 2 fathoms or less and mudflats. Winds are often out of the southeast and need to be considered when anchoring. There may be floating vegetation and debris in the harbor.

Semiahmoo Marina store and office, old water tower in back

Enter Semiahmoo Marina at the east end of the breakwater fuel float and moorage float "E." Tie temporarily to the breakwater and check at the office for a slip assignment.

Harbormaster Dale said its colder in the Blaine area than Bellingham, and when winds are 70 knots or more out of the south there may be problems in the harbor.

"Many people moor here from out of state and during bad weather we spend a lot of time on the docks checking mooring lines. Northeasters are cold, but we usually don't get those winds over 30 knots, except once in a great while. We're pretty well protected from north winds here. We have a great shipyard and we have a lot of people who outfit here before they go sailing offshore. This is also a great place for cruising to the San Juans or into B.C.," he said.

Semiahmoo Marina floats, Blaine in background

Facilities at Semiahmoo Marina

➤ 300 slip marina, sufficient guest moorage, accepts reservations
➤ Fees: 60¢ foot
➤ Fuel: diesel, gas, propane
➤ 30 amp shore power, water with moorage
➤ Restrooms, showers, laundry facilities, pumpout & porta-potty dump, no fee
➤ 35 ton capacity haulout, boat and engine repair, marine supplies, chandlery
➤ Boutique, basic store, two restaurants, lounge, lattes
➤ Semiahmoo Yacht Club offers reciprocal moorage
➤ Nearby: Semiahmoo Golf & Country Club golf course, hotel, hiking & cycling trails, *Plover* ferry ride in summer, daycare, museum
➤ Activities: walk, golf, swim, golf, tennis, bike & kayak, rental, picnic,
➤ Monitors: VHF Ch. 68
➤ Harbormaster: Dale Jensen, Tel.: 360-371-5700/FAX: 360-371-2422
➤ Address: 9540 Semiahmoo Parkway, Blaine, WA 98230

Historical Background of Drayton Harbor

Blaine and Semiahmoo have always been intricately linked. Semiahmoo Indians lived on Tongue Point long before the arrival of settlers, and the large cannery that was later built here.

A photo display in Semiahmoo Inn records the history of the area. There is also a harbor chart by the Wilkes' Expedition of 1841.

Drayton Harbor

"Drayton Bay" was named for Joseph Drayton, an artist with the Wilkes Expedition and the oldest member of the crew. Originally, the term included all of what is now called Semiahmoo Bay.

Because the Native Americans were so friendly and the bay surrounded by thick forests was so restful, the expedition stayed several days to rest, survey the coast, and assess the fishing.

Old scow used at fish traps

The photos include:

♦ 1858—Drayton Harbor, important as supply headquarters for prospectors before they left for the Fraser River, B.C., gold rush.
♦ 1870—First sawmill set up at Semiahmoo.
♦ 1884—Blaine, Washington Territory, was plat ted and recorded on Sept. 13. City named for James Blaine, R., who ran for president in 1884 against Grover Cleveland, D. Blaine lost, but won the hearts of citizens who kept his name for their town.
♦ 1893—15 canneries in Alaska formed Alaska Packers Association, APA, to market an over supply of canned salmon.
♦ 1894—APA purchased Drysdale Cannery at Semiahmoo.
♦ 1905—New $25,000 Victorian-style Coast Guard lighthouse opened at Semiahmoo Spit, justified because of increased amount of salmon and lumber shipped from Blaine and Semiahmoo. Dismantled in 1944, replaced with light tower, replaced in 1971 with present tower.
♦ 1918—Photo of APA "cannery girls," young women in black skirts, white blouses, long rubber aprons with hair tucked under hats, at work in the cannery by 7 a.m. each day. Typically women and children worked at the cannery along with men, and their jobs included work at "sliming tables."
♦ 1920—Male cannery workers lived in bunkhouses, including three-story China House and Indian House. Ages ranged from young boys to old men.
♦ 1930—Photo of unexpected huge run of salmon in Boundary Bay in August, workers knee-deep in salmon.
♦ 1944—Wooden ferry *M.V. Plover* built to carry workers from Blaine to Semiahmoo for the APA Cannery.
♦ 1964—Cannery operations at Semiahmoo phased out.
♦ 1984—Inn at Semiahmoo built.

Carl examines antique fish-cleaning machine at museum

Museum at Semiahmoo Spit

This is a terrific museum at the head of Semiahmoo Spit, filled with photos and displays which augment the information from the photo collection at the resort. The museum was originally one of the APA bunkhouses for cannery workers.

The cannery was there from 1893-1980, but commercial fishing started at Semiahmoo in 1876. Elaborate models of fish traps, outlawed by popular vote in 1934, are in the museum. China House, for Chinese workers, was on the site of the present marina and dismantled in the 1920s. Indian House was built for Indians who fished for APA and originally lived in tents on the spit. There was also a women's bunkhouse.

A fish processing machine invented by E.A. Smith in 1903 speeded up the process by cleaning one fish per second, replacing Chinese laborers who had hand-butchered the salmon. The machine, now outside the museum, revolutionized the canning industry, even saving floor space. It received an unfortunate and politically incorrect name in the early 1900s.

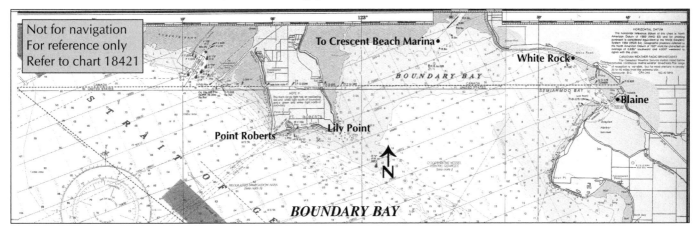

Not for navigation
For reference only
Refer to chart 18421

To Crescent Beach Marina

White Rock

BOUNDARY BAY

White Rock

Blaine

Lily Point

Point Roberts

N

BOUNDARY BAY

⚙ **UNDERWAY AGAIN,** and we're on our way to Point Roberts. However, before that, we take a quick detour into a bit of B.C. at Boundary Bay, just north of Blaine. Although we went to every place in this book in our boat, this is the one place we explored only by car, and here's what we found out.

WHITE ROCK & CRESCENT BEACH, B.C.

The resort city of **White Rock** is about two miles northwest of the entrance to

Drayton Harbor and along the east edge of Semiahmoo Bay. The city is easy to spot from the water because of the gigantic white rock on the beach. This favorite summer recreation area is called the "Riviera of British Columbia," with its three miles of sandy beaches.

The rock is charted about 600 feet east of a 1,500 foot long public pier with a large breakwater.

[Fl 15ft] flashing white light 15 feet high, is on a dolphin at the west end of the breakwater.

Two moorage floats are at the outer end of the pier just inside the breakwater. The west float is private moorage behind a locked gate. The east float, about 50 feet long, is for transient moorage. There are no other facilities. A sign on the float in both English and French advises, "Revenue Canada, customs and excise. All vessels entering Canada or returning must stop and report to customs, 1-888-CAN-PASS."

White Rock has a splendid brick promenade along miles of waterfront in constant use by walkers striding the path. Blue railings run along the path above the beach; yellow benches provide a bit of a rest.

The railroad tracks are also above the shore, with trains running between the two countries several times daily. Fish and chips eateries and gift shops are one block from the walkway along the main street of town. Homes, condos and apartments stair-step up the hills behind.

Boundary Bay is the shallow body of water that meets Semiahmoo Bay and indents the mainland between Kwomais Point, B.C., and Point Roberts. The bay is 11 miles wide from east to west along the International Boundary line. It runs about

Naming White Rock

This seaside city gets its name from an intriguing Indian legend.

The large white boulder was thrown into the air at Sidney by a Cowichan Indian sea god, according to legend.

The landing place was to be the home for the god and his mortal bride.

The white rock landed about 32 miles northeast on the beach at the city which was subsequently named White Rock.

➥ **NOTE:** U.S. Chart 18421, 1:80,000, shows channel markers and the southern part of the channel.

Chart 18400, 1:200,000, shows the first flashing red light, red daymarks, and a quick red flashing light on a dolphin near the river's mouth at Crescent Beach, although it's a very small scale.

Canadian Chart 3463, 1:80,00, shows the two flashing lights and two channel markers, and the complete area, including the railroad bridge and Crescent Beach Marina.

five miles north of the border to the B.C. shore.

Depths in the bay are from 7.5 to 1.5 fathoms for about one mile north of the boundary. Depths north of that area are under 2 fathoms, and much of the bay is mudflats and bares at low water and is called Mud Bay.

Channel to Nicomekl River & Crescent Beach Marina

A marked channel through the northern shallows of the bay is about 5.5 miles west of White Rock. The channel begins 0.7 mile north of the International Boundary, out in the middle of this seemingly empty, shallow, body of water, and leads northeast to the Nicomekl River and Crescent Beach and Crescent Beach Marina.

[FL R 4s 22ft] flashing red 4 second light 22 feet high in about 1 fathom *(shown on U.S. Chart 18421)* is the first navigation aid at the south end of the channel.

Triangular red unlighted daybeacons on dolphins or piles continue northeast in the bay for three miles to the next light.

[Q R] quick red flashing light is on a dolphin with a red daymark. It is one mile from the light to the turn at Crescent Beach, a recreation area near the mouth of the river on the south shore. The channel turns slightly southeast and continues up the river about 0.5 mile to a railroad swing bridge and the marina. A submarine pipeline is across the river east of the bridge.

Burlington Northern Railroad swing bridge over the Nicomekl River shows a red light when closed and green light when opened. The bridge is manned seven days a week from 6:30 a.m. to 10:30 p.m.

The bridge opens on demand and closes for train traffic. Opening signal is three blasts or phone the bridge tender at 604-538-3233.

When closed the vertical clearance of the swing span is 2.7 meters, and the trestle vertical clearance is 3.7 meters. There is a height clearance gauge on the northwest end of the bridge. *(Information from Canadian Sailing Directions 1999)*

Crescent Beach Marina is in a small basin immediately south of the railroad bridge. Mariners without recent local knowledge may wish to contact the marina for information regarding controlling channel depths, changes in markers, and to verify moorage availability for the size and draft of the boat.

Crescent Beach Marina, train crossing over swing bridge

Facilities at Crescent Beach Marina

➤ Limited guest moorage, call first, reservation needed; fees 75¢ foot
➤ 15 amp shore power & water included
➤ Fuel: diesel, gas
➤ Restrooms, no pumpouts
➤ Haulout up to 35 feet, boat & engine repair
➤ Marine chandlery, sells Canadian Charts, Charlie's Charts, Cruising Atlas, small craft nautical charts, fishing gear, bait
➤ Two-lane launch ramp, $7 fee
➤ Crescent Beach Yacht Club offers moorage to reciprocal clubs
➤ Customs port-of-entry, 1-888-CAN-PASS
➤ Nearby attractions: fish, swim, bicycle, walk, tennis, golf, bus service
➤ Marina manager: Al Endacott, Tel.: 604-538-9666/538-7433 FAX: 604-538-7724
➤ Address: 12555 Crescent Road, Surrey, B.C., Canada V4A-2V4

"How-to" Use the Channel

B.J. Chapman, former marina manager, gave us a tour of the facility, and told us his philosophy of entering the marina.

"It is a bit tight getting in and out of the marina, past the bridge and through the channel. Keep all those channel markers as close as possible, a couple of them almost go dry and you want to go straight between them. The north end of Boundary Bay is extremely shallow."

He "touched" bottom in the channel a couple of times in a sailboat with a 7 foot draft.

"If you get outside the channel it's so shoal you could practically walk clear to the highway (on the north shore several miles away). It can be kind of dicey coming in here if the wind is blowing: it blows hard over the shallows, especially if it's out of the north. If you're going with the tide it's not too bad, but if you're against it, with 3 or 4 knots of current and the wind, it can be tough. Prevailing and summer winds are southwest or west, while winter winds are generally out of the northeast," B.J. said.

Crescent Beach Boat Builders, large yacht builders, are also at the marina. Many of their yachts are launched at the marina ramp.

⚓**UNDERWAY AGAIN,** and we're on our way to Point Roberts, Washington.

The point is the U.S. peninsula south of the international boundary line at 49° North Latitude that juts south into Boundary Bay. It's cut off from the rest of the U.S. and Washington state and by land it can be reached only by driving 23 miles through British Columbia from Blaine.

By water, Point Roberts is about 12 miles west of the entrance to Drayton Harbor across Boundary Bay. Depths are less than 10 fathoms for the eastern two miles, and then it becomes 10 to 25 fathoms deep the rest of the way.

Point Roberts is about 12 miles northwest of Patos Island, the most northerly of the San Juans. It's an open passage across the Strait of Georgia, subject to the winds and currents of that body of water.

When the high bluffs of Point Roberts first become distinguishable they look almost like an island, because the bluffs are so high and the low shores north of Boundary Bay are so far away.

The entire Point Roberts peninsula, half Canadian and half United States, extends over four miles south into the Strait of Georgia. The American or south half, is 1.9 miles long by about 2.5 miles wide, with a land mass of less than five square *(statute)* miles.

The Strait of Georgia south of Point Roberts is heavily fished at night making the waters from Point Roberts to Blaine difficult for night navigation. In early morning daylight we counted—and dodged—more than three dozen purse seiners fishing the area. However, with new fishing regulations between the U.S. and Canada this fishery may be much smaller than in the past, or even abolished.

Lily Point, unnamed on charts, is the southeast point, with beautiful, white vertical cliffs 200 feet high topped by evergreen trees. The bluffs taper down from east to west along the south coast of Point Roberts, and from South Beach to the southwest tip of Point Roberts the shore is low or no-bank waterfront.

Naming Point Roberts

Spanish explorer Francisco Eliza thought the peninsula was an island when he first sailed past in 1791, naming it **Isla de Zepeda**.

When Spanish explorers Galiano and Valdez sailed by in 1792, they realized it was not an island and named it **Punta Cepeda.**

Capt. George Vancouver and his crew went ashore on the peninsula on June 22, 1792, naming it **Point Roberts** *for his friend and predecessor in the vessel* **Discovery,** *Lieutenant Henry Roberts.*

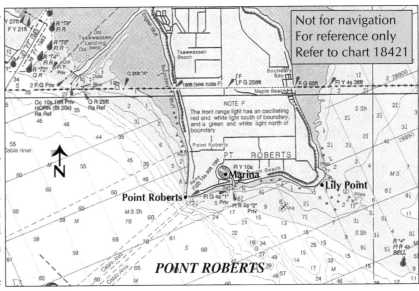

Not for navigation
For reference only
Refer to chart 18421

POINT ROBERTS

➥ **NOTE:** Canadian chart 3492, Roberts Bank, 1:20,000, shows the best details of the Point Roberts area northwest to the entrance to Fraser River.

Point Roberts Lighted Bell Buoy 4 [Fl R 4s Bell] flashing red 4 second bell buoy is two miles southeast of Lily Point, marking the outer edge of shoal areas surrounding much of southeast Point Roberts at Lily Point. The rocky toe extends southeast nearly one mile from the point.

A charted wreck is shown off South Beach about 0.5 mile offshore in approximately six fathoms.

Point Roberts Light [Fl(2) 15s 30ft 15M] two flashing 15 second lights on a red and white diamond-shaped dayboard on a 30 foot high skeleton tower visible 15 miles, is at the unnamed southwest point, locally called Point Roberts.

Lighthouse Marine County Park surrounds this beautiful point with 4,000 feet of shoreline along the Strait of Georgia, offering spectacular views of the strait, the Gulf Islands, some San Juan Islands, Mount Constitution and Mount Baker.

Point Roberts Marina is about 1.5 miles west of Lily Point, or 0.9 mile east of the southwest point of Point Roberts. The teardrop-shaped modern facility holds over 1,000 boats. It's a welcome sight for many returning U.S. boats, and for mariners possibly seeking shelter from rough Strait of Georgia waters.

A rock breakwater-jetty lies in a northeast-southwest direction across the narrow entrance channel.

Point Roberts Marina private navigation aids:

Basin Breakwater Light [Fl Y 10s] flashing yellow 10 second light, is 20 feet high on the northeast end of the breakwater.

Entering Point Roberts Marina

Basin Light 1 [Fl G 4s "1"] flashing green 4 second light 15 feet high, is on a pile less than 100 yards west of the southwest end of the breakwater.

Basin Light 2 [Fl R 4s "2"] flashing red 4 second light, is 20 feet high on the southwest end of the breakwater.

The channel entrance is at the southwest end between Lights "1" and "2," taking care to stay in mid-channel. Warning signs on pilings in the entrance note, "Caution, sandbars on either side of entrance. Stay in mid-channel," "Caution, sandbars west and east of channel entrance, stay in mid-channel," and "No Wake." That's enough to make us behave and keep us in mid-channel.

There's a slight jog in the channel and a break at the northeast end of the breakwater and another warning not to go through that break.

On an incoming tide there's a fair amount of current running in through the channel, and lines and fenders need to be ready for use as there's not much maneuvering room inside and mariners may need to dock quickly.

A commercial float, haulout, sling launch and fuel float are now in view. Visitors check in at the fuel dock for moorage assignment.

This modern marina holds an amazing 1,020 boats, over 90 percent of them Canadian-owned. Marina facilities, including a haulout, store, offices and restaurants, are in a red-roofed, two-story building on the east shore. There's also a public park. Canadian, U.S. and Washington state flags fly from tall masts over the facility.

Condos line the west side of the entrance channel.

Tulle Lagoon Becomes Marina

The marina location was once a tidal lagoon where there were lowlands called "tulle." An opening at the southwest corner of the lagoon allowed tidal water to move in and out.

The lagoon's entrance was adequate for a 50 foot sailboat to enter and tack back and forth several times without grounding.

Some called the north part of the basin a "stagnant pond" where cows once grazed.

Maps of Point Roberts community are at the marina and in local stores, making it easy to walk around this U.S. peninsula. The shopping center with most necessities is less than one mile north of the marina.

South Beach, east of the marina is lined with summer cabins and streets with familiar names such as Lopez, Orcas, Lummi, Sucia, Patos, Matia and Waldron.

Point Roberts cemetery is farther east along APA Road near the end, a fascinating historical look at the Point.

Inside Point Roberts Marina

Point Roberts Marina Facilities
➤ Guest moorage for 60-80 boats
➤ Fees: 50¢ foot, includes 30 amp shore power, water
➤ Fuel: diesel, gas, propane
➤ Restrooms with showers, laundry
➤ Pumpout & porta-potty dump, free
➤ Westwind Marine, Inc., boat & engine repair, 35 ton haulout
➤ Monorail sling boat launch
➤ U.S. Customs port-of-entry, Tel.: 1-800-562-5943; also Canadian Customs, 1-800-CAN-PASS
➤ Restaurant, cafe, lounge
➤ Chandlery, marine supplies, ice, fishing gear, bait, basic store
➤ Attractions: fish, shellfish, bicycle, walk, play area, picnic area, Point Roberts Yacht Club, reciprocal moorage for two boats per day
➤ Nearby: shopping center, post office, liquor store, motel, taxi service, Lighthouse Marine Park with camping, beach, launch ramp
➤ Monitors: VHF Ch. 68
➤ Marina manager: Bruce Gustafson
➤ Tel.: 360-945-2255/FAX: 360- 945-0927
➤ Address: 713 Simundson Dr., Point Roberts, WA 98281

The "Exclave" of Point Roberts

"Ex-clave," according to Webster: A section of a country set apart from the rest by surrounding alien territory.

While Point Roberts calls itself an exclave we note the term "enclave" means almost the same thing.

Webster: An outlying part of a country or a small autonomous territory entirely or nearly surrounded by the territory of another power.

Some residents of Point Roberts sometimes talk of their peninsula as the "un-island," the "Kingdom of Point Roberts," or even "Point Bob," but they say they don't want to form their own country.

Lighthouse Marine County Park is at the spectacular southwest tip of Point Roberts west of the marina, a pleasant, short walk. The park is accessible by both water and land, and there is a launch ramp. There are no mooring buoys.

⚓ Although depths are 2 to 5 fathoms around the point, anchoring for more than a brief period is not recommended because of the vagaries of the Strait of Georgia.

Winds and waves pound the gravel shores, especially in winter. Orca whales pass by frequently, often close to shore.

Views from here are unequalled. On a clear day you can see Mount Baker to the east, south across the Strait of Georgia to the San Juans, southwest to the Gulf islands, and to the west and northwest is Tswassen landing and the restless waters of Strait, all from a 30 foot tower as well as the beach. Sunsets are extravagant.

This is an intriguing park, with a long boardwalk, covered picnic areas sheltered from weather, a display with information about orca whales, a snack bar and restrooms. There's plenty of room to roam the park among driftwood and small hillocks, with even some random art displays and play areas. Beachcombing is good, but the lighthouse, for which the park is named, is simply an unimposing metal tower with a rotating beacon about 30 feet high.

Facilities at Lighthouse Marine County Park (Whatcom County)
➤ 22 acres with 4,000 feet of shoreline, no moorage
➤ Two-lane launch ramp with floats in summer
➤ Fees, county residents: trailered boat $5; car top $4; non-county residents: trailered boats, $7; car top $5
➤ 25 campsites, small RV's okay
➤ Picnic tables, shelters, fire grates, drinking water, restrooms, boardwalks
➤ 30 foot high viewing tower, play areas, information displays, snack bar
➤ Activities: whale watch, fish, dig clams, beachcomb, relax on beach, camp, picnic
➤ Tel.: 360-945-4911
➤ Address: 811 Marine Dr., Point Roberts, WA 98281

Continuing north along the west shore of the U.S. portion of Point Roberts, the bank rises to 160 foot high Boundary Bluffs, which, logically, continue across the border into Canada.

Monument County Park is at the northwest corner of the U.S., on the International Boundary at the 49th parallel.

Border Marker No. 1 is an unimposing stone obelisk at the park, the first of many border obelisks which mark the boundary between the two countries all across North America. The monument commemorates the Treaty of 1846 establishing the boundary between the U.S. and Canada. The obelisk cannot be reached from the beach below because the steep bluff has no usable trail. The only way to reach the monument is from land.

The park's tideflats at the bottom of the high cliff stretch over 0.5 mile from the shore and are accessible only by small, beachable boats.

Facilities at Monument County Park (Whatcom County)
➤ 8 acres, 500 feet of waterfront on the Strait of Georgia
➤ Park beach accessible only by beachable boat
➤ Land area atop the bluff can be reached by car, bike or walking the roads
➤ Activities: historical monument and magnificent views from the bluff, beachcombing and paddling along the shore

Originally Chil-tin-um

The Indian name for Point Roberts is Chil-tin-um. It was given to the place many hundreds of years ago, according to legend, when a large party of Indians was crossing the Gulf of Georgia in their war canoes. A gale blew them off their regular course and then a fog settled down on them. They kept padling until the cheif's canoe landed upon a sandy beach while he thought he was in deep water.

As each of the other canoes found themselves also grounded, the chief stepped ashore and said, "Chil-tin-um," because he couldn't see it! And that is the meaning of the word.

Snippets of Point Roberts History
The lower half of the 4.9 square mile *(statute miles)* peninsula is the enclave of Point Roberts where the international boundary at the 49th parallel is the northern border of this small part of Washington. The other three sides of the peninsula are coastline. The east side is Boundary Bay, the south and west borders are the Canadian waters of the Strait of Georgia.

When the international boundary line was set west of the mainland in 1846, it zigzagged from the 49th parallel south and west through various channels to the Strait of Juan de Fuca, giving Vancouver Island to British Columbia. It was not determined until 1872 just which channel would be the boundary. *(Pig War Ch. 1)*

Few of the treaty negotiators seemed to be aware that Point Roberts peninsula extended south of the 49th parallel, and this small portion of Washington state was left dangling.

First settlers of Point Roberts were Pacific Coast Salish Indians who named the peninsula Tceltenum (Cheltenum), meaning, "Couldn't see it," which sometimes happens in dense fog. They lived here thousands of years before settlers arrived.

After the Point Elliott Treaty of 1856 ceded "virtually all the land between Olympia and the Canadian boundary ... to the whites," many Indians were confined to reservations and began to leave Point Roberts.

Roberts Town at the southwest point, also known as Roberts City and Point Roberts, was born during the gold rush on the Fraser River in the late 1850s. The "city," comprising several huts, a liquor store, post office and a half-dozen buildings, was primarily concerned with supplying whiskey to those bound for the gold fields.

James Douglas stopped overnight at Roberts Town in November 1858 while enroute to Victoria to be sworn in as governor of the British Columbia Crown Colony.

Three months after American settler Lyman Cutler shot the British pig on San Juan Island in June 1859, which was the start of the Pig War—President James Buchanan ordered that Point Roberts be set apart as a U.S. Military Reserve. This essentially froze most social and business activity at the point.

In the meantime, even with the border "hostilities" in the San Juans, the obelisk marking the boundary between Canada and the U.S. was placed in Point Roberts in 1862. This is the longest undefended border in the world.

Stories abound about events occuring during construction. A wharf and ramp were built on the shore below the site and sailors and marines helped land the stone and erect the obelisk. The monument is the gravestone of a British soldier who was buried at its base when he died just as it was ready to be placed in position. When several Tsawwassen Indians assisted lifting the huge stone up the steep cliff it got loose and fell back to the beach.

The border between the two countries was finally settled in 1872 when Kaiser Wilhelm I of Germany established the boundary through Haro Strait ending the 1859 Pig War, and giving the San Juan Islands to the U.S.

Squatters began arriving at the point in earnest in the 1870s and 1880s, although settlers had been slowly sifting in for years. There were numerous squabbles and several murders during those early days. Until the late 1880s "the Point" was described in newspapers as a wild place, the hideout of smugglers and desperadoes from the mainland, the San Juans and Gulf islands.

Icelanders and others began moving to Point Roberts in the 1890s. Many had emigrated to Canada but in 1893 a Canadian depression caused unemployment problems and a number of them moved to Point Roberts.

Indians had been granted perpetual rights to operate reefnets in Point Roberts waters, but by 1894 commercial fishtraps had replaced the reefnets and the Indians were shut out.

In the early 1900s there were three fish canneries: at Lily Point, which earlier had been an Indian fishing station; the George and Barker Cannery on the west shore, and the Lighthouse Packing Company near the southwest corner of the Point. By 1905 there were 47 fish traps off the peninsula. The traps were outlawed in 1934.

Point Roberts was a booming community.

Obelisk #1, a monument to two countries, with a navigation aid facing the sea, information about the monument in front

Monumental History

Obelisk No. 1 in Monument County Park in Point Roberts was built from 40 tons of stone imported from Scotland and shipped around Cape Horn.

Coins were placed by stonemasons at the four corners of the base, which was made of locally mined stone.

It was finished in 1862 even though it is inscribed, "Erected 1861."

The obelisk cost $7,590.38, shared equally by the U.S. and Great Britain.

Point Roberts Cemetery

The fish canneries are long gone, there is a busy modern shopping center, library, community center, resorts, restaurants, a county park, marina, plus hiking, biking and walking on secluded roads and trails.

There's a primary school in Point Roberts, but youngsters from third grade on are bused daily through British Columbia to the high school in Blaine.

The Point is in the "sun belt," with annual rainfall of about 30 inches, about half that of Vancouver. The moderate climate and rural atmosphere are attractive to many. The population is just under 1,000, although in summer that rises to more than 5,000, when Americans and Canadians move into summer cabins. More than 20 percent of the permanent population is over 65 years old, and there is an active retirement community. Recreation and tourism are major draws to Point Roberts.

The cemetery reveals names of settlers and residents of the Point. It includes at least 20 pioneers born in 1850s, plus three persons born in the 1840s, and one woman born in 1832. Some of these settlers, of whom a large number lived into their 80s, were born in Iceland. Frank Odin was born at the point on March 24, 1863, possibly the first Caucasian born here, although he is not buried in the cemetery.

British Columbia

Tsawwassen Landing is immediately northwest of the border, where large B.C. ferries depart for Vancouver Island and the Gulf Islands. A causeway nearly two miles long extends southwest from English Bluff terminating at the deepwater ferry pier. The ferries and pier are easily visible from Lighthouse Park, and at night are quite a sight.

Roberts Bank is a huge shoal off the southwest mainland where the Fraser River enters the Strait of Georgia, about six miles northwest of Point Roberts. The bank extends as much as five miles offshore from Point Roberts to Point Grey near the southwest entrance to Burrard Inlet, about 23 miles to the north. The bank is marked by several bell buoys about four to five miles apart along its western edge.

⚓ **UNDERWAY AGAIN,** this time due to storm or other emergency beyond our control, driven north and west from Point Roberts we need to find a port of refuge.

Or possibly by whim or fancy we've decided to sail off the edge of NOAA Chart 18421 into the wonders of British Columbia.

We are now beyond our titled region of ***Gunkholing in the San Juan Islands*** to look at charts of overlapping or adjacent areas for potential ports of refuge or interest. Charts we suggest are:

Canadian Chart L/C 3463, Strait of Georgia, 1:80,000, metric

This was our preferred chart for the Crescent Beach and Crescent Beach Marina and Nicomekl River caper.

This chart provides an overview of potential destination options north and west of Point Roberts to Vancouver, Nanaimo and northern portion of the Gulf Islands.

Canadian Chart 3492, Roberts Bank, 1:20,000, metric

The 1:20,000 scale on this chart gave us a much closer look at Point Roberts for entering the Point Roberts Marina.

We can also check out the close-up details of Tswassen Yacht Club and Ferry Terminal and Deltaport/Westshore Terminals.

Canoe Passage seem highly questionable because of the lack of daybeacons, and without extraordinary local knowledge and high tide predictions. It is used by some locals. There is a marina near the swing bridge at the north end of Canoe Passage.

This chart ends at the south edge of the Steveston Jetty Entrance to Fraser River.

Canadian Chart 3490, Fraser River, Sand Heads to Douglas Island, 1:20,000, metric

This chart begins at the mouth of the Fraser River at Steveston Jetty in the Strait of Georgia. It details this major shipping channel's charted navigation aids, a variety of industrial facilities, public access, marina facilities and services and yacht clubs.

Inherent with using these charts are the following Canadian publications:

Sailing Directions British Columbia Coast (South Portion)
Canadian Tide & Current Tables Volume 5, Juan de Fuca Strait and Strait of
    Georgia
Pacific Coast List of Lights, Buoys and Fog Signals
Canadian Chart 1, Symbols & Abbreviations used on charts

That's it for this book. We've completed our cruise through the San Juan Islands, crossed Rosario Strait and visited islands and the mainland east of that body of water, checking out everything from Deception Pass to the Canadian border.

Thanks so much for coming along with us, exploring and gunkholing our way to new adventures. We've had a great time!

Bibliography

American Indians and the United States, a Documentary History, Vol. 4. Edited by Wilcomb Washburn, Smithsonian Institution. Random House, New York, N.Y. 1973.

Barkan, Frances B., Editor. *The Wilkes Expedition, Puget Sound and The Oregon Country.* Washington State Capital Museum, Olympia, WA. 1987.

Burn, June. *Living High, an Unconventional Autobiography.* Griffin Bay Book Store, Friday Harbor, WA. 1992.

Burn, June. *100 Days in the San Juans.* Edited by Theresa Morrow & Nancy Prindle. Longhouse Printcrafters crafters & Publishers, Friday Harbor, WA. 1983.

Clark, Richard E. *Point Roberts, USA, The History of a Canadian Enclave.* Textype Publishing, Bellingham, WA. 1980.

Dietrich, William. *Pacific Northwest, The Seattle Times Magazine.* Seattle, WA., Oct. 18, 1998.

Glidden, Helene. *Light on the Island.*

Islands Sounder weekly newspaper, Ted Grossman, editor. 1997-1998 editions. Friday Harbor & Eastsound, WA.

Henry, John Frazier. *The Midshipman's Revenge, or The Case of the Missing Islands.* Pacific Northwest Quarterly. October 1982.

Hilson, Stephen E. *Exploring Puget Sound & British Columbia.* Van Winkle Publishing Co., Michigan. 1975.

Jones-Lamb, Karen. *Native American Wives of San Juan Settlers.* Bryn Tirion Pub. 1994.

Kendrick, John. *The Men with Wooden Feet, The Spanish Exploration of the Pacific Northwest.* New Canada Publications, a division of NC Press Limited, Toronto, Ontario, Canada. 1985.

Kirk, Ruth, & Alexander, Carmela. *Exploring Washington's Past, A Road Guide to History.* University of Washington Press, Seattle and London. 1990.

McDonald, Lucile S. *Making History: The People Who Shaped the San Juan Islands.* Harbor Press, Friday Harbor, WA. 1990.

Meany, Edmond S. *History of the State of Washington.* The MacMillan Company, New York. 1946.

Mueller, Marge & Ted. *The San Juan Islands, Afoot & Afloat.* The Mountaineers, Seattle, WA. 1995.

Mueller, Marge & Ted. *North Puget Sound, Afoot & Afloat.* The Mountaineers, Seattle, WA. 1995.

Neil, Dorothy, & Brainard, Lee. *By Canoe and Sailing Ship They Came.* Spindrift Publishing Co., Oak Harbor, WA. 1989.

Richardson, David. *Pig War Islands.* Orcas Publishing Co., Eastsound, WA. 1971.

Sampson, Martin J., Chief, Swinomish Tribe. *Indians of Skagit County.* Skagit County Historical Society, Mount Vernon, WA. 1972.

Seven, Richard. *Pacific Northwest, The Seattle Times Magazine.* Seattle, WA., June 14, 1998.

Slotemaker, Terry. *Fidalgo Island Ferries, Chinese Laborer Facts, Mills, Deception Pass Bridge Facts, The Fidalgo Convict Camp, The Origin of Fidalgo and Guemes Island Area Place Names.* Anacortes Museum, Anacortes, WA, 1997.

Suttles, Wayne P. *The Economic Life of the Coast Salish of Haro and Rosario Straits. I: Coast Salish and Western Washington Indians.* New York: Garland, 1974.

Suttles, Wayne P. Talk on Orcas Island, May 31, 1987.

Thomas, Robert B. *Chuckanut Chronicles.* Chuckanut Fire District Auxiliary, Bellingham, WA., 1971.

Walbran, Captain John T. *British Columbia Coast Names, 1592-1906.* J.J. Douglas, Ltd., Vancouver, B.C. 1971.

Wilkes, Lt. Charles. *Diary of Wilkes in the Northwest.* Edited by Edmond S. Meany, reprinted from the Washington Historical Quarterly, 1925-1926. University of Washington Press, Seattle, WA. 1926.

Willis, Margaret, Editor. *Chechacos All, the Pioneering of Skagit.* Skagit County Historical Society, Mount Vernon, WA. 1973

Wood, Bryce. *San Juan Island: Coastal Place Names and Cartographic Nomenclature.* Published for Washington State Historical Society by University Microfilms International, Ann Arbor, Michigan. 1980.

Appendix

Whale Watching Guidelines

Whale watching is one of the exciting highlights of cruising this region. You're happily slipping through the water and suddenly spot a whale surfacing nearby. It's always a thrill. Orcas, grays and minkes swim in the area; the orcas are more common in the San Juans.

Dall's porpoises are also common throughout the region and we often find them diving across our bow.

Harbor seals seem to be everywhere, poking a curious head above the surface, sinking back under leaving scarcely a ripple. Report seal strandings to the Whale Hotline, 1-800-562-8832.

Sea lions don't breed in the area, they hunt and feed here.

The Federal Marine Protection Act passed in 1972, makes it illegal to kill, capture or harass marine mammals.

The following is a synopsis of the U.S. Federal Guidelines:

• Vessels should not approach within 100 yards/meters of marine mammals.

• Vessels should not be used to herd, chase or separate any groups of marine mammals.

• Vessels approaching marine mammals should approach cautiously from the side, travel parallel to the group, and at the same speed as the slowest animal.

• If you are approached within 100 yards by a marine mammal, you should:
  a. continue your course with little change in speed and direction, or
  b. stop the vessel and wait for the animals to move away.

• The 100 yards distance applies to other marine mammals

• Never separate a mother from its baby.

Report harassments and obvious violations to National Marine Fisheries Service, 800-853-1964.

While out on the water or beaches, you can feast on the sight of dozens of different waterfowl. If you're a "birder" you're bound to have plenty to keep you happy.

Avoid discharging any fuel, oil or petroleum products into the waters as even small amounts of oil have devastating impacts on marine life. Grab your camera and enjoy!

State Marine Parks

Nineteen state marine parks are in the area covered in ***Gunkholing in the San Juan Islands.***

These parks, accumulated by¡ the state over a period of as much as 50 years, give boaters an exceptional opportunity to enjoy many different aspects of ¡the Northwest, including the pristine peace of some undeveloped islands in the region.

Many of the parks are accessible only by water, others may be reached by land as well. There are underwater parks for divers; some launch ramps, docks, floats and mooring buoys; some have buoys only, some have neither. Many have overnight camping areas, others are day use only. Where overnight camping is allowed there are picnic areas and sanitary facilities.

Rafting is encouraged at mooring buoys in crowded moorages. The number of recommended boats that may tie to a buoy varies depending on boat length, location, currents and sea bottom. The information is printed on each buoy, fee $5 night.

Fees are charged year round at Cornet Bay, others charge from May 1 thru September 30. Fees at floats and docks are $8 per night or $50 per year for boats under 26 feet, and $11 per night and $80 per year for boats over 26 feet.

Mooring Buoy Diagram

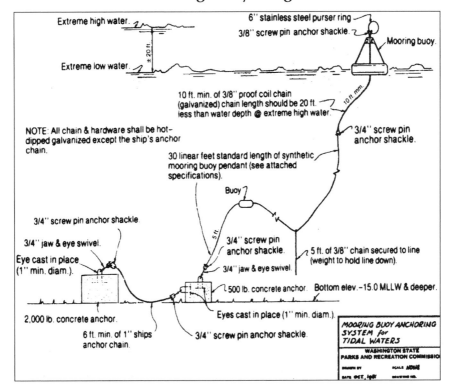

COUNTY, DNR, STATE & NATIONAL PARKS IN THE SAN JUAN ISLANDS AND MAINLAND AREAS ACCESSIBLE BY WATER AND VISITED IN THIS BOOK

Park	Address		Phone	Facilities
American Camp (Nat'l) Griffin Bay			360-378-2240	Anchor
Bay View (State)		Human powered boats	360-757-0227	High tide launch
Birch Bay (State)	5105 Helwig Rd., Blaine WA 98230		360-371-2800	Anchor
Blind Island (State)				Buoys/anchor
Clark Island (State)				Buoys/anchor
Cone Islands (State)				Beachable boats
Cypress Head, Lummi (DNR)			360-856-3500	Buoys/anchor
Deception Pass (State)	41229 State Route 20, Oak Harbor, WA 98277		800-562-0990	
Satellite parks, same address and phone number as Deception Pass Park:				
Bowman Bay				Ramp/ buoys/anchor
Sharpe Cove				Floats
Cornet Bay				Floats/ramp/anchor
Hope Island				Buoys/anchor
Skagit Island				Buoys/anchor
Doe Island (State)				Floats
Eagle Harbor, Lummi (DNR)			360-856-3500	Anchor
English Camp, Garrison Bay, (Nat'l)			360-378-2240	Dinghy dock/anchor
Freeman Island (State)				Anchor
Griffin Bay Campground (DNR)			360-856-3500	Buoys/anchor
Inati Bay (private, but open to public)				Anchor
James Island (State)				Buoys/float
Larrabee (State)	245 Chuckanut Dr., Bellingham, WA 98226		360-676-2093	Ramp
Jones Island (State)				Buoys/floats
Lummi Island Rec. Site (DNR)		Best for human powered boats	360-856-3500	Pull up on beach
Matia Island (State)				Buoys/floats
Obstruction Pass Campground (DNR)			360-856-3500	Buoys
Odlin (County) Lopez	Rt. 2, Box 3216, Lopez, WA 98261		360-468-2496	Buoys/ramp/anchor
Patos Island (State)				Buoys/anchor
Pelican Beach (DNR)			360-856-3500	Buoys
Posey Island (State)		Human powered boats	360-378-2044	Pull up on beach
Saddlebag Island (State)				Anchor
San Juan Park, S.J.Is., (County)	380 W. Side Rd N., Friday Harbor, WA 98250		360-378-8420	Ramp, anchor
Skull & Victim Islands (State)			360-378-2044	Undev./anchor
South Beach Park, Shaw Is. (County)				Ramp/ anchor
Spencer Spit (State)	Rt. 2., Box 3216, Lopez, WA 98261		360-468-2251	Buoys/anchor
Strawberry Island (DNR)		Human powered boats	360-856-3500	Pull up on beach
Stuart Island, Reid & Prevost Harbors (State)			360-378-2044	Buoys/floats/anchor
Sucia Island (State)			360-378-2044	Buoys/floats/anchor
Turn Island (State)			360-378-2044	Buoys
Upright Channel (DNR)			360-856-3500	Buoys/anchor
Young's Skagit (County) Park, Guemes				Anchor

Call 360-378-2044 for more information on these state parks in the San Juan Islands: Blind I., Clark I., Doe I., Freeman I., James I., Jones I., Matia I., Patos I., Saddlebag I., Skull & Victim I.

*Farley, our
Wonder Dog!*

*Dogs must be leashed in
all park lands.*

Public Tidelands—State Owned

A large number of parcels of state-owned tidelands are located throughout the San Juan Islands and the mainland areas discussed in this book. The state Department of Natural Resources (DNR) wants the public to know about them. As they point out, the public pays for them, the public should use them.

The state tideland ownership shown on the DNR State Public Lands Quadrangle Maps includes public use beaches, beaches which are leased to private parties, environmentally sensitive beaches and beaches otherwise not suitable for public use.

The state has made every effort to verify beach locations and property boundaries on these maps; however, the agency is not responsible for errors. Usually "boat-only access" beaches are publicly owned to the mean high tide line.

DNR staff said it's possible to anchor anywhere over saltwater bottom that is continuously wet as long as the boat is on a transient basis of a couple of nights, and not in a restricted area.

Beach users should first verify property boundaries— absence of posted signs does not mean public tidelands. Shellfish may not be taken from private tidelands without permission.

Some state tidelands are bounded on the water side by private oyster beds. Oyster Reserve Tidelands are managed by the State Department of Fisheries.

We urge all our readers to buy the maps in order to locate the state tidelands with accuracy and to take them ashore to avoid getting in trouble with private property landowners. Using dividers and a chart to complement the map, it's possible to scale off the locations of the public beaches.

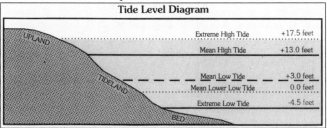

Diagram from Wash. State Public Land Quad map.

The maps are $5 each and they indicate public lands in each area. Contact DNR Photo and Map Sales, 1065 S. Capitol Way, M.S. AW-11, Olympia, WA. 98504, or call 1-800-527-3505; DNR, P.O. Box 68, Enumclaw, WA. 98022-0068.

Puget Sound Public Shellfish Sites is a booklet published by the State Game Department which gives information about locations of public areas for shellfish collecting and species at these various sites.

Consult the Washington State Department of Fisheries for the current sport fishing pamphlet and latest regulations and changes. Address: 1111 Washington St. S.E., P.O. Box 43144, Olympia, WA. 98504-3144, or pick one up from your local fishing license dealer.

To help locate these tidelands, the quad maps with a scale of 1:100,000 show where the beaches are, along with other items of interest. We have relied on three of these maps, San Juan County, Bellingham and Port Townsend regional maps, for information about state tidelands in the areas in this book. Public use of the tidelands range from extreme low tide to extreme high tide and the different ranges are shown in different colors on the maps.

For information about ordering maps contact DNR at:

Olympia Headquarters, 1111 Washington St. SE
P.O. Box 47000
Olympia, WA 98504-7000
360-902-1000

DNR Photo and Map Sales
P.O. Box 47031
Olympia, WA 98504-7031
360-902-1234

South Puget Sound Region
28329 SE 448th St.
P.O. Box 68
Enumclaw, WA 98022-0068

360-825-1631
Northwest Region
919 N. Township St.
Sedro Woolley, WA 98284-9395
360-856-3500

Shellfish—PSP

As early Puget Sound settlers learned, when the tide is out the table is set. There are many public places where shellfish can be harvested in Puget Sound. It's fun and delicious.

Shellfish are filter feeders which take in large volumes of water during feeding, contaminates and all. When boats anchor near shellfish beds and discharge sewage, shellfish may take up some of the disease-causing bacteria present in sewage. Eating contaminated shellfish can cause gastrointestinal disorders, nausea, diarrhea, infectious hepatitis or other diseases.

Mariners are asked to not anchor where there are known shellfish beds and to not discharge *any* sewage in shellfish areas. Don't harvest shellfish near marinas, popular anchorages, sewer outfalls or heavy industrial areas. When harvesting shellfish, watch for posted signs warning of possible contamination.

Paralytic Shellfish Poisoning (PSP), commonly known as "red tide," occurs when clams, oysters, scallops, geoducks and mussels consume a microscopic algae that contains a strong toxin. Eating infected shellfish can cause PSP which causes respiratory problems and even death.

PSP is rarely associated with a red tinge to the water. Reddish coloration of the water is more commonly associated with similar, but non-toxic organisms.

Infected shellfish do not look, smell or taste any different than those not infected. The only way to be certain the shellfish are safe is if they have been tested.

Rubbing them on your lips to see if your lips tingle is not a valid test of PSP.

Cooking will not kill the bacteria.

Early symptoms of PSP area tingling of the lips and tongue, which may begin with minutes of eating poisonous shellfish or may take and hour or two to develop. Depending upon the amount of toxin a person has ingested, symptoms may progress to tingling of fingers and toes and then loss of control of arms and legs, followed by difficulty in breathing. Some people have experience a sense of floating or nausea. If a person has consumed enough poison, death will result from paralysis of the breathing mechanisms in as little as two hours. Call for emergency assistance if you think you have PSP.

The state regularly tests shellfish and if there is any chance of PSP, the areas are posted. You can also call the PSP Hotline at 1-800-562-5632 for current information. (The above information from the State Department of Health, Environmental Programs, Office of Shellfish Programs.)

Puget Sound Pollution

Sound Information: A Boaters Guide, a booklet published by Puget Soundkeeper Alliance, an organization dedicated to protecting Puget Sound, is recommended reading for all boaters concerned about preserving our unique water environment.

With their permission, we reprint some of their information.

The Puget 10 Step: The Boaters Solution to Pollution.

1. Minimize use of toxic chemicals. Most marine stores carry a full line of non-toxic products for the bilge, holding tank and boat cleaning.
2. Buy only what is needed if you have to use a toxic chemical.
3. Be a good neighbor and see of others can use leftover chemical or paints rather than dispose of them.
4. Keep your dock box safe by lining bottom with tarps to contain spills. Store all chemicals in labeled closed containers.
5. Spills aren't slick. Recycle used oil, filters, paint and batteries. For the nearest locations call 1-800-RECYCLE.
6. Know where it goes. Puget Sound recreational boaters can dispose of hazardous wastes from routine maintenance at any household hazardous waste site.
7. Don't throw it away—recycle aluminum, plastic and paper.
8. Keep it out of the water. Use tarps or paper to keep paint, debris, cleaners out of water when doing slip-side maintenance9. Get involved in a group working to protect and enhance the Sound. Call 206-286-1309 or 1-800-42-Puget.
10. Don't keep it to yourself. Spread your knowledge of environmentally safe products and processes with others: "Pier" pressure really works.

Sewage Disposal—Do's & Don'ts

1. Don't discharge even treated sewage at the moorage. The same breakwaters that protect your boat also limit the flow of water through most moorages.
2. If you don't want to pump your holding tank, commercial pumpout companies will come to you. Check the phone book.
3. Not enough room for a holding tank? Use a portable toilet.

Sewage Disposal Locations

Anacortes:

Port of Anacortes (ST)	360-293-3134
Anacortes Marina (ST)	360-293-8200
Cap Sante Boat Haven (ST,DS,BT,BG)	360-293-0694
Skyline Marina (ST)	360-293-5134
Bellingham, Squalicum Harbor (ST,DS)	360-676-2500
Blaine (PT,DS)	360-676-2500
Deception Pass State Park (ST)	360-675-2417
Friday Harbor, Port of (DS,ST,PT)	360-378-2688
Islands Marine Center, Lopez (ST,DS)	360-468-3377
Point Roberts Marina (DS, ST)	360-945-2255
Rosario Resort	
Roche Harbor Resort (DS,ST)	360-378-2155

Semiahmoo Marina (DS,ST,PT)	360-371-5700
Snug Harbor Resort (PT)	360-378-4762
Stuart Island State Park (DS,ST)	360-378-2044
West Sound Marine (DS)	360-376-2314

(DS=Dump Station, ST=Stationary Pump, PT=Portable Pumpout, BG= Barge Pumpout)

Important Services & Agencies for Mariners at-a-glance

Department of Ecology:
   Northwest Region 206-649-7000
Puget Soundkeeper Alliance 206-286-1309
Puget Sound Water Quality Auth.
   ....360-493-9300 or 1-800-54SOUND
Reporting Oil Spills 1-800-OILS-911
Shellfish Advisory:
   Department of Health 360-753-5992
   Red Tide Hotline 1-800-562-5632
U.S. Coast Guard 206-217-6232
Washington State Parks and Recreation Commission:
   Boating Safety Program 360-902-8851
   Clean Vessel Act Pumpout Program 360-902-8551
   Boating Environmental Education 360-902-8551
Wildlife Services:
   Marine Animal Resource Center (MARC)
   Marine mammal strandings 360-285-SEAL or 360-775-1311
   Whale Hotline

Washington State Parks and Recreation Commission:

Ferry Information

There are about 212,000 ferry crossings in all Puget Sound and the San Juan Islands annually, carrying more than 25 million people. Consequently, all recreational boaters need to know what to expect in ferry crossing situations while cruising Western Washington inland waters.

We talked with personnel at both Washington State Ferries and the Coast Guard to gather the best information we could on what we need to know about ferry crossing situations.

Ferry skippers are extremely diligent and are as anxious to avoid confrontations or collisions as we are, and they need help from all of us.

Whether you are new to boating or an old hand, we hope you'll find this information useful.

Ferry Rules of the Road

1. **In narrow channels, small boats shall not impede deep-draft vessels**—such as ferries—in docking maneuvers or in channels. In open seas, however, sailboats do have the right of way over most other vessels.
2. **Five or more short rapid blasts** from the vessel's whistle means extreme alert—a collision is imminent—or a confusion over the other vessel's whistle signals.
3. **One short rapid blast** means vessel is altering its course to the right (starboard).
4. **Two short rapid blasts** means vessel is altering its course to the left (port).
5. **Three short rapid blasts** means vessel is reversing engines.
6. **Approaching another vessel head on, pass port to port.**
   We were cautioned:
   Always keep a sharp lookout.
   Be aware of where your boat is and other boats are.

For more information on commercial vessels, see the section on the Vessel Traffic System.

"Local Knowledge"

Local knowledge is best learned from experienced mariners cruising the area where they live. We make a point of meeting and talking with local mariners and others about their areas and experiences to glean as much local knowledge as possible.

We have cruised to, anchored in—usually overnight—or moored, at virtually every place of which we write, often many times. We have been to every marine park, checked out shorelines for public access, and visited all the marinas, public and private. We've also visited these areas by car, when possible. In addition, Jo was a liveaboard who cruised the San Juan Islands for 11 years. We have cruised our way around the Pacific Northwest separately or together for a combination of about 95 years.

We have contacted the Coast Guard, Harbor Patrol, NOAA, Washington State Parks, Department of Natural Resources (DNR), Department of Fisheries, Washington State Ferries, park rangers, various state and local park departments, marina owners and managers, local boaters, residents and others, for information.

None of this information is intended to replace official U.S. navigation charts, current charts, tide tables, tidal current tables, and other publications by NOAA and other services.

It is up to each boater to learn and use good seamanship and judgement. We encourage novice boaters to take Coast Guard Auxiliary and/or Power Squadron classes to help gain necessary skills for safe boating before casting off.

When afloat you're entirely on your own.

"Warning: The prudent mariner will not rely solely on any single aid to navigation, particularly on floating aids. See U.S. Coast Guard Light List and U.S. Coast Pilot for details."

Coast Guard on Law Enforcement:
Boardings and the Law

Many boaters are rankled by Coast Guard boardings and inspections, feeling their right to be secure "against unreasonable searches and seizures" is being violated.

"Basically boardings are to check for compliance with federal regulations. People see it as being a borderline encroachment on 4th amendment rights, and that's what gets them upset," said a Coast Guard officer.

"We're trained to come on board and say 'I'm here to just check for compliance.' If the boater has all the required equipment nothing thrills us more than to give the gold sheet that says 'you got it all, you look good.' Those in compliance aren't the ones we're talking about. Those without required equipment are the ones we need to check. We want to get that across to people.

"How do we decide who to board? We basically pick at random: fishermen, power boaters, sailors. Sometimes it comes down to the experience of the boarding team and officer. If we see faulty equipment or an unhealthy-looking situation, then we're likely to board. When a boat is being boarded, we ask for an INTEL check so the team knows what they're walking into."

A vessel underway, when hailed by a Coast Guard vessel is required to "heave to," or maneuver in such a manner that permits a boarding officer to come aboard.

The Coast Guard may impose a civil penalty up to $1,000 for failure to comply with equipment requirements, report a boating accident, or comply with other federal regulations.

A Coast Guard boarding officer who observes a boat being operated in an unsafe condition, specifically defined by law or regulation, and who determines that an especially hazardous condition exists, may direct the operator to take immediate steps to correct the condition, including returning to port.

An operator who refuses to terminate the unsafe use of a vessel can be cited for failure to comply with the directions of a Coast Guard boarding officer, as well as for specific violations which were the basis for the termination order. Violators may be fined not over $1,000 or imprisoned not over one year or both.

Patrolling Coast Guard cutters are always underway or on call year round. There are no more boats patrolling in the summer than in winter, but they are much busier in the summer with many more recreational boaters out on the water.

The Coast Guard does check to make certain that heads are in compliance. Which means that vessels under 65 feet may use Type I, II or III Marine Sanitation Devices which must be Coast Guard certified.

Generally, the Coast Guard will give a warning citation if all their requirements are not met and the citation will be forwarded to a hearing officer who will then decide on appropriate action.

Questions asked of the C.G. by recreational mariners:

"Why are we being boarded?"

The Coast Guard has the authority to board U.S. vessels anywhere, and can board foreign vessels in or near U.S. waters. Vessel inspection includes a check of registration papers and vessel's compliance with federal laws and regulations.

"What shall we expect if boarded by the Coast Guard?" A safety check will be conducted to be sure that equipment and machinery comply with U.S. regulations. The location of weapons must be identified for the safety of all concerned, but the intent is not to confiscate legal weapons.

"What do we do with expired flares?"

They can be kept on board (marked expired) as extras, or they may be left at a Coast Guard station. Do not fire them at any time, including July 4th, unless you are in need of immediate assistance.

If you want to practice using flares, request permission of the Coast Guard and they will issue a marine and land broadcast to alert the public that you are not in distress. Thousands of dollars and many hours are spent each year searching for false distress reports.

Boating While Intoxicated

Boating while intoxicated can now be prosecuted under civil tests, and Coast Guard vessels carry breathalyzer equipment on board.

"We do enforce the boating while intoxicated law. It's dangerously unacceptable to abuse alcohol and operate a boat. We want to get the drunks off the water.

"Boating accidents are even worse in Puget Sound because of the effects of 40°- 50° water," he said.

Yacht clubs are encouraging their members to abstain from drinking while running their boats.

Operating a vessel while intoxicated (blood alcohol content of 0.10 or higher) became a Federal offense on Jan. 13, 1988. Negligent or grossly negligent operation of a vessel which endangers lives and/or property is prohibited by law.

"Common Sense" Boating

• **Never cut between a tug and a tow:**

The cable/lines connecting the tow lie low in the water and are difficult to see and could rip your boat in half. The distance between the tugboat and the tow or barge may be as great as 1,000 feet.

• **Never pass closely behind a tugboat:**

Towed barges can also unexpectedly yaw from side to side. Log tows are deceptively dangerous with their "bundles," which may be difficult to see. Don't try to "out race" vessels with the intent of crossing ahead of them.

• **Other vessels, especially from afar, never appear to be as fast as they are actually traveling:**

• **Always maintain a sharp lookout.**

Dead heads (logs drifting upright), large vessels masked by background lighting from shore and fog banks—and other surprises—can make for unpleasant experiences.

• **A sailboat not under sail and under power:**

This is considered under the RULES OF THE ROAD to be a power driven vessel.

• **Carrying people in an unsafe manner:**

While it may be fun to dangle hands and feet in the water, it's easy to be crunched by another boat at a dock, or to fall off the boat and go into the propeller. There must be a sufficient railing for bow, gunwale or transom riding to be safe.

For more information on boating safety and boating courses, contact your State Boating Agency, Coast Guard District or the Boating Safety Hotline, or call 1-800-336-2628.

Vessel Traffic Service
General Information about VTS

There are close to 273,000 ship movements annually in all of Puget Sound, the San Juan Islands and the Strait of Juan de Fuca. That means approximately 750 plus ships transit some part of the area daily. This includes freighters, tankers, tugs and tows, Naval and Coast Guard vessels, including submarines and surface vessels. This figure includes the more than 212,000 ferry movements annually, or about 580 daily. It does not include the tens of thousands of recreational boats on the waters.

This kind of boat traffic almost makes you wonder if there's room enough for all of us, and helps us understand why the waterway traffic needs to be monitored and/or controlled.

The mission of the Puget Sound Vessel Traffic Service is to enhance safety on the waterways, particularly by preventing collisions, groundings and environmental damage, and to protect the beauty of the local waters. Certain laws apply to all vessels that ply the waters.

The more recreational boaters understand about the rationale behind the VTS, the safer the waterways will be for both commercial and recreational vessels.

What VTS Is

The Puget Sound Vessel Traffic Service (PSVTS) managed by 13th Coast Guard District is similar to air traffic control in monitoring vessel traffic, but 99% of the time it is advisory.

VTS was commissioned in 1972 as a voluntary system for vessel traffic; at that time about 140 boats transited the area daily. U.S. and Canada signed an international agreement in 1979 establishing the Cooperative Vessel Traffic Service; the Canadians monitor shipping in Haro Strait and west of Cape Flattery.

Full participation in VTS is required of those vessels over 132 feet (40 meters) in length to comply with VTS reporting requirements. "Passive participation" is required of vessels between 66 and 132 feet (20 and 40 meters) in length which must monitor designated VTS frequencies and comply with general VTS operating rules.

How it Works

The Traffic Separation Schemes (TSS) are shown on NOAA navigational charts in purple dashes. TSS is a two-lane water highway with each lane 1,000 yards wide. The lanes are separated by a 500 yard "median" or separation zone—pretty much like the freeway. Large vessels use the traffic lanes.

Lt. Dan Precourt gave us a tour of the Vessel Traffic Center in Building 1 at Pier 36, the C.G. Support Center in Seattle, for a complete briefing on how the system works.

Vessels in the TSS are monitored by round-the-clock crews in the Vessel Traffic Center. In a large, dimly-lit room three highly trained operators and one watch supervisor manage the 12 radar screens tracking the movements of all vessels in the TSS lanes. All personnel have instant recall of all the prominent geographic points in the entire VTS area. The same number of operators and supervisors are on duty during each of three daily watches in a highly labor intensive operation.

Vessels in the TSS are monitored by round-the-clock crews in the Vessel Traffic Center. In a large, dimly-lit room highly trained operators and one watch supervisor manage the 12 radar screens tracking the movements of all vessels in the TSS lanes. All personnel have instant recall of all the prominent geographic points in the entire VTS area. The same number of operators and supervisors are on duty during each of three daily watches in a highly labor intensive operation.

The center receives radar surveillance information from 12 strategically located radar sites in the area: Point Defiance, Point Robinson, Elliott Bay (at Pier 36), West Point, Point No Point, Point Wilson, Smith Island, Shannon Point (Guemes Channel), Village Point, Port Angeles, Clallam Bay and Cape Flattery.

"We have the authority to direct the movement of the vessels. In one percent of the time we will recommend or **urge**—such as telling them to pass port-to-port to avoid a collision. They can tell just by the tone of voice we use. First we **advise**, then **recommend**, then **tell** them what to do. We reserve that right as sometimes situations develop very fast with large vessels," Precourt said.

Colregs (Collision Regulations) Rule 10 details conduct within the TSS, which includes crossing the lanes at as close to right angles as possible.

Colregs Rule 10:

Any vessel in the TSS is bound by the TSS rules. The following is a summary of Rule 10. Actual copies of COLREGS Rule 10 are available in Rules of the Road books found in nautical bookstores.

1. A vessel shall, if possible, avoid crossing traffic lanes but, if obliged to do so, shall cross on a heading as nearly as practical at right angles to the general direction of traffic flow.

Crossing at right angles makes you much more easily detectable, both visually and by radar, by providing a beam view of your vessel. It also reduces the amount of exposure time to large vessels operating in the traffic lanes.

2. A vessel other than a crossing vessel or vessel joining or leaving a lane shall not normally enter a separation zone.

Separation Zones provide areas where a vessel can "bail out" in the event of an emergency. Fishing vessels, particularly in the Strait of Juan de Fuca, tend to fish in these "medians."

3. A vessel not using a TSS shall avoid it by as wide a margin as possible.

Recreational boaters are more maneuverable than a large vessel or a tug and tow. These vessels rely on the predictability of the traffic flow when following the traffic lanes. Recreational boaters that congest the TSS tend to reduce the predictability and therefore safety of vessel traffic.

4. Vessels, when leaving or joining traffic lanes, shall do so at as small an angle to the general direction of traffic flow as practicable.

This allows vessels to safely "merge" with existing traffic in the lanes and minimizes disruptions to existing traffic flow. Merging in this manner is similar to using a highway on/off ramp.

5. A vessel of less than 20 meters (66 feet) or a sailing vessel shall not impede the safe passage of a power-driven vessel following a traffic lane. A vessel engaged in fishing shall not impede the passage of any vessel following a traffic lane.

"Shall not impede" means a vessel MUST NOT navigate in such a way as to risk the development of a collision with another vessel (i.e., when a vessel following a TSS is forced to make an unusual or dangerous maneuver in order to avoid one of the vessels listed above, then the vessel following the TSS has been impeded).

The larger the vessel the more room and time it takes for that ship to maneuver or stop. Large vessels must maintain speed to steer. A 900 foot container ship or a tug with a cumbersome tow can't turn or stop on a dime. Stay well clear. The master or pilot must anticipate rudder commands or speed changes miles in advance. Remember, the master of a large vessel or tug and tow doesn't always know what YOU are going to do!

6. All vessels are required to keep the center of the precautionary area to port. A precautionary area is usually marked by a yellow lighted buoy and is clearly marked on all nautical charts.

This is an area where vessels following the TSS are negotiating course changes and where other vessels join or depart the TSS; therefore, all mariners must exercise caution in these areas. If you are in the TSS and encounter a large vessel, or a tug and tow in a precautionary area, BEWARE, for the vessel is most likely changing course and may be less able to avoid you.

Failure to comply with these regulations could create an unsafe navigational situation and may result in a civil penalty of up to $5,000.

Radio Contact with Vessel Traffic Services

VHF-FM channel 14 is the primary working frequency south of a line from Marrowstone Point to Lagoon Point, and across Possession Sound from Possession Point due east. North of these lines the primary frequency is VHF-FM channel 5A.

If unsure of your situation or another vessel's intentions you are urged to contact the vessel or PSVTS. The call sign is "Seattle Traffic" or simply "Traffic." Recreational boaters are asked to monitor the primary channel in their area—5A or 14—to get a feel for how congested the waterways are, offer radio assistance to disoriented mariners, relay distress calls to the appropriate Coast Guard rescue unit, and broadcast hazards to navigation—such as broken log booms, problems with the locks and other developing situations. Mariners are asked to report navigation aids they think may be missing or malfunctioning.

If you need to call VTS you should provide:
- Vessel name (not the call sign)
- Vessel type (sail/power)
- Vessel position (relative to a point of land or buoy)
- Nature of the distress or inquiry
- Keep your call short.

Miscellaneous Information

Heavy Traffic: The busiest times for heavy marine traffic are summer afternoons and weekends because of the increase in recreational boating traffic. There will often be 30 to 50 vessel movements in any shift, depending on weather, fishery openings, search and rescue operations and recreational boats. Sailboat races are also a busy time.

Unpredictable Peculiarities

During the winter of 1995, the very important Sierra Charlie buoy in Admiralty Inlet went underwater during an ebb current. Rains, swollen rivers, and quickly dropping tides caused the predicted four knot ebb current to run at closer to six knots. The buoy was pulled under water so far that someone reported it missing. When the current subsided the buoy surfaced, but the light was knocked out and had to be replaced.

For more information about the Vessel Traffic System, call 206-217-6040 and ask for a free PSVTS Users Manual. Or arrange for a tour any day of the week from 8 a.m. to 6 p.m. Boaters are encouraged to visit and view Vessel Traffic Center in operation. Vessel Traffic Services also provides speakers for boating organizations and yacht clubs.

Note: Sailboats do not have the right of way when following the traffic separation schemes—the Rules of the Road apply to everyone, not just those big vessels .

One Last Note

We've included the latest and most accurate information that we could find at the time the book went to the printer. That doesn't mean everything we've written will stay the same.

NOAA may make changes on the charts, navigation lights may be replaced, substituted or removed; marinas may change owners, adjust rates, close down; new marinas may come into existence; state and county parks may change fees or facilities; resorts and restaurants may change hands or go out of business.

This book is simply a guide for cruisers to explore the areas we've explored and to gunkhole their way to enjoyment.

If you encounter anything you think might be of interest to us please contact us and we'll use it to update our next edition.

Jo Bailey & Carl Nyberg, San Juan Enterprises, Inc.
3218 Portage Bay Pl. E., Seattle, WA 98102 206-323-1315
gunkholing@earthlink.net

Essential Current Tools for the San Juans

*NOAA Current Tables, Pacific Coast of North America
    and Asia*
Canadian Tide and Current Tables
Current Atlas, Juan de Fuca Strait to Strait of Georgia,
    Department Fisheries and Oceans, Canada
Washburne's Tables by Randel Washburne

NOAA Current Tables

Table 1 in the *Current Tables* lists daily current predictions showing slack, maximum flood and maximum ebb currents.

Current stations used in predicting currents in the San Juans and the areas covered in this book are at:

> Admiralty Inlet
> Deception Pass
> Rosario Strait
> San Juan Channel
> Active Pass

Table 2 in the *Current Tables,* "Current differences and other constants," lists over 70 "places" covered by this book where currents can be predicted based on Table 1 to determine max flood and max ebb currents and slack water.

Tidal currents refer to the horizontal motion of the water and not to the vertical rise and fall of the tide.

The relation of current to tide is not constant, but varies from place to place. The time of slack water does not generally coincide with high or low tides. The time of maximum speed of the current does not necessarily coincide with the time of the most rapid change in vertical height of the tide. *(From NOAA)*

Visualize during certain extreme tidal cycles that the change in water levels may reach or exceed 16 feet in the waters between the San Juan Islands north to Port Neville in Johnstone Strait.

There are only six restricted slots through which this combined tidal and river waters must flood or ebb twice daily into the ocean.

Johnstone Strait north of Port Neville connects to the ocean via Queen Charlotte Strait.

Haro and Rosario Straits, smaller San Juan and Swinomish Channels and Deception Pass, connect to the ocean via the Strait of Juan de Fuca.

The dynamics of the currents is awesome in the San Juans. Their enormous power and energy can be both useful and dangerous.

Knowing the direction of current and existing winds helps us to anticipate sea conditions, and often when to go or stay put.

Time and energy when afloat is precious, possibly more so to mariners in slower vessels and those opting to sail or paddle, as our Native Americans have long understood.

Current Atlas, Juan de Fuca Strait to Strait of Georgia, and Canadian Tide and Current Tables Volume 5

The current atlas is a spiral bound book with a total of 93 numbered current charts, plus other information. It covers the waters between Sooke to the west and Campbell River to the north. It includes the San Juan and Gulf Islands. The atlas is used with the **Canadian Tide and Current Tables Volume 5,** or in conjunction with separate annual private publications such as **Washburne's Tables**.

The direction of current flow is shown by hundreds of arrows on each of the 93 charts. Current speed in knots is shown visually by nine different sized arrows or a "+" when current is negligible. It illustrates where currents, large eddies and strong tidal flows may be encountered.

Using **Washburne's** the number of a specific chart representing the currents at a specific hour, day and date may be quickly identified.

Graphic review and representation of the constantly changing direction and speed of currents for the entire region is available at a glance.

Downstream from shoreline bulges or points useful backeddies tend to form. We can sometimes use these backeddies if the mainstream flow is adverse to our direction of travel.

This information also helps decide when to go or stay put or choose alternate courses to avoid adverse or dangerous sea conditions caused by winds and currents.

The charts show major backeddies but do not show lesser backeddies which form downstream of smaller obstructions.

On facing page 299 we show four representative current charts from the *Current Atlas*. They are examples of the current flow and directions during both strong floods and ebbs between the Strait of Georgia and Juan de Fuca Strait.

*(The four charts are from "Excerpts from **Current Atlas, Juan de Fuca Strait to Strait of Georgia,** reproduced with the permission of the Canadian Hydrographic Service, Department of Fisheries and Oceans.)*

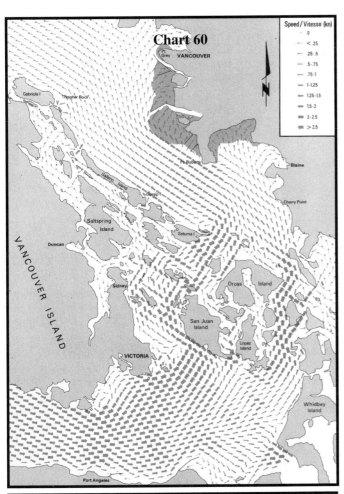

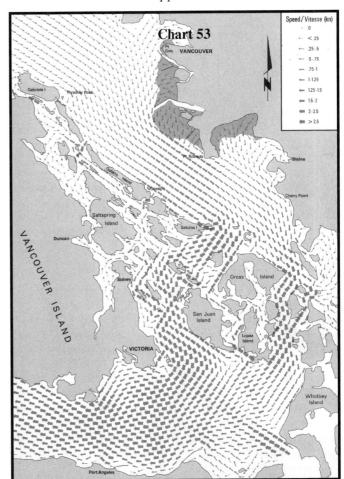

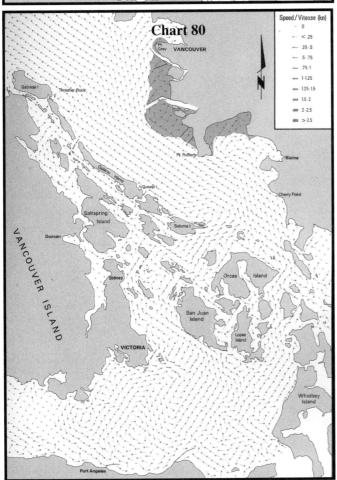

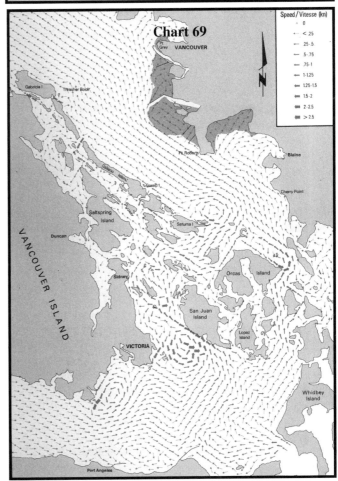

CRUISING NOTES

CRUISING NOTES

We have encountered a number of changes in some of the facilities at marinas, marine parks and other places, featured in *Gunkholing in the San Juan Islands*, published in 2000.

In this supplement we first note fee changes in state parks and some DNR changes; next we list county parks and launch ramps in San Juan, Skagit and Whatcom counties. The rest of the supplement is dedicated to changes at marinas, parks and resorts, which we list by chapters and pages.

Washington State Marine Parks

Washington state marine and other state parks are featured in the book. Many of the parks charge fees, although no fees are charged at unimproved state parks.

Washington State Parks has *designated sites* in which sharing camping space is mandatory in overflow conditions. Park buoys may be shared where boat lengths are listed on the buoys.

DNR, county and national parks are not included in the fee changes, any changes they have made are listed separately.

State parks fee structure as of 2001 follows.

Overnight moorage fees at floats:
➤ Boats under 26', $10/night
➤ Boats 26' to 34'11", $13/night
➤ Boats 35' and over, $16/night
➤ Mooring buoys, $7/night

Annual moorage permits:
➤ Boats under 26', $60/year
➤ Boats 26' to 34'11", $90/year
➤ Boats 35' and over, $110/year

Land camping:
➤ $6 per site, up to 4 persons
➤ $2 for each additional person over 18, up to 8 persons max/campsite
➤ If picking up friends who have driven to a state park, remind them there is a $5 per day parking fee at most parks.

Washington Water Trails

➤ Water trail campsites may be used only by persons arriving by human powered beachable water craft.
➤ Each person using trail sites must have $20 annual pass.

Water Trail maps are available through Washington Water Trails Association, 4649 Sunnyside Ave. N., Seattle, WA, 98103; Ph., 206-545-9161 or at www.wwta.org.

All DNR campgrounds are *listed* on Washington Water Trails, but DNR has no *designated* water trail campsites.

Wash. Department of Natural Resources (DNR) Parks

At this time, DNR does not charge for mooring buoys.

All campsites in DNR campgrounds are available on "first come, first served" basis.

Overflow camping, not in campsite, is not allowed. Tickets may be issued. DNR does not require sharing camp sites.

San Juan County Waterfront Parks & Launch Ramps

Two county parks have mooring buoys and ramps:
Buoys are $8/night, no launch fee.
➤ San Juan Co. Park, W. shore, San Juan Island, 2 buoys
➤ Odlin Co. Park, NW shore Lopez Island on Upright Channel, 4 buoys
➤ Eastsound on Orcas, day-use only dock with floats
County launch ramps are also at:

➤ **Obstruction Pass** on Orcas
➤ **Shaw Is. Co. Park** Shaw south shore at Indian Cove
➤ **Mackaye Harbor,** southwest shore, Lopez Island
➤ **Hunter Bay** in Lopez Sound, Lopez Island
➤ **Decatur Bay,** northeast shore Decatur Island

Launch Ramps in Skagit County:
➤ **Swinomish Channel,** N. of Rainbow Br. LaConner
➤ **Swinomish Channel** under Highway 20
➤ **Bay View** on Padilla Bay, high-tide only
➤ **Washington Park** in Anacortes

Launch ramps in Whatcom County:
➤ **Fairhaven,** South Bellingham
➤ **Squalicum Harbor Marina,** Bellingham
➤ **Blaine Harbor Marina,** Blaine
➤ **Lighthouse Marine County Park,** Point Roberts

VHF frequencies for pleasure boaters in the Northwest:
Ch. 16: international distress & calling
Ch. 22(A): Coast Guard Liaison
Ch. 66A: Port operations, marinas; do not call on 16
Ch. 78A: Intership, ship-shore for pleasure vessels only

Changes at Marinas, Parks and Resorts:

Chapter 1, San Juan Island

Page 10 — Griffin Bay DNR Campground
➤ Hand water pump no longer works. No plans to fix
➤ No designated Washington Water Trail campsite

Page 15 — Port of Friday Harbor Marina Facilities
➤ Breakwater A, moor either side
➤ Breakwater B, moor inside only
➤ Breakwaters C & D by reservation for vessels 44' & over
➤ C walkway—any open space
➤ G dock slips #20 & up, 40 feet, by assignment only
➤ H dock slips #16 & up, 30 feet, by assignment only
➤ Power at all locations except breakwater A & walkways
➤ There is no longer a walkway between C & E docks
➤ Call VHF 66A for slip assignment when entering

Moorage rates
➤ Sept. 15—April 30   60¢/foot
➤ May 1—June 30   70¢/foot
➤ July 1—Sept. 15   80¢/foot
➤ Vessels 75' and up $1.10/foot
➤ Reservations under 45' $1.05/foot
➤ Reservations 45' and up $1.30/foot
➤ Electricity   10¢/foot
➤ SJYC reciprocal/electric $4.80/foot
➤ Website: portfridayharbor.org

A major fire in May 2002 destroyed Friday Harbor Grocery (Whitey's) closest to marina, Mystical Mermaid, Hungry Clam, Friday Harbor Souvenir & Gifts, and San Juan Florists. No one was injured.

Page 21 — Battleship Island

Battleship Island, 0.5 mile northwest of the west tip of Henry Island, was charted by Cmdr. Wilkes as Morse's Island in 1841 after William H. Morse, purser steward on the brig *Porpoise*. The name was changed to Battleship in a 1925 government survey, but a Morse relative would like it changed back.

Page 26 — Roche Harbor Marina

- ➤ 20'x 20' open-sided shelter for all, no campsite
- ➤ Board walk connects four campsites and shelter
- ➤ New handicapped accessible toilet
- ➤ Six campsites, 7 picnic tables
- ➤ Listed Washington Water Trails campsite

It's possible to walk the beach around Cypress' north end; hikers need to know uplands are private, no trespassing.

Page 241–Strawberry Island DNR Site
- ➤ Listed Washington Water Trail campsite

Chapter 11, Bellingham Bay, including Chuckanut Bay
Page 247–Larrabee State Park Facilities
- ➤ 2,683 acres
- ➤ Boat launch ramp may be inaccessible to launch & retrieve watercraft at low tide
- ➤ No primitive camp sites

Page 252–Fairhaven Facilities
- ➤ Parking fee $5

Page 255–Squalicum Harbor Marina Facilities
- ➤ Launch ramp parking fee, $5 or $72 annually
- ➤ Address: 722 Coho Way, Bellingham, WA 98225

Chapter 12, Lummi I., Hale Passage, Blaine & Pt. Roberts
Page 266–Reil Harbor DNR Site
- ➤ Washington Water Trail campsite

Page 274–Birch Bay Park Facilities
- ➤ 167 campsites
- ➤ Designated hand launch for small boats
- ➤ Address: 5105 Helweg Road, Blaine, WA 98230

Page 277–Blaine Small Boat Harbor Facilities
- ➤ Contact Harbor office for moorage over 3 days
- ➤ Launch ramp fees, $5 U.S, $7 Canadian
- ➤ Monitors VHF Channel 68
- ➤ Marina Harbormaster: Pam Taft
- ➤ Ph.: 360-647-6176/FAX: 360-332-1043
- ➤ email: blaineharbor@portofbellingham.com
- ➤ Street address: 235 Marine Dr., Blaine, WA 98230

Page 279–Semiahmoo Marina Facilities
- ➤ Moorage fees: 80¢/foot
- ➤ Boutique, basic store, coffee bar
- ➤ Nearby: 2 golf courses, inn with 4 restaurants, spa, fitness center, hiking and cycling trails
- ➤ Activities: golf, swimming, tennis, racquetball rentals for bikes, rollerblades & kayaks, free concerts
- ➤ Harbormaster: Bill Tetreault

Page 282–Crescent Beach Marina Facilities
- ➤ 30 ton haulout up to 52'

Page 285–Point Roberts Marina Facilities
- ➤ Web page: www.pointrobertsmarina.com

Appendix, Page 291, Col. 1, Whale Watching guidelines:
- • Vessels should not approach within **400** yards/meters of whales, up from 100 yards, as motors may impair an orca's sonar ability from 95 to 99%.

San Juan Island emergency phone numbers

911—cell phones must dial 360-378-4151
San Juan County sheriff 360-378-4151
Medical Center 360-378-2141
Oil Spill 360-378-5322/800-424-8802
Red Tide Hotline 800-562-5632
Coast Guard 360-457-4404

Crossing the Border between the U.S. & B.C.
Entering Canada

When entering Canada report to a designated customs reporting site. Call toll-free at 1-888-226-7277, or contact Customs by VHF radio and you'll be told where to report. Canadian Customs has now become Canada Customs and Revenue Agency.

The first thing you need is to prove your citizenship. A passport is best. In lieu of that a birth certificate and a photo i.d. such as a driver's license may work. One Canadian Customs officer said, "without a passport you may have major problems." There is no fee for clearing Customs.

You must have with you:
- • Vessel registration number
- • Vessel name and length
- • Names, addresses, citizenship & birthdates of all on board
- • Estimated departure dates

Log your clearance number & post it on your boat. Vessels are subject to reinspection in Canadian waters.

Restrictions on what you can take into Canada:

Food enough for planned stay in Canada; no apples, potatoes, fresh corn; no pitted fruits: apricots, peaches, plums, quince, nectarines.

Dog & cat owners must have certificate from licensed veterinarian identifying pet & certifying rabies vaccination during previous 3 years.

Take in not more than 1.14 liters of hard liquor, or 1.5 liters of wine, or 24 12-ounce bottles of beer per person of legal age, which is 19 in Canada. Not more than one carton of cigarettes & 2 cans tobacco & 50 cigars per person 19 or older.

Firearms restrictions: call Canada Customs, 800-461-9999.

Is there an advantage to a CANPASS permit?

CANPASS permits were suspended following September 11, 2001. They were reinstated in April 2002. Permits have been extended six months from date of expiration on the permit. Cost is $25, Canadian funds.

A Canadian Customs officer told us, "We don't recommend CANPASS, there's no benefit to it, all boats must go to a 'designated' port-of-entry when entering Canada whether they have a CANPASS permit or not, and they will not be cleared by phone."

If you have a CANPASS permit you must call 1-888-CANPASS up to four hours before arriving in Canada. They will tell you your designated Port of Entry. You can not proceed to non-approved sites on the West Coast.

There are only three places where you **must** have a CANPASS permit to enter, Miners Bay & Horton Bay on Mayne Island & Townsite Marina in Nanaimo. No one seemed to know why you can't enter without the pass.

Designated reporting sites for clearing Customs in B.C:
Campbell River: Discovery Chevron, Discovery Marina
Mayne Island: Miners Bay, Horton Bay (CANPASS only)
Nanaimo: Brechin Pt. Marina, Nanaimo Harbour Commission, Townsite Marina (CANPASS Permit only)
Pender Island: Bedwell Harbour, 05/01/02—09/30/02
Prince Rupert: Fairview Government Dock, Rushbrook Government Dock, Prince Rupert Yacht Club
Sidney: Canoe Cove Marina, Port Sidney Marina, RVYC—Tseum Harbour, Van Isle Marina
Ucluelet: Dock location to be determined
Vancouver: White Rock Government Dock, Crescent Beach

Marina, Coal Harbour/Burrard Inlet, anywhere; False Creek, Steveston, either Chevron or Petro Canada gas station

Victoria: Royal Victoria Yacht Club, Victoria Customs Float-Inner Harbour, CFSA, Canadian Forces Sailing Association—Club members only

The following Customs offices at five previous ports of entry have been closed:

Anglers Anchorage
Bamfield
Port Alberni
Port Hardy
Powell River/Westview

U.S. Customs

(U.S. Customs is now the Bureau of Customs and Border Protection in the Dept. of Homeland Security.)

We'll go through clearing Customs as you return to the states and then tackle the confusing U.S. I-68 permit, called the "Canadian Border Boat Landing Permit."

Customs clearance is now "almost" back to normal and the PIN clearance system for recreational boats has been reinstated since the national threat level has gone down. Customs will check more boats and people this year and they could revoke the PIN clearance again if the threat level goes up.

All private boats returning to the U.S. are required to clear at a port-of-entry, such as Friday Harbor and Roche Harbor in the San Juans, or Anacortes, Bellingham, Port Angeles, Port Townsend, Point Roberts, Everett, Seattle, Tacoma.

A PIN (personal identification number) will be assigned to vessel operators on their first U.S. customs clearance. With a PIN you can report your arrival any time from one hour before leaving Canada to the time when you land in the U.S., or while underway by calling 1-800-562-5943 to clear by phone. The PIN telephone reporting system is in use 24 hours a day.

The following information is required:
• Vessel registration number
• Vessel name and length
• User fee decal number—this is issued the first time a boat over 30 feet enters or re-enters the U.S. The customs non-transferable decal costs $25, it's good for one year.
• Canadian clearance number, **required** for U.S. moored boats
• Carry positive citizenship identification, passport is best, or birth certificate and photo i.d.; driver's license does not prove citizenship
• Estimated date of departure required for B.C. moored boats

A release number will be issued on arrival; this must be logged with the date, time and place you cleared, and kept for a year.

It is still imperative to call Customs before entering the U.S. for clearance by boat and check for any change of procedures. The phone number is 800-562-5943.

There are restrictions on what you can bring back from Canada. U.S. doesn't allow citrus fruits, oranges, lemons, etc., because of the peels; Cuban cigars will be confiscated. Customs officers look for drugs: you are allowed only 100 doses Canadian codeine aspirin; no more than one liter of alcohol.

U.S. residents out of country for less than 48 hours can bring back $200 worth of merchandise without paying duty. If away longer you can bring in $400 worth of goods.

U.S. I-68 "Canadian Border Boat Landing Program"

The I-68 program allows certain applicants entering the U.S. by small pleasure boats to be inspected and issued a single boating permit for the entire boating season. This permit enables them to enter the U.S. from Canada for recreational purposes without the need to report to INS (U.S. Immigration Department) for further inspection. In other words, once you have an I-68 permit you can enter from time to time throughout the season without inspection, handy if you're fishing or cruising into B.C. more than once a year.

U.S. citizens, lawful permanent residents and Canadian citizens or landed Canadian immigrants are eligible to apply for Form I-68. There is not a requirement that boaters obtain form I-68.

Rules are that those who do **not** need an I-68 Boat Landing permit are those who enter the U.S. by reporting to a staffed Port-of-Entry each time they return. Conversely, those who **need a** valid permit are every boater who enters the U.S. **without** reporting directly to a staffed port-of-entry.

I-68 costs $16 per person or $32 for a family, and each family member 14 years old or more must have a separate form. Photos similar to passport photos are required, as are fingerprints of the applicants. Although you can look at the multi-page forms on the internet you must pick them up at a U.S. port-of-entry, and fill them out in person in the customs office.

Phil and Gwen Cole of Northwest Boat Travel have clarified some of the confusion in their website.

"In reality, U.S. Customs agents are NOT cross-trained and empowered by INS to act as Immigration Officers, so that none of the boater's Ports-of-Entry require the form." They further state that the "unofficial word" from boaters and Immigration officials speaking "off the record" is that INS lacks the funding and manpower to enforce I-68 rules.

The Coles write, "We cannot, in good conscience advise you to ignore these rules, but we also cannot fail to pass this information along. Our best suggestion, to be safe, is to either obtain valid, new (2002), I-68 forms or to enter the U.S. at a boater's Port-of-Entry that has Customs officers who are cross-trained and designated to act as Immigration officers." Also, be sure to have birth certificates or passports for everyone on board.

One Customs officer we spoke to said, "I don't think I-68 is a concern." Another said she hadn't even heard of it.

For more information on I-68 visit the Cole's website at www.nwboat.com., or the INS website at www.ins.usdoj.gov/graphics/lawenfor/bmgmt/inspect/boat.htm#faqs.

Other useful websites and phone numbers:
Recreational Boaters of Washington, newsletter@rbaw.org or WWW.RBAW.ORG
U.S. Customs office in Friday Harbor, 360-378-2080
U.S. Customs reporting number, 1-800-562-5943
Learn more about I-68 at www.ins.usdoj.gov/graphics/lawenfor/bmgmt/inspect/boat.htm#faqs
Canadian Customs and CANPASS, 1-888-226-7277 or 1-888-CANPASS

To order Washington State Public Lands Quad Maps for San Juan County or Bellingham areas, call state Department of Natural Resources at 360-902-1234. For more information on Washington State Parks go to www.parks.wa.gov.